In Search of Chinese Democracy

The Chinese quest for democracy dates back to the late nineteenth century, when concerned scholars spoke of the need for representative institutions to check the absolute powers of the Qing monarchy. Much of the scholarship on democratic movements and constitutionalism in China focuses on the 1911 Revolution and the heady but brief phase of competitive politics that followed, and on the May Fourth Movement of 1919, when science and democracy were championed by the country's new intellectuals. Edmund Fung contends, however, that the greatest momentum for democracy in China occurred between 1929 and 1949, during the Nationalist era, by means of civil opposition to the one-party rule of the Guomindang. This book, on the thoughts and actions of China's liberal intellectuals and political activists who pursued democracy, fills a gap in the historical literature concerning the period between May Fourth radicalism/the rise of Marxism and the accession to power of the Chinese Communists.

Why modern China has been unable to institutionalize democracy is a long-standing topic of debate and the ultimate subject of this book. The answer to this question – whether it is socioeconomic conditions, as some scholars believe, or China's political culture and institutional patterns, or authoritarian elements deeply rooted in the Chinese Confucian tradition – has important implications for the prospects for democratic government in China today.

Fung examines the internal and external factors that shaped democratic thought in the 1930s and 1940s. He argues that the reasons the growth of democracy was retarded and then ended during this period were ultimately more political than cultural. He questions the assumptions that Chinese liberal intellectuals were averse to political engagement, that they had little appreciation for the central principle of the liberal creed and little understanding of Western democratic thought, and that China lacked the intellectual foundations for democracy. He concludes that the Nationalist era contained the germs of a reformist, liberal order that had been prevented from growing by party politics, a lack of regime leadership, and bad strategic decisions. The legacy of China's liberal thinkers during this understudied era, however, can be seen in the prodemocracy movement of the post–Mao Zedong period.

Cambridge Modern China Series

Edited by William Kirby, Harvard University

尋求中國民主

馮兆基著

In Search of Chinese Democracy

In Search of
Chinese Democracy

Civil Opposition in Nationalist China,
1929–1949

EDMUND S. K. FUNG

University of Western Sydney

CAMBRIDGE
UNIVERSITY PRESS

PUBLISHED BY THE PRESS SYNDICATE OF THE UNIVERSITY OF CAMBRIDGE
The Pitt Building, Trumpington Street, Cambridge, United Kingdom

CAMBRIDGE UNIVERSITY PRESS
The Edinburgh Building, Cambridge CB2 2RU, UK   http://www.cup.cam.ac.uk
40 West 20th Street, New York, NY 10011-4211, USA   http://www.cup.org
10 Stamford Road, Oakleigh, Melbourne 3166, Australia
Ruiz de Alarcón 13, 28014 Madrid, Spain

First published 2000

Printed in the United States of America

Typeface Times New Roman 10/13 pt.   *System* QuarkXPress [BTS]

A catalog record for this book is available from the British Library.

Library of Congress Cataloging in Publication data
Fung, Edmund S. K.
In search of Chinese democracy : civil opposition in Nationalist
China, 1929–1949 / Edmund S. K. Fung.
p.   cm. – (Cambridge modern China series)
Includes bibliographical references.
ISBN 0-521-77124-2
1. Democracy – China.   2. Human rights – China.   3. China – Politics
and government – 1912–1949.   I. Title.   II. Title: Civil opposition
in Nationalist China, 1929–1949.   III. Series.
JQ1516.F86   2000
320.951'09'043 – dc21   99-36625

ISBN   0 521 77124 2   hardback

To Lucia and Eugene

Contents

Contents

Acknowledgments

Since the commencement of the "third wave" in the mid-1970s, and especially since the end of the Cold War, democracy and democratization have attracted a great deal of scholarly attention. Like many scholars, I have become keenly interested in these topics generally and Chinese democracy in particular since the Tiananmen tragedy of June 4, 1989. Tiananmen has unleashed a torrent of writings on Chinese democracy, raising many questions about the prodemocracy movement and the prospects for democracy in the post-Deng era. The literature is interesting and still growing. Little of it, however, has been historically informed, and little attention has been given to Chinese democratic thought. Andrew J. Nathan's excellent book *Chinese Democracy* (1986) has been a source of inspiration to me. But it skips not only the May Fourth Movement but also the whole of the democratic liberal tradition of the Nationalist period. For this reason, I thought I would write a book on that tradition and tell a hitherto little-known story about the prodemocracy movement in that period.

The research resulting in this book was supported by two separate grants from the Australia Research Committee during the periods 1992–1993 and 1995–1996, which enabled me to carry out fieldwork in China, Taiwan, England, and the United States. A period of academic study leave in the second half of 1996 provided me with the much-needed break from teaching and administrative duties to concentrate on research and writing. I am grateful to my employer, the University of Western Sydney.

The staffs of many libraries and archives have helped with this project: in Australia, the Menzies Library at the ANU, the Commonwealth Library, Fisher Library at the University of Sydney, Griffith University Library, and UWS Nepean Library; in China, the Chinese Academy of Social Sciences' Institute of Modern History Library, the Periodicals Library at Beijing University, Nankai University Library, Zhongshan University Library, the Yunnan Provincial Library, the Yunnan Normal University (previously the Southwest Associated University) Library, and the Library of the Department of History, Nanjing University; in Taiwan, Academia Sinica's Institute of Modern History Library; in England, the Library of the School of Oriental and African Studies; and in the United States, the Butler Library at Columbia University.

I should mention a number of academic colleagues, librarians, and archivists who have been especially helpful. These include, in China, Tang Yijie, Zhang Haipeng, Yang Tianshi, Bai Ji'an, Wei Hongyuan, Li Huaxing, Lin Jiayou, Zhang Xianwen, Zhu Baoqin, and Yang Hong; in Taiwan, Ch'en San-ching, Chang Peng-yuan, and Chang Yu-fa; in Australia, Elsie Leow and Chen Jie; and in the United States, Roger Jeans, who drew my attention to his latest works on Zhang Junmai and helped me in some other ways, and Frederic Spar, who has shared with me his book manuscript on Luo Longji based on his 1980 Ph.D. dissertation.

Regarding the book itself, I am extremely grateful to Peter Zarrow, John Fitzgerald, Colin Mackerras, Wang Gungwu, and David Goodman for their comments on an earlier draft of the entire manuscript. Their feedback has been invaluable in removing some of the book's deficiencies. In many cases, I have followed their advice, and I hope they will forgive me for the instances where I have persisted in my original views. I am equally grateful to the two anonymous readers who reviewed the manuscript for Cambridge University Press for their helpful and constructive comments and suggestions, all of which, as they will see, have been taken aboard. Needless to say, any shortcomings of the book are my responsibility alone. By way of a more impersonal debt, I feel bound to add that I have benefited greatly from every previous work on Chinese democracy that I cite, especially the works of Andrew Nathan, not least in cases where I have found myself in disagreement.

I would also like to thank Russell Hahn, the production editor for Cambridge University Press, who has been extremely helpful to me, and the copyeditor, Sara Black, for removing some of the stylistic infelicities and making the book more readable. This book has also benefited from the expertise of Nancy Hearst, who carefully proofread the book at the final stages. The artwork that provides the frontispiece is that of the eminent calligrapher Huang Miaozi (M. T. Wong). It is very much appreciated.

Acknowledgments

My secretary, Joy Kane, has helped me in numerous ways, especially when my personal computer was acting up. I cannot thank her enough for her assistance, patience, and understanding.

Last but not least, I am grateful to my wife, Lucia, for her patience and understanding over the years. The book is dedicated to her as well as to my son, Eugene, who seems to understand what an historian does to make a living.

Sydney
March 2000

A Note on Romanization

The *pinyin* system, the official romanization system in the People's Republic of China, is used throughout this book in place of the older Wade–Giles system except in cases where a person is better known in the West by a particular romanized form, such as Sun Yat-sen, Sun Fo, Chiang Kai-shek, T. V. Soong, and H. H. Kung. In the notes and bibliography, for reasons of consistency, the capital of Taiwan is spelled Taibei instead of Taipei.

Abbreviations

The abbreviations listed here are used in the text and the notes only, not in the bibliography.

CCP	Chinese Communist Party
DL	Chinese Democratic League
DLPL	*Duli pinglun* (The Independent Critic)
FRUS	U.S. Department of State, *Foreign Relations of the United States*. Washington, DC: Government Printing Office, relevant years.
GC	*Guancha* (The Observer)
GMCZH	Chongqingshi zhengxie wenshi ziliao yanjiu weiyuanhui, ed., *Guomin canzhenghui jishi* (A veritable record of the People's Political Council), 2 vols. Chongqing: Chongqing chubanshe, 1985.
GMD	Guomindang (Chinese Nationalist Party)
GWZB	*Guowen zhoubao* (National News Weekly)
JRPL	*Jinri pinglun* (Commentary Today)
LSMQJ	Liang Shuming, *Shuming quanji* (The collected works of Liang Shuming), 8 vols. Jinan: Shandong renmin chubanshe, 1993.
MMWX	Zhongguo minzhu tongmeng zhongyang wenshi ziliao weiyuanhui, ed., *Zhongguo minzhu tongmeng lishi wenxian, 1941–1949* (Documents on the Chinese Democratic League, 1941–1949). Beijing: Wenshi ziliao chubanshe, 1983.
MPG	Minor parties and groups
MZZK	*Minzhu zhoukan* (Democracy Weekly)
PCC	Political Consultative Conference
PPC	People's Political Council
PRC	People's Republic of China

SJPL   *Shiji pinglun* (Commentary This Century)
XY   *Xinyue* (The Crescent)
ZZXSHY   *Zhengzhi xieshang huiyi ziliao* (Source materials on the Political Consultative Conference), no editor. Chengdu: Sichuan renmin chubanshe, 1981.

Introduction

> The Chinese have aspired to democracy as they understood it
> for a hundred years, have claimed to have it for seventy, and
> for the last thirty-five years have lived in one of the most par-
> ticipatory societies in history.
>
> Andrew J. Nathan, 1986[1]

THE SEARCH for a way out (*chulu*) of China's predicament had
been a profound concern of Chinese intellectuals in the twentieth
century. How could China be saved from the twin incubus of foreign
imperialism and internal disorder? Where was she headed? Even if it
could be mapped out where the destination was, how was she going
to get there? Different options were canvassed. Some took what Lin
Yu-sheng calls the cultural–intellectualistic approach, assigning primacy
to intellectual and cultural reform as a first step toward the creation
of a new political order.[2] Others adopted an approach that placed a
premium on political engagement, stressing the possibility of simul-
taneous political reform and cultural change. For the liberal intellectuals of the Nationalist period, democratic and constitutional change
offered the best hope for a peaceful and modern China. They advocated
democracy (*minzhu*) and constitutionalism throughout the period, only
to find that the road to democracy was blocked. After 1949, "people's
democracy" under the People's Republic was a far cry from what they
had fought for.

---

[1] Andrew J. Nathan, *Chinese Democracy* (London: I. B. Tauris, 1986), p. x.

[2] In his study of the May Fourth intellectuals, notably Hu Shi, Chen Duxiu, and Lu Xun,
Lin Yu-sheng is concerned with their "iconoclastic totalism" which kept them preoccupied with cultural change prior to political action. See his *The Crisis of Chinese
Consciousness: Radical Anti-traditionalism in the May Fourth Era* (Madison: University
of Wisconsin Press, 1979).

This book is about the thoughts and actions of some particular groups of Chinese intellectuals and political activists who pursued democracy as they understood it by opposing the single-party system under Nationalist rule. Its purpose is threefold: first, to probe their understanding and advocacy of democracy and human rights; second, to examine the nature and complexity of the opposition movement that developed over two decades from thought articulation to organized political activism; and third, to study the role of middle politics, or the third force, during and after the war with Japan. This work is an attempt to fill a lacuna in the scholarship on the liberal intellectuals of the 1930s and 1940s who got lost between May Fourth radicalism/nationalism on the one hand and the growth of Marxism on the other. This is not merely a study of democratic thought but also a study of a political movement.

The title of this book uses the term *Chinese democracy* advisedly because some scholars have argued that *minzhu* is not democracy as the latter is understood in the West and that, therefore, it is almost a misnomer to call *minzhu* movements in China movements for democracy.[3] I do not follow this line of argument, nor am I concerned whether Chinese democracy is the same as democracy in the West or whether Chinese democrats were "true democrats." In this book I am only interested in understanding the kind of democracy envisioned by the middle-of-the-road intellectuals and the opposition movement in which their advocacy was located. The term *Chinese democracy* is used deliberately and perhaps also provocatively to invoke the remarkable blend of Chinese and Western thoughts that provided the theoretical underpinning for the movement. Civil opposition is defined as nonviolent opposition to the existing political order characterized by an authoritarian single-party system in a China dominated by militarists. It called for democratic and constitutional change without advocating the overthrow of the government by force of arms. By definition it did not include the anti-Chiang Kai-shek warlords and the armed opposition of the Chinese communist movement. Student activism, which may be considered part of civil opposition, is outside the scope of this book because it has been the subject of numerous books and articles. Civil opposition is treated

[3] See Lei Guang, "Elusive Democracy: Conceptual Change and the Chinese Democracy Movement, 1978–79 to 1989," *Modern China* 22:4 (October 1996): 417–447. In *Chinese Democracy*, Nathan has highlighted the differences between the Chinese version of democracy and the Western version, but he does not go so far as to say that Chinese democracy (*minzhu*) is not democracy.

here both in terms of ideas about democracy and in terms of a political movement. Our focus will be on elite opposition.

Historically, the Chinese quest for democracy can be dated back to the second half of the nineteenth century when concerned scholars spoke of the need for representative institutions to check the powers of the absolutist monarchy.[4] After China's humiliating defeat at the hands of Japan in 1894–1895, many scholar–officials, impressed with the achievements of Meiji Japan, espoused constitutionalism. In the period leading to the Revolution of 1911, reformers and revolutionaries alike wrote about constitutional alternatives and democracy in China. As Don Price has shown, their spokespersons had a clearer understanding of what democracy was about than even their counterparts in Britain.[5] Early twentieth-century China saw the first formally democratic institution in the City Council of Chinese Shanghai (as distinct from Shanghai's International Settlement), an institution that Mark Elvin has characterized as "gentry democracy."[6]

After the overthrow of the Qing Dynasty, new political parties, growing out of the pre-1911 revolutionary and constitutionalist camps, were formed, thus inaugurating the first, albeit short-lived, phase of competitive politics in modern China.[7] General elections were held which, though imperfect, were as free and fair as most first elections ever tended to be. Ernest Young has observed that "representative government and competitive elections among autonomous political parties came closer to dominating the political process . . . than at any other point in Chinese history."[8] The Nationalist Party (*Guomindang*, or GMD) led by Song Jiaoren won the elections in 1913. Had it not been for Song's assassination on the order of President Yuan Shikai and the political repression that followed, Song would have become premier and a responsible cabinet system might have been established.

---

[4] Xiong Yuezhi, *Zhongguo jindai minzhu sixiang shi* (History of modern Chinese democratic thought) (Shanghai: Shanghai renmin chubanshe, 1986), pp. 134–157.

[5] Don C. Price, "Constitutional Alternative and Democracy in the Revolution of 1911," in Paul A. Cohen and Merle Goldman, eds., *Ideas Across Cultures* (Cambridge, MA: Harvard University Press, 1990), pp. 199–260.

[6] Mark Elvin, "The Gentry Democracy in Chinese Shanghai 1905–14," in Jack Gray, ed., *Modern China's Search for a Political Form* (London: Oxford University Press, 1969), pp. 41–65.

[7] See Zhang Pengyuan, *Liang Qichao yu minchu zhengzhi* (Liang Qichao and early Republican politics) (Taibei: Shihuo chubanshe, 1981), ch. 3.

[8] Ernest P. Young, *The Presidency of Yuan Shih-k'ai: Liberalism and Dictatorship in Early Republican China* (Ann Arbor: University of Michigan Press, 1977), p. 76.

Despite the ascendancy of the military following Yuan's death in 1916, a vigorous movement, led by the enlightened gentry, was maturing. It advocated representative institutions and self-government at local and provincial levels,[9] coinciding with the New Culture and May Fourth Movements of 1915–1921 wherein science and democracy became the principal causes championed by China's new intellectuals. As Confucianism came under attack, individualism was advocated by such prominent figures as Hu Shi and Chen Duxiu, later a founder of the Chinese Communist Party (CCP).[10] Li Dazhao, also a founder of the CCP, understood democracy as the spirit of the age, linking it specifically with Marxism, in the wake of the Russian Revolution. Taking a democratic path to socialism, Li went on to develop a utopian theory of democracy during the 1920s.[11] And the anarchist Liu Shipei spoke of a concept of rights that seemed to lie at the core of his utopian vision. For the likes of Liu, anarchism, which held that the freedom of the individual should not be sacrificed in the interest of society, was a source of democratic thinking.[12]

The Nationalists in the 1920s adopted Sun Yat-sen's *Sanmin zhuyi* (Three Principles of the People) as its ideology. It seemed possible then to advance the antiimperialist and democratic causes simultaneously. But in 1928, when the Nanjing regime declared a period of political tutelage placing China under one-party rule, the Nationalist revolution was aborted and a counterrevolution began.[13] The result was to postpone

---

[9] John H. Fincher, *Chinese Democracy: The Self-Government Movement in Local, Provincial and National Politics, 1905–1914* (Canberra: Australian National University Press, 1980), ch. 8.

[10] Hu agreed with Henrik Ibsen's view that "No social evil is greater than the destruction of the individual's individuality." Cited in Jerome B. Grieder, *Hu Shih and the Chinese Renaissance: Liberalism in the Chinese Revolution, 1917–1937* (Cambridge, MA: Harvard University Press, 1970), p. 93. And Chen Duxiu insisted: "There is no higher value than that of the individual. All values depend on the individual. If there were no individuals (particulars) there would be no universe. Thus, it can be said that the value of the individual is greater than that of the universe. Thus there is no greater crime than to suppress the individual or to violate particularity." Quoted in Stuart R. Schram, ed., *Mao's Road to Power: Revolutionary Writings* (Armonk, NY: M. E. Sharpe, 1992), I, 208.

[11] See Ip Hung-yok, "The Origins of Chinese Communism: A New Interpretation," *Modern China* 20:1 (January 1994): 40ff; Arif Dirlik, *The Origins of Chinese Communism* (Oxford: Oxford University Press, 1989), pp. 43–52.

[12] For a scholarly treatment of Liu's anarchist thought, see Peter Zarrow, *Anarchism and Chinese Political Culture* (New York: Columbia University Press, 1990), pp. 83–95. For another recent study of anarchism in China, see Arif Dirlik, *Anarchism in the Chinese Revolution* (Berkeley: University of California Press, 1991).

[13] Lloyd E. Eastman, *The Abortive Revolution: China under Nationalist Rule, 1927–1937* (Cambridge, MA: Harvard University Press, 1974).

democracy almost ad infinitum. National disunity, political instability, civil strife, the communist challenge, the autocracy of Chiang Kai-shek, the ascendancy of the military, the escalating Japanese threat, and the "crisis of democracy" in Italy, Germany, Poland, and Spain, all contributed to a freezing of democracy by the Nationalist leadership.

Throughout the Nationalist period, many intellectuals, feeling the sting of political repression, criticized the GMD's political tutelage, one-party dictatorship, disregard of human rights, corruption, incompetence, and its many other failings. Democracy seemed to offer a prescription for China's political ills and bad governance. Of course, opposition to the regime was not necessarily or always motivated by a concern for democracy. For many, democracy was a convenient political weapon.

Until recently, few scholars considered the possibility of a liberal and democratic alternative in modern China,[14] even though they accepted the fact that liberalism was a significant strand in Chinese intellectual thought in the first half of the twentieth century.[15] Despite a large body of literature on modern China, the prodemocracy movement in the Nationalist era has been a neglected subject.

During most of the Nationalist era, China was under Japanese threat, which culminated in an eight-year war. The country was in crisis after 1931; consequently, national salvation was seen as a matter of great urgency. The idea of national salvation, or saving the nation (*jiuwang*), was not new; it had been a dominant motif in China's political and intellectual movements since the late nineteenth century when reformers and revolutionaries alike were anxious to find a way to save the country from external aggression and internal decay. This concern with *jiuwang* was in sharp contrast to the patterns of political and intellectual developments in Europe where the Enlightenment provided the intellectual underpinning and prepared the way for political movements aimed at the achievement of liberty, equality, and fraternity (for example, the constitutional movement in seventeenth-century England and the French Revolution

---

[14] In 1986, for example, when the authoritative *Cambridge History of China,* Volume 13, dealing with the Nationalist era was published, editors John K. Fairbank and Albert Feuerwerker and the five contributors took little notice of the minor parties and groups and hardly mentioned the constitutional and democratic movement during that era. Lloyd Eastman, who wrote the chapter on the Nanjing period, devoted less than a page to the question of Chinese democratization.

[15] See, for example, Elvin, "The Gentry Democracy"; Nathan, *Chinese Democracy*; and Grieder, *Hu Shih and the Chinese Renaissance.*

hina, enlightenment (*qimeng*), which found full expression
ourth Movement,[16] was preceded and overshadowed by

ıship between *jiuwang* – with its emphasis on antiim-
_, _____feudalism, antiwarlordism, and revolution – and *qimeng* –
which stressed science and democracy, reason and cultural criticism,
and individual freedoms and development – has been interpreted by
the eminent philosopher Li Zehou in terms of needs and priority. Li
argues that Chinese intellectuals' acceptance of Marxism–Leninism
and their rejection of anarchism and liberalism after the May Fourth
Movement was dictated by the imperatives of *jiuwang*, and was not the
result of an epistemological choice. Those imperatives – antiimperialism,
antiwarlordism, antifeudalism, and revolutionary wars against both
domestic and external enemies – left the intellectuals little time for a
thorough study of political ideologies prior to political engagement.
Jiuwang took precedence over everything else, including individual
emancipation and personal freedoms. What China needed was not "the
propaganda of such enlightenment thought as liberty and democracy"
nor "the encouragement and promotion of individual liberty and individuality" but "absolute obedience to the antiimperialist revolutionary
struggle," "iron discipline," "unified will," and "collective strength," compared with which individual rights and freedoms paled in importance.
For a while, during the May Fourth period, Li goes on, *qimeng* and
jiuwang were juxtaposed in a mutually reinforcing manner, but that
complementary relationship was short-lived. Events since 1919 were
such that the intellectuals felt compelled to embrace the authoritarian
regime in the process of *jiuwang*, which prevailed over *qimeng*.[17] Reviewing Chinese revolutionary thought in the early twentieth century, Li
concludes:

> Science and democracy of the May Fourth Movement made a sup-
> plementary lecture on the thought of the old democratic revolution,
> as well as providing the enlightenment chapter in [the era of] the
> new democratic revolution. However, because modern China still

---

[16] See Vera Schwarcz, *The Chinese Enlightenment: Intellectuals and the Legacy of the May Fourth Movement of 1919* (Berkeley: University of California Press, 1986).

[17] Li Zehou, "Qimeng yu jiuwang de shuangchong bianzou" (The double changes between enlightenment and national salvation), in Li Zehou, *Zhongguo xiandai sixiangshi lun* (Discourse on modern Chinese intellectual history) (Beijing: Dongfang chubanshe, 1987), pp. 25–41, esp. pp. 32–34.

found herself in a situation of foreign imperialism requiring salvation, the anti-imperialist task became extraordinarily outstanding, and the patriotic and revolutionary road was taken by generation after generation [of intellectuals]. Also because China was in a military and war situation for such a long time, . . . bourgeois democracy was placed in a secondary position from beginning to end.[18]

Li's *jiuwang*-prevailed-over-*qimeng* thesis captures the sense of urgency that Chinese intellectuals felt about China's crisis. It reflects that school of thought wherein Chinese nationalism is seen as the moving force in new China, stressing the centrality of antiimperialism. It also says something about the constraints of the historical moment in which enlightenment was forced to yield to the demands of national salvation. Many who could not wait to see the crisis resolved abandoned gradualism for radicalism and supported any regime that could move the country forward in the national interest. With the thesis's emphasis on war, revolution, and antiimperialism, we see an explanation, in part, for Republican China's failure to democratize.

The thesis has been influential in some quarters. He Baogang, taking a cue from Li, maintained that "[h]istorically, there was the trap in modern China: when the nation was in danger, the philosophy of the enlightenment was set aside."[19] Lincoln Li believed that "Nationalism, not democracy, remained the motivating force behind intellectual debates, student movements, and political reforms [in the Nationalist period]."[20] More recently, Marina Svensson asserted: "During the war [against Japan] national survival was the main concern, and questions of democracy and constitutionalism more or less faded into the background."[21] And Y. C. Wang has long argued that concern for China's survival in a world of imperialism had its antidemocratic potential, which added to the intellectuals' tendency to support statism.

---

[18] Li Zehou, "Ershi shiji chu Zhongguo gemingpai sixiang lungang" (An outline of Chinese revolutionary thought in the early twentieth century), in Li Zehou, *Li Zehou ji* (The collected works of Li Zehou) (Haerbin: Heilongjiang jiaoyu chubanshe, 1988), p. 205.

[19] He Baogang, *The Democratization of China* (London: Routledge, 1996), p. 89.

[20] Lincoln Li, *Student Nationalism in China, 1924–1949* (Albany: State University of New York Press, 1994), p. 145.

[21] Marina Svensson, "The Chinese Conception of Human Rights: The Debate on Human Rights in China, 1898–1949," unpublished Ph.D. dissertation, Lund University, 1996, p. 263.

Nationalism was pitted against individualism and, as a result, took precedence over it.[22]

No doubt there was tension between *jiuwang* and *qimeng*, and Li Zehou is correct in stating that the latter was overshadowed by the former and that ultimately *qimeng* lost out. But his thesis has some weaknesses and needs modification. For a start, his working definition of *jiuwang* emphasized the centrality of war and revolution to the neglect of other alternatives. Although he recognized both the internal and external dimensions of *jiuwang*, his main concern was the Chinese communist revolution. Thus, he acknowledged the role of violence in national salvation, stressing the protracted military situation in which there was little room for enlightenment. His definition of *qimeng* also was narrow, referring to individual liberation and dignity, personal freedoms, civil liberties, and many other things subsumed within liberalism in the classical sense. He distinguished between a political movement, *jiuwang*, and an intellectual movement, *qimeng*, failing to see that *qimeng* was also political in that many enlightenment intellectuals, contrary to popular belief, did not shun the politics of involvement. Not only were they ardent defenders of basic rights, but many were politically engaged as well, interested in a reordering of the political system in order to expand the scope for elite participation. Li's conception of *qimeng* ignored the persistent demand by government critics for political reform and *kaifang zhengquan*, an opening up of the regime. His thesis fails to link national salvation with institutional change, presupposing the incompatibility of *jiuwang* and *qimeng* and thereby overstating the dichotomy. As we shall see, critics argued that it was possible to recognize rights and to implement political reform even in times of national crisis and that an external war was no excuse for the state to trample upon human rights. The thesis assumes that the tension between *jiuwang* and *qimeng* was resolved simply by subordinating the aspirations of one side to the dictates of the other. It also assumes that enlightenment intellectuals were prepared to set aside their liberal and democratic aspirations for the sake of war and revolution. Both assumptions lack empirical foundations.

Two further points should be made here. First, since 1919, liberalism and democracy remained a part of the intellectual marketplace of ideas.

---

[22] Y. C. Wang observes that Chinese intellectuals had a tendency to support "statism," that is, a strong state to which the individual was subordinate. See his *Chinese Intellectuals and the West 1872–1949* (Chapel Hill: University of North Carolina Press, 1966), pp. 360–361.

In fact, both May Fourth veterans and activists of a younger generation held that China needed not only a strong state and Western science and technology but also a new form of government that was constitutional, representative, and responsible, in order to survive in a hostile international environment. For them, constitutional democracy was a means of nation building, ultimately achieving national wealth and power. No one favored a weak state. Nevertheless, a strong state could not be defined by a dictatorial regime that recognized no rights and civil liberties.

Second, the vocabulary of antiimperialism is so deeply colored by twentieth-century Chinese political concerns that it gets in the way of the search for a more accurate, credible reading of the liberal intellectual experience. To be sure, antiimperialism was a fact of life in China in the 1930s and 1940s and a potent force harnessed for political purposes by both the GMD and the CCP, as well as by all other political parties and groups. But *jiuwang* was not an external issue alone. (In fairness to Li Zehou, he never said it was.) That was why the Japanese factor did not divert all attention from domestic issues. Perhaps every thinking Chinese had an antiimperialist, nationalistic impulse, but not everyone was convinced of the need to put aside liberal and democratic values and accept authoritarian rule in the interest of national unity and antiimperialism.

Cherishing liberal and democratic values and demanding political and constitutional reforms were not necessarily incompatible with antiimperialist nationalism and a strong state. The Sino-Japanese War, rather than weakening the democratic forces, actually strengthened them to some extent. For the prodemocracy intellectuals, *qimeng* was concerned more with the democratic reordering of the political system than with cultural criticism, let alone cultural iconoclasm, as had been the case in the May Fourth period.[23] Though *qimeng* was overshadowed by antiimperialism, there was room within Chinese nationalism for loyalty to more than one political party. Because enlightenment did not impede national salvation, the liberal intellectuals tried to reconcile their values. Thus, the prodemocracy movement unfolded amid foreign imperialism, war and revolution, lasting nearly two decades before the Communists came to power. It was more significant than has been thought.

---

[23] In her book, *The Chinese Enlightenment*, Schwarcz has concentrated on the cultural aspect of *qimeng*, that is, the critical evaluation of traditional ethics and the cultural iconoclasm of the May Fourth era. In my present study, I am more interested in the democratic aspect of *qimeng*, that is, the priority of political reform of which May Fourth intellectuals had been suspicious.

The movement was directed, first and foremost, against one-party dictatorship and political repression. Democracy, alongside liberalism, became an ideology of opposition, demanding human rights, political pluralism, representative institutions, and constitutionalism. Civil opposition proceeded from the premise that a government should be empowered constitutionally and should act only within the bounds of well-defined legal procedures, with a commitment to a rule of law and the extension and protection of civil rights. It viewed liberalism not only as a philosophy of government and public life but also as a style of political criticism directed against any authoritarian regime. As a political weapon, democracy was used by "outsiders" to oppose the government, as well as by "insiders" agitating for political liberalization within the ruling party.

Second, the movement was nationalistic and antiimperialist, aimed at increasing China's capacity to fight Japanese aggression following the Manchurian crisis in the fall of 1931. It attacked the government's weak-kneed policy toward Japan, demanding armed resistance by forming a broad united front of all the political parties and groups and patriotic elements. From the opposition's point of view, there were no contradictions between struggle for democracy and armed resistance because democracy was conflated with nationalism.

Third, the movement represented a kind of middle politics seeking to steer a course between the two major parties and to serve as a bridge between them. Opposed to civil war, middle politics, or the third force, played a dual role as an agent of democratic change and a mediator.

It was, however, neither a populist nor a social movement. Although not indifferent to social issues, Chinese liberals were, as Jerome Grieder pointed out, "on the whole unsympathetic to a strategy of social change based on the idea of fundamental class antagonisms and conflict, choosing instead to emphasize qualities of individual character they assumed to be universal."[24] They were elitist and urban-based, devoid of the populism, revolutionary socialism, and militancy that characterized the Chinese communist movement.

Chinese intellectuals of the 1930s and 1940s were a differentiated class, far more diffuse than the handful of Beijing intellectuals who had risen to prominence in the late teens. They evinced varying degrees of

---

[24] Jerome B. Grieder, *Intellectuals and the State in Modern China* (New York: The Free Press, 1981), p. 283.

political activism and engagement. For analytical purposes, a typology may be offered as follows:

1. The elite of the major parties who belonged to, or were closely associated with, either the GMD (the governing elite) or the CCP (the adversarial elite).
2. The elite of the minor parties and groups (MPGs), who were interested in participating in the government under a multiparty system, either as loyal opposition or as a junior partner in a coalition regime. They were the principal prodemocracy activists.
3. The independent participatory elite who had no party or group affiliations (*wudang wupai*), that is, the nonpartisans or independents, "eminent persons of the community" (*shehui xianda*), from different walks of life. Some of them participated in the wartime People's Political Council (*Guomin canzhenghui*) and the postwar Political Consultative Conference (*Zhengzhi xieshang huiyi*). Some were progovernment, others were critics, but all were interested in political participation as independents.
4. The independent nonparticipatory elite who disclaimed political ambitions, contenting themselves as "impartial and disinterested critics." They were uncommitted in the sense that they did not ipso facto support one party or the other, depending on the issues. But they believed in a set of norms governing the transaction of public business, as well as a set of values, beliefs, and ideas that they reaffirmed from time to time. Principled, self-indulgent, and self-assured, they were concerned scholars, not political activists.

We are here concerned with the elites in the last three categories who have hitherto received relatively little scholarly treatment because of the traditional two-party paradigm into which the political studies of China from 1929 to 1949 have been cast. That paradigm emphasizes the "big picture" as it were – the power struggle between the GMD and the CCP – ignoring the third force and middle politics. The power struggle has been seen as a conflict between two competing ideologies, or between two equally authoritarian regimes. It was not until the early 1990s that the MPGs, the nonpartisans, and the issues of constitutionalism and democracy associated with them, emerged as a new area of historical research.[25] We will here redress this methodological bias by replacing the binary paradigm with a trinary framework taking into account the third force. We will study the thoughts and actions of those lesser-known

---

[25] See Roger B. Jeans, ed., *Roads Not Taken: The Struggle of Opposition Parties in Twentieth-Century China* (Boulder: Westview Press, 1992); Edmund S. K. Fung, "Recent Scholarship on the Minor Parties and Groups in Nationalist China," *Modern China* 20:4 (October 1994): 478–508.

figures – Hu Shi, who figured prominently in raising the human rights issue in 1929 and in defending democracy in 1934–1935, is a notable exception – who have been previously regarded as being outside mainstream Chinese politics.

They were primarily liberal intellectuals, returned students from the United States and Europe (some from Japan), many of whom became professors at universities and colleges. They included some of modern China's best minds and formed part of what Grieder calls "a conspicuous minority which was sufficiently perceptive and pensive to be aware of the push of change and the tug of tradition, and sufficiently well-educated and self-confident to hold and express opinions about the circumstances in which it found itself."[26] Anglo-American thought had a considerable influence on them. Others were schoolteachers, newspaper editors, publishers, writers, poets, artists, and the like. Still others were lawyers, engineers, and civil servants (some retired) in a variety of fields, including banking, trade and finance, transportation, and communications. The vast majority were on meager incomes, having no access to the country's financial and economic resources, as well as lacking political power and military muscle. Facing political repression, some were forced to seek asylum in warlord territory outside the jurisdiction of the GMD. By and large, they were remote from the peasantry and the laboring classes.

With the possible exception of the Third Party (*Disandang*), the MPGs were reformers, not revolutionaries. They were loyal critics in the tradition of imperial remonstrance (the duty of the scholar-officials to impeach corrupt officials and to speak out against injustices at any personal costs), but they distinguished themselves from the imperial scholars by their modern aspirations and opposition to the authoritarian system of government. They used different language and vocabularies, professing to represent public opinion. Until the 1940s, they were anti-communist on the grounds that communism was unsuited to China and that the CCP was violent and equally undemocratic, if not more so. Around 1947, more people began to feel as alienated from the government as did the independent, nonparticipatory elite who favored political reform.

The opposition elite here represents a new generation of Chinese liberal intellectuals who distinguished themselves by their political activism and cultural adaptability from the statism-oriented earliest

[26] Grieder, *Intellectuals and the State*, p. x.

12

transmitters of liberal thought to China (notably Yan Fu and Liang Qichao of the late Qing/early Republican period) and the cultural iconoclasts of the May Fourth era.[27] By and large, and with some exceptions, they were at ease culturally with the juxtaposition of East and West. Not only did they find Western liberal and democratic thought relevant to China, but they also saw compatibility between Western and Chinese values. Not torn intellectually between the East–West dichotomy, they were convinced of the possibility of "harmonization" to create a synthesis or syncretism suited to Chinese conditions and traditions. They did not rush to emulate Western models uncritically, nor did they blame Chinese culture per se for the lack of democracy in China. Instead, they blamed it on politics – the politics of one-party rule, of personal dictatorship, and of civil strife – the logic of their thinking being that a politics of democratization could be produced by changing the political system and the "rules of the game."

It is often said that Chinese democrats did not really understand democracy and that democracy was not suited to China. The late Lloyd Eastman, for one, observed that Chinese democrats of the Nanjing period "sometimes revealed a remarkably unsophisticated understanding of the true character of liberal democracy,"[28] that their "opposition to dictatorship stemmed ... from discontent with the Kuomintang [GMD] rather than from deep convictions in democratic values,"[29] and that "most Chinese, politicians and intellectuals alike, were weakly committed to the content of democracy, to the core values of liberalism."[30] He felt strongly that:

> Because of the nature of Chinese society and of its political traditions, *it is perhaps one of China's tragedies during the twentieth century that, in the quest for a viable political system, attempts had been made to erect democratic institutions* [emphasis added]. In a profound sense, Anglo-American democracy was not suited to China. This, I think, is not a value judgment. Democracy is still evolving, and neither its permanence nor ultimate preferability to other

---

[27] In making this point, I have benefited from Frederic J. Spar's study of Luo Longji. See his unpublished Ph.D. dissertation, "Liberal Political Opposition in Kuomintang and Communist China: Lo Lung-chi in Chinese Politics, 1928–1958," Brown University, 1980. In 1993, Spar revised his dissertation with a view to publication, giving it a new title "Human Rights and Political Activism: Luo Longji in Chinese Politics, 1926–1958."

[28] Eastman, *The Abortive Revolution*, p. 152.   [29] Ibid., p. 153.   [30] Ibid., p. 178.

systems of governance is yet assured, even in the countries of the West where it has developed. In China, an authoritarian system of rule is perhaps better able to produce the "greatest happiness of the greatest number."[31]

Following the lead of Eastman, most scholars in the West have held that during the Nationalist period democratic forces were underdeveloped and politically peripheral.

Eastman used Anglo-American democracy to judge China's democrats, a criterion that tends to dismiss all those who do not measure up to an idealized standard of values and institutions appropriate for democracy as undemocratic or not really democratic. The problem with this assessment is that it presupposes a universally accepted meaning, or precise definition, of democracy, as well as assuming that the best form of democracy for the world is liberal democracy, Anglo-American style. But that is a fallacy. Like nationalism, democracy is a protean term that has been analyzed by many Western theorists and thinkers. It has acquired many meanings and remarkably strong emotive overtones and is used in a bewildering variety of contexts. Liberal democracy has many apparent shortcomings both in theory and practice, as some Western scholars have pointed out.[32] Moreover, there are different types and models of democracy,[33] and it is possible to espouse democracy from conservative, elitist, corporatist, participatory, and paternalistic points of view, as well as from the perspective of socialism.

David Held has cautioned against treating the liberal component of liberal democracy simply as a unity. Different liberal traditions embody different conceptions of the individual, of rights and duties, and of the proper nature and form of community. Further, he has pointed out

---

[31] Ibid., pp. 179–180.

[32] See, in particular, the radical critique by the non-Marxist theorist, C. B. Macpherson, in his *The Real World of Democracy* (Oxford: Clarendon Press, 1966); *Democratic Theory: Essays in Retrieval* (Oxford: Clarendon Press, 1973); and *The Life and Times of Liberal Democracy* (New York: Oxford University Press, 1977). See also Andrew Levine, *Liberal Democracy: A Critique of Its Theory* (New York: Columbia University Press, 1981).

[33] C. B. Macpherson has written on four models, namely, protective democracy, developmental democracy, equilibrium democracy, and participatory democracy. See his *The Life and Times of Liberal Democracy*. More recently, David Held has dealt with three models: direct or participatory democracy; liberal or representative democracy; and one-party democracy. See his *Models of Democracy* (Stanford: Stanford University Press, 1987). For other variants of democracy, see also Graeme Duncan, ed., *Democratic Theory and Practice* (Cambridge: Cambridge University Press, 1983).

that the "celebratory" view of liberal democracy neglects the tensions between the "liberal" and the "democratic" components of liberal democracy. For example, the liberal preoccupation with individual rights or "frontiers of freedom" that "nobody should be permitted to cross" opposes the democratic concern for the regulation of individual and collective action. "An uncritical affirmation of liberal democracy," Held warns, "essentially leaves unanalyzed the whole meaning of democracy and its possible variants."[34]

Liberal democracy is paradoxical, and the relationship between liberalism and democracy is a profoundly ambiguous one. As David Beetham argues, liberalism has provided both a foundation for modern democracy and a constraint upon it in the modern world.[35] Bhikhu Parekh agrees. "Although in liberal democracy liberalism is the dominant partner, democracy, which has its own independent tradition and internal logic, has from time to time revolted against the liberal constraints."[36] Writing theoretically and also referring to India, Parekh argues that liberal democracy is specific to a particular cultural context and that any claims to universal validity made on its behalf ought not to be accepted uncritically. But he is not defending cultural relativism. He is only concerned with ways of reconciling the claims of cultural diversity with those of universalism in political thought. Because liberal democracy defines democracy within the limits of liberalism and represents only one way of combining them, Parekh sees no obvious reason why they cannot be combined in another way. He suggests that a political system might be democratically liberal rather than a liberal democracy, making democracy the dominant partner and defining liberalism within its limits. Political accountability can be sustained and defended without liberal democratic presuppositions.[37] His views are pertinent here because they are in line with the thinking of Chinese democrats who desired a variant of democracy combining liberalism nicely with democracy and Chinese cultural values.

---

[34] David Held, "Democracy: From City-states to a Cosmopolitan Order?" in David Held, ed., *Prospects for Democracy: North, South, East, West* (Cambridge: Polity Press, 1993), pp. 13–14. The quote is on p. 14.

[35] David Beetham has examined this duality and reassessed what limits liberalism might place on democracy and what limits democracy should place on liberal ambitions. See David Beetham, "Liberal Democracy and the Limits of Democratization," in Held, ed., *Prospects for Democracy*, pp. 55–73.

[36] Bhikhu Parekh, "The Cultural Particularity of Liberal Democracy," in Held, ed., *Prospects for Democracy*, p. 165.

[37] Ibid., pp. 156–175.

The relationship between liberalism and democracy is generally rendered as a nexus between liberty and equality. "Democracy is concerned with social cohesion and distributive evenness," writes Giovanni Sartori, "liberalism esteems prominence and spontaneity. Equality desires to integrate and attune, liberty is self-assertive and troublesome. . . . But perhaps the fundamental difference is that liberalism pivots on the individual, and democracy on society."[38] From that perspective, China's modern thinkers, drawing on the cultural resources of both Chinese and Western thought, were more inclined toward democracy, taking a greater interest in the insertion of popular power into the state than in the technique of limiting the state's power. They wanted to resolve the conundrum of how to combine the degree of individual initiative necessary for progress with the degree of social cohesion necessary for China's survival as a nation-state.

Although they were impressed with the Anglo-American system of government, Chinese democrats were not keen to embrace it without significant modifications. To the extent that they critiqued it, they would have agreed with Eastman that Anglo-American democracy was unsuited to China. But instead of accepting an authoritarian system of rule, as Eastman would have it, they wanted to adapt the Anglo-American model to China's conditions in the hope that a superior, distinctively Chinese system would evolve in the process. The question here, therefore, is not whether they understood "the true character of liberal democracy" but how they understood democracy generally.

What we are looking at in this book are, in the main, China's "liberal democrats," as distinct from the Marxist, socialist, and anarchist intellectuals of an earlier period. They were concerned first with *political* democracy, with a belief in popular sovereignty, constitutionalism, responsible government, competitive politics (but not excluding multiparty cooperation and coalition government), elite participation, thought liberation, and freedoms of the person, speech, publication, association, and assembly, all of which meet Joseph Schumpeter's minimalist criteria of political pluralism. According to Schumpeter, "democracy is a political *method*, that is to say, a certain type of institutional arrangement for arriving at political – legislative and administrative – decisions and hence incapable of being an end in itself, irrespective of what decisions it will

---

[38] Giovanni Sartori, *The Theory of Democracy Revisited* (Chatham: Chatham House, 1987), p. 384.

produce under given historical conditions."[39] The democratic method "is that institutional arrangement for arriving at political decisions in which individuals acquire the power to decide by means of a competitive struggle for the people's vote."[40]

Schumpeter's theory of democracy is compatible with a certain kind of elitism. Turning the traditional theory of democracy upside down, Schumpeter argued that a democratic system was not characterized by the translation of the "will of the people" into government action but by competing parties offering alternative policies and programs to the electorate who had little direct influence over those policies and programs. The people, or voters, were in fact limited to choosing and authorizing a government periodically. However, the difference between democratic and undemocratic regimes was nothing so pretentious as "government by the people" but rather the fact that, in a democracy, political competition existed and provided some minimal degree of accountability. A democratic regime also guaranteed some basic freedoms because political competition required the freedom to form associations and to propagate ideas.[41] Schumpeter distinguished between democracy as procedure and as result, between majority rule via popular elections and a society marked by equality and liberty.

As Andrew Nathan has suggested, Chinese democracy is best understood within a Schumpeterian framework,[42] which emphasizes free competition for the people's vote (but not necessarily universal suffrage), freedoms of speech and publication, the right to organize politically, accountability of the government, and mechanisms for the peaceful transfer of power. Defining democracy as a political method, or process, does not necessarily entail dealing with the problems of equal rights and of widening political participation. As a political method, its accent is on pluralism and peaceful means of conflict resolution without precluding the possibility of coalition government. Chinese liberal intellectuals were not interested in mass participation in the communist style, nor in the kind of broad participation on which Carole Pateman has written.[43] They

---

[39] Joseph Schumpeter, *Capitalism, Socialism and Democracy*, 3rd ed. (New York: Harper & Row, 1962), p. 242.

[40] Ibid., p. 269.

[41] Norman P. Barry, *An Introduction to Modern Political Theory*, 3rd ed. (London: Macmillan, 1995), p. 279.

[42] Nathan, *Chinese Democracy*, p. 226.

[43] Carole Pateman, *Participation and Democratic Theory* (Cambridge: Cambridge University Press, 1970).

were interested in a form of elite rule, resembling Max Weber's "bureaucracy,"[44] Robert Michels's "oligarchy,"[45] and Robert Dahl's "polyarchy."[46] For them, the best form of democracy was that found in elite consensus underpinned by a public philosophy.[47] Whereas Schumpeter's and Dahl's concerns were the illiberal and antidemocratic tendencies of the ordinary citizens and the possibility of participation-induced totalitarianism,[48] that of Chinese thinkers was the general ignorance of the masses.[49] The Chinese elite could easily defend democratic elitism, just as many Western thinkers defended it after the Second World War.

But a caveat must be entered for those who use the Schumpeterian framework for the study of Chinese democracy. Schumpeter was an economist for whom democracy is simply a market mechanism: the voters are the consumers, the politicians, the entrepreneurs. Because the market was used to explain the political behavior of the voters and the politicians alike, Schumpeterian democracy did not envision a kind of society with a set of moral ends.[50] By contrast, Chinese democracy, as we shall see, was as moralistic as it was elitist. Chinese intellectuals of the Nationalist period held a dim view of capitalism and would have little regard for politicians who operated on morally neutral ground.

One could be cynical about the political opportunism and ulterior motives of both the "outsiders" and "insiders" who attacked the Nationalist dictatorship under the banner of democracy. Indeed, many self-proclaimed democrats, motivated by self-interests, were, as the Chinese

---

[44] See Max Weber, "Bureaucracy," in *Max Weber: Essays in Sociology*, H. H. Gerth and C. Wright Mills, eds. and trans. (New York: Oxford University Press, 1964), part 2, ch. 8.

[45] See Robert Michels, *A Sociological Study of the Oligarchical Tendencies of Modern Democracies* (New York: Collier Books, 1962), pp. 364–371.

[46] Robert A. Dahl, *Preface to Democratic Theory* (Chicago: University of Chicago Press, 1963), p. 86; also Dahl, *Who Governs?* (New Haven: Yale University Press, 1961), pp. 85–86, 223–228, 315–325.

[47] Peter Zarrow has defined public philosophy as "an underlying consensus of values and goals." See his *Historical Perspectives on Public Philosophy in Modern China* (New York: Carnegie Council on Ethics and International Affairs monograph, 1997).

[48] Giovanni Sartori, *Democratic Theory* (New York: Praeger, 1967), pp. 72–95, esp. pp. 77–79.

[49] If Chinese elites exhibited a fear of the masses, they were not alone. Many liberals in the West felt the same. J. S. Mill, for one, believed that educated people should have more power than the uneducated and that an educated person should have several votes, an uneducated person, one only. See his "On Liberty," in Edwin A. Burtt, ed., *The English Philosophers from Bacon to Mill* (New York: The Modern Library, 1939), p. 956.

[50] Macpherson, *The Life and Times of Liberal Democracy*, p. 78.

saying goes, "selling dog's meat while hanging up a sheep's head" (*gua yangtou mai gourou*). But even if democracy were used as no more than a political weapon, good results could still be produced. As Sartori points out, democracy has often initially gained ground as an "oppositional ideal . . . a polemical notion whose function is to oppose, not to propose. The utterance of 'democracy' is a way of saying no to inequality, injustice, and coercion."[51]

The beginning of civil opposition was the utterance of democracy in terms of saying no to the GMD party-state and to the injustice, coercion, and political repression of the day. A commitment to the core values of liberalism – individualism and political equality – was desirable but not a precondition, let alone an absolute one. Let us not forget that democracy, defined as majority rule or government by popularly elected representatives, is not the same thing as liberty and may clash with it.[52] In the early nineteenth century, democracy was commonly seen as an enemy of liberty. It was once almost axiomatic that the two things are irreconcilably opposed. The evolution of democracy in Victorian England demonstrated that one could be a strong believer in constitutional democracy, like Walter Bagehot, without having to believe in political equality or social equity or to trust the masses. As Edward Friedman has observed, "the liberal West is not the fruit of long historical roots in a universalistic soil of free independent individualists."[53] "Democratic cultural commitments at the individual level tend to follow after the creation of a democratic polity."[54] Many democratic states were far from democratic in the beginning, and most political systems exhibit large gaps between theory and practice. For China, the important thing was to begin a process, that is, to make a democratic breakthrough and then consolidate it by building on democratic institutions gradually. Generating a democratic breakthrough was difficult, consolidating it was not easy either. But small steps had to be taken first. Each stage of the process,

---

[51] Giovanni Sartori, "Democracy," in *International Encyclopedia of the Social Sciences* (New York: Crowell Collier and Macmillan, 1968), p. 116.

[52] There was a whole library of nineteenth-century writings, led by W. E. H. Lecky's historical analysis *Democracy and Liberty* (1896), arguing for the eternal opposition between them. John Locke, often called the father of modern liberalism, stressed personal liberty and individual rights but did not favor democracy. Jean-Jacques Rousseau, often called the father of modern democracy, was no liberal.

[53] Edward Friedman, "Democratization: Generalizing the East Asian Experience," in Edward Friedman, ed., *The Politics of Democratization: Generalizing East Asian Experiences* (Boulder: Westview Press, 1994), p. 29.

[54] Ibid., p. 31.

for all its imperfections, should be seen as an improvement and appreciated for what it had accomplished. Democracy in China, as elsewhere, would be an incremental process.

The year 1929 has been chosen as the starting point for this book because it marked, approximately, the beginning of the prodemocracy movement rather than just an intellectual exegesis. For analytical purposes, the movement may be divided into four phases. The first, from 1929 to 1937, was a phase of thought articulation and was largely unorganized. It saw the raising of the human rights issue in 1929 by a handful of liberal intellectuals who set the opposition agenda. As the Manchurian crisis came to a head, this phase also witnessed the government's response to the Japanese threat by convening a National Emergency Conference in 1932. Even though patriotic elements demanded armed resistance, the democracy versus dictatorship debate of 1933–1935 sustained the momentum of the political discourse.

The second phase (1937–1940) saw more political action and limited cooperation between the government and the opposition parties. It witnessed also the opening of the People's Political Council, a wartime advisory body designed to bring together representatives of all the political parties and groups plus the "eminent persons from the community" to deal with the critical questions of war and reconstruction.

The third phase (1941–1946) was underscored by a third force movement, both within and outside the People's Political Council, featuring the Chinese Democratic League (*Zhongguo minzhu tongmeng*), which played a mediating role in resolving major party differences while pushing for constitutional rule. The opening of the Political Consultative Conference early in 1946 was a last attempt to resolve the problems of China by political means. From the outset, it may be noted, there was already a sense of fellowship – of democratic comrades of a sort – when the GMD became a nationwide target that could be held up to the standards of its own promises.

The fourth and last phase, from 1947 to 1949, marked the last stand of Chinese liberalism. Chinese democracy, hardly given a chance, was dead before the country plunged into all-out civil war. But a liberal forum, made up largely of the independent nonparticipatory elite, existed until the last year of the Nationalist rule, singing the swan song of liberalism as they faced a choice between the Nationalist Scylla and the Communist Charybdis. Alienated by the government, many supported the CCP under the banner of New Democracy.

This book will explore four sets of questions. The first set concerns the Chinese conceptions of democracy. What did democracy mean to them? What sort of democracy did they want? To answer these questions, we will study their thoughts and how their thinking was influenced by the internal and external circumstances in which they found themselves.

The second set of questions relates to the practicability of democracy in China in the 1930s and 1940s. Was democracy desirable during what the Chinese called a "national emergency" and amid a "crisis of democracy" in Italy, Germany, Spain, and Japan? Was democracy feasible in the war time when fighting the Japanese was a top priority and where elections could not be held? If not, what sort of a political system would be best suited to Chinese conditions? Was constitutional rule possible pending the adoption and promulgation of a constitution? To answer these questions, we will look at China's wartime democratic thought as well as the People's Political Council on which the opposition parties were represented.

The third set of questions concerns the third force movement. The middle-of-the-road intellectuals, standing between the government and the CCP, saw themselves as a mediator, peacemaker, and bridge. Without political and military muscles, was there any scope for a third force in Chinese politics? As political power grew out of the barrel of a gun – a Mao Zedong dictum with which Chiang Kai-shek could not have agreed more – what could a third force do to stop the civil war and advance the cause of democracy? If the cause was doomed to failure from the start, did it mean that the third force had no significance at all? To answer these questions, we will probe the meaning of a third force, study its role and place in Chinese politics, and consider its historical significance.

Finally, there is the question of why a democratic breakthrough did not take place. Why modern China failed to achieve a transition from authoritarianism to democracy is an oft-asked question. Many would blame it on the country's socioeconomic backwardness. Applying his theory of the social origins of dictatorship and democracy, Barrington Moore, Jr., has attributed Chinese dictatorship to the weaknesses of the bourgeoisie and the absence of a strong industrial base.[55] Lucian Pye, Richard Solomon, and Lloyd Eastman have blamed it on Chinese political culture, stressing the authoritarian family and state, the dependency relationship, and all the antidemocratic elements deeply rooted in

[55] Barrington Moore, Jr., *Social Origins of Dictatorship and Democracy* (Boston: Beacon Press, 1966), pp. 174–180, 187–189, 195–197.

Chinese tradition.[56] And Samuel Huntington, satisfied with cultural explanations, sees a correlation between Confucianism and authoritarianism, as well as a correlation between Puritanism and democracy.[57]

Evidence supporting the contention that the Confucian tradition is unfavorable to democracy is not lacking. The emphasis on authority, hierarchy, harmony, order, and stability is no doubt unhelpful to political modernization. However, critics of cultural explanations have argued that culture is not static, but open-ended, fluid, negotiable, and capable of transaction.[58] Some have drawn attention to early Confucianism's opposition to despotism[59] as well as to the existence of a number of pro-toliberal, protomodern, and protodemocratic values in the Chinese tradition – including the individual's moral autonomy, Mencius's *minben* thought (the primacy of the people, the thought that the just ruler and benevolent king must care for the welfare of the people),[60] opposition to despotism, the tradition of imperial remonstrance, and the literati's sense of responsibility for the fate of the country – values that, as Andrew Nathan says, "could conceivably serve as some of the building blocks of a Chinese democratic political culture."[61] Wm. Theodore de Bary has

[56] See, for example, Lucian W. Pye, *The Spirit of Chinese Politics. A Psychocultural Study of the Authority Crisis in Political Development* (Cambridge, MA: M.I.T. Press, 1968). Writing on the tragedy of Tiananmen in 1990, Pye commented: "The Chinese style of politics has again obstructed progress, and all the great hopes of the Beijing Spring have turned to despair." See his "Tiananmen and Chinese Political Culture: The Escalation of Confrontation," in George Hicks, ed., *The Broken Mirror: China After Tiananmen* (Harlow: Longman, 1990), p. 179; Richard Solomon, *Mao's Revolution and the Chinese Political Culture* (Berkeley: University of California Press, 1971), esp. ch. 9; Lloyd Eastman, *The Abortive Revolution*, ch. 7.

[57] Samuel P. Huntington, *The Third Wave: Democratization in the Late Twentieth Century* (Normal: University of Oklahoma Press, 1991). He believes that Western Christian influence has assisted democratization in the Philippines and Korea in recent times.

[58] For a critique of the political culture paradigm, see, for example, He Baogang, "A Methodological Critique of Lucian Pye's Approach to Political Culture," *Issues and Studies* 28:3 (March 1992): 92–113.

[59] Vitaly A. Rubin, *Individual and State in Ancient China: Essays on Four Chinese Philosophers*, Steven I. Levine, trans. (New York: Columbia University Press, 1976), pp. 27–28.

[60] For a historical study of the *minben* thought, see Jin Yaoji, *Zhongguo minben sixiangshi* (A history of the Chinese primacy-of-the-people thought) (Taibei: Taiwan Shangwu yinshuguan, 1993).

[61] These values include such ideals as the moral autonomy of the individual, the benevolence of the ruler, the responsibility of the literati to protest injustices at any personal costs, the responsibility of the government to care for the well-being of the people, and the people's responsibility for the fate of the country. See Andrew J. Nathan, "The Place of Values in Cross-Cultural Studies: The Example of Democracy in China," in Cohen and Goldman, eds., *Ideas Across Cultures*, p. 308. See also Thomas A. Metzger, *Escape from Predicament* (New York: Columbia University Press, 1977); Roger Des Forges,

gone too far in suggesting that there was a liberal tradition in late imperial China;[62] nevertheless, the question remains as to whether the authoritarianism or dependency of the Confucian tradition necessarily impeded democratization. Ramon Myers and Thomas Metzger are of the view that "the humanistic values of Confucianism should not be lumped together with those traditional institutional patterns admittedly blocking modernization."[63] Edward Friedman and others, referring to the increasingly institutionalized democracy in Korea, Taiwan, and Japan in recent decades, have challenged the traditional wisdom that Confucian political culture blocks democratization.[64] Historically, Confucian China, however hierarchical and authoritarian, was not inherently incapable of democratization; there was no reason why it should be trapped in history ad infinitum.[65]

Yet few would question the close nexus between culture and power in Chinese state institutions.[66] Politics and culture were inseparable in twentieth-century China, and we cannot ignore the political culture paradigm altogether. That paradigm can be modified. For my purpose here, two traditions of political culture in Republican China could be discerned. One was the mainstream authoritarian tradition, a legacy of the Confucian heritage and represented by leaders of the GMD and the CCP. The other was a minor liberal tradition of recent vintage represented by the liberal intellectuals whose contribution was to juxtapose their cultural vision against the less attractive culture of the major parties. Tang Tsou has written about Chinese politics being dominated throughout the twentieth century by the political game of "win all or lose all" (*quanying quanshu*), or "winner takes all." The rules of the game

---

"Democracy in Chinese History," in Des Forges et al., eds., *Chinese Democracy and the Crisis of 1989*, pp. 21–52; Merle Goldman, "Human Rights in the People's Republic of China." *Daedalus* 112:4 (Fall 1983): 111–112.

[62] Wm. Theodore de Bary, *The Liberal Tradition in China* (Hong Kong: Chinese University Press, 1983).

[63] Ramon H. Myers and Thomas A. Metzger, "Sinological Shadows: The State of Modern China Studies in the US," *Australian Journal of Chinese Affairs* 4 (1980): 5.

[64] Friedman, ed., *The Politics of Democratization,* Introduction and ch. 1.

[65] This is not to say that the Chinese cultural heritage did not create difficulties for political modernization. For a scholarly discussion of the familiar problems of continuity and discontinuity in modern Chinese history, see Thomas A. Metzger, "Continuities between Modern and Premodern China: Some Neglected Methodological and Substantive Issues," in Cohen and Goldman, eds., *Ideas Across Cultures*, pp. 263–292.

[66] This nexus is well demonstrated by Prasenjit Duara's empirical study of rural north China in *Culture, Power, and the State: Rural China, 1900–1942* (Stanford: Stanford University Press, 1988).

were that key political players showed no tendency to reach a compromise unless and until one side felt strongly enough that they could not win all or lose all. The pattern is that "a prolonged process of repeated negotiation and bargaining leading to a strategic compromise is possible only if there is a stalemate and only if there is a common perception that neither side can inflict a quick and total defeat on the other."[67] This pattern could be seen also in the conflict between the Nationalists and the Communists before 1949, which saw the escalation of a limited civil war to an all-out civil war. Caught between the two authoritarian parties, the liberal intellectuals opposed the dominant cultural tradition. That they failed under the conditions of the Nationalist period – the Chiang Kai-shek dictatorship, the communist insurgency, civil war, the weaknesses of civil opposition, and an illiberal age in the world at large – is not surprising. As a political project, democratization was, moreover, not helped by the constraints of the historical moment, including poverty, ignorance, and, above all, the Japanese invasion. What is significant is that they made an endeavor and, despite their failure, left a significant legacy to intellectuals in the period of the People's Republic.

The win-all-or-lose-all macrohistorical perspective on Chinese politics has one problem, however, namely, a tinge of determinism suggesting a teleological view of history.[68] Thus, Tang Tsou attempts to balance this perspective with a microaction analysis, drawing attention to such systems of ideas as game theory, rational choice theory, individual and/or collective actions and behavior theory, and the theory of the strategy of conflict.[69] The point here is that microactions and strategic decisions could change the macrohistorical pattern. The present study will show that the microactions of the liberal intellectuals were attempts to create mechanisms for negotiation, compromise, and peaceful conflict resolution. Strategic decisions different from those taken by the top National-

---

[67] See Tsou Tang, "The Tiananmen Tragedy: The State–Society Relationship, Choices, and Mechanisms in Historical Perspective," in Brantly Womack, ed., *Contemporary Chinese Politics in Historical Perspective* (New York: Cambridge University Press, 1991), pp. 320–321. This pattern is further explained in Zou Dang (Tang Tsou), *Ershi shiji Zhongguo zhengzhi: cong hongguan lishi yu weiguan xingdong jiaodu kan* (Twentieth-century Chinese politics viewed from the perspective of macro history and micro action) (Hong Kong: Oxford University Press, 1994), pp. 204–265, esp. pp. 260–261.

[68] For a critique of the teleological view of the Chinese revolution, see Myers and Metzger, "Sinological Shadows."

[69] Zou, *Ershi shiji*, pp. 206–222. For a study of the microaction analysis, see Adam Przeworski, *Democracy and the Market: Political and Economic Reforms in Eastern Europe and Latin America* (Cambridge: Cambridge University Press, 1991).

ist leaders before the final showdown with the Communists could have led to different results in terms of a democratic breakthrough.

This book will call into question a number of assumptions about modern China's political and intellectual history: that *qimeng* was set aside in the face of *jiuwang*; that Chinese intellectuals were averse to political engagement, had no stomach for the rough and tumble of political life, and were prepared to support any authoritarian party that offered a decent hope for national fulfillment; that Chinese thinkers were weakly committed to the core values of liberalism with a superficial understanding of Western democratic thought; and that modern China lacked the intellectual foundations for democracy. We will show that there were differing political views as well as common concerns in the intellectual community, that the MPGs and nonpartisans were a significant political and intellectual force, and that, above all, a tradition of liberal opposition was evolving in China's recent past.

Finally, it will be seen that civil opposition in the Nationalist period provides historical parallels and antecedents to the prodemocracy movement of the Deng Xiaoping era. There was no civil war, no foreign imperialism, and no national crisis in the Deng era. But there were common concerns about one-party rule, bad governance, official corruption and graft, a lack of rule of law, the overlapping of party and government, thought control, violations of human rights, and political repression. A reading of the pre-1949 opposition literature reveals some striking similarities with the prodemocracy literature of the post-Mao Zedong era. Fifty years later, the Chinese are still making similar demands, using similar arguments for democracy and almost the same language and repertoire (less the language of antiimperialism). It is hoped that this book will be welcomed also by students of contemporary China and general readers of other cultures interested in democracy and human rights.

1

The Dictatorial Regime

CIVIL OPPOSITION in the Nationalist period is best understood in a dual context: the repression of one-party rule and the imperatives of national salvation. It was the manifestation of a continued quest for democracy and a response to a national crisis brought about by a combination of internal and external problems. This chapter is concerned with the domestic context. It will examine first the dictatorial nature of the Nationalist regime and then Sun Yat-sen's conception of political tutelage, his democratic thought, the legacy of his doctrine, and finally Chiang Kai-shek's personal dictatorship and his constitutional designs that drew much criticism from the opposition elite.

THE NATURE OF THE NANJING REGIME

The GMD came to power in 1928 after completing the Northern Expedition, the success of which was more political than military. The new Nanjing regime, however, was unable to free itself from the influence of the military that had brought it into existence. By 1931, Nanjing controlled less than one-third of China, its writ being restricted to a constellation of provinces in the lower Yangzi River – Zhejiang, Jiangsu, Anhui, and Jiangxi, Henan, Hubei, and Fujian in varying degrees plus the financial center of Shanghai. In the first couple of years, Nanjing had to deal with the regional forces that had proclaimed their nominal allegiance – notably the Guangxi Clique led by Li Zongren, Bai Chongxi, and Li Jisen; Feng Yuxiang in the northwestern region of Gansu, Shaanxi, and Henan; and Yan Xishan in Shanxi.[1] These old warlords, now in

---

[1] James E. Sheridan, *Chinese Warlord: The Career of Feng Yu-hsiang* (Stanford: Stanford University Press, 1966), pp. 14–16.

Nationalist garb, had since been incorporated into the Party ranks. Aligned with one faction or another, they constituted a new but loose opposition within the Party, thus aggravating the factionalism endemic in Nationalist politics. During the years 1929–1931, they backed up the GMD Left led by Wang Jingwei and the Reorganizationists (Gaizupai),[2] who challenged Chiang Kai-shek's leadership.

After 1928, the GMD ceased to be a combat revolutionary party following the purge of the Communists and as it became the ruling party. It had lost its revolutionary élan as Chiang himself stated early in that year: "Now party members no longer strive either for principles or for the masses . . . the revolutionaries have become degenerate, have lost their revolutionary spirit and revolutionary courage."[3] In 1932, Chiang declared flatly, "The Chinese revolution has failed."[4]

Yet Nanjing was the most modern regime China ever had. It boasted a number of well-educated ministers and officials, some with doctorates from American and European universities, who were intelligent, competent, and very promising. From the start, it looked as if the government would be able to advance China in a modern style through gradual reform. But the reality was very different. Even though the Nanjing decade saw remarkable achievements in some respects, the government's overall performance was a source of disappointment to its well-wishers. For the liberal intellectuals, it was all the more disappointing because political reform was never on the agenda.

Lloyd Eastman maintained that the Nanjing regime was "neither totalitarian nor democratic, but lay uncertainly between those points on the political spectrum."[5] It was a "military-authoritarian regime" dominated by Chiang, who wielded ultimate authority "with minimal concern for formal chains of command." In contrast to Sun Yat-sen, who had regarded the GMD as "the ultimate locus of authority and as the trustee of the people's sovereignty during the preconstitutional phases of the revolution," Chiang, Eastman went on, "emasculated the party," turning it into

---

[2] For a detailed study of the GMD Left, see So Wai-chor, *The Kuomintang Left in the National Revolution, 1924–1931* (Hong Kong: Oxford University Press, 1991).

[3] Quoted in Lloyd E. Eastman, *The Abortive Revolution: China under Nationalist Rule, 1927–1937* (Cambridge, MA: Harvard University Press, 1974), pp. 4–5.

[4] Ibid., p. 1.

[5] Lloyd E. Eastman, "Nationalist China during the Nanking Decade, 1927–1937," in Lloyd E. Eastman, Jerome Chen, Suzanne Pepper, and Lyman P. Van Slyke, *The Nationalist Era in China, 1927–1949* (Cambridge: Cambridge University Press, 1991), p. 19.

a personal dictatorship backed by the army.[6] After the suppression of the left wing in 1930, the Party became a totally subservient machine to Chiang, who ruled like a patriarch having little regard for administrative procedures. It "became merely the propagandist, journalist and historian for the regime."[7] In like manner, John Fairbank observed that the Party "was unable to function as a party dictatorship."[8] Whereas Eastman's emphasis was on Chiang's emasculation of the Party, Fairbank's was on the dysfunction of the Party machinery that contributed to Chiang's dictatorship. The failure of the Party enabled Chiang to emasculate it.

Unlike the class-based Chinese communist revolution, the GMD proclaimed a commitment to an all-people revolution (*quanmin geming*), that is, a revolution not for any class or sectional interests, but for the interests of the entire population without class struggle. As Joseph Fewsmith notes, the GMD "did not deny the existence of classes in China, but it did deny the existence of irreconcilable differences between them."[9] The *quanmin geming* rhetoric was designed to counter the communist notion of class struggle and proletarian revolution. In 1927–1928, the GMD had enjoyed the support of the Shanghai business and financial community, but it was not a bourgeois party representing the interests of the commercial bourgeois and the comprador class as the Communists alleged. Parks Coble's study of the Shanghai capitalists has demonstrated that although capitalist interests overlapped with those of the regime, it was the regime that controlled the capitalists, not vice versa.[10] Nor was the GMD an instrument of the landlord class, even though it maintained the landlord system and failed to implement the moderate rent-reduction law enacted in 1934. The regime was made up of a diversity of disparate elements. Fairbank described it as having a dual character – "comparatively modern in urban centers and foreign contact, reactionary in its old-style competition with provincial warlords"; the

---

[6] Ibid., pp. 20–21. Eastman (p. 9) noted that of the members of the GMD's Central Executive Committee, forty-three percent in 1935 were military officers; twenty-five percent of the thirty-three chairmen of provinces controlled by Nationalists during the Nanjing decade were generals.

[7] Ibid., p. 21.

[8] John K. Fairbank, *China: A New History* (Cambridge, MA: The Belknap Press of Harvard University Press, 1992), p. 285.

[9] Joseph Fewsmith, *Party, State, and Local Elites in Republican China: Merchant Organizations and Politics in Shanghai, 1890–1930* (Honolulu: University of Hawaii Press, 1985), p. 93.

[10] Parks M. Coble, *The Shanghai Capitalists and the Nationalist Government, 1927–1937* (Cambridge, MA: Council on East Asian Studies, Harvard University, 1980).

regime existed "to perpetuate its own power, much in the manner of dynastic regimes."[11] Barrington Moore, Jr., proclaiming the social origins of modern political arrangements, observed that the main social basis of the GMD was "a coalition, or perhaps better, a form of antagonistic cooperation between the successors to the gentry and urban commercial, financial, and industrial interests. The Kuomintang [GMD], through its control of the means of violence, served as the link that held the coalition together."[12] The consensus among scholars is that the GMD had no interest in radical social change, in broadening political participation, or in confronting rural problems.

The GMD was authoritarian, not Leninist. Whereas Leninist parties emphasized party unity, iron discipline, organizational control, the party line, one common political center, and the absence of major factions, the GMD was a coalition of diverse and disparate elements and competing interests. Factionalism was endemic. There were two levels of factional politics. One level concerned rivalries at the top for control of the regime's legitimate authority and the organs for the exercise of this authority, notably the Central Executive Committee and Central Political Council. Another level involved groups within Chiang Kai-shek's own power structure competing over policy implementation and for the allocation of scarce resources.[13] At both levels, struggle for power and position, not ideological and policy differences, appeared to be the fundamental cause of factional strife. Instead of trying to stop factional strife, Chiang manipulated it, not averse to seeing the Party factionalized as long as all factional leaders within his own power structure were absolutely loyal to him.[14] Indeed, he thrived on his ability to mediate between divergent sectors and to arbitrate among conflicting interests as he was the sole link between them, the locus of loyalty, and, above all, the indispensable leader. Factionalism strengthened his position, but it had the effects of perpetuating the Party's organizational weakness and reliance on personalized, informal, and particularistic political processes.

[11] Fairbank, *China: A New History*, pp. 288–289.
[12] Barrington Moore, Jr., *Social Origins of Dictatorship and Democracy* (Boston: Beacon Press, 1966), p. 196.
[13] For details of the GMD factions, see Tien Hung-mao, *Government and Politics in Kuomintang China, 1927–1937* (Stanford: Stanford University Press, 1972), pp. 45–72; for an interpretation, see Hung-mao Tien, "Factional Politics in Kuomintang China, 1928–1937: An Interpretation," in Gilbert Chan, ed., *China at the Crossroads: Nationalists and Communists, 1927–1949* (Boulder: Westview Press, 1980), pp. 19–35.
[14] Ch'ien Tuan-sheng, *The Government and Politics of China, 1912–1949* (reprinted from 1950 Harvard University Press edition, Stanford: Stanford University Press, 1970), p. 132.

The regime owed much of its dictatorial tendencies to the legacy of Sun Yat-sen's doctrine and leadership style. To illustrate, let us review his notion of political tutelage and his thought on people's rights.

SUN YAT-SEN'S CONCEPTION OF POLITICAL TUTELAGE

Sun had intended the Nationalist revolution to undergo three phases: first, a phase of military rule during which all warlord regimes would be eliminated and China would be unified by force; second, a phase of political tutelage during which the GMD would prepare the people for constitutionalism; and finally constitutional rule that was supposed to be democratic. The first phase was completed in June 1928 after the warlord, Zhang Zuolin, had been dislodged from Beijing, followed by the second phase of political tutelage.

According to Sun's *Fundamentals of National Reconstruction* (*Jianguo dagang*, 1924), at the start of political tutelage, the government was to send trained and qualified persons to the various counties (*xian*) to assist in the preparation of self-government. The county, not the province, was to be the basic unit of self-rule. Citizens in a completely self-governing county would enjoy the rights of suffrage, recall, initiative, and referendum. In terms of its obligation to the central government, every county was to allocate a certain percentage of its annual revenue to the latter. The percentage was to be determined annually by the people's representatives, but it should not be lower than ten percent or exceed fifty percent of the county's revenues. After the establishment of self-government, every county would elect one delegate to the National Assembly. The stage of constitutional rule would commence in a province when all its counties had attained complete self-government. A governor would be elected. There was to be a balance of power between the center and the periphery, with matters of a national nature and those of a local character being the responsibilities of the central government and the provincial authorities, respectively. When more than one-half of the provinces had achieved local self-government, the National Assembly would be convened to adopt and promulgate a constitution, thus inaugurating constitutional rule. The National Government would be dissolved and a new government elected by the people, thereby accomplishing the task of national reconstruction.[15]

---

[15] Zhongguo Guomindang zhongyang weiyuanhui dangshi weiyuanhui, ed., *Guofu quanji* (The complete works of Sun Yat-sen) (Taibei: Zhongguo Guomindang zhongyang weiyuanhui dangshi weiyuanhui, 1981), I, 751–753.

The notion of political tutelage rested on several assumptions. The first was that, after coming to power, the GMD must continue to lead the Chinese revolution by educating the people in the idea and practice of democracy prior to constitutional rule. Second, constitutional rule must await the completion of local self-government in the provinces, a matter of years. Third, constitutionalism had run ahead of political tutelage in the early Republican period, which, according to the GMD elite, explained why party politics during that time had been an abject failure. Fourth, constitutional and democratic reform must, following the Chinese political tradition, remain the responsibility of the state that determined the pace of change and established the framework for it. These assumptions underscored the GMD's claim to the right to rule, to *dangzhi* – one-party rule. To ensure *dangzhi*, all other political parties and groups outside the GMD were outlawed (*dangwai wudang*), thereby putting the Party above the state (*dang gao yu guo*). Consequently, *dangzhi* became a party dictatorship, which in turn led to Chiang's personal dictatorship. These assumptions are questionable, as we shall see later.

For the moment, let it be noted that there was bound to be a gulf between rhetoric and reality. Political tutelage contained within itself the seeds of power corruption, producing a new self-serving elite that held on to power indefinitely, thereby blocking the transition to constitutionalism. There was a conflict of interest between Party power and central authority on the one hand and democratic rights and local self-government on the other. The moment the people were trained in the exercise of their rights, the authority of the Party at the local level would be undermined, and if the Party was not prepared to surrender its local power as it should, the regime's sincerity and real intentions would be called into question. Political tutelage also begged the question of whether the ruling party was equal to the task of educating and training the people. If the Party was as capable and enlightened as it claimed to be, why, then, was there no political liberalization within itself?

Sun did not state how long the period of political tutelage should last. Perhaps, he did not know himself, nor did anyone else. The leadership, nonetheless, declared at the Third National Party Congress in March 1929 that a six-year period would be in order. It was expected that a constitution would be adopted and promulgated in 1935 by the National Assembly, followed by the election of a new government.

SUN YAT-SEN'S DEMOCRATIC THOUGHT

The origins of Sun's Principle of People's Rights (*minquan zhuyi*) can be traced back to two sources: European Enlightenment and Chinese cultural heritage. One Western scholar wrote in 1937, with a bit of exaggeration, that Sun was "a more assiduous and widely read student of political science than any other world leader of his day except [Woodrow] Wilson."[16] More recently, one Chinese writer has argued that Sun was attracted to the nineteenth-century French notions of liberty, equality, and fraternity. Sun had incorporated the idea of equality into his *minquan* principle, subscribed to Abraham Lincoln's idea of "for the people, of the people, and by the people," equated democracy with people's rights, and upheld the Euro-American system of representative politics and republican system as a model for China.[17] Other scholars have contended that Confucian learning, to which Sun had devoted much attention, had a profound influence on him.[18] Still others have maintained that, on balance, Western liberal thought had been a stronger influence on him than had Chinese traditional thought.[19] The truth is that his doctrine was a curious amalgam of Confucian elements and Western liberal ideas.

That Sun was once impressed with the Western parliamentary system is unquestionable. In 1917, when he wrote the treatise "Primer of Democracy" (*Minquan chubu*), he left no doubt that China should learn the good things of Euro-American representative governments, especially

---

[16] Paul M. A. Linebarger, *Political Doctrines of Sun Yat-sen: An Exposition of the San Min Chu I* (Baltimore: John Hopkins University Press, 1937), p. 6. Linebarger observed (p. 8): "A German Marxian showed Sun to be a forerunner of Bolshevism; an American liberal showed Sun to be a bulwark against Bolshevism. A Chinese classicist demonstrated Sun's reverence for the past; a Jesuit father explained much by Sun's modern and Christian background."

[17] Zhang Lei, "Lun Sun Zhongshan de minquan zhuyi" (On Sun Yat-sen's principle of people's rights), *Lishi yanjiu* 1 (1980), cited in Wei Hongyuan, *Zhongguo jindai lishi de guocheng* (The process of Chinese history in recent times) (Guangzhou: Guangdong renmin chubanshe, 1989), p. 183.

[18] See, for example, Lü Shiqiang, "Lun Sun Zhongshan xiansheng de jicheng Zhongguo daotong yu fayang guangda" (On Sun Yat-sens's inheritance of Chinese traditions and their development), in Huang Wenfa, ed., *Sun Zhongshan sixiang yu dangdai shijie yan-taohui lunwenji* (Essays on Sun Yat-sen's thought and the contemporary world) (Taibei: Taipingyang wenhua jijinhui, 1990), pp. 233–245. See also Yu Ying-shih, "Sun Yat-sen's Doctrine and Traditional Chinese Culture," in Cheng Chu-yuan, ed., *Sun Yat-sen's Doctrine in the Modern World* (Boulder: Westview Press, 1989), pp. 79–102.

[19] Wei Hongyuan, *Zhongguo jindai lishi de guocheng*, pp. 183–184.

parliamentary procedures in the practice of democracy.[20] But he was no liberal democrat. In fact, he had been an autocratic leader throughout his revolutionary life, particularly in his last years when the GMD was reorganized with assistance from the Comintern. As *zongli* (director-general) of the GMD, he presided over the Party in a presidential style until his death in March 1925. My understanding of his democratic thought is informed by his six lectures on people's rights (*minquan*) delivered in March/April 1924 at a time of Party reorganization.

In his first lecture, Sun defined politics as "the management of public affairs."[21] Although he believed in Rousseau's theory of "the general will," he rejected his theory of natural rights, arguing that political rights "are created by circumstances of the times and [historical] tides." Rights, for him, were historical. He saw democracy as the "tide of the world today" (*xianzai shijie chaoliu*). In his view, the perennial problem with Chinese politics was that ambitious people, including the Taiping rebel leaders of the nineteenth century and, more recently, the warlords, had wanted to be emperor. To change this feudal, imperial mentality, it was necessary to establish a republic in which the only emperor was the people themselves who would practice local self-government and exercise four political rights, namely, election, initiative, recall, and referendum.[22]

In his formulation, popular sovereignty was to be exercised for the people by the National Assembly consisting of delegates from the counties in each province. The people would exercise the right of election only at county level. In other words, there would be no general elections. The remainder of their rights – initiative, recall, and referendum – would be exercised for them by the National Assembly, which would elect the President and heads of the five branches of government (called Yuan in

---

[20] *Guofu quanji*, I, 667–745. Bruce Elleman has argued that in 1918 Sun modeled the Principle of People's Rights on the United States, especially Lincoln's idea of "government of the people, by the people, and for the people." After 1923, however, Sun adopted a more Leninist interpretation of the term democracy. His new understanding of democracy, Elleman goes on, was based largely on the Comintern resolution of November 28, 1923, that Chinese democracy should serve "the interests of the workers of China" in their "struggles against imperialism." Sun's new democracy, then, was linked to anti-imperialism. See Bruce A. Elleman, *Diplomacy and Deception: The Secret History of Sino-Soviet Diplomatic Relations, 1917–1927* (Armonk, NY: M. E. Sharpe, 1997), p. 69.

[21] *Guofu quanji*, I, 65.

[22] Ibid., pp. 73–75, 77–79. On the four rights and the government's powers, see Sun's sixth lecture on *minquan zhuyi* delivered on April 26, 1924, in *Guofu quanji*, I, 151–155.

Chinese). The government, however, was not responsible to the National Assembly, which had no legislative power. That power rested with the Legislative Yuan, which was part of the government.

A Sunist government was elitist, moralistic, and paternalistic. Rejecting the notion that people are born equal, Sun understood equality as merely a political concept. He held that people were different in intelligence and ability and could be classified into three categories: those who are the first to know and to be enlightened (*xianzhi xianjuezhe*); those who are later to know and to be enlightened (*houzhi houjuezhe*); and those who are ignorant and incapable of enlightenment (*buzhi bujuezhe*). The first category consists of inventors; the second category, publicists; and the third category, "doers" who simply follow instructions. Human progress would be assured, we are told, if they all knew what they could or could not do and worked together in a complementary and cooperative manner, ready to serve one another.[23] It was this shared value of service to the community and the state that constituted Sun's "spirit of equality." This hierarchy of equality was based on intellect, ability, and public morality. He was interested in the moral–intellectual elite, the enlightened rulers, who were empowered to govern in the best interests of the governed.

Sun likened the management of public affairs to that of a large factory. The factory hires a specialist to be the managing director who is responsible to the shareholders. Although the shareholders have power, they leave the management to the managing director who takes all decisions and acts in their best interests. Similarly, in the management of public affairs, the President of the Republic was the managing director to whose government the people as shareholders entrusted the affairs of state. The President was in the driver's seat while the people were the car's owners; they could sit back, relax, and leave the driving to the driver who knew the way. There was no need to regard the President as an exalted one because the incumbent was only doing a job.[24] But, as Grieder comments, "Sun bequeathed to his followers no adequate notion as to how the destination chosen by the people was to be communicated to the government, which sat in the driver's seat, and which possessed the only map."[25] In fact, the people were never given the opportunity to choose

[23] Lecture 5, *Guofu quanji*, I, 127–128. On inequality generally, see Lecture 3, *Guofu quanji*, I, 91–105.

[24] Lecture 5, *Guofu quanji*, I, 133–136.

[25] Jerome B. Grieder, *Intellectuals and the State in Modern China* (New York: The Free Press, 1981), p. 345.

the destination. The moral–intellectual elite who controlled the political center chose it for them.

Even though he acknowledged the Euro-American origins of modern democratic thought, Sun was concerned about the shortcomings and deficiencies of liberal democracy and the problems arising from it. In particular, he despaired of its perceived administrative inefficiency, which explained why he did not think that the Euro-American systems were good models for China. The governments he most admired were the autocratic but efficient Prussian government of Bismarck and the oligarchy of Meiji Japan. He favored a strong state. The question for him, then, was how to achieve strong and efficient government that was also responsible. His answer, which he thought was his "new discovery," was the separation of *quan* (political rights) and *neng* (political ability).[26]

Underlying his *quan–neng* dichotomy were three different conceptions of power: sovereign power (*zhengquan*), administrative power (*zhiquan*), and people's power (*minquan*). Sovereign power, that is, popular sovereignty, was exercised by the state, administrative power by the government, and people's power by the populace. In exercising administrative power, the government entered into a social contract with the people, undertaking to provide efficient administration and good governance. The right to rule (*zhiquan*) was entrusted to the government, the sole trustee. Able personnel, the experts who ensured its efficiency, ran the "omnipotent government." The people exercising the four rights supervised it.

The *quan–neng* dichotomy had the effect of limiting political participation to the GMD elite. Yet their ability to rule was not proven. As Joseph Fewsmith has pointed out, the Party made solipsistic claims to "absolute" knowledge of the ills of Chinese society and *the* answer to them.[27] Sun's aphorism, "knowledge is difficult, action is easy," in sharp contrast to the Ming philosopher Wang Yangming's dictum "knowledge is easy, action is difficult," was an attempt to explain the failure of the early Republic and now to enhance the Party's authority over both the people and the state. If only the Party knew *the* answer to the ills of Chinese society, it alone held out hopes for the nation's salvation, and only it possessed the wisdom and power to rule.

Sun's view on liberty is well known. Emphasizing that personal freedoms should not be excessive, he argued that the problem with

---

[26] Lecture 5, *Guofu quanji*, I, 126.
[27] Fewsmith, *Party, State, and Local Elites*, pp. 89–90.

the Chinese people was not that they had no personal freedoms but that they enjoyed excessive liberty. The Chinese term for liberty (*ziyou*, possibly a Japanese loan word) was a nineteenth-century invention: the Western notion of liberty did not exist in Chinese classical texts or literature.[28] When Sun attempted to explain liberty by using the Chinese expression *fangdang buji* (behaving licentiously), he equated liberty with permissiveness and excessive individualism. In his view, traditionally Chinese had enjoyed a great deal of personal freedoms since imperial times without knowing it. China's youth, he feared, had become increasingly decadent and permissive in recent times, which gave rise to his theory of "a sheet of loose sand." He theorized that in feudal times, Europeans did not enjoy freedom, and so their revolutionary struggles had focused on the goal of individual liberty. Chinese society, by contrast, had enjoyed much more freedom since the Qin and Han Dynasties, and so the Chinese revolution was aimed, not at securing liberty that already existed, but at curbing it for the purpose of liberating China from the foreign yoke. It was the "loose sand" that kept China divided amid growing foreign economic and military pressures. He was critical of the students who demonstrated "irresponsibly" against all sorts of things on campus.[29] Emphasizing China's lack of unity and cohesion in an age of imperialism, he found a nexus between liberty and political tutelage. The people were to be trained politically before they could enjoy personal freedoms; otherwise, they would remain "a sheet of loose sand." This view is similar to what the eminent late Qing intellectual, Liang Qichao, had said: "They [Chinese] must be trained as citizens first; until then, freedom would lead only to disorder."[30] Indeed, Sun showed Liang's influence in the way he understood the relationship between individual freedom and national freedom in China.

Sun drew on John Stuart Mill's *On Liberty*. Yet what most impressed him was not Mill's emphasis on the fallibility of all thinking or his faith in the inalienable freedom of the individual but his reassertion, in the later years of his life, of the rights of society as a whole against the untrammeled liberties of the individual.[31] In other words, Sun admired Mill for putting limits on liberty. Thomas Metzger has argued that, for

---

[28] The Chinese term *ziyou zizai* meaning feeling free to act, to move around, and to do things in a relaxed manner without self-imposed or external restraints does not have the connotation of political rights as in the English word *liberty*.

[29] Lecture 2, *Guofu quanji*, I, 83, 87–88.

[30] Quoted in Andrew J. Nathan, *Chinese Democracy* (London: I. B.Tauris, 1986), pp. 62–63.

[31] Lecture 2, *Guofu quanji*, I, 86.

Sun, the limits were to be derived, as general principles, from "a determinate, teleological vision of history," a sense of "public morality," "reason," and "traditionally rooted core norms." Ultimately, the limits on freedom were to be derived from "rationally known principles, that is, the Three Principles of the People."[32] His conception of liberty was revolutionary, nationalistic, traditional, elitist, and moralistic all at once. To carry out the Chinese revolution, he asked people to sacrifice their personal freedoms. Until the revolution was won and national independence achieved, there was only freedom of the nation, not freedom of the individual. He made it clear that his people's rights were different from the natural rights (*tianfu renquan*) of the individual. A GMD government would grant rights, that is the four rights, to all the people, not just the bourgeoisie who were a minority in Chinese society. These were citizen's rights. But who were the citizens? The answer was, only those who were loyal to the Republic (ruled, of course, by the GMD) and who opposed the imperialists and warlords. All "traitors" who opposed the Republic and all those who supported the imperialists and warlords would be denied freedoms and rights.[33] The criterion for the enjoyment of rights was, therefore, political, though not class-based.

Moreover, as one distinguished scholar has observed, *minquan* did not mean personal freedoms, civil liberties, or individual autonomy. For Sun, the rights of the individual should be subordinated to those of the collectivity and the group to which one belonged.[34] Like Liang Qichao and the other well-known late Qing intellectual, Yan Fu, Sun stressed the need for a strong state capable of regulating and shaping society in the public interest, sharing with Mill a view of liberty in the context of knowledge, ethics, global history, and current policy prescriptions.[35] His vision of China was a perfect society, not only peaceful and prosperous but also moralistic in accord with the Confucian precepts of *ren'ai* (humanity and love) and *xinyi* (trust and righteousness), a society in which selfishness (*si*) gave way to a devotion to the public good (*gong*). In that vision,

---

[32] Thomas A. Metzger, "Did Sun Yat-sen Understand the Idea of Democracy? The Conceptualization of Democracy in the Three Principles of the People and in John Stuart Mill's 'On Liberty'," *American Asian Review* 10:1 (Spring 1992): 13–15.

[33] See the Manifesto of the GMD's First National Congress (1924), in *Geming wenxian* (Documents on the Chinese Revolution), ed. Luo Jialun (Taibei: Zhongguo Guomindang zhongyang weiyuanhui dangshi shiliao bianxuan weiyuanhui, 1955), VIII, 123–124.

[34] Wang Gungwu, *Power, Rights and Duties in Chinese History: The 40th George Ernest Morrison Lecture in Ethnology* (Canberra: Australian National University, 1979), p. 17.

[35] Metzger, "Did Sun Yat-sen Understand the Idea of Democracy?" pp. 22–29.

China would influence the world and ultimately lead to the great harmony on earth (*shijie datong*).[36]

THE LEGACY OF SUN YAT-SEN'S THOUGHT

After his death, Sun was canonized as the founding father of the Chinese Republic. A personality cult quickly grew up in his name as his sole heirs and interpreters of his thought tried to impose orthodoxy on the Chinese mind. He was idolized. What Lyon Sharman called a "lacquered image" had since been created out of an all too human and fallible man.[37] A great man or not, his influence on modern Chinese politics was profound. But his legacy did not enhance the liberal cause in that he bequeathed to his heirs and disciples an authoritarian party, an ideology that offered both a critique of and a program for transcending liberal democracy, and a leadership style with dictatorial tendencies. He left no notion as to how Chinese politics should be institutionalized, for his thought on public administration did not include ways of preventing those in authority from abusing their powers. There was neither mechanism for supervision of the GMD elite during the period of political tutelage nor guarantee for the successful transition to constitutional rule. As Jürgen Domes has observed, "[Sun's] systematic effort to develop a concept of democracy for China was more apt to provide a convenient legitimation for a system of developmental authoritarian dictatorship . . . than to promote the development of a pluralistic representative system."[38] There was no question of intraparty reform, for Sun assumed the intelligence and morality of the GMD elite in the public sphere. Consequently, his followers readily used his notion of political tutelage as a justification for one-party rule.

The Nationalist government showed all the shortcomings of Sun's five-power constitution. First, there was no separation of party and government. It was the Party that controlled the state through the Central Political Council. Both the Party center and its local branches interfered with the administrative authorities at both levels. Part of the problem was that senior Party members were also senior government

---

[36] This theme is apparent in Sun's sixth lecture on *minzu zhuyi*, or the principle of nationalism, delivered on March 2, 1924. See *Guofu quanji*, I, 53–64.

[37] Lyon Sharman, *Sun Yat-sen: His Life and Its Meaning* (reprinted from 1934 ed., Stanford: Stanford University Press, 1968), p. xi.

[38] Jürgen Domes, "China's Modernization and the Doctrine of Democracy," in Cheng, ed., *Sun Yat-sen's Doctrine*, p. 209.

officials, and vice versa.[39] Second, the five-power structure of government did not provide for a Montesquieuan separation of powers or any system of checks and balances such as that designed by the authors of the *Federalist Papers*. The five-power relationships, as well as Sun's conception of public administration, were vague, which even students of law, like the Yale-educated Wang Chonghui, the Justice Minister, found difficult to understand.[40] The crux of the matter was that the five Yuan were all parts of the government. The National Assembly, unlike the British Parliament or the United States Congress, had no legislative power, nor did it have the power to declare war, to approve the national budget, to debate issues of foreign policy and national defense, or to pass a vote of confidence. In the absence of a responsible cabinet system, the Nationalist government was absolutely free from popular supervision, responsible only to the highest Party authorities, and the locus of decision-making authority increasingly slid to the Military Affairs Commission headed by Chiang Kai-shek. The five powers in fact had collapsed into one – that is, the absolute powers held by the Central Political Council and, during wartime, by the Supreme National Defense Council, both chaired by Chiang. Party departments rivaled the ministries of the Executive Yuan with overlapping functions but unclear lines of authority, whereas the powerful Executive Yuan, where the vast majority of the functional ministries were located, overshadowed the Legislative Yuan, which had no independent powers. The Judicial Yuan, too, was anything but independent. The Examination Yuan, established to play a dominant role in all aspects of the civil service, was "a weak organization, with neither its own independent base of power nor the consistent backing of other entities in the government."[41] It had no integrity at all because recruitment into the civil service was, in reality, based not on a merit system or a policy of equal opportunity but largely on loyalty to the Party, old boy's networks, and nepotism, with appointments resting with the ministries concerned. That left the Control Yuan almost nonexistent as it had neither political clout nor power of judicial decision. Such was Sun's legacy. He had assumed that the various branches of government could work together in the public interest and that any disputes that might arise

---

[39] Ch'ien, *The Government and Politics of China*, p. 147.
[40] Eastman, *The Abortive Revolution*, pp. 167–168.
[41] Julia C. Strauss, *Strong Institutions in Weak Polities: State Building in Republican China, 1927–1940* (Oxford: Clarendon Press, 1998), p. 33.

could be resolved collectively by the government leaders under the direction of the President.[42]

It was a model of "bottom-up" democracy that Chinese democracy should begin in the form of local self-government at the county level and gradually work its way up. In theory, local self-government was meant to limit the penetration of state power. In practice, the penetration of GMD power was assured by political tutelage and assisted by the traditional *baojia* system of control through household registration.[43] Even if local self-government was practiced, the bottom-up approach supported movement in only one direction. There were no local government projects in the capital cities and other urban areas where, it could be argued, democratic practice would have a better chance of success because of a higher level of education and more favorable socioeconomic conditions.

On the center–periphery relationship, the Party's 1924 platform, following Sun's *Fundamentals*, declared a balance of power between them. In reality, a policy of centralization was pursued. It became a source of friction after 1928 as the central government sought to expand its power. The province, it should be noted, was not the basic unit of local self-government, but the link between central power and local authority.[44] The governor, while responsible for provincial matters, was under central direction in matters of a national nature, but the demarcation line was never clearly drawn. The Nationalists, true to the Chinese political tradition, were centralists allowing little scope for provincial autonomy.

Not least of all, the Party ideology was in many respects simplistic, incoherent, and incapable of being fully understood. Few Chinese would challenge it publicly, out of respect for Sun, but it was open to different interpretations. The Party had failed to retain control over its own ideology. Consequently, instead of being a "template for action," the ideology took on a regime "mentality."[45] This explained, in part, the regime's failure to implement the Three Principles of the People, thus contributing to the dictatorship of Chiang Kai-shek.

---

[42] Zhao Suisheng, *Power by Design: Constitution-making in Nationalist China* (Honolulu: University of Hawaii Press, 1996), p. 28.

[43] On the *baojia* system as a means of local control, see Michael R. Dutton, *Policy and Punishment in China: From Patriarchy to "the People"* (Cambridge: Cambridge University Press, 1992), pp. 85–88.

[44] Sun Ke, "Zhixian jingguo ji xianfa zhong de jige zhongyao wenti" (The constitution-making process and a few important issues), in Hu Zuoying, ed., *Xianzheng wenti yanjiu* (Study of constitutional issues) (Chongqing: Xinyishishe, 1940), p. 9.

[45] Fewsmith, *Party, State, and Local Elites*, pp. 184–185.

THE DICTATORSHIP OF CHIANG KAI-SHEK

Born in 1887 to a salt merchant-gentry family in Xikou, inland from Ningbo, Zhejiang Province, Chiang was a soldier, Confucian, and later Christian. He had acquired military training in north China and in Tokyo and, in Fairbank's words, "inherited a conventional Sino-Japanese Confucian (not liberal) outlook."[46] An admirer of the nineteenth-century scholar–official Zeng Guofan, who had assisted in the suppression of the Taiping Rebellion and contributed to the Tongzhi Restoration (1862–1874), Chiang was "the inheritor of China's ruling-class tradition: his moral leadership was couched in Confucian terms while the work style of his administration showed their old evils of ineffectiveness."[47] As a Confucian, he was outmoded; as a soldier, he relied on the use of force and coercion in conflict resolution; and as a dictator, he was ruthless. Not only did he regard his succession to the mantle of Sun as legitimate and well deserved, but he also avowed himself Sun's most faithful disciple, best suited to the task of implementing his ideas and plans for national reconstruction. Ambitious, manipulative, and strong-willed, Chiang was no ordinary man.

After 1928, the GMD leadership, collective for a couple of years following Sun's death, reverted to the Sunist style of monocratic leadership. Skilled in political manipulation, Chiang was able to ward off challenges from the GMD Left and some regional forces, thereby consolidating his position by early 1932. Like Yuan Shikai two decades before, he was convinced that Chinese politics demanded a dictator. Fascism had great appeal for him because it seemed capable of solving the problems of China.

Barrington Moore noted in 1967 the Nationalist regime's analogies to European fascism,[48] but it was Lloyd Eastman who demonstrated that a fascist movement did exist in China in the first half of the 1930s.[49] Studying the Blue Shirts – a fascist organization consisting of Whampoa military officers who pledged absolute loyalty to Chiang – Eastman argued that Chiang's conservatism had been misunderstood in that his aim was to strengthen China through a restructuring of the Chinese sociopolitical order. "The model for Chiang Kai-shek's ideal society lay not in the Chinese past, but in the specifically militaristic aspects of Japan, Italy and Germany."[50] There have been debates on how fascist Chiang's rule was:

---

[46] Fairbank, *China: A New History*, p. 284.   [47] Ibid., p. 292.   [48] Moore, Jr., pp. 197–199.
[49] Eastman, *The Abortive Revolution*, ch. 2.   [50] Eastman, "Nationalist China," p. 30.

in 1979, between Eastman and Maria Hsia Chang;[51] then in 1984, among Eastman, Fewsmith, and Bradley Geisert.[52] Fewsmith went on to publish a book in which he characterized the Nationalist regime as an "authoritarian regime" belonging to the same political species as Franco's Spain, Salazar's Portugal, and, to a slightly lesser extent, Mussolini's Italy.[53] More recently, Frederic Wakeman, Jr., studying the top-secret Society for Vigorous Practice (*Lixingshe*) and its front organizations, notes the differences between Chinese and European fascism, the key one being the fact that Chiang Kai-shek never wanted to create a mass movement. He labels the Nationalist organization of authoritarian political groups with personal loyalty to Chiang "Confucian fascism," stressing that the Chiang regime was a military dictatorship that showed itself to be more authoritarian in the Confucian fashion than fascist in the Nazi or Italian style.[54] In any case, fascism was a modern ideology at the time, thought by many to be at the forefront of historical progress and superior to parliamentary democracy. For Chiang, it was not so much a response to a developmental crisis[55] as a response to a crisis of legitimacy – the failure of Party rule, the communist insurgency, the challenge of the regional forces, liberal opposition, and student activism. Fascism, in whatever form, was used as a political method to revitalize the Party, to resurrect the nation, and to eliminate all political opposition. It abnegated individualism and Western liberalism, and it was repressive.

What Chiang most admired about Germany and Japan was their efficiency, national spirit, and, above all, social militarization.[56] As the New Life Movement, launched in 1934, demonstrated, he was interested

---

[51] Maria Hsia Chang, "'Fascism' and Modern China," *China Quarterly* 79 (September 1979): 553–567; Lloyd E. Eastman, "Fascism and Modern China: A Rejoinder," *China Quarterly* 80 (December 1979): 838–842.

[52] Lloyd E. Eastman, "New Insights into the Nature of the Nationalist Regime," *Republican China* 9:2 (1984): 8–18; Joseph Fewsmith, "Response to Eastman," *Republican China* 9:2 (1984): 19–27; Bradley Geisert, "Probing KMT Rule: Reflections on Eastman's 'New Insights'," *Republican China* 9:2 (1984): 28–39.

[53] Fewsmith, *Party, State, and Local Elites*, ch. 7.

[54] Frederic Wakeman, Jr., "A Revisionist View of the Nanjing Decade: Confucian Fascism," *China Quarterly* 150 (June 1997): 395–432.

[55] On the idea of fascism as a response to a developmental crisis, see A. James Gregor, *Interpretations of Fascism* (Morristown, NJ: General Learning Press, 1974), pp. 181–185. Gregor also uses the term *ideology of delayed development* to interpret fascism along with communism.

[56] A new relationship between Nanjing and Berlin was forged during the 1933–1936 period following the seizure by Hitler's National Socialist Party. For details, see William C. Kirby, *Germany and Republican China* (Stanford: Stanford University Press, 1984), ch. 5.

in the militarization of Chinese society so that the Chinese people who had been leading "a life of decadent frivolity" could discipline themselves to act in the national interest. He saw a facile identification of interests between fascism and Confucianism in the revitalization of Chinese society. Yet he was more suited to do a Zeng Guofan than a Adolf Hitler because he had no sense of mobilizing the middle class – be it an emergent class or a declassé – or the masses to create political power and to legitimize the regime. Despite his admiration for Western scientific and industrial progress, Chiang remained a traditionalist. What the New Life Movement also demonstrated was that Chiang reinvented Confucianism as a counterrevolutionary ideology to Chinese communism.[57] He was no generator of political reform and social change.

Yet Chiang was convinced of his selflessness and moral rectitude. In this regard, he was in the fine tradition of Confucianism in regard to the role of the Chinese elite. His ambitions were fueled not solely by a desire for personal gratification but also by a deep commitment to China's national interests, to which he perceived his power interests as being identical. Accordingly, he viewed anyone who opposed him or his policy as acting against the national interest, allowing no room in his world for a loyal opposition.[58] The idea of power sharing was alien to him. Thus, he outlawed all the other political parties and groups and did nothing to foster liberalization within his own party.

A dictatorship tolerates no opposition, guarantees no rights, curbs civil liberties, silences its critics, and relies on coercion to impose its will on the populace. The GMD dictatorship was no exception. Intellectuals, dissidents, students, and the ordinary people all felt the sting of its repression. Arbitrary arrests, detention without trial, and violations of human rights were commonplace. Many students, who demonstrated in 1931–1932 and again in 1935–1936 against the government's Japan policy, were harassed, arrested, or thrown into jail.[59] Any political movement

---

[57] Arif Dirlik, "The Ideological Foundations of the New Life Movement: A Study in Counterrevolution," *Journal of Asian Studies* 34:4 (August 1975): 945–980.

[58] Eastman, "Nationalist China," pp. 19–20.

[59] For student activism during this period, see Jeffrey N. Wasserstrom, *Student Protests in Twentieth-Century China: The View From Shanghai* (Stanford: Stanford University Press, 1991), and Lincoln Li, *Student Nationalism in China, 1924–1949* (Albany: State University of New York Press, 1994). For an earlier work, see John Israel, *Student Nationalism in China, 1927–1937* (Stanford: Stanford University Press, 1966). For a study of the GMD's policy toward student activism, see Huang Jianli, *The Politics of Depoliticization in Republican China: Guomindang Policy Towards Student Political Activism, 1927–1949* (Berne: Peter Lang, 1996).

not initiated or controlled by the GMD was distrusted and banned. People suspected of engaging in procommunist or antigovernment activities were terrorized, not least by the Blue Shirts's Special Service headed by the much-feared Dai Li, "China Himmler." Political repression was an instrument of Nationalist rule.

The repression, however, was neither thorough nor always effective. "During the Nanking decade," Eastman observed, "China enjoyed a considerable intellectual and political vitality" in areas outside Nationalist control, including the foreign-administered treaty-port concessions.[60] But the treaty-port concessions, including Shanghai's International Settlement, were not safe all the time.[61] Some dissidents felt compelled to seek political protection and support in warlord territory beyond the long reach of Nationalist power. Yet, despite political repression, some sort of civil society existed in the Nationalist period both in the strong sense of an arena of political opposition to the state and in the weak sense of a sphere of voluntary, autonomous, and associational activity located between state and society.

During the war with Japan, political repression continued after a brief period of relaxation. But the party-state was a weak dictatorship, a weak garrison state where control of the localities depended on suppression by means of violence. Although central power had expanded as a result of the Nationalist advance into hitherto hostile territory after 1937, there were limits to its authority and power. Technically, the means of control were either lacking or inadequate – railways, roads, telephones, radios, and other forms of communication. Intellectually, there was a flourishing of democratic thought, especially in Kunming, where Beijing University, Qinghua University, and Nankai University had been moved to form the Southwest Associated University. Political dissidents were able to seek shelter in Yunnan, where Governor Long Yun was no friend of the central government. Throughout the war, no other Chinese city enjoyed greater political freedom than Kunming, with the possible exception of Guilin. In the wartime capital, Chongqing, there was a body of literature critical of the government, despite official censorship. Outspoken critics refused to be cowed into submission. Those who were too afraid to speak out enjoyed what Hu Shi called "the freedom of

---

[60] Eastman, "Nationalist China," p. 23.

[61] For the state of law and order in Shanghai during the Nanjing period, see Frederic Wakeman, Jr., *Policing Shanghai, 1927–1937* (Berkeley: University of California Press, 1995). For Shanghai's gangsters, see Brian G. Martin, *The Shanghai Green Gang: Politics and Organized Crime* (Berkeley: University of California Press, 1996).

silence,"[62] a right not lost until after 1949. Or they could choose to be passive and indifferent, free from the politics of involvement. For all his faults, Chiang was not antiintellectual,[63] although he was said to have had little intimate contact with people of enlightenment.[64] There was no purge of intellectuals like the CCP's Rectification Campaign of 1942 or the Anti-Rightist Campaign of 1957. With some exceptions, the intellectuals survived the Nationalist rule.

There were liberal elements within the GMD, although in small numbers, led by Sun Fo, the only son of Sun Yat-sen and President of the Legislative Yuan from 1932 to 1948. Educated first at the University of California and then at Columbia University, where he earned a Master's degree, Sun was awarded a doctorate by Fudan University upon his return to China. He was a scholar, probably the best-read of the Nationalist elite.[65] It was his reading of Western political works that made him more progressive than most of his party colleagues. He thought and acted in Western terms and desired political reform. Because of his father, he feared no persecution and, almost alone in China, could say what he believed. He spoke publicly against oppression and corruption, saying what the people were thinking but did not dare to say. In 1932, as we shall see, he argued for an early termination of political tutelage and continued to adhere to that position. He had some supporters within the Party. But, observed one former American diplomat who had served in China, he lacked the wit or the strength to have any measurable influence, despite his good instincts and hard work.[66] A man of silk, not

[62] Hu Shi, disaffected with the Nationalist government, was reported to have told George Yeh, Vice-Minister of Foreign Affairs, in January 1949: "The only reason why liberal elements like us still prefer to string along with you people is that under your regime we at least enjoy the freedom of silence." Quoted in Suzanne Pepper, *Civil War in China: The Political Struggle, 1945–1949* (Berkeley: University of California Press, 1978), p. 227.

[63] The Nanjing government boasted a number of highly educated civilian administrators, including Wang Chonghui, Xiong Shihui, Wu Tingchang, Zhang Jiaao (Chang Kia-ngau), and Huang Shaohong, who would become leaders of the influential Political Study Clique (*Zhengxuexi*). Other GMD intellectuals included Wu Zhihui, Cai Yuanpei, and Ma Yinchu. A number of nonpartisan intellectuals also joined the government after 1935, notably Jiang Tingfu, Weng Wenhao, and Wu Jingchao. See Eastman, *The Abortive Revolution*, p. 158.

[64] Ch'ien, *The Government and Politics of China*, p. 123.

[65] Chen Lifu observed: "Of all the senior party members, I believed he [Sun Fo] was the one who had read the most Western works. He read daily about politics, economics, and science." See Chang and Myers, eds., *The Storm Clouds Clear Over China: The Memoir of Ch'en Li-fu, 1900–1993* (Stanford: Hoover Institution Press, 1994), p. 88.

[66] John F. Melby, *The Mandate of Heaven: Record of a Civil War, China, 1945–49* (Toronto: University of Toronto Press, 1968), p. 163.

of steel, he was no match in drive or vigor for the reactionary elements who controlled the Party and was sometimes snubbed by Chiang Kai-shek.[67] Other liberal GMD elements included Wang Shijie,[68] a member of the Political Study Clique, Shao Lizi,[69] Cai Yuanpei, former Beijing University President and a well-known educator, and others who enjoyed the support, outside the government, of Song Qingling (widow of Sun Yat-sen), He Xiangning (widow of Liao Zhongkai),[70] and Li Jishen, the Guangxi militarist. All of them wanted to see an early end to political tutelage, contrary to Chiang's constitutional designs.

CHIANG KAI-SHEK AND CONSTITUTION MAKING

In 1928, when the GMD was about to declare a period of political tutelage, there were calls from both within the Party and without for a provisional constitution. But the Party's right-wing leader, Hu Hanmin, considered it unnecessary on the ground that Sun Yat-sen had not required it. Chiang had no strong views one way or the other, and the matter was left undecided. In October 1930, however, Chiang

---

[67] Theodore H. White and Annalee Jacoby, *Thunder Out of China* (New York: William Sloane Associates, 1946), pp. 102–103.

[68] Wang Shijie, a native of Hubei, was one time Chancellor of Wuhan University (1929–1932) and Minister of Education (1933–1936). During the War of Resistance, he served as General Secretary of the People's Political Council (1938 to March 1943) and Minister of Information concurrently. After the war, he served as Minister of Foreign Affairs until 1948. In January 1946, he participated in the Political Consultative Conference as a government representative. After the failure of the Marshall mission, he pursued a strongly pro-United States foreign policy. When Chiang Kai-shek resumed the presidency of the National Government in Taiwan in 1950, Wang became General Secretary of the Presidential Office and a member of the GMD Central Advisory Committee. See Howard L. Boorman, ed., *Biographical Dictionary of Republican China* (New York: Columbia University Press, 1967–1971), III, 395–397.

[69] Shao Lizi was governor of Shaanxi in 1933–1936 and ambassador to the Soviet Union in 1940–1941. In 1943, he succeeded Wang Shijie as General Secretary of the People's Political Council and General Secretary of the Commission for the Inauguration of Constitutional Government. He played an important role in the 1945–1946 negotiations with the Chinese Communists, along with Wang Shijie. He also served as a GMD delegate to the Political Consultative Conference. Later he became Chairman of the National Assembly Preparatory Committee and took part in the drafting of the constitution. In 1947, he was elected to the State Council. And in January 1949, he led a five-man peace mission to Beijing. Following the failure of his mission, he decided to remain in Beijing. Subsequently he held a variety of posts in the People's Republic. See Boorman, ed., *Biographical Dictionary*, III, 91–93.

[70] Liao was a leftist, finance minister in the previous Nationalist government in Guangzhou, and head of the GMD's Labor Department when he was assassinated by right-wing elements on August 20, 1925.

unexpectedly proposed to the Central Executive Committee that a provisional constitution was necessary after all. His motive was political and blatantly opportunistic. The month before, the separatist regime of Wang Jingwei and the warlords Yan Xishan and Feng Yuxiang had adopted a Draft Provisional Constitution at the Enlarged Conference of the Central Executive Committee in Beijing. It contained articles guaranteeing personal freedoms, thus appealing to the intellectuals who resented Nanjing's political repression.[71] Wang and his military backers no doubt were using democracy as a political weapon in a power struggle. From the political right, Hu Hanmin again opposed the idea of a provisional constitution, contending that the time was not ripe.[72] In doing so, he antagonized Chiang and, as a result, was forced to resign as head of the Legislative Yuan and was put under house arrest early in 1931.

Henceforth, Chiang was interested in a constitutional design that would secure his powers as President of the Republic. As one scholar has documented, Chiang was intent on instituting a presidential rather than a cabinet form of government.[73] For the liberals, the aim of a constitution was to limit state power and to guarantee rights; for Chiang, it was to entrench and to legitimize his power constitutionally. A presidential system would allow him to rule as a monocratic leader and virtually turn the government into a constitutional dictatorship. Thus, the Provisional Constitution of May 1931 provided for a presidential system by empowering the President to appoint and dismiss the heads of the five Yuan and the various ministries. It did not envision competitive politics and allowed a single party to dominate. In the following years, when a draft constitution was prepared by the Legislative Yuan, factional politics led Sun Fo to pursue a cabinet alternative. But by 1935, the Chiang forces had gained the upper hand. The Draft Constitution, approved by the Fifth National Party Congress with some reservations in November 1935 and then promulgated by the government on May 5, 1936, provided for a strong presidency, but not a dictatorship.[74]

---

[71] Ch'ien, *The Government and Politics of China*, p. 137. On the Enlarged Conference, see So Wai-chor, *The Kuomintang Left*, pp. 138–148.

[72] Eastman believed that the actual cause of Hu's objection was the fear that Chiang Kai-shek meant to enhance his power by having himself named President under a new constitution. See Eastman, "Nationalist China," p. 13.

[73] On the differences between the presidential and the cabinet forms of government and Chiang's desire for the presidential system, see Zhao, *Power by Design*.

[74] Zhao, *Power by Design*, pp. 35–37; Eastman, *The Abortive Revolution*, p. 177.

The May Fifth Draft Constitution reflected the influence of the vice-chairman of the drafting committee, Wu Jingxiong (John C. H. Wu), an American-trained lawyer and jurisprudence thinker who "knew a particular kind of 'modern,' utilitarian, anti-natural law, historicist liberalism,"[75] which he combined with the thought of Sun Yat-sen. Indeed, the Draft Constitution betrayed the flaws of Sun's theory of the four rights and the five powers. It was not based upon democratic principles. Rather, its framers assumed the attitude that the granting of constitutional government was a kindness and a special favor to the people from the Party. To understand why it immediately became a subject of public criticism, let us look at its main features.

1. The form of the state. The Republic of China was called the Republic of the Three Principles of the People. In other words, a state ideology was enshrined in the Draft Constitution from which there could be no departure. Orthodoxy was imposed by constitutional means. This was objectionable to all those who believed in freedom of thought and who were still looking to the West for a more appropriate constitutional model. Moreover, as Thomas Greiff has noted, anyone who opposed the Three Principles of the People was denied his or her rights – a practice that represented a serious derogation of the principle of the rule of law, allowing the government to define arbitrarily on political grounds a category of citizens whose rights could be denied constitutionally on a systematic basis.[76]

2. The rights and duties of the citizens. The Draft Constitution hedged civil liberties with the phrase "in accordance with the law." The phrase was not a problem if there was already an established rule of law. But in China, where a modern rule of law was lacking and the administration of justice left much to be desired, the possibility of limiting by statue the liberties of the citizens was very real. The inclusion of the phrase diluted the notion of rights and undermined the constitutional protection of them against arbitrary government action. Critics were concerned that the rights granted by the state could be taken away at will by legislation. Grieder has observed: "The attempt to limit the exercise of state power by constitutional means turned upon itself when such phrases as 'except in accordance with the law' or 'as provided for in the Constitution' became themselves weapons in the arsenal of state power."[77] Using the law to restrict rights was similar to causing the law to diverge from the Constitution, which could easily lead to malpractice.

3. The National Assembly. It was to meet for one month every three years, its powers being limited to electing and recalling the President and

---

[75] Thomas E. Greiff, "The Principle of Human Rights in Nationalist China: John C. H. Wu and the Ideological Origins of the 1946 Constitution," *China Quarterly* 103 (September 1985): 443.

[76] Ibid., p. 446.   [77] Grieder, *Intellectuals and the State*, p. 337.

Vice-President and the heads of the five Yuan, initiating, holding refer-
enda, and amending the Constitution. But it had no legislative power, no
control over the purse strings of the government, and no say whatsoever
in the affairs of the government. And the Legislative Yuan, to be elected
by the National Assembly, had no power to bring the Executive Yuan to
account.

4. The powers of the President of the Republic. The Draft Constitution provided for a strong executive with little check on his powers. In particular,
he could decree legislation following the declaration of an emergency by
the Executive Council – a body comprising the head of the Executive Yuan
and government ministers. However, because all members of this Council
would be appointed and removed by the President, the requirement of
such a declaration would be no more than a formality. The only limitation
on his powers was a provision that all presidential decrees, to remain in
effect, required the ratification of the Legislative Yuan within three
months of being issued.[78]

5. The relationship between the central and local governments. The division
of powers between what were national affairs and what were local affairs
was maintained in principle. But this was a sheer platitude because the government was pursuing a policy of centralization.[79] Moreover, as the Guangxi
Constitutional Government Advancement Association criticized, even
though the provinces were empowered to execute the laws and orders of
the central government and to superintend local self-rule, the Draft Constitution failed to recognize the province as a unit of *political power* that
exercised local powers independently.[80]

The government intended to have the Draft Constitution adopted
by the National Assembly, scheduled for November 1937. However,
the Assembly was postponed indefinitely because war broke out. Consequently, the Provisional Constitution of 1931, with some changes,
remained in force until the end of 1946 when a new constitution was
adopted. As we shall see in later chapters, the May Fifth Draft provided
a battleground for constitutional change and a major weapon in the
power struggle both within the GMD and without.

Yet, regardless of the Draft Constitution, Chiang Kai-shek enjoyed
sweeping powers as President of the Executive Yuan, Chairman of the
Military Affairs Commission, Commander-in-Chief, and Chairman of
the wartime Supreme National Defense Council. To crown it all, at the
Extraordinary National Party Congress in March 1938, he was elected
zongcai (director-general) of the Party following an amendment of the

[78] Eastman, *The Abortive Revolution*, p. 177.
[79] Ch'ien, *The Government and Politics of China*, p. 304.
[80] Lawrence K. Rosinger, *Wartime Politics in China, 1937–1944* (Princeton: Princeton
University Press, 1945), pp. 108–109.

Party statute to establish that position. The supreme title of *zongcai* was not different in substance from that of *zongli*, which was reserved forever for the late Sun Yat-sen. As *zongcai*, Chiang had veto power over the decisions of the Central Executive Committee as well as those of the National Party Congress. He was also given emergency powers to deal expediently with all Party, government, and military affairs by decree during the war regardless of normal procedures and formal chains of command. At the Sixth National Party Congress in May 1945, he was reelected unanimously as the *zongcai*.[81] After the war, he retained the emergency powers in the name of communist suppression. Finally, in 1948, under the provisions of the new Constitution of 1947, he was elected President but not before the Communists had irrevocably weakened his position in the civil war.

CONCLUSION

The Nationalist regime was not only a one-party rule but also a personal dictatorship. It was military, repressive, corrupt, and incompetent; its dictatorial tendencies were, in no small measure, the legacy of Sun Yat-sen's doctrine. Sun's notion of political tutelage, his principle of people's rights, his conceptions of freedom and equality, and his presidential style of leadership bequeathed to Chiang and the ruling elite an ideology and a system that deprived China of a politics of democratization. Chiang, a conservative and a soldier by training, presided over a closed political system and a factionalized party at a time of growing civil opposition, communist insurgency, and external aggression. His instinct was to meet every domestic challenge as it arose by coercion, intimidation, bribery, force, or any other means he deemed expedient.

But the regime was a weak dictatorship, not least because of "residual warlordism" and national fragmentation. It was precisely for this reason that Chiang and the Blue Shirts tried in vain to establish a fascist state and that some government sympathizers advocated neo-dictatorship (see Chapter 3).

The quest for democracy was an indictment of the dictatorial regime. It was first concerned with human rights.

[81] Chinese Ministry of Information, comp., *China Handbook, 1937–1945* (New York: Macmillan, 1947), p. 40.

2

Setting the Opposition Agenda

The Issue of Human Rights, 1929–1931[1]

HUMAN RIGHTS are claims upon society that every individual should have, including the right to be free – both "free from" and "free to." They are thought to be inalienable, that is, they cannot be waived, transferred, or traded away, because they are implied in one's humanity. "Human rights," writes Louis Henkin, "enjoy at least a prima facie, presumptive inviolability, bowing only to important societal interests, in limited circumstances, for limited times and purposes, and by limited means."[2] They must, therefore, be protected against malevolence, corruption, and transgressions by the state. The contemporary view is that a liberal democratic system by far affords the best protection, and democratic social conditions are the most reliable vehicle for achieving happiness for the greatest majority. Conversely, constant violations of human rights by a repressive regime provide a cause for liberal opposition and political change. Democracy and human rights are not the same things, but the nexus between them is a significant one. Today, Westerners talking about democracy link it with human rights, calling governments that ban street demonstrations and censor newspapers undemocratic.

Writing on human rights in the People's Republic of China (PRC), Merle Goldman notes that concern for human rights is "neither alien to China nor merely a Western import" and that its roots "are deep in Chinese history and tradition." Confucianism, she further observes, contained a notion that people are entitled to what they need for material

---

[1] This chapter is based in part on my article, "The Human Rights Issue in China, 1929–1931," *Modern Asian Studies* 32:2 (May 1998): 431–458.

[2] Louis Henkin, "The Human Rights Idea in Contemporary China: A Comparative Perspective," R. Randle Edwards, Louis Henkin, and Andrew J. Nathan, *Human Rights in Contemporary China* (New York: Columbia University Press, 1986), p. 9.

survival and human dignity and that a fundamental tenet of government is to provide for the basic needs of the population.[3] In a similar vein, Franz Michael and Yuan-li Wu have written that "modern concepts of human rights were deeply embedded in certain ethical tenets fundamental to the Chinese creed."[4] Drawing on the Confucian tradition, especially the idea of morality, they argue that "contrary to what some in the West might believe, Chinese political history and political thought do not lack a well-developed, ever-refined concept of human relations that embodies human rights concepts."[5] For Michael and Wu, the Western conception of human rights is premised on four fundamental principles: (1) protection under law; (2) genuine popular participation in government, that is, democracy; (3) economic freedom of choice, which provides the material base for personal and political freedom; and (4) freedom of the mind, spirit, or will. In modern times, these ideas are enshrined in such documents as the Declaration of Independence, the Bill of Rights, and the United Nations Universal Declaration of Human Rights of 1948, to name just a few. Michael and Wu believe that these same ideals can be found in Chinese history.[6]

It is misleading, however, to equate Chinese humanism with the Western notion of human rights. Although the Chinese moral order was, broadly speaking, parallel to the Western theory of natural law, they were not the same. Goldman concedes that the Chinese conception of human rights "did not develop from theories of natural law such as those associated with the Judaeo-Christian tradition, nor did it put much emphasis on individualism and legal protection."[7] For the Chinese, moral order was created by human beings, not nature. Rather than limiting the ruler's power, it was intended to help him to be a virtuous king, or emperor. It contained no idea of individual rights as a constraint on state powers or any kind of authority, including that of the clan, family, parents, or husbands.[8] Chinese humanism did not follow the four fundamental principles mentioned earlier. There was no rule of law that protected individual rights and civil liberties (more of this later). Chinese human-

---

[3] Merle Goldman, "Human Rights in the People's Republic of China," *Daedalus* 112:4 (Fall 1983): 111.

[4] Franz Michael and Wu Yuan-li, "Introduction: An Overview," in Franz Michael, Wu Yuan-li, and John F. Copper, *Human Rights in the People's Republic of China* (Boulder: Westview Press, 1988), p. 2.

[5] Ibid., p. 3.   [6] Ibid.   [7] Goldman, "Human Rights," p. 111.

[8] Andrew J. Nathan, "Sources of Chinese Rights Thinking," in Edwards et al., *Human Rights*, p. 127.

ism did not encourage popular participation in government. Even though the traditional Chinese state was not totalitarian, it was, more often than not, despotic. Despite concerns for the well-being of the people, democracy either as a procedure, a political method, or a mode of thought hardly existed. Rebellions and local uprisings were directed at injustice, misgovernment, and official corruption and had nothing to do with individual claims on society or against the state. Economically, although the people enjoyed freedom of choice, in practice, the state and form of the economy, poverty, geographical factors, and logistic problems often limited their choice. Finally, whatever freedom of the mind, spirit, or will the Chinese literati might enjoy, they were constrained by the Confucian order and a social milieu where the pressures to conform were enormous. The tradition of remonstrance, in which righteous literati courageously criticized despotic rulers, lacked a popular and legal basis and thus offered no institutional protection to those who risked their lives by speaking their minds. Literary inquisitions were not lacking in China's long history. Thus, strictly speaking, the modern notion of human rights, first formulated in the West, is alien to traditional Chinese thought, which stressed state power, benevolent rule, social harmony, unselfishness, and the public good. There is a difference between the notion of human rights in Western thought and the language of benevolence in Confucian orthodoxy.[9] As Ann Kent writes, the attempt to link the humanist ethics of traditional China with the Western notion of human rights involves "a qualitative logical leap from the collective notion of 'well-being of the people', which they represent, to the notion of the quintessential value of the individual, which they do not."[10] On the other hand, the lack of human rights thinking in imperial China does not mean that Confucianism, or Chinese culture per se, was incompatible with human rights.

The idea of human rights came to China in the late nineteenth century, but its ideological base was quite different from the liberal thought from which it had originated. Discussions of the idea early in the twentieth century led some Chinese intellectuals to embrace it, while others, including Liang Qichao and Yan Fu, either rejected it or cast serious doubts on its relevance to China. During the 1911 revolutionary movement, human rights violations were blamed on the autocratic dynastic

---

[9] For a recent Confucianism–human rights discourse, see Wm. Theodore de Bary and Tu Weiming, eds., *Confucianism and Human Rights* (New York: Columbia University Press, 1997).

[10] Ann Kent, *Between Freedom and Subsistence: China and Human Rights* (Hong Kong: Oxford University Press, 1991), p. 35.

system, becoming part of the anti-Manchu propaganda. In the early Republican period, especially in the New Culture and May Fourth Movements, Confucianism was blamed, among other things, for China's lack of democracy and human rights. Human rights became a concern not only for the liberals seeking individual liberation but also for people like Chen Duxiu and Li Dazhao who were attracted to Marxism. Throughout the 1920s, human rights continued to be an important issue for those advocating science and democracy.[11]

In 1929, the human rights issue marked the beginning of a new prodemocracy movement. Arising after the conclusion in March of the GMD's Third National Party Congress, the issue was related to the wider questions of one-party rule, political tutelage, constitutional reform, the rule of law, public administration, political rights and civil liberties – questions that would be on the opposition agenda for the next two decades. Those who first addressed the issue were identified as the Human Rights Group (*Renquanpai*), a tiny group of independent Anglo-American-educated liberals who were loyal critics wanting to impress upon Nanjing the need to implement constitutional and political reforms. With just several members, the Group was short-lived. As individual critics, though, they maintained their rage after 1931.

We will concentrate on the thoughts of Luo Longji (1896–1965) and Hu Shi (1891–1962), the acknowledged leaders of the Group. Luo is of particular interest to us because he was closely associated with Zhang Junmai (better known in the West as Carsun Chang) and others who would establish, in 1932, the *Zaishengshe* (National Renaissance Society), which was to evolve into the National Socialist Party (*Guojia shehuidang*, which bore no relationship with the Nazis in Germany) three years later. Luo then became a National Socialist. He was equally critical of the Communists until the 1940s when he became increasingly sympathetic with them. Hu, always maintaining an independence of mind, never joined any political party. A May Fourth veteran, he was highly respected even by the government he criticized. From 1938 to 1942, he served as Chinese ambassador to the United States. Luo and Hu held similar views on a range of political issues but differed on others. In

---

[11] For a study of the human rights discourse in China before the Nationalist period, see Marina Svensson, "The Chinese Conception of Human Rights: The Debate on Human Rights in China, 1898–1949," unpublished Ph.D. dissertation, Lund University, 1996, chs. 5–6; see also Peter Zarrow, "Citizenship and Human Rights in Early Twentieth-Century Chinese Thought: Liu Shipei and Liang Qichao," in de Bary and Tu, eds., *Confucianism and Human Rights*, pp. 209–233.

examining their thoughts, this chapter will discuss several questions. What were their understanding and conception of human rights? What were their main concerns and demands? Considering the nexus between human rights and democracy, what sort of democratic system did they desire?

HU SHI'S OPENING SALVO

The human rights issue was raised by a small group of writers associated with the Crescent Society (*Xinyueshe*). Founded in Beijing in 1923 as a private club for returned students from England and the United States, the Society followed the May Fourth tradition of enlightenment, emerging in the late 1920s as "the most vigorous voice defending the transcendent values of reason and culture."[12] Its members, shocked by the outbreak of the White Terror following the accession to power of the Nationalists, "tried to shake off the burden of self-doubt by reasserting the supremacy of ideals over reality."[13] In March 1928, they launched a monthly magazine, *The Crescent* (*Xinyue*) (its head office was soon moved to Shanghai), with contributions from Xu Zhimo, Liang Shiqiu, Hu Shi, Wen Yiduo, and other graduates of the American-connected Qinghua University – all well-known literary figures who placed great emphasis on the freedom of thought and expression. Originally a literary review devoted to the study of fiction, poetry, translation, and literary criticism, *The Crescent*, from April 1929, expanded its scope to accommodate the interests of a number of political writers who, attracted to Fabianism, made some of the most cogent critiques of the Nanjing regime. The first political essay appearing in its pages was, however, not written by a Fabian socialist but by Hu Shi on human rights and the provisional constitution.

Enraged by a couple of recent developments, Hu was prompted to fire the first salvo. In March, Chen Dezheng, director of the GMD's Shanghai branch and of its propaganda department, proposed at the Party's Third National Congress that "counterrevolutionaries be severely punished." The term *counterrevolutionary* was broadly defined to include the Communists, other third party members, and all those who opposed the Three Principles of the People. Hu immediately complained to his friend

---

[12] Vera Schwarcz, *The Chinese Enlightenment: Intellectuals and the Legacy of the May Fourth Movement of 1919* (Berkeley: University of California Press, 1986), p. 202.
[13] Ibid.

Wang Chonghui, then President of the Judicial Yuan, about such a method of proving guilt or innocence.[14] As if Chen's proposal was not objectionable enough, on April 20, the government announced "An Order for the Protection of Human Rights" stating, inter alia, that "the highest authority of the GMD" would, if necessary, "restrict the freedoms of assembly, association, speech, and publication within the limits of the law." Chinese citizens, it added, must "obey and support" the GMD before they can enjoy their rights.[15]

Hu dismissed the April order as a farce, criticizing that political tutelage without constitutionalism was one-party dictatorship and, even worse, a personal dictatorship of Chiang Kai-shek.[16] His critique focused on three points. First, the government's narrow definition of human rights in terms of protecting one's "person, freedom, and property" ignored a whole range of other rights that could be considered human. Even within this narrow definition, the terms *freedom* and *property* were not defined, and the government failed to specify what rights were being protected. Second, even though the April order stated that "individuals or organizations" should not invade or impair anyone's "person, freedom, and property" by any illegal means, there was no mention of the Party organization, the government, or any official or quasi-official bodies. The real problem, Hu complained, was that it was often the government and the Party, or their agents, that violated human rights, and there was no law to provide sanctions against them in those situations. Third, no protection was accorded to those accused of being antirevolutionary or suspected of being communist; they were liable to arbitrary arrests, detention, or imprisonment without trial. Hu wondered, for example, whether the activities of the myriad anti-Japanese groups and associations in China came under the rubric of the April order – a question that had been raised by the Shanghai press.[17] Citing several cases of arbitrary arrests, he condemned the government's actions as illegal. He was particularly concerned about political interference with the administration of justice and the suggestion that the judiciary should be sub-

---

[14] Chou Min-chih, *Hu Shih and Intellectual Choice in Modern China* (Ann Arbor: University of Michigan Press, 1984), p. 128.

[15] For the full proclamation, see *Geming wenxian* (Documents on the Chinese revolution), Vol. 76, ed., Qin Xiaoyi (Taibei: Zhongguo Guomindang zhongyang weiyuanhui dangshi shiliao bianxuan weiyuanhui, 1978), p. 83.

[16] Hu Shi, "Renquan yu yuefa" (Human rights and the provisional constitution), *XY* 2:2 (April 10, 1929): 1. Note that the magazine often came out later than its official publication date and that each article had its separate numbering starting with page one.

[17] Ibid., pp. 2–3.

ordinated to the Party in cases involving "antirevolutionary elements." He deplored the continuation of *renzhi* (rule of man), arguing that if the government was serious about the protection of human rights, it was imperative that the foundations for a rule of law be laid. To that end, the first step should be to adopt a constitution or at least a provisional one for the period of political tutelage. He criticized Sun Yat-sen's *Fundamentals of National Reconstruction* for failing to see the need for a constitution and to specify the length of that period.[18]

Hu approached the human rights issue from a legalistic point of view. The government acted illegally when it violated human rights. Thus, only a rule of law (*fazhi*) could protect rights. "Not only should the powers of government be sanctioned by the law, but so should those of the Party. If the Party is not sanctioned by a provisional constitution, it means there is still a privileged class in the state above the law. How can there be a rule of law then?"[19] For Hu, any political tutelage that did not provide for a rule of law was an autocracy. Neither the Party nor the government should be above the law.

In a separate article, Hu continued his criticism of Sun Yat-sen for abandoning, after 1924, the idea of a provisional constitution. In his view, Sun's error lay in his mistaken belief that a constitution, provisional or not, and political tutelage need not go hand in hand.[20] Hu viewed constitutionalism as a means of limiting state powers and safeguarding rights against the incursion of the state. Constitutional rule was a symbol, in a historical sense, of the goal for which China had been fighting since the turn of the century. Several different versions of a constitution had been promulgated during the period 1911–1925: the Provisional Constitution of 1912, the Temple of Heaven Draft Constitution of 1913, the Draft Constitution of 1919, the Constitution of 1923, and the Draft Constitution of 1925. All these constitutions "granted" a common core of political rights consisting of speech, publication, assembly, and association, among other things. However, constitutionalism was not achieved by the mere promulgation of a constitution. Chinese constitutions were, as Nathan observes, programmatic – that is, they were presented as goals to be realized.[21] Even

---

[18] Ibid., pp. 4–12.

[19] Hu Shi, " 'Renquan yu yuefa' de taolun" (On human rights and the provisional constitution), *XY* 2:4 (June 1929): 4.

[20] Hu Shi, "Women shenme shihou caikeyou xianfa?" (When can we have a constitution?), *XY* 2:4 (June, 1929): 1–8.

[21] Nathan, *Chinese Democracy*, p. 111; see also his "Political Rights in Chinese Constitutions," in Edwards et al., *Human Rights*, pp. 77–92.

with a constitution in place, successive governments remained autocratic and repressive. But Hu was adamant that a provisional constitution would be better than no constitution at all because its existence could itself be an instrument in the hands of those working for greater democracy and human rights.

His human rights article drew some responses from readers of *The Crescent*, printed in the following issues of the journal. A short letter was also received from the respected educator, Cai Yuanpei, who praised him for speaking out courageously on such an important issue.[22]

At this juncture, Hu did not provide a conceptualization of human rights. That task was left to Luo, who, in Nathan's view, was "probably modern China's best-known rights theorist."[23]

LUO LONGJI'S CONCEPTION OF HUMAN RIGHTS

Born in 1896 into a family of gentry background in Jiangxi Province, Luo, five years Hu's junior, received a traditional education until the age of sixteen. In 1912, he went to Beijing, enrolled in Qinghua University, and lived there for nine years, becoming a May Fourth student activist. In 1921, at the age of twenty-five, he left for the United States on a Boxer Indemnity scholarship. In 1925, after earning his B.A. and M.A. degrees from the University of Wisconsin, he went to the London School of Economics and Political Science for graduate studies. One year at the L.S.E. was sufficient to turn him into a Fabian socialist under the influence of Harold J. Laski, the newly appointed professor of political science. (Laski's 1925 book *A Grammar of Politics*, widely used as a textbook in Western universities, was translated two years later into Chinese by Zhang Junmai, making a significant impact on a generation of Chinese liberal intellectuals.) In 1927, Luo returned to the United States to complete his doctorate at Columbia University with a dissertation on the British parliamentary system. He arrived back in China in 1928 to take up an appointment as professor of political science at Guanghua University in Shanghai. A frequent contributor to *The Crescent*, he was to become one of those responsible for transforming the magazine into a political review as well as

---

[22] Zhongguo shehui kexueyuan jindaishi yanjiusuo Zhonghua minguo shiliaoshi, comp., *Hu Shi laiwang shuxinxuan* (Selected correspondence of Hu Shi) (Hong Kong: Zhonghua shuju, 1983), I, 517.

[23] Nathan, "Sources of Chinese Rights Thinking," p. 156.

for its Fabianesque tone, earning a reputation as an incisive political critic.[24]

Luo had a profound knowledge of Western political systems and held deep liberal convictions. According to his political biographer, he "felt obliged neither to reconcile Occidental values with the weight of Confucian history as the first generation [of Chinese liberals] did, nor to repudiate the past as the second generation [the May Fourth iconoclasts] did."[25] He was able to conceptualize human rights from a Western perspective unfettered by Confucian values and traditions.

In his article on human rights in *The Crescent*, Luo proclaimed that the bankruptcy of human rights in China was a fact that could not be covered up, accusing the government of arbitrary arrests, imprisonment without trial, and secret executions. These actions, he went on, were not isolated incidents perpetuated by individual corrupt and cruel officials; rather, they were symptomatic of a bad system of government, for which the leadership should be held responsible.[26] His attacks on the government were direct and powerful, pulling no punches and mincing no words.

Luo defined human rights as "whatever conditions necessary for one to be human (*zuoren*)," the most important of which was the right to preserve life (*weichi shengming*). He did not distinguish between the right to live and the right to life.[27] But no doubt he appreciated that the right to life was only the lowest common denominator. To live, people need more than clothing, food, shelter, work, and personal safety. They should also enjoy the right to develop their individuality and capacities, to cultivate personality, to be happy, and to be at their best. Most important, they should be able to contribute to the attainment of the goal of the greatest happiness of the greatest number, or the wide community (*renqun*).[28] Luo's range of human rights was broad, enumerating a total

---

[24] For a brief outline of Luo's life, see Howard L. Boorman, ed., *Biographical Dictionary of Republican China* (New York: Columbia University Press, 1967–1971), II, 435–438. For a detailed political biography, see Frederic J. Spar, "Human Rights and Political Activism: Luo Longji in Chinese Politics, 1928–1958," a 1993 manuscript based on his 1980 Ph.D. dissertation.

[25] Ibid., p. 13.

[26] Luo Longji, "Lun renquan" (On human rights), *XY* 2:5 (July 10, 1929): 1.

[27] For a distinction between the right to life and the right to live made by contemporary scholars, see D. Premont, ed., *Essays on the Concept of a "Right to Live"* (Brussels: Bruylant, 1988). Olivier Yeyrat in that volume (p. 57) has suggested that "the right to life could appear as the lowest common denominator, the 'right to live' as the highest." Cited in Kent, *Between Freedom and Subsistence*, p. 16.

[28] Luo Longji, "Lun renquan," pp. 3–5.

of thirty-five rights, including popular sovereignty, personal freedom, equality, rule of law, basic civil liberties (such as freedoms of thought, speech, belief, the press, and association), an independent judiciary, social equity, nondiscrimination, equal opportunity, rights to work, property, and an education, and a number of bureaucratic and administrative reforms.[29] These rights did not seem to be listed in order of priority. Together, they were essential for a decent human life, good government, and a good society.

Luo did not owe his human rights ideas to the thought of Thomas Hobbes or of Jean-Jacques Rousseau. In fact, like Edmund Burke, Jeremy Bentham, and Karl Marx, he rejected Hobbes's theory of natural rights as well as the idea that rights are the satisfaction of all personal desires. He also dismissed Rousseau's notion of a state of nature in which human beings were free, equal, self-sufficient, and contented – the ideal of the "noble savage." But he acknowledged that rights were prior to the state, apparently accepting Rousseau's notion of the social contract and Hobbes's philosophy of government by consent.[30]

If Hu's approach to human rights was legalistic, Luo's was functional. A utilitarian liberal, Luo was profoundly influenced by Harold Laski, whose *A Grammar of Politics* was a major source of his rights thinking. It was Laski's view that "rights are those conditions of social life without which no man can seek, in general, to be himself at his best."[31] That does not mean to guarantee that one's best self will be attained; it means only that "the hindrances to its attainment are removed so far as the action of the State can remove them."[32] What, then, is the obligation or duty of the individual in return for his or her rights? For Laski,

> Rights . . . are correlative with functions. I have them that I may make my contribution to the social end. I have no right to act unso- cially [sic]. I have no claim to receive without the attempt, at least, to pay for what I receive. Function is thus implicit in right. In return for the conditions with which I am provided, I seek to make pos- sible a contribution that enriches the common stock. And that con- tribution must be personal, or it is not a contribution at all. . . . I

---

[29] Ibid., pp. 17–25.
[30] Ibid., pp. 5–6; also Luo Longji, " 'Renquan' shiyi" (Discourse on human rights), *XY* 3:10 (November 1930): 9–10.
[31] Harold J. Laski, *A Grammar of Politics*, 5th ed. (London: George Allen and Unwin, 1967), p. 91. The book was originally published in 1925 by Columbia University Press.
[32] Ibid., p. 98.

have to do something that is worth doing in order to enjoy that which the experience of history has proved to be worth enjoying. I may pay my debt to the State by being a bricklayer or an artist, or a mathematician. Whatever form my paying takes, it is essential that I should realise that the rights I have are given to me because I am performing some given duties.[33]

In a similar vein, Luo wrote:

I am only a member of the community. I do not exist independently of it. Rather my happiness is related to the happiness of the entire community. It is my responsibility to contribute to it to the best of my ability so that the whole community can be itself at its best, ultimately leading to the greatest happiness of the greatest number.[34]

Just as Laski talked about paying one's debt to the state for the rights one enjoys, so Luo spoke of one's responsibility to society. For both, the test of rights was social utility.

There were two essential elements in Luo's conception of human rights. One was personal freedoms and happiness, and the other was the individual as a responsible member of society. Even though the individual has a right to be free and happy, Luo dismissed John Locke's idea of the atomistic individual who may be left alone in society, protected in the creation of personal property. His liberalism was the new liberalism of Laski and the Fabians, not the laissez-faire liberalism of Locke and Adam Smith.[35] For Luo, human rights were both means to an end – the end being the common good, "the happiness of the largest number" – and an end in themselves, that is, developing one's human powers or capacities and being at one's best.

Although Luo shared with Bentham a disbelief in the notion of natural and inalienable rights,[36] he rejected the view that rights are the products of law – that is, people possess only such rights as are given them or allowed them by law. He was prepared to accept that the test of proper

---

[33] Ibid., p. 94.   [34] Luo Longji, "Lun renquan," p. 5.

[35] Terry Narramore, "Luo Longji and Chinese Liberalism, 1928–32," *Papers on Far Eastern History* 32 (1985): 173.

[36] Bentham called that theory "rhetorical nonsense upon stilts," maintaining that "Right is the child of law; from real laws come real rights, but from imaginary laws, from laws of nature come imaginary rights. . . . Natural rights is simple nonsense." Quoted in Maurice Cranston, "What Are Human Rights?" in Walter Laqueur and Barry Rubin, eds., *The Human Rights Reader* (New York: Meridian Book, 1977), p. 18.

law is the degree to which it promotes the greatest happiness of the greatest number, but he did not think that human rights were necessarily dependent on law. "From the law I can at the most know what rights I presently enjoy, but I cannot find what rights I *ought* [emphasis added] to have." He pointed out that law and justice were two separate things, the important thing being to ensure that laws were enacted to protect rights.[37] Here again, Luo acknowledged Laski, who held that "The State, briefly, does not create, but recognizes rights, and its character will be apparent from the rights that, at any given period, secure recognition."[38] Also invoking Rousseau's dictum that "law is the expression of the general will," Luo concluded that "the law protects human rights, and in turn human rights produce laws."[39] He disagreed with the Nationalist government's view that rights were granted by the state.

Luo held that the state exists to perform certain functions; once those functions are lost, the raison d'être of its existence is gone. The state is a trust whose duty it is to regulate and protect rights, including the right to private property. The authority of the state is limited, not absolute, as are people's obedience and duties to it.[40] If the state fails to protect rights, it is a human right to resist oppression. He invoked Locke's idea of the "right of revolution," which he understood as equivalent to Mencius's notion of the Mandate of Heaven, justifying rebellion against the oppressive king. Any rights could be transgressed by the state, but not the "right of revolution" – "a last resort" for the oppressed people. Sun Yat-sen, he added, had exercised this right to defend liberty and equality.[41]

Luo was not arguing for a weak state. He acknowledged that the state should enjoy extensive powers capable of commanding loyalty from its citizens, but he also maintained that both state and individual should fulfill the social contract. Like the Communists, he regarded the state as a tool, but, unlike them, he insisted that it should be used for promoting the happiness of all sections of the population and not the interests of the laboring classes alone. The state, he declared, is only one of the many kinds of human organizations whose relationship with the individual is one, not of domination, but of cooperation based on reciprocity, mutual constraints, and mutual responsibilities – the notion of a social contract and interaction between state and society.[42]

---

[37] Luo Longji, "Lun renquan," p. 6.
[38] Laski, *A Grammar of Politics,* p. 89; also quoted in ibid., p. 10.
[39] Luo Longji, "Lun renquan," p. 13.   [40] Ibid., pp. 7–10.   [41] Ibid., pp. 13–14.
[42] Luo Longji, "Women yao shenmeyang de zhengzhi zhidu" (What sort of political system do we want?), *XY* 2:12 (February 10, 1930): 5–7.

While he was talking about a Laskian social contract, at the back of his mind was perhaps also the Confucian tradition that emphasized loyalty of the people on the one hand and, on the other, the state's duty to care for them, if not actually to provide for their basic subsistence. Given his Anglo-American education, he had a profound understanding of liberalism and the sense of personal freedom associated with it. Frederic Spar has argued that "Luo unwaveringly placed the individual, not the state, at the center of his deliberations."[43] Spar is right to the extent that Luo believed that the state must protect individual rights. However, characteristic of China's liberal intellectuals at the time, Luo, while standing up for rights, disapproved of rampant individualism and social irresponsibility, insisting on the free individual's duties to society. He was not arguing that rights were derived from duties. The correlation between rights and duties was for him a matter of reciprocity, mutual benefit, not of competing interests, because it was possible for rights to be enjoyed and duties to be performed at the same time. What should one do in the event of a clash between them? Luo seems to have avoided this question. The challenge for him and other like-minded intellectuals was to strike a balance between personal liberties and state powers and to reconcile individual interests with those of society, a question that had been addressed by some Western liberal thinkers before.[44] Yet Luo did not feel compelled to reconcile his utilitarian concerns with the values of classic liberalism. Moreover, the idea of social utility allowed him to sit comfortably with the Chinese tradition that stressed duties and obligations. However, that idea is double-edged. On the one hand, it could be used to bolster an expansion of rights so that the free individuals could improve the quality and quantity of their contributions to society. On the other hand, it could be used by the authoritarian state to restrict rights ostensibly in the public interest.

Luo distinguished between human rights (*renquan*) and people's

---

[43] Frederic J. Spar, "Human Rights and Political Engagement: Luo Longji in the 1930s," in Roger B. Jeans, ed., *Roads Not Taken: The Struggle of Opposition Parties in Twentieth-Century China* (Boulder: Westview Press, 1992), p. 62.

[44] Nathan, "Sources of Chinese Rights Thinking," p. 137. Where liberty ends and where license begins was a worry for Cicero and his contemporaries. Centuries before, Plato also wrestled with this issue in considering the ideal form of government. Reflecting on the shortcomings of democratic rule, as he defined it, he said that "an excessive desire for liberty at the expense of everything else is what undermines democracy and leads to the demand for tyranny." Quoted in Phillip Gibson, "Asian Values, Western Values and Human Rights," keynote address delivered at the Twelfth New Zealand International Conference on Asian Studies, Massey University, November 26, 1997, p. 5.

rights (*minquan*). By the latter he meant rights conferred upon the citizenry by the state – in other words, citizen's rights. The difference between the two terms here was important for him, for he understood citizen's rights to be derived from the state, whereas human rights were prior to the law. It is possible, he pointed out, for a person to be stateless, but there can be no citizen who is not a human being. The scope of human rights, therefore, is broader than that of citizen's rights. He criticized Sun Yat-sen's *minquan* as being too narrowly defined in political terms, not including civil liberties like liberty, equality, and personal freedoms.[45]

Luo's distinction between *renquan* and *minquan* is a fine one, but human rights do include basic civil and political rights derived from the ancient notion, of Grecian origin, of the natural rights of the individual.[46] These rights have sometimes been called "first-generation" human rights, or "negative rights" (so called because they involve protection from harmful state action) and have been denigrated by socialists, communists, and nationalistic leaders of the underdeveloped societies as expressions of Western bourgeois culture and notions of individualism. These include neither "economic, social, and cultural rights" nor "positive rights" (so named because they generally require positive state action for their realization), which have come to be known as "second-generation" human rights.[47] Reflecting on the evolution of rights in England, France, and the United States from a historical perspective, Luo found that the meaning

---

[45] Luo Longji, "Renquan buneng liuzai yuefa li" (Human rights cannot stay in the provisional constitution), in "Miscellany," *XY* 3:7 (August 1930): 3–7.

[46] Civil rights may be defined as rights of immunity that the individual enjoys free from the interference of the state and others and independent of the general social conditions of society in which one lives. They include freedom of thought; freedom of conscience and religion; freedom of expression and association; freedom of residence and movement; the right to life; freedom from arbitrary killing, torture, or mistreatment; freedom from slavery, arbitrary arrest, or detention; and equality before the law. Political rights may be understood as rights of participation in politics, including the right of access to public service and the right of election and recall of government. See Kent, *Between Freedom and Subsistence*, p. 8.

[47] The Universal Declaration of Human Rights of 1948 added to the civil and political rights in the first twenty-one articles a set of new "economic and social" rights, or the second generation of human rights. "Group rights" were included in the 1966 International Covenant on Civil and Political Rights and the 1966 International Covenant on Economic, Social, and Cultural Rights. These rights stated that human beings form peoples who are entitled to political self-determination and control over their own natural resources as well as to live in a peaceful, healthy, and economically developing environment.

and content of human rights had changed over time and space since the eighteenth century. Thus, he acknowledged that human rights were both temporal and spatial and that demands for certain conditions necessary for human existence varied from time to time and from society to society. Although certain conditions existed at a given time in a given place, others did not because of different historical development and different circumstances.[48]

The view that human rights are historical, meaning that they could not be asserted abstractly of the entity human beings but must be related to the development of the society in which particular people live, was as acceptable to Luo as to Laski. Human rights are not unlimited and absolute. Like Bentham and Mill before him, Luo thought that different liberties fitted different stages of historical development, a view consistent with his rejection of the theory of natural rights. But he was not talking about cultural relativism. Rather, he was convinced more than ever that human rights, as distinct from unlimited freedoms, were now suited to China and could be put to good use. Yet his conception of human rights was in opposition to China's existing socioeconomic conditions. He stressed the right to an education and the right to work as well as the state's obligation to provide work and job opportunities for the citizens, in addition to relief and welfare in the event of natural disasters.[49] However, throughout the 1930s and until the mid-1940s, he paid little attention to social injustice and the economic plight of the Chinese masses, that is, to economic and social rights that the Communists emphasized. His chief concerns, which were shared by his group, were political and institutional, blaming violations of human rights on the shortcomings of the existing political system and the failings of the GMD regime.

CENTRAL CONCERNS OF THE HUMAN RIGHTS GROUP

The Human Rights Group set the liberal opposition agenda. Not all their concerns were fully articulated in 1929–1931, but these were identified at this point and would dominate the democracy discourse over the next twenty years.

[48] Luo Longji, "Lun renquan," pp. 14–17.
[49] See Nos. 16, 17, and 34 on his list of 35 rights referred to above in note 29 in this chapter.

Political Tutelage and One-Party Dictatorship

Political tutelage was inseparable from one-party rule. The GMD's argument for political tutelage, as noted previously, was anchored to the bedrock of Sun Yat-sen's three-stage revolutionary theory. Opposition to political tutelage inevitably entailed a critique of his democratic thought. With due respect for what he had done for China, critics were not impressed with his leadership style, or with his sheet-of-loose-sand theory. Liang Shiqiu, a literary critic, teacher, and translator of Western literature, attributed Sun's dictatorial tendencies partly to his frustration as a revolutionary leader and partly to Soviet influence after 1923. Questioning his theory, Liang argued cogently that individual liberty and state freedom were not mutually exclusive, both being desirable and necessary.[50]

Also called into question was the assumption that the GMD was equal to the task of political tutelage. When Hu argued that both people and government needed training in democracy, he was questioning the GMD's monopoly of power and its solipsistic claims to "absolute" knowledge of, and *the* answer to, China's ills. What the people needed, Hu argued, was not political tutelage but a "civic life in a civil society" (*gongmin shenghuo*) in which rights were enjoyed. He rejected Sun's argument that the early Republic had failed because constitutional rule had been ahead of national unification and political tutelage. The Republic had failed, Hu contended, because constitutional government was not established in the first place. "Without constitutionalism, political tutelage is nothing but autocracy. Surely that would not train people to go down the democratic road."[51] He was adamant that only a constitutional government was qualified for political tutelage. Apparently, he was not opposed to political tutelage per se. What he objected to was political tutelage without a constitution that guaranteed rights. He seemed to think, naïvely, that rights would be duly protected after a constitution was adopted.

Constitutional tutelage was acceptable to Hu as a temporary measure, but Luo would not consider it. Luo regarded political tutelage as part of a dictatorship, which, be it personal, party, or class, did not serve the purpose or function of the state. He further argued that just as the shareholders of a company did not need a period of managerial autocracy

---

[50] Liang Shiqiu, "Sun Zhongshan xiansheng lun ziyou" (Mr. Sun Zhongshan and liberty), *XY* 2:9 (November 10, 1929): 1–7.

[51] Hu Shi, "Women shenme shihou caikeyou xianfa?" pp. 5–8; the quote is on p. 5.

before participating in the affairs of the company, so the people did not need years of dictatorship before participating in the affairs of the state. He questioned that the people could be taught about political rights in a political system that did not allow them to exercise those rights. Like Hu, he contended that the political inexperience of the people was not a problem because political experience was incremental and democracy a learning process. They were both impressed with the Anglo-American model because it was one of trial and error that allowed learning from experience.[52]

Responding to concerns about the administrative inefficiency of Western democracy, Luo pointed out that political tutelage and authoritarianism did not make the Nationalist regime any more efficient. If anything, the regime was ineffective because of the incompetence of self-serving Party members. He singled out the malfeasance in the public service examination system. Instead of being open and competitive, it had become "a spoils system" whereby people joined the Party through personal connections, motivated by a desire to secure a government post and thereby enrich themselves (*shengguan facai*) like the imperial bureaucrats of old. Consequently, the best positions were held by Party hacks, not always the best persons for the jobs. He condemned that kind of public administration as "rule by Party members . . . a source of official corruption, a retrogressive step, political suicide, and a dead end for China."[53]

Nanjing was not only undemocratic and repressive but also inefficient and corrupt. From Laski, Luo learned that a working theory of the state must be conceived in administrative terms. Critics of government, Laski wrote, should

> concentrate attention less on the problems of power than on the problems of administration. . . . For so long as we deal with the concept of an intangible State, so long shall we miss the central fact that what is truly important is the relationships of those who act as its agents. It is the things they do and fail to do, the process in which their actions are embodied, that constitute the reality of political discussion.[54]

---

[52] Luo Longji, "Women yao shenmeyang de zhengzhi zhidu," pp. 10–13.

[53] Luo, Longji, "Wo dui dangwu shang de 'jinqing piping'" (My "thorough criticism" of Party work), *XY* 2:8 (October 10, 1929): 11–13.

[54] Quoted in Jerome B. Grieder, *Intellectuals and the State in Modern China* (New York: The Free Press, 1981), p. 342.

In other words, the state "is judged not by what it is in theory, but by what it does in practice. The state, therefore, is subject to a moral test of adequacy. There is no a priori rightness about its decisions."[55] Measuring the Nationalist government against this standard, Luo found it woefully inadequate. The problem lay with its monopoly of power and lack of popular supervision, resulting in official corruption and graft. Furthermore, like other authoritarian regimes, the GMD sought to control people's minds.

Thought Control and Freedom of Speech

One of the principles on which the Western notion of human rights rests is freedom of the mind, the spirit, and the will – an essential right that satisfies one's desire to express one's view. In this sense, it is an end in itself. But Luo, the utilitarian liberal, also saw social utility in freedom of speech; making contributions to society through reasoned public debate is a social responsibility. Conversely, suppression of such freedom destroys one's personality and individuality, which is tantamount to destroying one's life and, ultimately, the life of the wide community.[56]

Freedom of speech could pose a threat to the existing order, but Luo warned that its suppression was a far, far greater danger to the authorities. The only good thought was that which could be debated in a public forum and stand up against public scrutiny. Freedom of thought and expression must be absolute: "If there is no absolute freedom, there is absolutely no freedom."[57] Yet Luo did not judge any aspect of human

---

[55] Laski, p. 28.

[56] Luo Longji, "Lun renquan," p. 7. Luo acknowledged Laski, who wrote: "The view I am concerned to urge is that from the standpoint of the State the citizen must be left unfettered to express either individually, or in concert with others, any opinions he happens to hold. He may preach the complete inadequacy of the social order. He may demand its overthrow by armed revolution. He may insist that the political system is the apotheosis of perfection. He may argue that all opinions which differ from his own ought to be subject to the severest suppression. He may himself as an individual urge these views or join with others in their announcement. Whatever the form taken by their expression he is entitled to speak without hindrance of any kind. He is entitled, further, to use all the ordinary means of publication to make his views known. He may publish them as a book or pamphlet or in a newspaper; he may give them in the form of a lecture; he may announce them at a public meeting. To be able to do any or all of these things, with the full protection of the State in so doing, is a right that lies at the basis of freedom." See Laski, p. 120.

[57] Luo Longji, "Gao yabo yanlun ziyouzhe" (Advice to those who suppress freedom of speech), *XY* 2:6–7 (September 10, 1929): 9–10.

life in absolute terms. The question is whether he valued freedoms of thought and speech more for their social utility.[58] It would appear that he viewed them both as means to an end and an end in themselves.

Luo was as anticommunist as he was critical of the government. He saw a fertile ground for communism in China because of the Nationalist dictatorship and official corruption. To remove the cause for communism, he argued, it was necessary for the government to abolish one-party dictatorship, abandon any attempts at thought control, and effect administrative change. Sensitive political questions such as communism and political reform should be allowed to be discussed and debated in public. Suppression of free speech would only drive discussions of those questions underground to the detriment of the authorities.[59]

Thought control and the lack of freedom of speech in China constituted a national disgrace. Writing in a draft paper entitled "We Want Our Freedoms," Hu Shi felt a sense of mission. Intellectuals like himself, he declared, needed freedoms to fulfill their duties as citizens of the state. They must make constructive criticisms of the government by generating and participating in reasoned debates, as well as fostering a new culture in which China's scholars would concern themselves with the important public issues of the day. Hu wanted them to play the role of public supervisors of the government and leaders of political parties.[60] Like Luo, he saw social utility in free speech and a free press while holding dear the intrinsic value of such freedoms.

What alarmed the human rights activists was the government's attempt to unify people's thought (*sixiang tongyi*) under the Party ideology, politicizing education, literature, and art through a process of "Party-ization" (*danghua*). Liang Shiqiu, noted for his advocacy of the independence and aesthetic purposes of literary expression, immediately warned that thought control could only spawn radical opposition and create "enormous social chaos." What the Chinese needed was emancipation of thought and a liberal education, not unity of thought, which was impossible anyway.[61]

---

[58] Narramore, "Luo Longji and Chinese Liberalism 1928–32," p. 181.
[59] On Luo's critique of communism and the CCP, see "Lun gongchan zhuyi: gongchan zhuyi lilun shang de piping" (On communism: A critique), *XY* 3:1 (November 10, 1930): 1–22; and "Lun Zhongguo de gongchan" (On the communization of China), *XY* 3:10 (February 1931): 1–18.
[60] Geng Yunzhi, *Hu Shi nianpu, 1891–1962* (A chronology of Hu Shi's life, 1891–1962) (Hong Kong: Zhonghua shuju, 1966), p. 111.
[61] Liang Shiqiu, "Lun sixiang tongyi" (On unity of thought), *XY* 2:3 (May 10, 1929): 6–8.

Calls for the emancipation of thought, a free press, and a liberal education were refrains of the May Fourth era. In 1929, the human rights advocates rose again to defend the new culture. In a sharply worded essay entitled "The New Culture Movement and the GMD," Hu criticized the GMD as a party of the old culture, a reactionary party that had become petrified intellectually and alienated many a progressive thinker. He was particularly angered by the GMD's propaganda chief, Ye Chucang, who had started to glorify China's "golden age of virtues" prior to the Manchu Dynasty and spoken of the need to "restore" the nation from the "corrupting influences" of current times. Hu castigated the Nationalist regime as an enemy of freedoms of thought and speech, actively suppressing skepticism and the critical spirit. "One may deny God, but one cannot criticize Sun Zhongsan [Sun Yat-sen]. One does not have to go to the Church [on Sundays], but one cannot miss reading the will of the *zongli* or attending the weekly memorial ceremony [for him]."[62]

Thought control was only one aspect of the old culture. Another was the lack of a rule of law.

Rule of Law

In the Western legal tradition, law is binding on everyone, including the law makers themselves. It is meant to prevent arbitrary actions by those in authority and to guarantee a realm of freedom essential to the protection of life and human dignity against tyrannical oppression on the one hand and the regulation of human relations and activities in the community on the other. The rule of law means justice under a set of rules and guidelines applied equally to all, without the arbitrary swings to and fro that characterize both authoritarian and totalitarian regimes. It holds due process in as high regard as it holds outcome. And its starting point is protection of rights and limitation of state powers. The state's ability to coerce is limited by law that it cannot change at will, and rights may not be transgressed by others, including the civil authority, even for good reasons. The rule of law excludes the government from interfering with the citizenry within their private realm. Politically, it is related to proceduralism as a foundation for a democratic system of government. In terms of justice, it also means the rule of *just* laws (let it be noted, though, that many laws are less than just in democratic states).

---

[62] Hu Shi, "Xinwenhua yundong yu Guomindang" (The New Culture Movement and the Guomindang), *XY* 2:6–7 (September 10, 1929): 1–15; the quote is on p. 4.

Traditionally, Chinese political culture was characterized by *renzhi* (rule of man). The Chinese legal system was an amalgam of Legalism and Confucianism, based on a system of ethics and customs rather than on a system of formal, legal safeguards. Chinese laws were rules and regulations used to protect the ruling class and to maintain social stability and the existing order. They were also used as an instrument of crime control and punishment, not for the protection of the rights and interests of the subjects. There was no distinction between administrative commands and legal rules, nor between civil and criminal laws, nor a concept of separation between the functions of policing and the administration of justice. Because laws were made for the people to obey, they could be changed at the whim of the rulers who made them. The Western notion of equality before the law was alien to Chinese thought. Just as Confucian society was hierarchical, so Chinese laws were graded and unequal, with those in authority being above the law. Moreover, there was a well-established social tradition in which people dreaded litigation, preferring to settle disputes socially, that is out of court through mediation and conciliation so that social harmony could be maintained.[63]

Renzhi emphasized personal charisma (in the Weberian sense), benevolence, and good government. It was a style of politics and public administration that superseded institutions and recognized no political rules or mechanisms for conflict resolution and peaceful transfer of power. Because of its dependence on personalities, the way in which justice was administered varied from magistrate to magistrate, resulting in official corruption as well as arbitrary actions by those in authority. In short, *renzhi* impeded institutional development and the establishment of a modern rule of law.

The Nationalist rule was in the *renzhi* tradition. Thus, Hu insisted that just as the ordinary people needed a "civil life in a civil society," so the government should lead a life of rule of law (*fazhi shenghuo*).[64] He had personal reasons to be concerned about the government's abuse of power. Following the publication of his articles on human rights and constitutionalism, critics in the GMD attacked him for violating the Party doctrine and undermining the Party spirit.[65] On October 4, 1929, the Minister for Education, Jiang Menglin, who, ironically, was Hu's Columbia

---

[63] For the traditional Chinese legal system, see D. Bodde and C. Morris, *Law in Imperial China* (Cambridge, MA: Harvard University Press, 1967).

[64] Hu Shi, "Women shenme shihou caikeyou xianfa?" p. 6.

[65] See Zhang Zhenzhi, *Ping Hu Shi fandangyi zhu* (A critique of Hu Shi's anti-Party doctrine writings) (Shanghai: Guangming shuju, 1929).

University mate and one-time Beijing University colleague, reprimanded him for his "antirevolutionary," "old-fashioned," and "ridiculous" views. Hu was alleged to have misinterpreted the Party's ideology and the thought of Sun Yat-sen and was further criticized for his "arrogance," "ill-intentions," and "superstition about Western democracy." Most serious of all, he was accused of sabotaging the Party center and national unity. Consequently, he was dismissed from his position as principal of Shanghai's China Public Institute (*Zhongguo gongxue*).[66]

Hu's legalistic approach to human rights led him to insist that civil rights movements should proceed from a legal premise. He recognized the functions of law in an evolving political order and the need to educate people about the concepts of rights and freedoms and how these could be defended through a process of law. In December 1932, following the arrests by the government of a number of dissidents and Communists, an organization called the Chinese League for the Protection of Civil Rights was formed in Shanghai, under the leadership of Song Qingling, an outspoken critic of the GMD since 1927, and Cai Yuanpei. Its objectives were to secure the release of all political prisoners, to provide them with legal and other assistance, and to fight for the freedoms of speech, publication, assembly, and association. Early in 1933, a branch of the League was set up in Beijing, with Hu as chairman. While opposing the government's arbitrary arrests and suppression of civil liberties, Hu insisted that the aim of the League's movement should be twofold: first, to oversee the government, and second, to educate the people on the functions of the law in protecting their rights. "The law can only define our rights, but not protect them. The protection of rights rests solely on the individual efforts to cultivate a mind that refuses to forsake rights."[67] He did not endorse the League's demand for the "unconditional release of all political prisoners," arguing that all those who were branded revolutionary or antigovernment and who had been arrested on political grounds should be given the same legal protection as everyone else who had been arrested on different charges. He was highly critical of the habit of relying on personal relations (*renqing* and *guanxi*) to secure the release of the detainees. Not wishing to be part of the League's effort to turn what he thought was a legal issue into a political cause, he accepted

---

[66] Yang Tianshi, "Hu Shi yu Guomindang de yiduan jiufen" (Hu Shi's differences with the Nationalist Party), *Zhongguo wenhua* 9 (Spring 1991): 125.
[67] Hu Shi, "Minquan de baozhang" (The protection of civil rights), *DLPL* 38 (February 19, 1933): 2.

the government's right to deal with political opponents who sought to subvert it or overthrow it by force, provided that the due process of law was followed.[68] Seeing the political prisoners as a legal issue rather than a political one, he was out of tune with the other human rights activists, who did not believe that the government would follow the due process of law.

Luo recognized two broad categories of law in the West: constitutional law and the common law. He agreed with Hu that a constitution was important, but he feared that a constitution was sometimes used as a vehicle for violating rights by "certain individuals," "certain families," and "certain organizations."[69] Indirectly he was criticizing the GMD, its agents, and the big families connected with it. For these attacks, he, too, had to pay a price. On November 4, 1930, he was arrested in Wusong after a house search and taken to Shanghai, charged with expressing "reactionary" views and "insulting" Sun Yat-sen, which made him a communist suspect. Yet just as his arrest was sudden and arbitrary, so was his release. He was freed immediately after an unidentified powerful GMD figure (possibly Cai Yuanpei) intervened and bailed him out. He was so outraged by the incident that he later published an article about it in *The Crescent*.[70] There was more trouble ahead. In July 1931 police raided the premises of the Beijing office of *The Crescent*, made a few arrests, and confiscated over a thousand copies of the July issue, where Luo was alleged to have "denigrated" the Provisional Constitution, which the GMD had just adopted.[71] This provoked him to blast the authorities again in an article entitled "What Is Rule of Law?"

In that essay, Luo emphasized three points. First, rule of law meant that those in authority should obey the law themselves, that their prerogatives and arbitrary, or discretionary, powers should be curtailed, and that rulers and the ruled were equal before the law. Second, not only should rights be guaranteed constitutionally, but they should also be

---

[68] Ibid., pp. 2–5; Zhongguo kexueyuan jindaishi yanjiusuo, ed., *Zhongguo minquan baozhang tongmeng* (The Chinese League for the Protection of Civil Rights) (Beijing: Zhongguo shehui kexue chubanshe, 2nd ed., 1984), pp. 105–106; Jerome B. Grieder, *Hu Shih and the Chinese Renaissance: Liberalism in the Chinese Revolution, 1917–1937* (Cambridge, MA: Harvard University Press, 1970), pp. 277–278.

[69] Luo Longji, "Lun renquan," pp. 11–12.

[70] Luo Longji, "Wo de beibu de jingguo yu fan'gan" (My arrest and my disgust at it), *XY* 3:3 (January 10, 1931): 1–17.

[71] For Luo's critique of the Provisional Constitution of 1931, see "Dui xunzheng shiqi yuefa de piping" (Critique of the Provisional Constitution), *XY* 3:8 (July 10, 1931): 1–20.

spelled out in detail, emphasizing the due process of law. Third, all laws should be clear, delimited, and enforced.[72] The English sense of justice, the British legal system, and the notion of the absolute supremacy or predominance of regular law served as the underpinnings for his understanding of rule of law.

Sharing Hu's legalistic concerns, Luo went a step further to link human rights with institutional change. As a student of public administration, he was able to see that the fundamental problem with Chinese politics lay with weak institutions, which he blamed on the military ascendancy and official corruption. (It could be argued that military ascendancy and official corruption were the results as much as the causes of weak institutions.) "What sort of a political system do we want?" His answer, in short, was: "There is only one way for Chinese politics to go today, one that recognizes only institutions, not personalities. Once the system is on the right track, we support whoever is in power. Without a system in place that suits the [modern] time, we would oppose whoever is in government."[73] A sound system and strong institutions, he concluded, would reduce the chances for evil doings to a minimum, promote mutual cooperation, and exercise mutual restraints.[74] Institutional development was his prescription – and a right one – for China's political ills, a theme that he would ponder for many years.

Despite their slightly different approaches to human rights, Luo shared with Hu a profound belief in democratic institutions. Of course, democracy does not automatically ensure human rights, nor is it the panacea for all social and economic ills. The record of a number of Western democratic states over the last hundred years was pretty checkered. But democracy does provide the best safeguard against human rights violations. There being different variants of democracy, the question is, What model did Hu and company advocate?

DEMOCRACY AND "EXPERTOCRACY"

"Democracy is essentially a kind of education," wrote Hu in 1929, meaning that democracy involved a process of educating both government and people, a process of trial and error. The Chinese had no experience in democracy, but that was not a problem for Hu because they

---

[72] Luo Longji, "Shenme shi fazhi?" (What is rule of law?), *XY* 3:11 (December 1930): 1–17.
[73] Luo Longji, "Women yao shenmeyang de zhengzhi zhidu," p. 2.
[74] Ibid., p. 24.

needed the opportunity to gain the experience. Moreover, it was precisely for that reason that both rulers and ruled, like young kids needing education, should "go schooling" – a long process to be sure, but one that would produce the desired results over time.[75] Later, in 1933, Hu went so far as to argue that democracy was "kindergarten politics."[76] For the present, let us make a point about the education analogy. If everyone needs an education and is entitled to it, then everyone is entitled to be part of the democratic process. However, because not every Chinese had the opportunity to go to school, the elite would be the first to enjoy democratic rights, and the rest of the population just would have to wait. It was assumed that the modern elite who governed China would be enlightened and accountable. Chinese democracy would entail elections, political pluralism, and protection of human rights. But would there be universal suffrage and majority rule?

Luo was ambivalent in 1930, saying only that all those who had attained their majority could directly or indirectly participate in politics on an equal basis.[77] What he wanted to see was a representative government combining entrusted power with expert service. He called for the immediate opening of a National Constituent Assembly to adopt a constitution, advocating a democratic system of government not because it was perfect, but because, as Bertrand Russell had argued, it could control, contain, or minimize evil doings by those in authority. There could be no entrusted power without elections, competitive politics, and freedoms of thought, speech, publication, assembly, and association. Nor could there be expert service without an open and competitive civil service examination system, without legal safeguards for the terms of office, and without checking official corruption through legislation. On the question of representative bodies, Luo favored four categories: vocational bodies (including chambers of commerce, trade unions, peasant associations, educational associations, teachers associations, and the federation of student unions), local organizations (not stated exactly what these were), political parties, and the experts (professional societies).[78] However, no government, whatever its system, could be good without an able civil service. Emphasizing the importance of public administration, he shared Hu's view that politics was a "specialized science" (*zhuanmen*

---

[75] Hu Shi, "Women shenme shihou caikeyou xianfa?," pp. 4–5.
[76] See Chapter 4, pp. 115–119.
[77] Luo Longji, "Women yao shenmeyang de zhengzhi zhidu," p. 10.
[78] Ibid., pp. 15–24.

kexue), fit for the experts only, and not something for such laymen as many of those in the Nanjing regime.[79]

Hu took exception to Sun Yat-sen's adage that "knowledge is difficult, action is easy." Sun's thesis, he argued, overstated the dichotomy between knowledge and action, ignoring the fact that they are in a dialectical relationship where knowledge leads to action and action improves knowledge.[80] Hu was also concerned that it could encourage young people to develop an antiintellectual bias. If action is easy, why bother to acquire knowledge? It is no wonder that the military has an excuse to interfere with the business of government. To be sure, knowledge is difficult. But action is not easy either.

> The greatest danger today is that those in charge of the state do not understand their task is an absolutely complex and difficult one. Is there anything on earth more complex and difficult than having a group of men who have no modern academic training to govern a country that lacks the foundations of a modern materialist state? To undertake their task, there is no other way than to consult the experts and apply science [to China's problems].[81]

He rejected the assumption that the GMD alone knew how to govern China. If action was easy, why was the government's rhetoric not matched by actions?

Hu distinguished between popular participation in politics (*renmin canzheng*) and administering the state (*zhiguo*). The former did not require specialized knowledge because what the people needed was experience through participation, whereas the latter was a big enterprise involving the solution of specific problems through the application of specialized knowledge. Politically passive, the people should be induced to participate in politics (presumably through the ballot box).[82] After making this distinction, which really was a distinction between electing the government and running it, he was able to insist that the business of government was the responsibility of the experts, his message being that

---

[79] Luo Longji, "Zhuanjia zhengzhi" (Expert politics), *XY* 2:2 (April 10, 1929): 6. But Luo was much more critical of the Communists' ability to rule China should they win power. Observing that the CCP cadres had received only primary and secondary education, he characterized most of the junior party members as city rascals and country bandits. See his "Lun Zhongguo de gongchan," p. 5.

[80] Hu Shi, "Zhinan, xing yi bu yi" (To know is difficult, to act is not easy either), *XY* 2:4 (June 10, 1929): 12.

[81] Ibid., p. 15.   [82] Hu Shi, "Women shenme shihou caikeyou xianfa?," p. 4.

politicians should be advised and assisted by the specialists. This gave rise to the notion of "expert politics" (*zhuanjia zhengzhi*) and "government by experts" (*zhuanjia zhengfu*), or expertocracy.

It was left to Luo to provide the most scholarly analysis of the notion of expertocracy ever published in China. For a start, he understood "expert politics" in terms of the role of the state. Rejecting the laissez-faire liberalism of the eighteenth century, he viewed the state as an instrument of national development, especially in the areas of railways, telecommunications, transport, mining, reclamation, and the like, which, he believed, should not be left to the private sector. For him, the state was also an agent of social reform,[83] although it was not immediately clear what sort of social reform he considered necessary at this point. Further, taking a cue from Sun Yat-sen, he argued that just as a company needed a board of directors and expert managers, so a nation needed a capable president and an able government. Also drawing on Sun's *quan–neng* dichotomy, he maintained that expertocracy was composed of professional civil servants like a board of directors acting on behalf of the people, the shareholders:

> The legislative organ [of the government] is the company's board of directors, and the executive organ its administration charged with management. If the legislative organ commands the political authority entrusted to it, and if the executive organ employs men of specialized talents, then most of the problems that arise with respect to the political institutions of the state will be *ipso facto* resolved.[84]

There were, however, differences between Luo and Sun in four respects. First, whereas Sun's *neng* was the GMD elite, Luo's was from all quarters, hence the necessity of an open and competitive civil service examination system based on merit and equal opportunity. Sun had tried to enhance the standing and credibility of the Party government; nevertheless, Luo criticized its lack of administrative expertise. Second, Sun's board of directors and expert managers were responsible only to the Party and its leader, but Luo's were accountable to the people through representative bodies. Third, Luo's experts would face dismissal if they did not perform; Sun's would cling to power, and there was nothing to prevent them from corrupting themselves. Fourth, Luo was concerned with political and administrative reforms that alone could ensure

---

[83] Luo Longji, "Women yao shenmeyang de zhengzhi zhidu," pp. 5–7.
[84] Quoted in Grieder, *Intellectuals and the State,* p. 344.

expertocracy. His list of thirty-five human rights included overhauling the civil service examination system, banning military officers from holding civilian positions concurrently, introducing tax reform, and making government finances public.

Luo's criteria of good public administration were efficiency and cost-effectiveness.[85] He went so far as to say that he did not care what the ideology was as long as the administration was efficient.[86] He may have said that in a tongue-in-cheek manner; otherwise, it was a dangerous view to take because it could undermine the democratic cause he championed. If it could be demonstrated that democracy could not solve China's problems and that an authoritarian system could provide good governance and efficient administration, could a case not be made for neo-authoritarianism? Moreover, in the event of a conflict between democracy and efficiency, which should take precedence? These questions were not raised.

Luo linked human rights and democracy with political institutions. Hu was interested in his familiar homily that the scientific method, taught him by his mentor, John Dewey, offered the best solutions to China's problems, but Luo was convinced that institutional development offered the best hope for China's future. Additionally, Hu took a constitutional and legalistic approach to rights, whereas Luo was skeptical about the consummation of constitutional rule in the absence of administrative and political reforms. His emphasis on good governance and efficient administration reflected a major intellectual current of the Republican period – the attempt to link indirect democracy with elite systems of professional management. There was a danger that an expertocracy based on a small pool of talent – and China suffered from a dearth of talent – could give rise to a "new class" and an arrogant, if not oppressive, bureaucratic regime. Neither Hu nor Luo seemed concerned about this possibility, probably because they believed that as long as basic rights were enjoyed, especially free speech and a free press, the experts could be called to account.

The human rights advocates were concerned with political, not social, democracy. For them, democracy meant the broadening of the base of elite power and limited mass participation. The idea of majority rule was not entertained, nor was there any suggestion that the entire population would be politically empowered. Their conception of human rights was "negative" in the sense that rights must be protected from harmful state

[85] Luo Longji, "Zhuanjia zhengzhi," pp. 2–5.   [86] Ibid., p. 1.

action. It did not include membership of a political community in which effective participation was not only possible but also encouraged and facilitated. Little was written in 1929–1931 about universal suffrage by secret ballot, one person one vote, protection of the rights of the minority, or "positive rights."

The distinction between popular participation and administering the state betrayed tensions in Luo's and Hu's democratic thought. On the one hand, they rejected political tutelage and the argument that the people were not yet fit for democracy, thus standing up for them with a faith in their nativist wisdom and their ability to participate in the democratic process. On the other hand, they took an elitist view of the intellectuals' leadership role, having no time for the peasants and workers in matters of public administration and policy formulation, and sharing with Sun Yat-sen the wisdom of separating *quan* from *neng*. The business of government was a preserve for the moral–intellectual elite – the upper middle-class experts who would govern in the public interest. The idea was "for the people," "of the people," but not "by the people." Such elitism, however, need not be seen as "implicitly antidemocratic" as Grieder criticized.[87] Luo and company were not advocating democracy in the contemporary Millsian tradition. Their vision of democracy was that responsible elitism would be best suited to the Chinese tradition where the ordinary people (*lao baixing*) expected leadership from the civil elite and where, as John Fairbank observed, "the upper-class official had governed best when he had the true interests of the local people at heart and so governed on their behalf."[88] The notion of expertocracy was consistent with the traditional notion of selecting men of virtue and talent (*xuanxian yu neng*) for the civil service. What distinguished the new elite from the traditional literati was their enlightenment, their modern outlook, their defense of human rights (though not in the most liberal sense), and their insistence on representative institutions and responsible government. Equally important was their emphasis on a corpus of technically trained bureaucrats and administrators in whose hands necessarily lay the increasingly sophisticated operations of government, economics, industry, finance, and education, by which alone a modern state could function. Theirs was a kind of paternalistic democracy in which the enlightened government would work hand in hand with

---

[87] Grieder, *Intellectuals and the State,* p. 345.
[88] John K. Fairbank, *China: A New History* (Cambridge, MA: The Belknap Press of Harvard University Press, 1992), p. 319.

a technocratic elite, subject to popular supervision. They were strictly liberal in the classical sense of wanting to restrict government powers over the individual.

CONCLUSION

The issue of human rights was thrust into the political limelight in 1929–1931 not because of isolated incidents of transgression of rights, but because of wider questions about political tutelage and one-party dictatorship. In articulating their views in the pages of *The Crescent*, Hu and Luo represented public opinion, speaking for "the silent majority," as one of their friends put it.[89] They were critical of the Nationalist government, but they were also anticommunist. For this reason, writers in the PRC have interpreted the Human Rights Group as essentially a two-pronged bourgeois movement. On the one hand, it attacked the GMD dictatorship, exposing the government's "decadent, reactionary, and repressive" character; in this sense, it was positive and progressive in its advocacy of civil rights and liberties, rule of law, expertocracy, and popular supervision of government. On the other hand, it pinned high hopes on the government to carry out reforms and to eliminate the CCP. Moreover, it was constrained by class limitations and divorced from historical realities. Hu's insistence on reform and evolution is contrasted with the communist idea of change, whereas Luo is faulted for separating human rights from people's rights and for placing civil and political rights ahead of social and economic rights. Their legalistic and political approaches to the problems of China are described as "utopian" on the grounds that free speech, a free press, and democratic politics were neither sufficient to change the government nor substitutes for solutions to the most pressing problems facing the masses. Reflecting Beijing's current stand on human rights, the PRC writers have criticized that the Human Rights Group showed a lack of concern with the plight of the masses whose rights to clothing, food, and shelter, in short to subsistence, social justice, and economic equalities, were not given a higher priority.[90]

---

[89] A fellow liberal, Zhang Xiruo, wrote to Hu Shi in July 1929, lauding him for his "rare courage and seriousness in lecturing the government on such an important issue on behalf of the people, the silent majority." See Zhongguo shehui kexueyuan, comp., *Hu Shi laiwang shuxinxuan*, pp. 526–527.

[90] Qin Yingjun, "Zhongguo renquanpai sixiang qianxi" (A brief analysis of Chinese human rights thought), *Shixue yuekan* 6 (1986): 63–68; Liu Jianqing, "Renquanpai lunlüe" (An outline of the Human Rights Group), *Nankai xuebao* 2 (1987): 77–82; and Bao Heping,

There is some truth in these criticisms in that the Human Rights Group was interested in political, not social, democracy. In this chapter, we have seen a liberal philosopher (Hu) and a liberal student of public administration (Luo) trying together to prevail upon the authorities the need to carry out constitutional, legal, political, and administrative reforms. These reforms were on the agenda of civil opposition, an agenda set as early as 1929. Perhaps, basic human rights could be respected without a democratic form of government. Whether China was ready for democracy in the 1930s was open to debate. No one, however, would defend political repression. There was an elite consensus that basic rights and civil liberties should be guaranteed constitutionally and protected by law.

For all their critiques of the GMD regime, neither Hu nor Luo had much of an impact on the political process at this point. Human rights violations continued unabated. Early in 1932, Hu left Shanghai to take up an appointment as Dean of the College of Arts at Beijing University. There he soon launched a new magazine, *Duli pinglun* (The Independent Critic), but, as the Japanese threat to China escalated, he became less critical of the GMD, even though his passion for liberalism and democracy never diminished. Meanwhile, Luo had taken up a position as editor of Tianjin's independent newspaper *Yishibao* (Social Welfare). The Human Rights Group then disappeared before *The Crescent* ceased publication in July, by which time China had plunged into a crisis over Manchuria following the Mukden incident of September 18, 1931.

"Lun 'Renquanpai' de zhengzhi zhuzhang" (On the political platform of the Human Rights Group), *Minguo dang'an* 2 (1991): 79–87; Hu Weixi, Gao Ruiquan, and Zhang Limin, *Shizi jietou yu ta* (Crossroads and the tower) (Shanghai: Shanghai renmin chubanshe, 1991), pp. 285–293.

3

The National Emergency, 1932–1936

Political and Intellectual Responses

A FTER the outbreak of the Mukden incident, China's troubles had only just begun. Before the year 1931 was over, Japan had secured control of part of Manchuria. Then, on the night of January 26, 1932, Japanese naval forces, not to be outshone by the Kantong Army in Mukden, launched an attack on Shanghai. Four days later, the Nationalist government decided to remove its capital to Luoyang, where it remained until December. Early in February, Haerbin was captured by Japanese forces, after which the state of Manzhouguo (Manchukoku in Japanese) was formally set up on March 3, with its capital in Changchun (Jilin). Meanwhile, Chinese troops were forced to abandon Wusong near Shanghai, despite the stiff resistance of the Chinese Nineteenth Route Army and the Fifth Army Corps.

The onset of Japanese aggression brought about a "national emergency" (*guonan*), which again highlighted the issue of *jiuwang*. Of course, national salvation entailed resistance to the Japanese. The question was when to take up arms. Following the Mukden incident, the Nationalist government neither resisted the Kantong Army nor entered into any negotiations with Tokyo, choosing to turn to the League of Nations for help. Not wanting to fight the Japanese at this stage, Chiang Kai-shek pursued a policy of "first pacification, then resistance." Apart from his determination to eliminate the Communists first, Chiang was ill prepared for war against the Japanese army, which inspired awe and fear in him. He was also banking on the efficacy of the League of Nations in resolving the Manchurian problem. Even after the Japanese had advanced onto north China and consolidated their position there, Chiang still refused to take up arms, thinking that sooner or later Japan would clash with the Western powers, notably Britain and the United States, because of conflicts of interest.[1] Some regional forces, notably the Guangxi Clique led by Li Zongren, were quick to exploit the widespread anti-Chiang sentiment by calling for resistance.[2] The CCP, too, lost no time in capitalizing on the Japan issue, attacking the government in an effort to establish its nationalistic credentials. In the following years, numerous patriotic groups and organizations were formed, aimed at changing the government's policy and bringing about a broad anti-Japanese united front. Nanjing's nonresistance policy provided the ammunition that the opposition forces needed to attack Chiang in the name of antiimperialist nationalism.

But not every educated Chinese advocated immediate war at a time when China did not seem ready for it. Caution was voiced in some quarters. The British-educated geologist, Ding Wenjiang, then a professor at Beijing University, argued in 1932 that it was no good talking about recovering lost territory in Manchuria when the government ought to be defending what was under threat, like Rehe in the north. Following the Japanese seizure of Shanhaiguan, he urged Nanjing to compromise with the Japanese while seeking international support. Not opposed to resistance, he considered it imperative, though, that the GMD first be united, seek cooperation from all the military leaders around the country, and reach a truce with the CCP.[3] During the Rehe crisis of February 1933, he bluntly told an audience of Beijing University students that to advocate all-out war was irresponsible. He feared that war in 1933 would only lead to disastrous military defeat because China lacked the industrial and economic capacity to win a modern war. He urged them to concentrate

---

[1] Sun Youli, *China and the Origins of the Pacific War* (New York: St. Martin's Press, 1993), chs. 2–5. However, there was no lack of government members who favored resistance from the start. T. V. Soong, the Minister of Finance, was decidedly anti-Japanese. He had supported the Nineteenth Route Army and, after the conclusion of the Shanghai Truce on May 5, resigned from all government posts in protest and traveled to Shanghai where he issued a strong condemnation of Chiang Kai-shek's plans to proceed with the Fourth Extermination Campaign against the Communists. He did not resume office until July, having made his point. See Parks M. Coble, *Facing Japan: Chinese Politics and Japanese Imperialism, 1931–1937* (Cambridge, MA: Council on East Asian Studies, Harvard University, 1991), p. 60.

[2] The anti-Japanese theme of the Guangxi opposition is well treated in Su Mingxian, "The Regional Faction and Chinese Nationalism: A Case Study of Li Zongren and the Guangxi Clique During the Nanjing Decade," unpublished Ph.D. thesis, Griffith University, 1996.

[3] Ding Wenjiang, "KangRi jiaofei yu zhongyang de zhengju" (Resistance to Japan, extermination of the Communists, and the political situation in the center), *DLPL* 19 (September 25, 1932): 8–9; Ting Wenjiang, "Jiaru wo shi Jiang Jieshi" (If I were Jiang Jieshi), *DLPL* 35 (January 15, 1933): 3–4.

their efforts on training themselves as a skilled, modern elite instead.[4] After Rehe had been abandoned, he was willing to face heavy losses of Chinese territory to buy the time needed to build up China's defensive capacity. In 1935, he drew a parallel between Nanjing's predicament and that of Moscow just before Lenin made the Peace of Brest-Litovsk. Just as Lenin was prepared to abandon the Ukraine to the Germans in order to save the Bolshevik Republic, so the Nationalist leadership, Ding proposed, should be prepared to retreat to Hunan, Jiangxi, and Sichuan in order to save the Chinese Republic.[5]

Ding was not a voice in the wilderness. The diplomatic historian at Qinghua University, Jiang Tingfu, Ph.D. (Columbia), equally supported Nanjing's "first pacification, then resistance" policy. "To recover the lost territory by force is a no through road," he wrote in April 1934. "I think it is a dead road. . . . Our only way out is to rehabilitate the territory that is not yet lost, to which end the first step is to eliminate the Communists."[6] Hu Shi, initially opposed to negotiations with Japan, believed that China needed a long time to prepare for war, perhaps as long as fifty years, his message being that China could wait.[7] A pacifist, he approved of the unpopular Tanggu Truce of May 31, 1933, under which the Japanese agreed to withdraw voluntarily and completely to the Great Wall in return for the Nationalist government's cession of Heilongjiang, Jilin, Fengtian, and Rehe to Japan.[8] And Fu Sinian, the English- and German-educated Director of the Institute of History and Philology at the Academia Sinica and, like Hu Shi, a May Fourth veteran, advocated armed resistance because he did not trust the efficacy of the League of Nations in resolving the crisis. He warned that resistance must be "systematic," "organized," "protracted," and "cautious at every step" in view of China's

---

[4] Ding Wenjiang, "KangRi de xiaoneng yu qingnian de zeren" (The capacity to resist Japan and the youth's responsibility), *DLPL* 37 (February 12, 1933): 2–8; also cited in Charlotte Furth, *Ting Wen-chiang: Science and China's New Culture* (Cambridge, MA: Harvard University Press, 1970), p. 200.

[5] Ding Wenjiang, "Sue geming waijiao shi de yiye ji qi jiaoxun" (A page in the history of the foreign relations of the Russian revolution and its success), *DLPL* 163 (August 11, 1935): 15; also cited in Furth, *Science and China's New Culture*, p. 201.

[6] Jiang Tingfu, "Wei shiqu de jiangtu shi women de chulu" (The territory not yet lost is our way out), *DLPL* 47 (April 23, 1933): 5–8; Jiang Tingfu, *Jiang Tingfu huiyilu* (The memoir of Jiang Tingfu), ed. Xie Zhonglin (Taibei: Zhuanji wenxue chubanshe, 1979), p. 143.

[7] Hu Shi, "Women keyi denghou wushinian" (We can wait for fifty years), *DLPL* 44 (April 2, 1933): 4–5.

[8] Hu Shi, "Baoquan huabei de zhongyao" (The importance of protecting north China), *DLPL* 52–53 combined (June 4, 1933): 2–6. See also Grieder, *Hu Shih and the Chinese Renaissance*, pp. 252–253; Coble, *Facing Japan*, pp. 118–119.

military weaknesses and the people's lack of organization.[9] All these sentiments underscored the point that an all-out war was not an option favored by all patriotic Chinese intellectuals until around 1936.

Following the national emergency, the *jiuwang–qimeng* nexus was revisited. If coping with the crisis required an effective, powerful Chinese government, was a dictatorial regime not warranted? Some would argue that it was. But the antiimperialist nationalism of *jiuwang* obscured the unremitting demand for political and constitutional reforms amid growing external pressures. Scholars of Republican China, especially but not exclusively Chinese, have put so much emphasis on antiimperialism that they seem to have convinced themselves that it had so dominated the thinking of every educated Chinese since the May Fourth period that everything else was of secondary importance. To be sure, Chinese national consciousness was on the rise in the 1920s and 1930s. But it is often forgotten that not every educated Chinese blamed China's problems on imperialism. Again, Hu Shi's attitude was instructive. He played down the harmful effects of imperialism, holding that to solve China's problems, the "five great enemies" – poverty, diseases, ignorance, corruption, and disorder – must be confronted first.[10] His approach was introspective as well as prescriptive. Many others, while calling for an anti-Japanese united front, never lost sight of the failings of the party-state as the underlying cause of China's crisis.

Japan's actions in Manchuria only highlighted China's weaknesses that had contributed to foreign aggression in the first place. A weak and chaotic state was an invitation to foreign encroachment. China must put her own house in order, thereby saving herself from within. In other words, the answer to imperialism in general, and the Japan problem in particular, must ultimately be located within the Chinese state and society. Apart from Hu Shi's five great enemies, the corrupt and repressive Nanjing regime was part of the problem. The response to the national emergency, critics argued, was not merely military, it was, even more important, political, requiring the termination of one-party dictatorship and the development of democratic institutions. Democracy, the argument goes, would put Chinese politics on the right track, help to bring about national unity, resolve intraparty conflict, and provide oppor-

---

[9] Mengzhen (Fu Sinian), "Zhongguoren zuoren de jihui dao le" (The opportunity for Chinese to be men has arrived), *DLPL* 35 (January 15, 1933): 7–8.

[10] Hu Shi, "Women zou natiao lu?" (Which way are we going?), *XY* 2:10 (December 10, 1929): 1–16.

tunities for the minds to contribute to the state. The country then would be united behind the government in fighting the external foe.

The opposite view, however, was that China's difficulties could well be resolved by a new-style dictatorship more powerful and effective than the current regime. These two different approaches to Chinese politics – one reformist in the libertarian sense, the other dictatorial but not antireform – underscored the importance of domestic politics in China's response to Japanese imperialism. The debate between democracy and dictatorship in 1934–1935, on and off, in the pages of Beijing's *Duli pinglun* (The Independent Critic) and, to a lesser extent, Shanghai's *Dongfang zazhi* (Eastern Miscellany) and *Guowen zhoubao* (National News Weekly), and Tianjin's *Dagongbao* (L'Impartial) was more than of academic interest. Set against the background of a national emergency and a fascist movement, the debate concerned the *jiuwang–qimeng* relationship, raising serious questions about the GMD's political tutelage in one camp and about the government's limited powers in the other. Neither side was content with the political status quo.

Focusing on the internal issues, this chapter will first look at the Nationalist government's effort to seek public support by convening a National Emergency Conference in 1932. It will then provide a critique of the government's position on political tutelage from the opposition's point of view. Finally, it will examine the case for neo-dictatorship after some treatment of the minority reformist views within the GMD. The defense of democracy will be the subject of the next chapter.

THE NATIONAL EMERGENCY CONFERENCE

At the time of the Mukden incident, the GMD regime was in disarray, with a separatist movement afoot in Guangzhou led by Wang Jingwei, Hu Hanmin, and Sun Fo, and supported by the southern militarists. The Japanese threat served to bring the rivals to the negotiation table, resulting in a compromise – Chiang Kai-shek's resignation from all government posts in December 1931. In late January 1932, however, Chiang managed to make a comeback with, ironically, the support of Wang Jingwei, a formidable foe over the past three years. The so-called Chiang–Wang duumvirate was a marriage of convenience that lasted until Wang's defection to the Japanese in 1938. Wang replaced Sun Fo as head of the Executive Yuan on January 28, 1932, only to find his powers so restricted that he hardly had any say on military, financial, and foreign affairs, all of which were controlled by Chiang.[11] For his own political survival, Wang, notorious for his opportunism and capriciousness, abandoned whatever democratic ideals he might have had before, now supporting the status quo and political tutelage.

Before Chiang's return to power, the Nanjing regime had already drawn strong criticism over its handling of the Mukden incident. Much of the criticism was made in the context of domestic politics. The staunch anticommunist Chen Qitian of the outlawed Chinese Youth Party (*Zhongguo qingniandang*) warned that China was in danger of destruction if interparty strife did not cease. He called for the establishment of a coalition government to deal with the national emergency, proposing Britain's National Government of Ramsay MacDonald as a model.[12] Attacking Nanjing for failing to put the national interest ahead of party interests, he deplored the GMD's monopoly of power and the fact that people wishing to participate in national affairs were branded as "reactionary."[13] National salvation entailed resistance to Japan, continued suppression of the Communists, and termination of one-party dictatorship.[14] He accused the GMD of "causing unrest in the state," "usurping the state," and "going to destroy the state by selling it [to the Japanese]." He warned that unless the government took heed of public opinion, accepted popular supervision, abolished one-party dictatorship, and fought the Japanese, the people would be provoked into violence and revolution.[15] His idea of a coalition government, not well developed at this point, reflected the desire of the opposition elite for political participation. He also represented a popular opposition view when he proclaimed: "There is a party state, but no people's state. There are party rights, but no civil rights; there are party members, but no citizens; and there is party strife, but no national politics. . . . Only when one-party

---

[11] So *The Kuomintang Left*, p. 205.

[12] Chen Qitian, "Guonan yu dangzheng" (The national emergency and party politics), *Minsheng zhoubao* 6 (November 7, 1931): 1–2. Chen did not mean to include the Communists in a coalition government as he remained staunchly anticommunist at this point. He advocated a policy of resisting the Japanese and eliminating the Communists at the same time. See his article, "Liangchong guonan jiagong xia de Zhongguo" (China under the dual threat of national emergency), *Minsheng zhoubao* 7 (November 14, 1931): 1–2. *Minsheng zhoubao* was one of the Youth Party's publications.

[13] Chen Qitian, "Wei guonan gao guomin" (Advice to the citizens on the national emergency), *Minsheng zhoubao* 10 (December 5, 1931): 6–8.

[14] Chen Qitian, "Guomin jiuwang yundong de sanda mubiao" (The three main goals of the national salvation movement), *Minsheng zhoubao* 12 (December 19, 1931): 1–2.

[15] Chen Qitian, "Guomin jiuwang yundong" (The national salvation movement), *Minsheng zhoubao* 11 (December 12, 1931): 1–2.

dictatorship is abolished can the national emergency be resolved."[16] The historian Zuo Shunsheng, also a Youth leader, blamed the national emergency on the GMD, calling on the people to "keep an eye on the Nanjing regime."[17] Meanwhile, party colleague Chang Yansheng maintained that to stop civil war, it was necessary to establish a democratic system so that political battles could be fought in a legal and peaceful fashion.[18]

The Youth Party was not alone. Early in 1932, Luo Longji, now the new editor of Tianjin's *Yishibao*, wrote a number of editorials calling on the government to "open up the regime" by carrying out political, constitutional, and administrative reforms.[19] In one of them, he declared:

> It is time to return politics to the people (*huanzheng yu min*). Three years ago, opposition to one-party dictatorship might have been a bit too radical or emotional. Now the achievements of one-party dictatorship and the state of affairs in the Nanjing government are all before our eyes. On what justification can one-party dictatorship continue? So far the GMD has failed to achieve what fascist Italy and Soviet Russia have accomplished. It is time to find a new way out for China. The issue is not the administrative powers of the ruling party, but the fact that the Party has placed itself above the state.[20]

Luo also supported the idea of a coalition government, proposing that no single party should hold more than three-fifths of its seats.[21] He echoed the widely held opposition view that the GMD dictatorship should be replaced with a national government led by virtuous and able men who would represent the views of the entire nation. Such a government should be above party lines and assemble the best minds from all parties and groups to work with a sense of national purpose.[22]

[16] Chen Qitian, "Guonan yu dangzhi" (The national emergency and one-party rule), *Minsheng zhoubao* 21 (April 1, 1932): 3–9.

[17] Zuo Shunsheng, "Wenti zainei bu zaiwai" (The problem is internal, not external), *Minsheng zhoubao* 15 (January 9, 1932): 1–2.

[18] Chang Yansheng, "Wei feizhi neizhanzhe jin yijie" (A word on the cessation of civil war), *Minsheng zhoubao* 28 (June 12, 1932): 1–2.

[19] See, for example, editorials on January 13, 16, 17, 18, 1932.

[20] *Yishibao*, editorial, January 20, 1932.

[21] *Yishibao*, editorial, February 1, 1932.

[22] Luo Longji, "Gao Riben guomin he Zhongguo de dangju" (A word to the Japanese and also the Chinese authorities), *XY* 3:12 (n.d. possibly November 1931): 14–17.

For the GMD regime, it was one thing to seek the cooperation of other political parties and groups in meeting the Japanese threat, it was quite another to share power with them. A politics of democratization was lacking in the Party's inner circles. The government was only prepared to maintain a semblance of national unity. To that end, a National Emergency Conference, intended to accommodate some prominent figures outside the GMD, was convoked in Luoyang in April 1932.

The origin of the conference can be traced back to November 1931, when it was first suggested by Cai Yuanpei at the GMD's Fourth National Party Congress. The proposal was approved by the Central Political Council and endorsed by Wang Jingwei. Toward the end of January 1932, invitations were issued over the joint signatures of the Chairman of the Government, Lin Sen,[23] and the then head of the Executive Yuan, Sun Fo, to attend the conference, scheduled for February 1. At this point, it was understood that the conference would be given broad-ranging powers, including the power to adopt resolutions on foreign policy, financial administration, military affairs, and "all matters concerning the national emergency."[24] Apparently, it was Sun Fo's wish to begin to open up the regime gradually.

The conference was later postponed because of the fighting in Shanghai, the removal of the capital to Luoyang, and Wang Jingwei's appointment to the presidency of the Executive Yuan. In mid-March, the number of delegates was increased to more than 450, representing a broad spectrum of China's social and political elites, including, but not limited to, former Beijing militarists and bureaucrats; diplomatic luminaries; leaders from industry, commerce, and finance; educational, cultural, and literary figures; Revolution of 1911 veterans; the Youth Party; the news media; former Manchu and Mongol royal families; and overseas Chinese communities.[25] There were neither Communists nor representatives from the pro-CCP Third Party.

Reaction to Nanjing's initiative was mixed. Duan Qirui, a former premier of Beijing's warlord government, was suspicious of Nanjing's ulterior motives. He declined the invitation, dismissing the conference as impractical. Zhang Boling, President of Nankai University, endorsed it but warned that it would be difficult to send the delegates home after

---

[23] Lin was appointed to that office after Chiang Kai-shek's forced resignation of all his positions in the government in December 1931.

[24] Shen Yunlong, *Minguo shishi yu renwu luncong* (Reflections on Republican historical events and personalities) (Taibei: Zhuanji wenxue chubanshe, 1981), p. 331.

[25] Ibid., pp. 336–337.

they had convened, his message being that the government would be well advised to take them seriously. Former Beijing parliamentarian Sun Hongyi expressed the hope that constitutional reform would be on the agenda and that an All-People Representative Conference be formed to frame a constitution for a future elected government. The Youth Party, while supporting the initiative, continued to push for an early "return of politics to the people."[26] Luo Longji was hoping that the conference, as a temporary solution, would provide some sort of popular supervision of government; the permanent solution, however, must lie in the opening of a National Assembly in which to adopt a constitution guaranteeing rights. He had no doubt that the GMD would win the government comfortably in a free election and would have nothing to lose by abandoning one-party dictatorship.[27]

The conference was presided over by Wang Jingwei, who restricted the agenda to three specific items: defense against Japanese aggression, suppression of the Communists, and flood relief. The restriction was contrary to Sun Fo's original idea of giving the conference a broad-ranging mandate to discuss a wide range of issues, including domestic politics.[28] The exclusion of internal political issues incensed many invitees. Li Huang, a Youth Party leader, recalled a conversation he and others had with Wang Jingwei in Shanghai prior to the conference:

> As soon as we saw Wang Jingwei, we all felt very unhappy. From the start, he had a preconceived idea that all those advocating resistance to the Japanese were making troubles for the government and that to talk about politics was to show an intention to usurp power from the government. Thus he said to the four of us loudly and severely: "The Nationalist regime was established with bloodshed in a revolution over many years. If you want to abolish one-party rule, you had better go and start another revolution now!" The meeting broke up unpleasantly on that note. . . . The National Emergency Conference was held perfunctorily as scheduled. All the seven invited comrades of the Youth Party refused to attend, and so did over half of Shanghai's leading figures.[29]

---

[26] Ibid., pp. 338–339.

[27] *Yishibao*, editorials, January 20, and March 30, 31, 1932.

[28] For Wang's speech made in Shanghai on April 3 and 4, 1932, see *GWZB* 9:14 (April 11, 1932), major news.

[29] Li Huang, *Xuexunshi huiyilu* (The memoir of Li Huang) (Taibei: Zhuanji wenxue chubanshe, 1973), p. 180.

The conference, which opened in Luoyang on April 7 and lasted six days, was boycotted by the Youth Party and many others from Beijing and Tianjin.[30] Only about one-third of the invitees were present, of whom over eighty percent belonged to the GMD. But the conference turned out to be more exciting than the government would have liked it to be. Among the GMD members were a few reformers who, in defiance of Wang Jingwei's "no-politics" directive, proposed an early end to political tutelage and the formation of a coalition government. A strong body of opinion emerged, favoring the establishment of a representative body in the political center to provide for popular supervision. A motion that political tutelage be shortened from the six-year period was lost. But a separate motion was carried by a large majority. It proposed that political tutelage should last as long as originally intended and that, pending the opening of the National Assembly, a National People's Representatives Congress (*Guomin daibiao dahui*), with the powers of resolution, approving the budget and national debts, and ratifying important treaties, should be held on October 10, 1932.[31] Finally, the conference also resolved to prevail upon the government to establish safeguards for the basic civil liberties in order to foster democracy and to prepare for constitutional rule.[32]

The conference proved to be a mere facade of political participation. Tianjin's independent newspaper *Dagongbao* commented in a leader:

> The abolition of one-party dictatorship is a matter of time, not a matter of right or wrong. There is nothing unlawful in discussing it publicly. . . . Most people have accepted political tutelage faithfully since 1928. But now they feel they have learned nothing from the tutor. Instead, they find a shattered country crying out for salvation, and feel compelled to speak out for reforms in order to save themselves. . . . The National Emergency Conference did not adequately represent the [will of the] people. Worse still is the attitude of the government [toward political and constitutional reforms].[33]

Not everyone who had attended the conference thought so. Independent delegate Jiang Tingfu accused some delegates of playing politics and not supporting the government sufficiently in dealing with the external threat. He criticized their demands for the termination of one-party dictatorship and the establishment of a National People's Representatives

---

[30] Ibid.   [31] *GWZB* 9:15 (April 18, 1932), major news, pp. 3–4.
[32] Ibid., p. 5.   [33] *Dagongbao*, editorial, April 13, 1932.

Congress prior to constitutional rule as "untimely and inappropriate." Nanjing was not a very good government, but it was not the cause of Japan's actions in Manchuria. He did not think that political reform would be of any help to the government in the current crisis, nor that the government leaders were inferior to their opponents in terms of education and morality. Skeptical from the start about the utility of such a conference and pessimistic about its outcome, he thought it would have been more productive had the delegates been united behind the government. Nanjing was procrastinating with constitutional reform, but he doubted that the people wanted constitutionalism at this point. There had been division among government members at the conference, with some being "leftists." (He was implying Sun Fo and company.) His high regard was reserved for Wang Jingwei, "a born-leader of the masses and China's [Leon] Gambetta."[34] It was Wang who, no longer a leftist, drew a good deal of criticism for his defense of political tutelage.

A CRITIQUE OF WANG JINGWEI'S VIEWS ON POLITICAL TUTELAGE

Wang's defense of the GMD's position was mounted on several grounds. The first was the oft-repeated argument that Chinese, left alone, were too uneducated to know how to exercise their democratic rights. Second, because the Republic of China was established by the GMD – previously the Revolutionary Alliance (*Tongmenghui*) – to "sabotage" political tutelage was to sabotage the GMD, which in turn meant sabotaging the Republic. Third, China's previous record of constitutionalism was so bad that it should not be implemented at the present time. And fourth, some of the current advocates of constitutionalism were former bureaucrats and politicians who were, therefore, unqualified to talk about it.[35]

Critics were quick to refute those arguments. Wang Zaoshi, a leading member of the National Salvation Association (*Quanguo gejie jiuguo lianhehui*, or *Jiuguohui* for short), while not denying that the majority of Chinese were ignorant, raised questions about the GMD's suitability as

---

[34] Jiang Tingfu, "Canjia guonan huiyi de huigu" (Looking back at my participation in the National Emergency Conference), *DLPL* 1 (May 22, 1932): 9–12. Leon Gambetta was the French Minister of War in 1870; he tried to save the French Republic from Prussian invasion.

[35] Cited in Wang Zaoshi, "Duiyu xunzheng yu xianzheng de yijian" (My views on political tutelage and constitutionalism), *Zaisheng* 1:2 (June 20, 1932): 2.

a political tutor. (Wang was a political scientist with a doctorate from the University of Wisconsin and one-time research fellow at the London School of Economics and Political Science, where he came under the influence of Harold Laski.)[36] He asked rhetorically whether the GMD itself was a sound party, whether its members were the most talented people in the country, and whether it had a track record of political tutelage. The GMD, he pointed out, was awfully divided, with many new and old bureaucrats and militarists incorporated into its ranks. Not only were its members not talented, but a good many of them were actually bad elements. Political tutelage, he added, should be based on "good-man politics" (*xianren zhengzhi*), but the GMD rulers did not derive their power from their knowledge, education, and talents. Few were good men, and few were fit to be political tutors. As for the claim that people's rights would increase and expand as political tutelage unfolded, he pointed out that after three years of tutelage the people were still denied democratic rights. Again, he asked rhetorically: "Look at world history. Is there any country that enjoys democracy as a result of political tutelage? Is there any country where democracy is not the result of a people's struggle? It is human nature that, once in power, people, either as individuals or groups, are unwilling to give it up."[37] The GMD was no exception.

Zhang Junmai, leader of the newly formed National Socialist Party, questioned why only members of one political party should be tutoring the rest of the population. Like Luo Longji and Wang Zaoshi, he did not think that GMD members were qualified and sufficiently educated for the task they set for themselves, nor were the people's lack of education and the country's vastness and backward transport infrastructure compelling arguments against constitutional rule.[38] Fellow National Socialist Zhu Yisong argued that, even if political tutelage was necessary, it should not be the GMD's monopoly, nor should it be separated in time from constitutional rule. Political tutelage was a contradiction in terms in that there was "a conflict of ethics" between one-party dictatorship and democracy.[39] To philosophy professor Zhang Dongsun, the theory of

---

[36] Zhou Tiandu, ed., *Qi junzi zhuan* (The seven honorable persons) (Beijing: Zhongguo shehui kexueyuan chubanshe, 1988), p. 624.

[37] Wang Zaoshi, "Duiyu xunzheng yu xianzheng de yijian," pp. 3–4.

[38] Zhang Junmai, "Guomindang dangzheng zhi xin qilu" (Guomindang rule at a new crossroads), *Zaisheng* 1:2 (June 29, 1932): 3–4.

[39] Zhu Yisong, "Zhongguo guojia de lunli jichu wenti" (The question of the foundations of Chinese national ethics), *Zaisheng* 1:6 (October 20, 1932): 20–23.

political tutelage was fundamentally flawed because it failed to provide a democratic model for China's future. "Since the undemocratic system during the period of political tutelage is different from the democratic system that is supposed to be established under constitutional rule, how can the people learn to practice democracy?"[40]

The claim that without the GMD there would not have been the Republic and that opposing political tutelage was to oppose the GMD and the Republic was patently illogical, absurd, and an insult to intelligence. Wang Zaoshi pointed out that the Republic was brought into being in 1912 by a combination of factors, the GMD being only one of them. The Republic could survive without the GMD, and perhaps, he added, the overthrow of the GMD might not be a bad thing after all as a way of defending the Republic.[41] The suggestion that the GMD might be overthrown, coming as it did from a noncommunist, was radical. But Wang did not seem to be serious about it. What he wanted were political and constitutional reforms leading to a peaceful transformation of Chinese politics from a monocracy to representative government.[42] A pointed remark was also made by Zhang Junmai that, even if the GMD had been instrumental in establishing the Republic, the Republic was dead; what remained was a party-state.[43]

On the failure of constitutionalism since 1912, Wang Zaoshi argued like Hu Shi that the reason was because constitutionalism had not been implemented; otherwise, Parliament would not have been dissolved, Yuan Shikai would not have proclaimed himself emperor, and warlordism would not have prevailed. The early Republican experience only demonstrated that there were "wicked people" who had opposed and sabotaged constitutionalism.[44] A leader in Tianjin's *Yishibao* (penned by Luo Longji) attributed the failure to the lack of expert knowledge and sincerity on the part of those in authority.[45] And Chen Qitian, seeing striking similarities between the current party-state and the late Qing Dynasty in their lack of sincerity about constitutional reform, predicted that the GMD regime would meet the same fate as the Manchu regime.

---

[40] Zhang Dongsun, "Dang de wenti" (The party's problem), *Zaisheng* 1:3 (July 20, 1932): 6–10.

[41] Ibid., pp. 4–6.

[42] Wang Zaoshi, "Wo weishenme zhuzhang shixing xianzheng" (Why do I advocate the implementation of constitutional rule?), *Zaizheng* 1:5 (September 20, 1932): 1–10.

[43] Zhang Junmai, "Guomindang dangzheng zhi xin qilu," p. 6.

[44] Wang Zaoshi, "Duiyu xunzheng yu xianzheng de yijian," p. 6.

[45] *Yishibao*, editorial, April 8, 1932.

Just as China had survived the fall of the Manchus, so she would survive the demise of the current party-state.[46]

To the charge that some of the present advocates of constitutionalism were former Beijing bureaucrats and politicians who were unfit to talk about it, the response was that they were not entirely responsible for its failure. Moreover, they were no worse than Nanjing's present bureaucrats and politicians who failed to see the need for constitutionalism during the period of political tutelage. Nanjing's leaders had no right to attack them when the GMD failed to do better.[47]

All this was a powerful rebuttal of Wang Jingwei's arguments. By far the most cogent counterargument was that the notion of political tutelage was fundamentally flawed – conflicts of interest between one-party dictatorship and democracy – and that the people were far from learning to practice democracy because no local self-government was actually in place. Clinging to one-party dictatorship, the GMD reinforced the popular view that it had been corrupted by power and that the obstacle to constitutional rule was not widespread illiteracy and popular ignorance but the ruling party itself. "The people are innocent," Zhang Dongsun protested. Likening China to a block of land, and constitutionalism to a beautiful tree, he said that the reason why this beautiful tree could not grow in this land was because the land was full of poisonous weeds. Until the weeds were thoroughly removed, nothing good could grow out of it. Zhang singled out the warlords and the bureaucrats as the main obstacles to constitutionalism, adding that the GMD had failed to remove those obstacles and to lay down procedures for the transition to constitutionalism, despite the decree that constitutional rule should commence in 1935.[48] It is not hard to understand the frustration of the loyal critics. If the aim of political tutelage was really to train the population in democratic praxis, it had failed thus far. By 1932, four years into tutelage, local self-government still had not been established, and the people enjoyed no more rights than before.

---

[46] Chen Qitian, "You manqing lishi shuodao 'dangguo' xianzhuang" (From Qing history to the present state of the party-state), *Minsheng zhoubao* 26 (May 29, 1932): 5–6, continued in 27 (June 5, 1932): 7–9.

[47] Wang Zaoshi, "Duiyu xunzheng yu xianzheng de yijian," pp. 6–7.

[48] Zhang Dongsun, "Guomin wuzui: ping Guomindang de xianzheng lun" (The people are innocent: a critique of the Guomindang's theory of constitutionalism), *Zaisheng* 1:8 (December 20, 1932): 6–7.

The liberal elements outside the GMD were not the only ones who were frustrated. Some progressives within the ruling party also were calling for political and constitutional reforms.

SUN FO'S REFORMIST VIEWS

On April 24, 1932, less than two weeks after the conclusion of the National Emergency Conference, Sun Fo, who had moved for an earlier end to political tutelage, announced a draft Program for Resistance to Japan and National Salvation (*KangRi jiuguo gangling*). It consisted of three parts: Party affairs, external affairs, and internal affairs. On Party affairs, he advocated the cessation of government subsidy to the Party apparatus. On foreign affairs, he called for strong ties with China's neighbors and thorough resistance to the Japanese. And, on internal affairs, he renewed the proposal for an early end to political tutelage with the following seven points:

1. To begin preparations for constitutionalism;
2. To convene in June 1932 the Third Plenum of the Central Executive Committee to consider Party reform;
3. To authorize the Legislative Yuan to begin drafting a constitution in October 1932;
4. To convene in April 1933 the First National Assembly to adopt a constitution and to set a date for its promulgation;
5. To carry out local self-government earnestly following the promulgation of the constitution;
6. To allow the people to enjoy the freedoms of political organization and political participation as well as the rights of election and running for public office, provided that this was not at variance with the Three Principles of the People; and
7. To hold elections for the First National Assembly in the provinces and municipalities based on population distribution.[49]

It is interesting to note that, contrary to his late father's idea and the Party line that the effective establishment of representative assemblies and local self-government in at least half of the nation's counties was a prerequisite to constitutional government, Sun Fo proposed that these be carried out simultaneously.

Sun had lost out in the new Chiang–Wang duumvirate, after serving as president of the powerful Executive Yuan for only one month. As the new head of the weak Legislative Yuan, his powers were extremely limited.

---

[49] *GWZB* 9:17 (May 2, 1932), major news, p. 9.

But his reformist views were well received in liberal circles, despite skepticism that the first National People's Representatives Congress would be given sufficient powers to do its job.[50] Zhang Junmai, while acknowledging that local self-government could contribute significantly to the democratic process as the Japanese and Prussian experiences had demonstrated, rejected suggestions that constitutionalism in the political center needed to await local success. The locality and the center were neither mutually exclusive nor in a causal relationship, he wrote, citing the example of Great Britain to support his argument that constitutional rule could precede local self-government and that these could also take place simultaneously. The people were not actually learning to exercise the four rights because they simply had no opportunity to do so, just like being asked to learn swimming without being allowed to go into the water. It was unnecessary to await the completion of a census, a land survey, a police force, and road construction before the people could exercise their democratic rights.[51] Those tasks, added fellow National Socialist Zhu Qinglai, were the responsibilities of the local authorities; local self-government was impossible unless it was constitutionally empowered.[52]

Not surprisingly, Sun Fo's views did not prevail in the GMD's inner circles. The day October 10, 1932, passed without the National People's Representatives Congress being held. In mid-December, when the Third Plenum of the Fourth Central Executive Committee met, there was renewed talk of concentrating the nation's strength on resistance. Sun and T. V. Soong, the Finance Minister, led a group of politicians in proposing that the government follow the example of the Nineteenth Route Army and the Fifth Army Corps in gallantly resisting the Japanese and make an attempt to recover lost territory in Manchuria.[53] On domestic issues, Sun managed to pass a resolution that the pace of local self-government be stepped up, that the National Assembly be convened in March 1935 to adopt and promulgate a constitution, that the Legislative Yuan be asked to commence work on a Draft Constitution, and that the convocation of the National Assembly be preceded by a people's political council, all of which would lay the foundations for democratic

---

[50] See, for example, Zhang Junmai, "Guomindang dangzheng zhi xinqilu," pp. 5–6; Ding Zuoshao, "Ping Sun Ke kangRi jiuguo gangling caoan" (Comments on Sun Ke's anti-Japanese national salvation proposal), *Minsheng zhoubao* 26 (May 29, 1932): 7–8.

[51] Zhang Junmai, "Guomindang dangzheng zhi xin qilu," pp. 2–3.

[52] Zhu Qinglai, "Xianzheng pingyi" (A critique of constitutionalism), *Minsheng zhoubao* 27 (June 5, 1932): 13.

[53] Coble, *Facing Japan*, p. 67.

rule.[54] Early in 1933, the Legislative Yuan commenced work on the drafting of a constitution. A thirty-seven-member Constitution Drafting Committee, chaired by Sun, was appointed, with two vice-chairmen, Wu Jingxiong and Zhang Zhiben, both jurists.[55] Because Sun was intent on proposing a cabinet system of government, the constitution became an instrument in the struggle for power.

But formidable forces within the Party were opposed to democratic reform. It was a time when a.fascist movement was under way, aimed at installing Chiang Kai-shek as the dictator. Among the intellectuals themselves, a voice crying out for neo-dictatorship was also heard in some quarters.

THE ADVOCACY OF NEO-DICTATORSHIP

It is often said that the 1930s were not a prosperous decade for liberalism and democracy in the world at large. Jerome Grieder speaks of a "crisis of democracy" in Italy, Germany, Poland, Spain, and Japan,[56] whereas Eugene Lubot writes on Chinese liberalism in an illiberal age.[57] Soviet communism was on the rise, even though some Western intellectuals joined the famous Fabians, Sidney and Beatrice Webb, in declaring Soviet Russia to be really more democratic than the decaying capitalist West. And, because of the Great Depression, many Western countries, including Britain and the United States, were under considerable economic pressures, confronted with a host of problems, especially unemployment and social division. British writers like Bertrand Russell, Harold Laski, and H. G. Wells were beginning to question whether the European democracies were capable of solving the severe twentieth-century problems of economic privilege, nationalist rivalry, and technological change.[58]

In China, the first half of the 1930s saw civil strife, military separatism, social unrest, a growing communist movement, the specter of war with Japan, and a central government unable to assert its authority in the periphery. Nationalist China was a weak state operating in a hostile

---

[54] See Sun Fo, *China Looks Forward* (London: George Allen and Unwin, 1944), pp. 81–82; Wu Jingxiong and Huang Gongjue, *Zhongguo zhixianshi* (History of Chinese constitution making) (Shanghai: Shangwu yinshuguan, 1937), pp. 717–722.

[55] Sun, *China Looks Forward*, p. 82; *GWZB* 10:4 (January 23, 1933), major news, p. 4.

[56] Jerome B. Grieder, *Intellectuals and the State in Modern China* (New York: The Free Press, 1981), p. 345.

[57] Eugene Lubot, *Liberalism in an Illiberal Age: New Culture Liberals in Republican China, 1919–1937* (Westport: Greenwood Press, 1982).

[58] Furth, *Science and China's New Culture*, p. 216.

environment under external and internal pressures. In these circumstances, it seemed to many that the creation of a strong government
capable of uniting the country and commanding its human, financial, and
material resources must take precedence over political and constitutional
reforms. When they advocated neo-dictatorship, the idea itself was not
new. Two decades earlier, Liang Qichao had advocated enlightened
despotism in the later years of his life. What was new now was a sense of
crisis, urgency, and utter despair at China's internal disorder in the face of
escalating external threat. The Nanjing regime was already a dictatorship
for all intents and purposes, but it was a weak and incompetent one. The
urge for neo-dictatorship sprang from a desire to transform Nanjing into
a strong and effective government capable of national salvation.

Neo-dictatorship was advocated against the backdrop of the fascist
movement launched by the Blue Shirts and the Society for Vigorous
Practice referred to in Chapter 1. In 1933, it was fashionable to talk about
fascism in China. A large number of publications were advertised in the
Shanghai newspaper *Shenbao*, "reflecting widespread public interest in
the Black and Brown Shirts."[59] It must be stressed, however, that the
advocates of neo-dictatorship described next did not articulate their
views in fascist terms because they were not fascists.

When the American-educated diplomatic history professor Jiang
Tingfu advocated dictatorship in an article entitled "Revolution and
Autocracy," published in *Duli pinglun* in December 1933, his argument
rested on a notion of "historical necessity." The timing of his article is
noteworthy. Earlier, on November 20, the Fujian Rebellion had broken
out, led by Chen Mingshu, Commander of the Nineteenth Route Army,
who proclaimed the establishment of the Republic of China People's
Revolutionary Government in Fuzhou. The rebellion was supported by
a curious mix of anti-Chiang Kai-shek elements, including the CCP, the
Third Party, the Trotskyites, the Youth Party, the National Socialist Party,
the Guangxi Clique, and nonpartisan intellectuals from around the
country. Opposing the GMD regime, the rebellion possessed a socialist
character with a political platform calling for resisting the Japanese as
well as professing democracy.[60] With such a makeup, the rebellion hardly

---

[59] Frederic Wakeman Jr., "A Revisionist View of the Nanjing Decade: Confucian Fascism,"
China Quarterly 150 (June 1997): 426.

[60] Fighting broke out between the Nationalists and the rebel forces on December 16. But
in just a little more than a month, government troops were able to crush the rebellion.
For details, see Lloyd E. Eastman, *The Abortive Revolution: China under Nationalist
Rule, 1927–1937* (Cambridge, MA: Harvard University Press, 1974), ch. 3.

inspired confidence. The overthrow of the Nationalist government in these circumstances would not appear to be in the national interest.

Subconsciously reacting to the rebellion, Jiang Tingfu argued that China's problem, first and foremost, was lack of unification – a problem caused not so much by the warlords, who were but products of circumstances, as by Chinese particularism and the country's backwardness. He theorized that there were only civil wars in China, not revolutions, because Chinese had neither the capacity nor the qualifications for revolution. Every time a revolutionary movement was launched, including Sun Yat-sen's, it was without fail used by the foreign powers as an imperialist tool, resulting in the loss of Chinese rights and territory. Jiang then went on to make a case for dictatorship from a historical perspective. Reviewing the modern histories of Britain, France, and Russia, he "discovered" that their histories were divided into two broad periods. The first period related to nation building; the second, to the promotion of the people's well-being by the state. Likening present-day China to England before the Tudors, France before the Bourbons, and Russia before the Romanovs, he was of the opinion that China was still a dynastic state, not a nation-state, because the family- and region-oriented Chinese still lacked a sense of loyalty to the state. Imperial China left no legacy that could be used either as "revolutionary capital" or as "a new ruling class for the political center." In contrast to Czarist Russia, moreover, imperial China's material civilization had lagged far behind. In his view, autocracy had contributed to the formation of the nation-state in Britain, France, and Russia, but not in imperial China. China was yet to go through a stage of nation building under autocratic rule. Revolution was a big obstacle to nation building, he concluded. What China needed was the "power of unification," which was being destroyed by civil war.[61]

If Jiang Tingfu was correct in stating that China's old autocracy had failed in nation building, how could he be justified in thinking that a new dictatorship could do better? For a historian, his interpretations of British, French, and Russian histories are amazingly superficial. As Hu Shi was quick to point out, the making of the British nation-state owed nothing to the autocratic monarchy, and dictatorship was not a necessary stage in nation building. Hu argued, not persuasively though, that China since the Han and Tang Dynasties had already become a nation-state in

---

[61] Jiang Tingfu, "Geming yu zhuanzhi" (Revolution and autocracy), *DLPL* 80 (December 10, 1933): 2–5.

that the Chinese had fostered a complete notion of themselves as a distinct race-nation (*Zhonghua minzu*). What Jiang had demonstrated was only the shortcomings and legacy of the old society and old politics. As regards China's material backwardness, Hu blamed it on a general lack of education and shortages of talent, insisting, in short, that unification must be political, not military, without counting on dictatorship.[62]

In a rejoinder to Hu's critique, Jiang reiterated his position by emphasizing, on the one hand, Chinese particularism and its tendency to impede the growth of national consciousness and, on the other, poverty, which ultimately allowed the warlords to maintain their private armies to enrich themselves. Even though he had initially compared imperial China with Tudor England, Bourbon France, and Romanov Russia with a view to learning a lesson from them, he said that Western politics and Chinese politics were two entirely different things; hence, there was no need to copy from the West. "The more we talk about Western 'isms' and political systems, the more disorderly and the more disintegrated China will become."[63] Jiang thought that the Chinese people had no desire for a national representative body because representatives tended to represent no one but themselves, and parliament could not resolve civil conflict as long as the military was in power. The only way to solve China's domestic problems was to establish a personal dictatorship as a transitional method to rid the country of the tens of "small dictatorships" (meaning local warlord regimes). He criticized those who opposed dictatorship as either reciting from Western textbooks or feeling like "second-class warlords" (meaning Nanjing's regional opponents). The target of dictatorship was not the people, but the "second-class warlords" – the "real enemies of unification." A personal dictatorship would be a good thing for the people because it offered the best chance of unifying the country.[64]

Concerned with unification under a strong and effective central government, Jiang did not demand that the unified government be enlightened; enlightened rule was a bonus. But at least it should be capable of maintaining stability and order throughout the country. Only then could civil war be eliminated and China modernized.[65] For all its faults, the Nanjing regime should be supported because "the prerequi-

---

[62] Hu Shi, "Jianguo yu zhuanzhi" (Nation building and autocracy), *DLPL* 81 (December 17, 1933): 2–5.
[63] Jiang Tingfu, "Lun zhuanzhi bing da Hu Shizhi xiansheng" (On autocracy and a response to Mr. Hu Shi), *DLPL* 83 (December 31, 1933): 2.
[64] Ibid., pp. 3–6. [65] Ibid., p. 4.

site to good government is having a government first; unless the country is unified, no government could be a good government."[66] He was tired of war and revolution.

Earlier, in an extraordinary manner, Jiang had blamed the intellectuals, not the warlords, for China's domestic problems, accusing them of seeking power by colluding with the anti-Chiang Kai-shek forces in the name of democracy.[67] His accusation was a veiled criticism of the leaders of the Youth Party and the National Socialist Party who had supported the Fujian Rebellion. In his view, China's problem was, fundamentally, economic, not political. "Our problem is not a problem of ideology or system. Our problem is one of rice bowl, of peace. This is the ABC of politics. Before the alphabet is learned, there is no need to speak of grammar, let alone diction."[68] He no longer approved of Nanjing's attempts to suppress the Communists by force, now convinced that the answer to the communist insurgency lay in a recognition of the necessity of land redistribution.[69] Yet there were contradictions between his weariness of war and revolution and his belief in the efficacy of military unification. He was unduly confident that a dictatorship would promote China's economic development, thus removing the root cause of communism. The question of legitimacy facing a dictatorship did not seem to worry him.

Jiang's belief in dictatorship was strengthened in 1934–1935 after his visits to Soviet Russia and Germany, which left him with a good impression of both countries, particularly Soviet Russia. He found Russia to be a country with a bright future, an egalitarian society striving to achieve excellence, and Russian workers to be hardworking, notwithstanding the lack of private property.[70] However, as he visited other European countries, he began to waver between dictatorship and democracy, observing that, of all the European states, Britain was the most stable socially and politically. Neither the extreme left nor the extreme right had any

---

[66] Jiang Tingfu, "Geming yu zhuanzhi," p. 2.

[67] Jiang Tingfu, "Zhishi jieji yu zhengzhi" (The intellectual class and politics), *DLPL* 51 (May 21, 1933): 16.

[68] Ibid., p. 17.

[69] Jiang Tingfu, "Dui gongchandang bixu de zhengzhi celüe" (The strategy necessary for dealing with the Communist Party), *DLPL* 11 (July 31, 1932): 6–8.

[70] For his recollections of his trips to Russia and Germany, see Jiang Tingfu, *Jiang Tingfu xuanji* (The collected works of Jiang Tingfu) (Taibei: Zhuanji wenxue chubanshe, 1978), III, 569–599; Jiang Tingfu, *Jiang Tingfu huiyilu*, pp. 151–170. For his views on a comparison of Soviet Russia and Nazi Germany, see *Jiang Tingfu xuanji*, pp. 601–608.

prospects in British politics. In the summer of 1935, he revised his view that the end of the British Empire was in sight. Not only was Britain the pillar of Europe, but, forgetting the United States for the moment, he thought Britain was also the pillar of the entire world.[71] There were three competing ideologies in the world: communism, fascism, and liberalism. In his judgment, fascism had the gloomiest prospect, so that its ultimate failure was only to be expected. Liberalism had proved itself superior to communism. On liberalism he wrote:

> I am no admirer of liberalism and its political system. I still think that the liberal system is unsuited to Chinese conditions. But after my visit to Britain, I have come to realize that citizens brought up under the British political system are the most valued treasures of a nation. . . . The ideology of the Britons is a powerful locomotive. In the event of emergency and disaster, the people of a liberal state would be united in integrity and sincerity. Because such unity is free, its power is greater than otherwise.[72]

Yet China remained to him a case sui generis. Writing in October 1936, Jiang still thought that a start of constitutional rule was not all that important, insisting that, from the people's point of view, land remained the most important issue. What's more, from the modernizing experiences of China, Soviet Russia, Japan, and Turkey, he concluded that countries with the greatest concentration of state powers were the most successful and effective. Thus, in China's case, apart from achieving unification, a concentration of state powers would serve the purpose of modernization.[73]

Torn between the strengths of liberal democracy and the perceived utility of dictatorship, Jiang in the end decided to stand firmly on the side of the latter because of economic considerations. In his memoir thirty years later, he wrote:

> The poverty of the Chinese people was a problem demanding urgent solution. Thus, I considered that immediate action should be taken in the economic sphere without awaiting China's democratization.

[71] Jiang Tingfu, "Maodun de Ouzhou (xia)" (Europe in contradictions [part 2]), *DLPL* 166 (September 1, 1935): 10.

[72] Jiang Tingfu, "Sanzhong zhuyi de shijie jingzheng" (The world competition of three ideologies), *GWZB* 12:38 (September 30, 1935): 5–8; the quote is on p. 7.

[73] Jiang Tingfu, "Zhongguo jindaihua de wenti" (On the question of China's modernization), *Dagongbao*, October 10, 1936, reprinted in *DLPL* 225 (November 1, 1936): 10–13.

I thought economics should take priority over politics. In economics, I thought, two tasks were essential. One was to engage in production and [to improve] transport by using modern science and technology, and the other was socialization or a fair distribution of wealth. I considered constitutionalism and parliamentary democracy to be a secondary question. The creation of more wealth and its equal distribution were the most important things. I never thought Hu Shi opposed the development of the economy for the sake of prosperity. At the same time, I also hoped that he never suspected me of opposing democracy. Our differences were not a matter of principle, but a matter of priority.[74]

Jiang never argued for dictatorship by assaulting the basic values of liberalism. No autocrat at heart, he thought Hu Shi was naïve in ignoring the "corruption, rottenness, waste, stupidity, and indifference that existed behind the scenes in many democratic countries" as well as China's experience with democratic institutions.[75] Dictatorship for Jiang was a means of unification, a response to modernization, and an ideology of delayed development.

He was not alone in understanding China's problems from a historical perspective. The sociologist Wu Jingchao also saw a cycle that kept repeating itself in Chinese history. It consisted of three phases: (1) from harsh rule to the overthrow of the existing regime; (2) from struggle of power by the military to unification; and (3) from good administration to the restoration of peace. Currently, China was still trapped in the second phase; the only way that unification could be achieved was by force of arms. This led Wu to think that the time was not ripe for democracy. A federation of self-governing provinces would only add to regional and military separatism, and reconstruction without unification was impossible.[76] For Wu, history repeated itself. He was ambivalent about dictatorship, but in arguing for military unification, he lent it implicit support.

By far the most prominent figure who responded positively to calls for dictatorship was Ding Wenjiang. In a 1932 article on Chinese politics, he criticized the Nationalist government, making three "minimum demands": respect for the freedoms of thought and speech; cessation of state funding for the GMD's provincial, district, and city branches; and

---

[74] Jiang Tingfu, *Jiang Tingfu huiyilu*, p. 142.   [75] Ibid., pp. 141–142.

[76] Wu Jingchao, "Geming yu jianguo" (Revolution and nation building), *DLPL* 84 (January 7, 1934): 2–5.

the establishment of procedures for the transfer of political power.[77] Yet, for all its faults, Ding could see no viable alternative to the Nanjing regime. Rather than trying to overthrow it, he would ask it to reform itself, sharing with Jiang Tingfu a profound concern about China's political fragmentation. The reason why China had not been unified since the early Republic, Ding averred, was because of the lack of a common belief. But a common belief was only the lowest common denominator for people interested in politics. Ding was arguing, not for unity of thought, but for an underlying consensus on the basic political, economic, and social values and goals pertinent to China. In his view, the political conflicts since 1912 had been largely conflicts of belief. (He meant to say, I think, that the political conflicts had been caused by ideological differences.) Thinking that the Three Principles of the People had few true believers, he hoped that a common belief could be fostered among the GMD, the CCP, and the Third Party (he made no mention of the Youth Party).[78] How? He did not say.

In terms of his own beliefs, Ding held that whatever action satisfied most of the desires of the largest number in the wide community was beneficial to society. His utilitarian bent was matched by his absolute faith in science. "Any conclusion not derived by scientific methods is not knowledge. In the realm of knowledge, the scientific method is omnipotent."[79] He did not believe in God or in the existence of the soul, separate from the body, because these could not be scientifically proved. To him, the principle of science was invariably a question of possibility, and nothing was to be believed if it conflicted with scientific knowledge.[80] No one would question his scientific credentials. He was able to declare that he had no blind faith either in democracy, notably the parliamentary system, or in dictatorship. He found the responsibilities of the dictator so onerous that no person, however talented, would be equal to the task. Moreover, a dictatorial system had many problems. For it to be permanent, all political opposition would have to be eliminated, and all criticisms and public debates, banned. It would be just a matter of time before the dictator became corrupt, turning a blind eye to what he did not want

---

[77] Ding Wenjiang, "Zhongguo zhengzhi de chulu" (The exit for Chinese politics), *DLPL* 11 (July 31, 1932): 4–5.

[78] Ding Wenjiang, "Gonggong xinyang yu tongyi" (A public faith and unification), reprinted from *Dagongbao* in *GWZB* 11:5 (January 22, 1934): 1–2.

[79] Ding Wenjiang, "Wo de xinyang" (My beliefs), reprinted from *Dagongbao* in *DLPL* 199 (May 13, 1934): 10.

[80] Ibid.

to see. At this point, it was not apparent that Ding was inclined toward dictatorship. But he added that if the leader could unite the few talents around the country for the purpose of good governance, it would hardly matter what political system was adopted. He rejected the view that revolution was China's only solution. But he sympathized with the Communists, asking the government to recognize them for what they were – an armed, organized political opposition, not "bandits" (*fei*).[81]

It was not until December 1934, months after his visit to the Soviet Union in the summer of 1933,[82] that Ding advanced the idea of a new-style dictatorship in an article published in Tianjin's *Dagongbao*. He began by raising a double-barreled question. Was dictatorship possible in China presently? If not, was democracy possible? As with the GMD elite, Ding argued that because over seventy-five percent of the population were illiterate, democracy was impossible; what's more, they were largely uninterested in politics. He invoked H. G. Wells and Bertrand Russell to make the point that true democracy in such circumstances was impossible. He also criticized Hu Shi's idea that democracy was kindergarten politics,[83] arguing that democratic states that had made remarkable achievements were all politically experienced. In China, he concluded, neither dictatorship nor democracy was possible, but, relatively speaking, democracy was "more impossible." In view of China's existing conditions – low level of general education, inadequate systems of transport and communication, unsound political parties, and economic backwardness – any talk of democracy was unrealistic. What China needed was a "new-style dictatorship" that would distinguish itself from the "old-style autocracy" in the following manner:

1.   The dictator must be completely devoted to the national interest;
2.   The dictator must have a thorough understanding of a modern nation state;
3.   The dictator must draw on the nation's talents, experts and specialists; and
4.   The dictator must use the national emergency to rally behind the nationalist banner the allegiance of all those capable of participating in politics.[84]

---

[81]   Ibid., p. 11. For his views on communism and the CCP, see his articles "Suowei <jiaofei> wenti" (On the so-called "bandit elimination" question), *DLPL* 6 (June 26, 1932): 3–4; "Pinglun gongchan zhuyi bing zhonggao Zhongguo gongchan dangyuan" (A critique of communism and advice to members of the Chinese Communist Party), *DLPL* 51 (May 21, 1933): 5–14.

[82]   For Ding's Russian experience, see Furth, *Science and China's New Culture*, pp. 208–212.

[83]   See Chapter 4, pp. 115–119.

[84]   Ding Wenjiang, "Minzhu zhengzhi yu ducai zhengzhi" (Democratic politics and dictatorial politics), reprinted from *Dagongbao* in *DLPL* 133 (December 30, 1934): 4–7.

In using the term *old-style autocracy*, Ding implied that Nanjing's rule had been a failure, a regime far from modern and efficient. To expand the regime's powers, already dictatorial, without further alienating the people required a change of leadership style and substance by meeting the previously mentioned conditions. Unlike Jiang Tingfu, however, Ding did not advocate unification by force,[85] or a personal dictatorship. His neo-dictatorship was a technocracy of the moral–intellectual elite, united in the task of transforming the current regime. "Consistent with his Confucian heritage," observes Charlotte Furth, "[D]ing continued to imagine that the ruler and the educated bureaucracy are the structural pivots of any political system, but by the mid-1930s he had infused into these forms another final change of meaning: the elite had become a technocracy and the ruler the director of a brain trust."[86]

Ding's choice of dictatorship over democracy underscored his hopes that it would help China overcome the current crisis, which neither revolution nor the gradual and peaceful route to democracy could do. Because he felt compelled to choose, he made no assault on the basic values of liberalism and democracy. In fact, if he were free to choose, he would rather be a worker in Britain or the United States than an intellectual in Soviet Russia, and rather be a geologist in Soviet Russia than a White Russian in Paris. Facing the Japanese aggression, he would also rather be a technician in a dictatorial China than a submissive subject of the Japanese Empire.[87] In other words, he would not forsake his belief in Western liberal values but would forfeit liberty rather than face China's extinction at the hands of Japanese imperialism. Ding was a liberal at heart, and a nationalist. But finding himself in a national emergency, he thought it necessary to make a choice, and he chose the Soviet model. In so doing, he did not show a lack of central concern for political liberty as Furth thought.[88] Rather, he was sanguine about neo-dictatorship being scientific and progressive and capable of extricating China from her predicament. It was not intended to be a permanent

---

[85] For Ding's view on the cessation of civil wars, see his article "Feizhi neizhan de yundong" (The movement for a cessation of civil war), *DLPL* 25 (November 6, 1932): 2–5.

[86] Furth, *Science and China's New Culture*, pp. 218–219.

[87] Ding Wenjiang, "Zailun minzhi yu ducai" (Again on democracy and dictatorship), reprinted from *Dagongbao*, in *DLPL* 137 (January 27, 1935): 19–22.

[88] Furth has written: "His views of Communism, of the USSR, and of dictatorship all illustrate [Ding's] lack of central concern for political liberty as it is understood in the West. He moved from an elitist and instrumentalist view of the democratic process in the 1920s to the frank advocacy of enlightened dictatorship for China after 1933." See *Science and China's New Culture*, p. 219.

feature of Chinese politics but merely a response to the national emergency. Ding would hope that as soon as the crisis was over, dictatorship would give way to democracy.

For many, the choice was not an easy one. Frustrated, one scholar wrote: "Only if someone could break the stalemate by positively and seriously engaging in reconstruction and producing concrete results for everyone to see, I believe dictatorship is possible and that the majority of the people would welcome it."[89] He noted that the Chinese had no concepts of rule of law, of rights and obligations, of freedom and equality, and of popular representation. He agreed with much of what Jiang Tingfu said, but differed from him in emphasizing reconstruction, not military unification, as a means of nation building, adding that with reconstruction, especially in the area of public transport and communications, China's material conditions would improve, and local particularism also would diminish. He despaired of Western democracy's shortcomings: inefficiency, "false assumptions" about equality, "pretense" of public opinion and majority rule, and corruption and intimidation at the ballot box. Above all, he saw a world trend toward dictatorial rule and would support enlightened despotism in China.[90]

The Harvard-trained political scientist Qian Duansheng, then a professor at the National Central University in Nanjing, best represented the perception of such a world trend. Early in 1930, he wrote in defense of democracy, arguing that democratic rule was relatively beneficial to the people and that dictatorship was fundamentally an unstable form of government that would ultimately fail.[91] By 1934, however, he had changed his mind, seeing a "decline of Western democracy" due to two factors: first, the growth of proletarian consciousness and distrust of democracy and, second, democracy's inability to deal with the economic problems of a modern state. His argument was based on economic nationalism: all modern states desired to strengthen and expand their economies, having problems of one kind or another and waging economic wars among themselves. Democratic states could not cope with all these problems because their powers were limited and their capacity for prompt actions was constrained by party politics and the parliamen-

---

[89] Zhang Hong, "Zhuanzhi wenti pingyi" (An appraisal of the question of dictatorship), *DLPL* 104 (June 10, 1934): 10.

[90] Ibid., pp. 4–5, 9–10.

[91] Qian Duansheng, "Demo kelaxi weiji ji jianglai" (The crisis and future of democracy), *Guoli Wuhan daxue shehui kexue jikan* 1:1 (March 1930), cited in Eastman, *The Abortive Revolution*, p. 146.

tary system. By contrast, dictatorship had the powers to develop the national economy for the benefit of the people. Examining the modern dictatorships and totalitarian states in Italy, Germany, Turkey, and Soviet Russia, Qian came to the conclusion that, with the possible exception of Germany,[92] all had performed well economically and politically. Amid growing economic nationalism around the world, a command economy was necessary, thus rendering the decline of the democratic states inevitable and helping the world trend toward dictatorship. Even Britain and the United States, he thought, were heading for a planned and controlled economy, and Anglo-American democracy would be reduced to "a dictatorship of intellectuals and capitalists." He now considered dictatorship a necessary transitional system for reasons of economic production. But he did not like personal dictatorship because there would be succession problems but no mechanisms for a smooth transfer of power. What he favored was one-party dictatorship, well organized, effective, and committed to furthering the interests of the people. He wrote thus:

> China urgently needs to become a strong country within a short period of time. It would be impossible to industrialize the whole country in ten to twenty years. But within that space of time, the coastal provinces must achieve a high level of industrialization, complemented by agricultural growth in the inland regions. Only then can we resist the enemies in the next world war and be taken seriously by friendly states. To achieve the goal of industrializing the coastal regions, [our] country must possess the powers of a totalitarian state, which in turn will depend on a popular dictatorial system.[93]

Qian envisaged that system to be "a coalition dictatorship of the educated class and the bourgeoisie aimed at developing the national economy"; it was ideologically compatible with the Three Principles of the People. He subscribed to Sun Yat-sen's sheet-of-loose-sand theory. The Chinese needed to be organized.[94]

For Qian, then, dictatorship was a response to economic modernization, a view shared by those who assumed that a planned economy was

---

[92] Qian did not think highly of Germany's economic achievements, and was particularly critical of Hitler's anti-Semitism. See Qian Duansheng, "Minzhu zhengzhi hu? Jiquan guojia hu?" (Democracy? Dictatorship?), *Dongfang zazhi* 31:1 (January 1, 1934): 21.
[93] Ibid., pp. 17–25; the quote is on p. 24.   [94] Ibid., pp. 22, 25.

the superior method of development. One Stanford-trained political scientist thought that in reaction to the world depression, "people inevitably rise together and cry for 'controls' and 'planning'." "Dictatorships," he continued, "sweep aside yesterday's planless, unorganized, anarchic conditions, and implant social, economic, and political controls that are organized and planned."[95]

Qian was too quick to accept the achievements of Italy, Turkey, and Soviet Russia. In perceiving the "decline of Western democracy," he overlooked the fact that Russia and Turkey were undemocratic in the first place and that Italy and Germany did not have as long a democratic tradition as England and the United States did.[96] If dictatorial states were better equipped to deal with economic problems, why did Russia and Turkey not become economic powers?

The ways in which the United States and Britain were responding to the Great Depression added to the perception of a world trend away from democracy. The New Deal of President Franklin D. Roosevelt appeared to be creating an economic dictatorship, while the government of Ramsay MacDonald, with an all-party cabinet, also seemed to be taking Britain down the same track. "Democracy is in trouble. Even the United States, Britain, and France are moving toward dictatorship," said one writer, "Mussolini and Hitler have become the most outstanding figures in the world." World War I had been fought for the survival of democracy, he continued. "In the Second World War of the future, it will be a war between Bolshevism and fascism. Which will win only time can tell. But democracy will have been dead and buried."[97] All these perceptions were, of course, far from the truth, but they did reflect a sense of despair at China's economic backwardness.

Economic management apart, there was an erosion of confidence in Western democracy in general. One writer thought that the majority of the world's populations, including Americans, were far from equal and free and that the "collapse of democracy" would be permanent.[98] Another expressed strong skepticism about the reality of democracy,

---

[95] Zhang Jinqian, "Ducai zhuyi lun" (On dictatorship), quoted in Eastman, *The Abortive Revolution*, p. 147.

[96] Zhu Yisong, "Guanyu minzhu yu ducai de yige da lunzhan (xia)" (The great democracy versus dictatorship debate [part 2]), *Zaisheng* 3:4–5 combined (July 15, 1935): 29–40.

[97] Zhu Weiru, "Demo kelaxi de qiantu" (The future of democracy), *Shidai gonglun* 3:7 (May 11, 1934): 8–14; the quote is on p. 14.

[98] Zhang Jinjian, "Minzhu zhuyi zai jinri" (Democracy today), *Dongfang zazhi* 31:4 (February 16, 1934): 43–47.

citing the example of the United States, where the blacks, ethnic Chinese, and other people of color were discriminated against and where the gulf between big capitalists and small employees made a mockery of liberty and equality. Calling into question the basic assumptions about democracy, he declared: "Democracy, basically, is a formula that deceives; it is a sheer fantasy."[99] The dictatorship proponents were agreed that what China needed was a strong state; neo-dictatorship offered the best hope, at least for the time being, and no other party could do a better job than the GMD in the existing circumstances. They were also convinced that China lacked the necessary conditions for democracy and that only a dictatorship could cope with the current crisis and eventually resolve the nation's socioeconomic problems.[100] Finally, there was a sense of cultural despair and self-doubt regarding the qualities of Chinese as a race, once thought to be superior, to meet the challenges of the modern world. China seemed to have tried everything to regain her pride and greatness, all to no avail. For some scholars, the 1930s were "a period of painful, remorseless national self-flagellation."[101] Neo-dictatorship would offer China the last chance.

In the final analysis, the case for neo-dictatorship was built on its perceived utility. For Jiang Tingfu, it was a necessary stage in the process of nation building. For Ding Wenjiang, it was the only hope for China, led by a technocracy in a new-style administration. For Qian Duansheng, it was a world trend and the best system of economic management. For others, it was a reaction against the deficiencies of democracy as well as the grim realities of social, political, and economic inequalities. For all of them, it was the only system whereby immediate measures could be taken to tackle China's pressing problems. Like fascism, neo-dictatorship was a response to the national emergency, to the "failure" of democracy, to modernization, and to delayed development. Many would hope that ultimately it would be replaced by democracy.

The question of what conditions must be met if neo-dictatorship were to produce the desired results was not well considered. Ding Wenjiang's

---

[99] You Huansheng, "Minzhu zhengzhi hu?" (Democratic politics?), *DLPL* 135 (January 13, 1935): 7–9.

[100] See, for example, Xu Daolin, "Xianfa caoan chugao shangdui" (On the draft constitution), *DLPL* 94 (April 1, 1934): 10; Shuo Ren, "Zhengzhi wenti de taolun" (Discussion of the question of political institutions), *DLPL* 164 (August 18, 1935): 17–18; Li Pusheng, "Guomindang weishi jinbiaodui zige" (The Guomindang has not yet lost its qualifications as a champion team), *DLPL* 176 (November 10, 1935): 6–9.

[101] Eastman, *The Abortive Revolution*, p. 158.

four conditions were insufficient and sounded Confucian. Moreover, as Zhang Junmai criticized, these conditions applied to a democratic government as much as to a neo-dictatorship.[102] Even worse, Ding failed to insist on a rule of law, or on any mechanisms for checking abuses of power, official corruption, and political repression. It was simply assumed that neo-dictatorship would be enlightened, benevolent, and responsible. As to the availability of the dictator, or the Supreme Leader (*zuigao lingxiu*), Chiang Kai-shek's name was hardly mentioned by Jiang and Ding, suggesting that they had doubts about him. Hu Shi's insistence that nobody in China was eminently qualified for the job forced Jiang to concede that he was not sure himself.[103] Qian Duansheng was perhaps the only one who mentioned Chiang Kai-shek as the best candidate on the grounds that Chiang had been transformed over the years from a militarist into a great leader "enjoying high prestige and popular support."[104]

Another question not discussed was how power could be centralized in the political center in view of the recalcitrant regions that guarded their interests jealously. What was the trade-off that could induce them to give up their powers to the center? Clearly, the case for neo-dictatorship was by no means strong. It fed on China's chaos, division, and internal weaknesses. It sniped at the deficiencies of Western democracy and assumed the achievements of Soviet Russia and the fascist regimes of Europe. Above all, it failed to show how it was possible when Nanjing was detested by the regions and, even more important, how it could succeed where the old dictatorship had failed.

CONCLUSION

The national emergency, which highlighted the relationship between *jiuwang* and *qimeng*, called for a Chinese response that went beyond armed resistance and antiimperialist nationalism. National salvation, as much internal as external in nature, was not separate and distinct from enlightenment, from the issue of constitutionalism and democracy. The 1932 National Emergency Conference failed precisely because, from the

---

[102] Zhang Junmai, "Minzhu ducai yiwai zhi disanzhong zhengzhi" (A third kind of politics besides democracy and dictatorship), *Zaisheng* 3:2 (April 15, 1935): 11–12.

[103] Hu Shi, "Zhengzhi tongyi de tujing" (The route to political unification), *DLPL* 86 (January 21, 1934): 2.

[104] Qian Duansheng, "Duiyu liuzhong quanhui de qiwang" (My expectations of the sixth plenum), *DLPL* 162 (August 4, 1935): 6, 8.

perspective of its critics, the government was unsympathetic to their demands for political and constitutional reforms. The progressives within the GMD were a small minority whose views were easily ignored. But the quest for democracy continued, despite escalating Japanese imperialism.

There was another perspective, however. Some intellectuals, who had been disillusioned with the result of China's experience with democratic institutions since 1912, considered the immediate implementation of constitutional rule both impossible and undesirable. They were not Party hacks, having been critics of the government, but they now viewed neo-dictatorship as a transitional system best suited to China in the midst of a national emergency. Their understanding of neo-dictatorship was also informed by "the decline of Western democracy," developments in Europe, Stalin's Five-year Plan, the Great Depression, President Roosevelt's New Deal, and a perceived world trend toward autocratic rule. Retreating from liberalism and democracy, they succeeded in putting democracy on the defensive.

4

In Defense of Democracy,
1933–1936

THE PASSION of enlightenment intellectuals in defending democracy was not diminished by the Japanese threat. "China was once again ready to listen to educated young men and women who sought to combine national salvation with a deeper commitment to intellectual emancipation," writes Vera Schwarcz. "As in the May Fourth movement at Beida [Beijing University], a vocal minority arose to do battle with cultural conservatives, both those inside and outside the Guomindang."[1] Prodemocracy writers were a vocal minority who rose to do battle with the dictatorial regime in the intellectual marketplace of ideas, convinced that democracy was relevant to the national emergency, the foreign threat being no justification for dictatorship, new or old.

Writing on the democracy versus dictatorship debate of 1933–1934, Lloyd Eastman commented that the debate was "mundane, a trifle stodgy" and that democracy's defense was "faltering" and "poor." "The advocates of democracy seldom articulated a comprehensive defense of their position and instead sniped at the shortcomings of the [GMD's] system of party rule."[2] Particularly unimpressed with Hu Shi's kindergarten politics argument, Eastman was adamant that Chinese democrats lacked "a sophisticated understanding of the true character of liberal democracy."[3] He overlooked the fact that the great debate went beyond 1934 and the pages of *Duli pinglun* to become a wider democracy discourse. Other liberal writers wrote elsewhere at about the same time and also later on the possibility of a state both democratic and strong.

---

[1] Vera Schwarcz, *The Chinese Enlightenment: Intellectuals and the Legacy of the May Fourth Movement of 1919* (Berkeley: University of California Press, 1986), p. 197.
[2] Lloyd E. Eastman, *The Abortive Revolution: China Under Nationalist Rule, 1927–1937* (Cambridge, MA: Harvard University Press, 1974), pp. 141, 151.
[3] Ibid., p. 152.

Chinese liberalism, or democracy for that matter, was not associated with a weak state and an absence of national purpose. Although the proponents of democracy lacked originality in their thinking and their arguments suffered from occasional lapses of judgment and inconsistencies, they were never dull. To be sure, few seemed to have a good grasp of democratic theory and its philosophical basis, but some did show an appreciation of democracy's basic values, strengths, and weaknesses. Their conceptions of democracy, as we shall see in this and other chapters, reflected an interesting combination of utilitarianism and utopianism.

This chapter begins with a discussion of Hu Shi's and other liberal views on democracy. It will then examine the thoughts of those who advocated democratization within the GMD and political reform within the existing framework of single-party rule. In a national emergency demanding a strong and effective government, an important issue for Chinese intellectuals was the tension between democracy and concentration of powers. The last part of the chapter is devoted to an exploration of this issue with special reference to the views of the National Socialists.

HU SHI'S KINDERGARTEN POLITICS

Against the onset of a spate of articles advocating neo-dictatorship, the defense of democracy was mounted on three grounds: as a means of unifying the country and uniting all the political parties and groups and the general population in the face of the external threat; as a means of reforming the government; and as an end in itself. Democracy was possible in China, it was argued, despite the widespread illiteracy of the population.

The most eminent defender was Hu Shi, who, it will be recalled, had attacked the government for its violations of human rights, for the absence of a provisional constitution during the period of political tutelage, and for the lack of a rule of law. We also have noted his critiques of Jiang Tingfu's misreading of British, French, and Russian histories and of Wu Jingchao's cyclical view of Chinese history in their advocacy of dictatorship. True to his liberal convictions, Hu insisted that unification must be achieved politically.[4] Thus, he advocated a political system that provided for a close relationship between the center and

---

[4] Hu Shi, "Wuli tongyilun" (On military unification), *DLPL* 85 (January 14, 1934): 3–7.

the periphery based on mutual interests. That was a parliamentary system – "the raison d'être for, not an outcome of, unification."[5] Whereas Jiang and Wu viewed China's political fragmentation and disorder as a justification for dictatorship, Hu saw these as compelling reasons for parliamentary democracy. He could not see anybody, any party, or any class in China capable of enlightened dictatorship, nor could he think of any issue big enough to rally the entire population behind a dictatorship (not even the Japanese threat).[6] Although constitutionalism alone could not save China, he was convinced that it could put Chinese politics on the right track. There were no secrets to constitutionalism, he declared, only two principles: a rule of law and government responsibility to the people.[7]

All these were reasonable arguments. But Hu provoked the most derision and criticism when he expressed the following view:

> Constitutional democracy is only a kind of kindergarten political system best suited to the training of a people and race lacking in political experience. . . . Many kindergarten races already had democracy a long time ago. That is not strange at all. The merits of democracy lie in its need for no outstanding talents, in its flexibility in gradually enlarging the base of political authority, in "bringing together talents for the general good," . . . in giving the majority of the people who are mediocre opportunities for political participation so that they can be trained to value their rights. In short, whereas democracy is the politics of common knowledge, enlightened despotism is the politics of the specialized elite. Whereas the specialized elite is difficult to come by, common knowledge is relatively easy to train. In a country like ours so lacking in talents, the best political training is a constitutional democracy that can gradually enlarge the base of political authority.[8]

He claimed that even though England and the United States were the original homes of modern democracy, "think-tank politics" was a recent development. Modern dictatorship requiring specialized skills and

---

[5] Hu Shi, "Zailun jianguo yu zhuanzhi" (Again on nation building and autocracy), *DLPL* 82 (December 24, 1933): 2–7; "Zhengzhi tongyi de tujing" (The route to political unification), *DLPL* 86 (January 21, 1934): 2–6; "Zhengzhi tongyi de yiyi" (The meaning of political unification), *DLPL 123* (October 21, 1934): 2–4.

[6] Hu Shi, "Zailun jianguo yu zhuanzhi," pp. 4–5.

[7] Hu Shi, "Xianzheng wenti" (The constitutional question), *DLPL* 1 (May 22, 1932): 7.

[8] Hu Shi, "Zailun jianguo yu zhuanzhi," p. 5.

knowledge was the politics of advanced research. China was not ready for it.[9]

Hu's kindergarten politics argument was flawed and embarrassing to his friends. Ding Wenjiang was quick to point out that England, the United States, and all other accomplished Western democracies were politically experienced in contrast to the inexperience of the Russians, Italians, and Germans. Moreover, talents, advanced skills, and expert knowledge were needed in all modern societies, irrespective of their political systems.[10] Hu's contention – that most people in the world, including Americans and Britons, were not interested in "political interference" and that the good thing about democracy was that periodically the people, however ignorant they might be, had the chance of saying yes or no at the ballot box[11] – cut no ice with his readers because he ignored what it took for someone to make an informed decision at election time. Furthermore, just as dictatorship required specialized knowledge and expertise, so did democracy. If democracy was gradual and incremental, from kindergarten to graduate school, then dictatorship should never be the politics of the research institute. Clearly his defense of democracy was uncharacteristically incompetent.

Yet we can make some sense of Hu's kindergarten politics by putting it in perspective. He was arguing with his friends Jiang and Ding, who had abandoned the liberal cause, and with others who viewed Chinese democracy as a distant goal unattainable for a long time to come, not the least because of the widespread illiteracy of the masses. The illiteracy argument, though refuted by democracy proponents, still carried much weight. To counter it further, he felt compelled to contend that even ignorant people were capable of exercising their rights at the ballot box because democracy was "common sense" politics. In essence, he was saying that the Chinese as a race were capable of governing themselves democratically. He was concerned with a democratic breakthrough, or the initial stage of constitutional democracy – a project beginning with the kindergarten through the high school to the university and the research institute, ultimately reaching the advanced Anglo-American stage. He was also speaking of minimalist democracy with its emphasis on electing a government. In trying to cut democracy down to a man-

[9] Hu Shi, "Zhongguo wu ducai de biyao yu Keneng" (The unnecessity and impossibility of dictatorship in China), *DLPL* 130 (December 9, 1934): 4–5.

[10] Ding Wenjiang, "Minzhu zhengzhi yu ducai zhengzhi," pp. 5–6.

[11] Hu Shi, "Da Ding Zaijun xiansheng lun minzhu yu ducai" (A response to Mr. Ding Zaijun on democracy and dictatorship), *DLPL* 133 (December 30, 1934): 7–8.

ageable size, he reduced it to something that even the illiterate could understand – that is, saying yes or no at the ballot box. His message, in other words, was that democracy was not an unattainable goal, that it was about electing a government, and that the best democratic training was the practice of democracy itself. He was standing up for basic rights, despite his elitism in governance; like Schumpeter, he viewed democracy as a political method first and foremost.

Others shared this view. The Princeton-educated historian Hu Daowei, also reducing democracy to a political process, contended that in the twentieth century even illiterates could cast their votes by pressing an electric button that used colors to represent the candidates, as some Americans were said to have done before. Widespread illiteracy was, therefore, no longer an obstacle to democracy.[12] Eastman criticized that this was "an inane retort to the critics who perceived democracy not merely as a question of casting ballots but as a political practice inseparable from the whole cultural environment."[13] But Hu Daowei went on to say, "the only condition for the right to vote is that the people possess political knowledge. And the only way to train people in political knowledge is to give them the opportunity for political participation – in other words, to practice democracy."[14] On this point, the two Hus were speaking on the same wavelengths, without trying to separate democratic practice from the whole cultural environment. Hu Shi, in particular, had spoken of a "civic life in a civil society" for both rulers and the ruled. There could be no cultural environment conducive to democracy without some sort of democracy being practiced at the same time.

Hu Shi also put forward his idea of *wuwei* (nonaction) politics (not to be confused with *wuwei* philosophy to which he was opposed). He did not like big government, least of all an interventionist one that was incompetent, corrupt, reactionary, and incapable of modern transformation. He would rather see people being left alone to pursue their own goals with the role of the government being reduced to that of a law enforcement agency.[15] *Wuwei* politics was the politics of small government.

---

[12] Hu Daowei, "Zhongguo de qilu – wei minzhi yu ducai wenti jiushang yu Ding Wenjiang xiansheng ji shixia zhuxian" (China at the crossroads – A response to Mr. Ding Wenjiang and other scholars on the issue of democracy and dictatorship), *GWZB* 12:6 (February 18, 1935): 1–10. This article was continued in the next issue of *GWZB* 12:7 (February 25, 1935): 1–9.

[13] Eastman, *The Abortive Revolution*, p. 153.

[14] Hu Daowei, "Zhongguo de qilu," pp. 3–4.

[15] Chou Min-chih, *Hu Shih and Intellectual Choice in Modern China* (Ann Arbor: University of Michigan Press, 1964), pp. 134–135.

Hu Shi further defended democracy from two premises: functionalism and individuality. As a loyal critic, he saw that great benefits would accrue to the government if it became a constitutional democracy. Democracy could make the GMD more progressive by forcing it onto the reform path. While acknowledging that political openness and competition could lead to its loss of power, he thought the GMD was most likely to become a better and stronger regime as a result. Additionally, democracy would place the government on a constitutional footing, thereby legitimizing it. Because there was no party that could compete with it successfully, the GMD need not feel threatened,[16] a point Luo Longji had made before. Hu was correct in stating that a legitimate and reformed government would be a better place to cope with the national emergency. That was another way of saying that to legitimize a dictatorship, even a new-style one in Ding Wenjiang's image, was not easy.

Given his May Fourth credentials, there could be no question about Hu Shi's commitment to independence of thought, the freedoms of speech and publication, and the free and autonomous development of individuality – to what he called "healthy individualism."[17] But in this debate, his articulation of the intrinsic values of individualism was overshadowed by his Schumpterian concerns.

ZHANG XIRUO'S DEFENSE OF LIBERAL VALUES

At this point, it was Zhang Xiruo, a professor of political philosophy at Qinghua University and a friend of Hu Shi's (Zhang, too, held a Ph. D. from Columbia University), who rose to defend the basic values of liberalism more vigorously than anyone else. Embarrassed by Hu's notion of kindergarten politics, Zhang feared that, instead of advancing the cause of democracy, Hu had done considerable damage to it.[18] Invoking Plato, he attributed the failure of institutional development in China's long history to a lack of knowledge and ethics – the two essential things that formed the basis of all political institutions. The problem did not lie

---

[16] Hu Shi, "Zhengzhi gaige de dalu" (The wide road to political reform), *DLPL* 163 (August 11, 1935): 3–4.

[17] Hu Shi, "Geren ziyou yu shehui jinbu – zaitan wusi yundong" (Individual liberty and social progress – The May Fourth Movement revisited), *DLPL* 150 (May 12, 1935): 2–5.

[18] For Zhang's full critique of Hu's kindergarten politics, see Zhang Xiruo, "Minzhu zhengzhi dangzhen shi youzhi de zhengzhi ma?" (Is democracy really kindergarten politics?), *DLPL* 239 (June 20, 1937): 3–6.

with the ruling class alone, he wrote, it had much to do with the low status of the individual vis-à-vis the family and the collectivity in Chinese society.[19] Drawing attention to individualism from the Western point of view, he emphasized that without individual liberation there would have been no modern science and modern culture. Individual liberation was "a great historical tide," "an irresistible conquering force," and "unavoidably contagious."[20] To his mind, the greatest merit of individualism was that the individual's conscience is the ultimate judge of what is right and what is wrong in politics:

> Only if individuals have the chances to give full expression to what their conscience considers to be wrong, and only if they have the liberty to express what their rationality opposes, could they discover their close relationship with the state, discover the dignity and value of their existence, and love their country. How noble are such individuals and how valuable are they as citizens of the state! A state that claims such citizens is far more advantageous than a state that claims thousands and thousands of people as its tools.[21]

Thus, he attached great importance to individualism, the development of individuality, and the fostering of the personal integrity (*renge*) of the citizenry, which would help to lay a new foundation for China's reconstruction. He defended the May Fourth enlightenment which, he thought, had been on the wane of late.[22] Although he launched no direct attack on dictatorship, his reaffirmation of the core values of liberalism left no doubt where he stood. Democracy seemed to him to be the best political system the world had ever known because it was government based on consent, its power derived from reason, not force. Invoking Bertrand Russell, H. G. Wells, Harold Laski, and John Dewey, he argued that the success of democracy depended on two variables: first, the people's knowledge and their ability to understand general political issues and, second, their interest in politics and political participation; both could be promoted through education. How could democracy be

---

[19] Plato was of the opinion that the disorders of a state were due largely to ignorance and selfishness. See Zhang Xiruo, "Yiqie zhengzhi zhi jichu" (The foundations of all politics), *GWZB* 12:6 (February 18, 1935): 1–4.

[20] Zhang Xiruo, "Guomin renge zhi peiyang" (Cultivation of the national integrity), *DLPL* 150 (May 12, 1935): 15.

[21] Ibid.

[22] Zhang Xiruo, "Zailun guomin renge" (Again on the national integrity), *DLPL* 152 (May 26, 1935): 2–5.

implemented, given the widespread illiteracy of the population? His answer was that the people must still learn to practice it at once because democracy was something worth learning about, and not hard to learn if only they tried.[23] He supported the view that democracy was intrinsically valuable and an important learning process.

Zhang Xiruo's defense of liberal values struck a responsive chord with Hu Shi, who quickly reaffirmed the May Fourth spirit and his faith in the intrinsic worth of the individual, personal freedoms, and the liberation of thought, all of which were important also for social progress.[24]

OTHER PRODEMOCRACY VIEWS

Hu Daowei, whom we have just met, also embarrassed his colleagues by attempting to distinguish between dictatorship (*ducai*) and autocracy (*zhuanzhi*) in three respects: first, dictatorship was based on *fazhi* (rule of law), whereas autocracy was based on *renzhi* (rule of man); second, dictatorship was a process and a tool, whereas autocracy was an end in itself; and third, dictatorship involved the monopoly of political power, whereas autocracy involved the monopoly of both political and economic powers.[25] His argument is flawed. A rule of law is a basis for democracy rather than a condition for dictatorship. There is not a great deal of difference between dictatorship and autocracy. What's more, he showed a lack of clear thinking when he wrote at one point that China since ancient times had never practiced democracy and at another that before the Revolution of 1911 China had been tyrannical (*baonue*) but rarely autocratic (*zhuanzhi*).[26] Nonetheless, if he meant to say that a new-style dictatorship would not work unless it was based on a rule of law, he was correct, as was his premise that democracy safeguards rights.

Following the rights thinking of the French Revolution, Hu Daowei was convinced that people were born free and equal and that the purpose of the state was to protect the rights to liberty, property, personal safety, and resistance to oppression. He also thought Europeans had long

---

[23] Zhang Xiruo, "Wo wei shenme xiangxin minzhi" (Why do I believe in democracy?), *DLPL* 240 (June 27, 1937): 4–5.

[24] Hu Shi, "Geren ziyou yu shehui jinbu," pp. 2–5.

[25] Hu Daowei, "Lun zhuanzhi yu ducai" (On autocracy and dictatorship), *DLPL* 90 (March 4, 1934): 5–11.

[26] Hu Daowei, "Zhongguo de qilu (xu)" (China's future [continued]), *GWZB* 12:7 (February 22, 1935): 4.

abandoned the theory of natural rights in favor of the English school of thought that held that rights were stipulated by the law. He was particularly impressed with the English writ of habeas corpus and the British system of an independent judiciary whereby not only were rights protected, but those in authority could be sued for violations of rights and for compensation. It was important for him that rights included the possibility of redress.[27]

The human rights theorist Luo Longji did not enter the debate at this point, but he had penned a number of pungent editorials in *Yishibao* criticizing the Nanjing regime. Later, in 1935, he published an article taking Ding Wenjiang and Jiang Tingfu to task for failing to understand that the purpose of politics was to nurture and develop the individual's personality and character and to ensure "the greatest happiness of the greatest number." He reiterated his previous views on human rights, adding that rights were respected in a democracy but violated in a dictatorship. There was nothing like "ideal dictatorship," he declared. Ultimately, dictatorship, by focusing on the authority of the dictator, meant the rule of man, not of law. He pointed out that there already existed a seven-year-old dictatorship in the name of political tutelage. Worse still, it had degenerated into a personal dictatorship. If the Chiang Kai-shek regime was not already a dictatorship, Luo wondered what it was. Overseas, he saw only a "readjustment," not a weakening, of democratic institutions in Britain, France, and the United States, aimed at rendering the executive government more efficient, their governments being all popularly elected.[28] In a separate essay on Chinese constitutional reform, he argued that the difference between democracy and dictatorship boiled down to a difference between the "politics of peace" and the "politics of violence," between *fazhi* and *renzhi*. The transformation of China from one kind of politics to the other required a modern legal system, a depoliticized civil service, protection of civil rights and liberties, equal opportunity for political participation, and a cessation of government funding for the ruling GMD,[29] things he had included in his 1929 list of human rights. He was adamant that neo-dictatorship would not make the GMD regime any more efficient, nor would it provide mechanisms for peaceful conflict resolution.

[27] Hu Daowei, "Quanli shi shenme?" (What are rights?), *DLPL* 45 (March 26, 1933): 10–14.

[28] Luo Longi, "Wo dui Zhongguo ducai zhengzhi de yijian" (My opinions on Chinese dictatorship), *Yuzhou xunkan* 2:3 (June 5, 1935): 1–11.

[29] Luo Longji, "Women yao shenme de xianzheng?" (What sort of constitutionalism do we want?), *Ziyou pinglun* 1 (November 22, 1935): 3–9.

Chinese liberals were inclined toward elitist, technocratic democracy. For many, the quintessence of democracy was not rule by the people but popular supervision of government. For all its faults, democracy, wrote political scientist Zou Wenhai, is the "most reasonable," "most just," and "most useful" political system designed to promote the well-being of the entire population, all classes, groups, and organizations, as well as individual interests; and it ensures equal opportunity. But in a democracy, he added, the people remain the governed, and the governing elite is of necessity a small minority. Democratic elitism and popular government are not incompatible. A popular government is popular because it is popularly elected and accountable. Popular supervision of government is possible, even though most people lack political and specialized knowledge, because there could be only one criterion with which to judge the government: popular interests. A good government promotes the popular interest; a bad government neglects the people and corrupts itself. To oversee the government, the people must enjoy basic freedoms, especially thought liberation and freedom of speech, which make public opinion possible. Public opinion is a powerful weapon in that it offers a critique of government policies and actions. Although not everyone can be part of the governing elite, everybody is capable of defending one's rights. Zou also stressed the importance of free elections. China had had elections and a Parliament before, but politicians, the military, and vested interests had rigged those elections, and Beijing's short-lived Parliament had never worked. If China was to become a truly democratic state, he concluded, elections had to be clean, free from political corruption, and representative institutions must be developed. He was optimistic that both were attainable.[30] In emphasizing the importance of periodic elections and free speech as the means of popular supervision of government, he echoed the view of many contemporary liberal thinkers both at home and abroad.[31]

---

[30] Zou Wenhai, "Xuanju yu daibiao zhidu" (Elections and the representative system), *Zaisheng* 2:5 (February 1, 1934): 1–32.

[31] More recently, John Plamenatz has observed: "There is democracy where rulers are politically responsible to their subjects. And there is political responsibility where two conditions hold: where citizens are free to criticize their rulers and to come together to make demands on them and to win support for the policies they favor and the beliefs they hold: and where the supreme makers of law and policy are elected to their offices at free and periodic elections." See his *Democracy and Illusion: An Examination of Certain Aspects of Modern Democratic Theory* (London: Longman, 1973), pp. 184–185.

In defense of democracy some scholars invoked John Stuart Mill,[32] hardly realizing that Mill also had argued for the possibility in some special circumstances of a legitimate "benevolent despotism."[33] Their point was that democracy was important for China not merely because it would help to unify the country and unite all political parties in an anti-Japanese united front, but also because it was the best system in its own right. "Even without the national emergency," argued one writer, "constitutional democracy should not be postponed, let alone abandoned."[34]

Others rejected suggestions that Western democracy was on the wane. They questioned the achievements of Europe's dictatorial regimes, pointing out that Soviet Russia, Germany, Italy, Spain, Poland, Lithuania, Hungary, and Yugoslavia had all failed to solve their political, economic, and unemployment problems and that civil strife showed no signs of abating in some of these countries. Dictatorial regimes were threats to world peace, as in the cases of Germany and Italy. There was, moreover, a recent movement to abandon dictatorship and to restore democracy in Portugal.[35] Britain, France, and the United States all held steadfastly to their democratic institutions, in spite of the Great Depression. As Tao Menghe, a Japanese- and British-trained professor of sociology and Director of the Institute of Social Sciences at Academia Sinica, put it, Europe's dictatorial regimes were "crisis governments" located in societies that had no long democratic traditions. Far from retreating, Western democracies were holding their ground.[36]

Back home, the defense of democracy was not impregnable by any means. Apart from the stupidity of Hu Shi's kindergarten politics, many questions were left unanswered. How would constitutional democracy stop the regional militarists from opposing the political center? How would it check the communist movement and resolve the country's socioeconomic problems? How would it ensure a cessation of civil strife?

---

[32] See, for example, Minsheng (a pen name), "Shuangzhou xiantan (6)" (Fortnightly talks [6]), *DLPL* 133 (December 30, 1934): 9–14.

[33] See Gerald F. Gans, *The Modern Liberal Theory of Man* (New York: St. Martin's Press, 1983), p. 221.

[34] Song Shiying, "Zhongguo xianzheng zhi qiantu" (The future of Chinese constitutionalism), *DLPL* 234 (May 16, 1937): 15.

[35] See, for example, Du Guangxun, "Qingkan Ouzhou ducai zhengzhi de jieguo" (Have a look at the consequences of European dictatorships), *DLPL* 146 (April 14, 1935): 9–13.

[36] Tao Menghe, "Minzhu yu ducai" (Democracy and dictatorship), *GWZB* 12:1 (January 1, 1935): 4.

And how would it bring about national unification? The same questions could be asked of neo-dictatorship, too.

The great debate was perhaps a draw, inconclusive and with no clear winners, prompting Hu Shi to make an impassioned plea for a "common political belief." Whatever political system might be adopted, it was important to resolve China's domestic problems politically, not militarily, and to maintain constitutionalism as the political ideal.[37]

Although the debate had little force either to moderate or to change the character of the GMD regime, opposition to dictatorship from a section of the intellectual community lent support, and perhaps also some legitimacy, to the anti-Chiang Kai-shek movement in warlord territory. This forced Chiang and his lieutenant Wang Jingwei to declare in a joint cable on November 27, 1934, that "the people and all social organizations would enjoy the freedoms of speech and association according to the law" and that these liberties, "provided that they are not against the background of violence and riots," would be protected by the government. The declaration added that "in view of China's current situation and the times there really is no necessity or possibility of an Italian or Soviet form of political system."[38] Nanjing's leaders had decided to postpone the Fifth National Party Congress, scheduled for early 1935, which Chiang had hoped to use to consolidate his political dominance. To be sure, Chiang did not mean what he said when he denied having any intention of becoming a dictator. Moreover, as Hu Shi pointed out, the statement that people could enjoy personal freedoms only if such freedoms were not set against "the background of violence and riots" was too ambiguous to inspire confidence.[39] But at least for the time being, Chiang felt compelled to back away from his dictatorial designs.

For many intellectuals, the choice was not cut and dried. Even Jiang Tingfu and Ding Wenjiang aspired to democracy as the ultimate goal. Wu Jingchao later denied that he had ever supported dictatorship.[40] In the meantime, some would explore the possibilities of democratization within the existing framework of political tutelage.

---

[37] Hu Shi, "Cong minzhu dao ducai de taolun li qiude yige gongtong xinyang" (Seeking a common political belief from the democracy versus dictatorship debate), *DLPL* 141 (March 10, 1935): 16–19. Reprinted from *Dagongbao*, February 17, 1935.

[38] Cited in Hu Shi, "Wang Jiang tongdian li tiqi de ziyou" (The liberty mentioned in the telegram from Wang and Jiang), *DLPL* 131 (December 16, 1934): 4.

[39] Ibid.

[40] Wu Jingchao, "Zhongguo de zhengzhi wenti" (The question of China's politics), *DLPL* 134 (January 6, 1935): 18; "Xingqi lunwen" (Weekly featured article), *Dagongbao* (Tianjin), December 3, 1934.

DEMOCRATIZATION WITHIN THE FRAMEWORK OF
POLITICAL TUTELAGE

There were two possibilities here. One was to lift the ban on the other parties and to introduce some form of multiparty politics, with the GMD still being predominant, that is, a competitive dominant party system. The other was political liberalization within the ruling GMD itself. Both recognized the reality of political tutelage.

The view that democratization should begin with the legalization of the opposition parties was widely supported in intellectual circles. Tao Xisheng, a professor of politics at Beijing University (later private secretary to Chiang Kai-shek), wrote in 1932 that dictatorship was "the wrong idea of an era." He did not think national salvation could be achieved even if the GMD was united and given concentrated powers; rather, it was necessary to "open up the regime" by lifting the ban on the minor parties.[41] Writing again early in 1935, Tao, frustrated at the fact that the GMD was already a dictatorship for all intents and purposes, began to wonder whether the parliamentary system could ever be put into practice.[42] He remained convinced that, once legalized, the opposition parties would give up the idea of armed struggle and rally behind the government against foreign aggression, and the National People's Representatives Congress, yet to be established, would be the new arena for political opposition.[43] The single-party system would remain in force as long as political tutelage lasted, but he saw the possibility of incorporating multiparty politics into it, adding that the GMD could expect to enjoy the support of the minor parties and groups if they were legalized.[44]

Multiparty politics in a single-party system is not necessarily a contradiction in terms. It was Zhang Foquan, the American-educated editor of Tianjin's *Dagongbao* and correspondent for Shanghai's *Guowen*

---

[41] Tao Xisheng, "Yige shidai cuowu de yijian" (A view on the error of an era), *DLPL* 20 (October 2, 1933): 2–3.

[42] Tao Xisheng, "Minzhu yu ducai de zhenglun" (The debate between democracy and dictatorship), *DLPL* 136 (January 20, 1935): 12.

[43] Tao Xisheng, "Lun kaifang dangjin" (On lifting the ban on political parties), *DLPL* 237 (June 6, 1937): 9.

[44] Tao Xisheng, "Zailun dangjin wenti" (Again on the ban on political parties), *DLPL* 239 (June 20, 1937): 14; "Budangzhe de liliang" (The strength of the non-Party elements), *DLPL* 242 (July 11, 1937): 10. Tao was close to the GMD and later became a member of that party. His democratic views were sometimes inconsistent. Nonetheless, a recent Taiwanese scholar has categorized him as a democracy advocate during the first half of the 1930s. See Chen Yishen, <*Duli pinglun*> *de minzhu sixiang* (The democratic thought of the *Independent Critic*) (Taibei: Lianjing chubanshe, 1989), p. 107.

zhoubao, who gave the loudest voice to the idea of multiparty politics during the period of political tutelage. He did not support democracy or dictatorship unconditionally, but he was strongly opposed to personal dictatorship, claiming a middle ground between fascism and parliamentary politics.[45] Like the late Qing reformers, he favored a constitutional preparatory period, having no objection to political tutelage per se, which was not the same thing as dictatorship. He criticized Nanjing for not practicing real political tutelage and for misinterpreting Sun Yat-sen's thought, pointing out that Sun had never said that during the period of political tutelage there should be "no parties outside the ruling party." The Nanjing regime had been "largely a failure" because the Party was put above the state. One-party rule was not good for China because Chinese politicians showed a lack of "political ethics" and "religious fervor" (meaning, probably, a sense of commitment). The masses were perhaps not ready for parliamentary democracy. But, on balance, he argued that democracy was still "less dangerous" than dictatorship, and not necessarily inefficient because there could be a strong and effective government without being undemocratic.[46] Considering the political inexperience of the Chinese people, he favored an oligarchy and limited suffrage based on education during the constitutional preparatory period.[47] But the preparatory period would differ from the existing political tutelage in one important respect: all nonviolent political parties should be legalized and allowed to compete freely for the popular vote. (Presumably the CCP was to be excluded because of its violence.) It was to be a fixed four- or six-year period, during which elections would be held, but there would be no rights of referendum, initiative, and recall. This was not full constitutional rule, only a start of the democratization process, beginning in the cities with the educated, spreading in the course of time to rural areas, and ultimately achieving universal suffrage. Education was the a priori condition for the right to vote.[48]

---

[45] Zhang Foquan, "Jidian piping yu jianyi – zaitan zhengzhi gaige wenti" (A few criticisms and suggestions – Again on the question of political reform), *GWZB* 12:38 (September 30, 1935): 2.

[46] Zhang Foquan, "Jianguo yu zhengzhi wenti" (Nation building and the question of political institutions), *GWZB* 11:26 (July 2, 1934): 3–8.

[47] Zhang Foquan, "Xunzheng yu zhuanzhi" (Political tutelage and autocracy), *GWZB* 11:36 (September 10, 1934): 4.

[48] Zhang Foquan, "Zhengzhi gaizao de tujing" (The path to institutional reform), *GWZB* 12:34 (September 2, 1935): 6; "Women jiujing yao shenmeyang de xianfa?" (What sort of constitution do we really want?), *DLPL* 236 (May 30, 1937): 3–4.

Preparations for full constitutional rule should be made by reorganizing the GMD and the government. Among other things, Zhang Foquan called for the adoption of a British-style cabinet system.[49] Yet he had little faith in the Montesquieuan notion of separation of powers. He desired a strong government alongside Parliament, the ultimate means of control, likening the powerful executive government to the legendary Monkey Sun Wukong and Parliament to the Tang Monk. The Monkey had the power to do what his Master wanted him to do, but it was the Master who had the ultimate power to restrain and control the Monkey.[50] He was critical of Sun Yat-sen's five-power structure of government.[51] But he failed to articulate how the GMD and the government should be reorganized and what system of checks and balances should be instituted. His idea of a Tang Monk-like parliament, reflecting the influence of Chinese popular culture, was too vague to be of any real use.

The significance of his thought lay in his hopes that a reformed GMD would play the role of a mentor fostering the growth of other parties that would compete for the popular vote. That role should be played during, not after, the period of political tutelage so that popular interest in politics could be aroused and a knowledge of politics infused in the people's minds through democratic practice.[52] Apart from the peaceful coexistence of multiple parties, all governments, central and local alike, should accept popular supervision and public criticism.[53] Freedom of speech was as important for him as for Hu Shi and other democracy exponents.

Not everyone agreed that conditions in China were ripe for multiparty competition. Samuel Huntington has observed that "a multiparty system is incompatible with a high level of political institutionalization and political stability" and that in "modernizing countries multiparty systems are weak party systems."[54] Lifting the ban on the opposition parties might

---

[49] Zhang Foquan, "Zhengzhi gaizao de tujing," pp. 1–10; "Jidian piping yu jianyi," pp. 1–6.

[50] Zhang Foquan, "Jianguo yu zhengzhi wenti" (Nation building and the question of political institutions), *GWZB* 11:26 (July 2, 1934): 5.

[51] Zhang Foquan, "Minyuan yilai woguo zai zhengzhi shang de chuantong cuowu" (The traditional error that we have made in politics since the beginning of the Republic), *GWZB* 10:44 (November 6, 1933): 5–8; also Zhang Foquan, "Zhengzhi gaizao de tujing," pp. 7–8; "Jinhou zhengzhi zhi zhanwang" (A look at the future of politics), *DLPL* 219 (September 20, 1936): 2.

[52] Zhang Foquan, "Jianguo yu zhengzhi wenti," p. 3.

[53] Zhang Foquan, "Women wei shenme yao shuochang daoduan" (Why should we be talking long and short?), *DLPL* 230 (April 18, 1937): 12.

[54] Samuel P. Huntington, *Political Order in Changing Societies* (New Haven: Yale University Press, 1968), p. 423.

not be as useful as effecting political liberalization within the ruling GMD itself. The exponent of this view was American-educated Chen Zhimai, B.A. (Illinois) and Ph.D. (Columbia), professor of history and politics at Beida and later also at Qinghua and Nankai. (He became a distinguished diplomat and ambassador later in his life.) Writing in January 1935, Chen agreed with Hu Shi that "China's domestic problems should be resolved politically rather than by force and that there was absolutely no reason for blindly imitating dictatorship."[55] His sympathy appeared to lie in the prodemocracy camp. Although the democratic system could be cumbersome, it could still produce the most efficient government, as attested by the experiences of England, the United States, France, and Switzerland after the First World War. Like many of his contemporaries, he did not think that universal suffrage, impossible in China's existing conditions, was a necessary requirement of democracy, pointing out that during the French Revolution, the French were divided into the "positive" and "negative" categories – only the former enjoyed the right of political participation. England, he added, did not have universal suffrage until 1929, and in many Latin countries, with the exception of Spain, women's suffrage was yet to be achieved. Considering China's conditions, the ideals of democracy should not be set too high. It was important to grasp the fundamentals of democracy and to develop it step by step. Each step forward, for all its inadequacies, would produce good outcomes.[56] Democracy held strong appeal to him because it provided mechanisms for the peaceful transfer of power. Moreover, he was sanguine about its capacity to stamp out official corruption.[57]

By mid-1936, however, Chen had become less sure about the superiority of democratic rule. Democracy no longer seemed fashionable, or appropriate for China and the times. But he did not want to throw all his weight behind dictatorship. In fact, he dismissed dictatorship's claim to efficiency:

> We think that China's existing conditions will not allow us to defend old-fashioned Western thought. We should immediately

---

[55] Chen Zhimai, "Minzhu yu ducai de taolun" (Discourse on democracy and dictatorship), *DLPL* 136 (January 20, 1935): 10.

[56] Ibid., pp. 4–11.

[57] Chen Zhimai, "Lun zhengzhi tanwu" (On political corruption), *DLPL* 184 (January 5, 1936): 2–6; "Shangguidao de zhengzhi" (Politics on the right track), *DLPL* 237 (June 6, 1937): 3.

abandon our previous superstition about democracy. . . . We need a government with centralized powers, one that is capable and efficient and which draws on the talents the country could offer. *. . . But the most efficient government is not necessarily a dictatorship* [emphasis added]. A dictatorial government is, in some respects, extremely incompatible with the principle of efficiency. We think that for China's political system [we should] abandon the democratic thought of nineteenth-century Europe on the one hand and, on the other, construct a system on the following principles.[58]

The first principle was the peaceful transfer of power. Drawing on Reginald Basset's *The Essentials of Parliamentary Democracy* (1935), Chen maintained that democracy was a political mechanism for conflict resolution. The second was the protection of civil liberties, whereas the third principle was nonrecognition of political equality. From Maurice A. Pink's *The Defense of Freedom* (1935), he learned that limited suffrage would be more suitable for the Chinese, insisting that the right of political participation should be determined by the level of education. There was no need to identify democracy with the politics of the whole population, or *Ländesgemeinde* as the Swiss called it.[59]

Chen had no time for lofty principles that he considered impracticable. The reality of GMD rule was not going to be changed easily. Calls for neo-dictatorship while one-party rule was already in place reflected badly on the Party itself. The problem, in his view, lay with the Party system and organization, not the theory of political tutelage. What the Party needed was internal reform, including reform of the Central Political Council. All the GMD factions, he suggested, should be put on a policy footing so that they could compete openly for power over policy issues. The successful faction would form a government, supervised by the Central Political Council, which also should be reorganized. The factions not in power then became the opposition, thus democratizing the Party organization. Should the ruling faction fail to deliver, others could try to oust it in an open, competitive manner. Yet he did not believe that ending one-party rule would be appropriate at this point because of the low level of literacy and the people's lack of national and constitutional consciousness. There was no viable alternative party,

[58] Chen Zhimai, "Zailun zhengzhi de sheji" (Again on institutional designs), *DLPL* 205 (June 14, 1936): 4.
[59] Ibid., pp. 4–5.

none sufficiently strong to pose much of a threat to the GMD. To "open up the regime" by organizing more political parties, he warned, would repeat the fiasco of the early Republic.[60] "Democracy within the ruling party" (*dangnei minzhu*) was a viable alternative to him because it sanctioned a kind of competitive politics. Facing the reality that factionalism was endemic in Chinese politics, he dismissed the call for party unity as a "fantasy," pleading instead for open intraparty competition based on policy issues.[61]

The notion of *dangnei minzhu* rested on the assumption that China could not be democratized until the GMD democratized itself first. As such, it is best understood as a democratizing strategy. However, Chen's idea of turning GMD factionalism into an opportunity, or a mechanism, for open competition under one-party rule would undermine the position of Chiang Kai-shek as the sole link between the factions, the locus of loyalty, and the indispensable leader. Certainly Chiang would not endorse it.

Both Chen and Zhang Foquan accepted the reality that the GMD was predominant, both desired political reform, both saw the need for some political competition prior to constitutional rule, both favored limited suffrage based on education, and both held dear the freedom of speech. But they differed over the extent and framework of reform. Whereas Zhang stressed the importance of tolerance and political pluralism by recognizing the existence of the minor parties and groups, Chen emphasized the utility of intraparty competition as a first step toward democratization.

So far we have looked at democracy's defense. It was a difficult task trying to convince those on the other side of the debate that Chinese politics were ready for pluralism and that Chinese society was ready to allow the people to hold real power. It was the inconclusive outcome of the debate that raised questions about the relationship between democracy and dictatorship. Were they diametrically opposed and mutually exclusive? If not, could they be reconciled? These questions were taken up by some opposition scholars in an attempt to find a middle ground.

---

[60] Chen Zhimai, "Zhengzhi gaige de biyao" (The necessity of institutional reform), *DLPL* 162 (August 4, 1935): 3–4; "Zailun zhengzhi gaige" (Again on institutional reform), *DLPL* 166 (September 1, 1935): 3, 7; "Xianzheng wenti yu dangzheng gaige" (The constitutional question and party reform), *DLPL* 175 (November 3, 1935): 2–6.

[61] Chen Zhimai, "Zailun zhengzhi gaige," p. 6.

ARE DEMOCRACY AND DICTATORSHIP
MUTUALLY EXCLUSIVE?

One of the points emerging from the debate was the perception that the democratic system was inefficient and ineffective, whereas dictatorship was quite the opposite. Would it not be perfect if a kind of democracy could be found that would provide for a strong and effective government? Was such a system not what China needed in a national emergency and perhaps also after? In this section, we study the views of a particular group of liberal intellectuals, the National Socialists, who were groping for just such a system.

The National Socialist Party was a lineal descendant of Liang Qichao's Research Clique (*Yanjiuxi*) and the Progressive Party (*Jinbudang*) of the early Republican period. Perhaps it can be dated back even further to Liang's Emperor Protection Party (*Baohuangdang*) of the late Qing period. Before Liang's death in 1929, Zhang Junmai and Zhang Dongsun had attempted in vain to persuade him to form a new political party as a counter to the two major parties.[62] In 1931, they formed the *Zaishengshe* (National Renaissance Society) with about one hundred other scholars and college professors. The name was chosen to indicate their belief that the Republic could be re-created with a Chinese Renaissance. In May 1932, the Society launched a scholarly journal with the same title *Zaisheng* (with an English title *National Renaissance*). In the autumn of 1934, at a national convention in Tianjin, the Society was reorganized under the new name National Socialist Party.[63] It was made up of a diversity of scholars, articulate and conservative, but not as far right as the Youth Party. Though it never developed a mass following, it was quite influential among its constituency of educated, middle-aged moderates.[64] At the time of formation, it had only about one hundred members.[65]

---

[62] For their association with Liang Qichao, see Zhang Pengyuan, *Liang Qichao yu minchu zhengzhi* (Liang Qichao and early Republican politics) (Taibei: Shihuo chubanshe, 1981), pp. 267–270.

[63] According to National Socialist Party histories, it was founded on April 16, 1932, contrary to GMD accounts that it was not officially established until 1934. See Roger B. Jeans, *Democracy and Socialism in Republican China: The Politics of Zhang Junmai (Carsun Chang), 1906–1941* (Lanham: Rowman & Littlefield, 1997), p. 203.

[64] Lyman P. Van Slyke, *Enemies and Friends: The United Front in Chinese Communist History* (Stanford: Stanford University Press, 1967), pp. 172–173.

[65] In 1947, its leaders claimed that membership in Shanghai alone was 30,000. See Roger B. Jeans's entry "Chinese Democratic Socialist Party," in Haruhiro Fukui, ed., *Political Parties of Asia and the Pacific* (Westport: Greenwood Press, 1985), p. 213.

Zhang Junmai, who had studied and traveled in Japan (1906–1910), Germany and England (1913–1916), France and Germany (1919–1921), and Germany again (1929–1931), was a proponent, like Liang Qichao, of the blending of Eastern and Western thought.[66] Early in 1923, he sparked off a lively intellectual debate by raising doubts about following the Western path of industrialism, capitalism, and scientism. He held that science was powerless to solve the spiritual problems of human life and was leading Western civilization to materialism and moral degeneracy, and that a sound philosophy of life should not rely upon the determinism of scientific laws, but on one's intuition and free will.[67] Aware of the strengths and weaknesses of both East and West, he sought a synthesis, or cultural syncretism, an enterprise that would occupy his attention for the next twenty years or so. A cultural conservative, he conceived of the National Socialist Party as a party of intellectuals rather than an organization in need of a mass following.[68] In 1936, reelected as secretary-general of the party, he published a book entitled *Mingri zhi Zhongguo wenhua* (China's Culture Tomorrow), a comparative survey of the cultures of Europe, India, and China. In it, he argued that Chinese were distinguished from Europeans and Indians by their humanistic concerns and ethics, and that Chinese ethics should be used as the point of departure for the construction of a new culture as the foundation for developing new political and economic systems.[69] In 1938, he published another book *Liguo zhi dao* (The Way to Build the Nation), illuminating his conception of a new culture that was eclectic and different from May Fourth iconoclasm. The construction of such a culture, which adopted selected liberal values of the West, was the raison d'être of the National Socialist Party. A nationalist and patriot, he took the Chinese race (*minzu*) and Chinese ethics (*lunli*) as the basis of Chinese society that transcended classes. Like Sun Yat-sen, he was concerned about the shortcomings and dangers of unbridled capitalism, opposing class struggle and social revolution.

---

[66] For a scholarly biography of Zhang, see Jeans, *Democracy and Socialism*.

[67] Zhang thought that Chinese youth since 1919 had shown too much faith in the ability of science to solve all problems, including social and personal ones. He believed that problems of the human soul, of morality, of the aesthetic nature, could not be solved by mere rationalism. He provided a critique of Western modernization, warning against the ugliness, injustice, and cruelty of industrialized urban society. See Guy S. Alitto, *The Last Confucian: Liang Shu-ming and the Chinese Dilemma of Modernity* (Berkeley: University of California Press, 1979), p. 78.

[68] Van Slyke, *Enemies and Friends*, p. 172.

[69] Howard L. Boorman, ed., *Biographical Dictionary of Republican China* (New York: Columbia University Press, 1967–1971), I, 33.

The other Zhang – Dongsun – who was a few months younger than Junmai (b. 1887), was a scholar of Western philosophy who had been closely associated with Liang Qichao and editor of several magazines and newspapers, including Shanghai's *Shishi xinbao* (China Times) in the 1920s. Earlier, in 1920, when the Comintern agent Gregory Voitinsky arrived in Shanghai to meet with Chen Duxiu, he had taken part in some of the secret discussions that led to the formation of a communist preparatory group. Later he withdrew from the group because he did not believe in class struggle, clashing with Chen several times over the question of capitalism and industrial development. He was on Junmai's side in the science versus philosophy debate. From 1925 to 1930, he was professor of philosophy and Dean of the College of Arts at Shanghai's Guanghua University. In the summer of 1930, he moved to Beijing to take up an appointment at Yanjing University, where he remained for the rest of his teaching career. As a thinker, he was interested in an epistemological synthesis, or pluralism, that formed the basis of his theory of knowledge. As a founding member of the National Socialist Party, he was a frequent contributor to *Zaisheng*, writing on a wide range of political issues, including the Japanese threat, and supporting calls for all-out war against Japan.[70]

The National Socialists stood for nationalism, democracy, and state socialism, echoing the GMD's Three Principles of the People. Although Zhang Junmai was profoundly influenced by German social democracy, he and his party colleagues favored Anglo-American democracy as well, opposing the GMD dictatorship and suppression of human rights.[71] They also advocated an independent judiciary and direct general elections to representative bodies at all levels, especially the National People's Representatives Congress.[72] Prior to 1937, the National Socialist Party was the only minor party capable of articulating its political views systematically through the *Zaisheng*.[73] One of the themes running through the early articles in that magazine was that the GMD could have transformed itself into a democratic party as soon as it came to power in 1928. Until 1928, the GMD had built a democratic, nationalistic, and antiimperialist platform. High hopes had been pinned on the Nanjing regime, and it could have won the support of the scholars and the peasants, without which no Chinese regime could expect to last long. Many *Zaisheng* writers believed that had the regime put in place a democratic

---

[70] Ibid., pp. 129–132.

[71] Jeans, *Democracy and Socialism*, p. 203.

[72] Zhongguo dier lishi dang'anguan, ed., *Zhongguo minzhu shehuidang* (The Chinese Democratic Socialist Party) (Beijing: Dang'an chubanshe, 1988), p. 73.

[73] By comparison, the writings of the Youth Party members in their short-lived magazine *Minsheng zhoukan* were brief and superficial.

system, it would have easily won power by the popular vote, dominated Chinese politics, governed in a parliamentary style, and set itself up as a model for the rest of the country.[74] If the GMD had feared a loss of power, it had been misguided as the minor parties would have been too weak to pose any serious threat. In choosing one-party rule, the GMD appeared to have abandoned its democratic aspirations, sought power for power's sake, and shown a poor understanding of democracy.[75] These views were not new. Hu Shi and Luo Longji had articulated something similar before.

Zaisheng writers realized that as a political system democracy was not perfect. But they still regarded it as the best system history had ever known. More important, they were convinced that it could be improved to suit China's conditions. How? Put in the context of the great debate, this was a question of whether democracy was capable of developing the strengths often attributed to dictatorship.

Zhang Dongsun was sanguine that it was. Aware of China's political fragmentation and the ascendancy of the military, he shared with Jiang Tingfu and others a desire for a strong and efficient government capable of national unity and central planning. He distinguished between two kinds of dictatorship: "legal" and "moral." The former was established legally by those in authority who constituted a privileged class above the law; it was undemocratic. The latter referred to a concentration of powers in the government with the consent of all the political parties; it was democratic and suited to a national emergency because it had the capacity to make quick decisions unhampered by bureaucracy and undue opposition. But, he hastened to add, even in a crisis, the democratic system must remain intact, the only change being that the government was given extraordinary powers temporarily to cope with an extraordinary situation. This would be made possible by the democratic process, especially when the ruling party enjoyed a huge majority in Parliament, or when the opposition was prepared to give full cooperation in the public interest.

Zhang Dongsun was not convinced that a democratic state was necessarily inefficient and ineffective, nor that the democratic process would have to be jettisoned before the government could enjoy

---

[74] Typical of this line of thinking was Zhang Dongsun, "Minzhu yu zhuanzhi shi bu xiangrong de me?" (Are democracy and autocracy mutually exclusive?), *Zaisheng* 1:7 (November 20, 1932): 2–3.

[75] Wu Guanyin, "Minguo chengli ershiernian shang zai taolunzhong zhi xianfa" (The constitution still talked about twenty years after the establishment of the Republic), *Zaisheng* 1:11 (March 20, 1933): 6.

"autocratic powers." In his view, the roots of China's current problems lay in the poor quality of the ruling party. If the GMD were good, honoring its commitment to democracy eventually, it could well establish a "moral dictatorship" quite acceptable to the people. He went on to differentiate between "operational autocracy" and "institutionalized autocracy." Needless to say, he was opposed to the latter, but regarded the former, which could be democratic in spirit, as being necessary in extraordinary times. To make it work, democracy (read: Western-style democracy) would have to be "revised."[76]

Zhang's distinctions between legal dictatorship and moral dictatorship and between operational autocracy and institutional autocracy were contrived and convoluted. Some would argue like Luo Longji that any form of dictatorship was unacceptable. Others would take exception to his suggestion that a strong and effective government in extraordinary times was similar in spirit to a dictatorship. As one reader criticized, the term *moral dictatorship* was in conflict with the spirit of democracy.[77] But Zhang was not arguing for moral dictatorship in normal times; he was only trying to say, rather clumsily perhaps, that democracy and autocracy were not mutually exclusive during a national emergency provided autocracy was legitimized by the people through the democratic process. Even more important, moral dictatorship was, for him, a contingency measure that would have the best of all possible worlds – a strong, efficient, and effective government as well as protection of basic rights. The problem with this argument, though, is that it underestimated the danger of moral dictatorship becoming a permanent feature of Chinese politics, thereby blocking the development of democratic institutions.

Some *Zaisheng* writers also discussed the familiar question of the relationship between liberty and rights. Notwithstanding the necessity of a powerful central government in the midst of a national emergency, they considered it important that the government did not degenerate into a dictatorial regime. Taking an introspective view of the national emergency, Zhu Yisong saw the crisis as the result of "a nation in total bankruptcy, morally, religiously, economically, educationally, and administratively," adding that it was "unprecedented." To cope with it, he wrote, the state must be able to play a constructive role in economic development, education, and national defense through the socialization of key industries and enterprises. Considering China's conditions, he feared that

---

[76] Zhang Dongsun, "Minzhu yu zhuanzhi shi bu xiangrong de me?" pp. 2–11.
[77] See Sun Baogang's critique of Zhang's article and Zhang's rejoinder in ibid. In response, Zhang agreed to drop the term *moral dictatorship* altogether.

the Anglo-American system would create enormous difficulties in policy implementation because that system often led to a rapid succession of governments, hence political instability. But he did not find the systems in Soviet Russia and fascist Italy good either. The system he proposed was a powerful coalition government, to be made up of "multiparty talents" and based on "a politics of national consensus" and "popular support." Only such a government, strong yet democratic, offered the best future for Chinese politics.[78]

But a coalition government could be just a coalition of diverse elements motivated by a desire to divide up the spoils of office. How would liberty be guaranteed? Zhu's answer was that, first, the powers of a coalition government should be spelled out in detail in the constitution, the government should be responsible to the National People's Representatives Congress, and the Congress should have no power to dismiss the government during the period of national rehabilitation. Second, basic rights and civil liberties must be protected by the state. He challenged Sun Yat-sen's view that Chinese had enjoyed excessive personal freedoms, arguing that Sun had confused liberty with licentiousness. What had existed in imperial China was not democratic politics, but the politics of *minben* (the primacy of the people), which had been a constraint on the monarchy and the ruling classes. With the imperial system gone and Confucianism under attack, *minben* politics had lost its restraining influence. What should now be put in place was democratic politics that guaranteed rights, in return for which the people should fulfill their obligations, including supervision of government. He called on them to take an active interest in public and national affairs, to understand those affairs, and to take part in public debates. Only then could they train themselves politically, and only then could democracy be fostered.[79]

It was important that liberty and rights be safeguarded not only for personal gratification and the development of individuality but also for popular supervision of government through a national representative institution. Zhu's articulation of democracy showed a greater clarity and sophistication than Zhang Dongsun's. Yet both had been influenced by Zhang Junmai's idea of "revisionist democracy" (*xiuzheng minzhu zhengzhi*), which provided the ideological underpinning for the National Socialist Party.

---

[78] Zhu Yisong, "Xinshidai de minzhi zhuyi" (Democracy in a new era), *Zaisheng* 1:9 (January 1, 1933): 72–75.
[79] Ibid., pp. 76–80.

REVISIONIST DEMOCRACY

Zhang Junmai jointly wrote the leading article, "The Words We Want to Say," for the inaugural issue of *Zaisheng* (May 1932)[80] and went on to publish in the next two issues a two-part essay on national democracy and state socialism.[81] The first of these articles marked him as a Nationalist Socialist arguing for a "revisionist democracy," which required the adaptation of foreign models to Chinese conditions by "removing [from those models] what is unsound and rectifying what is excessive." Although he appreciated popular government and the necessity of party politics in a democracy, he was concerned that the "common will" was often not represented by the political parties that manipulated representative institutions. So that the common will could be truly represented, he advocated a political system, democratic in principle and spirit and capable of guarding itself against political manipulations, and one that was free from multiparty strife on the one hand and one-party rule on the other.[82]

Reviewing the fortunes of prewar parliamentary democracy and the emergence of the proletarian dictatorship in Soviet Russia and fascism in Italy after 1919, Zhang Junmai saw the prewar trend toward popular government being challenged by a new trend toward concentration of powers and authoritarianism. He understood that phenomenon in terms of the tension between personal freedoms and state powers, due to lack of limits being placed on both sides. To his mind, Europe's parliamentary democracy would face enormous problems in times of difficulty because of a host of inherent problems, including inefficiency, rhetoric rather than action, excessive interparty wrangling, rapid succession of governments rotating between political parties, and subordination of the national interest to party interests. He saw concentration of powers in Britain's MacDonald government, America's Roosevelt administration, and France's "Holy Alliance," all because of the Great Depression. Other writers had drawn attention to all these before in making a case for dictatorship. But he drew different conclusions: Britain and the United States were not going down the dictatorial track, despite more powers being given to their governments. What China needed was what he

---

[80] "Women suo yaoshuo de hua" became the Manifesto of the National Socialist Party in April 1938. It has since been published separately and also as part of a documentary study of the party. The citation here is based on Zhongguo dier lishi dang'anguan, ed., *Zhongguo minzhu shehuidang*, pp. 40–79.

[81] Zhang Junmai, "Guojia minzhu zhengzhi yu guojia shehui zhuyi" (National democracy and national socialism), *Zaisheng* 1:2 (June 20, 1932): 1–38; continued in 3 (July 20, 1932).

[82] Zhongguo dier lishi dang'anguan, ed., *Zhongguo minzhu shehuidang*, pp. 48–49.

called "democracy on the basis of national concentration" (his English) (*jizhong xinli zhi guojia minzhu zhengzhi*).[83]

Contrasting the liberalism of John Stuart Mill with German idealism, Zhang Junmai took a position somewhere in between. On the one hand, he argued for a strong state and a powerful executive government in order to achieve efficiency, flexibility, and unified command. On the other hand, he defended personal freedoms and independence of thought as essential for individual development, creativity, and self-actualization. To safeguard individual liberty, he drew a line between the powerful executive and the autonomous individual and free society. Yet he considered the balance between state powers and personal freedoms to be variable, depending on the needs of the time. Finding China in the midst of a national emergency, he was opposed to laissez-faire individualism, which he equated with personal licentiousness, even suggesting that, for the sake of social justice, personal wealth and property should be regulated. Chinese democracy for him was a question of delimiting the respective boundaries of and striking a balance between liberty and authority.[84] "Power (*quanli*) is for efficient administration. Liberty is for the protection of social culture and individual thought."[85] They could be "nicely harmonized."[86]

To cope with the national emergency, Zhang Junmai advocated a "national consensus government" (*juguo yizhi zhi zhengfu*), or "unified government" (*tongyi zhengfu*), with a mandate to rule for a term longer than most governments in the West. It would have three salient features: a spirit of national unity, a capacity to act forcefully, and a concentration of powers. The Executive Yuan, he proposed, should be made up of members from different parties elected by the National People's Representatives Congress, which should have legislative power as well as the power to approve the national budget. The government should be judged on its actions and performance, not its rhetoric, but it should also be given sufficient power to do its job. Efficiency could be achieved by limiting the powers of the National People's Representatives Congress vis-à-vis the Executive Yuan. Once a five-year administrative plan (*xingzheng dagang*) had been formulated by the government and approved by Congress, it should remain in effect within the five-year period, regardless of any change of government. Unless the plan failed to be implemented, Congress should have no power to dismiss the government by passing a vote of no confidence. The government's performance should be subject to an annual review by Congress or at the end of a specified period. In the

---

[83] Zhang Junmai, "Guojia minzhu zhengzhi yu guojia shehui zhuyi," pp. 24–27.
[84] Ibid., pp. 28–29.   [85] Ibid., p. 25.
[86] Zhongguo dier lishi dang'anguan, ed., *Zhongguo minzhu shehuidang*, p. 58.

event of unsatisfactory performance, the responsible personnel or ministers should be dismissed. At the same time, a nonpoliticized civil service system should be established. To prevent a division of spoils by politicians and party hacks, officials below the rank of vice-ministers should not be replaced, except for unsatisfactory performance or criminal offense, by an incoming administration.[87] He also proposed that a proportion of the seats in Congress be given to independent specialists from industry, commerce, agriculture, the sciences, and other fields, while elections to public office should be based on experience, qualifications, and perhaps also on tests and examinations. In this way, he would rule out the illiterate, the uneducated, and the military, noting that limited suffrage had been quite common in democratic states since the nineteenth century.[88] His elitism in regard to public administration was similar to that of Luo Longji and Hu Shi.

Economically, revisionist democracy was a variant of state socialism. Zhang Junmai saw poverty as the cause of China's economic problem, the resolution of which required the generation of wealth for a start. He assigned to the state an important role in developing the national economy and state capitalism in juxtaposition with private enterprise in a mixed economy. The state should own all the nation's natural resources, mining, electricity, railways, transportation, and other key public utilities, and the rest should be privately owned. Above all, the state should have a special responsibility for central planning. But central planning, he feared, would add to the "bureaucratic capitalism," already being developed by well-placed government members for their own interests. To prevent its further growth, he favored a division of labor between the planner and the manager: central planning being the responsibility of the state, whereas management of the economy and state enterprises was entrusted to the guilds and other professional bodies.[89] In short, his economic program was a combination of capitalism and socialism, emphasizing public ownership as well as recognizing private property. It was not significantly different from the GMD's economic platform. Where they differed was over implementation. In his formulation, the private and the public sectors were unified under a state-managed plan, aimed at the "popularization of private ownership" alongside state ownership

---

[87] Zhang Junmai, "Guojia minzhu zhengzhi yu guojia shehui zhuyi," pp. 30–33; also "Minzhu ducai yiwai zhi disanzhong zhengzhi" (A third kind of politics besides democracy and dictatorship), *Zaisheng* 3:2 (April 15, 1935): 18–22.

[88] Ibid. pp. 31 and 19, respectively; Zhongguo dier lishi dang'anguan, ed., *Zhongguo minzhu shehuidang*, p. 51.

[89] Zhongguo dier lishi dang'anguan, ed., *Zhongguo minzhu shehuidang*, pp. 54–59.

and the realization of "land to the tillers" with compensations paid to the landlords.[90]

The significance of the National Socialists' democratic thought did not lie in its originality or brilliance; it was lacking in both. The significance lay in its attempts to find a middle way, or balance, between democracy and dictatorship, between personal freedoms and state powers, between rights and duties, and between liberalism and statism, taking into account the necessity of a strong and efficient state and the intrinsic values of the autonomous individual and a free society. Zhang Junmai greatly valued social justice on the basis of which he formulated his economic policies. Unlike Luo Longji, he subscribed to the theory of natural rights, but he shared with Luo a belief in a rule of law as the foundation on which to maintain human rights and dignity. A rule of law, combined with a "rational will," would provide the best mechanisms for checking abuses of power on the one hand and for restraining permissive individualism on the other. It was a combination of modern law and traditional virtues. Revisionist democracy, in the round, was "a third kind of politics apart from democracy and dictatorship,"[91] which would provide equal opportunity for elite participation and a rule of law.[92]

Zhang Junmai's faith in this "third kind of politics" was a manifestation of Chinese "intellectual utopianism," to use Thomas Metzger's term. Modern Chinese intellectuals had a utopian vision of society, believing as Rousseauists and Marxists did that good governance entailed "a fusion of knowledge, morality, political power, and individual freedom."[93] They desired not just a free society but a perfect one under democratic rule that worked for both state and society. Consistent with that tradition, Zhang searched for a perfect system, free of political manipulations and selfishness, which would work in normal times, whether under multiparty rule or single-party rule, and would also achieve, in the event of an emergency, "the concentration of national strengths and the common will."[94] His intellectual utopianism, however, did not mean that he was unaware that even in a democracy electoral politics typically involved the cunning, partisan machinations of politicians and the corrupting

---

[90] Ibid., pp. 61–63.

[91] Zhang Junmai, "Minzhu ducai yiwai zhi disanzhong zhengzhi," pp. 14–24.

[92] Jizhe, "Women yao shenmeyang de zhidu" (What sort of system do we want?), *Zaisheng*, 2:9 (July 1, 1934): 9. The author was actually Zhang Junmai.

[93] Thomas A. Metzger, "Modern Chinese Utopianism and the Western Concept of the Civil Society," in Chen Sanjing, ed., *Guo Tingyi xiansheng jiuxu danchen jinian lunwenji* (Essays commemorating the ninetieth birthday of Professor Kuo Ting-yee) (Nangang: Zhongyang yanjiuyuan jindaishi yanjiusuo, 1995), II, 302ff.

[94] Zhongguo dier lishi dang'anguan, ed., *Zhongguo minzhu shehuidang*, p. 49.

influence of vested interests. Such machinations and corrupting influence had characterized the elections in the early Republic, and it was precisely for that reason that Zhang and his associates wanted a system free of those things. From the liberal democratic perspective, such a system is, of course, inconceivable because democracy is about power and maximization of interests and utilities according to morally neutral "rules of the game" that allow almost unlimited competition by political parties and groups for votes as well as almost unlimited interest brokerage.

CONCLUSION

We have looked at the differing approaches to the national emergency by the Nationalist government, its critics, and its sympathizers. The crisis, brought to a head by Japan's actions in Manchuria, was aggravated by China's domestic problems. For the government, those problems were the communist insurgency and the recalcitrance of the regional militarists. The critics, however, saw greater problems. Much more problematic were one-party dictatorship, political tutelage, and the failings of the regime – a disease that constitutional democracy could best cure in the long term. Enlightenment was part of national salvation.

Government sympathizers, on the other hand, viewed the domestic problems from a different perspective. Even though they conceded that the government was inefficient, incompetent, and by no means good, they thought that it could be reformed and that no other party could do a better job in the circumstances. The advocates of neo-dictatorship blamed the problems on China's political and military fragmentation as well as on its poverty and backwardness, attributing the government's inability to deal with those problems to limited powers and an insufficient command of the nation's resources. What China needed, so the argument goes, was a strong and effective regime capable of unifying the country, maintaining order, and governing in the national interest. Moreover, there seemed to be a world trend toward dictatorship and "a decline of Western democracy."

Put on the defensive, the other camp argued that dictatorship could not achieve unification, that there was no political party equal to a new-style dictatorship, that no dictator could command the loyalty and obedience of the entire nation, and that democracy was practicable. Some strongly defended the core values of liberalism and the intrinsic worth of democracy, which should be fostered regardless of the national emergency. The liberal views of Zhang Xiruo, Luo Longji, Hu Shi, and many others whom we shall meet do not support Eastman's claim that Chinese intellectuals "were attracted to democracy less because it provided guarantees of individual freedoms than because they were disillusioned with the ineffectiveness of Kuomintang [GMD] authoritarian rule."[95] Opposition to the dictatorship stemmed from both discontent with the GMD and strong convictions that democratic values were not incompatible with Chinese values.

Although Hu Shi's kindergarten politics was a poor rebuttal of the dictatorship argument, his point that democracy was a political method, a learning process, and a matter of trial and error was articulated also by many others. Some suggested a constitutional preparatory period in which all political parties were legalized so that they could compete freely with the ruling party. No one would expect the GMD to lose power in an open contest. The important thing here was open competition, even within the framework of political tutelage. It is in this light that Chen Zhimai's notion of "democracy within the ruling party," with its emphasis on competition among the GMD factions on the basis of policy issues, is best understood.

Chinese liberalism was associated with a strong state and a national purpose. Some intellectuals, such as the National Socialists and *Zaisheng* writers, were intent on combining the strengths of dictatorship with those of democracy, thereby reconciling *jiuwang* with *qimeng*. Zhang Junmai found a middle path in revisionist democracy. His "third kind of politics" would, in times of national emergency, take the form of a unified government based on a national consensus and, at all times, would operate according to a rule of law protecting human rights and a "rational will" restraining permissive individualism.

The great debate did not polarize the intellectual community because neither side was extremist. The likes of Jiang Tingfu and Ding Wenjiang were not antidemocratic at heart, whereas the other camp was aware of the difficulties facing Western democracies. That explained why *Zaisheng* writers argued for a middle ground, as would many other intellectuals (see Chapters 6 and 7).

An organized prodemocracy movement did not unfold prior to the outbreak of the Sino-Japanese War, but the democracy discourse had begun, and the opposition agenda was set long before 1937. The war created a new situation, internally and externally, demanding national unity and multiparty cooperation. The battlefield for democracy, alongside the war, was shifted from the intellectual marketplace of ideas to the political arena of the People's Political Council.

---

[95] Eastman, *The Abortive Revolution*, p. 153.

5

An Abortive Democratic Experiment

The People's Political Council, 1938–1945

FOLLOWING the Marco Polo Bridge incident of July 7, 1937, China went to war with Japan. Earlier a second GMD–CCP united front had been formed after the Xi'an incident of the previous December. On July 15, Chiang Kai-shek convened a conference at Lushan, a mountain resort in Jiangxi province, attended by delegates from the MPGs, non-partisans, and other leading lights of the community, with the exception of the Communists; Chiang held separate talks with them. The conference sent a clear signal to the nation that the government was prepared to accommodate the opposition parties and to hear their views on the question of war.[1] Because resistance to the Japanese demanded national unity, all political parties and groups accepted the government's authority and the necessity of a strong state.

The outbreak of war imposed constraints on Chinese party politics, forcing all the parties concerned to seek temporary compromises. Wartime politics, played out in the People's Political Council (PPC), showed how the opposition parties tried to work with the government in a quasi-representative national body. The first of its kind in China's history, the PPC, created in accordance with Article 12 of the government's 1938 Program of Armed Resistance and National Reconstruction,[2] was intended to be a special wartime institution, charged with advising the government on the questions of war and reconstruction. It

[1] Zuo Shunsheng, *Jin sanshinian jianwen zaji* (A record of the events of the last thirty years) (Taibei: Zhonghua yilin wenwu chubanshe, 1976), pp. 55–56.
[2] Article 12 stated: "An organ shall be set up for the people to participate in affairs of state, thereby unifying the natural strength and collecting the best minds and views for facilitating the formulation and execution of national policies." See Chinese Ministry of Information, comp., *China Handbook, 1937–1945* (New York: Macmillan, 1947), p. 80. For the Chinese text, see *GMCZH*, I, 36.

brought together representatives from all political parties and groups, the provinces, and eminent figures from the wide community – the best talent the country had to offer. A symbol of national unity, it was viewed by some foreign observers as a "wartime parliament."[3]

The PPC is given much attention here because it illustrates the theme of a democratic breakthrough not achieved. The opposition elite called it a "public opinion institution" (*minyi zhiguan*), which provided mechanisms for "public opinion" to be articulated and channeled to the government. It was not nearly as representative as a parliament, but there was some sort of representation, and it held out hopes of a transition to an interim coalition government. In this sense, it was a democratic experiment and was hailed as such at the outset by civil opposition.

The PPC established a framework for a limited dialogue and limited multiparty cooperation during the war period. The dialogue and cooperation operated on two levels: between the two major parties under the terms of the second united front on one level and, on the other, between the government and all the other political parties and groups, including the CCP, in the form of political consultation. What happened in the GMD–CCP relationship would have implications for the PPC itself. The war provided the MPGs with opportunities for limited political participation and new power realignments. They were given provisional recognition by the government, that is, recognition without legal rights. But the cooperation was limited because the new framework fell far short of power sharing, and the PPC ultimately failed as a democratic experiment not so much because of the war as because Chiang Kai-shek chose not to expand its powers, a strategic decision based on partisan considerations.

From the standpoint of civil opposition, the PPC improved the prospect of harmonizing the values of national salvation and enlightenment. The conduct of war necessitated restrictions on personal freedoms, but it did not mean that democratic and human rights should be sacrificed on the altar of anti-Japanese nationalism. The goals of the liberal opposition were twofold: saving the nation from the Japanese invasion and liberating it from the authoritarian regime. Even the Nationalist government felt compelled to promise at the outset of the war that freedoms of speech, publication, assembly, and association would be protected "in

---

[3] Wang Yunwu, *Youlu lun guoshi* (Wang Yunwu on national affairs) (Taibei: Taiwan shangwu yinshuguan, 1965), p. 5. Wang was an independent delegate and, as of the Fourth PPC, a member of the presidium.

accordance with the law," provided that these did not contravene the Three Principles of the People.[4] Although these promises were not kept, the government did, for a year or so, adopt a more liberal and tolerant attitude toward political dissent, relaxing controls on speech, publication, and assembly, releasing political prisoners, and tolerating the activities of patriotic mass organizations.[5] The PPC concerned itself with a broad range of issues, from military campaigns through national defense to diplomatic relations, international affairs, financial and economic matters, rural reconstruction, education and culture, and matters of a general nature. It also provided the platform from which to push for constitutionalism, democracy, and human rights.

Because the MPGs were to play an important part in the PPC, an outline of them on the eve of the war is in order.

THE MPGS ON THE EVE OF THE SINO-JAPANESE WAR

We are here concerned with what came to be known as the "three parties and three groups" (*sandang sanpai*), namely, the Chinese Youth Party, the National Socialist Party, the Third Party, the National Salvation Association, the Rural Reconstruction Group (*Xiangcun jianshepai*), and the Vocational Education Society (*Zhonghua zhiye jiaoyushe*). They would later coalesce to form the Chinese Democratic League (*Zhongguo minzhu tongmeng*).

The Youth Party was founded in Paris in December 1923 by a group of patriotic Chinese students with the objectives of "internally eliminating the national robbers [meaning the Communists and the warlords] and externally resisting the foreign powers." Despite its name, the Youth Party was not a party of young people, but it sought to rejuvenate China as the Young Turk Party did in Turkey. Initially known as the Nationalism China Youth Corps (*Guojia zhuyi qingniantuan*), it was opposed to both the GMD and the CCP during the period of the first united front (1924–1926). Led by Zeng Qi, Li Huang, Zuo Shunsheng, and others who had returned early in 1924 to China to set up headquarters in Shanghai, the party held its first National Congress in the summer of 1926. In 1928,

---

[4] See Articles 25 and 26 of the 1938 "Program of Armed Resistance and National Reconstruction," Chinese Ministry of Information, comp., *China Handbook, 1937–1945*, pp. 80–81; *GMCZH*, I, 37.

[5] Lyman P. Van Slyke, *Enemies and Friends: The United Front in Chinese Communist History* (Stanford: Stanford University Press, 1967), pp. 154–155.

after declining an invitation to join the GMD, it was outlawed by the Nanjing regime, forcing Zeng Qi and others to flee to Sichuan and the northeast provinces controlled by anti-Chiang warlords. It remained an underground organization with its Youth Corps acting as a front until 1929.[6] Ideologically, it was staunchly anticommunist and strongly nationalistic, but not fascist as Marilyn A. Levine would have it.[7] Its members were recruited mainly from the educated class, having weak links with the business community and the masses. The leadership was conservative and oligarchic. The party structure consisted of the national congress, committees, regional branches, and affiliated groups. Its political platform, developed in later years, was compatible with the GMD's, but differed in its advocacy of parliamentary democracy, far less economic planning and more private enterprise, and provincial autonomy under a federal system.

When the Manchurian crisis came to a head, the Youth Party declared itself ready to support the government, provided that Nanjing took up arms against Japan and put an early end to one-party dictatorship. Zeng Qi stated in December 1931 that the prerequisite to national unity was the dismantling of the single-party system and the establishment of a provisional representative assembly to formulate national policies and other measures to deal with the Japanese.[8] In January 1932, Youth Party activists took part in the defense of Shanghai and Wusong against the Japanese invasion and, in the following years, joined the volunteer corps in fighting the Japanese in the northeast. Others remained in Sichuan, then under the control of General Liu Xiang; still others, hunted by GMD agents, led a perilous existence in treaty-port foreign settlements and concessions. In a country dominated by militarists, the Youth Party and others like it had to seek protection from anti-Chiang warlords as a

---

[6] For a more detailed study of the Youth Party, see Edmund S. K. Fung, "The Alternative of Loyal Opposition: The Chinese Youth Party and Chinese Democracy," *Modern China* 17:2 (April 1991): 260–289; Chan Lau Kit-ching, *The Chinese Youth Party, 1923–1945* (Hong Kong: Centre of Asian Studies, University of Hong Kong, 1972); Marilyn A. Levine, "Zeng Qi and the Frozen Revolution," in Roger B. Jeans, ed., *Roads Not Taken: The Struggle of Opposition Parties in Twentieth-Century China* (Boulder: Westview Press, 1992), pp. 225–240; and Ch'ien Tuan-sheng, *The Government and Politics of China 1912–1949* (Stanford: Stanford University Press, 1970), pp. 351–353.

[7] Levine's contention that the Youth Party in its early years was fascist is unsustainable. She concedes (p. 235) that it "lacked a racial basis of discrimination against foreigners" and that "there is little evidence to indicate that they were anti-parliamentarian or anti-democratic, a genuine feature of most fascist groups."

[8] Fung, "The Alternative of Loyal Opposition," pp. 264–265.

matter of survival. It was not until 1935, when Chiang was seriously contemplating resistance to Japan, that GMD agents approached Zuo Shunsheng and Li Huang with a view to cooperation in anticipation of all-out war. Subsequently, Youth representatives participated in the Lushan Conference, leading to an exchange of letters in April 1938 between Zuo, who had assumed the Youth leadership, and the government leaders. In his letter to Chiang and Wang Jingwei, Zuo referred to freedoms of speech, publication, assembly, and association as a basis for constitutional rule in the years to come.[9] Thereafter, the Youth Party became the largest party after the GMD and CCP.[10]

Similar letters were also exchanged between leaders of the National Socialist Party and the government.[11] Zhang Junmai, who had been extremely critical of both major parties, was on good terms with Zeng Qi, Li Huang, and Zuo Shunsheng, and they would cooperate in the years ahead. Since its inception, the growth of the National Socialist Party had been slow because it had great difficulties in recruiting new members. According to Qian Duansheng, "the party organization was extremely weak. Their adherents were either Carsun Chang's personal friends, mostly fellow followers of Liang [Qichao] in earlier times, or former students."[12] Qian criticized him as "neither an organizer himself nor a man able to pick capable men able to organize for him."[13] The American diplomat John Melby found Zhang Junmai as "unrealistic" as his brother Jiaao (Chang Kia-ngau, a financial and economic wizard, incorruptible in the Shanghai cesspool) was hard-headed. As a scholar, Zhang was "highly intelligent and well educated"; as a politician, he was "utopian [and] ineffectual."[14] The National Socialists held their first party congress in 1934 and their second in 1936. While maintaining their position as a third force between the GMD and the CCP, they had links with some

---

[9] Zuo Shunsheng, *Jin sanshinian jianwen zaji*, pp. 37–40; Chen Qitian, *Jiyuan huiyilu* (The memoir of Chen Qitian) (Taibei: Taiwan Shangwu yinshuguan, 1972), pp. 164–166, 266; Li Huang, *Xuedunshi huiyilu* (The memoir of Li Huang) (Taibei: Zhuanji wenxue chubanshe, 1975), pp. 168–170, 173–205; Liu Xia, *Shibanian lai zhi Zhongguo qingniandang* (The Chinese Youth Party over the past eighteen years) (Chengdu: Guoyun shudian, 1941), p. 50.

[10] By the end of 1948, membership of the Youth Party was around 300,000. See Chen Qitian, *Jiyuan huiyilu*, p. 306.

[11] Chinese Ministry of Information, comp., *China Handbook, 1937–1945*, pp. 73–74.

[12] Ch'ien, *The Government and Politics of China*, p. 354. Throughout the wartime period, there were no more than several hundred National Socialists.

[13] Ibid., p. 355.

[14] John F. Melby, *The Mandate of Heaven: Record of a Civil War, China, 1945–49* (Toronto: University of Toronto Press, 1968), pp. 162, 166.

regional militarists, notably Chen Jitang in Guangdong, Yan Xishan in Shanxi, and the Guangxi Clique. A party organ, *Yuzhou xunkan* (The Universe), a trimonthly, was launched for South China to parallel *Zaisheng* in the north.[15] As far as Zhang Junmai was concerned, his anti-communism outweighed his dislike for the GMD because of the CCP's violence.

The Third Party had its origins in the Provisional Action Committee of the Guomindang (*Guomindang linshi xingdong weiyuanhui*), an offshoot of the GMD formed in November 1927 as a result of the GMD–CCP split. Its leader, Deng Yanda, had served under Chiang Kai-shek as the GMD's political commissar in the General Headquarters of the Nationalist Revolutionary Army. In forming the Committee, Deng enjoyed the support of the left-wing Wuhan faction, including Song Qingling and Chen Youren (Eugene Chen, the former Nationalist Foreign Minister). The group was soon joined by two former communists, Tan Pingshan and Zhang Bojun, as well as others of the GMD's radical (far more left than the Wuhan) faction. In the spring of 1928, when Deng was still in Europe on an extended tour, the faction rallying behind Tan Pingshan renamed the Committee the China Revolutionary Party (*Zhonghua gemingdang*) because they wanted closer association with the CCP. When Deng returned to China in May 1930, he and Song Qingling managed to restore the previous name.

Proclaiming a revolution of the common people (*pingmin geming*), the Provisional Action Committee leaders considered themselves the only faithful disciplines of the Three Principles of the People and the "three cardinal policies" of the GMD reorganization period.[16] They declared that their objectives were to fight imperialism, feudalism, and capitalism and to establish a "people's regime" with the workers and the peasantry at its core. Their political platform included "land to the tiller," the abolition of all the unequal treaties, restoration of diplomatic relations with the Soviet Union, and demolition of the foreign economic regime in China, although foreign investment that did not seek to control China's

---

[15] For details, see Roger B. Jeans, *Democracy and Socialism in Republican China: The Politics of Zhang Junmai (Carsun Chang), 1906–1941* (Lanham: Rowman & Littlefield, 1997), pp. 206–216.

[16] These policies were alliance with the Soviet Union, alliance with the Chinese Communists, and support for the peasantry and the working class. In practice, the Committee remained committed only to the third policy of organizing a mass revolutionary base. See J. Kenneth Olenik, "Deng Yanda and the Third Party," in Jeans, ed., *Roads Not Taken*, p. 117.

economy would be welcome.[17] In many respects, these policies bore a close resemblance to those of the CCP. But Deng rejected the communist notion of the dictatorship of the proletariat because he did not believe that one form of dictatorship would be better than another. He also disapproved of the CCP's method of turning one section of the peasantry against another through intimidation and violence, even though he set as much store on armed uprisings as did the CCP.[18] During the years 1930 and 1931, the Committee plotted to overthrow the Nanjing regime by organizing a military coalition of anti-Chiang forces. "What distinguished the [Provisional Action Committee's] challenge to Nanjing from others," writes Kenneth Olenik, "was a distinct ideology and the fact that, for a brief moment, it stood a very good chance of succeeding."[19]

The Nationalists immediately cracked down on the Committee. On August 17, 1931, Deng was arrested in Shanghai. A jail term led to his secret execution on November 29. His death unleashed a torrent of factional disputes that nearly destroyed the party organization. Even though the Committee was in shambles, one faction in Fujian was still strong enough to play a role in the abortive Fujian Rebellion of 1933–1934.[20] In 1935, the organization was changed to the Chinese Liberation Action Committee (*Zhongguo minzu jiefang xingdong weiyuanhui*), better known as the Third Party, and was under the leadership of Zhang Bojun, Peng Zemin, and others who supported calls for an anti-Japanese united front.[21] (In 1947, the Third Party was renamed the Chinese Peasants and Workers Democratic Party [*Zhongguo nonggong minzhudang*].)

The National Salvation Association was formed in Shanghai in May 1936. It was, as Parks Coble has shown, a "single-issue group" of patriotic Chinese from many walks of life, including educators, academics, students, journalists, bankers, businessmen, workers, women's groups, other professionals, and city dwellers of differing political persuasions. The issue that concerned them was resistance to Japanese impe-

---

[17] Qiu Qianmu, *Zhongguo minzhu dangpaishi* (A history of the Chinese democratic parties and groups) (Hangzhou: Zhejiang jiaoyu chubanshe, 1987), pp. 1–19; Olenik, "Deng Yanda," pp. 111–134; Chien, *The Politics and Government of China*, pp. 355–356.

[18] Qiu Qianmu, *Zhongguo minzhu dangpaishi*, pp. 19, 21; Olenik, "Deng Yanda," p. 118.

[19] Olenik, "Deng Yanda," p. 111.

[20] Qiu Qianmu, *Zhongguo minzhu dangpaishi*, pp. 27–34; Lloyd E. Eastman, *The Abortive Revolution: China Under Nationalist Rule, 1927–1937* (Cambridge, MA: Harvard University Press, 1974), pp. 93, 96.

[21] Qiu Qianmu, *Zhongguo minzhu dangpaishi*, pp. 44–49.

rialism, all wanting the government to fight the Japanese by stopping civil war and forming a broad united front. The Association was a patriotic movement tapping the powerful force of nationalism and popular sentiment for resistance. Not a political party, it had an informal organization and a loose structure admitting members of all political coloration. Among its leaders were three notable women, Song Qingling, He Xiangning, and Shi Liang (a lawyer). This diverse group of anti-Japanese activists drew its unity from a branch in the north headed by Zhang Shenfu (a professor of philosophy at Qinghua University and former member of the CCP) and a branch in the south led by Zou Taofen (a journalist); Shen Junru (a legal scholar), and Tao Xingzhi (a former student of John Dewey). Much of the Salvationist writings were published in Zou's journal *Dazhong shenghuo* (Life of the Masses), which, until its suspension by Nanjing in late February 1936, had a circulation of 200,000 copies per issue on average. Because of its clamor for a cessation of civil war and an anti-Japanese united front, the Association had been accused by the GMD as a communist front organization. Nevertheless, it was an autonomous movement, despite its sympathies and support for the CCP.[22] Even more important, it was a popular force to be reckoned with. Its leftist views and association with the CCP made it, of all the MPGs, the most persecuted, both during and after the war.[23] The most sensational persecution was the arrest on the night of November 22, 1936, of seven key figures: Shen Junru, Zou Taofen, Zhang Naiqi, Sha Qianli, Li Gongpu, Wang Zaoshi, and Shi Liang, dubbed by the Chinese press the "seven honorable persons" (*qi junzi*).[24] The arrests and the trials that followed received wide publicity, which had the effect of enhancing their cause and standing. They were not released until July 9, 1937, two days after the Marco Polo Bridge incident. So far the Salvationists had shown no interest in politics other than the politics of armed resistance. During the war, however, as we shall see, some of them were among the most vociferous in demanding constitutional reform and human rights.

---

[22] Parks M. Coble, "The National Salvation Association as a Political Party," in Jeans, ed., *Roads Not Taken*, pp. 135–150.

[23] Ch'ien, *The Government and Politics of China*, p. 357. See Zou Taofen, *Taofen wenji* (The collected works of Zou Taofen) (Hong Kong: Sanlian shudian, 1959), III, 261–315, for details of that persecution.

[24] For details of the incident, see Parks M. Coble, *Facing Japan: Chinese Politics and Japanese Imperialism, 1931–1937* (Cambridge, MA: Council on East Asian Studies, Harvard University, 1991), pp. 335–342, 353.

The Rural Reconstruction Group represented those who considered the educational, administrative, and productive reconstruction of the village the starting point for national reform. The key figure was Liang Shuming, a philosopher and cultural conservative, portrayed by Guy Alitto as "the last Confucian" in the Chinese dilemma of modernity.[25] A critic of Hu Shi, two years his senior, Liang was not a great admirer of Western culture. A self-taught India scholar, he had lectured on Indian philosophy and religion at Beijing University at the same time Hu was Dean of Arts. He had a deep loathing for modern urban and industrial life. Chinese society, Liang averred, was "a village society," the problems of which should be resolved through a process of rural reconstruction. His program for rural reconstruction was a kind of agrarianism, "an attempt to prevent the China of the future from becoming what the great treaty port of Shanghai had already become."[26] Many of his ideas, such as antiurbanism, anticonsumerism, a general emphasis on overall rural development (closing the urban–rural gap and the intellectual–peasant divide), local initiative, and self-reliance, showed a striking resemblance to Mao Zedong's populism. But he rejected Mao's notion of class conflict on the grounds that, although rural reconstruction was ultimately a kind of revolution, it was one that could be carried out without class struggle and violence.[27] Liang was extremely critical of the Nationalist government's failure to improve the lot of the peasantry, among other things, but he did not see an immediate need to seize political power. In his view, China's crisis was essentially cultural rather than political, and rural reconstruction was not about taking power.[28]

In 1931, Liang launched the Shandong Rural Reconstruction Research Institute as a means of peacefully resolving the problems of class and social relationships. Believing that the proper kind of education could obviate the need and causes for revolution, he attempted to create an enlightened leadership of intellectuals and an educated peasant mass on the one hand and institutions integrating the functions of local self-government and economic cooperation on the other.[29] Through his work in Shandong, he came into intimate contact with some CCP leaders and experienced at first hand the extent and quality of their administrative

---

[25] For a most scholarly intellectual-political biography of Liang, see Guy S. Alitto, *The Last Confucian: Liang Shu-ming and the Chinese Dilemma of Modernity* (Berkeley: University of California Press, 1979).

[26] Ibid., p. 196.   [27] Ibid., pp. 215–225.   [28] Ibid., pp. 204–205.

[29] For details, see ibid., pp. 238–278.

system behind the Japanese lines. In 1937, Shandong's rural reconstruction collapsed under the Japanese occupation of that province.

Liang represented only one stream of the rural reconstruction movement. Another stream was those associated with Yan Yangchu, better known in the West as James Y. C. Yen, and the Dingxian experiment in Hebei. Less politically engaged than Liang, Yan stressed the necessity and efficacy of education in the very fundamentals of village life – administration, economics, technology, sanitation, and health.[30]

The Vocational Education Society was organized in Jiangsu in 1917 by Huang Yanpei, an educator and social reformer. It promoted the construction of a system of American-style industrial arts schools as the instrument for training people to rebuild China. Although primarily engaged in educational work, the Society did engage in some political activities. Huang and his associates utilized the Jiangsu Provincial Education Society as a forum for the discussion of Jiangsu provincial affairs and Chinese national affairs. Following the outbreak of the Manchurian crisis, he was among those who strongly opposed Nanjing's nonresistance policy; he also was instrumental in launching the journal *Jiuguo tongxin* (National Salvation Communication) (later shortened to *Guoxin*). In 1932, during the Nineteenth Route Army's defense of Shanghai, the Society led the local people in supplying and supporting the Chinese troops. Huang actively campaigned for war against Japan by making speeches and publishing journal articles, but he was not opposed to Nationalist rule. Throughout the early 1930s, his relations with the government were not good because some of the education organizations with which he was associated became fronts for anti-GMD groups.[31] Relations did not improve until the outbreak of the Sino-Japanese War.

These MPGs demanded political reform, but not everyone wanted immediate constitutional democracy. Liang Shuming, for one, had no illusions about what a constitution could do for China. In his view, Chinese society, so different from Europe in culture and history, was not ready for constitutionalism because it lacked the political customs and tradi-

---

[30] See Charles W. Hayford, *To the People: James Yen and Village China* (New York: Columbia University Press, 1990).

[31] Zhang Qifeng, "Huang Yanpei: Zhongguo zhiye jiaoyu zhi xianju" (Huang Yanpei: Pioneer in Chinese vocational education), unpublished M.A. thesis, National Taiwan Normal University, 1990, pp. 129–130; Wang Huabin, *Huang Yanpei zhuan* (Biography of Huang Yanpei) (Jinan: Shandong wenyi chubanshe, 1992), pp. 139–143; Howard L. Boorman, ed., *Biographical Dictionary of Republican China* (New York: Columbia University Press, 1967–1971), II, 212.

tions on which democracy was built.[32] Huang Yanpei thought that China was not yet ready for Western democracy, and was content, until 1945, to let the Nationalist government fulfill its promise to carry out constitutional reform in due time. What he envisaged was a "nursery-style democratic government" that gave the people the opportunity to learn the habits of democracy while practicing it on a limited scale.[33] Neither Liang nor Huang was antiliberal, nor would they make concessions to freedoms of thought, speech, and publication.

The MPGs never had a large active membership or much real power. But, as Lyman Van Slyke has observed, "in one way or another they represented, spoke for, or influenced nearly all educated Chinese who were not irrevocably committed to the [GMD] or CCP. The minor parties were also involved in clique politics, and hence exerted a pull on disaffected members of the [GMD]. For all these reasons, the various minor parties had a collective importance far beyond their actual numbers."[34] Viewed with suspicion by the GMD, the MPGs were wooed by the CCP as allies in a united front strategy designed to build hegemony and to isolate the ruling party.[35]

The PPC provided a public forum where the MPGs, along with the independents, could exert their influence collectively.

FORMATION OF THE PEOPLE'S POLITICAL COUNCIL

The precursor to the PPC was the National Defense Advisory Council (*Guofang canyihui*), formed on August 17, 1937, under the jurisdiction of the Supreme National Defense Council, which had replaced the peacetime Central Political Council as the highest policy-making body in the party-state. An outgrowth of the Lushan Conference, the new

---

[32] Liang Shuming, "Tan Zhongguo xianzheng wenti" (On the question of Chinese constitutionalism), *LSMQJ*, VI, 491–492.

[33] Thomas D. Curran, "From Educator to Politician: Huang Yanpei and the Third Force," in Jeans, ed., *Roads Not Taken*, p. 91.

[34] Van Slyke, *Enemies and Friends*, p. 169.

[35] See Gerry Groot, "Managing Transitions: The Chinese Communist Party's United Front Work, Minor Parties and Groups, Hegemony and Corporatism," unpublished Ph.D. thesis, University of Adelaide, 1997, chs. 1–2. Groot studies the united front strategy by using the Italian communist Antonio Gramsci's principles for the winning and maintaining of "hegemony." Gramsci defined hegemony in terms of a class or part of a class "which gains the consent of other classes and social forces through creating and maintaining a system of alliances by means of political and ideological struggle," and not by exercising the power of coercion alone.

council was welcomed by the opposition parties as a vehicle for multi-party cooperation.[36] Its initial membership of sixteen was later increased to twenty-five, not counting Chiang Kai-shek (chairman), but including leaders of the "three parties and three groups" and the CCP, plus several independents.[37] Hu Shi also was a member, but he was soon sent abroad to drum up international support for China in the war against Japan.[38]

At its first meeting, Acting Chairman Wang Jingwei clarified the purposes of the new council: to listen to the views of the delegates, to report government plans for discussion, and to report developments at the war front and in the international arena. Its duties and responsibilities, however, were ill defined. As a matter of fact, the council meetings were rather informal, and the atmosphere was positive and friendly. It was a small body. Of the twenty-five members, almost half were unable to attend for a variety of reasons. Neither Mao Zedong, who was in Yan'an, nor Zhou Enlai attended a single meeting. Consequently, not much was achieved, apart from exchanging views and hearing reports from the government representatives on the military and diplomatic fronts.[39] Li Huang recalled that "there was a lot of empty talk and discussion."[40] But Zuo Shunsheng remembered it as a "good organization" and Wang Jingwei as a "good chairman" and that its members discussed concrete issues in an "excellent" atmosphere of "spiritual unity against the enemy [Japanese]."[41]

What was not in dispute was that it was too small and insufficiently representative of the broad united front of anti-Japanese organizations.

---

[36] Liang Shuming, "Wo nuli de shi shenme?" (What have I been working hard for?), *LSMQJ*, VI, 184.

[37] They were Zeng Qi, Li Huang, Chen Qitian, Zuo Shunsheng, Zhang Junmai, Zhang Dongsun, Liang Shuming, Yan Yangchu, Huang Yanpei, Shen Junru, Zou Taofen, Mao Zedong, Zhou Enlai, Lin Zuhan, Qin Bangxian, Hu Shi, Jiang Baili, Fu Sinian, Tao Xisheng, Jiang Menglin, Ma Junwu, Zhang Boling, Zhang Yaozeng, Shi Zhaoji, and Chen Bulei. See Zhou Tiandu, ed., *Qi junzi zhuan* (The seven honorable persons) (Beijing: Zhongguo shehui kexueyuan chubanshe, 1988), p. 109; Li Yibin, ed., *Zhongguo qing-niandang* (The Chinese Youth Party) (Beijing: Zhongguo shehui kexue chubanshe, 1982), p. 272.

[38] Carsun Chang, *The Third Force in China* (New York: Bookman, 1952), p. 110.

[39] Liang Shuming, "Wo nuli de shi shenme?" *LSMQJ*, pp. 188–188; Shen Pu and Shen Renhua, eds., *Shen Junru nianpu* (A chronology of Shen Junru's life) (Beijing: Zhongguo wenshi chubanshe, 1992), pp. 190–191; Zhou Tiandu, ed., *Qi junzi zhuan*, pp. 109–110.

[40] Li Huang, "The Reminiscences of Li Huang," Lillian Chu Chin, trans., 1971, p. 543. Chinese Oral History Project, Special Collections, Butler Library, Columbia University.

[41] Zuo Shunsheng, "The Reminiscences of Tso Shun-sheng," as told to Julie Lien-ying How, 1965, p. 140. Chinese Oral History Project, Special Collections, Butler Library, Columbia University.

The delegates were all invited by Chiang Kai-shek. Because it was solely concerned with national defense, there was no political agenda. Liang Shuming recalled that, when he proposed some political and administrative reforms, he was literally gagged.[42] Worst of all, it lacked a legal and constitutional basis, existing informally at the mercy of the government. For all these reasons, the delegates demanded a properly constituted body with wider powers and wider representation. The government's response was to transform it into the PPC.

The PPC rested on four principles: concentration of the nation's best minds in an advisory capacity; national unity; a start of democratization; and national reconstruction. For the government, the PPC was not intended to be the representative institution that the opposition parties desired. Like its precursor, it was an advisory body, albeit legally constituted. Any advice given would be accepted or rejected as the government deemed fit. There was no question of its replacing the Supreme National Defense Council as the state's highest wartime policy-making body. It had no authority whatsoever over any organ of the government, nor would the government be responsible to it in any way.

Nonetheless, the PPC provided the link between war and democracy, a vehicle for limited political participation and a training ground for multiparty politics and parliamentary-style debate. For the MPGs, it was the thin end of the wedge. And for the Communists, it was an instrument of the united front and the New Democratic Revolution. They supported the MPGs, calling for their legal recognition.

Under the initial Organic Law, the First PPC was to consist of 150 elected members in four categories, but the number was later increased to 200. The four categories were:

A. Eighty-eight representatives from the provinces and municipalities who were prominent figures having served for more than three years in a community organization, a private body, or in the civil service in the cities;

B. Six prominent figures (four Mongols and two Tibetans) who had served in Mongolia and Tibet;

C. Six prominent figures representing overseas Chinese communities where they had worked for more than three years; and

D. One hundred prominent figures who had served for more than three years in important cultural, educational, and economic organizations.[43]

---

[42] Liang Shuming, "Wo nuli de shi shenme?" *LSMQJ*, p. 189.   [43] *GMCZH*, I, 46–49.

There was no separate category for the opposition parties and groups. It was understood, however, that the leaders of those parties and groups would be "elected" under Category D and that a few extra members would be designated under Category A. The list of nominees for Category D was subject to approval by the GMD's Central Executive Committee. Students, peasants, and workers also were excluded, reflecting the PPC's narrow base. The inclusion of CCP delegates was insufficient in terms of peasant–worker representation because there were rural organizations in areas not under communist control, whereas the absence of student representatives betrayed the government's fear of youthful radicalism.

As far as opposition politics was concerned, Category D was the most important. The First PPC drew one hundred members from this category. The representation of the political parties and groups is shown in Table 5.1. Although there were twenty-three GMD delegates, the MPGs, combined with the CCP,[44] the independents, and those from educational circles and the media, made up sixty percent. (Additionally, another National Socialist, another Rural Reconstructionist, two more National Salvationists, and two more Vocational Educators were elected under Category A.) These delegates represented the important sections of China's urban society. Although no MPG was allowed to send more than seven delegates, the non-GMD delegates collectively constituted a force to be reckoned with. Qian Duansheng noted that Category D "included some of the most outspoken critics of the government, as well as some of the most outstanding leaders of China."[45] They regarded themselves as representing the public interest and the opinion of the "silent majority."[46] The Nationalists constituted a majority in the First PPC, but they were not predominant, a fact that contributed to the goodwill in the beginning.

Those in Category A came from twenty-eight provinces and six municipalities. Some provinces had four delegates each, and some cities had two each. Of special significance was the inclusion of ten women, who

---

[44] The CCP delegates were Mao Zedong, Chen Shaoyu, Qin Bangxian, Dong Biwu, Wu Yuzhang, Lin Zuhan, and Deng Yingchao. Mao, however, never attended the sessions.

[45] Ch'ien Tuan-sheng, "War-time Government in China," *American Political Science Review* 36:5 (October 1942): 857.

[46] Lawrence N. Shyu, "China's 'Wartime Parliament': The People's Political Council, 1938–1945," in Paul K. T. Sih, ed., *Nationalist China During the Sino-Japanese War, 1937–1945* (Hicksville, NY: Exposition Press, 1977), p. 280.

Table 5.1. *Distribution of Category A delegates to the First PPC*

Chinese Nationalist Party 23	Independents 7
Chinese Communist Party 7	Former Beijing parliamentarians 5
Chinese Youth Party 7	Educational circles 18
National Socialist Party 7	Financial and industrial circles 6
National Salvation Association 4	News media 5
Third Party 2	Catholic Church 1
Rural Reconstruction Group 2	Overseas Chinese communities 2
Vocational Education Society 1	Miscellaneous 3

Sources: Shen Yunlong, *Minguo shishi yu renwu luncong* (Reflections on Republican historical events and personalities) (Taibei: Zhuanji wenxue chubanshe, 1981), pp. 378–379; Wang Yunwu, *Youlu lun guoshi*, pp. 11–12.

accounted for five percent of the total delegates. Even though women were represented by a small percentage, this was the first time that they occupied seats in a national political body like the PPC. Deng Yingchao (Zhou Enlai's wife) observed that they participated in it not as advocates of women's rights and gender interests, despite their concerns about the fate of women in Japanese-occupied areas, but as equals to men in the anti-Japanese movement and the reconstruction program.[47]

The term of the PPC members was for one year, renewable for another. Later, an amendment was made to make further extensions possible, if necessary. There were regulations for elections, but no elections were actually held because of wartime difficulties. The government simply allocated a number of seats to each party, group, and community organization and approved the lists submitted for consideration. It also nominated and appointed the independents as well as the provincial and city delegates. The total number of delegates increased from 200 in the First PPC (1938–1940) to 220 in the Second PPC (1941) to 240 in the Third PPC (1942–1943) and to 290 in the Fourth PPC (1945–1948).[48] Government officials, as distinct from GMD members, were barred from becoming PPC members, but they were eligible for appointment to the small five-person presidium that replaced the Speaker after the First PPC.[49]

[47] *GMCZH*, I, 81–82.
[48] See the Revised Organic Laws of the Second, Third, and Fourth PPCs, *GMCZH*, II, 768, 1049, and 1415.
[49] *GMCZH*, II, 770–771. The first presidium consisted of Chiang Kai-shek (chairman), Zhang Boling, Zuo Shunsheng, Zhang Junmai, and Wu Yifang. See ibid., p. 780.

THE EARLY PHASE OF THE PPC

At the outset, the opposition parties greeted the PPC with enthusiasm. Zuo Shunsheng expressed the hope that it would "mark the beginning of democracy" and an improvement on "the hollowness of the previous National Emergency Conference."[50] Wang Zaoshi thought it could become "a channel of communication between the government and the masses," and "a transitional stage" in the development of democratic institutions.[51] And Yan Yangchu expected it to become "the organ and soul of the peasant masses."[52] The public mood was captured by a leader in the *Wuhan ribao* (Wuhan Daily) on June 18, 1938, hailing the PPC as "the organization that will bring a new life to the nation."[53] Hankou's *Dagongbao* (L'Impartial) greeted it as a "manifestation of the spirit of democracy," laying "the foundations for future constitutional rule," and paving "the way for democracy."[54] The communist *Xinhua ribao* (New China Daily) welcomed the delegates as "the people's representatives entrusted with great responsibilities."[55] The left-wing weekly *Qunzhong zhoukan* (Masses Weekly) defined those responsibilities in terms of promoting democracy and prosecuting the war to the very end.[56] Not least of all, Mao Zedong approved of it:

> In the current extreme circumstances of war, the opening of the PPC is a clear indication of the progress our nation's political life has made toward democracy, and of the unity achieved by our nation's political parties and groups, ethnic groups, classes, regions, and areas. Although, as a representative body, the PPC is unsatisfactory considering the way in which it is brought into existence and of its powers, its functions and significance are not to be lost. Its functions are to make every endeavor to unite further the various forces committed to the War of Resistance and national salvation. Its significance lies in its attempts to make a start of democracy in China's political life.[57]

What united the delegates was their desire to present a broad united front to Japanese aggression.

Initially, the PPC was given only four powers: to approve all the important policies of the government; to make proposals; to receive government reports, and to interpellate government officials. To these were

---

[50] *GMCZH*, I, 87. [51] Ibid., p. 92. [52] Ibid., p. 100. [53] Ibid., p. 133.
[54] Editorial, June 18, 1938, ibid., p. 131.
[55] Editorial, June 29, 1938, ibid., p. 115. [56] *GMCZH*, I, 120–121. [57] Ibid., p. 76.

added the power to conduct investigations in March 1943 and the power to assess, but not to approve, the state budget in September 1944. Five committees examined government reports and resolutions from the floor that dealt with military affairs and matters relating to national defense, foreign affairs and international events, domestic affairs, financial and economic problems, and educational and cultural matters. If necessary, special committees could be set up to investigate specific problems or to draft special reports.[58] However, these committees were not nearly as powerful as the parliamentary committees of a Western democracy because the PPC could only investigate matters entrusted to them by the government, and the government decided what to do with the recommendations. As for the assessment of the state budget, the PPC could not amend, let alone reject, it. In any case, the wartime budget was such a complicated matter that it was simply left to the supreme Party authorities to prepare and decide. By far the single biggest difficulty for the PPC was its lack of legislative power. PPC resolutions had no binding force; again, it was up to the authorities concerned to implement them, as they deemed fit. As chairman of the Supreme National Defense Council, whose approval was required for all PPC resolutions, Chiang Kai-shek was given emergency powers to issue decrees on important matters that could easily override those resolutions.[59] The government was free to determine what were important measures and policy plans and what were not.[60] Moreover, the President of the Executive Yuan was not liable to impeachment, thus making it impossible to bring him to account.[61]

Finally, there were considerable time constraints. The PPC was required to sit every three months (every six months as of the Second PPC), each time ten days (fourteen days as of the Third PPC). When it was not sitting, powers were vested in a twenty-five-member Residential Committee (*zhuhui weiyuanhui*). Because of logistic problems and the

---

[58] Chinese Ministry of Information, comp., *China Handbook, 1937–1945*, p. 113.

[59] When Wang Shijie, the PPC Secretary, was asked to draft the PPC's Organic Law, he intended to give the Council legislative power in an attempt to rectify the situation that the Legislative Yuan, since its inception, had become an appendage to the Executive Yuan. This, however, was not entertained by Sun Fo because it would marginalize his position and influence as President of the Legislative Yuan. Consequently, Wang's draft was significantly amended. See Wen Liming, "Wang Shijie yu guomin canzhenghui (1938–1944)" (Wang Shijie and the People's Political Council), *KangRi zhanzheng yanjiu* 3 (1993): 171.

[60] Chien, "War-time Government in China," pp. 857–858; Shyu, "China's 'Wartime Parliament,'" p. 277.

[61] Chen Qitian, *Jiyuan huiyilu*, p. 182.

war situation between 1938 and 1941, it sat only twice a year on average and had met only once a year since 1941.[62] Every plenum began with a few lengthy government reports, followed by questions and answers, all of which took up a great deal of time. Large numbers of proposals were put forward. Few were considered thoroughly and with the care they deserved, as the delegates often complained afterward. Furthermore, few resolutions were put into effect because either the authorities were unwilling to do so or the war presented difficulties or both.

These limitations on its powers notwithstanding, the PPC was perhaps the most representative body ever assembled in Nationalist China, functioning in a way more democratic than the country had known for many years. Only a majority quorum was required for holding a plenum, and only a majority vote of all those present was required for adopting a resolution. The delegates enjoyed freedom of speech inside the PPC as did members of parliament in the West. Outside, of course, they were answerable to the same laws as ordinary citizens with regard to public utterances and writings.[63]

The PPC had a promising start, but its success would depend on how seriously the government took it. The following comment by Zou Taofen at the opening of the First PPC was rather perceptive:

> The powers of the PPC are limited. However, if its three functions
> – resolution, recommendation, and hearing government reports or
> raising questions – can be amply carried out, it would at least, on
> the one hand, enable people to understand the government's policy
> directions, both internal and external, and how these policies are
> implemented and, on the other, enable public opinion and positive
> suggestions to be forwarded to the government. In this way, the
> barrier between government and people can be removed and the
> conduct of national affairs facilitated. Clearly all this would be of
> great use during the period of war resistance. However, the extent
> to which this objective can be achieved depends as much on the
> importance the government attaches to public opinion represented
> by the PPC as on the concrete work of the PPC itself.[64]

---

[62] Shyu, "China's 'Wartime Parliament,' " p. 278.

[63] Chinese Ministry of Information, comp., *China Handbook, 1937–1945*, p. 113. I am not aware of any delegates who were persecuted by the government for what they had said *inside* the PPC, though several strident critics were not "reelected" after serving a term.

[64] Quoted in Mu Xin, *Zou Taofen* (Zou Taofen) (Hong Kong: Sanlian shudian, 1978), p. 236.

This set the tone for the next nine years. Zou likened the nongovernment members to "invited guests" (*laibin*) and the GMD delegates to "companions for the guests" (*peike*). The former were expected to be polite, entertained by the latter on behalf of the host. In Zou's view, the PPC resembled a representative body, but was far from it.[65]

The First Plenum of the First PPC was held in Hankou from July 6 to 15, 1938. A total of 167 delegates out of 200 were present, the remainder being absent because of illness, overseas travel, or logistic problems. Opened by Speaker Wang Jingwei (President of the Executive Yuan), the occasion was marked with pomp and ceremony, being attended by the heads of the other Yuan, government ministers, and a number of foreign diplomats including the British and American ambassadors, the Swedish minister, the French chargé d'affaires, and various legation secretaries.[66] The presence of the foreign diplomats sent a signal to the outside world that China was united behind the government and deserving of international support. Wang's opening speech emphasized the gravity of the national crisis, the need for national unity and resistance, and the complementarity of democracy and concentrated powers. He maintained the Party line that armed resistance and national reconstruction would be carried out simultaneously.[67] Lin Sen, President of the National Government (a figure head), spoke of the extraordinary times in which the PPC was created, as well as the extraordinary spirit and determination that ought to be displayed in discharging the enormous duties with which the PPC was entrusted.[68] And Chiang Kai-shek, as Chairman of the Military Affairs Commission, reiterated in his speech that the sole purpose and significance of the PPC was "to concentrate the nation's strength in order to fight aggression to the death and thereby to achieve national reconstruction." It was to accomplish two tasks, he went on to say. The first was to strengthen national unity and to consolidate unification; the second was to lay the foundations for a democratic state.[69] There could be no doubt about Chiang's sincerity with regard to the first task. His commitment to the second, however, was highly suspect.

The delegates unanimously expressed their full support for the

---

[65] Ibid., p. 235.

[66] Guomin canzhenghui mishuchu, ed., *Diyijie diyici huiyi jilu* (Record of the inaugural meeting of the People's Political Council) (Chongqing: Guomin canzhenghui mishuchu, 1938), pp. 3–4.

[67] *GMCZH*, I, 157–158.   [68] Ibid., p. 161.   [69] Ibid., pp. 164–165.

government's Program of Armed Resistance and National Reconstruction. Accepting the leadership of the GMD and the Three Principles of the People as the "highest guiding principle during the war," they were keen to play a constructive role. The CCP, too, had every desire to cooperate at this point. There was a consensus that wartime China needed a strong and powerful government led by Chiang, now hailed as the national hero. There was also more freedom of speech than China had known for many years. National unity was at a high level, and the times were generally propitious for the PPC to be a sounding board of public opinion.

A number of important issues were on the MPGs' agenda from the outset. These included the establishment of provincial and district assemblies within a specified period of time; reform of the local political structure as a means of speeding up local self-government; protection of the freedoms of speech, publication, assembly, and association; relaxation and standardization of the censorship law; legalization of all the MPGs and the CCP; and a strengthening of all the patriotic, anti-Japanese mass organizations.[70] Most of these issues were taken up in the First Plenum of the First PPC, with many proposals approved by the PPC and later also by the government with or without amendments. The First Plenum concluded on a cordial note. The delegates had spoken freely and enthusiastically on a wide range of matters. All seemed to be going well.

Yet beneath the outward display of cordiality lay the discomfort that some delegates were beginning to feel. One delegate was literally gagged when he expressed dissatisfaction with the performance of Wang Jingwei as President of the Executive Yuan and asked for his replacement. Another, who proposed a liberalization of the censorship law, was subsequently reprimanded by the authorities.[71] What's more, it did not appear that the PPC resolutions would be carried out, prompting renewed calls for the speeding up of local self-government and a review of the censorship law at the next two plenums. A new proposal, recommending the establishment of a modern legal system as a basis for national reconstruction, also was put forward.[72]

---

[70] See Guomin canzhenghui mishuchu, ed., *Diyijie diyici huiyi jilu*, pp. 183–187; Fudan daxue xinwenxi yanjiushi, ed., *Zou Taofen nianpu* (A chronology of Zou Taofen's life) (Shanghai: Fudan daxue chubanshe, 1982), p. 113.

[71] Luo Longji, "Banian lai Zhongguo minzhu de dongxiang" (The Chinese democracy movement in the past eight years), *MZZK* 2:9 (September 16, 1945): 7.

[72] Guomin canzhenghui mishuchu, ed., *Diyijie dierci huiyi jilu* (Record of the second plenum of the First People's Political Council) (Chongqing: Guomin canzhenghui mishuchu, 1938), pp. 59, 61–62; *GMCZH*, I, 325.

In December 1938, the PPC received a setback from Wang Jingwei's defection to the Japanese, but no other senior GMD figures had followed suit, and China's war resolve remained strong. When the First PPC ended in October 1940, after holding five plenums, the independent newspaper *Yishibao* spoke optimistically about China's political future, describing the PPC as "a transitional representative institution."[73] Zuo Shunsheng thought the morale of the delegates was "excellent" and Chiang Kai-shek's attitude toward the other parties "not prejudiced."[74] But all this disguised the political differences that had begun to emerge. Some delegates were becoming very critical, and, of course, the government did not like it. Consequently, two of them, Third Party leader Zhang Bojun and Zhang Shenfu, a notable National Salvationist – both well known for their pro-CCP views – were dropped from the Second PPC, scheduled for March 1941.[75] Then came the New Fourth Army incident in January 1941;[76] it caused a serious breach in the united front.

When the Second PPC opened in March, relations between the government and the CCP were so strained that all seven communist delegates refused to attend after the government had rejected their twelve-point demand. It looked as though national unity, delicate and fragile from the start, was going to fall apart. Anxious to maintain a semblance of it, Chiang indicated that he had no intention of taking military action against the Communists and asked their delegates to return to the PPC. Dong Biwu and Deng Yingchao, two of the CCP delegates, resumed their seats at the Second Plenum, partly on the persuasion of some MPG leaders.[77] But the tension remained. Moreover, there was growing concern about the government's inability to implement any PPC resolutions.[78] Its sincerity was called into question, and the initial goodwill from both sides gave way to mutual suspicions.

---

[73] *GMCZH*, I, 763.

[74] Zuo Shunsheng, "Reminiscences," p. 161.

[75] See Category D's membership of the Second PPC in *GMCZH*, I, 784–786.

[76] On January 4, some 9,000 New Fourth Army troops moved to Maolin in Jingxian (Anhui). They were attacked by a large Nationalist force on the following day, with clashes continuing into the next ten days. As a result, virtually the whole New Fourth Army contingent was killed or captured, and the communist commander Ye Ting was taken prisoner. For a detailed account of the incident, see Ch'en Yung-fa, *Making Revolution: The Communist Movement in Eastern and Central China 1937–1945* (Berkeley: University of California Press, 1986), pp. 64–75.

[77] Shen Pu and Shen Renhua, eds., *Shen Junru nianpu* (A chronology of Shen Junru's life) (Beijing: Zhongguo wenshi chubanshe, 1992), p. 239.

[78] See, for example, the editorial of Chongqing's *Guomin gongbao* (National news), dated February 22, 1939, in *GMCZH*, I, 502–503.

As of the Second PPC, provincial delegates were "elected" from the newly formed provisional provincial political councils.[79] Their numbers increased from 88 to 90 in the Second PPC, to 164 in the Third PPC, and to 199 in the Fourth PPC, whereas the numbers of those designated or appointed by the central government were reduced, ostensibly to make the system more democratic.[80] The government, however, had no problem in stacking the extra seats with progovernment elements, given that the Nationalists controlled most of the provisional provincial assemblies.[81] A few MPG delegates, reputed for their critical tongues, were removed after the Second PPC; they included Luo Longji and five National Salvationists, namely, Zou Taofen, Wang Zaoshi, Shen Junru, Shi Liang, and Tao Xingzhi.[82]

In the Third PPC, there were fewer than twenty opposition members, including the Communists but not the independents.[83] Chen Qitian recalled that as the number of non-GMD members decreased, "people came away with the feeling that the influence and reputation of the PPC declined council after council."[84] Very concerned, Liang Shuming wrote in November 1941 that the PPC was facing a question of whether it should go on in its current state or be abolished altogether. In his view, it had failed as "a public opinion institution," resulting in a serious erosion of national unity. Even if it were not abolished, its future was bleak because the government was not prepared to increase its powers.[85] Luo Longji, who lost his seat after the Second PPC, complained that by the time of the Third PPC (October 1942), it had become "a mere decoration." Representatives of the Youth Party and the National

---

[79] In September 1938, two months after the first PPC had held its inaugural plenum, the Nationalist government promulgated the Organization Regulations of the Provisional Provincial Council. By March 1945, such councils had been formed in nineteen provinces. See Chinese Ministry of Information, comp., *China Handbook, 1937–1945*, p. 113.

[80] See the membership lists, *GMCZH*, II, 781–784, 1056–1059, 1422–1425.

[81] Chen Qitian, *Jiyuan huiyilu*, pp. 182–183.

[82] See the membership lists in Category D for the Second and Third PPC in *GMCZH*, II, 784–786, 1060, respectively; Shen and Shen, eds., *Shen Junru nianpu*, p. 243. Note that the membership lists in Category D, whereas the numbers had increased from 100 in the First PPC to 118 in the Second PPC, were substantially reduced to 60 in the Third PPC before clawing back to 75 in the Fourth PPC.

[83] See the membership list, *GMCZH*, II, 1060; see also Luo Longji, "Banian lai Zhongguo minzhu de dongxiang," p. 8.

[84] Chen Qitian, *Jiyuan huiyilu*, pp. 182–183.

[85] Liang Shuming, "Zailun Guomin canzhenghui" (The People's Political Council revisited), *LSMQJ*, VI, 309–311.

Socialist Party expressed their displeasure by boycotting the First Plenum of the Third PPC; others who attended "did not speak a word." By then, relations between the government and the Communists had gone from bad to worse, rendering the PPC increasingly ineffective.[86]

When the Third PPC opened in October 1942, the European War had been raging for nearly three years, and the Pacific War, for nearly one. Earlier in January of that year, the Western powers had renounced their extraterritorial rights in China, thereby ending the century-old unequal treaty regime. China was now anointed as one of the "Big Four" by the United States and perceived by the Allies as a freedom fighter. It was hard to reconcile the image of a Big Four with the poverty and backwardness of China, and even harder to juxtapose the image of a freedom fighter against Chiang's repressive regime.

While the Nationalists might have been enjoying the international accolade they did not deserve, their differences with the Communists continued to tear at the delicate fabric of national unity, prompting concerned MPG leaders to take on the role of a mediator over the next few years.[87] When the Fourth PPC began sitting in July 1945, the CCP delegates again refused to attend, accusing the government of failing to consult them and the MPGs on the election of the provincial delegates to the Fourth PPC and for unilaterally setting a date (November 12, 1945) for the National Assembly.[88] The constitutional issue was thrust back in the political limelight.

RENEWED PUSH FOR CONSTITUTIONALISM

The campaign for constitutionalism had been brought to a temporary halt at the start of the war as civil opposition cooperated with the government. But in September 1939, it was renewed at the Fourth Plenum of the First PPC. Two factors contributed to the revival. The first was Wang Jingwei's defection to the Japanese who had set up a puppet regime in Nanjing, promising constitutional rule in an attempt to win popular support in the occupied areas. Although Wang's collaboration with the Japanese did not formally commence until March 1940, he had begun to appeal to other political parties and groups to join him.[89] His

---

[86] Luo Longji, "Banian lai Zhongguo minzhu de dongxiang," p. 8.
[87] See Chapter 7, pp. 255–258.   [88] *GMCZH*, II, 1428–1429.
[89] Responding to Wang's calls, some members of the National Socialist Party and the Youth Party defected in 1940. See Roger B. Jeans, "Third-Party Collaborators in Wartime

defection put the Nationalist government, now relocated in Chongqing, under a great deal of pressure, challenging it to match his constitutional reform and to do better.

Another factor was the GMD's tightening controls of political organizations, groups, and individuals suspected of being subversive. After an initial period of relative tolerance of political dissent, the jail was once again filled with political prisoners during the winter of 1938–1939. Zou Taofen's leftist Life Book Company was ordered closed. Communist and radical literature was confiscated. Several communists and ultraliberals were reported to have been detained. Even the Chinese industrial cooperatives were placed under close surveillance because it was feared that these organizations might be subject to communist influence.[90] Differences with the CCP resurfaced, especially following the establishment of the Shen-Gan-Ning and Jin-Ji-Chao border regions, where separate Soviet governments had been formed. Friction took place in Hebei, Shandong, and Shanxi, causing the GMD leadership to develop at the Fifth Plenum of the Fifth Central Executive Committee held in January 1939 a secret strategy aimed at "preventing," "restricting," and "dissolving" communism as part of a broader strategy to control the activities of all "dissident parties."[91] In April, there were reports of clashes between government and communist forces in Shandong. In that summer, the Shen-Gan-Ning border region was encircled by a large government force. Fighting soon broke out in Hebei, Henan, Anhui, Shanxi, Shandong, Hubei, and Hunan.[92] By then, the GMD had put in place a series of measures designed to "restrict the activities of other parties," "to deal with the communist problem," and "to guard against communist activities in Japanese-occupied areas."[93] These measures had implications for all political dissidents. As Qian Duansheng recalled, the position of the

---

China: The Case of the Chinese National Socialist Party," in Lawrence Shyu, ed., *China During the Anti-Japanese War, 1936–1945* (Berne: Peter Lang, forthcoming 2000); Li Yibin, ed., *Zhongguo qingniandang* (The Chinese Youth Party) (Beijing: Zhongguo shehui kexue chubanshe, 1982), pp. 276–280.

[90] *FRUS* (1939), III, 209–210. Chen Lifu, the Education Minister, was reported to be working assiduously through the Party and his ministry to popularize the GMD with the youth of China. The activities and organization of the Three Principles of the People Youth Corps were being greatly expanded in an endeavor to attract the youth from similar communist organizations.

[91] Van Slyke, *Enemies and Friends*, p. 97.

[92] Harrison E. Salisbury, *The Long March: The Untold Story* (London: Macmillan, 1985), p. 280.

[93] Shen and Shen, eds., *Shen Junru nianpu*, p. 216; Van Slyke, *Enemies and Friends*, p. 97.

MPGs "was growing progressively worse by the end of 1939" after they had been rather well treated by the GMD for a brief period.[94] The renewed constitutional campaign was a response to the latest round of political repression.

Interestingly, leading the campaign in the PPC was a Nationalist, Kong Geng from Hubei, who urged the government to act on the resolution of the 1938 Extraordinary National Party Congress regarding the opening of the National Assembly to adopt a constitution. Supporting the Kong proposal, MPG leaders Zuo Shunsheng, Zhang Junmai, and Zhang Bojun proposed three courses of action: (1) set up a Constitution Drafting Committee made up of members elected from the ranks of the PPC with the government's approval; (2) make the Executive Yuan responsible to the PPC and the provincial and district governments responsible to the provisional political councils at the respective levels pending the opening of the National Assembly; and (3) promulgate a constitution within a short period of time, thus ending one-party dictatorship and recognizing the legality of all the existing political parties and groups.[95]

A separate proposal initiated by Zhang Junmai demanded immediate political reform, including the formation of a wartime Executive Yuan modeled on the British wartime cabinet. Similar proposals were submitted by the Vocational Educator Jiang Hengyuan, the National Salvationists Wang Zaoshi and Zhang Shenfu, and the CCP delegates led by Chen Shaoyu, calling for the legal protection of all anti-Japanese parties and groups.[96] Others renewed their demand for the safeguard of civil liberties, or human rights. On all these issues, the MPGs, the independents, and the CCP were at one. After two years of cooperation with the government, the question of one-party dictatorship was brought back into sharp relief.

Not all the delegates supported early constitutionalism, however. In fact, a heated debate took place, with the progovernment members arguing vehemently that constitutionalism was unnecessary and inappropriate in the midst of a war. A compromise was reached on September 16, when the following resolution was passed: "That, as a short-term solution, the government be asked to set a date for the convocation

---

[94] Ch'ien, *The Government and Politics of China*, p. 358. [95] *GMCZH*, II, 583–585.

[96] See Guomin canzhenghui mishuchu, ed., *Diyijie disici huiyi jilu* (Record of the fourth session of the First People's Political Council) (Chongqing: Guomin canzhenghui mishuchu, 1939), pp. 92–95; *GMCZH*, I, 586–588.

of the National Assembly and, in the meantime, to set up a Constitution Promotion Committee (*xianzheng qichenghui*) composed of PPC members to assist the government in this matter; and that, as a long-term solution, the government be asked to proclaim immediately the political equality of all Chinese citizens (with the exception of those who have defected to the Japanese) and to improve substantially the various government organs so that the talents around the country can be utilized and concentrated on the tasks of resistance and reconstruction."[97]

The coupling of the short-term solution with the long-term one in the resolution suggested that the legal recognition of the parties and groups outside the GMD and the strengthening of the legal basis of individual liberties were the main objectives sought by the opposition parties.[98] These basic rights should have been granted a long time before.

The government was procrastinating. Two days earlier, the GMD organ *Zhongyang ribao* (Central News) had stated in a lead article entitled "Today's Constitutional Question" that, although it was "harmless" to talk about it, constitutionalism was not central to the pressing problems facing the country. Even if it were, constitutionalism was a "question of method," not a "question of principle." The method was for the people to defend the Provisional Constitution of 1931, which remained the Basic Law for the period of political tutelage, and the 1938 Program of Armed Resistance and National Reconstruction. The editorial concluded, rhetorically, that it was the substance of constitutionalism, not the document by itself, that mattered.[99] Yet, even though the people were asked to stand by the Provisional Constitution of 1931 and the 1938 Program, the government failed to safeguard the civil liberties embedded in those documents.

The government only agreed to set up the Constitution Promotion Committee consisting of twenty-five members appointed from the ranks of the PPC to review the Draft Constitution of May 5, 1936. The Committee would report back to the Fifth Plenum, scheduled for April 1940.

---

[97] *GMCZH*, I, 593.

[98] Lawrence K. Rosinger, *Wartime Politics in China, 1939–1944* (Princeton: Princeton University Press, 1945), p. 57.

[99] *GMCZH*, I, 597–599. In another leader on November 25, entitled "Constitutionalism during the War Period," the *Zhongyang ribao* reiterated the Party line on the prerequisites to constitutional rule and criticized those who engaged in "pure talk." Only after the war was won could constitutional rule commence. It was a question of timing, the paper stressed, warning that it was extremely dangerous to forget about China's most pressing needs. See ibid., pp. 600–602.

Of the twenty-five members, fourteen were MPG leaders and independents, one was a communist, and several were legal experts and political scientists, who would convene a series of public symposia on constitutionalism in Chongqing. The co-convenors of the Committee were Huang Yanpei, Zhang Junmai, and Zhou Lan (probably an independent).[100] With such a makeup, it raised the prospect of marked changes to the Draft Constitution. Zou Taofen, however, feared that the members were not at liberty to draft a new constitution and that only minor changes would be allowed.[101]

The Committee did report back to the PPC, recommending changes to the Draft Constitution that would limit the powers of the executive government while expanding those of the National Assembly and its recess committee. A divergence of opinion ensued between the GMD and the opposition members on three issues: (1) the contents of the constitution, (2) the composition of the National Assembly, and (3) the convocation date of the Assembly. On the first issue, greater limits to the powers of the Executive Yuan but more powers to the future Assembly were recommended. It was further proposed that when the Assembly was in recess, there be a standing committee to oversee the government. Not surprisingly, this was unacceptable to the GMD delegates who argued that if the Assembly could meet once a year, there would be no need for a standing committee.[102]

On the second issue, there was strong opposition to the government's position that the membership of the Provisional National Assembly of 1936–1937 was still valid. The "elections" of 1936–1937 were neither free nor competitive. In fact, the Assemblymen, nearly all GMD members, had been designated by the government, and the Assembly, therefore, was unrepresentative. Moreover, times and circumstances had changed since then, and new developments such as the emergence of the MPGs

---

[100] The MPGs and the independents included Huang Yanpei, Shen Junru, Shi Liang, Zhang Lan, Chu Fucheng, Zhang Shenfu, Wang Zaoshi, Zhang Bojun, Li Huang, Zuo Shunsheng, Hu Zhaoxiang, Luo Longji, Zhang Junmai, Fu Sinian, and Luo Wengan. The CCP member was Dong Biwu. See Huang Yanpei, "Wo suo shenqin zhi Zhongguo zuichuqi ji zuijinqi xianzheng yundong" (My experience of the very early and the very recent Chinese constitutional movement), *Xianzheng yuekan* 1 (1944): 10–11. According to another source, only twelve were MPG and independent members. See Zhou Tiandu, ed., *Shen Junru wenji* (The collected works of Shen Junru) (Beijing: Renmin chubanshe, 1994), p. 411.

[101] Zou Taofen, *Taofen wenji* (The collected works of Zou Taofen) (Hong Kong: Sanlian shudian, 1959), III, 188–189.

[102] Wen Liming, "Wang Shijie," p. 175.

and the existence of the PPC should be taken into account. The prewar election laws, therefore, should be changed to reflect the new realities. In short, it was argued that the new Assembly should include members of all political parties and groups and the independents, which only new elections could ensure.[103] The concerns of the opposition parties were warranted. A National Assembly made up of GMD members and pro-government elements would see the adoption of a constitution having no regard for opposition views.

Concerning the convocation date of the Assembly, the opposition parties wanted it as soon as practicable, but Chiang Kai-shek would only agree to convene as soon as the war was over. Meanwhile, he would consider making some administrative changes to the Executive Yuan. But, according to the PPC Secretary Wang Shijie, Chiang was not prepared to withdraw GMD party cells from schools or to cease government funding for the Party.[104]

The Constitution Promotion Committee was dissolved after submitting its report. It has been suggested that, as a result of the government's displeasure at the Committee's recommendations, the whole question of constitutionalism was postponed for the next three years.[105] That is misleading. There was no loss of momentum as far as the opposition parties were concerned, nor was the issue of civil liberties "forced into the background in the face of the more basic immediate problem: the future of the state itself" as Lawrence Shyu would have it.[106] Constitutionalism, democracy, and human rights, along with the GMD–CCP tensions, remained the hot political issue of the day. Thus, in November 1941, under pressure from the MPG delegates, the Second PPC's presidium, chaired by no less an authority than Chiang himself, put forward a proposal to "promote democratic rule and to strengthen the War of Resistance." The proposal included stepping up efforts at local self-government, opening the National Assembly as soon as the war was over, expanding the powers of the PPC, recruiting government officials based on merit, and protecting civil rights.[107] The government approved it, but

---

[103] Hui Yiqun, "Tuixing xianzheng de jige juti wenti ji juti renwu" (A few concrete questions and concrete tasks concerning the implementation of constitutionalism), in Hu Zuoying, ed., *Xianzheng wenti yanjiu* (Study of constitutional issues) (Chongqing: Xinyishishe, 1940), pp. 29–30.

[104] Wen Liming, "Wang Shijie," pp. 174, 178.

[105] Lawrence N. Shyu, "China's Minority Parties in the People's Political Council," in Jeans, ed., *Roads Not Taken*, p. 163.

[106] Ibid., pp. 161–162.   [107] *GMCZH*, II, 992.

no date was set for the National Assembly. Subsequently, some changes were made: an increase in the PPC's membership, "election" of provincial delegates to the PPC, and expansion of the PPC's powers to include investigation.

But the government was not becoming more liberal or democratic. The publication in March 1943 of Chiang's manifesto, *Zhongguo zhi mingyun* (China's Destiny), widened the intellectual gap between the liberal intellectuals and GMD ideologues. Chiang cursed liberalism along with communism, blasting both as noxious manifestations of the May Fourth Movement that had led to denigration of things Chinese and widespread adulation of things foreign. By promoting these alien things, he alleged, Chinese liberals had aided and abetted "cultural aggression."[108]

In September of that year, the Eleventh Plenum of the GMD's Fifth Central Executive Committee passed a resolution that the National Assembly be convened within one year after the conclusion of the war.[109] At the same time, quite separately, the Second Plenum of the Third PPC passed a motion moved by the presidium that a Commission for the Inauguration of Constitutionalism (*Xianzheng shishi xiejinhui*) be set up, with Sun Fo, Wang Shijie, and Huang Yanpei as co-convenors.[110] On November 12, the Commission was established by the Supreme National Defense Council. In addition to the full complement of presidium members and a few GMD leading lights, it was composed of thirty-eight non-GMD members, including two Communists, Zhou Enlai and Dong Biwu, and such MPG activists as Huang Yanpei, Zhang Bojun, Zuo Shunsheng, Zhang Junmai, Liang Shuming, and Wang Zaoshi. Chiang made himself chairman.[111] The formation of the Commission marked the "second wave" of the wartime constitutional movement.

The functions of the Commission were (1) to make proposals to the government concerning preparations for the establishment of constitutional rule; (2) to investigate the progress of local self-government and to make reports thereon to the government; (3) to investigate the enforcement of laws and regulations concerning constitutional rule and to make reports thereon; (4) to serve as a link between the government

---

[108] Chiang Kai-shek, *China's Destiny and Chinese Economic Theory* (New York: Roy Publishers, 1947), pp. 98–100.

[109] Chinese Ministry of Information, comp., *China Handbook, 1937–1945*, p. 61.

[110] Ch'ien, *The Government and Politics of China*, p. 309.

[111] Ibid.; Shen and Shen, eds., *Shen Junru nianpu*, pp. 247–248; Xu Hansan, ed., *Huang Yanpei nianpu* (A chronology of Huang Yanpei's life) (Beijing: Wenshi ziliao chubanshe, 1985), p. 154.

and the people in connection with the question of constitutional rule and related political problems; and (5) to deliberate on matters relating to the constitution as mandated by the government.[112] Although there was no mention of the Draft Constitution, over which there remained considerable differences, it certainly was on the agenda.

It is possible to see the role of international influences on the respective positions of the opposition and the government. The European War saw the German forces in retreat in the latter half of 1943. The real possibility of an Allied victory, presumably a victory of democracy over fascism, was no doubt a source of tremendous encouragement to the forces of enlightenment in China. But far more important was the role of the Americans. For some time, there had been criticism in American newspapers and periodicals of the GMD regime because the United States was concerned about conditions in China and wanted to see some political reform in the Chinese government. Huang Yanpei revealed that Chiang, in a speech to the Eleventh Plenum of the Fifth Central Executive Committee, had mentioned President Roosevelt's advice to his government, including "early constitutional rule" and "the GMD's retreating to an equal legal position vis-à-vis the other political parties in order to resolve the political conflict."[113] Apparently, Chiang felt a need to appear to be doing something. To improve a badly tarnished image, his government thus appeared more conciliatory, relaxing the virtual ban on political activity during the years 1943–1944.[114]

Domestically, there was a growing voice within the GMD calling for an early end to political tutelage, with Sun Fo making several political speeches in as many months. On January 21, 1944, in an address to the Senior Party Affairs Class of the Central Training Corps, Sun said that China should become a constitutional democracy and lead the other Asian states that would gain independence from their colonial masters after the war. Turning to domestic politics, he declared that after constitutionalism was implemented, the GMD would change its current "special status" to an "ordinary position" and be equal before the law to any other political party or group. He added that the Party could expect to remain in power but must tolerate criticism from the opposition

---

[112] Chinese Ministry of Information, comp., *China Handbook, 1937–1945*, p. 119.
[113] Huang's diary, September 10, 1943, quoted in Wen Liming, "Huang Yanpei yu kangRi zhanzheng shiqi de dierci xianzheng yundong" (Huang Yanpei and the second constitutional movement during the war against Japan), *Jindaishi yanjiu* 5 (1997): 148.
[114] Van Slyke, *Friends and Enemies*, p. 177.

parties and compete for votes by convincing the people that it deserved their support. Although the various tasks associated with political tutelage were still unfinished, he saw no need to wait any longer because those tasks could be completed while constitutionalism was carried out. He was critical of the Party. After sixteen years of political tutelage, he pointed out, the people were still not exercising the four rights, and there was still not a single member of a county political council or a county magistrate who was popularly elected (they were all designated or appointed by the government). The five-power structure, he continued, was a far cry from the Western concept of separation of powers. "After the promulgation of the constitution, such bodies as the Supreme National Defense Council should cease to exist. That is to say, apart from the National Assembly, there should be no higher authority."[115] An edited version of his speech was subsequently published in Chongqing's *Xianzheng yuekan* (Constitutional Monthly).

On February 23, Sun addressed the Central Training Corps again, and this time a copy of the translation of his speech entitled "Democratization of the Government and Planned Economy" was handed, a few weeks later, to the American embassy in Chongqing by a member of the Legislative Yuan apparently with his approval. A summary of it by embassy officials is worth reproducing here:

> In order to transfer sovereignty to the people, the [GMD] and the Government must make changes in their present practices – particularly the [GMD], which has forgotten the very substance and method of democracy. The [GMD] has unfortunately assumed the attitude and habits of a ruling-caste and has come to regard itself as the sovereign power entitled to a special position and to suppression of all criticism. To achieve democracy we must take action as follows: First, the [GMD] must reorientate its psychology and correct its attitude of intolerance; second, the [GMD] must show a democratic spirit in action as well as in attitude; and third, the [GMD] must learn democratic methods. The existing suspicion in the United States and Great Britain that China is moving toward dictatorship and fascism is a danger to China's future. We need constructive aid from the Allies both now and after the war and they might refuse cooperation and leave China isolated if they think that

---

[115] Sun Ke, "Youguan xianzheng zhu wenti" (Various questions concerning constitutionalism), *Xianzheng yuekan* 3 (1944): 5–12; the quote is on p. 12.

China under the [GMD] will be fascist rather than democratic. Sympathy in those countries for the [CCP] does not arise from liking of Communism but because they feel that the [GMD] cannot carry out democracy and rejects the existence of other parties. This can be corrected through the realization of [*minquan zhuyi*] (democracy). A free economy, such as that in the United States and Great Britain, has been shown to be inconsistent with China's needs; China must, therefore, adopt a planned economy slightly similar to that of the Soviet Union. China must concentrate her total effort on all monopolistic and basic industries and national defense industries and leave light industry and production of consumers goods to private capital, with restrictions on the production of unnecessary luxuries and consumers goods. The present international situation and that which will follow after the war demand an emphasis on national defense reconstruction. Only through democracy in government and planned economy can China's future be assured.[116]

Ambassador C. E. Gauss noted that this was "the first instance that has come to the Embassy's attention of outspoken semi-public criticism by a [GMD] and Government leader of the fascist tendencies of the [GMD] and the Chinese Government."[117] Unlike the January speech, this one did not find its way into the Chinese press.

On April 15, Sun Fo launched yet another attack on the Party in an address to the Legislative Yuan, the thrust of which was that:

The [GMD] has claimed for 30 [sic] years [that] it has been carrying out political tutelage in China but actually it has assumed [a] form of party dictatorship. . . . The [GMD] has no right to monopoly of political activity. We have now developed from [a] system of party dictatorship to one of personal dictatorship and while claiming to be [a] democratic country have no democracy even inside [the] party. If democracy cannot be established in [GMD] headquarters at [Chongqing], where can it be established? Suggestions have been made that I make complaints against [the] Government and [the] party directly and privately. I have done this many times without effect. People accuse me of being talkative idealist but if I do not say these things no one else will and I say them for China's sake. Unless I say these things now and unless China goes democratic now it will be too late.[118]

---

[116] *FRUS* (1944), VI, 385.   [117] Ibid.   [118] Ibid., p. 410.

Sun's speeches constituted a strong indictment of the Party, resonating with the MPGs. Chiang was said to have discussed with a couple of senior Party members the issues raised in those speeches and to have issued orders that local self-government be established throughout the country within two years.[119] Still dissatisfied with the leadership, Sun continued to criticize the Party government every now and then during the remainder of the war period, expressing his "leftist" views on a range of issues, including democracy and the communist question.[120]

Outside the government, the constitutional momentum was sustained by the MPGs sponsoring a series of public seminars, symposiums, and meetings at which the Draft Constitution was often the topic of discussion. Other topics of interest included the rule of law, democracy, and civil liberties. A number of magazines and journals were launched in Chongqing and Kunming. Chief among these was the *Xianzheng yuekan*, which first appeared on New Year's Day 1944. By the time it went out of business in March 1946, a total of twenty-seven issues had been published, with contributions from liberal intellectuals, politicians, and progressive government members advocating constitutional democracy, a rule of law, and human rights. Also worthy of note was the formation in Chongqing in September 1944 of a nongovernmental Constitutional Democracy Promotion Association.[121] The question now was no longer whether constitutionalism was necessary, but what sort of constitution should be adopted and how best to implement it. The constitutional movement, hitherto confined to the educated elite, was now being popularized.[122]

The Commission for the Inauguration of Constitutionalism had a much higher profile and a larger membership than the previous Constitution Promotion Committee. But what could it achieve, where the previous body had failed, unless the government was serious about it? Huang Yanpei seemed optimistic. Wang Shijie, on the government's side, was not, as he knew privately only too well how far Chiang Kai-shek would go.[123]

---

[119] Ibid., p. 393.

[120] See Gao Hua, "Lun kangzhan houqi Sun Ke de 'zuoqing'" (On Sun Fo's "leftist tendencies" during the latter half of the war of resistance), *Minguo yanjiu* 2 (1995): 206–221.

[121] Shen and Shen, eds., *Shen Junru nianpu*, pp. 249–253.

[122] Liu Simu, "Xianzheng de ⟨qicheng⟩yu ⟨chujin⟩" (The promotion and implementation of constitutionalism), in Hu Zuoying, ed., *Xianzheng wenti yanjiu* (Study of constitutional issues) (Chongqing: Xinyishishe, 1940), pp. 18–19.

Although there was a public movement for the study of the Draft Constitution, it was carefully controlled by the GMD, intended largely for publicity purposes both at home and abroad, and the draft was not expected to undergo any marked changes.[124] Thus, when the Commission produced a report containing thirty-two points and departing significantly from the draft, it received little attention from the government.

In a dramatic twist on New Year's Day 1945, Chiang announced that the National Assembly would be convened before the end of the year, unless untoward and unexpected military developments should intervene.[125] Then in May, the Sixth National Party Congress set a date for its opening (November 12).[126] This was inconsistent with the earlier decision that constitutional rule would be implemented one year after the conclusion of the war. In his opening address to the Fourth PPC in July, Chiang indicated that all matters relating to the convocation of the National Assembly were open to discussion, adding that measures had been put in place in preparation for constitutionalism. These included the abolition of Party cells in the army and schools, elections of provincial and county assemblies within six months, and the legalization of all non-GMD political organizations "in accordance with the law."[127]

In July 1945, the Communists boycotted the Fourth PPC over the issue of the National Assembly. They suspected that the putting forward of the date was due to pressures from the U.S. Ambassador to China, General Patrick Hurley, who was alleged to be anticommunist. For some time, the Communists had joined with the MPGs in calling for the convocation of a political consultative conference for the purpose of forming an interim coalition government. They now feared that an early opening of the National Assembly would give the GMD the opportunity to adopt a constitution that would have the effect of legitimating the existing regime.[128]

Surprisingly, the MPG leaders became the incredible backsliders, opposing its early opening. The Youth Party delegates summed up their objections on the following grounds: half of the country was still under Japanese occupation; the members of the Provisional National Assembly of 1936–1937 were GMD-controlled; the MPGs were yet to be legalized; there were no freedoms of speech, publication, assembly, and

---

[123] Wen Liming, "Wang Shijie," pp. 184–185.
[124] Observation by Ambassador Gauss. See *FRUS* (1944), VI, 364.
[125] Chinese Ministry of Information, comp., *China Handbook, 1937–1945*, p. 72.
[126] Ibid., pp. 52, 59–60.   [127] *GMCZH*, II, 1449–1450.   [128] Ibid., pp. 1428–1429.

association and no freedom of the person; and the CCP had decided on a boycott. They asked the government to do three things first: legalize all political parties and groups, protect basic rights, and open a political consultative conference to consider a reorganization of the government and to set a new date for the Assembly.[129]

Another and more compelling reason for their volta-face was that the increasing tension between the government and the CCP was threatening to destroy what remained of national unity. China was once again in danger of plunging into a civil war in the summer of 1945. A six-man PPC delegation had just been to Yan'an to meet with Mao Zedong.[130] Two of them (Huang Yanpei and Leng Yu), plus a provincial delegate from Jiangsu (Jiang Hengyuan), declined to take part in the PPC debate on the issue of the National Assembly, after expressing in writing their opposition to the government's plans.[131] Third Party leader Zhang Bojun, also just returned from Yan'an, called for the immediate opening of a political consultative conference.[132] Others added that November was only four months away, too short a time for adequate preparation for the Assembly.[133]

Support for the government's May decision was not lacking, however, thus splitting the PPC. Consequently, an ambivalent resolution was passed, acknowledging a lack of consensus and recommending that the government give further consideration to all matters relating to the question of the National Assembly. Prior to its opening, it added, all political parties should be legalized, civil rights should be protected, efforts should be continued to resolve the government's differences with the CCP, and the process of local self-government should be expedited by establishing representative bodies at various levels.[134]

Strong opposition from the MPGs and the CCP forced the GMD leadership to back down. But the issues remained unresolved. Would there be new elections to the National Assembly? What should its powers be vis-à-vis the Executive Yuan? Would a new government be elected immediately after a new constitution was adopted and promulgated? The opposition parties took the view that all these questions should be dealt with in a political consultative conference rather than in the now ineffectual PPC.

After the war, the PPC continued to lead an official, if insignificant,

---

[129] Ibid., pp. 1469–1471.   [130] See Chapter 7, pp. 257–258.
[131] Ibid., pp. 1465–1466.   [132] Ibid., pp. 1467–1468.   [133] Ibid., pp. 1478–1479.
[134] Ibid., pp. 1483–1484.

existence until March 28, 1948, just one day before the opening of the First National Assembly. It had a checkered history of nearly ten years, having held a total of thirteen sessions.

EVALUATION OF THE PPC

In conclusion, we feel compelled to ask the question, was the PPC a quasi-democratic institution or a mere facade of political participation? To answer this question, it should first be appreciated that the PPC began with an abundance of goodwill from both sides of politics, greeted by civil opposition as a "public opinion institution," an instrument for laying the foundations for a democratic state, and a symbol of national unity. Qian Duansheng, a PPC member himself, wrote in 1942: "The existing People's Political Council is a promising instrument for introducing more and more non-[GMD] participation in government. If some real power is given it, and if the politically articulate elements outside the [GMD] are given more adequate representation on it, there is no reason why the Council should not develop into something from which a future assembly of the nation may very well derive lessons."[135] As late as September 1943, Chongqing's independent newspaper *Dagongbao* still called the PPC "a ladder to democracy," born with "a Heavenly mission."[136] It was not a representative institution in a popular sense, and there were no real elections. But there was a good mix of delegates from the various groupings in the political arena, plus the independents, provincial representatives, and others. In terms of their quality, one would agree with Qian that "on the whole they have been on a high level and perhaps as good a lot as a purely elected body can show in China at present [1942]."[137] The U.S. Department of State shared this view, observing: "Although the People's Political Council was purely advisory, the prestige of its members and the caliber of its discussions made it a significant body."[138]

Although the PPC was not a "wartime parliament" by any means, it had some protoparliamentarian features. Its members enjoyed freedom of speech inside it, and the sessions were never dull or placid. Presidents

---

[135] Chien, "War-time Government in China," p. 870.
[136] Editorial, September 20, 1943, *GMCZH*, II, 1195.
[137] Chien, "War-time Government in China," p. 857.
[138] U.S. Department of State, *The China White Paper (August 1949)*, originally issued as *United States Relations with China with Special Reference to the Period 1944–1949*, reissued with a new introduction by Lyman P. Van Slyke (Stanford: Stanford University Press, 1967), I, 52.

of the Five Yuan and government ministers often attended council meetings, reporting orally or in writing on their portfolios and fielding questions from the floor. The delegates enjoyed the power of interpellation. For example, in one plenum of the Third PPC, Finance Minister H. H. Kung (Kong Xiangxi) and Education Minister Chen Lifu were questioned vigorously by opposition members about policies and matters in their respective portfolios. Official corruption and the government's price policy also came under attack.[139] Sun Fo wrote in 1944: "Ministers in the Government have more and more to pay heed to the P.P.C. Not a few of the important and otherwise powerful ministers have found themselves in uncomfortable positions when P.P.C. members indulged themselves in straight talk and outspoken criticism. This is a hopeful trend in China's march towards democracy."[140] Zuo Shunsheng recalled that even such senior ministers as H. H. Kung and T. V. Soong "were afraid of being questioned" and "lost color on the spot."[141] Allowing opposition and independent members to bring government policies under the microscope was an unprecedented, albeit healthy, development in Chinese politics and governance. But none of the ministers could be impeached, and Chiang Kai-shek would ensure that any criticism of them would not go too far. When too many questions were raised about the work of H. H. Kung, one delegate recalled, Chiang came to his defense, cutting short all questioning, thus saving him "much embarrassment."[142]

Thus, despite its limited powers, the PPC had been a training ground for parliamentary politics and a valuable learning experience for its members. Independent Wang Yunwu recalled that, in the latter half of the PPC's existence, indirect elections had been held in some provinces. He believed that had elections been held from the start, the vast majority of the PPC members would have been elected by virtue of their qualifications, experience, and social standing. In other words, there could have been elections, which could have been institutionalized. Speaking highly of their performance, he was convinced that PPC members had an impact on the Executive Yuan as well as a salutary effect on the Legislative Yuan.[143] Zuo Shunsheng, speaking from personal experience, also thought that the PPC demonstrated that democracy was not only necessary but possible.[144]

[139] Wen Liming, "Wang Shijie," p. 182.
[140] Sun Fo, *China Looks Forward* (London: George Allen and Unwin, 1944), p. 89.
[141] Zuo Shunsheng, *Jin sanshinian jianwen zaji*, pp. 70–71.
[142] Chang, *The Third Force in China*, p. 112.   [143] Wang Yunwu, *Youlu lun guoshi*, p. 5.
[144] Zuo Shunsheng, *Jin sanshinian jianwen zaji*, p. 69.

In this sense, the PPC was a democratic experiment, not an exercise in futility. Its significance is best understood in perspective. Before the war, all the opposition parties and groups had been outlawed, leaving no room for loyal opposition, let alone multiparty cooperation. With the onset of the war, the government, making a virtue of necessity, reached some sort of accommodation with the opposition. In return, the latter was prepared to cooperate in the hope that a democratizing process would develop. The delegates, involving themselves in a broad range of political, social, economic, and educational issues, were serious and enthusiastic about their role. Many had traveled a long way from various parts of the country. For the first time, they were able to debate issues in a parliamentary fashion. They had some success in mobilizing human power and resources for the war effort and in getting the government to implement some of their resolutions on financial, economic, and educational matters, though not on political, military, and administrative matters.[145] In the final analysis, the PPC could be viewed as a first step toward a democratic breakthrough. Again, one is inclined to agree with Qian Duansheng that:

> It would be extravagant to claim that in it [the PPC] Chinese democracy has found anchor, or even to claim that through it China has made a long stride along the road to democracy. But if the function of a democratic assembly is to voice the opinion of the people and to make the government feel obliged to respect that opinion, the People's Political Council is not to be dismissed as a nonentity merely because it is not a fully elected assembly or because it has yet to acquire the power of compulsion.[146]

The PPC could have marked the start of a democratization project had its powers been widened to bring the government to account. Unfortunately, it ended up as an abortive democratic experiment, abortive in that it was prevented from growing in stature and from becoming more broadly representative. Consequently, it remained an instrument by which the Nationalists "provided a safety-valve for opposition without touching the apparatus of its own power," as one American writer put it.[147] As far as Chiang Kai-shek was concerned, the PPC was a mere advi-

---

[145] Shyu, "China's 'Wartime Parliament,' " pp. 292, 291–297.

[146] Ch'ien, "War-time Government in China," pp. 858–859.

[147] Paul M. A. Linebarger, *The China of Chiang K'ai-shek: A Political Study* (Boston: World Peace Foundation, 1941), p. 72.

sory body from beginning to end, a mere facade of political participation, albeit an improvement on the National Emergency Conference of 1932. Its creation had been driven by the imperatives of war, not by a desire to "open up the regime." Hostage to the mainstream political culture tradition, Chiang was unable to understand modern political pluralism and to appreciate the liberal alternatives presented by the opposition elite. As long as the PPC was cooperative, he had no problem with it. But as soon as the non-GMD delegates became sharply critical of his regime, he had no qualms about reducing their numbers markedly beginning with the Third PPC. Thereafter, the PPC was reduced to "an empty showcase of democracy, wielding no power that could in a meaningful way alter the policies and practices of the reigning elite."[148]

For the PPC's failure as a democratic experiment, party politics as well as Chiang's strategic decisions and "rational choice" were largely to blame, to which must be added the communist problem. Yet the government frequently spoke of "laying the foundations for a democratic state." In the rhetoric, there was a nexus between war and democracy on both sides of politics, as we shall see in the next chapter. In the midst of a foreign war, democracy was still a rallying cry in national politics.

[148] Lloyd E. Eastman, *Seeds of Destruction: Nationalist China in War and Revolution, 1937–1949* (Stanford: Stanford University Press, 1984), pp. 43–44.

6

Wartime Democratic Thought

CHINESE INTELLECTUALS from the 1920s through the 1940s were torn between antiimperialist nationalism and cultural critique, between the external imperatives of *jiuwang* and the internal prerequisites of *qimeng*.[1] When full-scale war with Japan broke out in 1937, they felt compelled to support *jiuwang* first, accepting that to be patriotic was not to attack China's "greatness," its culture and civilization. Vera Schwarcz has written of the early war period: "For a brief interval, there was a common cause between intellectuals who were convinced that China must pursue internal self-emancipation simultaneously with resistance to external aggression and activists whose top priority was national salvation."[2] She draws attention to a New Enlightenment movement (1936–1937) led by May Fourth veterans and young communist theoreticians who departed from the "old" enlightenment path of cultural critique to call for a more systematic and rational synthesis of Chinese and Western cultures. As China suffered defeat after defeat in the first two years of the war, pressures mounted on May Fourth veterans to cease attacking Chinese traditions while the fight for national survival was so perilous. Overwhelmed by a sense of nationalism, some attempted to redefine the Chinese national identity that diminished the appeal of cultural iconoclasm.[3]

But both May Fourth veterans and the liberal intellectuals of a younger generation soon reasserted the priority of *qimeng* in the midst of the pressure to concentrate on *jiuwang*. For the prodemocracy activists, the most important thing about *qimeng* was not cultural critique

---

[1] This is the theme of Vera Schwarcz's book, *The Chinese Enlightenment: Intellectuals and the Legacy of the May Fourth Movement of 1919* (Berkeley: University of California Press, 1986).
[2] Ibid., p. 197.   [3] Ibid., pp. 222–236.

and iconoclasm. The most important thing was political reform as an internal prerequisite to *jiuwang*. Sustaining the democratic impulse, they engaged in a search for a kind of democracy based on a systematic and rational synthesis of Chinese and Western cultures. Indeed, far from stifling the democratic discourse, the Sino-Japanese War brought vitality to it in the rear areas, especially in Kunming, where a number of liberal magazines were published,[4] with contributions from scholars of different persuasions.[5] For civil opposition, democracy was both a goal and a political weapon, inseparable from the war itself. Prior to the war, the opposition elite had hoped in vain for democratic change. With the outbreak of war, they hoped that, when it was won, China would be liberated from the twin shackles of imperialism and dictatorship. "That was why all pro-democracy elements insisted on war [with Japan]," wrote Luo Longji eight years later, "and those who fought it did believe in democracy."[6] The war was viewed as a facilitator of democracy, and democracy also became a means of survival for the minor parties and groups (MPGs).

The theme of the wartime political discourse was unity, resistance, reconstruction, and democracy – a theme that, on the surface of it, transcended party lines. Unity was essential for resistance and reconstruction, with democracy being perceived as the link between them. The democratic thoughts of the MPGs and the independents were influenced

[4] The most notable among these were *Jinri pinglun* (Commentary Today), *Minzhu zhoukan* (Democracy Weekly), and *Ziyou luntan* (Liberal Forum). Appearing for the first time in Kunming on New Year's Day, 1939, *Jinri pinglun* was probably founded by the faculty members of the Southwest Associated University. The editor appears to have been Qian Duansheng. The weekly was also joined by intellectuals from Yunnan University and other institutions. Prominent contributors included Pan Guangdan and popular writers Zhu Ziqing and Shen Congwen. Published in the early years of the war, the weekly contained detailed reports and analyses of the international situation, as well as discussion and analysis of China's wartime politics, economy, education, and foreign policy, which formed the basis for immediate proposals for a reform of the Nationalist government. In November 1939, it was joined by Luo Longji. The magazine ceased publication in April 1941. *Minzhu zhoubao* was beholden to the Democratic League while *Ziyou luntan* was an independent magazine.

[5] Hu Shi made no contribution to the discourse because he was out of the country after July 1938 when he became a special envoy of Chiang Kai-shek, launching a diplomatic offensive in Europe and the United States aimed at mustering Western support for the war against Japan. In September, Hu was appointed as China's ambassador to the United States, a position he held until 1942. Afterward, he stayed in New York and later at Harvard University, returning to China in June 1946 to take up the presidency of Beijing University. See Geng Yunzhi, *Hu Shi nianpu, 1891–1962* (A chronology of Hu Shi's life, 1891–1962) (Hong Kong: Zhonghua shuju, 1966), pp. 164–186.

[6] Luo Longji, "Banian lai Zhongguo minzhu de dongxiang" (The Chinese democracy movement in the past eight years), *MZZK* 2:9 (September 16, 1945): 6.

partly by the contingencies of war, partly by international developments, partly by their understanding of democracy, and partly by their strong conviction that the most appropriate political system for China was not one based on unreserved or ill-informed borrowing from the West, but one that took account of Chinese conditions and traditions.

The ideology of the Democratic League will be treated in the next chapter. But first let us look at the GMD's rhetoric as well as the CCP's New Democracy.

THE GMD'S WARTIME DEMOCRATIC RHETORIC

From the outset of the war, the GMD proclaimed a commitment to democracy. The 1938 Program of Armed Resistance and National Reconstruction stated that the foundations for reconstruction and a democratic state would be laid during the war. Accordingly, Chiang Kai-shek established the PPC, as we have seen, and the Party set itself several political tasks: speeding up local self-government, improving the Party organization at various levels to increase administrative efficiency, and dealing with corrupt officials by confiscating their property.[7]

The GMD's wartime rhetoric reflected certain motifs that recurred time after time in modern Chinese democratic thought. One of these was the compatibility of democracy with strong government. Addressing the inaugural PPC on July 6, 1938, Speaker Wang Jingwei stated that reconstruction and war were the two sides of the same coin, the most important task in reconstruction being the erection of a democratic system on the "strength of the masses" in connection with their struggle for liberation from foreign oppression and "remnant feudalism." (By remnant feudalism he meant the regional militarists still opposed to the central government.) Here, the archetypal theme of antiimperialism and antifeudalism found full expression, as in communist propaganda. "China needs a strong, powerful central government that can concentrate the strength of the masses, train them, and lead them," Wang declared. "Only then can [we] resist aggression, achieve [national] independence and liberate [ourselves]. And only then will there be hopes for the realization of democracy."[8] Invoking Sun Yat-sen's *quan–neng* dichotomy, he reaffirmed the Party's position that liberty and reunification, like democracy and concentration of powers, were not incompatible. "China is at a critical moment of life and death," Wang proclaimed:

---

[7] *GMCZH*, I, 36.   [8] Ibid., p. 157.

Without an able government [*neng*], the current difficult situation cannot be coped with; without popular sovereignty [*quan*], the nation's strengths and resources cannot be concentrated in the hands of the government for the purpose of resistance and reconstruction. Not only will unification not hamper freedom, but it is freedom's safeguard. Not only will concentration of powers not hamper democracy, but it is the necessary condition for democracy.[9]

The notion that democracy and concentrated powers were complementary was not new. It was, as we have seen, central to Zhang Junmai's revisionist democracy. But whereas Zhang stressed the safeguard of civil rights, Wang used the promise of democracy to legitimate the authoritarian regime.

Another motif of modern Chinese democratic thought was the primacy of the state and the subordination of the individual to the collectivity. In his address to the First PPC, Chiang Kai-shek stated that democracy was liberty that did not infringe upon the freedoms and rights of others. His accent was on individual discipline, not personal freedoms.

Especially at this critical moment of life and death for the entire nation-state (*minzu*), our real democratic freedom is definitely not the freedom of the individual or the freedom of a minority. It is the freedom of the entire country and nation-state, to which the freedom of the individual and freedom of a minority must be sacrificed. It can be said that to seek freedom, we need to recognize where the nation and the individual stand in relation to each other, as well as the needs of the time and the circumstances, so that the laws of the land can be enforced, the War of Resistance advantaged, the democratic structure established, and the foundations for the freedom of the entire nation-state laid.[10]

---

[9] Ibid., pp. 157–158.

[10] Ibid., p. 163. This view of democracy informed the government's position on constitutionalism. Wu Jingxiong, a drafter of the May Fifth Draft Constitution in the Legislative Yuan, seemed to be following the government's line when he noted that the constitutional movements in Europe and the United States had been aimed at personal freedoms, whereas the movement in China was aimed at national salvation. In other words, the starting point of Euro-American constitutionalism was the individual, that of the Chinese movement, the collectivity, or the nation-state. See Wu Jingxiong and Huang Gongjue, *Zhongguo zhixianshi* (A history of Chinese constitution making) (Shanghai: Shangwu yinshuguan, 1937), pp. 609–610.

Linking democracy with national unity and independence, Chiang asked the people to make personal sacrifices. His notion of democracy, like Sun Yat-sen's, recognized not the sanctity of individual rights and interests, but the primacy of the state and the collectivity.

This is best illustrated by the Program for the National People's Spiritual General Mobilization (*Guomin jingshen zongdongyuan gangling*) launched on February 20, 1939, in which Chiang spoke of the "ethics of national salvation," based on the Confucian ethics of loyalty, filial piety, benevolence, righteousness, and integrity. To defend China's independence and territorial integrity, he demanded absolute unified command, politically and militarily. A revised version of the New Life Movement of 1934, the National People's Spiritual General Mobilization sought to remold Chinese by changing their old habit of loose living ("without a purpose and motivation") and nurturing a new lively and enterprising spirit coupled with a national consciousness. As in the New Life Movement, the people were asked to develop a healthy psychology, to be physically fit by exercising, to be hygienic, clean, tidy, and to get up early in the morning, and so on. Chiang called on them to "destroy their private and selfish designs" in the national interest, to correct all "diverse and complex" thoughts contrary to the Three Principles of the People, and to refrain from expressing any views that would endanger the nation-state, sabotage the unified military and administrative commands, and undermine the government's war effort. They would enjoy freedom of speech, but within the limits of the national interest and wartime needs.[11]

The National People's Spiritual General Mobilization was designed to enhance nationalist sympathies in the midst of the war; it was not about democracy. Critics were cynical about its intentions. How could the people be expected to make personal sacrifices unless those in authority were exemplary? As the editor of Chongqing's independent newspaper *Dagongbao* put it:

> The real spirit of democracy consists in meeting the needs of national victory. What I am talking about is not the form of institution, but the spirit of politics. The spirit of democracy is anti-bureaucratic, [entailing] a rule of law, fulfillment of duties and obligations, and making sacrifices for the nation.[12]

The spirit of democracy transcends rulers and the ruled. A rule of law is important even in times of war because it alone could provide safeguards

---

[11] Ibid., pp. 445–453.   [12] Ibid., p. 493.

against the authoritarian state. The editor's point was a potent one: in carrying out their duties, those in high places should display the same spirit that they expected of the ordinary people.[13]

THE CCP'S NEW DEMOCRACY

Writing on the anti-Japanese united front in May 1937, Mao Zedong said:

> ... democracy is the most essential thing for resistance to Japan, and to work for democracy is to work for resistance to Japan. Resistance and democracy are interdependent, as are resistance and internal peace, [and] democracy and internal peace. Democracy is a guarantee for resistance, while resistance provides favourable conditions for the development of the democratic movement. . . . It is correct and indisputable that the day-to-day struggle against Japan and the people's struggle for a better life must be linked up with the movement for democracy. Nevertheless, the central and essential thing at the present stage is democracy and freedom.[14]

In emphasizing the role of democracy in the war, Mao shared the GMD's instrumentalist view of democracy as a method of mobilization and of democracy's links with antiimperialism. An editorial of the *Xinhua ribao* (New China Daily) dated September 16, 1939, stated thus:

> Without democratic rights, the necessary condition for mass mobilization for fighting the war is lost, as are the enormous strengths of an all-out national and racial war of resistance. In short, when the people are denied freedoms of speech, publication, assembly, and association and the right of armed resistance, it would be impossible to mobilize them into fighting the war, and this [in turn] would make it impossible to achieve full democracy gradually.[15]

Similarly, Yan'an's *Xin Zhonghuabao* (New China News) editorialized ten days later:

> Only democracy can really mobilize the entire population into the great enterprise of armed resistance and national reconstruction

---

[13] Ibid.
[14] Mao Tse-tung, *Selected Works of Mao Tse-tung* (Peking: Foreign Languages Press, 1967), I, 288–289.
[15] *GMCZH*, I, 611.

and overcome all kinds of difficulties. Only democracy can really bring about the genuine unity of all the political parties and groups around the country, concentrate talents, and engage them in the struggle for the New China of the Three Principles of the People. And only democracy can really reform the old and all that is inappropriate for the wartime political structure, and eliminate all corrupt officials and degenerate elements.[16]

CCP democracy at this point was neither the bourgeois democracy of the West nor the proletarian, socialist democracy of the Soviet Union, but the "democracy of the war of liberation."[17] Mao called it New Democracy, referring to a stage in the Chinese revolution – a long period of "bourgeois-democratic struggle against imperialism, feudalism and bureaucratic-capitalism" prior to the achievement of socialism. Early in 1940, he published an important treatise on that subject, at a time when ominous cracks were beginning to appear in the structure of the GMD–CCP united front. In that treatise, he refuted both "bourgeois dictatorship" and "proletarian dictatorship," speaking of a "joint dictatorship of all the revolutionary classes" and a system of government based on "democratic centralism."[18] In April 1945, in an essay entitled "On Coalition Government," he wrote:

> It is a law of Marxism that socialism can be attained only via the stage of democracy. And in China the fight for democracy is a protracted one. It would be a sheer illusion to try to build a socialist society on the ruins of the colonial, semi-colonial and semi-feudal order without . . . a thoroughgoing bourgeois-democratic revolution of a new type.[19]

And in July, he reiterated:

> The new democracy that China wishes to practice is nothing else than the joint democratic dictatorship [*minzhu de lianhe zhuanzheng*] of all the anti-imperialist and all the anti-feudal classes; of course, it is neither American bourgeois dictatorship nor the proletarian dictatorship of the Soviet Union.[20]

---

[16] Ibid., p. 618.   [17] Ibid., pp. 611–612.

[18] Mao, *Selected Works*, II, 347–352, 354–360.

[19] Ibid., III, 233. In the 1967 edition, the phrase "led by the Communist Party" was added.

[20] Quoted in Stuart R. Schram, *The Political Thought of Mao Tse-tung*, revised and enlarged edition (New York: Praeger, 1969), p. 403.

While accepting the Three Principles of the People and supporting Chiang Kai-shek and his government in fighting the Japanese, Mao clearly was interested in a "joint dictatorship." But, as Stuart Schram has noted, Mao's view from the time he first used the term *New Democracy* in 1939 was that, after 1919, leadership of the Chinese revolution rightfully belonged to the proletariat.[21] Mao defined democracy in terms of the class character of the state, not as a political method, giving "little thought to the establishment of a political system democratic in its structure and mechanisms, and not merely in the sense that it was held to represent 'the people.' "[22] He did not link democracy with institutions.

New Democracy provided the theoretical underpinning for the CCP's united front strategy designed to win hegemony and to isolate the GMD. As long as the united front was in force, the CCP supported a strong and powerful wartime government and also regarded the MPGs and the independents as important allies because of the role of the intellectuals as the ultimate "agents of hegemony."[23] Supporting the "struggle for democracy and freedom" while fighting the Japanese would enhance the CCP's nationalistic and democratic credentials. There were common concerns about rights and civil liberties and the legalization of all anti-Japanese parties, groups, and organizations. In particular, the Communists demanded the right to bear arms, which was crucial to the expansion of their power. As with the civil opposition elite, they declared that the aim of wartime democracy was to enhance China's military capabilities through a concentration of multiparty strengths.[24] They also echoed the opposition view that the masses, denied civil liberties, would be hard to mobilize. Ironically, in Yan'an, the revolutionary base, civil liberties were hardly protected under Mao's rule.

THE DEMOCRATIC THOUGHTS OF THE MPGS AND THE INDEPENDENTS

A number of themes emerged from the literature of the MPGs and the independents. For analytical purposes, these themes may be outlined

---

[21] Stuart R. Schram, *The Thought of Mao Tse-tung* (Cambridge: Cambridge University Press, 1989), p. 78.

[22] Ibid., p. 108.

[23] Gerry Groot, "Managing Transitions: The Chinese Communist Party's United Front Work, Minor Parties and Groups, Hegemony and Corporatism," unpublished Ph.D. thesis, University of Adelaide, 1997, p. 11.

[24] Schram, *The Thought of Mao Tse-tung*, p. 108.

in question form. Was democracy necessary, desirable, and practicable during the war? How could the powers of a strong and effective wartime government be reconciled with the values of democracy? Were the single-party and multiparty systems mutually exclusive? What sort of democracy was best suited to China both during and after the war?

Unity, Resistance, and Reconstruction

From the outset, prodemocracy activists considered the prosecution of the war to be as much political as military, with some going so far as to say that it was political first and military second. Shi Fuliang, a former Nationalist, now an independent, represented a widely held opposition view when he wrote that the political question during the war was about democracy. Military affairs, he contended, were part of politics, and war was an extension of it. The thrust of his argument was that China's ultimate victory would depend on getting her politics right. The government would be able to command the nation's resources – human, financial, and material – to fight and win the war if a democratic political structure and correct policies were put in place. Militarily and economically, the war effort must rely on mass support, and the masses must be mobilized. Mass mobilization, however, was a political issue. "There must be political reform so that the government can rest on a popular basis. With mass support, it will become a really strong and powerful government capable of resisting the Japanese to the very end."[25] For Shi, democracy was an instrument of mass mobilization. To enlist popular support, the government must be prepared to broaden the scope for political participation by establishing representative institutions. The tone of wartime politics was set.

Resistance and reconstruction were regarded as mutually reinforcing. Qian Duansheng, then editor of the short-lived but influential wartime weekly *Jinri pinglun* (Commentary Today), averred:

Without *kangzhan* (resistance) there won't be a nation to reconstruct. Without *jianguo* (national reconstruction), even when the war is won, it will only be a short-term victory as the world is still the same where the strong bullies the weak. Therefore, *jianguo* must

---

[25] Shi Fuliang, *Minzhu kangzhan lun* (On democracy in the war of resistance) (Shanghai: Jinhua shuju, 1937), pp. 18–37; the quote is on p. 21.

take on a meaning not divorced from national security; it is best understood as an extension of *kangzhan*.[26]

The idea of reconstruction during the war was not as ludicrous as it might sound. After 1940, the war became a military stalemate, with the Japanese occupying north China and the eastern coast and the Nationalist government relatively secure in Chongqing. Reconstruction of some sort was possible. Thus, Zhang Shenfu declared that reconstruction was more important than fighting the war. The war was short-term and would come to an end sooner or later, but reconstruction was long-term and must continue after the war. The groundwork for reconstruction, therefore, should be laid during the war, not after.[27]

The question of national unity, or unification – a recurring theme in Chinese politics – concerned the power relations between the political center and the recalcitrant regions. A resolution of this question would require appropriate political and institutional arrangements to be made. The idea of unification by force as historically inevitable prior to reconstruction, once entertained by Jiang Tingfu and Wu Jingchao, was now categorically rejected by thinking people of all political persuasions. "Unification must be built on the general will, the common desire of the people," proclaimed Rural Reconstruction leader Liang Shuming.[28] Unification did not mean unity of thought, but a unity of mind in prosecuting the war to a successful end. There was no room for traitors. Resistance was not the government's responsibility alone, it was also the obligation of every citizen. There was a sense of citizenship, of public ownership and responsibility, which, once aroused, could galvanize the people into action in support of the government's war effort.[29]

The Case for Wartime Democracy and Human Rights

Many would argue that because democracy needed peace it was impossible to carry out political reform when the government was preoccupied with national survival. Against this, the case for democracy was made on a number of grounds. First, democracy was a vital part of *jiuwang*. The

---

[26] Qian Duansheng, "Guojia jinhou de gongzuo yu zeren" (The task and responsibility of the nation from now on), *JRPL* 4:13 (September 29, 1940): 197.

[27] *GMCZH*, I, 526.

[28] Liang Shuming, "Zhongguo tongyi zai hechu qiu?" (Where is Chinese unification to be searched?), *LSMQJ*, VI, 586.

[29] Luo Longji, "Qicheng xianzheng de wojian" (My view on the realization of constitutionalism), *JRPL* 2:22 (November 19, 1939): 339–344.

argument was made at the very outset of the war that *jiuwang* was two-dimensional: China's external and internal problems were crying out for solutions simultaneously. From that perspective, *jiuwang* and *minzhu* (democracy) were not two separate issues. As one Shanghai writer put it, *jiuwang*, apart from resisting Japanese imperialism, was also a democratic movement aimed at the establishment of a democratic republic. "Democracy is the political line in the *jiuwang* movement. To complete the *jiuwang* movement is to carry out the mission for democracy."[30] These were not contradictions, he argued. To save the nation, it was not necessary to bring the democratic movement to a halt. Instead, the two movements should go hand in hand. "The victory of the *jiuwang* movement, therefore, is the victory of going down the democratic path."[31] This contradicts the view that democracy must, of necessity, be subordinated to antiimperialist nationalism. May Fourth veteran philosopher Zhang Shenfu, well known for his writings on Bertrand Russell, spoke of wartime philosophy and a wartime culture fostering science and democracy: "Simply put, science and democracy are the mutually independent, inseparable goals of philosophy. Both are needed in the war of resistance and for the sake of national construction. The formation of science and the implementation of democracy are the preconditions for carrying out the united front and the war of resistance."[32]

Second, democracy was justified on the grounds that it could mobilize human and material resources for prosecuting the war and position China alongside the Allies in the fight against fascism.[33] It was also contended that constitutional democracy would have the effect of reassuring the people of the nation's survival, a much-needed reassurance following the defection of Wang Jingwei to the Japanese in December 1938. From this standpoint, democratic change was a necessary political concession in return for popular trust and support.[34] Unless there was some sort of power sharing, it was argued, the great minds around the country would not be inclined to rally behind the government. Without their support, national unity was unattainable.[35]

---

[30] Fu Yushen, *Minzhu zhengzhi yu jiuwang yundong* (Democratic politics and the national salvation movement) (Shanghai: Guangming shuju, 1937), p. 18.

[31] Ibid., p. 45.

[32] Vera Schwarcz, *Time for Telling Truth Is Running Out: Conversations with Zhang Shenfu* (New Haven: Yale University Press, 1992), pp. 177–183; the quote is on p. 182.

[33] Zhang Shenfu, "Women wei shenme yao minzhu yu ziyou" (Why do we want democracy and liberty), *Xinhua ribao*, September 12, 1944.

[34] See the joint proposal submitted by Zuo Shunsheng et al., *GMCZH*, I, 584–585.

[35] See the joint proposal submitted by Zhang Junmai et al., *GMCZH*, I, 586–588.

War was no barrier to constitutional reform, wrote Chen Qitian of the Youth Party, noting that constitutional change had been achieved in England during times of civil war and by Americans in the War of Independence and that, even in China, the Provisional Constitution of 1912 was the result of civil war. Chen could be faulted for misreading the vastly different situations in England and the United States when the constitutional movements unfolded there. But he was anxious to drive home the message that a successful war of resistance depended absolutely on mass support and that there was no better way of securing such support than an offer of constitutional rule. In his view, people finding themselves in a national crisis could survive only on hopes, and nothing could hold out greater hopes than constitutional rule.[36] He ignored the more immediate problems of survival facing the people to which democracy offered no solutions.

Liang Shuming spoke of the utility of wartime democracy in terms of mass mobilization involving mass participation and popular supervision of government. Defining democracy as a form of "political corporate life," "a process of transforming the majority of the people from passivity to activity," he thought it was the people's spontaneity, voluntarism, and initiative that made mass mobilization work.[37] In his Shandong years of rural reconstruction, he had viewed democracy as "a step in organizational technique," which was underdeveloped in China, and a mechanism for mass participation in village affairs. Like Mao, he was interested in organizing the masses. Defined in those terms, democracy would assist in wartime conscription, which hitherto had been widely resented. Specifically, he wanted mass mobilization units to be part of any wartime representative institutions.[38]

The National Salvationist lawyer Shen Junru maintained that constitutionalism was necessary in times of war because it was important that every citizen and every party concerned – rulers and the ruled, center and periphery, and individual and community – knew what their rights and obligations were under the constitution. Restrictions on rights might be warranted for the sake of national security, but a rule of law and safeguard of civil liberties, particularly free speech and a free press, were not

---

[36] Chen Qitian, *Minzhu xianzheng lun* (On constitutional democracy) (Taibei: Taiwan Shangwu yinshuguan, 1966), pp. 147–149.

[37] Liang Shuming, "Dongyuan yu minzhu" (Mobilization and democracy), *LSMQJ*, VI, 514–515, 518–519, 524–526.

[38] Ibid., pp. 538–539. Liang criticized that members of the PPC and the provincial councils were mostly designated or appointed by the government.

only desirable but also necessary in sustaining the war effort.[39] Shen's argument, emphasizing both rights and obligations, proceeded from a legalistic premise. Deprived of rights, people would feel no obligations toward the state. John Plamenatz has observed: "Democracy is a matter of rights and obligations and of procedures that secure rights and ensure that obligations are, or can be, fulfilled."[40] Shen complained about the deprivation of personal freedoms when citizens were asked to fulfill obligations and to make personal sacrifices. The question, then, was not how much freedom should be curtailed, but how little of it should be enjoyed and safeguarded. What is interesting about Shen's legalistic approach is that obligations to the state requiring personal sacrifices in times of national crisis should be rights-based.

Third, following the utilitarian argument, the case for democracy rested on national imperatives. In May 1944, the Democratic League issued a warning to the government: "If democracy is not realized during the war, then what we will have after the war will not be democracy but the division and ruin of our country. The pain will be ten times of today's."[41] Democracy was considered to be a matter of urgency that could ill afford to wait any longer. Zhang Lan, the League's chairman, went so far as to suggest, naïvely, that democracy would be a panacea to all China's ills: "We believe that if democracy is not realized in China, none of the problems – political, interparty, economic, prices, national resistance, military, and all the others in the social, educational, and cultural areas – can be settled satisfactorily."[42]

An editorial in Kunming's liberal magazine *Ziyou luntan* (Liberty Forum) responded to suggestions that rights and freedoms should be significantly restricted during the war by quoting Harold Laski, who posited that liberty should be enjoyed in times of war as well as in normal times. Otherwise, the people would not want to fight the war or make any contributions to it. The military defeats of Italy and Germany in 1944 were cited as evidence of their citizens not supporting their own governments because they were deprived of their rights and freedoms.[43]

---

[39] Zhou Tiandu, ed., *Shen Junru wenji* (The collected works of Shen Junru) (Beijing: Renmin chubanshe, 1994), pp. 411–436.

[40] John Plamenatz, *Democracy and Illusion: An Examination of Certain Aspects of Modern Democratic Terror* (London: Longman, 1973), p. 181.

[41] *MMWX*, p. 18.

[42] See Zhang Lan's foreign press conference in Chongqing on August 3, 1945, *MMWX*, p. 53.

[43] *Ziyou luntan* 3:2 (October 1, 1944): 1.

There was also an international factor in their argument. The Second World War was perceived to be a global struggle between democracy and fascism. China was on the side of the Allies, which had the effect of enhancing the cause of Chinese democracy and strengthening the forces of enlightenment. It would appear that only a China aspiring to be democratic could find a place in the ranks of the democratic states and enjoy their support. National salvation, which was more than fighting the Japanese, would be assured if only China became enlightened, modern, and democratic.

The case for wartime democracy was inseparable from the campaign for human rights that resurfaced in the summer of 1941. The campaign was launched in the pages of the magazine *Shidai pinglun* (Modern Critique), which was first published in Beijing and later in Hong Kong under the editorship of Zhou Jingwen, a member of the Democratic League. Numbers 73 and 74 of volume 3 of *Shidai pinglun* came out as a special issue on the subject and were later reprinted as a book.[44] The articles there dealt with various aspects of human rights, including their nature, origins, and status as a movement in China. For our purpose, it is interesting to look at their thoughts on the relationship between the war and democracy and human rights.

Their arguments for human rights were not different from those for democracy, the common theme being that resistance to the Japanese required popular support. If the Chinese people enjoyed the freedoms of the person, residence, religious belief, speech, publication, assembly, and association, wrote one article, they would be willing to make substantial contributions to the government's war effort in numerous ways, thereby consolidating national unity.[45] Zou Taofen, who had been clamoring for a relaxation of the press censorship and other civil liberties in the PPC, argued that there was a correlation between human rights protection and multiparty unity in the conduct of the war. Only with protection of human rights could there be unity, and only with unity could people from different political backgrounds work together, and only when they worked together could human rights continue to be safeguarded.[46] Human rights were linked with democracy. "Human rights are

---

[44] See Zhou Jingwen, ed., *Renquan yundong zhuanhao* (Special issue on the human rights movement) (Hong Kong: Shidai piping she, 1941). I use this book for the following citations.

[45] Lin Guanping, "Renquan yundong yu tuanjie kangzhan" (The human rights movement and unity in the War of Resistance), in ibid., pp. 35–36.

[46] Zou Taofen, "Dangpai yu renquan" (Party and groups and human rights), in ibid., pp. 5–7.

the most basic content of democratic politics," one writer maintained. "The human rights campaign is the preliminary step of democratic politics. It can also be said to be democracy's enlightenment movement."[47] The writer feared that a constitution alone was no guarantee for human rights; the only guarantee was the establishment of a democratic system. He rejected suggestions that human rights and democracy were unwarranted in times of war, contending that China was fighting a war of national liberation in which there was an identity of interests between the people and the state. To protect popular interests and human rights therefore could only enhance the people's capacity for resistance.[48] The war, said another writer, was also a struggle for democracy. Unless this struggle was successful, there was no way of protecting human rights. Thus, the positive goals of the human rights movement were a rule of law and democracy.[49] According to another article, the war of national liberation was related to democracy and human rights because the people wanted to be free. They did not wish to find at the end of the war that they remained "domestic slaves" (*jianu*) while the same privileged class continued to hold the reins of power. Why should they be making endeavors and personal sacrifices to save the nation from imperialism only to benefit the ruling class? The human rights campaign must develop to ensure that when the war was won, the people would be free also from the shackles of autocratic rule.[50]

War is, more often than not, the enemy of civil and political rights suppressed ostensibly in the national interest. In making their case for democracy, Chinese liberals and democrats conflated it with nationalism. Lucian Pye has noted: "Nationalism provides not just the basis of loyalty of a people to their nation-state but also defines the role of leaders, and in so doing sets limits on their conduct."[51] Nationalism also defines citizen's rights and obligations and, in the process, the relationship between rulers and the ruled. The sense of citizenship helps to focus loyalty on the nation-state, especially during a national crisis. The vexed

---

[47] Han Qiutong, "Renquan yundong yu minzhu zhengzhi" (The human rights movement and democratic politics), in ibid., p. 37.

[48] Ibid., pp. 38–39.

[49] Xiao Zhongna, "Dangqian renquan yundong de tezheng ji qi zhongxin renwu" (The current human rights movement and its characteristics and central tasks), in ibid., pp. 74–77.

[50] YCS (pseudonym), "Renquan yundong yu kangzhan" (The human rights movement and the war of resistance), in ibid., pp. 88–89.

[51] Lucian W. Pye, "How China's Nationalism Was Shanghaied," in Jonathan Unger, ed., *Chinese Nationalism* (Armonk, NY: M. E. Sharpe, 1996), p. 88.

question in the present case is, was constitutional democracy practicable in the midst of an all-out war?

The Practicability of Constitutional Democracy in Wartime

Dison Poe, a government member, observed that, even in the West, there was "a conspicuous shrinkage of democratic practices" during the war. Both the British wartime cabinet and the American president were given extraordinary powers. The British Parliament was extended time and again, and President Franklin Roosevelt was reelected to the White House a fourth time. There was no "acute and immediate need" for China to pursue democracy. What China needed was a strong and powerful government capable of asserting its authority and getting things done.[52]

In the opposition camp, the terms *democracy* and *constitutionalism* were used interchangeably. Thus, to be democratic was to implement constitutional rule, meaning local self-government, a rule of law, protection of rights and civil liberties, recognition of all the political parties, depoliticization of the nation's armies, separation of party and government, and so on. Then again, the question arose: was constitutional rule feasible pending the adoption and promulgation of a constitution? An editorial in *Ziyou luntan* thought so:

> Do not view constitutional rule as a lofty ideal beyond our reach. It is only the politics of obeying the law. In the constitutional states generally, governments rule by the law, and people act in accordance with the law, while civil liberties are protected. . . . From government to people . . . everyone is equal before the law. *Constitutional rule is not necessarily democratic rule, but it must manifest itself in a rule of law* [emphasis added]. . . . It is not a complicated matter, and it can be put into effect at any time.[53]

Reduced to a rule of law, constitutional government was not out of reach. But the nexus between the rule of law and democracy was not lost

---

[52] Dison Hsueh-feng Poe, "Comments on Lawrence N. Shyu, 'China's 'Wartime Parliament': The People's Political Council, 1938–1945,'" in Paul K. T. Sih, ed., *Nationalist China During the Sino-Japanese War, 1937–1945* (Hicksville, NY: Exposition Press, 1977), p. 315. Poe was a member of the wartime Supreme National Defense Council.

[53] Leading article, "Tan xianzheng" (On constitutionalism), *Ziyou luntan* 2:2 (February 1, 1944): 1. The author's name was not stated.

on the democracy advocates. Echoing the general sentiment of his liberal colleagues, Wu Zhizhuang, a professor at the Southwest Associated University, wrote that a rule of law must rest on the notions of human rights and democracy; maintaining law and order was only part of it. Citing the example of Britain, he explained that Britons had great respect for the rule of law because it had developed simultaneously with democracy. In other words, it was democracy that underpinned the British legal system. The same was true of the Americans and their legal system. To Wu, a rule of law presupposed democratic rule.[54]

Democracy, John Keanes has observed, is a process for arriving at collective decisions in which interested parties and their representatives participate. Democratic procedures include a rule of law and constitutional guarantees of a whole range of freedoms and liberties.[55] Laying down procedures and requiring everyone and every interested party, especially those in authority, to follow them is an essential part of the rule of law. Procedures, like laws, can be changed through the democratic process, but not at the whim of those in authority. The opposition elite was convinced that a rule of law, as a basis for constitutional government, could be established, in spite of the war.[56]

Distinguishing between constitution (*xianfa*) and constitutional rule (*xianzheng*), Wu Zhizhuang noted that the road to constitutional rule varied from society to society. In some countries, constitutional rule was a sham. Only those that "practice the *substance* of constitutional rule" could be said to be constitutional states. All fascist states had constitutions, he observed, but that did not stop them from becoming dictatorships. In such countries as Britain, the United States, and Canada, constitutional rule was built on social customs and practices. The thrust of his argument was that a constitutional culture – what he called "the constitutional life of the people" – should be fostered while a constitution was being framed. In this sense, constitutional rule – in a very informal sense – was possible pending the promulgation of a constitution. It was useless to have a constitution without the substance of constitutional

---

[54] Wu Zhizhuang, "Zhongguo de fazhi yu minzhu" (China's rule of law and democracy), *Ziyou luntan* 1:5–6 combined (August 30, 1943): 3–5.

[55] John Keanes, "Democracy and the Media: Without Foundations," *Political Studies* 40 (1992): 124.

[56] See Wu Zhizhuang, "Zhongguo de fazhi yu minzhu." See also Wang Gongyu, "Fazhi minzhu yu tongyi" (Rule of law, democracy, and unification), *JRPL* 1:16 (April 16, 1939): 6–8; Lou Bangyan, "Dangzhi yu fazhi" (Party rule and rule of law), *JRPL* 5:2 (January 1941): 10–12; and Wu Han, "Zhiren yu zhifa" (Rule of man and rule of law), *Ziyou luntan* 2:3 (March 1, 1944): 19–21.

rule. The constitution, in his view, should be an instrument of reform in a rapidly changing society, with popular sovereignty, liberty, and equality being the key to constitutional rule. He did not underestimate the length of time needed for China to become a constitutional state – a matter of years – but he thought that the protracted war against Japan and the rapid changes taking place in China would produce "new strengths" to assist in the process.[57]

To be sure, there were preconditions for constitutional democracy. But, argued Zhang Shenfu, these were not absolute, depending on circumstances and the stage of historical development. Democracy, like science, is a trial, an experiment; perfect democracy could not be achieved in a short time, and people must enjoy civil liberties before they can talk about democracy.[58] From this perspective, a small step toward democracy could be taken in spite of the war.

But the war did militate against any attempts at democratization, a point not lost on those who were torn between ideal and reality. Writing in May 1940, Luo Longji conceded that in the existing circumstances popular sovereignty was less important than administrative efficiency. Drawing on the Chinese classic *Li Yun*, which contained a precept that "the Great Way is to regard all under Heaven as public and to select the virtuous and the able [for government] (*da dao zhi xing ye, tianxia weigong, xuanxian yu neng*)," he gave a narrower meaning to "opening up the regime." In the midst of the war, he explained, "opening up the regime" did not mean the election of a popular government under a new constitution, which was impossible, but rather the formation of a "national consensus government" into which were brought the best minds, regardless of their party affiliations. These people, described as political experts in his earlier writings, were to replace the current incumbents who were inefficient and unqualified for their jobs. Such "personnel adjustment" was to be coupled with "administrative restructuring" pending constitutional rule. Luo cited the British wartime cabinet as a good model of a multitalented wartime government. A temporary expediency in China's case would be to trade off a popularly elected government for good governance, the latter being consistent with the centuries-old tradition of moralistic and paternalistic rule. Meanwhile,

---

[57] Wu Zhizhuang, "Zhuanbian shehui zhong de Zhongguo xianfa yu xianzheng" (The Chinese constitution and constitutionalism in a changing society), *Ziyou luntan* 2:3 (March 1, 1944): 2–7.

[58] Zhang Shenfu, "Minzhu yu zhexue" (Democracy and philosophy), *Ziyou luntan* 3:3 (November 1, 1944): 9–10.

a little democracy could be achieved by increasing the powers of the PPC without a further broadening of political participation.[59]

In this trade-off, the wartime government was to enjoy extraordinary powers. The question remained: how could it be reconciled with the values of democracy?

Tensions Between Powerful Government and Democratic Values

The question of tension in this regard applied to peacetime and wartime alike, although it is more relevant to the latter. A powerful government, almost by definition, was one with concentrated powers (*jiquan*). In Chinese politics, the traditional form of *jiquan* was simultaneously bureaucratic and autocratic, with its powers coming from the top down. What the democrats wanted was a modern form of *jiquan*, with its powers derived from below, representing the general will, the outcome of a democratic process involving the participation of "the conscious masses." This was, they argued, what China needed during the war.[60] The legitimacy of a powerful wartime government must rest on popular consent. In this way, there could be no tension between *jiquan* and *minzhu*.[61] It seemed convenient simply to ignore the tension by dwelling on their mutually reinforcing capacity. Thus, one scholar likened leadership of the state to the head of a body, the government structure to the arms, and the people to the hands and fingers. For the body to function effectively, the head, the arms, the hands, and the fingers must coordinate and work in unison. Without democracy, there could be no real, effective concentration of powers.[62]

Zhang Junmai, who had written on the idea of a "national consensus government,"[63] was impressed with what he saw in wartime Britain, too. He found there "a politics of leadership" that enjoyed the support of Parliament. The wartime prime minister exercised extraordinary powers with the consent of the people, Parliament, and all political parties. In normal times, he noted, British politics were characterized by a free play

---

[59] Luo Longji, "Lun gongkai zhengquan" (On opening up the regime), *JRPL* 3:21 (May 26, 1940): 323–326.

[60] Shi Fuliang, *Minzhu kangzhan lun*, pp. 171–174.

[61] Wang Gongyu, "Jiquan yu minzhu" (Concentrated powers and democracy), *JRPL* 3:1 (January 7, 1940): 9–11.

[62] Zhang Zhirang, "Zhongguo xianzheng yundong yu shijie minzhu chaoliu" (The Chinese constitutional movement and the democratic world tide), *Xianzheng yuekan* 1 (1944): 4.

[63] See Chapter 4, pp. 139–140.

of individual and party interests and respect for personal freedoms. During a war or national crisis, however, partisan interests were put aside. The citizens were willing to forgo some of their liberties for the good of the nation, displaying what he called "a spirit of great patriotism" (*da aiguoxin*) by placing the national interest above personal, party, or group interests. It was their ability to mobilize, support, and sacrifice for the country that enabled Britain to turn initial defeats into ultimate victory. This sense of great patriotism transcended party lines. It rested on the notion of rule of law emphasizing, politically, the "rules of the game" (*gongtong guize*), which he understood to be political ethics entailing fair competition free from violence and military interference. In Britain, the Magna Carta provided a legal foundation for the state and continuity for the political system as it evolved through the centuries. There were peaceful means of adjusting and coordinating the plans and proposals of individuals and parties, as well as a commitment to personal freedoms. What most impressed Zhang was the British democratic tradition that made a powerful wartime cabinet possible and temporary restraints on personal liberties acceptable to the British people. He saw a lesson for China in British politics. It was important to tackle the political problems at hand by recognizing the freedom of speech, legalizing all other political parties, expanding the powers of the PPC, and implementing political reform, all of which would promote "a spirit of great patriotism" supporting a strong wartime Chinese government.[64] It follows that the problem with China was its lack of a democratic tradition, and that was precisely why such a tradition should be fostered. Until then, there could be no resolution of the tension between concentration of powers and democratic values.

Could good governance ease the tensions? Perhaps. But, as Luo Longji pointed out, the Nationalists could not provide good government without effecting personnel and structural reforms. Such reforms underscored the importance of political institutions, or "the institutionalization of politics" (*zhengzhi zhiduhua*), the topic of a few articles in *Jinri pinglun*,[65] highlighting the lack of institutional development as the basic

[64] Zhang Junmai, "Da aiguoxin" (Great patriotism), *Minxian* 1:2 (May 31, 1944): 1–4.
[65] See, for example, Fu Mengzhen (Fu Sinian). "Zhengzhi zhi jigouhua" (The institutionalization of politics), *JRPL* 1: 1 (January 1, 1939): 3–5; Qian Duansheng, "Zhengzhi de zhiduhua" (The institutionalization of politics), *JRPL* 1:7 (February 12, 1939): 4–5; Zhang Foquan, "Lun zhengzhi zhi zhiduhua (On the institutionalization of politics), *JRPL* 1:19 (May 7, 1939): 4–5; and Luo Wengang, "Lizhi zhiduhua" (The institutionalization of public administration), *JRPL* 1:24 (June 13, 1939): 3–4.

problem with Chinese politics and public administration. Both rulers and the ruled were to blame for that: the rulers because they took advantage of the traditional *renzhi* (rule of man), and the ruled because they obeyed only those in authority, not the law itself. "Whatever systems may be in place, there is no respect for institutions, only fear of those in authority," Qian Duansheng complained, calling on the government to develop institutions and to foster an institutional culture.[66]

Samuel Huntington uses institutionalization as a basis for evaluating whether a government is strong and modern or weak and backward.[67] Measured against this criterion, the Nationalist government must be judged as weak and backward. Institutional reform would strengthen and modernize the regime, reduce the tension between concentrated powers and democracy, and, in the process, boost the political stocks of the GMD itself. If good governance was produced as a result, could a case not be made for continued one-party rule even after the war?

Single-Party System or Multiparty System?

Qian Duansheng took the lead in this debate. In a June 1940 article, he wrote that, even though China should adopt a multiparty system in the future, for the present all the MPGs should recognize the leadership of the GMD (which they did actually) and adopt the Three Principles of the People, subject to differing interpretations, which allowed for policy differences. Competition was good because it would force the GMD to lift its game. There remained the communist problem, which, he suggested, could be dealt with in two ways. First, the Red Army and the border regions ought to be abolished because there should be only one Chinese government and army. Second, communism should be allowed to compete with the state and other ideologies in the marketplace of ideas. Qian was confident that communism would be rejected by the bulk

---

[66] Qian Duansheng, "Zhengzhi de zhiduhua," pp. 4–5. Qian identified two other areas of reform: government structure and personnel. In terms of structural change, his emphasis was on the central government, where powers should be concentrated in the appropriate authorities with functional differentiation and no duplication of offices. In terms of personnel, the emphasis was placed on a nondiscriminatory recruitment policy based on ability, discipline, and personal character so as to eradicate official corruption and to ensure getting the best person for the job. See Qian Duansheng, "Kangzhan zhisheng de tujing" (The path to war victory), *JRPL* 1:11 (December 3, 1939): 5–7.
[67] Samuel P. Huntington, "Political Development and Political Decay," *World Politics* 17 (April 1965): 386–430.

of the population when they realized what it was all about; particularly they would find communist violence repugnant. He desired to see one-party rule abandoned after the opening of the National Assembly, scheduled for November 12, 1940 (postponed in the event).[68]

Four months later, Qian confronted the decades-old conundrum of what sort of political system China needed. He thought it should be one that was operational, endurable, compatible with the national character, and, most important, capable of resolving China's pressing problems. He was convinced that it was neither the old-style Chinese bureaucracy nor Anglo-American democracy and that only a government with extraordinary powers could be efficient, up to the tasks of resistance and reconstruction, and generate national wealth and power. But he feared that it would be repressive. So the best government should be both "authoritarian and humanistic," respecting "individuality and human dignity." That was not a tall order for him, for he had high regard for Chiang Kai-shek, who could be given concentrated powers, provided that he was assisted by a representative body.[69]

Qian now came out strongly in favor of the single-party system *even after the war*, for he believed that the multiparty system was going to wither in the world.

> If Germany, Italy, and Japan win this world war, Euro-American democracy and all the systems associated with it, including the multiparty system, will be abandoned. . . . Conversely, if China, Britain, and the United States win, the victorious nations, in order to maintain their national strengths and redress internal class inequalities, will also replace the multiparty system with the single-party system.[70]

If President Roosevelt were reelected, he went on, there would be a further increase in state powers, a prospect that would be welcomed by the Democratic and Republican Parties alike, thereby rendering party differences insignificant. And if Britain won the European War, she would become an "advanced socialist state," where the existence of multiple parties would be in doubt.[71] His predictions could not have been farther from the mark.

---

[68] Qian Duansheng, "Lun dang" (On political parties), *JRPL* 3:23 (June 9, 1940): 355–358.
[69] Qian Duansheng, "Women xuyao de zhengzhi zhidu" (The political system we need), *JRPL* 4:15 (October 13, 1940): 228–230.
[70] Qian Duansheng, "Yidang yu duodang" (Single party or multiple parties), *JRPL* 4:16 (October 20, 1940): 246.
[71] Ibid., p. 247.

Once again, international influences played a part in Chinese political thinking. Qian's articles immediately followed the German *blitzkreig* and the fall of France in June 1940, which helped to revive the prewar perception that dictatorship was superior after all. What attracted Qian to the single-party system, in view of the latest German successes, was its assumed capacity to change society, to boost production, and to improve the people's livelihood, as well as the perception that the multiparty system weakened the authority of the state – arguments that he had made in support of neo-dictatorship six years before. Now he held that a government with extraordinary powers would not inevitably clash with democracy if the ruling party was a truly democratic party "respecting individuality and human dignity" and "promoting the public good, peace, and universal harmony."[72]

Qian wrote off the minor parties, notably the Youth Party and the National Socialist Party, on the grounds that they were too small, too ineffective, and ideologically indistinguishable from the GMD. All things considered, he believed, the GMD, for all its faults, was still best suited to lead the country, a view with which most critics would agree. It needed reform, however, and must respect civil liberties. A reformed GMD would enjoy popular support, and, with good policies in place, would stay in power for a long time to come. The world had entered upon an era of single-party politics, he concluded, and China should be part of it.[73]

Qian's articles provoked a sharp critique from Luo Longji. Questioning Qian's understanding of the political trend in the West, Luo rejected his predictions about future developments in Britain and the United States and expressed a positive view of the prospect of multiparty systems in the postwar world order. It was premature to say who would eventually win the European War, despite the French and British setbacks. Moreover, Luo argued, the European situation had nothing to do with the political systems of the belligerent states, pointing out that Germany enjoyed military superiority to Britain and France, but not to the United States, whereas Italy was inferior to both Britain and France. The Germans were scientifically advanced and possessed many national character traits that contributed to their war efforts. The temporary setbacks of Britain and France were caused by their diplomatic failure to induce the Soviet Union to fight alongside them. Finally, Luo contrasted the failure of the GMD dictatorship with the success of Hitler's Germany: China had a longer history of one-party dictatorship than

---

[72] Ibid., p. 246.   [73] Ibid., p. 247.

Germany, and yet, despite some achievements, the GMD regime was a failure overall.[74]

As others had done before, Luo challenged the assumption that dictatorship promoted efficiency where democracy did not. He made three points: (1) power was not the only condition for efficiency; (2) China's inefficiency was not due to a lack of dictatorial powers; and (3) democracy could accommodate political forces that were real, endurable, and expandable. In China's case, the way to achieve efficiency was not to give more powers to the existing regime but to implement political reform and establish a sound system so that those in authority could not be self-serving. Efficiency meant not only a capacity to make decisions and to carry out policies quickly and flexibly but also the economy of time, energy, and resources. It was efficient to make decisions and implement policies with a minimum of time, energy, and resources. By the same token, it was efficient to minimize social sacrifices to achieve maximum benefits for the largest number. Efficiency had much to do with the quality of the organization and the caliber of the people who did the work. Traditionally, Chinese politics were authoritarian, and yet Chinese administration had always been inefficient. Luo concluded that good personnel and good organization made a difference.[75] The question of expertocracy was revisited.

Concerning the tension between democracy and concentrated powers, Luo's argument was, first, theoretical: a truly democratic party cannot preside over a dictatorship, a dictatorship cannot respect "individuality and human dignity," and democracy is inseparable from the multiparty system.[76] Then, turning to Chinese politics, he agreed that the GMD was still the most appropriate party to rule China and that Chiang Kai-shek was the best person to lead it. He also concurred that the Youth Party and the National Socialist Party were too small, too weak, and too ineffective. But he thought that they should not be written off but rather be accorded legal recognition immediately so that they could compete for power openly and peacefully, which would be for the betterment of Chinese politics. There was no dispute that competition would be good for the GMD, the consensus being that if the Nationalists would live up

---

[74] Luo Longji, "Ouzhan yu minzhu zhuyi de qiantu" (The European War and the future of democracy), *JRPL* 4:1 (July 7, 1940): 10–13.

[75] Luo Longji, "Quanli yu xiaolu" (Power and efficiency), *JRPL* 4:9 (September 1, 1940): 134–137.

[76] Luo Longji, "Zhongguo muqian de zhengdang wenti (shang)" (China's current problems with political parties [part 1]), *JRPL* 4:24 (December 18, 1940): 376–379.

to their democratic promises, they could retain power for a very long time to come.[77]

In a rejoinder to Luo's critique, Qian reaffirmed his position on the single-party system, but he also challenged the GMD to revitalize its ideology, to improve the quality of its members, to make itself self-sufficient rather than depend on state funding, and to separate the Party from the government. He also argued for the legal rights of the minor parties, but reiterated that if the GMD provided good government, not only would it be popular but the rationale for the existence of the other parties would also diminish.[78] In 1942, writing for an American readership, Qian thought it "unthinkable" to expect the GMD to "practice self-denial and give up political power to its rivals or opponents."[79] But political liberalization within the Party was important for the future of Chinese democracy. "Perhaps to practice democracy inside the [GMD] is of more real significance than to try vainly to establish democracy for the country at large. If during the period of reconstruction the country shall continue in the hands of the [GMD], as it is not unlikely to do, it is evident that it will not be democratized before the Party itself is democratized."[80] His argument calls to mind the idea of *dangnei minzhu* that Chen Zhimai had articulated before the war.[81]

The fall of France in June 1940 was capable of a different interpretation: it did not represent a victory of fascism over democracy, as the dictatorship advocates would have it. One professor at the Southwest Associated University pointed out that Britain's defense against the Nazi invasion remained quite strong.[82] Another contended that the "successes" of the Soviet Union, Germany, and Italy demonstrated not the failure of democratic experiments but the fact that the experiments had not been given full play. It was a myth that dictatorship could deal with the economy more effectively. Witness the dictatorial regimes of Europe that were actually facing more economic difficulties. Even though the good professor acknowledged that Western democracies had shortcomings and deficiencies that needed some readjustment and reform, he was

---

[77] See the second part of Luo's article, *JRPL* 4:25 (December 25, 1940): 392–397.
[78] Qian Duansheng, "Lun dangwu" (On party affairs), *JRPL* 5:14 (April 13, 1941): 234–236.
[79] Ch'ien Tuan-sheng, "War-time Government in China," *American Political Science Review* 36:5 (October 1942): 869.
[80] Ibid., p. 871.   [81] See Chapter 4, pp. 129–131.
[82] Li Shuqing, "Lun minzu zhuyi" (On democracy), *JRPL* 4:18 (November 3, 1940): 282–284.

optimistic about democracy's survival and prospects.[83] He expected to see a multiparty system installed in postwar China, adding that a start of constitutional rule during the war would prepare the country for a peaceful transfer of power.[84]

In the latter half of 1943, German forces were in retreat. Then came the D-Day invasion in June 1944, followed by the encircling of Germany in July. By the end of the year, Belgium and France were almost entirely liberated. In mid-December, the Germans launched a considerable counteroffensive in the Ardennes, but this Battle of the Bulge was the last major effort in the west. At the end of January 1945, the Germans were again driven out of France and, two months later, were pushed back to their western frontiers of 1919. On the China front, the Japanese attacked the defenses of the Yellow River near Zhengzhou in April 1944, marking the beginning of a general offensive in central Henan and of the transcontinental Ichigo Offensive, which lasted until December. The Japanese offensive was quite successful throughout 1944, although it was not without resistance. Nonetheless, the Chinese were encouraged by developments in Europe, especially after the Yalta meeting of Roosevelt, Churchill, and Stalin in February 1945. (Chiang Kai-shek was not told about the secret agreement whereby Russian troops would be sent to Manchuria after the end of the European War on the condition that the status quo was preserved in Outer Mongolia, that the port of Dalian was internationalized, and that Port Arthur (Lüshun) was leased to the Soviet Union for use as a naval base.)

With the end of the war in sight, democracy seemed to be the future toward which the world was inexorably moving. Chinese democrats were reinforced in their view that China should stand at the forefront of that future by becoming a democracy. To be democratic was to be progressive and to ride on the crest of the world tide. Yet many thought that China was a case sui generis, where foreign models could not be copied straightaway. Toward the end of the war, the question was not whether a democratic form of government was good, but whether there was a middle path between the single-party and multiparty systems. The view of Liang Shuming in this respect deserves some attention.

---

[83] Wang Gongyu, "Tantan ducai zhengzhi" (On dictatorship), *JRPL* 5:9 (March 9, 1941): 143.

[84] Wang Gongyu, "Zoushang xianzheng zhi lu" (Going down the constitutional road), *JRPL* 2:23 (November 26, 1939): 359.

Liang Shuming's Single–Multiple Inclusive System

As a founder of the Democratic League, Liang was a cultural conservative and not nearly as liberal as Luo Longji or Zhang Junmai. He had
written numerous articles on Chinese politics during the war period, even
though his ideas were at times inconsistent and not well articulated.[85]
Earlier (1930 and 1931) he had expressed the view that European
democracy was "the first no-through road for Chinese politics," and
Soviet communism was "the second no-through road."[86] He did not
approve of parliamentary politics and Western-style elections for China
under the existing conditions and had no objections to one-party rule
per se in a changing society where a new order was yet to be established.
In 1941, speaking of political parties, he divided them into two broad categories. One consisted of revolutionary parties, such as the GMD, the
CCP, the Soviet Communist Party, and Italy's Fascist Party, all of which
sought to overthrow the ancien regime and to establish a new political
order. Representing revolutionary movements, these parties attempted
to accomplish certain historical missions. Another category consisted of
political parties competing freely for power according to established
rules and procedures, and representing sectional interests and different
social forces with their own political ideals, platforms, policies, and
agendas – such as those in Britain and the United States. A single-party
system was suitable where a new political order was just being
constructed, whereas a multiparty system was appropriate where the
political order was already well established.[87] In revolutionary China, a
case could be made for one-party rule. However, Liang was concerned
about the shortcomings of the GMD, not the least because of the
ambiguities of its class base and revolutionary targets. In his view, the
government had been an abject failure.[88] The existence of the opposition
parties, including the CCP, was a reality that ought to be recognized.

---

[85] This is my personal view based on my reading of his writings.

[86] Liang Shuming, "Women zhengzhi shang de diyige butong de lu" (The first no-through
road for Chinese politics), and "Women zhengzhi shang de dierge butong de lu"
(The second no-through road for Chinese politics), *LSMQJ*, V, 133–173 and 261–294,
respectively.

[87] Liang Shuming, "Zhongguo dangpai wenti de qiantu" (Questions on the future of
Chinese party politics), *LSMQJ*, VI, 569–572.

[88] The government had failed to unify the nation, to carry out the plan of land equalization, and to eliminate warlordism, and it was divorced from the masses. See Guy S. Alitto,
The Last Confucian: Liang Shu-ming and the Chinese Dilemma of Modernity (Berkeley: University of California Press, 1979), p. 204.

Thus, he was searching for a system for China that would have the best of both worlds – what he called a "single–multiple inclusive system" (*yiduo xiangrongzhi*) having two tiers. The first tier was where the GMD stood above all the others. The second tier was made up of all the other parties and groups representing sectional interests but all supporting the GMD; they would have a voice in the affairs of state by being involved in the policy-making process. Between the two tiers there was constant interaction and close cooperation. Multiparty consultation and deliberation would resolve policy differences in a spirit of tolerance. For Liang, this was a Chinese way of problem solving. Convinced that Chinese society was culturally unique, he was not interested in foreign solutions to Chinese problems, showing his distaste for foreign models.[89]

Liang's two-tiered system approximates Samuel Huntington's dominant-party system. Huntington has observed: "In a dominant-party system only one party has the capacity to govern, but two or more opposition parties, usually representing more specialized social forces, are sufficiently strong so that they can affect the political process which goes on within the dominant party. The dominant party, in short, does not monopolize politics; it must, in some measures, be responsive to other groups of political actors."[90] In Nationalist China, only the CCP would be "sufficiently strong" to "affect the political process which goes on within the dominant party" even if the GMD did not monopolize politics. Liang's prescription rested on a different assumption that fierce competition, Western-style, would lead to division, antagonism, and confrontation, thus weakening the state, undermining national solidarity, and impeding reconstruction. Chinese political parties, he further assumed, had a good deal in common regarding broad policy objectives and were capable of mutual trust and developing strategies to reach the common goal.

These assumptions create three problems. First, the common good was a myth, the reality being that each party was fighting for its own interests in a political game where the rules were not predetermined. Second, the GMD was not prepared to share power. Third, Chinese politics were conflict-prone and personalistic. Although one-party rule, as distinct from one-party dictatorship, was acceptable to him, Liang

---

[89] Liang Shuming, "Wo nuli de shi shenme," *LSMQJ*, VI, 222–224.
[90] Samuel P. Huntington, *Political Order in Changing Societies* (New Haven: Yale University Press, 1968), p. 419.

feared that without support and inputs from the second tier it would be dictatorial, repressive, and incapable of unification and reconstruction. His inclusive system depended for its success on the sufferance and good conscience of the dominant party on the one hand and the cooperation of the second tier on the other. It had no vision of institutionalized opposition.

Nor can it be fully understood in political terms, for it grew out of Liang's culturalist view of democracy. Guy Alitto has suggested that Liang's theory of political democracy was informed by his own "explicitly anti-liberal, anti-Marxist theory of China's unique culture."[91] Recently, Ip Hung-yok has challenged his portrayal of Liang as a reluctant supporter of Western values and Westernization who proposed a "contradictory solution" to "the Chinese dilemma of modernity." Her controversial view is that Liang "pointed precisely to the compatibility of Chinese and Western cultures" and that this cultural defender "could appreciate the individual-oriented value embedded in democracy as a kind of value both precious and alien." Liang, Ip continues, "could recognize the autonomous moral value of liberty and rights, and advocate integrating them into what the Chinese esteemed most highly – the realm of morality."[92] Yet Liang held a strong conviction that the root cause of China's political problems since the early Republic was fundamentally cultural. He argued that even though China's old culture had been eroded by the new influences of the West, a new culture absorbing the best of Western values while remaining distinctively Chinese was yet to be created. Apart from the modern cultures of Britain and the United States, there also was the culture of the Soviet Union, which was making an impact around the world. China should study these alien cultures with a view to developing a new Chinese culture that would have the best of all possible worlds. The failure to do so thus far had caused what Liang called "a loss of cultural harmony" (*wenhua shitiao*).[93] He posited that democracy entailed the recognition of other people (*chengren pangren*) as well as of oneself, of equality, of reason, and of majority votes, and the respect for individual liberty, all of which were compatible with the Confucian values of *shu* (forgiveness), *qian* (modesty), and *rang* (concession). But he also believed that the manifestations of democracy

---

[91] Alitto, *The Last Confucian*, p. 297.

[92] Hung-yok Ip, "Liang Shuming and the Idea of Democracy in Modern China," *Modern China* 17:4 (October 1991): 469–508; the quotes are on pp. 473 and 474.

[93] Liang Shuming, "Zhengzhi de genben zai wenhua" (The roots of politics lie in culture), *LSMQJ*, VI, 686–689.

varied from society to society, depending in no small part on the cultural traditions of each society.[94]

Liang feared that, in China's case, the ideas of "the individual being at the center position" (*geren benwei*) and of free competition, Western style, would exacerbate the "looseness" of the Chinese people. Here he subscribed to Sun Yat-sen's sheet-of-loose-sand theory. Because of significant historical and cultural differences between China and the West, he did not consider British-style constitutionalism appropriate for China. He would speak later in 1947 of an "election disaster" (*xuanzai*), arguing that competitive elections of the Western type, which required aggressiveness and self-exhibition, were neither Chinese style nor good for China. Although he had no problem with the Anglo-American systems for Britons and Americans themselves, he thought that Chinese civilization, compared with other world civilizations, was so "premature" (*zaoshu*, meaning that spiritually China had advanced far ahead of its socioeconomic development)[95] that constitutionalism was not something that should be copied from the West. Although he concurred that China needed democracy and constitutional rule as the cure for one-party rule and personal dictatorship, he was convinced that constitutional democracy in China must grow out of Chinese culture, reflecting the best of Chinese values and recognizing China's realities. He believed in government by a minority of virtuous men and experts, scoffing at the idea of majority votes in policy and decision making. He would have agreed with the eighteenth-century European Enlightenment thinkers who held that a good form of government was based not on the caprice of the majorities but on reason and right as found in the eternal order of things, and that the correct policy was not derived from a vote of hands. He warned against borrowing *blindly* from the West, adamant that the West, too, should learn from China. Indeed, he looked forward to a Chinese Renaissance, convinced of the ultimate superiority of Chinese culture.[96]

This kind of culturalism influenced the development of Liang's single–multiple inclusive system. But his view that the parliamentary system and competitive politics were incompatible with Chinese cultural

---

[94] See his 1949 book *Zhongguo wenhua yaoyi* (The essence of Chinese culture), in *LSMQJ*, III, 1–316, esp. pp. 240–245.

[95] This is the thrust of his 1921 book *Dongxi wenhua ji qi zhexue* (The cultures and philosophies of East and West), in *LSMQJ*, I, 321–540.

[96] Liang Shuming, "Yugao xuanzai, zuilun xianzheng" (Warning on the disaster of elections and reflection on constitutionalism), *LSMQJ*, VI, 699–722. This article, in two parts, was originally published in *Guancha* in September 1947.

traditions was not prevalent among China's liberal intellectuals. Luo Longji, Hu Shi, Zhang Junmai, and other Western-educated scholars would have rejected it. Nevertheless, Liang's desire for multiparty cooperation could be reconciled with the idea of pluralistic politics entertained by other MPG leaders who had been calling for the formation of an interim coalition government that would allow room for both opposition and cooperation. We shall write more on coalition government in the next two chapters. For the moment, Liang's culturalist view of politics raises questions about the opposition elite's understanding of democracy.

UNDERSTANDING DEMOCRACY

So far we have seen that Chinese liberal intellectuals approached democracy from an instrumental vantage point. There was little theoretical exposition of it, and not a great deal of thought had been given to the more abstract philosophical concepts underpinning the establishment of a democratic state. To many political activists, democracy meant unrelenting opposition to one-party dictatorship and Nationalist repression. It would be all too easy to conclude that they were incapable of a normative understanding of democracy. But that is misleading. In an article dealing with Liang Shuming and the idea of democracy in modern China, Ip Hung-yok has challenged Andrew Nathan's thesis that the central tradition of modern Chinese democratic thought was the perception of democracy as an effective means to state power and national development. The case of Liang Shuming, Ip argues, has demonstrated that modern Chinese intellectuals were capable of making "multiple commitments" to democracy – a "nation-oriented utilitarian" commitment (in terms of national wealth and power), an "individual-oriented utilitarian" commitment (in terms of individual happiness), and an "autonomous value" commitment (in terms of individual autonomy).[97] Although I found some of Ip's judgments on Liang's democratic thought to be questionable, her idea of multiple commitments is useful in appreciating the democratic aspirations of China's liberal intellectuals. Those commitments were neither contradictory nor mutually exclusive. It was possible to be utilitarian about democracy in terms of serving China's national purposes and to speak in the same breath of the liberal values of democracy. There is nothing inconsistent about that. What do democrats not say about the

---

[97] Ip, "Liang Shuming."

utility of democracy? Today, Western democrats and human rights champions want the authoritarian states of Asia to democratize in the belief that democracy can reduce official corruption and graft, eliminate cronyism, ensure peaceful conflict resolution, and so on. They don't simply ask Asians to enjoy democracy as an end in itself. A functional approach to democracy does not preclude a normative understanding of it.

Take Luo Longji for example. We have probed his thoughts on human rights and administrative reform. What should be noted, too, is his understanding of democracy as a way of life, a principle of human existence, and a philosophy. "Democracy is absolutely more than political and economic democracy. It is a kind of faith (*xinnian*) to everybody."[98] Harking back to his human rights thought, he maintained that every human being has one's own values, dignity, individuality, and integrity, all of which are respected in a democracy. Everyone can try to achieve one's best. "People are all equal in terms of their intrinsic worth and dignity because they all seek to be human beings."[99] He concluded:

> Democracy believes that people are an end in themselves. The slogan of democracy is "I am a human being." Democracy's enemy is "treating people as anything but human beings." Therefore, all institutions in society, be they political, economic, or anything else, are mere means to an end. The means cannot run counter to the end itself. Therefore any institutions that do not treat *ren* as human beings should be overthrown.[100]

Here the term *ren* had a dual meaning: the individual and people. Luo would have agreed that any governments that did not respect human rights were undemocratic. His belief in the core values of liberalism is unquestionable.[101]

Luo was not alone. Vocational Education leader Huang Yanpei viewed democracy as a "conceptualization of freedom" as much as a system of government, placing high values on personal freedoms, although he also warned against "irresponsible individualism."[102] Also stressing democracy's liberal values, one independent scholar wrote:

---

[98] Luo Longji, "Minzhu de yiyi" (The meaning of democracy), *MZZK* 1:1 (December 9, 1944): 5.

[99] Ibid., p. 1.   [100] Ibid., p. 5.

[101] This is the thrust of Frederic J. Spar's study of Luo. See his "Human Rights and Political Activism: Luo Longji in Chinese Politics, 1928–1958," manuscript, 1993.

[102] Huang Yanpei, *Minzhuhua de jiguan guanli* (Organizational management of democratization) (Shanghai: Shangwu yinshuguan, 1948), pp. 1–2.

Democracy is a philosophy of hope, an optimism. . . . Democracy's view of life holds that every person has his or her worth and independent individuality. Each respects the other's individuality and expects others to respect his or hers. . . . The most obvious merit of democratic life is that people understand that there can be a variety of viewpoints. Truth can be discovered only through the cooperation of intelligence and knowledge. To appreciate the worth of other's independent thinking sustains an attitude of tolerance.[103]

The National Salvationist lawyer and feminist Shi Liang of the "seven honorable persons" fame, who had been campaigning for democracy and women's rights during the war, further illustrates our point. Apart from the familiar emphasis on popular sovereignty and democracy as a political method, Shi also stressed the worth of the individual, equality, mutual respect, tolerance, and justice, turning the traditional relationship between rulers and the ruled upside down by injecting a notion of egalitarianism into human relationships. In a 1945 public lecture on "Women and Democracy" marking Woman's Day (March 8), she said:

To speak of democracy seems so simple, just like asking the people to be their own masters. If only it were so simple. In fact, democracy is the way of being human beings. It is a method for people living together in a community. It can also be said to be a philosophy of life. Democracy consists not only in politics and economics. Its fundamental meaning is: "We are all human beings. I respect my own view and also others." . . .

By virtue of the worth of the individual and individuality, human beings are the superior form of life. We cannot say, "I have my individuality. Others don't." Instead, we should say, "I have my individuality, so have others." Not to force others to be like us is true democracy. On the other hand, democracy is the content of democratic politics, only democracy constitutes true political spirit.[104]

Why did China want democracy? It was not just because democracy was "a world trend." China needed democracy because of its own conditions. Drawing attention to democracy on the operational level, Shi maintained that it was not good enough to put democratic institutions in place;

---

[103] Wu Wenzao, "Minzhu de yiyi" (The meaning of democracy), *JRPL* 4:8 (August 23, 1940): 120.

[104] Quoted in Zhou Tiandu, ed., *Qi junzi zhuan* (The seven honorable persons) (Beijing: Zhongguo shehui kexueyuan chubanshe, 1988), p. 560.

these needed to be operational, just as the exercise of rights by the people must be real. Not least of all, Chinese democracy should not be a carbon copy of a foreign model. As a political system, democracy was something that the Chinese must decide for themselves because it was a process of adaptation based on China's needs and conditions.[105]

Zhang Dongsun, drawing on a range of secondary Anglo-American works, as well as on the Chinese classics, viewed democracy as "everybody managing one's own affairs."[106] He followed C. D. Burns's interpretation that "government is a method of education, but the best education is self-education, and therefore the best government is self-government which is democracy."[107] Under a system of self-government, wrote Zhang, everybody is a ruler and a subject at once; hence, there is a unity in the ruler–ruled relationship. No one is in the governing position permanently, nor is anyone being governed forever. To be democratic is to reject the adversarial relationship between rulers and the ruled and to implement the general will, the latter being often a difficult task. There is bound to be a diversity of views in every aspect of human life, but a system that tolerates diversity and encourages free discussion of public affairs permits some sort of agreement and reconciliation to be achieved out of reason (*lixing*). Democracy, therefore, is, in part, "government by free discussion" (his English).[108] But, for Zhang, it is much more than a political system. It is also a principle, a spirit, a mode of thought, a way of life, a culture, and an ideal. Of course, the spirit cannot be separated from the system itself. No democratic system in history has ever reached the stage of perfection. He subscribed to A. F. Hattersley's view that "democracy is a matter of degree and that no complete expression has yet been given to democratic ideals."[109]

Viewed as a principle, a spirit, and an ideal, democracy sets the highest standards for democratic institutions. But the standards are not fixed and can only be reached gradually and incrementally; the higher the standards, the more democratic the institution. Zhang Dongsun noted that it is always better to have a little democracy than no democracy at all; a

---

[105] Ibid., p. 561.

[106] Zhang Dongsun, *Lixing yu minzhu* (Reason and democracy) (Hong Kong: Longmen shudian, 1968), pp. 147–148. This book was originally published by Shanghai's Shangwu yinshuguan in March 1946. The manuscript was prepared during the war, and some of Zhang's thoughts were conceived while he was imprisoned in Beijing by the Japanese.

[107] C. D. Burns, *Democracy* (1935), quoted in ibid., pp. 147–148.

[108] Ibid., p. 143.

[109] A. F. Hattersley, *A Short History of Democracy* (1930), quoted in ibid.

little each time will accumulate and amount to a great deal over time. To be democratic, a society must be democratic in habit and culture. Liberty and equality are vital parts of society. But liberty is not licentiousness, he pointed out, and individual liberty must not lead to actions that harm others. Nor is equality a natural endowment. He agreed with E. G. Conklin that "democratic equality does not mean equality of heredity, environment, education or possessions; least of all does it mean equality of intelligence, usefulness, or influence. . . . Democracy alone permits a natural classification of men with respect to social value, as contrasted with all artificial and conventional classifications."[110] Upholding the democratic ideal, each democratizing society needs to develop in its own way, taking into consideration its conditions and cultural traditions. In his view, which he would elaborate in the postwar years, China must go down the track of "socialistic democracy" (his English) without a radical, violent revolution. That road was neither Anglo-American nor Soviet Russian but one with Chinese characteristics, with the intellectuals, the modern literati, leading the way, followed by the peasantry. In any event, the democratization of China was not merely a question of institutional change; it also had significant implications for the whole of Chinese culture.[111]

Taking a holistic sociocultural approach toward democracy, Zhang Dongsun was correct in stating that democracy involves the whole of society, culture, and the population.[112] Indeed, he regarded any political system devoid of a democratic social culture as not truly democratic, even if it included a constitution. He also believed that a democratic social culture could be developed even in the absence of formal democratic institutions. He appreciated Rousseau's idea of a social contract and regarded autocracy and dictatorship as a "malaise" because a dictatorial government was based on force, coercion, and deception.[113] Individual liberty was important for him, and the individual should be treated as an end withal and with respect. Here he acknowledged Immanuel Kant, who held that humanity should be treated as an end in itself, never simply as a means.[114] Human beings are rational; thus, there is a com-

[110] E. G. Conklin, *Direction of Human Evolution* (1921), quoted in ibid., p. 129.
[111] Ibid., pp. 186, 188.
[112] Zhang Dongsun devoted a whole chapter to democracy in his book, *Sixiang yu shehui* (Thought and society) (Hong Kong: Longmen shudian, 1968), pp. 157–180. This book was also originally published in Shanghai in 1946, and the manuscript was prepared during the war.
[113] Ibid., pp. 164–166.   [114] Ibid., p. 175.

monality of values between democracy and rationalism, the "two greatest treasures of Western civilization," in Zhang Dongsun's opinion.[115] It is human instinct to pursue individual happiness. Taking a cue from Bentham, he argued that everyone is the judge of his or her own utility; otherwise, one would not be a rational agent.[116] Treating liberty as a social concept, he was able to argue that liberty must be rational. Because people are rational, they enjoy democracy, freedom, and equality and are capable of making contributions to society and the world at large.[117]

National Socialist leader Zhang Junmai also developed the theme that democracy respects human dignity and individual liberty. He was convinced that the Kantian principle applies to politics as well as to morality and that any political act that treats people merely as a means should be rejected, regardless of how good the results may be. A human rights advocate, he understood democracy as a mechanism for "overthrowing authoritarianism by applying the principle of human dignity and theory of natural rights and for constructing [a kind of] politics that is compatible with human dignity."[118]

Middle-ground Democracy

Writing on Liang Qichao and Chinese democratic thought, Andrew Nathan draws attention to Liang's assumptions, widely shared by contemporary thinkers, of the *natural* harmony of social roles and relations and of the compatibility of public and private interests.[119] A careful reading of the prodemocracy literature of the war period (and also the civil war period that followed) indeed shows that the compatibility of public and private interests was a common theme. But there is little in the literature to suggest that the collectivity need not worry about granting rights and freedoms to the individual, or that the problem of antisocial motivations on the part of the individual did not exist. Most liberal writers, while trying to identify some broad common interests between the individual and the collectivity, were cognizant that conflicts of interest are inherent in a democratic state and society. It is human nature to be selfish, but it is not desirable; so they decried selfishness and warned

---

[115] Ibid., p. 168.   [116] Ibid., p. 166.   [117] Ibid., pp. 178–179.

[118] Zhang Junmai, "Minzhu zhengzhi de zhexue jichu" (The philosophical basis of democracy), in Li Huaxing, ed., *Zhongguo xiandai sixiangshi ziliao jianbian* (A brief compilation of materials on modern Chinese political thought) (Hangzhou: Zhejiang renmin chubanshe, 1983), V, 363.

[119] Andrew J. Nathan, *Chinese Democracy* (London: I. B. Tauris, 1986), pp. 51–55.

against rampant individualism. They saw a need to reconcile the differences between state powers and individual rights, between public and private interests, and between the values of statism and democracy, harping on the theme not so much of *natural* harmony as of a necessary harmonization of social roles and relations. Reconciliation and harmonization did not come easy; these could be achieved only through social cooperation, made possible not by following instincts but by leading a "civil life in a civil society" enriched by civic education. What distinguished the liberal thinkers of this period from Liang Qichao was their insistence that rights and personal freedoms should be enjoyed *before* the individual could make contributions to the state and the public good and *before* they could cooperate socially.

The notion of social cooperation was not unique to the Chinese of course. Bertrand Russell once wrote: "Where democracy does not exist, the government mentality is that of masters towards dependents; where there is democracy it is that of *equal co-operation* [emphasis added]."[120] Harold Laski, with his brand of "liberal socialism," would have thought much the same thing.

It is important to differentiate between what democracy is and what democracy would be. Liberal Chinese thinkers understood Anglo-American democracy generally, but they wanted Chinese democracy to be something different and superior, something that I would call middle-ground democracy. From their standpoint, Chinese values were a catalyst for democracy, not an impediment to it.

Let us probe their thoughts more deeply by looking at the work of Pan Guangdan, a Columbia-educated professor of sociology, Dean of the Faculty of Arts at Qinghua of the Southwest Associated University, and a National Socialist. In a 1944 essay entitled "The Individual, Society, and Democracy," Pan dismissed the dictatorships of Germany, Italy, and Japan as anachronistic because they treated society as an organism in which the individual was suppressed in the name of the state. In particular, he condemned Hitler's treatment of the individual. In the same breath, he also criticized Anglo-American democracy as unsound because of its strong bias toward individualism. Drawing on the works of John Stuart Mill, Herbert Spencer, Harold Laski, and Max Weber, he argued that democracy obsessed with individualism was no more democratic than socialism; nor was it a true democracy. The Anglo-American

---

[120] Bertrand Russell, *Power: A New Social Analysis* (London: Allen and Unwin, 1938), pp. 202–203.

systems were not good for China because *"the individual and individualism are not the same* [emphasis added], nor are freedom and free competition. Individualism and free competition in China have created a few 'financial lords' (*caifa*) who ignore ninety-nine percent of the population. How can this be [a] healthy [development]?"[121]

The distinction between the individual and individualism, between freedom and free competition, was important for Pan. He reasoned that the individual, while seeking self-fulfillment, should also care for the public good; otherwise, individual development would become a sort of "unhealthy individualism." And competition, when it gets too fierce as it will in capitalism, would pose a danger to the competitors themselves as well as to the poor masses who are in no position to compete in the first place.[122] Pan betrayed Laski's influence when he wrote: "The individual is also a member of the community who should act in a dual capacity, developing oneself and contributing to the collectivity at the same time."[123] But he went further than Laski to insist on a balance and harmony between individuality and communality. "Such balance and harmony are the demands of all civilized persons. When these demands are met, all civil strife, revolutions, and international wars would disappear. And only democracy could meet these demands."[124] Chinese and Western thinkers alike advocated peaceful conflict resolution. But if the latter were rational and methodological, Pan was idealistic and prescriptive.

A firm believer in eugenics,[125] Pan's *xianren zhengzhi* (politics of the men of virtue) was elitist, similar to the expert politics articulated by Luo Longji. Like Sun Yat-sen, Pan graded people according to their intelligence: those in politics should come from the upper grade with a few from the middle grade and none from the lower grade. He believed in representative government, but, mindful of China's conditions, he wanted only those with outstanding intelligence and qualities to repre-

---

[121] Pan Guangdan, "Geren, shehui, yu minzhi" (The individual, society, and democracy), *MZZK* 1:4 (December 30, 1944): 6.

[122] Pan's apprehensions about capitalist competition call to mind the view of the English founders of the Fabian Society that "the Competitive system assures the happiness and comfort of the few at the expense of the suffering of the many and that society must be reconstituted in such a manner as to secure the general welfare and happiness." Quoted in Lawrence C. Wanlass, *Gettell's History of Political Thought*, 2nd ed. (London: George Allen and Unwin, 1961), p. 347.

[123] Pan Guangdan, "Geren, shehui, yu minzhi," p. 7.   [124] Ibid.

[125] For Pan's thoughts on eugenics as a way of national salvation, see his "Yousheng de chulu" (Eugenics as a way out), *XY* 4:1 (December 1931): 1–33.

sent the people. Politics was not for the average person, and Chinese democracy meant government by virtuous men who came from the wide community, representing part of public opinion, and only the part that was educated, intelligent, and sensible. Like some Western thinkers, he questioned the notion of the general will[126] because he recognized only the voice of those who were well qualified and suited to speak for the people. Contrasting such Chinese traits as passivity with the activism of Britons and Americans, Pan argued that democracy could only be developed in China through the adaptation of its principles to the conditions and characteristics of Chinese life.[127]

Chinese democracy was Confucian in its humanistic expressions. Zhang Shenfu, who had led the New Enlightenment movement of 1936–1937 on which Schwarcz has written,[128] defined it as a kind of pluralist politics that allowed people to accommodate one another magnanimously and inclusively (*yuren weishan*). Chinese democracy would also provide everyone with equal opportunity to develop one's potential to the utmost (*jinqi zaiwu*) and to one's satisfaction (*gede qisuo*). He pleaded not only for the freedoms of speech, publication, assembly, organization, thought, academic study, and research, but also for freedoms from wants, fears, and unemployment. True to the May Fourth tradition, democracy was coupled with science because democracy also builds on critical analysis, a faculty of differentiation, and tolerance of differing and opposing views. Just as science looks for common patterns and universal principles, so democracy explores the common ground among individuals and groups. Zhang held that philosophically democracy came close to the Chinese notions of universalism (*tianxia weigong*), or great harmony (*datong*), of *ren* (benevolence, or humanity), *zhong* (the golden mean), and of *shu* (forgiveness), all resting on rationality.[129] His contribution to the political discourse lay in his rejection of the culturalist view that Western democratic thought and Chinese values were incompatible,

---

[126] Long before modern scholars launched attacks on the classical theory of democracy, Bentham was making fun of the notion of the general will. Equally skeptical of that notion, Schumpeter spoke instead of "the manufactured will." For a more recent critique, see Plamenatz, *Democracy and Illusion*, pp. 7–8, 39–40.

[127] Pan Guangdan, "Minzhu zhengzhi yu Zhongguo shehui sixiang beijing (shang)" (Democratic politics and the background of Chinese social thought [part 1]). *Ziyou luntan* 2:3 (March 1, 1944): 8–16.

[128] Schwarcz, *The Chinese Enlightenment*, pp. 222–230.

[129] Zhang Shenfu, "Women wei shenme yao minzhu yu ziyou" (Why do we want democracy and liberty), *Xinhua ribao*, September 12, 1944; "Minzhu tuanjie de jingshen tiaojian" (The spiritual conditions for democratic unity), *Wencui* 1:1 (October 9, 1945): 2.

arguing instead that democratic values were consistent with Chinese ethics and the central tenets of Chinese thought. His democratic thought was in line with his New Enlightenment view that jettisoned cultural iconoclasm in favor of a systematic and rational synthesis of Chinese and Western cultures.

Even Luo Longji, who rarely felt obliged to "justify his intellectual and political position in terms of Chinese traditional values,"[130] contended in one of his 1940 essays that, while the terms *popular sovereignty* and *political regime* were new to the Chinese, and democracy in the sense of political participation had never existed in China, a "politics of public opinion" (*minyi zhengzhi*) had not been lacking. Invoking Mencius's *minben* thought, he went on to say that Chinese emperors often paid heed to the voices of the people because to ignore them would be dangerous and could lead to justifiable rebellions. He thought that the "politics of public opinion" was an imperial legacy on which modern Chinese democracy could build.[131] In another essay, he argued that the traditional civil service examination system had been an open regime embodying the true spirit of democracy in contrast to the current exclusive regime based on loyalty to and connections with the GMD.[132] In both essays, he drew on the Chinese classics. His argument that there was a "politics of public opinion" in imperial China ignores the gap between words and deeds. Chinese emperors rarely listened to the voices of the people. Respect for *minben* and "public opinion" was merely a ruling class proclamation, a thought, unmatched by actions. But his oblique references to Chinese humanism and the tradition of remonstrance were an attempt to drive home the message that there were aspects of Chinese political life that were democratic in spirit. In other words, Chinese political culture was not entirely antidemocratic. Democracy was compatible with Chinese political and philosophical thought, the latter being no obstacle to democratization.

Likewise, anticommunist stalwart Chen Qitian saw in democracy an embodiment of both *ren* (people) and *ren* (benevolence), between which there was a facile identification. There were protodemocratic elements

---

[130] Spar, "Human Rights and Political Activism," p. 13.

[131] Luo Longji, "Zhongguo yu minyi zhengzhi" (China and the politics of public opinion), *JRPL* 4:21 (November 24, 1940): 320–322. He elaborated on this point in a later essay, "Minzhu zhengzhi yu minyi zhengzhi" (Democratic politics and the politics of public opinion), *MZZK* 1:6 (January 20, 1945): 3–5.

[132] Luo Longji, "Lun gongkai zhengquan" (On the opening up of the regime), *JRPL* 3:21 (May 26, 1940): 323–326.

in Confucianism, but he noted that democracy had failed to develop in China because Confucianism, instead of emphasizing the rule of law, extolled the notion of the sage king (*shengwang*).[133] To promote a democratic culture, Chen would tap into the cultural resources of both Chinese and Western thought. Despite being Chinese-educated, he had read some of the works of Bertrand Russell and Harold Laski (in Chinese translations) and seemed quite comfortable sitting between the cultural worlds of East and West. Democracy promotes good government, and good government for Chinese intellectuals was moralistic. That rulership should be moral was a central Confucian precept. Chen reflected a view prevalent among Chinese intellectuals when he wrote:

> The politics of democracy is the politics of morality; it should not be unscrupulous. . . . Political parties that apply morality will win popular sympathy and maintain solidarity within themselves. Such a principle might seem pedantic to the selfish elements. But for the state and the people, even for the future of the parties themselves, it is necessary to establish party ethics. If a political party does not concern itself with morality, it will become an intriguing and self-serving cabal (*pengdang*) incapable of assuming the important duty of national salvation.[134]

But it does not follow that the leader is morally superior. To reject the notion of the sage king is to accept the basic assumption of modern political theory that people, being fallible, can be corrupted by power. To guard against the ruler's abuse of office, institutional checks and restraints are necessary.

As with many fellow intellectuals, Chen Qitian's vision of democracy extended beyond the confines of a political system. Democracy for him was "a political and social ideal" in which the individual and the state, rulers and the ruled, the public sphere and the private realm, all interacted in a mutually beneficial way.[135] A nice balance between them was a goal pursued by all those who accepted the intrinsic worth of the free individual. "Neither sheer selfish individualism nor sheer autocratic corporatism is good for democracy. This is because the ideal of democracy lies in mediation between the individual and the state, between liberty and order, and between equality and organization."[136] Power and liberty

---

[133] Chen Qitian, *Minzhu xianzheng lun* (On constitutional democracy) (Taibei: Taiwan Shangwu yinshuguan, 1966), pp. 58–59.
[134] Ibid., p. 108.   [135] Ibid., pp. 15–16.   [136] Ibid., pp. 16–17.

in a democracy should be treated as a unity, but with a balance. "Only then could there be discipline in politics and a capacity for improvement and progress."[137] There was a sense of optimism about the prospect of resolving the tension between power and liberty through social cooperation.

In short, the dominant Chinese democratic thought stressed not so much the *natural* harmony as the harmonization of interests by holding the middle ground. Whereas Western liberal democrats emphasize rights and personal freedoms and see nonviolent conflicts and self-interests as a normal part of political and economic life, the Chinese value obligations, duties, and self-restraints, seeing conflicts and selfishness as undesirable and destructive. Moreover, Western scholars have focused on the individual–collectivity dichotomy, but Chinese thinkers are more interested in a complementary and mutually beneficial relationship.

Middle-ground democracy was a moderate critique of Anglo-American democracy and an attempt to provide a Chinese alternative to laissez-faire liberalism and the Western capitalist system. It drew on the Chinese principle of the "golden mean" (*zhongyong zhi dao*), extolling the virtues of not going to the extreme in political, economic, and social life alike. In the context of wartime Chinese nationalism, wherein Chinese culture was praised rather than criticized, middle-ground democracy could also be interpreted as a Sinification of liberal democracy. To Sinify a foreign idea or model was to adapt it to Chinese conditions and to make it distinctively Chinese. Nationalism apart, the Sinification of liberal democracy also sprang from a deep conviction that Chinese values were capable of reformulation and reconstruction to assist in political change, that these values were compatible with Western values, and that a synthesis of Chinese and Western cultures was not only possible but also desirable. Few, however, seemed to be aware that middle-ground democracy could be just an abstraction in that it was hard to establish where exactly the middle ground was and what institutional arrangements were most appropriate. The golden mean could turn out to be lackluster after all. Luo Longji could only look to Fabianism, and Zhang Junmai was drawn to German social democracy, whereas some tried to improve the thought of Sun Yat-sen. Finally, as a construct, middle-ground democracy was eclectic and moralistic – an expression of Chinese intellectual utopianism – in contrast to the Millsian vision of democracy based on competition among parties and interest groups

[137] Ibid., pp. 44–45.

according to morally neutral political procedures while legally pursuing selfish ends.

A Dim View of Capitalism and the Question of Conflict of Interest

Middle-ground democracy revealed a dim view of capitalism taken by Chinese intellectuals generally in the twentieth century. Such a view was held partly because of the legacy of World War I (seen by many as a war over markets) and, more recently, the anticapitalist trend of the world in the 1930s and the Great Depression. Another reason was because of the legacy of the antiimperialism of earlier decades, especially a leftover from the radical antiimperialism of the Nationalist Revolution period from 1924 to 1927. After all, the imperialists, especially Britain, represented capitalism in their minds. The Nationalist Revolution had seen the beginnings of the pressure to force the British imperial retreat, and the demands to abolish extraterritoriality and to undertake treaty revision were still going strong even after Chiang Kai-shek turned to the right and toned down the GMD's antiimperialist rhetoric.[138] Under those circumstances, a dim view of capitalism might not be too surprising.

A third reason was that China's liberal, democratic movement was not preceded by an industrial revolution that would have produced a powerful capitalist class. Chinese liberals and democrats were neither a product of capitalist development nor, in the main, associated with big business, which was almost nonexistent. From their standpoint, they could not see the need for a struggle between the capitalists and the working class because both were weak. The conundrum for them was how to industrialize and democratize China without the inequalities engendered by unbridled capitalism. We shall return to this conundrum in Chapter 9.[139]

But there were deeper cultural reasons as well. There was a pronounced bias in Confucian culture against merchants (although it was not always observed in practice). The liberal intellectuals, even as they rejected the mainstream tradition of political culture, saw themselves as the inheritor of the role of the imperial literati. There was something unseemly about an intellectual in the 1930s or 1940s championing capitalism, wherein com-

---

[138] See Edmund S. K. Fung, *The Diplomacy of Imperial Retreat; Britain's South China Policy, 1924–1931* (Hong Kong: Oxford University Press, 1991).
[139] See pp. 317–327.

225

petition was not only fierce but sometimes also immoral though legally permissible. Capitalism inevitably meant the pursuit of individual profits, a scramble for markets, a concentration of wealth, surplus production, exploitation of the workers, and the neglect and destitution of the vast majority of the people. It was hard for Chinese intellectuals not to be critical of the social injustice, class exploitation, consumerism, permissiveness, and gulf between rich and poor that is so evident in the capitalist countries and yet so inconsistent with Chinese humanistic values. Capitalism could easily be the handmaid of bourgeois power in a society where the bourgeoisie was a very small minority. The moving force in capitalism is individual drive. Chinese intellectuals desired the unleashing of individual energy, but they feared rampant individualism because it was irresponsible and harmful to the public good. Zhang Junmai's concern in his "revisionist democracy" illustrates this point, and Pan Guangdan's misgivings about fierce competition in the marketplace of free enterprise were perhaps typical of the thinking of Chinese "liberal democrats." Competition for the maximization of interests meant greed, and greed, like selfishness, is decried in Confucian culture (again it may not always be observed in practice). Although impressed with the achievements of the industrialized West, they were afraid of the social problems and injustice associated with capitalism. In this respect, they were not very different from the Nationalist elite who followed the anticapitalist bias of Sun Yat-sen's Principle of the People's Livelihood (*minsheng zhuyi*).[140] Where they differed significantly was in their insistence on the right to private property and individual liberty.

Middle-ground democracy, and its underpinning intellectual utopianism, also masked a reluctance on the part of Chinese thinkers generally to discuss the question of conflict of interest. It is not suggested that they believed such conflicts were inconceivable. That they dwelled on the need for institutional restraints to guard against the ruler's abuse of power as well as on the theme of harmonization of interests through social cooperation is indicative of their awareness of those conflicts. They simply could not bring themselves to discuss them positively in a morally neutral manner. There are three plausible explanations for that. First, despite their Western education (that is, those who were Western-educated), the liberals and democrats of the 1930s and 1940s had no

---

[140] For the GMD's critique of capitalism, see Joseph Fewsmith, *Party, State, and Local Elites in Republican China: Merchant Organizations and Politics in Shanghai, 1890–1930* (Honolulu: University of Hawaii Press, 1985), pp. 100–103.

desire to divest themselves of the legacy of their Confucian heritage.[141] They were not cultural iconoclasts. Even though they drew on Western works on liberalism, democracy, constitutionalism, and human rights, they were also interested in the protoliberal, protomodern, and protodemocratic values in the Chinese tradition that were compatible with Western thought. Unlike the radical intellectuals of the May Fourth period, they did not attack Confucianism per se (although they did critique it) but instead demanded a reordering of the political system. Many occasionally invoked the Chinese classics to reinforce their points. Others like Liang Shuming, who showed distaste for Western models, had deep-seated fears of violence, political instability, and social disorder. They seemed more interested in the marketplace of ideas (freedoms of thought and speech) than in the marketplace of politics (competing for power in a *morally neutral* playing field) or simply the marketplace (free enterprise).

Second, there were cultural reasons here, too. Traditionally, a distinct and strong element of pacifism and aversion to war ran throughout Chinese culture, in contrast to the martial spirit and military virtues extolled in Japanese and European societies. Likewise, there was something unbecoming about a Chinese intellectual dwelling on the question of conflict of interest and being seen as selfish, greedy, aggressive, and socially uncooperative.

Third, the liberal intellectuals had their attention and energy so resolutely focused on creating a marketplace in which differing interests could compete that they never got around to deciding how to handle the conflicts when those interests were allowed to be expressed. The answer always seemed to be harmonization, which, in politics, did not mean that one did not have to vote but that a consensus to be achieved through negotiation was preferable to confrontation and not being able to reach a decision. Thus, Chinese notions of democracy were more "consensual" and more "substantive" than Western "procedural" notions.

Zhang Dongsun seems to be the only one to have written on the question of conflict of interest around this time. In an essay on China's past and future, he identified ten categories of conflict (*chongtu*), both internal and external, in Chinese society and polity, including social antagonisms (he did not like the term *class conflict*). Conflicts, he acknowledged, were endemic in Chinese social and political life. "It must be realized

---

[141] I would include Luo Longji among them, notwithstanding his commitment to the core values of liberalism and his many years of Anglo-American education.

that societal conflict is a kind of social process, the opposite being the so-called social harmony." But he added that a society had no feet to stand on if there was only conflict and no harmony. Because Chinese society was conflict-prone, mechanisms for peaceful conflict resolution were necessary. To reduce conflict was not to eliminate some contestants but to make "appropriate arrangements" based on reason so that all contestants could operate within a predetermined scope (that is, following the already agreed upon rules of the game). In this way, conflict could be contained, and harmony could be achieved.[142]

CONCLUSION

The war period was far from sterile in the democratic discourse. Insofar as democracy was concerned, the internal prerequisites of *qimeng* were not diminished by the external imperatives of *jiuwang*. Both the government and civil opposition spoke of democracy as a means of strengthening resistance to Japan and laying the groundwork for national reconstruction. For the government, democracy, or rather the promise of it, was a method of elite mobilization, a means of bringing together the nation's best minds, and a basis for multiparty support for its war effort. For the Communists, democracy was part of the strategy of the united front. For civil opposition, it was a political method and a world tide of which China should be part. And for the true believers, it was desirable even in times of war and need not be entirely sacrificed to the demands of antiimperialist nationalism. The defense of rights, personal freedoms, and civil liberties was not in conflict with national survival.

Democracy was best served by peace. In the midst of a war, it was difficult to imagine how democracy could be practiced, and it was only natural that democracy should be sheer rhetoric for the government and a goal for civil opposition. Indeed, the Nationalists were long on words and short on actions: democracy was conspicuous by its absence. For their part, the MPGs and the independents were unable to offer any specific solutions to China's pressing problems other than a slogan. In their analysis of China's situation, democracy had become the sole factor, and the problems of the nation were pinned down to a lack of it.

Moreover, democracy was conflated with nationalism. Yet the utility of democracy in mobilizing popular support was a myth. As the CCP's experience demonstrated, the rural masses in the border regions

---

[142] Zhang Dongsun, *Lixing yu minzhu*, pp. 154–173, esp. pp. 172–173.

were motivated to take up arms against the Japanese and to support the Communists for a variety of reasons, including patriotism, nationalism, land reform, rent and interest reduction, and coercion.[143] Democracy in the form of local elections or in any other form was not a crucial factor in winning popular support. The Chinese masses knew almost nothing about democracy as a political process, let alone as a spirit and a way of life, nor did they care about it because they had more pressing problems to worry about.

To think that democracy was a panacea for all China's ills was naïve. The problems of China were complex and perhaps more economic than political, as many discovered. In a wartime situation where a powerful government was necessary, administrative and personnel reforms were perhaps more important than ending one-party rule. The existing conditions in the country did not help the cause of democracy. On the other hand, it is fair to say that the opposition demands were minimal and justifiable because constitutional democracy had been reduced to a rule of law, the safeguard of basic rights and civil liberties, and a recognition of the legal status of the MPGs and the CCP. Furthermore, because China was fighting on the side of the Allies, some movement toward constitutionalism and democratization would stand it in good stead in the international community. Political reform was a possibility if only the ruling party adopted the correct policy.

Because Anglo-American democracy was considered unsuited to China, the possibility of a middle path between the single-party and multiparty systems was explored. Even though their approach was functional, China's liberal intellectuals were capable of understanding the normative conception of democracy and did not fail to reaffirm the core values of liberalism from time to time. They searched for a way of resolving the tension between concentration of powers and democratic values, between the individual and the state, and between rights and duties, and they found it in middle-ground democracy. They held a dim view of capitalism and were generally reluctant to discuss the question of conflict of interest, choosing to harp on the theme of social harmony consistent with the Chinese tradition but not with Chinese realities.

Meanwhile, they also sought to bridge the gap between the GMD and the CCP. In so doing, civil opposition constituted a third force movement in Chinese politics.

---

[143] There is a new body of revisionist literature on Yan'an communism, which is beyond the scope of this book.

7

The Third Force Movement

The Chinese Democratic League, 1941–1945

J UST ONE YEAR into the First People's Political Council (PPC), the MPGs, frustrated at the renewed tension between the two major parties, were caught in the cross fire in a limited civil war. But, instead of ducking for cover, they took upon themselves a dual role as a mediator and a motor in the movement for democratic and constitutional change. Mediation was a difficult mission, but it was important for them because only reconciliation through negotiations could bring about China's unification, provide a framework for pluralist politics, and thereby ensure their own survival in the postwar period. Portraying themselves as a third force in Chinese politics, the MPGs' mission was to explore the possibility of a third road that was neither Nationalist nor Communist.

Earlier writers have employed the third force paradigm in a variety of ways. James Seymour has characterized the MPGs as "small middle parties" composed of middle-of-the-road intellectuals who sought to be "a liberalizing influence" but who were impotent through a lack of military power.[1] Roger Jeans defines the third force in terms of opposition to both the Nationalists and the Communists, stressing the MPGs' attempts to offer political alternatives and their being caught in the cross fire between the major combatants.[2] For Thomas Curran, the third force was "a loose coalition of intellectuals, educators, businessmen, and professional politicians dedicated to the introduction of democratic reforms and the maintenance of national unity in the interest of fighting the Japanese."[3] Considering its mediating role, he emphasizes its attempt

---

[1] James Seymour, *China's Satellite Parties* (Armonk, NJ: M. E. Sharpe, 1987), pp. vii, 5.
[2] Roger B. Jeans, "Introduction," in Roger B. Jeans, ed., *Roads Not Taken: The Struggle of Opposition Parties in Twentieth-Century China* (Boulder: Westview Press, 1992), p. 2.
[3] Thomas Curran, "From Educator to Politician: Huang Yanpei and the Third Force," in Jeans, ed., *Roads Not Taken*, p. 86.

"to chart a middle course, weaving a path between the Scylla of the GMD and the Charybdis of the CCP."[4]

In the 1940s, the Chinese themselves gave the term *the third force* several shades of meaning. First, it referred to a coalition of MPGs and nonpartisans who met from time to time to share their thoughts on the national issues of the day, and it distinguished the "middle politics" of moderation, impartiality, and independence, stressing the importance of compromise and peaceful conflict resolution. Second, the term, lending itself to a class interpretation, denoted a "middle" force representing what Chinese writers called the national bourgeoisie and the petty bourgeoisie. Third, the term referred to an ideological position somewhere between Anglo-American democracy and Soviet socialism. The third force was a coalition of disparate elements, with a diversity of beliefs and interests. By 1947, it had become a spent force.

Writing in 1952 for an American readership, Zhang Junmai defined the third force as:

> ... something which grows out of the needs and context of Chinese politics and society. It has nothing to do with any policy of neutralism or aloofness from the Western democracies and the U.S.S.R. Rather it is sympathetic towards a rational study of Western political and social ideals so that a proper evaluation and a judicial [sic] selection can be made for the progressive development of Chinese society.[5]

For Zhang, the third force was not a product of the Cold War, but an internal politico-intellectual force seeking to transform China into a modern society through a judicious selection of Western political and social ideals that could blend harmoniously and profitably with Chinese culture. It represented a synthesis of Chinese and Western thought, an eclecticism embracing the principles of constitutional democracy and the spirit of Chinese culture. It also was a reminder of the revisionist democracy on which he had written in the 1930s.

To illuminate the third force movement that developed in the 1940s, several questions may be asked from the outset. Was there a third road for China? If so, how did it relate to Chinese democracy? If not, were the middle-of-the-road intellectuals naïve and out of touch? If their efforts were doomed to failure from the start, did the third force have

---

[4] Ibid.
[5] Carsun Chang, *The Third Force in China* (New York: Bookman, 1952), p. 14.

any significance? We shall begin discussing these questions here by focusing on the Chinese Democratic League (DL) during the period 1941–1945. A full investigation must await the unfolding of the events of 1946 covered in Chapter 8. The DL is of particular interest to us here because it was a coalition of MPGs and independents, a movement that illustrates the diversity, complexity, and weaknesses of the third force. Furthermore, many DL leaders were also members of the PPC at one time or another. The DL was the vehicle for civil opposition outside the PPC, but it did not represent the totality of the third force. There were independent, nonparticipatory liberal elements who were critical of the government but not politically engaged.

FORMATION OF THE CHINESE DEMOCRATIC LEAGUE

The forerunner of the DL was the United National Reconstruction Comrades Association (*Tongyi jianguo tongzhihui*), formed in Chongqing in October 1939 by a number of MPG leaders serving on the PPC. Liang Shuming was instrumental in setting it up after he had made an eight-month tour of the communist border areas in north and east China, the scenes of armed clashes between government and communist troops in 1939. He met with Mao Zedong and other CCP leaders, became sympathetic to their movement, and thought cooperation with them a possibility, despite his disapproval of class struggle and their violent methods. The name of the Association, suggested by him, underscored the importance of national unity and solidarity in the war against Japan.[6] Its aims were set out in a twelve-point covenant, or twelve "articles of faith" (*xinyue*) as the Chinese called them. These included recognition of the Three Principles of the People as "the highest principle for the War of Resistance," support for Chiang Kai-shek's leadership, constitutionalism, official recognition of the minor parties, nationalization of all the nation's armed forces, and academic and thought freedoms.[7] The Association was not antigovernment by any means, and the twelve articles of faith contained nothing subversive. It had no intention of antagonizing the gov-

---

[6] Liang held that rather than proceeding from constitutionalism to unity and unification, that is, using constitutionalism as a means of achieving them, it should be the other way around. See Liang Shuming, "Wo nuli de shi shenme?" *LSMQJ*, VI, 250. Some people referred to the Association as the Resistance and Reconstruction Comrades Association (*Kangzhan jianguo tongzhihui*). See Yi Sheng, "Zhongguo minzhu tongmeng" (The Chinese Democratic League), *Zaisheng* 104 (May 1, 1946): 14–15.

[7] For the twelve articles of faith, see *MMWX*, pp. 2–3.

ernment but only sought its understanding. In fact, Liang went to see Chiang, showing him the covenant, which the latter approved on the condition that the Association did not develop into a political party. To set Chiang's mind at ease, the membership list shown to him left out the National Salvationists, who were thought to be too procommunist. But subsequently, the Association, claiming more than thirty PPC members, did include the National Salvationists.[8] It was a small, low-key group, with only four or five people initially involved, apart from Liang. They were Zhang Junmai, Huang Yanpei, Zuo Shunsheng, and Zhang Bojun, who met informally to discuss and exchange views among themselves with no immediate plans for political action.[9] The idea of a third force had not yet emerged at this point.

As more armed clashes between government and communist troops took place in the north, culminating in the New Fourth Army incident, third party mediation seemed desirable. When the CCP delegates served notice that they would boycott the Second PPC, scheduled for March 1941, over the incident, Liang Shuming, Zuo Shunsheng, Luo Longji, Huang Yanpei, and a few others attempted in vain to convince them to return.[10] According to a DL source, the government, somewhat embarrassed by the boycott, asked the MPG delegates to mediate in an attempt to maintain a semblance of national unity.[11]

Earlier in December 1940, the group had met at Zhang Junmai's Chongqing residence and decided to expand the Association by launching a newspaper, *Guangmingbao* (Bright News) in Hong Kong, as its organ. Liang Shuming was given that task and went there early in 1941. In March, he was back in Chongqing and, along with sixteen other people, renamed the Association the Chinese League of Democratic Political Groups (*Zhongguo minzhu zhengtuan tongmeng*).[12] The name

---

[8] Lyman P. Van Slyke, *Enemies and Friends: The United Front in Chinese Communist History* (Stanford: Stanford University Press, 1967), p. 170; Anthony Joseph Shaheen, "The China Democratic League and Chinese Politics, 1939–1947," unpublished Ph.D. dissertation, University of Michigan, 1977, p. 13.

[9] Zuo Shunsheng, *Jin sanshinian jianwen zaji* (A record of the events of the last thirty years) (Taibei: Zhonghua yilin wenwu chubanshe, 1976), p. 79.

[10] The CCP's twelve demands over the incident were rejected by Chiang Kai-shek. For details of the group's good offices, see Liang Shuming, "Wo nuli de shi shenme," *LSMQJ*, VI, 162–173.

[11] Tseng Chao-lun, "The Chinese Democratic League," *Current History* 1:33 (1946): 32. The author was a DL member and professor at Beijing University.

[12] Liang Shuming, "Zhongguo minzhu tongmeng shulue" (Brief history of the Chinese Democratic League), *LSMQJ*, VI, 598; Luo Longji, "Cong canjia jiu zhengxie dao canjia

change was kept a secret for fears that the government might see it as a political party in breach of Chiang's condition. A thirteen-strong Central Executive Committee was set up. Five of them formed the Standing Committee, chaired by Huang Yanpei, who resigned a few months later,[13] succeeded by Zhang Lan, with Zuo Shunsheng as general secretary. Chiang soon learned about it, but not the names of its leaders. He then sent Sun Fo and Wu Tiecheng to Hong Kong to curtail its activities, declaring it an "anonymous organization," forcing Zhang Junmai to state in the PPC who the responsible persons were.[14] Still, Chiang was not happy about it, and the powerful CC Clique within the GMD was particularly hostile. Nothing, however, was done about it probably because he did not think highly of Liang and company as political organizers and saw no immediate threat to his regime.[15]

On October 10, 1941, the League's existence was formally announced in Hong Kong. A manifesto and a ten-point statement on the current situation in China were published in *Guangmingbao*, with English editions subsequently appearing in England and the United States for foreign consumption, the most important points being the "democratization of politics" and the "nationalization of the armies."[16] No mention was made of support for Chiang's leadership, but there was no hint of opposition to him either. The statement only committed the League to "supervising and assisting the GMD in thoroughly implementing the Program of Armed Resistance and National Reconstruction" (Point 4). The manifesto distinguished the League from the major parties by rejecting violent means of conflict resolution and highlighting freedom of speech and popular support. It sought unity of action among the MPGs and the independents themselves, as well as cooperation with the two major

---

Nanjing hetan de yixie huiyi" (Some recollections of the events from my participation in the old Political Consultative Conference to my participation in the Nanjing peace negotiations), *Wenshi ziliao xuanji*, no. 20 (Beijing: Zhonghua shuju, 1961), p. 195; Chang, *The Third Force in China*, p. 114.

[13] Huang Yanpei appears to have been pressured by the government to resign. His vocational education schools depended on the government's goodwill and he was then also chairman of the National War Bonds Sales Committee. When he resigned from the chair of the DL, he denied publicly that he was a member. See Shaheen, "The China Democratic League," p. 77.

[14] Chang, *The Third Force in China*, p. 114.

[15] Zuo Shunsheng, "The Reminiscences of Tso Shun-sheng," as told to Julie Lien-ying How, 1965. Chinese Oral History Project, Special Collections, Columbia University, pp. 182–184.

[16] For the full-text of the manifesto and the ten-point statement, see *MMWX*, pp. 5–9.

parties. With its public appearance, the idea of a third force crystallized, but it was not conceived in terms of holding the balance of power, let alone winning government.

As its name suggested, the League was made up of a number of political groups, the "three parties and three groups," to which we have referred previously.[17] Although their leaders joined as individuals, they represented their own parties and groups, thus maintaining a dual identity and divided loyalty. All the same, membership was open also to those having no party affiliations. Zhang Lan, who had replaced Huang Yanpei as Chairman of the Central Executive Committee, was a case in point. A native of Sichuan province, elderly (b. 1872), one-time civil governor of Sichuan under the Duan Qirui Government, and a former president of Chengdu University (1918–1931), Zhang was an independent without a power base. He was made head of the organization because of his standing, his liberal views, and his ability to raise funds.[18]

The League was a conglomeration of disparate and diverse elements, not a unitary organization. As stated in its 1941 manifesto, it was "a preliminary integration of parties and groups with democratic thought."[19] In Zhang Lan's words, it was not a political party, but "a coalition of groups driving the democratic movement."[20] That is, it was a movement as well as a political alliance, aimed at maintaining national unity by reconciling the major parties' differences and generating a democratic breakthrough. These aims, expressed in simple language, were supported by all liberal elements across the country.

Yet from the outset, the League was beset by rivalries among its constituent groups and between the left and the right. On the right was the Youth Party, the largest group within it. Until September 1944, the Youth Party, led by Zuo Shunsheng and Li Huang, managed to dominate the organization in Sichuan, a Youth base for years.[21] On the left were the National Salvation Association and the Third Party, both close to the Communists. Somewhere between them were the National Socialist Party, the Rural Reconstruction Group, and the Vocational Education Society.

---

[17] See Chapter 5, pp. 146–154.
[18] Zhao Xihua, *Minmeng shihua, 1941–1949* (History of the Democratic League, 1941–1949) (Beijing: Zhongguo shehui kexue chubanshe, 1992), p. 32.
[19] *MMWX*, p. 5.
[20] Quoted in Yi Sheng, "Zhongguo minzhu tongmeng," p. 15.
[21] Luo Longji, "Cong canjia jiu zhengxie," p. 197.

ORGANIZATION AND LEADERSHIP

Since 1941, with its headquarters in Chongqing, the League had established branches in various regions, provinces, and cities. The first city branch was formed in Kunming in May 1943 by Luo Longji, Pan Guangdan, and others. The following years saw the formation of the Sichuan branch, the Yunnan branch, the Chongqing city branch, and the Southeast regional branch. After the Provisional National Congress of October 1945, regional branches were also established in north, northeast, northwest, and south China, and city branches were set up in Hankou, Changchun, Guangzhou, and Guilin.[22] In particular, the Kunming and Yunnan branches attracted large numbers of nonpartisan adherents, notably professors from the Southwest Associated University and Yunnan University and their students. Others were writers, editors, artists, and the like whose memberships greatly increased the proportion of individual members.[23] In Hong Kong, the League's operation came to an end following the Japanese occupation of the colony three months after the outbreak of the Pacific War. During the years 1941–1943, it was also brought to a standstill in government territory. After 1945, branches were formed in Southeast Asia and the United States as well.

Although the headquarters remained in Chongqing, Kunming was a League stronghold. These two main centers of activity revealed a deep split within the organization. The Chongqing group was made up mostly of such elements as those in the Youth Party who were generally older, more conservative, more realistic, and somewhat readier to compromise with the government. Many of them had been in and out of public life for a long period of time and were quite familiar with the political facts of life. The Kunming group, on the other hand, was composed mainly of younger writers, teachers, and students who tended to be more idealistic, more radical, and more antigovernment, possessing the spirit and sentiment of the 1935 Beijing student December Ninth Movement. This explained the power struggle and anti-Youth Party sentiment at the

---

[22] Zhao Xihua, *Minmeng shihua, 1941–1949* (History of the Democratic League, 1941–1949) (Beijing: Zhongguo shehui kexue chubanshe, 1992), pp. 33–35.

[23] It is difficult to ascertain the percentage of the independents. Yi Sheng, "Zhongguo minzhu tongmeng," p. 15, estimated it at seventy percent. According to Luo Longji, the ratio between the independents and those with party affiliations was twenty to one. See Luo, "Cong canjia jiu zhengxie," p. 198.

National Representative Conference, held in Chongqing in September 1944.[24]

At that conference, the name of the organization was shortened by dropping the two Chinese words *zhengtuan* (political groups). This move recognized the reality that the organization had become larger and more heterogeneous as a result of the admission of large numbers of non-partisans and individuals from a broad section of the urban population having liberal and democratic aspirations.[25] The influence of the Youths was significantly curtailed, as was that of the National Socialists to a lesser extent. Of the thirty-three members of the newly elected Central Executive Committee, only five were Youths (previously nine) and four were National Socialists, including Luo Longji, who later declared himself an independent. Of the thirteen members of the Standing Committee, three were Youths and four were National Socialists (again including Luo). Zhang Lan remained Chairman of the Central Executive Committee and the Standing Committee; being a nonpartisan, his position was meant to be above party lines.[26] But he was more a figurehead than an executive leader, leaving the day-to-day affairs to the other office bearers, including Zuo Shunsheng (General Secretary), Zhang Bojun (Chief of Organization), Luo Longji (Chief of Propaganda), Zhang Shenfu (Chief of Culture), Liang Shuming (Chief of Internal Relations), and Zhang Junmai (Chief of International Relations). Zhang Lan's only real role was as treasurer thanks to his fund-raising ability.[27] According to a well-informed source, Zuo's position was in name only because the Youth Party was now divested of the control of the secretariat after a power struggle.[28] Other key figures, but not office bearers, included Shen Junru and Tao Xingzhi (both National Salvationists); Ma Zemin, Zhou Jingwen, and Dong Shijin (all independents); and Zhou Xinmin (an independent later found to be a communist). The influence of individual members was on the rise, although the key positions were still filled by leaders of the "three parties and three groups." Since the National Representative Conference, real control of the DL had slid into the hands of the more radical groups. At the Provisional National Party Congress in October 1945, memberships of the Central Executive Committee and the Stand-

---

[24] Van Slyke, *Enemies and Friends*, pp. 179–180.
[25] Yi Sheng, "Zhongguo minzhu tongmeng," p. 15.
[26] Luo Longji, "Cong canjia jiu zhengxie," p. 197.
[27] Zhao Xihua, *Minmeng shihua*, p. 32; Van Slyke, *Enemies and Friends*, p. 180.
[28] Ch'ien Tuan-sheng, *The Government and Politics of China, 1912–1949* (Stanford University Press, 1970), p. 359.

ing Committee were increased to sixty-six and eighteen, respectively.[29] Of the extra thirty-three Central Executive Committee members, only two were from the Youth Party, and of the eighteen Standing Committee members, only Zuo retained a seat for his party. By then, the Youth Party had lost nearly all its influence in the League.

Democratic League leaders were all intellectuals, including some of China's best known and most highly respected scholars, whose approach to politics exhibited a combination of literati-ism – the spirit of the critical imperial scholar – and modern liberalism. Melville Kennedy has commented that they "had inherited the long tradition of China's scholar-government for moralizing on state affairs. The intellectual tradition was to indulge in lofty political exhortation while doing little actively to support it."[30] However, Kennedy continues, "there is evidence that the Democratic League leaders regarded themselves as a good deal more than irresponsible perfectionists or the conspicuous but useless conscience of the government. Individually, they were tirelessly active. Moreover, they felt themselves to be politically influential."[31] His conclusion is that "the political impracticality, the perfectionism, and even ingenuousness of these modern-day literati in dealing with organized and concentrated power accounted for their general ineffectiveness as much as did [GMD] terrorism. As a would-be political party facing determined and powerful opposition, the League left a record of rather pathetic political ineptitude."[32] The problem with them was that they were "political amateurs" (to borrow Jerome Grieder's term), scholars, thinkers, and philosophers, but not professional politicians whose only common ground was opposition to the repressive regime and a desire for democratic change.

The organization lacked any men of stature capable of leadership. Chu Anping, editor of the postwar liberal journal, *Guancha* (The Observer), noted that some DL leaders, such as Zhang Lan and Shen Junru, were elderly, belonging to "a previous generation." The most politically experienced leader, in his view, was Huang Yanpei, but Huang, too, was a "yesterday's man." Zhang Junmai would make a good parliamentarian, but was not suited to a position of executive responsibility. Zhang Dongsun, a political philosopher, was no politician. The only person suited to an

---

[29] Zhao Xihua, *Minmeng shihua*, pp. 32–33.
[30] Melville T. Kennedy, Jr., "The Chinese Democratic League," *Papers on China* 7 (1953): 148.
[31] Ibid.   [32] Ibid., pp. 137–138.

active political life was Luo Longji, who was truly bilingual (Chinese and English), articulate, and passionately interested in politics. But Luo's major weakness was that "he is not as virtuous as he is talented." (Chu was implicitly referring to Luo's private life, which had been the subject of gossip and criticism in some quarters.)[33] The coalescence of these men into a political movement was the outcome of a hostile political environment in which they found themselves. The leadership was fragile.[34]

Not surprisingly, the DL suffered from serious organizational weaknesses. Not being a political party, there was no party discipline to speak of. No sanctions were put on the independent activity of its constituents. As the organization was unable to define itself, it faced an identity crisis. It was not always clear when members were acting individually, for their own parties and groups, and for the DL. There did not seem to be a clear vertical or horizontal relationship, or a command structure at the regional, provincial, and city branches. Membership was not strict. People joined individually, without having to resign from their parties, and could come and go as they pleased. Nobody seemed to know how many rank-and-file members each branch really had, nor was it clear who the cadres were at the lower levels. Those having party affiliations tended to act on their own while wearing the DL hat. Rivalries and jealousies abounded among the branches in recruiting new members. At the upper and middle levels, there was little organizational control. Many had joined simply because of their discontent with the government and the CCP. Some were motivated by a desire to be associated with the Communists without having to join the CCP.[35]

By the end of the war with Japan, the DL claimed a membership of about 3,000, of whom seventy percent were without party affiliations and eighty percent were based in Chongqing and other parts of Sichuan. Of the sixty-six Central Executive Committee members, over ninety percent were intellectuals, and two percent were "national capitalists," "enlightened gentry," and "patriotic military officers." Of the intellectuals, over ten percent were communists.[36] (The membership increased substantially

---

[33] For a relatively objective view of Luo Longji by a long-time associate, see Liang Shiqiu, "Luo Longji lun" (On Luo Longji), *SJPL* 1:15 (April 12, 1947): 5–10.

[34] Chu Anping, "Zhongguo de zhengju" (China's political situation), *GC* 2:2 (March 8, 1947): 7.

[35] Wang Fei, "Minzhu tongmeng jiepou" (Anatomy of the Democratic League), *Ziyou tiandi* 1:8 (April 30, 1947): 6–7; Luo Longji, "Cong canjia jiu zhengxie," p. 196.

[36] Zhao Xihua, *Minmeng shihua*, pp. 32, 393; Yi Sheng "Zhongguo minzhu tongmeng," p. 15.

between 1945 and 1947, when it was outlawed by the government, the total number being estimated at 100,000.)[37] Even though the rank and file were mainly nonpartisans, the leadership still counted on the elite of the "three parties and three groups." Differences among them persisted, as, for example, between Zuo Shunsheng and Luo Longji. Considering its small membership, the DL's claim to represent "the silent majority" of Chinese society was extremely weak. It never managed to attract or represent the peasants and the laboring classes, despite the knowledge that a democratic movement must be based on popular support.

With respect to funding, DL branches were largely self-reliant, but the headquarters relied on contributions from a variety of sources, including its own members. Zhang Lan was personally responsible for part of the operating funds, and the CCP was known to have made some "private" contributions.[38] According to an American diplomatic source, after the DL's reorganization in September 1944, the CCP provided a subsidy of one million *yuan* (Chinese dollar) in a lump sum, plus 60,000 *yuan* per month, paid through the Third Party leader Zhang Bojun.[39] The regional militarists, who had differences with Chiang Kai-shek, were also a source of financial aid, such as Long Yun, Governor of Yunnan; Liu Wenhui, Governor of Xikang; and Li Jishen, former Governor of Guangdong and currently head of Chiang's headquarters in Guilin.[40] Apart from financial considerations, their backing was important as a counter to Chiang's dictatorial regime.

VIEWS ON DEMOCRACY AND THE POLITICAL PLATFORM

Here we shall analyze the DL's views expressed in its official pronouncements, rather than the views of individual members some of which we probed in the previous chapter.

---

[37] Roger Jeans's estimate, without citing his sources. See his entry on the DL in Fukui Haruhiro, ed., *Political Parties of Asia and the Pacific* (Westport: Greenwood Press, 1985), p. 169.

[38] Wang Fei, "Minzhu tongmeng," p. 7.

[39] Cited in Van Slyke, *Enemies and Friends*, p. 183; see also Shaheen, "The China Democratic League," p. 193.

[40] For a study of Long Yun's relations with Chiang Kai-shek during the war, see Lloyd E. Eastman, *Seeds of Destruction: Nationalist China in War and Revolution, 1937–1949* (Stanford: Stanford University Press, 1984), ch. 1; also Eastman, "Regional Politics and the Central Government: Yunnan and Chungking," in Paul K. T. Sih, ed., *Nationalist China During the Sino-Japanese War, 1937–1945* (Hicksville, NY: Exposition Press, 1977), pp. 329–362.

We have noted Chairman Zhang Lan's naïveté in thinking that democracy would be a cure-all for China's ills. He seems to have underestimated the length of time before democracy could be institutionalized and operational in China. Yet his view of democracy was conventional at the time. For him, democracy is politics in which the people are sovereign. He laid down five conditions for the attainment of "true democracy" in China: (1) political sovereignty should reside in the people and not in one person or party; (2) the people should either directly or indirectly manage public affairs and supervise the government through their representatives; (3) these representatives should be elected freely and directly by the people; (4) the people and their representatives in the central government should exercise the four rights (election, recall, initiative, and referendum) without fears or favors; and (5) a democratic constitution defining the rights and duties of the people as well as the powers and responsibilities of the government should be framed by a body of elected representatives and adopted and promulgated by the National Assembly.[41] These were the ABCs of Chinese democracy, and here Zhang's emphasis was on procedures and political method. But he also called on his followers to "make an effort to realize democracy even in our daily life and habits. We must not disregard what is good in other people, or disguise what are really our own flaws."[42] He preached tolerance and equality, viewing democracy as an egalitarian order in which everyone has an equal opportunity to develop his or her potential irrespective of class and gender.[43]

In October 1945, at the Provisional National Representative Congress, the DL provided in a political report a powerful reaffirmation of liberal–democratic values:

> The term *democracy* originally meant "the rule of the people." It was a political system. However, the definition of this term has evolved to the point where nowadays it has a broader [meaning] than a political system. Democracy is a way of human existence; it is a principle for people to be human (*zuoren*). This principle posits human beings as the goal. In society all political and economic organizations are only tools for people to attain the goal of being human.

---

[41] Zhang Lan, "Zhongguo xuyao zhenzheng de minzhu zhengzhi" (China needs true democratic politics), in Sichuan shifan xueyuan, comp., *Zhang Lan wenji* (The collected works of Zhang Lan) (Chengdu: Sichuan jiaoyu chubanshe, 1991), pp. 185–196.
[42] Quoted in Shaheen, "The China Democratic League," p. 340.
[43] Ibid.

People are the masters of all organizations and systems. In accordance with this principle, therefore, the American, Lincoln, said that government should be "of the people, by the people, and for the people." Because human beings are the goal, the numerous necessary conditions for people to be human are inviolable. These necessary conditions are usually referred to as habeas corpus and the freedoms of thought, belief, speech, publication, assembly, association, etc. Because democracy recognizes that people are their own masters, it also recognizes that they are equal in respect of their dignity and worth. According to this principle, therefore, everyone's opportunity to be a human being should be equal. When everyone is free and equal and one's own master, when everyone can attain the goal of being human, and when everyone can realize one's full potential, that is democracy. In a society where all political and economic organizations are instruments for the purpose of everyone being human and being one's own master, that is democracy. According to this principle, therefore, the people are the masters of the nation. The sole purpose of organizing the state is to promote the wellbeing of the entire population. According to this principle, if politics in a state become the dictatorship of one person or one section of the population, and if economics becomes the monopoly of one person or one section of the population, the meaning of democracy is lost. The politics and economics of a democracy must be the politics and economics of the entire population.[44]

The linking of democracy with human rights, the individual, and the entire population reflected the influence of Luo Longji and perhaps also that of Zhang Junmai, who held that human rights are rights with which people were born, inalienable (*buke yirang*), enjoyed by everybody, irrespective of race, creed, and beliefs, and should be respected at all times and places.[45] Thus, human rights were described in the political report as "the numerous necessary conditions for people to be human" which were "inviolable" (*buke qinfan*). In the early 1930s, Chinese rights thinking had focused on civil and political rights. Fifteen years later, the DL went further to demand economic and social rights as well, arguing that economic liberty and equality were more important than political liberty

---

[44] See the political report, *MMWX*, pp. 74–75.
[45] Marina Svensson, "The Chinese Conception of Human Rights: The Debate on Human Rights in China 1898–1949," unpublished Ph.D. dissertation, Lund University, 1996, p. 278.

and equality for the poor people who had no job security and no means of livelihood. After an eight-year war, economic reconstruction was regarded as a higher priority, putting the government under pressure to provide immediate relief for the refugees and jobs for the returned service men, retired soldiers, and unemployed.[46] Now attention was also given to workers' rights and welfare, the right to an education, and the right to gender equality. Not least of all, the political platform included a social welfare system designed to secure personal safety against diseases, old age, disabilities, unemployment, and so on.[47]

The importance of individual autonomy was duly recognized, though not at the expense of the interests of the wider community. While recognizing the tensions among the individual, society, and state, the DL elite held that individual liberty and personal development need not be in conflict with the well-being of the population at large. Juxtaposing personal freedoms with community interests in a complementary relationship, they conceived of democracy in Fabian, democratic socialist, and Chinese humanist terms, all at once.

The meaning and system of democracy had evolved over time and space, and in establishing a modern democratic system, no country could wipe out its historical past or ignore the conditions prevailing at home. The democratic system the DL wanted was "absolutely not going to be a carbon copy of either the Anglo-American or the Soviet system." Instead, it would be a system that, learning from the Anglo-American and Soviet experiences, would be biased toward neither capitalist democracy nor socialist democracy. In any case, according to the political report, Chinese democracy must, as a minimum, respect the freedoms of speech, publication, assembly, association, and so on. There must be elections, which required the formation and legalization of political parties, representing different constituencies and different points of view and competing for the popular vote. The political report acknowledged the superiority of the Anglo-American systems but also noted their shortcomings and deficiencies in the socioeconomic domain where "adjustment" was necessary to extend political freedom and equality to the economic sphere. In short, the report saw the possibility of "using Soviet economic democracy to enrich Anglo-American political democracy."[48] How?

The answer may be found in the DL's political platform, which, based on a number of statements issued between 1941 and 1945, illustrates the

---

[46] *MMWX*, pp. 83–84.   [47] Ibid., p. 86.   [48] Ibid., pp. 75–77.

organization's ideology and democratization project.[49] Such persistent demands as termination of one-party dictatorship, nationalization of the armed forces, establishment of a rule of law, and protection of basic freedoms were part and parcel of the prodemocracy repertoire. An important thing to note was the call for the establishment of a "national affairs multiparty consultative body" pending the adoption of a constitution. The call, first made in October 1941,[50] was repeated time and again. In November of that year, the MPG delegates to the PPC succeeded in passing a resolution to the effect that such a body be established. Nothing came out of it, however, because the GMD's Central Political Council found it unacceptable and was only prepared to set up a wartime administrative committee consisting of leaders from all political parties who would have no real powers. Infuriated, Zhang Lan, Zhang Junmai, and Zuo Shunsheng refused to attend the PPC in protest, not resuming their seats until the Commission for the Inauguration of Constitutionalism was formed in November 1943.[51] They enjoyed the support of the CCP delegates who, in September 1944, urged the formation of a coalition government.[52] On October 10, the DL issued a statement calling, inter alia, for the establishment of a unified wartime national government,[53] similar to the coalition government on which Mao Zedong had written recently.[54]

Upholding the principle of popular sovereignty, the DL viewed the state as an instrument for the promotion of the common good, not an end in itself. High on the political platform were the protection of basic rights and civil liberties and a rule of law with an independent judiciary. These were familiar refrains. More specifically, it called for a bicameral system, with a Senate elected by the provincial assemblies and a popu-

---

[49] For the full text of the political platform, see ibid., pp. 66–70.
[50] See the League's statement of October 10, 1941, ibid., p. 8.
[51] Liang Shuming, "Zhongguo minzhu tongmeng shulüe," *LSMQJ*, VI, 609.
[52] *GMCZH*, II, 1342–1349.   [53] *MMWX*, p. 32.
[54] On April 24, 1945, Mao Zedong wrote an essay on coalition government, in which he said, among other things: ". . . the urgent need is to unite representatives of all political parties and groups and of people without any party affiliation and establish a provisional democratic coalition government for the purpose of instituting democratic reforms, surmounting the present crisis, mobilizing and unifying all the anti-Japanese forces in the country to fight in effective co-ordination with the allied countries for the defeat of the Japanese aggressors. . . . After that it will be necessary to convene a national assembly on a broad democratic basis and set up a formally constituted democratic government, which will also be in the nature of a coalition and will have a still wider representation of people from all parties and groups or without any party affiliation." See Mao Tse-tung, *Selected Works of Mao Tse-tung* (Peking: Foreign Languages Press, 1967), III, 205.

larly elected House of Representatives with powers similar to those of a Western parliament. The President, as head of state, was to be a ceremonial one as executive powers were to be vested in a cabinet system responsible to the House of Representatives. On local self-government, the DL advocated direct democracy below county level, empowering provincial assemblies to make provincial constitutions following the promulgation of the state constitution, with a division of powers between the center and the periphery. There was to be universal suffrage without discrimination on the grounds of property, education, beliefs, gender, and race, contrary to the view of some intellectuals that there should be a graduated system of voting rights based on the level of education. Toward the national minorities, the policy was quite liberal, offering them equal treatment and state protection of their languages, cultures, and minority interests, including self-government with their own constitutions that did not conflict with the state's.

Economically, the political platform emphasized "equalization of wealth," aimed at assuring adequate livelihood, eliminating great inequalities of wealth, and ensuring economic security by enhancing productivity. The state was to safeguard the rights to life, work, and leisure; to care for the old, the weak, and the disabled; and to protect both private and state property. A planned economy was envisioned, combined with a policy of nationalization in the areas of banking, public transport, mining, forestry, waterworks, electricity, and other public amenities, leaving other enterprises to the private sector. In both the private and state sectors, management was to be democratized through worker participation. In industry, the emphasis was laid on people's livelihood and national defense. Foreign investment would be welcome, to be facilitated by new legislation. In agriculture, a policy of rents reduction aimed at protecting land use by poor peasants was to be adopted, with a ceiling on private land ownership, above which private land was subject to purchase by the state in accordance with the law. Through cooperative and state farming, agriculture production was to be industrialized and modernized, the ultimate goal being gradual nationalization of agricultural land. Furthermore, there was to be an equitable taxation system. On foreign trade, both state and private ventures were to be encouraged according to the nation's needs. And on foreign affairs, the platform called for complete independence and self-reliance while cooperating with the democratic nations of the world to fulfill the peace mission of the United Nations.

Militarily, the DL was committed to depoliticizing the country's armies by putting their command, including the communist troops, in the hands of the state. The military was to be barred from executive positions and not to interfere in politics. Conscription was advocated, along with a system of national service. The quality of the soldiers was to be enhanced by improving their working conditions and educational standards. Disabled war veterans were to be looked after by the state. No suggestion was made, however, as to the size of the standing army.

In the field of education, the emphasis was laid on popular education, vocational training, and compulsory education at elementary level. The elimination of illiteracy was an important long-term goal. The accent on vocational education, reflecting the influence of Huang Yanpei, was a corrective to the government's strong bias to tertiary education during the Nanjing period. Nevertheless, great importance was attached to research at universities and academic freedom.

On social policy, the platform stressed the importance of social welfare and security, including child care, public hygiene, and a public hospital and health system. China's population was to be kept at an appropriate level, though there was no indication of what that level was, or whether birth control would be practiced. Probably reflecting the influence of Pan Guangdan, eugenics was mentioned. There was a labor policy advocating an eight-hour working day and minimum wage. Finally, the platform included a plank on women – apparently reflecting the influence of Shi Liang and other feminists – emphasizing gender equality, economically, politically, socially, and legally. Women's rights of political participation, as well as their right to an education, to work, and to rest and recreation were to be protected by the state. Moreover, state crèches, mess halls, and the like were to be provided so that women could be more independent economically. There was no mention of equal pay or affirmative action.

The political platform was an interesting mix of ideas and influences, designed to gain the widest possible acceptance by the intellectual community. Reflecting the DL's diverse constituents, it was the product of a compromise rather than a systematic synthesis. Some of the policies were compatible with the CCP's; others were similar to those of the GMD that had remained on paper. Neither capitalism nor socialism was embraced, but there seemed to be a bit of both, indicating an attempt to combine Anglo-American democracy with Soviet socialism. In 1945, Luo Longji thought that the DL offered a third road featuring a planned economy under a system that protected private property. He recalled sixteen years later: "At the time we had illusions about finding a new road between

Anglo-American capitalism and Soviet socialism. And that was the so-called third road."[55]

Struck by more similarities than differences among China's political parties, Qian Duansheng commented on the DL's policies as follows:

> [The] Democratic League emphasizes democratic ideals as they are known in the West. In that, it is more outspokenly Western than the [GMD] claims to be. In economics, it is to the left of the Youth Party and the Democratic Socialist Party but to the right of the Third Party. It is perhaps quite close to the economic principles of the [GMD]. This is another proof that *as far as the professed principles of parties are concerned there is little choice between the parties of China. They are all democratic. They all tend to be socialistic* [emphasis added]. No believer in free enterprise could find any satisfaction in the economic planks of any party.[56]

True, they all held a dim view of capitalism, the marketplace of free enterprise. But the DL distinguished itself from the ruling Nationalist Party by its belief in modern pluralist politics for which nothing in Chiang's experience had prepared him.

Melville Kennedy has criticized that "Nowhere in the Democratic League's program was there a proposal for direct action by minority parties or a strategy for bringing pressure to bear in support of the democratic program which the League was urging on the government."[57] His observation is correct if by direct action he means going to the people and making a social revolution. But DL leaders called repeatedly for the convocation of a political consultative conference and the formation of an interim coalition government to resolve political differences, a proposal that they genuinely thought was their greatest contribution to peace.[58]

RELATIONS WITH THE CCP AND THE GMD

From the start, the DL was not hostile to the CCP, despite the fact that the Youth Party was stridently anticommunist. (The Youth Party toned down its anticommunist rhetoric after the outbreak of the war.) The National Salvation Association was manifestly procommunist, as was the

---

[55] Luo Longji, "Cong canjia jiu zhengxie," p. 204.
[56] Ch'ien, *The Government and Politics of China*, p. 362.
[57] Kennedy, "The Chinese Democratic League," p. 152.
[58] Tseng Chao-lun, "The Chinese Democratic League," pp. 33–34.

Third Party, which had been enjoying good relations with the CCP since the Fujian Rebellion. The Rural Reconstructionists were prepared to work with the Communists in mobilizing the rural masses. Respected by Mao Zedong, Liang Shuming was one of the very few who could argue with him without being intimidated. In July 1943, Liang told Arthur Ringwalt, the U.S. consul at Guilin, that there was close contact between the DL and the CCP because both desired a successful prosecution of the war and also because the CCP had asked the DL to lead a campaign for continuing the united front.[59] Since then, the Communists had infiltrated the DL, filling the ranks at middle and lower levels.[60] Not surprisingly, writers in the PRC have emphasized the DL's close relationship with the CCP.[61]

The CCP's activities in Yunnan illustrate the extent of communist support for the DL's Kunming branch. According to a 1992 CCP source, intended for internal circulation only, the Communists exploited the long-standing differences between Long Yun and the central government. Early in 1939, when the CCP's Southern Bureau was formed, communist agents made contacts with Long's close associates. Following the New Fourth Army incident, the Nationalist authorities wanted to arrest communist suspects and agents in Yunnan but received no cooperation from Long. Toward the end of 1942, when Luo Longji came to Kunming to establish a local branch, the Southern Bureau sent Zhou Xinmin, who had earlier joined the DL, to assist Luo. In May 1943, when the Kunming branch was formed, a number of Communists joined as individual members. Zhou Xinmin later became a member of the DL's Central Executive Committee. In August, Luo met with Long Yun, who asked that Zhou Enlai be invited to visit Kunming. In October, the Southern Bureau appointed Hua Gang as envoy to establish direct but secret links with Long. As a result, the CCP was allowed to establish radio stations in Yunnan and Guizhou for communication with the Southern Bureau. Other communists arrived on Hua's heels, making contacts with liberal elements in the educational and cultural circles, including Wen Yiduo, Pan Guangdan, Fei Xiaotong, Wu Han, and Zeng Zhaolun. By then, the DL had tilted heavily to the CCP as the influence of the leftist groups and communist members grew, and an extraordinary triangular relationship among the Kunming branch, the CCP, and Long Yun had

---

[59] Cited in Shaheen, "The China Democratic League," p. 191.
[60] Wang Fei, "Minzhu tongmeng," pp. 7, 9.
[61] See, for example, Zhao Xihua, *Minmeng shihua*, pp. 2–4, 438–439.

developed. In this context, the Communists hailed Kunming as the "democratic fortress in the great rear area."[62] The 1992 CCP source supports the complaints of the Nationalist authorities that Long "harbored leftist elements, causing Kunming to become a hotbed of Communism."[63]

The tilt toward the CCP culminated in the signing of a pact in November 1945. Under the pact, reportedly signed by Zhang Shenfu (the DL's Chief of Culture) and Zhang Bojun (the Third Party leader working for the CCP's Organization Department), the DL and the Communists undertook to fight together "to overthrow the Nationalist dictatorship and to realize a democratically governed new China." They agreed not to compromise or cooperate with the Nationalists separately. In case of negotiations with the Nationalists, they were obligated to inform each other, and only when there was mutual consent might either party reach an agreement with them. The DL was also obligated to support the CCP's stand in all future conferences as long as it did not contravene DL principles. Individual members were not to be restricted by that. But in the event of complete disagreement, this might not be publicly made known. For its part, the CCP undertook to recognize and assist the DL in setting up branches in the "liberated areas"; these branches might also exchange information with local CCP branches.[64] The pact seems to have been the result of individual efforts. It was not binding on individual DL members, nor did it represent the DL's official position. Zhang Lan does not appear to have approved of it. Van Slyke thought it "may have been a personal or factional step taken by some parts of the League on their own."[65] What seems certain is that the more influential and radical Kunming group had acted independently of the Chongqing headquarters.

Why did the DL choose to cooperate with the CCP? There were three reasons for that, according to American-educated Zeng Zhaolun, a leading DL figure, who was writing for a foreign readership in 1946. First, just as the United States had cooperated with the Soviet Union in the European War, so the DL could cooperate with the CCP:

> Communism, with all the possible criticism that might be piled on it, is at least very much better than fascism. It is fundamentally different in quality. Without the cooperation of Russia, the Allies

[62] Zhonggong Yunnan shengwei tongzhanbu, comp., *Yunnan tongyi zhanxian ziliao huibian* (Collection of materials on the CCP's Yunnan provincial committee's united front) (Kunming, 1992), *neibu ziliao* (for internal distribution only), pp. 1–4, 9–10.
[63] Cited in Eastman, *Seeds of Destruction*, p. 27.
[64] Van Slyke, *Enemies and Friends*, p. 192.   [65] Ibid., p. 193.

would not have been able to defeat Nazi Germany. For similar reasons, without the cooperation of the Chinese Communist party, it would be impossible to emancipate the Chinese people from the yokes of the Gestapo service and to give them the minimum amount of freedom so essential for the establishment of a democratic state.[66]

Second, there was no need to be afraid of the Communists because, despite their belief in communism as the ultimate world order, they had "no intention of introducing communism – nay, not even the Russian type of socialism – into China at the present stage, nor for a generation to come."[67] Third, "in any country where there are more than two political parties, it is only natural that the opposition parties would [sic] often stand together and oppose the rule and policies of the ruling party."[68] There had been no serious conflict between the DL and the CCP, Zeng added, and provision had been made for settling any such differences in case they should arise.

With its independence probably compromised,[69] the schism within the organization deepened, with the Youth Party particularly dissatisfied. There were signs of a breakaway. The crunch came toward the end of 1945 when the government, in an attempt to exploit the discord within the DL, offered the Youth Party five seats at the upcoming Political Consultative Conference, as opposed to nine for the other parties and groups that remained in the DL. The Youth Party accepted the offer, thus seceding.[70] A year later, the National Socialist Party, now renamed Democratic Socialist Party (*Minzhu shehuidang*) following a merger with the America-based Democratic Constitutional Party (*Minzhu xianzhengdang*), also seceded after deciding to participate in the National Assembly, which was boycotted by the CCP–DL alliance.[71] In October 1947, the DL was outlawed by the government.

The Nationalists and progovernment elements accused the DL of being a communist front. It is interesting to note the appearance in Hong Kong in 1947 of a little book, *A Critique of the Democratic League*. The

---

[66] Tseng Chao-lun, "The Chinese Democratic League," p. 35.
[67] Ibid.   [68] Ibid.
[69] Van Slyke, *Enemies and Friends*, p. 194, thinks that "to a very great extent, League members who favored collaboration with the CCP did not think that they were sacrificing their independence and integrity." They were "of genuinely independent convictions."
[70] Ch'ien, *The Government and Politics of China*, p. 359.
[71] One section of Democratic Socialists, led by Zhang Dongsun, remained with the DL and refused to have anything to do with the National Assembly. See ibid., pp. 355, 360.

editor and principal contributor, Huang Ganyin, apparently a Nationalist, began by attacking the DL as "a meeting place of political flies," referring to the large number of frustrated politicians and military figures, former corrupt bureaucrats, and all those who had joined "in order to overthrow the government without wishing to be extensively engaged in politics or to join the CCP." By fraternizing with the Communists, the DL lost its "middleness" and independence, as well as diminishing its role as a mediator.[72]

Huang criticized that the DL was always critical of the government but hardly of the CCP, ignoring the lack of civil liberties and personal freedoms in communist territory, where, ironically, DL activity was prohibited.[73] Liang Shuming, succeeding Zuo Shunsheng as the DL's general secretary in 1946, explained why they did not criticize the CCP: "Let me say this. We must wait until peace is secured. At the present time, our aims are the same. [The CCP] cannot be criticized."[74] The DL leaders believed that they were of one mind with the Communists in trying to find a peaceful resolution to the conflict at hand.

Huang was skeptical of the democratic pretensions of the DL leaders, accusing them of wanting to advance their own interests and seeking public office. From that perspective, he could see no distinct political philosophy, no central political thought, no vision, and no clear strategies to achieve China's long-term goals. He further criticized that the DL was divorced from the masses and had done nothing to represent their interests.[75] These criticisms were not altogether unfair. The DL leaders were not politically disinterested. Like all aspiring politicians the world over, they sought power and public office. However, that did not mean that they were all "political flies" devoid of good intentions. Some, like Luo Longji, held deep-rooted liberal convictions.

Until late 1947 or early 1948, it was a mistake to portray the DL as a communist stooge. The Chongqing group was not procommunist, and leading figures like Zuo Shunsheng, Zhang Junmai, and Huang Yanpei maintained independence of thought and action. The DL was very different from the CCP in terms of social base, historical background, and

---

[72] Huang Ganyin, ed., *Minmeng pipan* (A critique of the Democratic League) (Hong Kong: Zhongbaoshe, 1947), pp. 1–2.

[73] Ibid., pp. 16–17.

[74] Liang Shuming, "Zhongguo minzhu tongmeng daibiao Liang Shuming shuoming minmeng dui zhonggong taidu" (The Democratic League representative Liang Shuming's statement on the League's attitude towards the CCP), *LSMQJ*, VI, 634.

[75] Huang Ganyin, ed., *Minmeng pipan*, pp. 6–7.

political philosophy, even though they were in full agreement on certain policy issues and strategies. Their close association should not obscure the fact that government actions had pulled them together. As one writer noted, both were victims of repression; hence, they had a common cause.[76] Moreover, the CCP had moderated its radical policies, postponed the socialist revolution, and adopted many "middle" policies that appeared identical to those of the third force. The DL's fraternity with the CCP had more to do with alienation by the government than with the appeal of Chinese communism.

Chu Anping, although critical of the DL's leadership, defended its leftist tendencies:

> All progressive political groups are, of course, a little leftist. That is a world trend. To say that the DL has been a CCP tail is a malicious insult. It should be appreciated that practical politics could not be completely free of manipulation (*quanshu*). Tactically, the DL and the CCP have supported each other, which is only to be expected because their common aim is to weaken the GMD. With that aim, it is natural that they should be closely associated. If we say that the DL has been used by the CCP, we must also say that the DL has used the CCP, too.[77]

In another way, Luo Longji explained the DL's position to John Melby, the Second Secretary at the American embassy in Nanjing, in a conversation on April 13, 1947:

> The Democratic League stands for a liberal, middle-of-the-road policy and that it is, therefore, opposed both to the [GMD] and to the Communists, though political exigencies of the moment require it to follow a course of action largely in support of the Communist position.[78]

In the final analysis, the DL–CCP alliance was a tactical one. It was, noted one American scholar, "a united front against the [GMD] Government for the realization of democracy and the cessation of the civil

---

[76] Li Pingxin, "Lun disan fangmian yu minzhu yundong" (On the third party and the democracy movement), in Li Huaxing, ed., *Zhongguo xiandai sixiangshi ziliao jianbian* (A brief compilation of materials on modern Chinese political thought) (Hangzhou: Zhejiang renmin chubanshe, 1983), V, 497.

[77] Chu Anping, "Zhongguo de zhengju," p. 7.

[78] *FRUS* (1947), VII, 97; John F. Melby, *The Mandate of Heaven: Record of a Civil War, China, 1945–49* (Toronto: University of Toronto Press, 1968), p. 202.

war."[79] Without such an alliance, the DL would not have been taken seriously by the government, but the alliance did constrain its independence of action at times. On balance, the CCP had more to gain than the DL. In 1955, Chen Yi, the PRC's Foreign Minister, speaking at a memorial service for Zhang Lan, paid tribute to the DL, acknowledging that in 1941 and thereafter it had assisted the CCP by sustaining the anti-Chiang struggle in the rear area.[80]

Relations with the Nationalists, therefore, were unsatisfactory at all times. The DL was never afforded legal recognition and was always treated with suspicion by the government. The feeling was mutual. The DL viewed the government as fascist, which explained, in part, its collaboration with the Communists.[81] It also sought to cooperate with the progressive elements within the GMD who were themselves at the mercy of the right wing of the Party. Zeng Zhaolun claimed that a few Nationalists had joined the organization and become "important leaders."[82] He did not reveal their names, and I have been unable to identify them or verify his account. But it appeared that Sun Fo had some sympathy for the DL and was reported to have addressed one of its open forums in 1944.[83] The American consul-general in Kunming, Wm. R. Langdon, also occasionally mentioned some "well-placed [GMD] liberals" who were critical of Chiang Kai-shek and his government.[84]

The DL had been accused of conspiring to overthrow the Chiang regime in 1944. There was indeed such a conspiracy as part of an anti-Chiang movement in the provinces of which there were two vortices. One was in Guangxi led by Li Jishen with the support of various southern commanders, including Long Yun and Zhang Fakui. Another was in Kunming, where the prime movers were the radical group allegedly led by Luo Longji, who established contacts with a number of regional militarists.[85] The conspirators were an extraordinarily heterogeneous group of regional militarists, radicals, idealists, opportunistic politicians, and

---

[79] It became a full alliance after 1946. See Shaheen, "The China Democratic League," p. 408 and ch. 9.

[80] Cui Zongfu, ed., *Zhang Lan xiansheng nianpu* (A chronology of Zhang Lan's life) (Chongqing: Chongqing chubanshe, 1985), p. 4.

[81] Tseng Chao-lun, "The Chinese Democratic League," pp. 34–35; Melby, *The Mandate of Heaven*, p. 202, quoting Luo Longji.

[82] Tseng Chao-lun, "The Chinese Democratic League," p. 37.

[83] *FRUS* (1944), VI, 456.   [84] Ibid., pp. 476, 493.

[85] Eastman, *Seeds of Destruction*, pp. 29–30. For Luo's involvement in the conspiracy, see Frederic J. Spar, "Human Rights and Political Activism: Luo Longji in Chinese Politics, 1928–1958," manuscript, 1993, pp. 196–202.

feudal barons. There was much plotting and planning for concerted action in the event of a collapse of the central government in Chongqing. According to the American consul in Guilin, a meeting was planned for October 10, 1944, in Chengdu, the chief purpose of which would be to call into being a provisional Government of National Defense (*guofang zhengfu*). That government would unite the country and prosecute the war against Japan to the end. It would be democratic under the direction of some nationally known and respected leaders yet to be selected. The Communists had not been consulted on the plans, but after the new government was formed, they would be asked to participate in it along with the democratic elements of the Nationalist elite.[86] In the end, nothing came of all this conspiring because the opposition, being the heterogeneous group that it was, could not work concertedly in the creation of a viable alternative government.[87]

The conspiracy raised several interesting questions. Did the DL ever contemplate the use of force, supplied by the disaffected regional militarists, to overthrow the central government? Did its association with the militarists not make a mockery of what they stood for as a liberal third force and represent a radical departure from the principles of civil opposition? Was the conspiracy directed at both Chiang Kai-shek personally and the Nationalist government? To answer these questions, it is important to bear in mind that the conspiracy was hatched in anticipation of a collapse of the central government in the circumstances prevailing in the country. To be sure, the regional militarists would always avail themselves of any opportunity that might arise to weaken central government authority. But, as Lloyd Eastman noted, the strategy of the DL's Kunming group was formulated on the assumption that the Chiang regime, in the midst of the Japanese Ichigo Offensive in 1944, was on the verge of collapse. The group leaders "thus thought it possible *to avoid violence* [emphasis added] and concentrated instead on preparing to fill the void that would be created by the approaching fall of the Nationalist government."[88] There was no intention of turning civil opposition into organized violence. The DL had not contemplated the use of force to topple the government. Its aim was to democratize the regime, not to overthrow it.[89] The thought of the government's imminent demise in 1944 was not as

---

[86] *FRUS* (1944), VI, 415–416. [87] Eastman, *Seeds of Destruction*, pp. 31–32.

[88] Ibid., p. 31. For details of the dissident movement and the involvement of individual DL activists, see Shaheen, "The China Democratic League," ch. 5.

[89] Shaheen, "The China Democratic League," pp. 181–182.

wild as it might seem, considering the Japanese offensive, official corruption and ineptitude, inflation, widespread discontent, and the debilitating effects of seven years of war.

If the opposition had taken on a serious dimension in 1944, it was because the conspirators now took the position that Chiang Kai-shek was solely responsible for China's critical situation. The DL thought that the GMD under his leadership would not really carry out any reform in the central government and that he and his regime were doomed. Such views revealed the serious decline of Chiang's prestige among Chinese liberals, including some frustrated GMD members. Less than a year before, many thinking Chinese still believed that Chiang would be China's only leader, but now he was strongly criticized even by those who did not support the conspiracy and who did not believe it could succeed.[90] The only difference between the conspirators and other "well-informed" liberals not associated with the movement was that the latter thought that Chiang was too firmly established to be overthrown and that it was American support alone that could influence the GMD regime into paths of democratic reform.[91]

The local militarists stood for the very opposite of the ideals of democracy and freedom for which civil opposition was fighting. But it is easy to understand why the minor parties turned to them. Because the local warlords were opposed to increasing central government authority, their support was thought to be necessary to the success of the democratic movement. One National Salvationist told an American embassy official in Chengdu that if "this policy of fighting fire with fire" enabled the joint opposition to break the power of the "fascist elements" in the government, the warlords themselves would be much more likely than the Nationalists to allow the gradual development of a less centralized and more democratic government, not least because many of the subordinate officers of the warlords held liberal views.[92] For the minor parties, it was also a matter of survival in the face of political repression.

MEDIATION AND OPPOSITION TO CIVIL WAR

Since its inception, the DL had set itself two tasks: mediation and democratization. Linking them was the conviction that conflict should be resolved politically and that a political solution was possible only if there was a widening of the base of government.

[90] *FRUS* (1944), VI, 492, 493–494. [91] Ibid., pp. 490–491. [92] Ibid., p. 442.

Previously we dealt with the vigorous push for constitutionalism and civil liberties in the PPC.[93] Many of the MPG delegates to the PPC were also DL leaders while maintaining their party/group identity. The DL's approach to mediation was not "strongly traditionalist" as Melville Kennedy criticized,[94] for it proceeded from the premise that Chinese politics should be demilitarized and democratized and that all the armies should be nationalized under one unified command. These were important principles. But the Communists could not be expected to give up their troops to the state without guarantees for their regional autonomy and involvement in the processes of government. Even with such guarantees, it was extremely doubtful that they would. And why should they give up their troops as long as the GMD regime was a military dictatorship?

Good offices were first made when the MPG delegates tried to dissuade the Communists from boycotting the PPC following the New Fourth Army incident. Between 1941 and 1943, there were further attempts at a political settlement. In September 1943, Chiang gave explicit instructions to the Party's Central Executive Committee that the communist problem was a purely political one that should be solved by peaceful means.[95] Following that, General Lin Biao, representing the CCP, conducted negotiations in Chongqing in November on the reorganization of the communist forces. Further negotiations took place in Xi'an in May 1944 and lasted through September when the details were reported to the PPC.[96] Within the Nationalist camp, there were elements favoring reconciliation and continued cooperation with the Communists in order to finish the war with Japan. The Political Study Clique, for one, though declining in importance in Nationalist politics, was believed to be advocating that in the summer of 1944.[97]

The U.S. Department of State acknowledged that the "minor parties played an important, if unsuccessful, role in negotiations between the Communists and the [GMD] prior to the offer of American good offices in 1944 by Major General Patrick J. Hurley, the Personal Representative of President Roosevelt."[98] In June 1944, when Vice-President Henry A. Wallace came to Chongqing, he met with DL representatives.[99] Liang

[93] See Chapter 5, pp. 166–179.   [94] Kennedy, "The Chinese Democratic League," p. 157.
[95] Chinese Ministry of Information, comp., *China Handbook, 1937–1945* (New York: Macmillan, 1947), p. 67.
[96] *The China White Paper (1949)*, I, 54–55; *GMCZH*, II, 1323–1364.
[97] *FRUS* (1944), VI, 456.   [98] *The China White Paper (1949)*, I, 54.
[99] Liang Shuming, "Zhongguo minzhu tongmeng shulüe," *LSMQJ*, VI, 608.

Shuming, then the DL's resident representative in Guilin, asked Consul Arthur Ringwalt to forward a letter to the vice-president, in which he set out the DL's position on the Chinese situation.[100] In August, Ambassador Clarence Gauss, in a personal interview with Chiang Kai-shek, said that he appreciated that the difficulty of one-party rule could not be overcome on a broad basis to give representation in the government to the MPGs. But he thought "perhaps a limited solution might be found under which able representatives of the [minor] parties or special groups might be . . . invited to share in some form of responsible war council which planned and carried out plans to meet the serious war crisis taking place in China."[101] The ambassador's idea was that in such sharing of responsibility there could be developed a disposition toward cooperation for China's unification. That was in line with the thinking of the MPGs and independents.

One of the terms of the mission of General Hurley, who succeeded Gauss as the U.S. Ambassador to China, was to unify all the Chinese military forces for the purpose of defeating Japan. To that end, on November 7, 1944, he flew to Yan'an for a two-day conference with Mao Zedong and, in January of the following year, brought Zhou Enlai and others to Chongqing for negotiations. In June 1945, Hurley was also providing assistance to a group of seven persons to meet with the Communists in Yan'an.[102]

The mission of the group illustrates not only the DL's involvement but also the ambiguous status of those concerned. According to Hurley, the "committee of seven," as he called the group, was appointed by the government following the Sixth GMD National Congress (May 1945). They called on him on June 27, informing him that three independents had been appointed by the PPC and that the others had volunteered their services. They sought his advice and were told that they should go over all the proposals and counterproposals made by both sides and make their own decisions.[103] On July 1, the group consisting of Huang Yanpei, Zuo Shunsheng, Zhang Bojun, Leng Yu, and two independents, Chu Fucheng and Fu Sinian (less the third independent Wang Yunwu due to illness) went to Yan'an by air for a five-day conference with Mao and other communist leaders. There was no government member in the group, contrary to what Hurley had thought. Huang, Zhang, and Zuo were leading DL figures, of course, but they were also leaders of their

---

[100] *FRUS* (1944), VI, 458–459.   [101] *The China White Paper (1949)*, I, 62–63.
[102] Ibid., pp. 73–82, 102–105.   [103] Ibid., pp. 102–103.

own parties and groups. What hats were they wearing? In what capacity did they visit Yan'an? Zuo recalled that it was "a sort of private trip," not representing the government but endorsed by it and assisted by the American embassy, which paid for their return airfares. He did not regard himself or the others as representing either the government or the PPC.[104] Zuo was not entirely correct. It would appear that the visit was a PPC initiative with the apparent approval of Chiang Kai-shek and the blessing of the American embassy and a sort of "parliamentary" delegation with no official status. Whatever the case may have been, the outcome was the same. After the visit, some came away with the impression that the CCP was pragmatic, flexible, and down to earth in dealing with the problems of rural Shaanxi;[105] however, Fu Sinian was disillusioned.[106]

Hurley wished to see the DL develop into a liberal force, which was precisely how the DL viewed itself. While playing the role of a mediator, the DL was also vigorously engaged in campaigning for constitutionalism. From May 1944 until late summer 1945, the journal *Minxian* (Democracy and Constitutionalism) was published in Chongqing. In 1945, the influential *Minzhu zhoukan* (Democratic Weekly) appeared in Kunming as a DL organ. And in mid-November, the DL launched a nationwide anti-civil-war campaign, holding mass rallies and opposing American intervention in China's internal affairs. Notable among those involved were high-profile professors from Kunming's Southwest Associated University. This was a remarkable university that proudly regarded itself as the "bastion of democracy" and "guardian of the liberal heritage of the New Culture." Many of its academic staff had, by now, established new bonds with Chiang Kai-shek's less-than-loyal opposition.[107] They had

---

[104] Zuo Shunsheng, *Jin sanshinian jianwen zaji*, p. 80. See pp. 81–93 for his account of the visit.

[105] Upon his return, Huang Yanpei wrote a short book, *Yan'an guilai* (Return from Yan'an) recording favorably what he saw in Yan'an. "What I have seen . . . is very near to my ideals. The Communists are not interested in high-sounding theories. Instead, they are interested in finding out what the people need and in practical knowledge and practical work." Quoted in Spar, "Human Rights and Political Activism," p. 236. See also Curran, "From Educator to Politician," pp. 96–97.

[106] See Howard I. Boorman, ed., *Biographical Dictionary of Republican China* (New York: Columbia University Press, 1967–1971), II, 45.

[107] John Israel, "Southwest Associated University: Preservation as an Ultimate Value," in Sih, ed., *Nationalist China During the Sino-Japanese War, 1937–1945*, p. 146. For a full treatment of this university, see John Israel, *Lianda: A Chinese University in War and Revolution* (Stanford: Stanford University Press, 1999).

a great deal of influence on the students who organized a DL Democratic Youth Corps to demonstrate against civil war.[108] Not to be outshone, twenty-eight activists in Chongqing jointly made a plea to both Chiang and Mao to settle their differences politically.[109]

Before the year was over, Kunming was the scene of the December First Movement. On November 25, students in Kunming, which had a large concentration of schools during the war, attempted to hold a gathering to protest against armed clashes between the government and the Communists. The police, firing over the heads of the demonstrators and cutting off the electricity supply to the public-address system, disrupted the gathering. In retaliation, the students boycotted classes. Many took to the streets, confronting the police and demanding an end to civil war and freedoms of speech and assembly. On December 1, armed police invaded a number of campuses and opened fire on demonstrating students, leaving three students and a music teacher dead and more than a hundred others injured. The incident sparked off more demonstrations in Kunming and other cities.[110] DL activists and prominent intellectuals supported the students, attending rallies, delivering antigovernment speeches, demanding democracy, and opposing civil war.[111] By the end of 1945, civil opposition, the student movement, and the anti-civil-war campaign had merged into a big movement.

CONCLUSION

Civil opposition was transformed into a third force movement early in the 1940s in response to widening cracks in the structure of the united front. To prosecute the war against Japan, an end had to be put to civil strife, for which purpose the MPG leaders appointed themselves to a peace-making mission while campaigning for constitutional and

---

[108] Zhao Xihua, *Minmeng shihua*, pp. 59–60.

[109] Shen Pu and Shen Renhua, eds., *Shen Junru nianpu* (A chronology of Shen Junru's life) (Beijing: Zhongguo wenshi chubanshe, 1992), p. 267.

[110] For the details, see Israel, *Lianda*, pp. 369–375; Lincoln Li, *Student Nationalism in China, 1924–1949* (Albany: State University of New York Press, 1994), pp. 121–129; Suzanne Pepper, *Civil War in China: The Political Struggle, 1945–1949* (Berkeley: University of California Press, 1978), pp. 42–93.

[111] Liu Zhi, "Shishu minmeng zai "yier.yi" yundong de lishi yiyi he jiben jingyan" (An attempt to describe the Democratic League's role in the December First Movement), in ⟨Yier.yi⟩ yundong yu xinan lianda bianweihui, ed., ⟨*Yier.yi*⟩ *yundong yu xinan lianda* (The December First Movement and the Southwest Associated University) (Kunming: Yunnan daxue chubanshe, 1996), pp. 252–262.

democratic reforms. To pull themselves together, they called the DL into being.

The DL illustrates the weaknesses rather than the strengths of the third force movement. If China needed a third major party in the 1940s as some thought,[112] the DL failed to fill the bill. The MPGs failed to band together into a single, liberal organization capable of national leadership. Thomas Curran has commented that the third force movement "was doomed from the start, because its leaders lacked the vision even to try to create a sustainable base of power."[113] China was essentially an agrarian society where the middle class was small, conservative, and politically unorganized. Coming from that class and aloof from the rural masses, the third force movement was not inclined to take direct action in the social revolution. The DL failed as an organization and a movement for a combination of factors: lack of leadership and cohesion, political inexperience, mutual rivalries and personal differences among its leaders, financial difficulties, lack of popular support, and Nationalist repression. But the single most important factor was the fact that the DL, having no control of the means of violence, was incapable of competing with the major parties on the same terms and in the same playing field. The playing field was not level. Even if there had been a Chinese liberal party devoted to the public good, it would have been no match for the Nationalists and the Communists who were entirely different political animals.

The reality was that in Chinese politics, which were violent and unstable, there was little room for a third force. Does that mean there was no need for it at all? It is all too easy to answer in the affirmative. One is tempted to ridicule the middle-of-the-road intellectuals as naïve and ineffectual and their efforts as an exercise in futility. But the third force movement had a deeper significance than has been recognized. It represented a minor but important tradition of political culture juxtaposed against the authoritarian cultures of the GMD and the CCP. It produced the germs of a reformist, liberal order in the Nationalist era. It further developed the democratic impulse of the May Fourth period, drawing strength from reason, tolerance, and a proclivity for negotiation and compromise. It also belied the conventional wisdom that Chinese intellectuals had no taste for political engagement. It was not naïve, but coura-

---

[112] See, for example, Luo Longji, "Zhongguo xuyao disan ge da zhengdang" (China needs a third large political party), *MZZK* 1:16 (April 9, 1945): 4–7.
[113] Curran, "From Educator to Politician," p. 87.

geous, to advocate nonviolent means of conflict resolution in a violent and illiberal setting. The American diplomat John Melby wrote in his diary on November 17, 1945:

> They [DL leaders] were almost all educated abroad, call themselves the intellectuals of China, make a precarious sort of living writing ambiguous editorials for [GMD] papers, and discuss the situation in their spare time. They believe the civil war will be continued . . . and advocate discussion groups as the way out of all troubles, possibly because they do not have an army and are mostly unlikely to get one. Despite the tremulous and ineffectual air about them, I have to admire their guts. They never stop their criticism of the Government, even though they know they are under continual secret police surveillance. Every so often one of them disappears, and his death is seldom quick or gentle; they also know it could happen to them all at any time.[114]

DL activity was nothing, if it was not political. Yet its leaders were political amateurs, easily out-maneuvered by the big players of the major parties for whom the rules of the game were to win all. Nevertheless, some held liberal convictions, genuine in the belief that they could be a bridge between the Nationalists and the Communists. It was only natural that they should view democracy from a Chinese standpoint. They could be faulted for many things, but not for wanting to adapt Western democracy to Chinese conditions.

The DL did not represent the totality of the third force. There were liberal elements not associated with any antigovernment movement but equally critical of the Chiang regime. They may be classified as the exponents of the Western liberal tradition in the Chinese scene, although the ruling elite viewed many of them as "radicals." Some had been on the fringe of governmental affairs through their participation in the PPC. There were also liberal elements within the government who shared the democratic aspirations of the opposition, feeling frustrated at their inability to contribute to the government as policies were dictated by Chiang.

The third force was searching for a way for China to go forward. Some called it a third road. But if Chinese politics were reduced to a choice between authoritarianism and democracy, it could be argued that there was no third road, not even a second road because the Nationalists and

---

[114] Melby, *The Mandate of Heaven*, p. 34.

the Communists were equally authoritarian. In that perspective, there could be only one road – democratization – that underscored the relationship between democracy and middle politics.[115] But Chinese politics were too complex to be reduced to such simple terms.

The third force movement did not come to a stop at the end of 1945. By then, the last chance of averting civil war lay in the forthcoming Political Consultative Conference.

---

[115] Wu Dange, "Minzhu luxian yu zhongjian luxian" (The democratic line and the middle line), *Shi yu wen* 1:8 (May 2, 1947): 3–4, continued on p. 15.

8

"Peace, Democracy, Unification, and Reconstruction," 1946

IN AUGUST 1945, the Chinese won the war but did not win the peace. National salvation was partially, and only partially, achieved. No sooner had the Japanese surrendered than the threat of a renewed civil war loomed large. Reflecting the mood of the intellectual community, civil opposition took on the slogan "peace, democracy, unification, and reconstruction."[1] The order of these words was significant. First, there must be peace – only then could there be democracy – then, democracy, and only then could there be unification, or national unity. And only with peace, democracy, and unity could there be reconstruction. This was similar to the CCP's slogan "peace, democracy, and unity," portraying the government as an obstacle to peace. For its part, the government insisted on unity, or unification, prior to democracy, meaning that the Communists must give up their armed opposition first.[2] As for the masses, after a devastating eight-year war, the last thing they wanted was civil war.

This chapter is largely a narrative. The facts are laid out here to add to the themes of this book. The Political Consultative Conference (PCC) and the subsequent peace efforts of the third force illustrate the theme of peace, democracy, unification, and reconstruction. The PCC, especially, sheds lights on the way in which civil opposition conducted itself as it attempted to translate its ideas into policies. (Chief among those ideas was the Democratic League's slogan "democratization of politics and nationalization of the armies.") With public opinion on its side, the PCC

---

[1] The DL published a collection of official documents in late 1945 entitled *Heping minzhu tongyi jianguo zhilu* (The road to peace, democracy, unification, and national reconstruction) (Chongqing: Minxian yuekanshe).

[2] This theme had been developed during the war by GMD writers who blamed the absence of democracy on the country's disunity and separatism. See Ye Qing, *Tongyi yu minzhu* (Unification and democracy) (N.p.: Duli chubanshe, 1940).

held out hopes of a political settlement. The Communists did not seem to be irrevocably committed to civil war early in 1946. The Nationalists were facing many problems and might be willing under certain circumstances to reach a settlement. Internationally, the United States desired to see a united and peaceful China, and the Soviet Union did not want a Chinese civil war either.

Unfortunately, despite some initial success, the PCC proved to be a failure, prompting the third force to resume its mediating role. The peace effort is outlined here not merely for the record but, more important, to illustrate once again the juxtaposition of the minor but challenging tradition of liberal opposition against the win-all-or-lose-all tradition of Chinese political culture. In the end, as the limited civil war escalated into an all-out civil war, the dominant mainstream political culture, not surprisingly, prevailed, thus blocking the road to democracy.

THE POLITICAL CONSULTATIVE CONFERENCE

The Chongqing talks between Mao Zedong and Chiang Kai-shek in the summer of 1945 under General Patrick Hurley's auspices resulted in the signing of the "Double-Tenth Agreement" (October 10) on twelve issues. General principles were agreed on democratization, unification of the armed forces, and recognition of the CCP and all other political parties as equal before the law. The government further agreed to guarantee the freedoms of person, religion, speech, publication, and assembly: to release political prisoners: and to permit only the police and law courts to make arrests, conduct trials, and impose punishments. A political consultative conference was to be held on November 20 for the implementation of the agreed principles.[3] Three vital issues were left unresolved, however: representation on the National Assembly, the redesignation of the communist troops, and the legality of the communist base areas and their administrations. These issues were to be resolved at the PCC, which had been postponed to early January 1946 because of growing tensions in Manchuria.

On January 10, when the PCC opened, a cease-fire agreement was reached through the efforts of the Committee of Three composed of General George C. Marshall, President Truman's special envoy with the personal rank of ambassador, as adviser; General Zhang Zhizhong representing the government; and Zhou Enlai representing the CCP.

[3] For a summary of the negotiations, see *The China White Paper (1949)*, I, 105–110.

Under the agreement, a general cease-fire, to be supervised by an Executive Headquarters in Beijing led by three commissioners representing the government, the CCP, and the United States, was to take effect from January 13. It was to bring to a halt all troop movements in North China, with certain exceptions included in the stipulation regarding the cease-fire order. The stipulation provided for the movement of government troops into Manchuria to restore Chinese sovereignty and to the south of the Yangzi River in connection with the government's military reorganization plans.[4]

The PCC was a litmus test with which to gauge the sincerity of the conflicting parties in trying to settle their political differences.[5] The delegates represented all the groupings in the Chinese political arena: after hard bargaining, there were eight from the GMD,[6] seven from the CCP,[7] nine from the DL,[8] five from the Youth Party,[9] and nine independents,[10] a total of thirty-eight participants, twenty-two of whom were concurrently members of the PPC. By then, the third force had split into three distinct political groupings, namely, the DL (less the Youth Party), the Youth Party in its own right, and the independents. The Youths and most of the independents were progovernment, whereas the DL was in a tactical alliance with the CCP. The PCC lacked any legal authority to enforce its decisions. Morally, all parties represented

---

[4] Ibid., pp. 136–137.

[5] Qian Jiaju, "Ping zhengzhi xieshanghui" (Comment on the Political Consultative Conference), *Ziyou shijie banyuekan* 1:5 (January 1, 1946): 159–160.

[6] They were Sun Fo, Zhang Chun, Wu Tiecheng, Wang Shijie, Chen Lifu, Zhang Lisheng, Chen Bulei, and Shao Lizi.

[7] They were Zhou Enlai, Dong Biwu, Wu Yuzhang, Lu Dingyi, Ye Jianying, Deng Yingchao, and Wang Ruofei.

[8] They were Zhang Lan, Shen Junru, Zhang Junmai, Zhang Dongsun, Zhang Bojun, Huang Yanpei, Zhang Shenfu, Luo Longji, and Liang Shuming.

[9] They were Zeng Qi, Chen Qitian, Yu Jiaju, Chang Naide, and Yang Yongjun. Surprisingly, Li Huang was not a delegate. Zuo Shunsheng claimed in his memoir (*Jin sanshinian jianwen zaji*, pp. 98–99) that he was not interested because he did not think that a conference of this kind could resolve the problems. The fact, however, was that Zuo had been ousted from the leadership of the Youth Party by former leader Zeng Qi. Zeng was believed to be instrumental in taking his party out of the DL and was more willing to cooperate with the government. See Luo Longji, "Cong canjia jiu zhengxie dao canjia Nanjing hetan de yixie huiyi" (Some recollections of the events from my participation in the old Political Consultative Conference to my participation in the Nanjing peace negotiations), *Wenshi ziliao xuanji*, No. 20 (Beijing: Zhonghua shuju, 1961), pp. 213–214; Liang Shuming, "Wo canjia guogong hetan de jingguo" (My participation in the GMD–CCP negotiations), *LSMQJ*, VI, 908.

[10] They were Shao Congen, Mo Dehui, Wang Yunwu, Fu Sinian, Qian Yongming, Mou Jiaming, Hu Lin, Guo Moruo, and Li Zhuchen.

at the conference were obliged to accept its decisions, but legally those decisions were subject to approval by the central executive committees of those parties.

At the opening session of the PCC, Chiang Kai-shek renewed the government's "four promises": (1) guarantees for the freedoms of person, creed, speech, publication, assembly, and association; (2) equal legal status for all political parties that operated openly within the law; (3) the holding of popular elections and implementation of local self-government; and (4) the release of political prisoners, except traitors and those found to have committed definite acts injurious to the Republic.[11] Chiang was, as usual, long on rhetoric and short on action. Nonetheless, the PCC got off to an exciting start, with the delegates placing high hopes on it.[12]

The PCC was concerned with five specific issues: (1) revision of the 1936 Draft Constitution; (2) convocation of a constituent national convention for the purpose of adopting a new constitution; (3) reorganization of the government; (4) formulation of a political program to end the period of political tutelage and to commence national reconstruction; and (5) reorganization of all the armed forces under unified command. All these were to be dealt with separately by five subcommittees meeting in closed sessions, each made up of two representatives from each of the five constituent political groupings. In addition, there was a Steering Committee, which continued to meet after the adjournment of the PCC on all questions relating to the five problem areas. It was the expectation of the opposition parties that an interim coalition government would be formed to devise details of implementing the PCC resolutions prior to the convocation of the National Assembly.

In the event, five resolutions were passed before the PCC adjourned on January 31. In his address to the closing session, Chiang Kai-shek promised that the resolutions would be fully respected and carried out by his government as soon as the prescribed procedures had been completed. He also pledged to uphold the national reconstruction program faithfully and to see to it that all the military and civil authorities would follow it strictly.[13] "Uphold the PCC resolutions" became an opposition

---

[11] *ZZXSHY*, pp. 129–133; Lyman P. Van Slyke, ed., *Marshall's Mission to China, December 1945–January 1947: The Report and Appended Documents* (Arlington, VA: University Publications of America, 1976), I, 24–25.

[12] Luo Longji recalled how excited and hopeful he was when he attended the conference. See Luo Longji, "Cong canjia jiu zhengxie," p. 219.

[13] *The China White Paper (1949)*, I, 138.

slogan thereafter. Let us now look at the five problem areas in some detail, focusing on the role of the opposition parties.

The 1936 Draft Constitution

The question of the Draft Constitution revealed the clearest divergence of views between the GMD and the opposition parties. The GMD wanted the four rights – election, recall, initiative, and referendum – to be exercised by a 2,000-strong National Assembly; a powerful President; a strong central government; and a five-Yuan structure. The Draft Constitution provided for all that. Specifically it empowered the National Assembly to elect the President and Vice-President, the heads of the five Yuan, and members of the Legislative and Control Yuan. But the National Assembly was not designed to be the supreme law-making body to which the government would be responsible. As Zhang Junmai criticized, the Draft Constitution "provided for a system whereby the people had no rights while the President was omnipotent."[14]

Sun Yat-sen had favored a plebiscite democracy at county level, but he had also wanted the National Assembly to exercise the four rights for the people, that is, indirect democracy through the people's representatives. Was it possible to juxtapose the two types of democracy? The CCP and the DL wanted the four rights to be exercised by the people themselves, leaving the National Assembly as a synonym for "the electorate"; a President with extremely limited powers; an American-style system of checks and balances; a decentralized federal system; and a tripower government again similar to that of the United States.[15] The Youth Party's position was similar, proposing a cabinet system, a bicameral legislature, a more effective five-Yuan structure, and a fair division of powers between the central government and provincial authorities.[16] The challenge for the Draft Constitution Subcommittee was to devise a system that could reconcile direct and indirect democracy and bring the executive government to account.

The Subcommittee found an answer in Zhang Junmai's notion of an "invisible National Assembly." (Zhang, it may be noted, was not a member of the Subcommittee.) His idea was to abolish the proposed National Assembly as an organic body, retaining its name only. The four rights were to be exercised through the ballot box without the actual con-

---

[14] Quoted in Luo Longji, "Cong canjia jiu zhengxie," p. 227.
[15] Van Slyke, ed., *Marshall's Mission to China*, I, 31.   [16] *ZZXSHY*, pp. 252–255.

vocation of the National Assembly. The President was to be elected directly by the county, provincial, and central political assemblies, free from the control of the central government. The remainder of the four rights was to be exercised in a similar way. The essence of a British-style parliamentary system would be assured if the functions of the five Yuan were redefined according to the principle of checks and balances. Specifically, Zhang suggested that the Control Yuan should be turned into something like the Upper House, the Legislative Yuan into the House of Commons, and the Executive Yuan into the cabinet. The Executive Yuan should be responsible to the Legislative Yuan, which should have the powers to pass votes of no-confidence in the cabinet and to order the formation of a new one. The Executive Yuan, for its part, should have the power to dissolve the Legislative Yuan and to hold new general elections.[17] The crux of Zhang's proposal was a responsible cabinet system, with the five powers being reduced to three – executive, legislative, and control – plus an independent judiciary, a depoliticized Examination Yuan, and a civil service based on merit. The proposal enjoyed the support of the opposition parties.

With respect to provincial self-government, the MPGs favored a system under which the province was the highest local self-governing unit, with a directly elected governor and a provincial constitution. The idea was to establish a federal system giving a large degree of autonomy to the provinces, thereby resolving the issue of the communist "liberated areas." The National Salvationist lawyer Shen Junru pointed out that the "liberated areas" were a legacy of the war and that their legal status, along with their achievements, should be recognized.[18] Meanwhile, it was also suggested that the position of Vice-President be created and that there be a Standing Committee when the National Assembly was in recess. There was also a move to have the phrase "in accordance with the law" removed from the clause relating to civil liberties.[19] Sun Fo and Shao Lizi, the government's representatives on the Subcommittee, were understood to agree with their overall position.[20]

Consequently, the PCC resolution recommended a number of major amendments to the Draft Constitution based on the following principles:

---

[17] Carsun Chang, *The Third Force in China* (New York: Bookman, 1952), pp. 204–205; Liang Shuming, "Wo canjia guogong hetan de jingguo," *LSMQJ*, VI, 900.

[18] *MMWX*, pp. 136–137.   [19] *MMWX*, pp. 137–138.

[20] Liang Shuming, "Wo canjia guogong hetan de jingguo," *LSMQJ*, VI, 900, 903.

1. The National Assembly. The entire electorate, when it exercises the rights of election, recall, initiative, and referendum, shall be called the National Assembly. Pending the extension of universal suffrage, the President shall be elected by the district, provincial, and national representative assemblies. The recall of the President is to be effected by the same means as that employed in his election.
2. The Legislative Yuan. This Yuan is to be the supreme law-making body of the State and will be elected by the electorate. Its functions are to correspond to those of a parliament in a democratic country.
3. The Control Yuan. This Yuan, to be elected by the provincial assemblies and the assemblies of the self-governing areas of minority peoples, will exercise the functions of consent, impeachment, and supervision.
4. The Judicial Yuan. This Yuan shall be the Supreme Court of the State but shall not be responsible for judicial administration. The justices shall be without party affiliations and shall be appointed on the nomination of the President with the consent of the Control Yuan.
5. The Examination Yuan. This Yuan, whose members shall be appointed on the nomination of the President with the consent of the Control Yuan, shall examine candidates for civil service. The members shall be without party affiliations.
6. The Executive Yuan. This Yuan shall be the supreme executive organ of the State. The President of the Executive Yuan shall be appointed on the nomination of the President of the National Government and with the consent of the Legislative Yuan. The Executive Yuan is to be responsible to the Legislative Yuan, and if the latter expresses no confidence in the former, the Executive Yuan may either resign or may ask the President of the National Government for the dissolution of the Legislative Yuan for a second time.
7. Presidency of the National Government. The President may promulgate emergency decrees according to law when the Executive Yuan has so decided, but the action must be reported to the Legislative Yuan within one month. The right of the President to call the heads of the five Yuan into conference need not be written into the Constitution.
8. The System of Local Government. The province is to be the highest unit of local government, the division of powers with the National Government to be decided according to a "fair distribution." The governor will be elected by the people, and the provinces may have their own constitutions, which must not, however, contravene the provisions of the National Constitution.
9. The Rights and Duties of the People. All those freedoms and rights generally enjoyed by people in democratic countries should be protected by the Constitution. The right of self-government must be guaranteed to minority peoples who live together in one particular locality.
10. Elections. A separate chapter on elections shall be provided into the Constitution. Only those twenty-three years of age or over will have the right to be elected.
11. Fundamental National Policies. A separate chapter in the Constitution

should be devoted to fundamental national policies, including items on national defense, foreign relations, national economy, culture, and education.

12. Amendments to the Constitution. The right to amend the Constitution shall be vested in a joint conference of the Legislative and Control Yuan, the proposed amendment then being subject to approval by the same body which has the right to elect the President of the National Government.[21]

In short, the PCC resolution provided for a cabinet system in which the executive government was responsible to the legislature, closely approaching the French system. On the other hand, the tripower government and the system of checks and balances were similar to the Anglo-American model. Subsequently, a twenty-five-member Constitutional Review Committee was set up with five representatives from each of the five political groupings, assisted by ten coopted members who were constitutional experts.

The National Assembly

As noted before, there was disagreement over the legality of the "elected" membership of 1935–1936. The DL reinstated its opposition to the old membership, proposing that the old members stand for reelection and that, as an alternative, the constitution might be framed by experts and put to a referendum.[22] To break the impasse, independent delegate Wang Yunwu suggested a compromise, namely, that the old membership be retained on the proviso that (1) supplementary elections would be held in provinces where either no elections had taken place before or earlier elections had been incomplete; and (2) extra seats be created for representatives from all MPGs and prominent community leaders as well as for the GMD's Central Executive Committee members and other functionaries. This would increase the total number of delegates from 1,200 (the old membership) to 2,050, including 700 new members and 150 representatives from Taiwan and Manchuria.[23] The proposal was acceptable to all the parties concerned, and a resolution was passed to that effect.

---

[21] For the full text of the resolution, see *ZZXSHY*, pp. 282–285; *The China White Paper (1949)*, II, 620–621; *China Handbook, 1937–1945*, pp. 746–747. According to Zhang Junmai, he suggested most of the twelve principles in the name of the DL. See Chang, *The Third Force in China*, p. 154.

[22] *MMWX*, pp. 130–134.

[23] Wang Yunwu, *Youlu lun guoshi* (Wang Yunwu on national affairs) (Taibei: Taiwan Shangwu yinshuguan, 1965), p. 177.

Another problem associated with the National Assembly related to the approval of the revisions to the Draft Constitution. As the government would try to amend the revised constitution, the opposition parties insisted that any amendments must require a three-fourths majority, and the non-GMD delegates control one-quarter of the seats, thereby holding the veto power. The CCP–DL alliance was determined to "prevent Chiang Kai-shek from turning the National Assembly into his veto machine and passing a constitution that would provide for a personal dictatorship."[24]

Finally, the PCC resolved that the National Assembly should be convened on May 5, 1946, to adopt the constitution, ratified by a vote of three-fourths of the delegates present. The 1,200 geographical and vocational delegates should be retained, and delegates from the northeast provinces and Taiwan should be increased by 150. The extra 700 seats should be apportioned among the various parties and social leaders on a ratio to be decided later.[25] Subsequently, after much maneuvering and bickering between the Youth Party and the DL, the apportionment was as follows: GMD, 220; CCP, 190; DL, 120; Youth Party, 100; and independents, 70.[26]

Reorganization of the Government

The MPGs expected a reorganization of the government pending the convocation of the National Assembly. Reorganization would provide for effective multiparty participation in government and improve administrative efficiency, with a cabinet system and a responsible Executive Yuan.[27] For the government, however, it meant something different. The GMD representatives, led by Sun Fo, submitted a seven-point proposal for an "enlargement" (*kuoda*) of the government. The proposal provided

---

[24] Luo Longji, "Cong canjia jiu zhengxie," p. 227.

[25] *ZZXSHY*, pp. 272–273; *The China White Paper (1949)*, II, 619.

[26] According to Wang Yunwu, the Youth Party demanded that because it was the third largest political party in the country, it should be apportioned more seats than the DL. The bickering did not come to an end until the CCP, in an attempt to woo the DL, negotiated with the GMD, proposing that the Youth Party and the DL be apportioned an equal number of seats (one hundred) but that the DL would receive an extra twenty seats, ten from the GMD and ten from the CCP. The GMD accepted the proposal. See Wang Yunwu, *Youlu lun guoshi*, pp. 204–205; also Ch'ien Tuan-sheng, *The Government and Politics in China, 1912–1949* (Stanford: Stanford University Press, 1970), p. 319; Chang, *The Third Force in China*, p. 155.

[27] Luo Longji's statement in the PCC on January 14, in *MMWX*, p. 121.

for an expansion of the State Council and the Executive Yuan by making a number of non-GMD appointments. The enlarged State Council was to be the state's "supreme political guiding body." The President was to have emergency powers, although he would be required to report to the Council on actions he had taken within a specified period of time. State Council members were to be nominated by the President and approved by the GMD's Central Executive Committee.[28]

The difference between reorganization and enlargement was significant because the latter was not designed to curtail the powers of the current regime. Speaking to the item, Wang Shijie, Minister of Foreign Affairs and a cosignatory to the proposal, stated unequivocally that enlargement was intended to be an interim system prior to constitutional rule and that, therefore, the transition must entail no changes to the existing legal system.[29] Under the existing legal system, of course, supreme power rested with the GMD's Central Executive Committee, which approved all appointments to the State Council, including the non-GMD members being proposed. With Chiang Kai-shek's control of the Central Executive Committee, his powers were not to be diminished in any way. On Wang's own confession, the idea of the State Council being "the highest guiding organ of the state" was "an abstraction." In fact, its powers, still those of an advisory body, were limited to consideration and resolution of legislative principles, policy implementation directions, military administration, financial planning and the state budget, and exchange of views between the President and other members.[30] The presidential system of government would be a far cry from the supreme multiparty policy-making body that the opposition parties demanded.

The Youth Party, while agreeing that reorganization was an interim measure lasting between six months and a year, insisted on two conditions. One was participation by the MPGs and the independents, and the other was the substantive powers of the new regime. The Youth delegates proposed replacing the Supreme National Defense Council, chaired by Chiang Kai-shek, with a new multiparty Central Political Council, as well as a reorganization of the Executive Yuan, with non-GMD members included in all the ministries. Lastly, they proposed an increase of the PPC's membership from its current 290 to 500, with expanded powers, so that it could become an effective supervisory body.[31] The proposal was not an attempt to undermine the GMD's

[28] *ZZXSHY*, pp. 175–176.   [29] Ibid., p. 177.
[30] See point 4 of the proposal, in ibid., p. 175.   [31] *ZZXSHY*, pp. 181–183.

authority because, as Youth Party leader Zeng Qi added, Chiang Kai-shek would remain the link between the state, the ruling party, and the proposed Central Political Council.[32]

The DL took a similar stance, maintaining that reorganization should be based on three principles: a common political platform acceptable to all parties, a collective policy-making body, and mechanisms for multiparty involvement in policy implementation.[33] There was strong opposition to a presidential system and cosmetic change.

After considerable deliberation, a resolution was adopted, providing for a revision of the Organic Law of the National Government to make the State Council the supreme organ in charge of national affairs. The State Council would be competent to discuss and decide on legislative principles, administrative policies, important military measures, financial schemes and the budget, appointment and dismissal of ministers of state with or without portfolios, appointment of members of the Legislative Yuan and the Control Yuan, matters submitted by the President for consideration, and proposals submitted by three or more Council members. In the event of a State Council decision being difficult to be carried out, the President might submit it for reconsideration. Should three-fifths of the Council members, upon reconsideration, uphold the original decision, it should be implemented accordingly. General resolutions before the Council were to be passed by a majority vote. Should a resolution involve changes to administrative policy, it must be passed by a two-thirds majority. Whether a given resolution involved such changes was to be decided by a majority vote. Concerning the Executive Yuan, all its ministers were ipso facto ministers of state, of whom there might be three to five without portfolios; non-GMD members were eligible for appointment. Of the forty State Council members, half were to be from the GMD, and the remainder were from the other parties and independents. The presidents of the five Yuan were to be ex-officio members. The specific allotment of the non-GMD seats was to be the subject of separate discussion after the PCC's adjournment. Non-GMD representatives were to be nominated by their own parties. However, if they were unacceptable to the President, they could be replaced. The independents were to be nominated by the President and could be vetoed by a one-third vote of

---

[32] Ibid., p. 184; see also Zeng Qi, *Zeng Muhan (Qi) xiansheng yizhu* (The posthumous works of Mr. Zeng Muhan [Qi]) (Taibei: Wenhai chubanshe, n.d.), pp. 174–176.

[33] Luo's statement in the PCC on January 14, *MMWX*, p. 121.

the State Council members, in which case alternative nominations were required.[34]

The allocation of the twenty seats to non-GMD members was an important matter for the CCP–DL alliance. Because any changes to the government's administrative policy required a two-thirds vote of the State Council members present, the alliance sought to control at least fourteen seats (out of forty) between them. They were given to understand by Wang Shijie that Chiang Kai-shek had agreed verbally to give seven seats each to the CCP and the DL.[35] If that were true, Chiang was quick to renege on it, for the GMD was willing to allocate them thirteen seats only. Subsequent talks among the non-GMD groups reached no agreement. The Youth Party strongly opposed giving fourteen seats to the alliance, vowing not to participate in the government if the CCP was given ten seats, or if the DL received more seats than the Youth Party itself.[36] Up to the summer of 1946, this issue remained a stumbling block to government reorganization.[37]

Reflecting on the matter almost two decades later, Wang Yunwu regretted that the question of the non-GMD seats had not been settled before the PCC adjourned. That was a "big mistake" because to leave the matter to later consideration missed the opportunity of reaching a compromise at a time when the atmosphere was not poisoned. He believed that the Communists, then not yet in a powerful position, seemed prepared to make concessions and probably would have accepted a total of twelve or thirteen seats between them and the DL. An interim coalition regime could have been formed afterward. Perhaps the Communists would still want to seize power by revolutionary means at a later stage, but at least in the first half of 1946, they would have taken account of the positions of the other parties as well as public opinion, which was strongly opposed to civil war.[38] Wang's view was all the more pertinent as he was widely thought to be progovernment.

Why was the veto power thought to be such an important issue? Liang Shuming offered an insight into the opposition's thinking. To restore peace on a permanent basis, it was imperative to nationalize all the armies, but the Communists would not give up control of their troops without a trade-off, that is, trading military control for political gains. It

---

[34] *ZZXSHY*, pp. 270–271; *The China White Paper (1949)*, II, 610–611.
[35] Luo Longji, "Cong canjia jiu zhengxie," pp. 225–226; Ch'ien, *The Government and Politics of China*, p. 378.
[36] Van Slyke, ed., *Marshall's Mission to China*, I, 30.   [37] Ibid.
[38] Wang Yunwu, *Youlu lun guoshi*, pp. 182–183.

would appear that the only guarantee for the CCP's political space was to formulate and to carry out a program of peaceful reconstruction, to protect rights, and to reorganize the government on terms that would give all political parties and groups, not the least the CCP, fair and effective representation. To ensure that the constitutional principles established by the PCC were followed, that the State Council was consultative, that rights and civil liberties were safeguarded, and that the program of peaceful reconstruction was not changed unilaterally by the government, it was important for the opposition parties to hold the veto power in the State Council.[39] The same argument applied to the veto power in the forthcoming National Assembly. Liang was naïve to think that, given the veto power, the CCP would turn in its troops to the state. Mao Zedong did not trust Chiang Kai-shek, and the feeling was mutual. There was no way that the CCP could be induced to lay down its arms in 1946.

The Program of National Reconstruction

The program of national reconstruction was to be comprehensive in scope, covering a whole range of matters from democratic and administrative reforms through local self-government to rehabilitation and relief. One of the most important issues concerned the communist "liberated areas" and the status of the Red Army (renamed the People's Liberation Army in July 1946). The Communists wanted local self-government and the recognition and reorganization of their troops in phases, with designated areas and equal treatment by the government. To the Nationalists, however, this would constitute an *imperium in imperio* and a new form of regionalism.

The PCC resolution on national reconstruction began with a preamble reaffirming the delegates' desire for multiparty cooperation and participation in government. Four general principles were laid down: first, recognition of the Three Principles of the People as "the supreme guiding principles of national reconstruction"; second, construction of a new united, free, and democratic China "under the guidance of President Chiang Kai-shek"; third, national reconstruction by means of democratization, nationalization of the armed forces, and recognition of the equality and legality of all political parties; and fourth, peaceful conflict resolution. The freedoms of person, thought, religion, belief, speech, the

---

[39] Liang Shuming, "Tan guofu weiyuan ming fenpei wenti" (On the question of the allocation of the State Council seats), *LSMQJ*, VI, 671–673.

press, assembly, association, residence, movement, and communication were to be guaranteed. Any existing laws that contravened those freedoms were to be revised or repealed. No one other than the law enforcement agencies was to have the right to arrest, try, and punish offenders, and the political, social, educational, and economic equality of women was to be guaranteed.

The resolution was also intended to achieve administrative efficiency, bureaucratic streamlining, and differentiated responsibility, with a sound, meritorious system of civil service, an independent judiciary, and mechanisms for supervision. The powers between the central and local governments were to be fairly distributed, and popular elections were to be held at local levels. On military affairs, the main provisions were the nationalization of the armies under unified command; separation of army and party, and troop reductions. On foreign affairs, the emphasis was put on China's active participation in the United Nations and the development of friendly relations with the United States, the Soviet Union, Britain, and France. In addition to all these, there were references to economics and finance, education and culture, rehabilitation and relief, and Chinese residents overseas. The annex to the resolution included a provision for the maintenance of the status quo in the "liberated areas," where the local government was under dispute, until a settlement was made by the National Government after its reorganization.[40]

The CCP made a significant concession by recognizing the Three Principles of the People as the "highest guiding principles of national reconstruction" and Chiang Kai-shek's leadership, as well as accepting the provision for armed reductions according to the military reorganization plans. This led Luo Longji to believe that the CCP was genuinely interested in seeking peace, democracy, and unification.[41] Luo was biased, of course. But he was not alone in thinking that the CCP had no wish to take China down the communist path in the short or medium term, a point to which we shall return.

Army Reorganization under Unified Command

The Youth Party representatives submitted a proposal in two parts. The first part called for an immediate cessation of hostilities, the maintenance of rail communications in North China by a special body to be set up by

---

[40] *ZZXSHY*, pp. 273–280; *The China White Paper (1949)*, II, 612–617.
[41] Luo Longji, "Cong canjia jiu zhengxie," p. 230.

a reorganized government, and the formation of inspection teams to investigate the situation in the disputed areas and to report back to the PCC. The second part dealt with the nationalization of the armies, stressing fair reductions on both sides; separation of military and civil administrations; separation of army and party; conscription; creation of a National Defense Ministry administrating all the three forces; and popular supervision of the military establishment.[42] The major concern here was the perennial problem of military intervention in politics. Speaking to the item, Chen Qitian said that to promote democratization, it was necessary to nationalize the troops first,[43] a view taken by the government also.

A separate proposal from the DL representatives asked that all soldiers on active service resign their party memberships and owe their loyalty to the state. It recommended also that massive troop reductions be made so that more efforts and resources could be devoted to scientific research, industrial construction, and military training of citizens. A troop reduction committee was to be set up consisting of military personnel and civil representatives from the GMD and the CCP plus representatives from the other parties. The committee, to be assisted by several American military advisers, was to formulate a policy within one month for implementation by a reorganized government.[44] The DL's position was similar to that of the Youth Party generally, but it differed significantly in the order it gave to "democratization of politics" and "nationalization of the armies." The DL wanted democratization first.

The deliberations really boiled down to these two issues, and the position of the CCP was as crucial as the government's. The Communists agreed with the thrust of the Youth Party's proposal but disagreed with Chen Qitian's "personal view" that nationalization of the troops should precede political democratization. All the troops, Zhou Enlai insisted, should belong not only to the state but also to the people; all those forces that had contributed significantly to the eight-year war should be recognized and reorganized; and local security and law and order should be the responsibility of local security or self-defense forces. On the other related questions, Zhou, supporting the principle of civil administration, proposed that military administration should come under the jurisdiction of the Executive Yuan, effectively dissolving the wartime Military Affairs Commission. Interestingly enough, he also proposed that reform of the military institutions should model on the democratic states,

---

[42] *ZZXSHY*, pp. 212–216.   [43] Ibid., p. 217.   [44] *MMWX*, pp. 123–124.

especially the United States, and that military education should be stripped of the ideologies of the GMD and the CCP alike.[45] To nationalize the troops was to put them under the sole unified command of the state. For the CCP, the crucial question was, Who represented the state? Certainly not the Nationalist government as far as the Communists were concerned. As the *Jiefang ribao* (Liberation Daily) editorialized, the communist troops could only be put under the command of a democratic coalition government that denied any political parties special privileges.[46] Thus, army reorganization was linked with coalition government and democratization.

Finally, it was resolved that the question of army reorganization and cease-fire be referred to the Committee of Three for further consideration. Two fundamental principles were agreed upon: separation of army and party, and separation of civil and military authorities. Under the first principle, all political parties would be forbidden to carry on party activity, openly or secretly, in the army. All soldiers on active service who had party affiliations would be forbidden to take part in party activity at the district in which they were stationed, and no party or individual could use the army as a political weapon. Under the second principle, no soldiers on active service would be permitted to serve concurrently as civil officials. Military districts should be separate and distinct from administrative districts, and the army should be strictly forbidden to interfere in politics. With respect to the reorganization of the communist forces, it was also agreed that the task should be completed within six months, after which the entire country's armies would be reorganized into fifty or sixty divisions.[47]

On February 25, agreement was reached on massive troop reductions on both sides; it was to be completed within eighteen months, at which time there would be roughly 840,000 government troops in fifty divisions, and 140,000 communist troops in ten divisions integrated into the national army. It was also agreed that the majority of the communist divisions would be deployed in North China, the area of their greatest strength and concentration.[48] The conclusion of this agreement improved the prospects of peace because it provided a basis for unification. But the implementation of all this was not helped by the lack of a "superior

[45] *ZZXSHY*, pp. 198–204.   [46] Cited in ibid., pp. 304–312.
[47] Liang Shuming's clarification of the DL's proposal, in *MMWX*, pp. 125–126. For the full text of the PCC resolution, see *ZZXSHY*, pp. 280–281; for an English translation, see *The China White Paper (1949)*, II, 617–619.
[48] *The China White Paper (1949)*, I, 140–143; Wang Yunwu, *Youlu lun guoshi*, pp. 196–201.

authority capable of enforcing either the cease-fire or the military and political accords."[49]

THE PCC'S ULTIMATE FAILURE

The PCC was a success insofar as agreements had been reached on the five key issues described earlier. The resolutions were the results of reasoned debate, compromise, and a willingness to cooperate among the delegates. Provided that they were carried out, multiparty cooperation, which could be seen as an initial stage in the process of democratization, appeared to be a real possibility. The fact that representatives of the opposition parties were able to meet with government members on the vital issues facing the country was a welcome development. Opposition delegates had been remarkably constructive, whereas government members, notably Sun Fo, Wang Shijie, Shao Lizi, and Zhang Qun also had acted in good faith. The PCC adjourned on January 31 in an atmosphere of jubilation. Public reaction to the resolutions was one of enthusiastic approval, hailed by Luo Longji as "the Magna Carta of Chinese liberty,"[50] and by Chongqing's communist newspaper *Xinhua ribao* as the "new direction of Chinese history."[51] Many welcomed the mediation of the United States, placing high hopes on General Marshall's peace mission.[52] They saw the first distinct rays of hope for peace since the civil war had threatened in the fall of 1945. In like manner, General Marshall endorsed the agreements reached by the PCC as "a liberal and forward-looking charter, which then offered China a basis for peace and reconstruction."[53]

But the signs were ominous. Earlier, while the PCC was still in session, special GMD agents had ransacked the homes of three delegates and opposition figures, Huang Yanpei, Zhang Shenfu, and Shi Liang.[54] On February 10, a meeting held in Jiaochangkou on the outskirts of Chongqing to celebrate the successful conclusion of the PCC was disrupted, leaving several people injured. Twelve days later, the premises

---

[49] Suzanne Pepper, "The KMT–CCP Conflict, 1945–1949," in Lloyd E. Eastman et al., eds., *The Nationalist Era in China 1927–1949* (Cambridge: Cambridge University Press, 1991), p. 299.

[50] Luo's conversation with Melby, *FRUS* (1947), VII, 98.

[51] Editorial, February 2, 1946.   [52] Luo Longji, "Cong canjia jiu zhengxie," p. 232.

[53] *The China White Paper (1949)*, II, 688.

[54] Shen Pu and Shen Renhua, eds., *Shen Junru nianpu* (A chronology of Shen Junru's life) (Beijing: Zhongguo wenshi chubanshe, 1992), p. 271; Xu Hansan, *Huang Yanpei nianpu* (A chronology of Huang Yanpei's life) (Beijing: Wenshi ziliao chubanshe, 1985), p. 178; *ZZXSHY*, pp. 446–447.

of *Xinhua ribao* and the DL's *Minzhubao* (Democracy News) were attacked. Both incidents were believed to have been the work of thugs hired by right-wing elements within the GMD opposed to the PCC resolutions.[55]

From March 1 to 17, when the Second Plenum of the GMD's Sixth Central Executive Committee met in Chongqing, approval of the PCC resolutions, though in toto, was hedged by reservations. Even worse, the "irreconcilable elements" (General Marshall's words), notably the CC Clique and the powerful group of Whampoa generals, were particularly opposed to the principles for the revisions to the Draft Constitution.[56] Zhang Qun, Wang Shijie, and Shao Lizi, three of the GMD representatives at the PCC, came under ferocious attack, forcing Chiang Kai-shek to come to their defense because they had acted entirely at his behest.[57] Chiang appealed to the "reactionary elements" several times to support the PCC resolutions, assuring them secretly that as long as he was alive, he would never let the CCP join the government. It was possible, suggested Lloyd Eastman, that Chiang publicly wanted to be seen, especially by the United States government, to be supporting the PCC resolutions and that he was forced to reveal his hand to a few party colleagues about his true intentions.[58]

Consequently, the Central Executive Committee decided that Sun Yat-sen's *Fundamentals of National Reconstruction* should be taken as the basis for the making of the constitution. It also made a number of objections to the principles for the revisions of the Draft Constitution. The Draft Constitution Subcommittee then met on March 15 to consider those objections.[59] The Youth representatives and the independents were prepared to budge, but the CCP and the DL were not. After several meetings, the CCP–DL alliance eventually agreed to compromise by dropping the idea of an "invisible" National Assembly and the suggestion that the Legislative Yuan be empowered to pass votes of no-confidence in the Executive Yuan, and the Executive Yuan to dissolve the Legislative Yuan. But the chief CCP delegate, Zhou Enlai, insisted that the Executive Yuan should still be responsible to the Legislative Yuan and be overseen by the Control Yuan. Finally, the Communists also

---

[55] *ZZXSHY*, pp. 448–450, 457–461; *MMWX*, pp. 100–101.
[56] Van Slyke, ed., *Marshall's Mission to China*, I, 63–64.
[57] *FRUS* (1946), IX, 154, 158, 161.
[58] Lloyd E. Eastman, *Seeds of Destruction: Nationalist China in War and Revolution, 1937–1949* (Stanford: Stanford University Press, 1984), pp. 116–117.
[59] Chang, *The Third Force in China*, p. 189; *The China White Paper (1949)*, I, 144.

agreed to drop the demand that the provinces be empowered to make their own constitutions.[60] But significant differences remained over provincial autonomy and the powers of the Presidency.

Convinced that the GMD had acted in bad faith, the CCP and the DL refused to nominate members to the State Council for participation in a reorganized government until the GMD published a statement of any revisions of the PCC resolution and pledged to implement the program as revised. Under these circumstances, the Constitutional Review Committee was unable to proceed with the preparation of a revised constitution for the National Assembly, scheduled for May 5.[61]

By June, the GMD still had not carried out the PCC resolutions or the "four promises" regarding civil liberties. This led Luo Longji, Shi Liang, and eighty-seven other concerned scholars to publish a joint letter addressed to "the people of the nation" criticizing the government's inaction and "fascism."[62] There was an atmosphere of terror in Kunming, the scene of an anti-civil-war, prodemocracy movement. On July 11, Li Gongpu was assassinated. Four days later, Wen Yiduo, an American-educated poet and scholar, was also gunned down. Both victims were members of the DL's Central Executive Committee, and both had been vociferous critics of the government. The assassinations, apparently carried out by the GMD's special agents so senselessly and unnecessarily, shocked the intellectual community. The DL immediately lodged a protest, denouncing Chiang Kai-shek in a cable on July 18.[63] Li and Wen became martyrs and instant icons of "democracy fighters." Memorial services held in Kunming and various other cities became the occasions for inflammatory antigovernment activity.[64]

The ultimate failure of the PCC could be attributed in no small measure to the recalcitrance of the CC Clique and other "irreconcilable elements" within the GMD who wanted to sabotage the PCC agreements. Chiang seems to have had no intention of carrying them out in the first place and had deliberately violated them.[65] Another underlying reason for the failure was the hostilities in Manchuria, for which both the government

---

[60] Luo Longji, "Cong canjia jiu zhengxie," p. 229; Wang Yunwu, *Youlu lun guoshi*, p. 212.

[61] Van Slyke, ed., *Marshall's Mission to China*, I, 65–66.

[62] *MMWX*, pp. 177–178. The letter was dated June 16.

[63] *MMWX*, pp. 182–183, 191–193, 198–199.

[64] The Li–Wen assassinations were the subject of numerous articles in *Minzhu zhoukan*. Liang Shuming was immediately asked to conduct an independent investigation into the murders. His report is included in *LSMQJ*, VI, 640–669.

[65] Luo's conversation with Melby, *FRUS* (1947), VII, 98.

and the Communists were to blame.[66] Reflecting on this in 1952, Zhang Junmai wrote that had the five resolutions been carried out, they

> would have meant a secure future for China, because they repre-sented assent achieved through negotiation, and not by violence and war. They also represented the mutual tolerance and moderation of the parties concerned. It was a great pity that after only one and a half months, *civil war broke out again in Manchuria between the [GMD] and the Communist army and nullified all the resolutions* [emphasis added].[67]

Despite its ultimate failure, the PCC had a profound significance. Wang Yunsheng, editor of Shanghai's *Dagongbao*, called it "originally the ideal and artistic progressive road for China in the current situation."[68] Qian Duansheng described it as representing "the democratic path," "the coalition road," and "the only road to peace and unification."[69] And inde-pendent observers viewed the principles of the PCC as democratic, resting on the notion of coalition government.[70] The PCC sessions dis-played a spirit of cooperation, moderation, and compromise so essential for peaceful conflict resolution. There was a rare opportunity to resolve China's problems politically, only to be passed up by the government. The consensus in the intellectual community in 1946 was that a coalition government was what China needed for a transition to democracy.

THE NOTION OF COALITION GOVERNMENT

Coalition government, from the standpoint of civil opposition, rested on the notion of pluralistic politics and power sharing. For years, the MPGs had been calling for the formation of an interim regime consisting of multiparty representatives who need not be popularly elected. In due course, it would be replaced by a popular government that might or might not still be a coalition. Wang Yunsheng described the process of change thus:

---

[66] Wu Shichang, "Hetan yinian" (One year after the peace talks), *GC* 1:24 (February 8, 1947): 10–11.

[67] Chang, *The Third Force in China*, p. 156.

[68] Wang Yunsheng, "Zhongguo shiju qiantu de sange chuxiang" (Three trends for China's current situation and future), *GC* 1:1 (September 1, 1946): 5.

[69] Qian Duansheng, "Wei heping keyi tongyi lun" (Only peace can achieve unification), *GC* 2:4 (March 22, 1947): 7.

[70] Wu Shichang, "Hetan yinian," p. 12.

Because all of the various political parties were to participate in the reorganization of the government, it was to be a coalition. The coalition government would convene the National Assembly and draft the constitution. It would be transitional and be replaced by a constitutional government through general elections. In this way, the [political] line of the PCC would be transformed into the way of a democratic constitutional government.[71]

One very important thing about coalition government prior to an elected constitutional government was its provision for a system of checks and balances of sorts. This view was best articulated by Zhang Dongsun, who saw coalition government as an instrument for reshaping the major parties in a democratic fashion, hopeful that the MPGs would, in the process, act as a buffer and a bridge between the two major parties and thus encourage their cooperation. Criticizing the GMD as an "organization that no democratic state could tolerate," Zhang wanted it to be changed from a "special" (read: privileged) (*tebie*) political party to an "ordinary" (*putong*) one. This could be accomplished either by expecting the GMD to reform itself or by bringing outside pressures to bear on it. Voluntary reform, he feared, would not achieve the desired results because the GMD would only make "superficial, cosmetic change." So the GMD had to be pressured into changing itself, and the pressures would best emanate from a coalition government. Seeing the GMD as an immediate obstacle to China's democratization, he considered its transformation a high priority. And believing that Mao Zedong was not bent on realizing communism in the foreseeable future, he would also expect the CCP, once involved in the processes of government, to change from a revolutionary party to an ordinary one. Together with the MPGs, the CCP could provide the checks and balances that the Chinese system of government badly needed. Would an interim coalition regime be undemocratic because it was not going to be popularly elected? Zhang did not think so, arguing that, among them, the GMD, the CCP, and the DL represented the interests of all sections of Chinese society.[72]

---

[71] Cited in Suzanne Pepper, *Civil War in China: The Political Struggle, 1945–1949* (Berkeley: University of California Press, 1978), p. 189.

[72] Zhang Dongsun, "Zhuishu women nuli jianli 'lianhe zhengfu' de yongyi" (A recount of the purpose of our efforts at establishing "coalition government"), *GC* 2:6 (April 5, 1947): 6–7. There was another reason why Zhang favored a Chinese coalition government. He thought it would be acceptable to both the United States and the Soviet Union, thus enjoying their support in a Cold War era.

Like democracy itself, coalition government was viewed as a postwar trend. Zeng Zhaolun of the DL described it as a "common phenomenon" in the democratic states, citing the examples of Winston Churchill's cabinet and the Roosevelt administration during the Second World War and now some of the victorious countries of Europe. Struck by the deficiencies in the Anglo-American two-party system, Zeng thought that the days might be over when elected governments were ruled by a succession of political parties.[73] Another professor, writing after V-J Day, greeted coalition government as a "new achievement" of the Second World War. "If the greatest achievement of the First World War was the Russian Revolution, that of the Second World War is the coalition government of new democracy." The good professor envisioned expanded political and economic democracy under coalition governments, drawing attention to the postwar regimes in Poland, Romania, and Yugoslavia. Those regimes had representatives from all classes, including enlightened capitalists, workers, and the Church, and it was such broad representations that made bloodless social revolution possible, he added. In short, coalition government was "a current tide, a driving force behind the backward and conservative countries in a new direction toward a peaceful and happy new world. Today, it is the key to a new world as well as the key to a new China."[74] From this perspective, coalition government was seen not as a transition to, but as a variant of, democracy. Not only was it a "world trend," but it also seemed eminently suited to China. It was, moreover, consistent with Chinese notions of democracy being more consensus-oriented and more "substantive" than "procedural." The Chinese did not like a quick succession of alternating party governments as in some Western democracies for fear of political instability. Coalition government did not guarantee political stability to be sure, but it allowed room for multiparty cooperation and political consultation, provided that the various parties could agree on the rules of the game.

The Chinese notion of coalition government approximates Arend Lijphart's model of "consociational democracy," the distinguishing characteristic of which is elite cooperation. The political leaders of the different segments of the population, writes Lijphart, "cooperate in a grand coalition to govern the country. It may be contrasted with the type

---

[73] Zeng Zhaolun, "Banian lai de shijie minzhu langchao" (The world democratic tide over the last eight years), *MZZK* 2:1 (July 7, 1945): 7–8.

[74] Tui Zhi, "Lianhe zhengfu" (Coalition government), *MZZK* 2:8 (September 8, 1945): 10–11.

of democracy in which the leaders are divided into a government with bare majority support and a large opposition."[75] Like the consociational democracy model, which is applicable to the Third World, coalition government from the MPGs' perspective was intended to achieve stable government during a transition to democracy through the cooperation of the political elites of significant segments of Chinese society, even though the GMD remained the dominant party.

This was, of course, different from Mao Zedong's idea of coalition government. Mao's was related to the united front strategy and underpinned by his theory of New Democracy, which preached "the joint democratic dictatorship of all the antiimperialist and all the antifeudal classes." But the difference was not immediately clear from his wartime rhetoric. Earlier in April 1945, he had written:

> We Communists propose two steps for the termination of the [GMD] one-party dictatorship. First, at the present stage, to establish a provisional coalition government through common agreement among representatives of all parties and people with no party affiliation. Second, in the next stage, to convene a national assembly after free and unrestricted elections *and form a regular coalition government* [emphasis added]. In both cases there will be a coalition government in which the representatives of all classes and political parties willing to take part are united on a democratic common programme in the fight against Japan today and *for national construction tomorrow* [emphasis added].[76]

Delete the word *Communists* from the preceding statement, and you can be forgiven for thinking that a minor party leader penned it. Furthermore, the liberals could be easily misled by Mao's assurance that the Communists were not "opposed to the development of individual initiative, the growth of private capital and the protection of private property."[77] Mao supported coalition government during and immediately after the war because the CCP was not strong enough militarily to "win all," and he did not wish to "lose all." Rather, he wanted to win over the MPGs and the independents as the ultimate "agents of hegemony."

---

[75] Arend Lijphart, *Democracy in Plural Societies: A Comparative Exploration* (New Haven: Yale University Press, 1977); the quote is on p. 25.

[76] Mao Tse-tung, "On Coalition Government," in Mao Tse-tung, *Selected Works of Mao Tse-tung* (Peking: Foreign Languages Press, 1967), III, 242.

[77] Ibid., p. 231.

As for Chiang Kai-shek, coalition government, be it provisional or regular, had no appeal for him. He would have no problem in coopting some noncommunist elements, such as the Youths and the National Socialists, into the administration, but definitely would not accommodate the Communists. He was convinced that the real purpose of the CCP was not to abolish one-party rule, but rather to overthrow the GMD control and to establish a one-party dictatorship by the CCP itself. (Subsequent events proved him right.)

The failure to form an interim coalition government in 1946 reinforced the perception that the Nationalist government, apparently backed by the United States, was fascist. When the PCC exited from the political stage, the peace process was derailed, but not before the third force had made a last effort at mediation.

MEDIATION OF THE THIRD FORCE

The third force sometimes acted on its own and sometimes with the encouragement, advice, and assistance of General Marshall and J. Leighton Stuart, the newly appointed U.S. Ambassador to China. We shall keep the narrative to a minimum.

The civil war was going to start in Manchuria, the control of which would decide its outcome.[78] But the cease-fire agreement of January 10, 1946, did not apply because the Nationalist government considered Manchuria to be a matter of "recovering Chinese sovereignty," meaning effecting Soviet evacuation. (The Soviet Union had entered the Pacific War by attacking the Japanese army in Manchuria on August 8, 1945, just one week before the Japanese surrender.) The issue had international repercussions in the Cold War era that had just begun, which explained why Washington was prepared to assist in transporting the American-equipped Nationalist forces to Manchuria.[79] On January 20, General Marshall proposed that field teams from the Executive Headquarters in Beijing be sent to Manchuria in order to stop possible hostilities and to establish a basis for the demobilization of the armies under the plan for military reorganization and integration. It was not until March 11 that Chiang Kai-shek agreed to the entry of the field teams. But the numer-

---

[78] The communist victory in Manchuria would set the stage for their conquest of China. See Steven I. Levine, *Anvil of Victory: The Communist Revolution in Manchuria, 1945–1948* (New York: Columbia University Press, 1987).

[79] For an account of Soviet-American rivalry in Manchuria, see ibid., ch. 2.

ous conditions he attached prevented the teams, which arrived early in April, from bringing about a cessation of hostilities.[80]

It was against this background that early in April the DL and the CCP jointly called for a cease-fire in Manchuria and asked that the PCC be reconvened to consider the Manchurian question. On April 10, at a meeting with the GMD representatives held in Nanjing, the DL put forward a three-point peace proposal designed to permit government occupation of Changchun.[81] Zhou Enlai acquiesced in the proposal but wanted the cease-fire to be comprehensive and permanent. When General Chen Cheng on the government's side insisted that Manchuria was outside the parameters of the cease-fire agreement, the talks broke down as soon as they started.[82]

On April 18, communist forces entered Changchun after engaging an advance unit of Nationalist troops and local militia for three days. On the same day, General Marshall, who had left for Washington the previous month, arrived back in Chongqing and immediately contacted Luo Longji and Zhang Junmai with a request that they renew the DL's mediation effort. General Marshall's idea, according to Zhang, was to persuade the Communists to pull out of Changchun, while he tried to prevail upon Chiang Kai-shek the wisdom of a comprehensive and lasting cease-fire.[83] Between April 24 and 29, Luo and Zhang met with the GMD and CCP representatives numerous times. Meanwhile, Chiang insisted on the evacuation of Changchun as the sine qua non for talks, which the CCP rejected categorically. Zhou Enlai accused Chiang of reneging on the PCC resolutions and the United States of assisting Chiang in the civil war. General Marshall, temporarily withdrawing from formal mediation, was hoping that the DL could bring the conflicting parties back to the negotiating table. But the DL backed the CCP's position, demanding that any cease-fire be unconditional, comprehensive, and permanent.[84]

Nonetheless, the DL was able to come up with a new proposal,[85] which Chiang rejected while Zhou Enlai agreed to consider, subject to instructions from Yan'an. Luo Longji and Zhang Lan then went to see General Marshall. Before the general had a chance to look at it, he had

---

[80] *The China White Paper (1949)*, I, 145–146.

[81] For the three points, see *MMWX*, p. 155.

[82] Luo Longji, "Cong canjia jiu zhengxie," pp. 236–237.

[83] Ibid., pp. 239–241; Chang, *The Third Force in China*, p. 175.

[84] Luo Longji, "Cong canjia jiu zhengxie," p. 240.

[85] Van Slyke, ed., *Marshall's Mission to China*, I, 105.

flown to Nanjing, to which the Nationalist government returned on May 5.[86]

On May 23, government troops entered Changchun following a communist withdrawal from that city. The occupation of Changchun strengthened Chiang Kai-shek's position. Continued negotiations resulted in a fifteen-day truce in June. On June 20, an agreement was reached by the Committee of Three for a cease-fire in Manchuria, extending the truce period to the end of the month. But the extended talks collapsed in mid-July over the unsettled question of north Jiangsu, among other things.[87]

Early in August, Ambassador Stuart proposed the formation of a special committee, which subsequently came to be known as the Committee of Five (including government and CCP representatives but, for obscure reasons, none from the DL), with himself as chair. Its purpose was to reach an agreement for the immediate reorganization of the State Council. Chiang Kai-shek acquiesced in Stuart's proposal, but stipulated five military demands that the Communists would have to meet and carry out within a month to six weeks. The Communists rejected those demands prior to the discussion of political matters,[88] prompting Chiang to deliver on August 13 a public assessment blaming the CCP for the breakdown in negotiations and for the failure to implement the PCC resolutions.[89] The Committee of Five never met.

On August 14, Chiang announced that the National Assembly would be convened on November 12, 1946. The PCC resolution on the National Assembly provided for its convocation on May 5. But an earlier agreement had been reached on April 24 in discussion between representatives of all parties, including the GMD, to postpone it, on the understanding that the date would be decided by discussion among all parties.[90] The GMD's unilateral decision, therefore, was contrary to the spirit of the PCC. Late in September, pressed by the government to submit a list of their delegates to the National Assembly, the DL leader Zhang Lan and others cabled Chiang, criticizing his decision and urging that hostilities be stopped and peace restored first.[91]

On October 10, government forces captured the Communist-held city of Kalgan (Zhangjiakou), northwest of Beijing. The next day, the gov-

[86] Luo Longji, "Cong canjia jiu zhengxie," pp. 240–241.
[87] For the details of the negotiations, see Van Slyke, ed., *Marshall's Mission to China*, I, 119–176.
[88] *The China White Paper (1949)*, I, 174–176.   [89] Ibid., p. 177.
[90] Ibid., p. 197.   [91] *MMWX*, 233–234.

ernment issued a mandate announcing that the National Assembly would be convened on November 12, as planned. The DL received the news of the fall of Kalgan with sadness and regret. "The capture of Kalgan," wrote Luo Longji, "was not a victory for Chiang, but the beginning of his big political failure."[92] Zhou Enlai had made it clear to General Marshall that if government troops did not cease attacking Kalgan, the CCP would be compelled to presume that the government had abandoned a peaceful settlement. The fall of Kalgan, followed closely by the government's issuance of an order for the convocation of the National Assembly, caused Zhou to refuse to return to Nanjing for continued negotiations. Liang Shuming, then the DL's general secretary, told Ambassador Stuart that the CCP and the minor parties were convinced that the government's action was "the initial step toward Fascism." He also thought "the possibility of the resumption of peace negotiations . . . is now a thing of the past."[93] Meanwhile, Chiang intimated that he could not agree to an unconditional cessation of hostilities unless the CCP agreed to participate in the National Assembly by submitting a list of delegates, among other things.[94]

At this point, General Marshall believed that, under the circumstances, American mediators should stand aside and encourage Chinese efforts to reach a settlement, with a third party group as the middle man.[95] It was inconceivable that the Chinese themselves could succeed where General Marshall had failed. Marshall's recourse to a Chinese third party group was an implicit admission that American mediation had failed. The group he had in mind included not only the DL but also the Youth Party, the Democratic Socialist Party (formerly the National Socialist Party), and some prominent independents. Thereupon, Ambassador Stuart asked Liang Shuming to persuade Zhou Enlai, who had left for Shanghai earlier, to return to Nanjing for talks.[96] Of all the third party activists, Liang was by far the most enthusiastic and most sincere in his attempts to bring about peace and unification. Zhang Junmai, too, was enthusiastic.[97] Zuo Shunsheng of the Youth Party, who had not participated in

[92] Luo Longji, "Cong canjia jiu zhengxie," p. 259.
[93] Liang Shuming, "Wo canjia guogong hetan de jingguo," *LSMQJ*, VI, 936; *FRUS* (1946), X, 362, 366; *The China White Paper (1949)*, I, 196–197.
[94] Van Slyke, ed., *Marshall's Mission to China*, I, 314.
[95] *The China White Paper (1949)*, I, 199–200.
[96] Liang Shuming, "Wo canjia guogong hetan de jingguo," *LSMQJ*, VI, 936.
[97] Luo Longji, "Cong canjia jiu zhengxie," p. 264. Roger Jeans is convinced that Zhang was "a key member" of the Third Party Group. See Roger B. Jeans, "Last Chance for Peace: Zhang Junmai (Carsun Chang) and Third-Party Mediation in the Chinese Civil War,

the PCC, was indifferent, but he joined the Third Party Group (*disan fangmian*) along with Li Huang as the Youth representatives.[98]

It is unnecessary to go into the details of the Group's mediation efforts.[99] Suffice it to say that the Group managed to persuade Zhou Enlai to return to Nanjing for talks on October 21. Proposals and counterproposals followed, but the time for talks had already run out. On October 26, Nationalist troops occupied the city of Andong in Manchuria, causing Zhou Enlai to say that the Communists should break off all negotiations and that he must await instructions from Yan'an.[100] By then, it had become clear that further talks would be futile, though the Group continued to meet with Zhou Enlai.

Flush with military successes, Chiang Kai-shek was keen to gain a political victory as well by getting all the other parties to participate in the National Assembly. He agreed to delay its opening for three days so that the CCP and the DL could submit their lists of delegates. On November 8, he issued a cease-fire order setting the stage for the convocation of the National Assembly against a background of peace rather than civil war. His approach to the National Assembly was not sufficiently in accordance with the PCC agreements. As General Marshall commented, if all the delegates turned up, a simple majority vote of the overwhelming GMD members could determine the character of the constitution without much consideration of the fundamental guarantees agreed to in the PCC.[101]

On November 12, the CCP informed the government that it would neither participate in nor approve of the National Assembly on the grounds that it had been called unilaterally. Two days later, the DL also announced a boycott of the Assembly.[102] But the Youths, the Democratic Socialists, and the independents all agreed to take part, prompting Zhou Enlai to state that the door of negotiations had been "slammed" by the government.[103] On November 15, the National

---

October 1946," in Larry I. Bland, ed., *George C. Marshall's Mediation Mission to China, December 1945–January 1947* (Lexington, VA: George C. Marshall Foundation, 1998), p. 325.

[98] Zuo Shunsheng, *Jin sanshinian jianwen zaji* (A record of the events of the last thirty years) (Taibei: Zhonghua yilin wenwu chubanshe, 1976), p. 102.

[99] See Jeans, "Last Chance for Peace," pp. 293–325; Van Slyke, ed., *Marshall's Mission in China*, I, 317–359; Chang, *The Third Force in China*, pp. 179–186. The best Chinese accounts may be found in Liang Shuming, "Wo canjia guogong hetan de jingguo," *LSMQJ*, VI, 934–946; and Luo Longji, "Cong canjia jiu zhengxie," pp. 258–283.

[100] Van Slyke, ed., *Marshall's Mission to China*, I, p. 343.

[101] Ibid., p. 369.   [102] *MMWX*, p. 246.   [103] *The China White Paper (1949)*, I, 208.

Assembly adopted the new constitution, later promulgated on New Year's Day 1947.[104]

The new constitution was quite liberal in some respects. It provided for protection of property; freedoms of speech, religion, association, and assembly; freedom to choose residence; and secrecy of correspondence. It also granted the four political rights and the right to petition the government, as well as enacting the institution of habeas corpus and a number of limitations on arbitrariness in the criminal process. The Bill of Rights was impressive, if all those rights were to be given full effect. The phrase "such freedoms shall not be restricted except in accordance with law," which had appeared in the 1936 Draft Constitution, was deleted. Equal, direct, and secret voting was stipulated. The National Assembly was to be popularly elected under various categories, geographical and vocational. In addition, women were to be included in a separate category. The head of the Executive Yuan was to be appointed by the President of the Republic with the consent of the Legislative Yuan. For its part, the Legislative Yuan was to be a full-fledged parliament. But the Constitution was ambiguous on the question of whether the system of government was to be presidential or cabinet. There were provisions that could be used either to perpetuate a dictatorship or to bring about a more democratic government, depending on the personality and wishes of the President. Even though the Constitution had incorporated some of the revisions of the 1936 Draft Constitution, it failed to provide for the all-important checks on the powers of the President. Overall, it was a "fairly good document, better in craftsmanship, more democratic in spirit, and more satisfactory in the framework of government that it purports to build up than any other constitution . . . the Republic has had, with the possible exception of the ill-fated [Cao Kun] Constitution of 1923."[105]

The drafter of the new constitution, Zhang Junmai, described it as "a document which represents the Chinese concensus [sic] in matters of government, including the compromise position of the Chinese Communists."[106] Chen Qitian, speaking for the Youth Party, also

---

[104] For an English translation of the Constitution, see Ch'ien, *The Government and Politics of China*, pp. 447–461.

[105] Ibid., pp. 325, 329.

[106] Chang, *The Third Force in China*, p. 221. He found support for his view in General Marshall, who had noted: "In fact, the National Assembly has adopted a democratic constitution which in all major respects is in accordance with the principles laid down by the all-party Political Consultative Conference of last January. It is unfortunate that the

welcomed it as a "glorious result of tolerance and compromise between the government and various political parties," "a consensus constitution." Framing the constitution was not difficult, he added; what was difficult was giving full effect to it, which was the responsibility of the government.[107]

By the end of 1946, the third force had split hopelessly. The Youth Party had gone to the government's side, and the Democratic Socialist Party had been split, too, before it was "expelled" from the DL. From the leftist point of view, the Youths and the Democratic Socialists led by Zhang Junmai had been "bought off." On the other hand, those who chose to join the government with a view to reforming it from within under the new constitution were convinced that the DL had become a communist fellow traveler. The collapse of the peace talks marked the end of the third force movement. As Zhang Junmai discovered, there was no room for a middle path; under those circumstances, one must take a stand.[108] One might withdraw from politics altogether, as Huang Yanpei did when he decided to fade into a position as a senior fellow in the educational establishment to await the outcome of the inevitable civil war. But abandoning politics was not a real option as Huang soon discovered. In the end, he chose the CCP, as did many others.[109]

REFLECTIONS ON THE THIRD FORCE PEACE EFFORTS

In 1946, civil opposition was keen to take every opportunity to translate its ideas into action. The DL's slogan "democratization of politics and nationalization of the armies" was widely supported by the intellectuals, irrespective of their party and group affiliations. These were the issues about which they felt very strongly, and the resolution of which would

Communists did not see fit to participate in the Assembly because the constitution that has been adopted seems to include every major point that they wanted." See *The China White Paper (1949)*, II, 688.

[107] Chen Qitian, *Jiyuan huiyilu* (The memoir of Chen Qitian) (Taibei: Taiwan Shangwu yinshuguan, 1972), p. 215.

[108] Zhang Junmai rejected Zhou Enlai's allegation that the new constitution to be adopted in the National Assembly was designed to legalize dictatorship or to legalize the split of the country. He thought that he and his party should support the government because it was at least prepared to have the constitution to adopt a rule of law while the CCP was out to overthrow the government by force. See Chang, *The Third Force in China*, p. 186.

[109] Thomas D. Curran, "From Educator to Politician: Huang Yanpei and the Third Force," in Roger B. Jeans, ed., *Roads Not Taken: The Struggle of Opposition Parties in Twentieth-Century China* (Boulder: Westview Press, 1992), pp. 86–87.

pave the way for a peaceful and democratic China. Civil strife must be stopped in the national interest.

In playing the role of a peacemaker, the third force was encouraged and assisted by General Marshall, who saw it as a potential liberal force serving as a balance between the two major parties.[110] But considering the fact that his own mediation had been unsuccessful, there was no reason to believe that the third force could have done better. This begs the question: were the peace efforts doomed to failure from the start? The argument for an affirmative answer is compelling. Both the CCP and the GMD were revolutionary parties, both were authoritarian, both believed in violent means of conflict resolution, and both represented the mainstream tradition of Chinese political culture. There was a complete lack of faith and a feeling of distrust on both sides, with each seeing behind all proposals from the other an ulterior motive. The long-standing conflict had reached a point where the two combatants really had to fight it out, once and for all. Both tried to buy time through nego-tiations, and, after the spring of 1946, peace talks could only prolong the conflict and be used by both sides as a cover to attack each other. Finally, Chiang Kai-shek was a soldier who could see only a military solution to the communist problem, and Mao Zedong believed that political power grew out of the barrel of a gun.

There was, therefore, an air of inevitability. But at what point did all-out civil war become inevitable? It was not ordained in late 1945 or early 1946, when the CCP was not irrevocably committed to civil war, according to Van Slyke.[111] He agrees with Edmund Clubb that it was not until March or April 1946 that both sides were committed to the assumption that their differences would be settled on the battlefield. "From now on, negotiations would be geared to the needs of the armed struggle."[112] Suzanne Pepper, commenting on the cease-fire agreement of January 10 and the troop reduction agreement of February 25, 1946, writes:

> Perhaps the two main parties to the agreements were sincere in con-cluding them. From the hindsight of history, they appear rather to have been a cynical maneuver entered into by both rivals in order to pacify Chinese public opinion and the American ally, while buying time for the most advantageous possible deployment of their

[110] *The China White Paper (1949)*, I, 213.
[111] Van Slyke, *Enemies and Friends*, p. 188.   [112] Ibid., p. 189.

mutual armed forces. In fact, the truth may lie somewhere in between, since both Chiang Kai-shek and Chou En-lai subsequently indicated that genuine disagreement had existed within their respective parties at this time on the merits of working out a compromise accommodation between them. *The implication is that the two parties were perhaps still undecided in early 1946, and that the resolve to settle their differences through full-scale war emerged only with the progressive breakdown of the agreements reached at that time* [emphasis added].[113]

Some MPG leaders genuinely believed that the CCP was prepared to reach a political settlement early in 1946. Asked by General Marshall why the CCP seemed willing to compromise, Luo Longji said that the CCP and the Soviet Communist Party were quite different in that the former focused on land reform.[114] He shared the view of many foreign observers at the time that the Chinese Communists were merely land reformers who did not insist on abolishing private ownership.[115] He thought the Communists were sincere in wishing to enter into a coalition until July 1946, though he had some doubts that any coalition government involving elements as divergent as the Nationalists and the Communists could really be expected to work except under extreme threat from abroad.[116] Zhang Junmai, for all his anticommunism, found it wrong to refuse to work with the Communists so long as their demand was limited to a coalition government.[117] Liang Shuming, too, was convinced that they were sincere at the negotiation table, pointing out that Zhou Enlai had agreed to several compromises at the PCC sessions aimed at avoiding all-out war.[118] In June 1947, reflecting on the events of the past twelve months, Liang wrote:

> In the previous July, it was the GMD that wanted civil war. At last year's end and early this year, the CCP wanted it. The initial intentions of both parties had been a limited war. Last July, the GMD's objectives were to capture certain strategic points and railway lines, not to fight to the bitter end. Later, when the CCP wanted war, it

---

[113] Pepper, "The KMT–CCP Conflict, 1945–1949," p. 299.
[114] Luo Longji, "Cong canjia jiu zhengxie," p. 232.   [115] Ibid., p. 230.
[116] Luo's conversation with Melby on April 13, 1947, *FRUS* (1947), VII, 99.
[117] Chang, *The Third Force in China*, p. 185.
[118] Liang Shuming, "Shiju qiantu da kewen" (Answers to questions about the future of the situation), *LSMQJ*, VI, 680.

also sought to make it even as a way of realizing peace. Unfortunately, despite their limited objectives, the reality was that the situation had developed beyond their control.[119]

Early in 1949, again recalling the failed talks of 1946, Liang concluded that the CCP was not responsible for the civil war at all,[120] a view not widely shared by government critics.[121]

The likes of Luo Longji and Liang Shuming could be faulted for being naïve and easily misled by communist propaganda. But they desperately wanted peace for democracy and unification. No doubt, their attitudes were influenced, in part, by Mao's rhetoric on coalition government and the CCP's recruitment of intellectuals, assuring them that there was a place and a role for them in the new society.[122] However, there were good reasons why the CCP would be willing to compromise early in 1946. Its troops, inadequately trained in conventional warfare, were outnumbered and outgunned by the better-equipped government forces. The prospect of a CCP victory in a full-scale civil war did not look bright, and it might lose all in a final showdown. Moreover, as the Chinese people were weary of war, a peaceful settlement, backed by the third force and public opinion, would be in the CCP's best interest. The Communists did not take the third force lightly, for they would lose public support if they spurned the peace overtures. It was good politics and good propaganda for the CCP to portray itself as committed to peace, democracy, and unity, and the government not.

---

[119] Liang Shuming, "Zhonggong linmo weihe jujue hetan" (Why did the CCP refuse to talk toward the end?), *LSMQJ*, VI, 726.

[120] Liang Shuming, "Guoqu neizhan de zeren zaishui?" (Whose responsibility was it for the previous civil war?), *LSMQJ*, V, 790–795.

[121] Suzanne Pepper found that many liberal intellectuals thought that both the CCP and the GMD were equally responsible for the civil war and that the Communists probably did not want peace any more than did the GMD. Many also condemned both parties for pursuing their own selfish ends at the expense of the nation as a whole. See her *Civil War in China*, p. 170.

[122] In December 1939, Mao told the intellectuals that, despite their petty bourgeois shortcomings, they could play an important role as a revolutionary vanguard or serve as a link with the masses. See "The Chinese Revolution and the Chinese Communist Party," in Mao, *Selected Works*, II, 321–322. And in April 1945, Mao wrote: "[We] need large numbers of educators and teachers for the people, and also people's scientists, engineers, technicians, journalists, writers, men of letters, artists and rank-and-file cultural workers. . . . Provided they serve the people creditably, all intellectuals should be esteemed and regarded as valuable national and social assets." See "On Coalition Government," *Selected Works*, III, 282–285.

From the peacemaker's point of view, hopes ought not to be abandoned until all avenues for peace had been exhausted. The DL believed that twice the government had passed up a good opportunity to reach a negotiated settlement. The first time was in late April and early May 1946 when the government refused to reopen the PCC to consider the Manchurian question. The second time was during the three-week truce in June when talks floundered on the question of north Jiangsu.[123] If all-out civil war was inevitable after June, any subsequent effort at mediation was an exercise in futility.

In a statement made on his return to the United States in January 1947, General Marshall said, inter alia, that the political and military elites in the GMD and the government had frankly told him that it was inconceivable to cooperate with the CCP and that the only solution to the problem at hand was by force of arms.[124] The reason for the government's hard line was its anticommunism. Mao Zedong's "On New Democracy" and "On Coalition Government" did nothing to allay Nationalist fears of an ultimate communist seizure of power. After all, government forces enjoyed a clear superiority over the Communists in numbers, arms, equipment, transport capability, and training and might also expect American assistance when the going got tough. Chiang Kai-shek was confident that he could eliminate the Communists once and for all within eight to ten months; then he would win all, and the Communists would lose all. While peace talks were being held, government troops waged campaigns to strengthen their military and bargaining positions. As General Marshall observed, the government had been using the negotiations largely for its own purposes.[125] (To be sure, the same could be said about the CCP.) It was difficult to separate Chiang from the reactionary and "irreconcilable elements" in the Party because of his own deep feelings and long associations.[126] He was convinced that the CCP's support for a coalition government was merely tactical and short term.

The failed mediation brought to an end the third force movement begun six years before. It marked a defeat for peace, for democracy, for unification, and for the nascent tradition that civil opposition represented. After 1946, the middle road of Chinese politics was closed. Facing a choice, some stayed with the government. Others considered

---

[123] *MMWX*, pp. 213–214.
[124] For the full report, see *The China White Paper (1949)*, II, 686–689.
[125] *The China White Paper (1949)*, I, 209.   [126] Ibid., p. 213.

the CCP to be the lesser of the two evils. Still others saw the choice in terms diametrically opposed – between prodemocracy and antidemocracy, between good and evil – believing that the CCP was a benign and prodemocracy force. That was an error of judgment, for democracy was already dead, and the Communists were just waiting to bury it.

9

The Last Stand of Chinese Liberalism

FOLLOWING the failure of the Political Consultative Conference, China soon plunged into an all-out civil war. It was a hopeless situation for all those who pleaded for peace and democracy. To vent their anger and frustration, they could take to the streets, demonstrating against civil war, hunger, and the government, and in so doing risk arrests and their lives. Other than that, there was not much they could do. Yet in the intellectual marketplace of ideas, there remained a liberal forum at the center of which were the independent, nonparticipatory elite plus some MPG thinkers who had withdrawn from political engagement. Standing on the sideline, claiming impartiality, disclaiming self-interests, pondering the future of China, and wondering where Chinese liberalism was headed, these liberal elements were a diffuse and unorganized coterie of university professors and intellectuals fighting a battle already lost. Theirs was the last voice, a swan song, or perhaps a requiem. Maintaining their faith in liberalism, they still spoke, desperately, of the continued necessity of a middle force representing the will of the people. Finding themselves at a crossroads, they could not help but wonder where they were going. The tragedy was that, as they faced the prospect of a final CCP victory and pondered what it meant for them, the road to democracy was closed long before they realized.

Earlier works on the civil war period have shown that the Nationalist government drove the liberals to the communist camp rather than the CCP winning them over. Suzanne Pepper, in her excellent work on this period, has treated at great depth the intellectuals' critique of the government. The critique was directed at a whole range of issues, including the form of Nationalist rule; political repression, violation of human rights, official corruption, and incompetence; the economic and political consequences of the civil war and responsibility for it; and the liberal ideal of a middle path between socialism and democracy.[1] Yet there were considerable misgivings about the CCP. A more recent study of the liberal writers of Shanghai's influential weekly *Guancha* has noted their concern that under communism they would suffer more than they had under the current regime.[2] Few looked forward to political life under CCP rule.

This chapter focuses on the last stand of Chinese liberalism, the dilemma facing the noncommitted intellectuals, and their search for "new liberalism," "new democracy," and "new socialism" that would enable them to come to terms with Chinese communism. It will show that sympathy for the CCP was driven not only by profound disillusionment with the Nationalist government but also by wishful thinking that socialism and democracy could be achieved simultaneously under the rule of the CCP. Some felt able to reconcile their liberal and democratic thoughts with Mao Zedong's New Democracy. Others came to an appreciation that China needed a fair political system to ensure equality before liberty. Seeing the severity of China's economic problems and social injustice, they wittingly or otherwise endorsed the CCP's peasant revolution, despite their disapproval of the violence used in the implementation of the land reform program. Still others were convinced that China's only *chulu* (way out) now was the revolutionary road and could only hope that revolution and enlightenment were not necessarily incompatible. Eventually, those who elected to stay on the mainland, willingly or reluctantly, or because it was a Hobson's choice, went down a track that took liberalism and democracy to a dead end.

THE POSTWAR PRODEMOCRACY SETTING

The political discourse of 1939–1945 in the West had upheld democracy as the opposite of Nazism. Democracy was a Cinderella whose humble virtues shone forth after the gaudy sisters, fascism and communism, turned out so badly. "Their fanaticism," Bertrand Russell wrote after the war, in the end "roused the hostility of the world" against the Nazis and led to their defeat. One-time elitist Gaetano Mosca, after living under

---

[1] Suzanne Pepper, *Civil War in China: The Political Struggle, 1945–1949* (Berkeley: University of California Press, 1978), ch. 5.
[2] Wong Young-tsu, "The Fate of Liberalism in Revolutionary China," *Modern China* 19:4 (October 1993): 485.

Mussolini, came to appreciate that "the defects of parliamentary assemblies are merest trifles compared to the harm that inevitably results from abolishing them."[3]

After the war, democracy was hailed by many educated Chinese as a world trend, of which their country must be part, in the belief that only democracy could bring about China's unity and reconstruction and save the GMD regime in the process. A new China must be peaceful, united, free, democratic and a cooperative member of the family of nations.[4] "In today's world," proclaimed the philosopher Zhang Shenfu, "a real victory in the War of Resistance requires democracy. In today's world, if national reconstruction is to be a real success, then we need democracy even more. Without democracy there can be no unity, without unity there can be no unification, and without unification how is national reconstruction possible?"[5] No one, however, thought that Chinese democracy would be anything but a long and tortuous road.

By mid-1946, when civil war became inevitable, the quest for democracy had become part of a wider antiwar, antihunger, antioppression, and anti–United States movement. There was a resurgence of student activism begun the year before with the December First Movement. From 1946 through 1947 to 1948, students joined their college and university professors in demanding an end to the civil war, formation of a coalition government, cessation of American interference, and peaceful reconstruction.[6]

The postwar period saw a proliferation in the major cities of a number of liberal magazines and journals, some new, some old, with titles reflecting the general mood of the intellectual community. The most notable and influential of these was *Guancha*, an independent journal beholden to no political group. Starting as a weekly on September 1, 1946, *Guancha* was the most widely read journal around the country, with a circulation, by the end of 1948 when it was closed down by the government, of sixty thousand with its actual readership estimated conservatively at double

---

[3] Quoted in Roland N. Stromberg, *Democracy: A Short, Analytical History* (Armonk, NY: M. E. Sharpe, 1996), p. 116.

[4] See, for example, Sun Jiyi, "Zhanhou Zhongguo zhengzhi wenti" (The question of postwar Chinese politics), *Minzhu zhengzhi* 6–7 combined (November 1945): 25–27.

[5] Zhang Shenfu, "Minzhu tuanjie de jingshen tiaojian" (The spiritual conditions for democratic unity), *Wencui* 1:1 (October 9, 1945): 2.

[6] On postwar student activism, see Pepper, *Civil War in China*, ch. 3; Jessie G. Lutz, "The Chinese Student Movement of 1945–1949," *Journal of Asian Studies* 31:1 (November 1971): 89–110.

this figure.[7] Another notable journal was *Shiji pinglun* (Commentary This Century), launched in Nanjing in January 1947. Equally critical of the government and the CCP, *Shiji pinglun* writers repeatedly expressed the hope that the government would recognize its failings and introduce reform because they did not believe that the CCP could do a better job in the circumstances.[8] Other independent journals included *Minzhu* (Democracy, Shanghai), *Minzhu luntan* (Democratic Forum, Shanghai), *Ziyou luntan* (Liberal Forum, Kunming), *Ziyou shijie banyuekan* (Free World Bimonthly, Guangzhou), *Minzhu banyuekan* (Democracy Bimonthly, Beijing), *Minzhu zhengzhi* (Democratic Politics, Chongqing), and *Minzhu shenghuo* (Democratic Life, Chongqing). As for liberal journals beholden to particular groups, the most important was the DL's *Minzhu zhoukan* (Democracy Weekly, Kunming). Some small magazines, like Shanghai's *Zhoubao* (Weekly), *Xiaoxi* (News), and *Shenghuo zhishi* (Knowledge for Living) were short-lived, closed by the authorities in mid-1946. A year later, Shanghai's *Minzhu* met the same fate. Throughout 1946 and 1947, these magazines carried articles demanding peace, unity, nationalization of the armies, popular elections, rule of law, legalization of all political parties, a depoliticized civil service, and, above all, "return of the reins of government to the people" – familiar refrains.[9] Chiang Kai-shek was constantly reminded of his four promises, which were made at the opening session of the Political Consultative Conference. Human rights continued to be a critical issue, to which the last number of the ill-fated *Minzhu* (August 1947) was devoted.[10]

The postwar period also witnessed the formation of a number of minor political groups. In December 1945, the Chinese Democratic National Construction Association (*Zhongguo minzhu jianguo hui*) was formed in Chongqing – a business group made up of industrialists, merchants, business persons, and the like. Among its founders were Huang Yanpei, Shi Fuliang, and the banker and financier Zhang Naiqi. Also formed in December 1945 was the Association for the Promotion of Chinese

---

[7] Pepper, *Civil War in China*, p. 134; Wong Young-tsu, "The Fate of Liberalism," p. 488, note 1.

[8] See, for example, editorials in 1: 3 (January 18, 1947) and 1: 9 (March 1, 1947).

[9] See, for example, the editorial board, "Zhanhou Zhongguo zhengzhi wenti" (The postwar China question), *Minzhu zhengzhi* 6–7 combined (November 1945): 16–24; Wu Han, "Lun kuoda zhengfu zuzhi fang'an" (A proposal on the enlargement of the governmental structure), *MZZK* 2:24 (January 20, 1946): 3–4.

[10] See *Minzhu* 49–50 combined (August 24, 1947).

Democracy (*Zhongguo minzhu cujinhui*). Based in Shanghai, its members were recruited from two sources: the cultural, publishing, and literary circles and, to a lesser extent, the Shanghai business community. In July 1947, it merged with the Guomindang Association for the Promotion of Democracy (*Guomindang minzhu cujinhui*), a regrouping of the anti-Chiang forces within the GMD dating back to 1927. Formed in March 1946, it was led by Li Jishen and He Xiangning, with the stated aim of carrying out the political and economic policies of the late Sun Yat-sen.

Two other new groups may be mentioned. One was the September Third Study Society (*Jiusan xueshe*), which came into being in Chongqing in May 1946. A society of prominent scientists and educators, it was led by Xu Deheng, a former Beijing University professor and a member of the People's Political Council. Apart from the familiar prodemocracy demands, it was particularly concerned with academic freedom, a liberal approach to university administration and research centers, and the application of science to problem solving. Another new group was the Three Principles of the People United Comrades Association (*Sanmin zhuyi tongzhihui*), a splinter group of the GMD established in October 1945 by Tan Pingshan.[11] All these groups supported the PCC resolutions. Sympathetic with the Communists, if not openly pro-CCP, they were welcomed by the latter as part of the CCP's united front strategy. With small memberships and no political clout, they were insignificant in postwar politics and more ineffectual than the MPGs of the war period.

The Nationalist government came under constant attack. Some assaults were extremely ferocious. Zhang Xiruo, the Columbia-trained political scientist at the Southwest Associated University, likened the regime to a gang of violent armed bandits:

> A feudal clique that is politically impotent, ignorant, stupid, reactionary, corrupt and autocratic monopolizes the present regime. This regime is as stupid as a cow and as ferocious as a tiger.... If the Communists are "red bandits," then the Nationalists are "white bandits." Perhaps we may call the Nationalists "black bandits" since

---

[11] Qiu Qianmu, *Zhongguo minzhu dangpaishi* (A history of the Chinese democratic parties and groups) (Hangzhou: Zhejiang jiaoyu chubanshe, 1987), pp. 142–159; Wang Tianwen and Wang Jichun, *Zhongguo minzhu dangpai shigang* (Outline of the Chinese democratic parties and groups) (Kaifeng: Henan daxue chubanshe, 1988), pp. 127–153, 161–180, 291–304.

"white" implies purity. . . . This regime is a "black gang" that maintains itself in power by means of violence and guns. It is most unfortunate for the country's future. The consequences would be to send China's destiny to hell.[12]

No one, however, called for its overthrow. There was no conspiracy. Rather, they desired to see a coalition government, in the hope that the GMD would reform itself. One frequent contributor to Shanghai's *Minzhu*, for example, made it clear every time he wrote that his hope was that the GMD would tackle its problems and thereby retain power.[13] Critics still acknowledged the leadership of the GMD and Chiang Kai-shek. After the collapse of the peace talks in 1946, Zhang Dongsun still maintained that he wanted to save the Nationalist regime from self-destruction.[14]

The consensus was that the problems of China could not be resolved by force or external intervention, that the Communists could not be easily defeated, and that the civil war, if not stopped, would only ruin the country and add to the people's suffering. The government had not yet run out of time and could still do the right things, if only it had the political will.[15] It was widely believed that the problem with the GMD was not the lack of a sound ideology but the fact that the ideology had not been translated into action. Economically, for instance, instead of carrying out the policy of land equalization and restriction of capital, the GMD had entrenched landlord interests and fostered bureaucratic capitalism. Feudal landlords and bureaucratic capitalism were Marxist jargons. But as one recent scholar has pointed out, Chinese liberals had used these terms long before the CCP made them part of its vocabulary.[16] There was deep resentment against official corruption and the "financial lords" (*caifa*) who had links with the most powerful figures in the government.[17]

---

[12] Zhang Xiruo, "Zhengzhi xieshang huiyi yinggai jiejue de wenti" (The questions that should be resolved in regard to the Political Consultative Conference), *MZZK* 2:24 (January 20, 1946): 9–10.

[13] Ma Xulun, "Guomin de zeren yinggai shuohua" (It is the citizen's duty to speak up), *Minzhu* 8 (December 1, 1945): 173–181.

[14] Zhang Dongsun, "Zhuishu women nuli jianli 'lianhe zhengfu' de yongyi" (An account of the purpose of our efforts at "coalition government"), *GC* 2:6 (April 15, 1947): 6.

[15] Kang Yongren, "Cong renxin ji guoji jushi kan Zhongguo qiantu" (China's future seen from public support and the international situation), *SJPL* 1:14 (April 5, 1947): 5.

[16] Wong Young-tsu, "The Fate of Liberalism," p. 480.

[17] Zheng Xuejia, "Lun minzhu yu jingji jianshe" (On democracy and economic construction), *Minzhu yu tongyi* 4 (June 10, 1946): 3–4.

Even progovernment independents were convinced that such "noble houses" as the Soongs and the Kungs, which enjoyed a monopoly in many state enterprises resulting in inefficiency and cronyism, should be "eliminated."[18]

As repression increased, the issue of human rights kept coming up. In February 1947, following the arrest of over two thousand people, including professors, teachers, doctors, publishers, shopkeepers, and students, in the course of a so-called census investigation in Beijing, thirteen professors issued a joint statement demanding respect for human rights. This was followed early in March by a declaration of human rights issued over the names of 192 academics of Beida, Qinghua, Yanjing, and other universities. In May, 130 journalists belonging to the North China Correspondents Association met in Beijing, demanding freedom of the press and safeguards for civil liberties.[19]

In some quarters, the idea of a third force, despite the setbacks of previous years, was revisited, focusing on the question of whether there really was a third road for China.

THE THIRD FORCE REVISITED

Leading the discourse in 1946–1947, Shi Fuliang and Zhang Dongsun used the terms *middle party* and *middle politics* rather than third force or third party. Early in 1946, Shi, a former Nationalist economist, wrote that China's best way forward was to democratize and to have three major political parties, not two. If a powerful middle party were formed, not only would it "harmonize" the relations between the two major parties, but it would also become a stabilizing force influencing the policies of both the left and the right. He assigned the middle party a historical mission to democratize and industrialize China and, in the process, to enhance the position and interests of the peasants and the laboring classes. It would represent a middle road (*note*: not a third road) and the best hope for China's future.[20] His view was later reiterated in a

---

[18] Fu Mengzhen (Fu Sinian), "Lun haomen ziben zhi bixu chanchu" (On the necessary elimination of noble house capitalism), *GC* 2:1 (March 1, 1947): 6–8. Fu was particularly critical of T. V. Soong.

[19] Pepper, *Civil War in China*, pp. 141–142.

[20] Shi Fuliang, "Lun zhongjianpai" (On the middle party), *Guoxun* 405 (January 1, 1946): 12–13.

feature article published in Shanghai's *Wenhuibao* in July, reducing the problem of Chinese politics to a conflict between the democratic and antidemocratic forces. For him, there was no third road.[21]

Although Shi appreciated the Anglo-American systems, he rejected the kind of democracy controlled by a small privileged minority of bureaucratic capitalists, compradors, and big landlords. Cast in the mode of new democracy, middle party opposed all forms of dictatorship and foreign dependence. Economically, he went on, it represented a form of new capitalism anchored in liberalism, albeit with a socialist bent, and it could be a friend, or an enemy, of the two major parties, depending on their policies.[22] Shi was hoping against all odds that the idea of a middle party would grow in strength. But he exaggerated its independence of thought, action, and policy, claiming, unconvincingly, that it represented the bulk of the population.

Zhang Dongsun gave a dual meaning to the term *middle politics*. First, in the context of Cold War politics, middle politics meant a position between the United States and the Soviet Union where China could play the role of a mediator. (He was extraordinarily naïve about China's ability to play that role.) Second, in terms of domestic politics, it meant the differentiation between the major and minor parties and the positioning of the latter somewhere between the GMD and the CCP. Ideologically, it denoted a space between capitalism and socialism. But he hastened to add that this duality might be misleading in that the GMD was not really a capitalist party, nor was the CCP an advocate of communism for the present.[23]

Zhang's conception of middle politics was informed in part by Cold War politics. China, he argued, must be acceptable to both the United States and the Soviet Union by adopting a "middle" system between capitalism and communism. Such a system would resemble Anglo-American democracy politically and Soviet socialism economically. "This is to adopt democracy without capitalism and to adopt socialism without a proletarian revolution. We want liberty, not licentiousness; cooperation,

---

[21] Shi Fuliang, "Hewei zhongjianpai" (What is meant by middle party?), *Wenhuibao* (July 14, 1946), reprinted in Li Huaxing, ed., *Zhongguo xiandai sixiangshi ziliao jianbian* (Hangzhou: Zhejiang renmin chubanshe, 1983), V, 298–301.

[22] Ibid., pp. 299–301.

[23] Zhang Dongsun, "Yige zhongjian xing de zhengzhi luxian" (A political line of a middle nature), *Zaisheng* 118 (June 22, 1946), reprinted in ibid., V, 202–207.

not conflict. Because we don't want licentiousness, we reject capitalist control and domination. Because we don't want conflict, we reject class struggle."[24] Here Zhang reflected the dim view of capitalism so widely held by Chinese intellectuals. His vision of a democracy without capitalism and socialism without a proletarian revolution ignored the immensely complex and delicate political task of actually working out such a system.

Internally, middle politics sought to draw the two major parties closer together by pulling one to the left and the other to the right through consultation, mediation, and compromise. "This is the middle road for every party to take," Zhang declared. "It is the only road. There is no other road. . . . And it is a democratic road. But it is neither purely Anglo-American nor purely Soviet."[25] To restore peace, middle politics had to be "extremely strong" and "completely independent" and must seek to bridge the gap between the conflicting parties in a coalition government.[26]

In short, Shi and Zhang represented a body of opinion in the postwar period that rejected suggestions of a third road. In their view, there was only one road – democratization and industrialization. Chinese politics were then reduced to a conflict not between the two major parties, but between the forces of democracy and industrialization and those of authoritarianism and bureaucratic capitalism. This reductionism did not preclude either of the parties from becoming democratic and industrialized. As one Beijing professor pointed out, liberalism did not lie between the Three Principles of the People and Chinese communism; it was at odds with the latter and a critique of the former.[27] Yet if liberalism was "a historical motor of change," it was on the side of leftist politics.[28] And that was why young students, discontented with the status quo, were inclined to the left.

If there really were only one road for China ahead, would it be taken by the Nationalist government? And if the government were incapable of going down that path, where would the liberals be going?

[24] Ibid., p. 204.   [25] Ibid., pp. 206–207.

[26] Zhang Dongsun, "Heping heyi hui si le?" (Why is peace dead?), *Shi yu wen* 1:3 (March 28, 1947): 3–4; and "Zhuishu women nuli jianli 'lianhe zhengfu' de yongyi," pp. 5–7.

[27] Yang Renbian, "Guanyu ⟨Zhonggong wang hechu qu?⟩" (On "Where the CCP is going?"), *GC* 3:10 (November 1, 1947): 11.

[28] Yang Renbian, "Zailun ziyou zhuyi de tujing" (Again on the path of liberalism), *GC* 5:8 (October 16, 1948): 4.

WHERE ARE THE LIBERALS HEADED?

By mid-1947, the Nationalist government had absolutely lost its legitimacy and moral leadership. This was a serious problem because the government was so corrupt and so incompetent that even its sympathizers were dismayed. Progressive elements within the GMD were equally concerned about the ultraconservatism of the leadership. Earlier, in August 1945, in a public lecture delivered at the Southwest Associated University, Qian Duansheng, a long-time supporter of Chiang Kai-shek, had spoken of the need for "a new political leadership" that was "progressive and forward-looking." Such a new leadership must be injected with new blood from younger members. Although not wishing to challenge Chiang's authority, Qian pointed out that the current leadership was old and tired and badly in need of revitalization if the Party were to stay in power. Of all the elderly leaders in the Party government, Shao Lizi, in his view, was perhaps the only progressive. The leadership would benefit from an injection of liberal elements from both within and outside the Party, as well as from a coalition government including the Communists whose rural achievements over the past few years made a profound impression on him.[29] Qian did not mention Sun Fo. But it was understood that the liberal group in the GMD could play a more active role. Some non-GMD members known to hold liberal views could also be brought into the government.

General Marshall, after dealing with Chiang Kai-shek for a year, also thought that the Nationalist government, if it were to stay in power, would have to liberalize. On his departure from China early in 1947 after his failed mission, he made a statement, in which, inter alia, he called for a liberal leadership composed of liberal elements from within the GMD and the two minor parties that had joined the government. He believed that American advice to the Nationalist government could be helpful in many matters, but not in the elimination of official corruption without an effective opposition party. He had met with the MPG leaders and some independents about the need to organize a liberal group to serve as a balance between the two major parties. Such an organization should be devoted to the welfare of the people and not to the self interests of the MPG leaders themselves. They would then be able to exert political influence that would increase as the organization gained prestige.

---

[29] Qian Duansheng, "Jiangju ruhe dakai: lun Zhongguo zhengzhe de qiantu" (How to break the stalemate: On China's political future), *MZZK* 2:7 (August 20, 1945): 12–13.

Neither the GMD nor the CCP could then take a decisive step without its support.[30] In short, he wrote:

> The salvation of the situation, as I see it, would be the assumption of leadership by the liberals in the Government and in the minority parties, a splendid group of men, but who as yet lack the political power to exercise a controlling influence. Successful action on their part under the leadership of Generalissimo Chiang Kai-shek would, I believe, lead to unity through good government.[31]

Marshall's advice went unheeded, of course. But honestly he did not himself think that the liberals had "the remotest chance for leadership" in China.[32] It was only natural that the liberals, disappointed and perhaps also disenchanted, should be left wondering what the future held for them.

They were confused, depressed, and anxious. Already some individuals and groups had made a choice by joining one camp or the other, which raised a question in the minds of some independent scholars: Who were the true liberals and who were not? There was a view, articulated by Beijing University Professor Yang Renbian, that a distinction should be made between liberals and progressives. It followed that there were progressives, but not liberals, in the major parties. "Liberalism is a creative force seeking progress. To seek progress is to oppose stagnation, which means opposing the status quo."[33] True liberals were those who, discontented with the status quo, pursued progress in an uncompromising spirit. They were ridiculed by the CCP as "little people" (*xiao shimin*) or "petty bourgeoisie." But being little people had the advantage of being able to mix with the poor masses and to understand their needs. Those who had joined the GMD and the CCP were not liberals because the Nationalists protected the status quo, whereas communism was irreconcilably opposed to liberalism.[34] True liberals found themselves in an awkward position, accused on the one hand by the left of having no "ism"

---

[30] Marshall regretted that the MPGs "had allowed themselves to be divided and were consequently unable to influence the situation or prevent the use of military force by the Government or the promotion of economic collapse by the Communists. In the midst of this deplorable situation stood the Chinese people alone bearing the full weight of the tragedy." See *The China White Paper (1949)*, I, 213–214.

[31] Ibid., II, 688.   [32] Ibid., I, xxiv–xxv.

[33] Yang Renbian, "Ziyou zhuyizhe wang hechu qu?" (Where are the liberals headed?), *GC* 2:11 (May 10, 1947): 5.

[34] Ibid.

and being progovernment, and, on the other, by the right of being a "tail" of the CCP and communist travelers.[35]

Divided on where they were going and about what they could do, some remained optimistic that they could serve the country independently without participating in government, let alone winning power. Thus, Shi Fuliang wrote:

> Under China's specific circumstances, the liberals perhaps will never win power, they may even never participate in government. The "liberal road" is not necessarily a road to a seizure of political power, especially in China. The liberals should take the success-not-for-ourselves attitude, striving hard to achieve their goals but not thinking of making personal gains. What they should strive for is practical work, not superficial achievement. Therefore, their success or failure cannot be judged by their ability or otherwise to seize power.[36]

This moral disclaimer of interest in power was, in fact, an admission of their predicament and political impotence.

Many were still hoping that a new liberal force could lead the revolution and carry it to completion; they emphasized a new force because the liberals had come to realize the need to understand the masses better than they had before.[37] Chu Anping, editor of *Guancha* and a former student of Harold Laski, wrote in March 1947 that it was the liberal intellectuals who alone could shake the corrupt GMD regime and, at the same time, repulse the violent CCP, which the people feared. Considering the extremes of the two major parties, only the liberal intellectuals, using morality and liberal thought, could provide political leadership, stabilize the situation, and save the nation. He asked his fellow liberals not to abandon hopes but to rise up from their state of depression and anxiety about the nation's future to fulfill their "historical responsibility."[38] A sense of desperation was unmistakable.

---

[35] Ibid. See also Zhou Shouzhang, "Wei zhenzheng de ziyou zhuyi fenzi daqi" (Cheering for the true liberal elements), *SJPL* 4:10 (September 4, 1949): 5–7. For Zhou, the true liberals were those who held liberal convictions, and who were peaceful, progressive, nationalistic, and independent-minded.

[36] Shi Fuliang, "Lun ziyou zhuyizhe de daolu" (On the road of liberalism), *GC* 3:22 (January 24, 1948): 4.

[37] See, for example, Zhou Zhongqi, "Lun geming" (On revolution), *GC* 3:22 (January 24, 1948): 10.

[38] Chu Anping, "Zhongguo de zhengju" (China's political situation), *GC* 2:2 (March 8, 1947): 8.

Indeed, conscious of their own weaknesses, many were not so sure about their capacity to influence Chinese politics. One Beijing professor bluntly stated that it was a sheer fantasy to expect the Chiang Kai-shek regime to provide liberal leadership because the old guard was jealous of its vested interests and would defend those interests at all costs. His critique was meant as much for the liberal intellectuals themselves as for the regime. Unlike modern Europe, he reasoned, modern China lacked the basis of a powerful new bourgeoisie. Imperialist aggression and civil war had destroyed the foundations of China's "petty bourgeoisie." By and large, Chinese intellectuals led a miserable and perilous existence under Nationalist rule, had no opportunity for personal development, and were denied freedoms of expression and publication. Frustrated and repressed, they could only turn to the CCP if they were not anticommunist. In short, he concluded, what the liberals should do now was not to try to provide political leadership but to keep pace with the masses by "sharing their wisdom with them, helping them, and cooperating with them."[39] How this could be done was not immediately clear. But he put his finger on the soft spot of the Chinese liberal movement when he said that it had failed to mobilize support at the grass-roots level. Chinese intellectuals had always operated in small circles, talking among themselves rather than to the ordinary people. Frankly, he did not think that the liberals could do better than previously.[40]

The liberal force sought to be independent and neutral. But even if it could be independent, there was no room for neutrality. What's more, no useful purpose would be served by adhering to a neutral position. Neutrality, even if possible, was unhelpful and unproductive. One liberal writer argued thus:

> The combination of liberalism and an attitude of neutrality is absolutely wrong. True liberals should consider the principles of all the questions at hand and decide what is progressive and rational. ... They should choose between right and wrong, attack what deserves to be attacked, and support what ought to be supported. They need action and unity! Action promotes unity, and unity facilitates action.[41]

---

[39] Huang Hai, "Ziyou fenzi neng lingdao Zhongguo ma?" (Can the liberal elements lead China?), *Minzhu banyuekan* 2 (January 25, 1947): 6–7.

[40] Shi Fuliang, "Lun ziyou zhuyizhe de daolu," pp. 3–5.

[41] Wang Gongliang, "Ziyou zhuyizhe yu zhongli taidu" (The liberal elements and their neutral attitude), *SJPL* 4:20 (November 13, 1948): 9–10.

His point was that, depending on the issues, the liberals should support the party that did the right things.

The liberals were not helped by their inability to form a strong political organization like a liberal party.[42] There were several reasons for that. First, it was widely held that liberalism transcended party lines; hence, there was no need for a strong organization claiming liberalism alone. Yang Renbian noted that Chinese liberals were accustomed to being unorganized, citing the example of the May Fourth Movement, which was not organization driven. He wondered how Chinese liberals, unconstrained by political dogmas, could form a large, tightly knit organization, which he did not think necessary anyway.[43]

Second, there were problems inherent in the character of Chinese intellectuals. Chu Anping noted that Chinese intellectuals were dispersed and potentially strong, more concerned with morality than power and self-interests. They had a sense of integrity, putting much value on personal relationships, but they were narrow-minded and individualistic, belittling one another in the tradition of the arrogant literati. Politics required leadership, vision, magnanimity, organization, and discipline, all of which were lacking in Chinese intellectuals who easily quarreled over minor issues at the expense of bigger ones. In addition, the political and economic restrictions and thought controls that the Nationalist regime had imposed on them over the past twenty years rendered any attempts at effective political organization extremely difficult.[44]

Third, Chinese intellectuals were, in the main, armchair scholars lacking political skills. Their good education did not translate into effective political leadership.[45] Finally, their distaste for power detracted from their effectiveness as political organizers. Regime control was not important for those who were convinced that to lead the people and to educate them in the current prodemocracy movement; they would be more effective in opposition than in government.[46]

Alone and unaided, there was little they could do to change the

---

[42] Wong Young-tsu, "The Fate of Liberalism," pp. 467–468, 486; Eugene Lubot, *Liberalism in an Illiberal Age: New Culture Liberals in Republican China, 1919–1937* (Westport: Greenwood Press, 1982), p. 49.

[43] Yang Renbian, "Ziyou zhuyizhe wang hechu qu?" p. 5.

[44] Chu Anping, "Zhongguo de zhengju," pp. 7–8.

[45] In 1946, after Hu Shi's return from the United States, there were rumors that he was planning to organize a new political party. Some responded to the rumor by questioning Hu's ability to offer effective leadership in spite of his education. See Pepper, *Civil War in China*, p. 191.

[46] Yang Renbian, "Ziyou zhuyizhe wang hechu qu?" p. 6.

Chinese situation, prompting some desperate souls to seek foreign help. In February 1947, there was talk in Beijing of forming a "patriotic democratic united front" as part of the world's democratic movement that would enjoy the support of people around the world, including Americans.[47] In July, a group of ten professors called on the United States to establish a Democratic International (*minzhu guoji*) to act as a counterweight to the Communist International.[48] Reaction to the call at home was mixed. Some found the idea "constructive and worthy of consideration" but were concerned about suggestions that the United States financially support the Democratic International and all parties and groups professing to be democratic.[49] Others, appalled, found it "dangerous" and "objectionable" because it was anti-Soviet, anti-CCP, and pro-American.[50] They blasted the ten professors as "disgraceful" and "fake liberals" who failed to see that the United States was seeking to expand her global influence just like the Soviet Union and that both were partly responsible for the civil wars in many parts of the world. There was serious concern about American interference in China's internal affairs.[51]

Paradoxically, the United States, far from being a source of support, harmed the Chinese liberal and democratic cause by following a policy designed to assist Chiang Kai-shek, although it did criticize his government. The perception that the United States was propping up a repressive regime was reinforced by the American military presence in China. The behavior of some American marines was appalling, including drunkenness, theft, rape, and even murder. Criticism of American policy had escalated since the failure of the Marshall mission, which was not seen to be impartial from the start. There was, moreover, a strong view that China should steer an independent course rather than be turned into an

---

[47] Chu Yi, "Lun aiguo minzhu tongyi zhanxian" (On the patriotic democratic unification front), *Minzhu banyuekan* 3 (February 15, 1947): 2. This theme was also developed by many contributors to the Shanghai journal *Minzhu*.

[48] Yang Guangshi et al., "Women duiyu daju de kanfa yu duice" (Our views and strategies on the current situation), *GC* 2:21 (July 19, 1947): 3–4.

[49] Wu Shichang, "Lun 〈minzhu guoji〉" (On the Democratic International), *GC* 2:22 (July 26, 1947): 5.

[50] Yi Qiwen, "Yizai suowei 〈minzhu guoji〉!" (Wonderful! The so-called Democratic International), *Shi yu wen* 1:21 (August 1, 1947): 10–11.

[51] Ouyang Changhong, "Cong suowei 〈minzhu guoji〉 shuoqi!" (Speaking on the so-called Democratic International), *Shi yu wen* 1:22 (August 8, 1947): 7–8; Bo Qi, "Wei ziyou zhuyizhe de zhen mianmu" (The real face of the fake liberal elements), *Shi yu wen* 1:22 (August 8, 1947): 9–10.

anti-Soviet base, which was what Washington was thought to be doing. Finally, the ascendancy of the right wing in postwar American politics also served to undermine the Chinese democratic cause by strengthening Chiang's hard line toward the Communists without fears of a backlash from the United States. The 1947 Wedemeyer mission to China and Korea to conduct an on-the-spot survey as a basis for a reappraisal of American policy in China was widely seen as evidence of a radical shift of American policy to the right. It appeared that Washington was a friend not of Chinese democracy, but of Chiang and his repressive regime.[52]

Within China, the mood about the future of democratic institutions was increasingly pessimistic.[53] There was widespread cynicism about politicians at all levels: they were thought to be "corrupt," "depraved," "deceptive," and "incapable of leading the country." Members of the provincial political councils were found to have no concern for the national good and the well-being of the people. Far from representing the people and leading the country, they were alleged to be greedy and selfish, prostituting themselves to the authorities.[54] Faith in constitutionalism eroded rapidly in some quarters. Liang Shuming, who never disguised his distaste for British-style constitutionalism and Western political models that did not take account of Chinese cultural traditions, was convinced that "competitive elections" for a new government in the existing conditions would be a disaster.[55] Zhang Dongsun agreed, adding that elections since the early Republic had always been used and manipulated by "special forces" and that constitutionalism, Anglo-American style, was unsuited to China.[56] The real problem was not with constitu-

---

[52] Wong Young-tsu, "The Fate of Liberalism," pp. 475–479. General Albert C. Wedemeyer was sent by Marshall, who had become the new Secretary of State upon his return to the United States.

[53] Compare my observation with Suzanne Pepper's that the pessimistic mood was not widely shared. Pepper, *Civil War in China*, p. 187, cites only two liberal writers, one of whom lived in the United States.

[54] See, for example, Situ Yiheng, "Zhongguo minzhu de zhanwang" (The prospect of Chinese democracy), *Minzhu luntan* 2:3 (September 20, 1947): 9–11.

[55] Liang Shuming, "Yugao xuanzai, zhuilun xianzheng" (Predictions about an election disaster, and a critique of constitutionalism), *LSMQJ*, VI, 699–722. Liang had made no contribution to the discussions of the Draft Constitution at the Political Consultative Conference. He chose to be reticent because he was adamant that the Western multiparty system, with its emphasis on competitive politics and rule by the majority party, was not appropriate for China. What he desired to see in China was a government above party lines to be established by a multiparty body. See "Yan'an guilai" (Return from Yan'an), *LSMQJ*, VI, 626–627.

[56] Zhang Dongsun, "Wo yi zhuilun xianzheng jianji wenhua de zhenduan" (I also want to talk about constitutionalism and cultural diagnosis), *GC* 3:7 (October 11, 1947): 3–6. With

tionalism itself, or with Chinese culture, but with the facts that Chinese constitutions were programmatic and that there was no way of ensuring that those in authority would not act unconstitutionally. As the civil war raged, some came to feel that it was pointless to talk about democratic and constitutional rule.[57]

Disaffection with the government certainly helped the communist movement. But in 1947, liberal intellectuals were not driven to the communist camp in droves because they feared the establishment of a totalitarian form of government, the abolition of private property, and the danger of China's becoming a puppet of the Soviet Union.[58]

By and large, the liberals were evenhanded in their critiques of the two major parties. Some were particularly critical of the CCP on the question of liberty, having no illusions about personal freedoms under a communist regime, which would be more interventionist than the GMD.[59] They dreaded the thought of stricter press censorship and tighter controls of literature and art.[60] They had no doubt that the CCP was antidemocratic, believing in *dangzhu* (the party being the master), not *minzhu* (the people being their own masters). Under the current regime, critics could still criticize the government and sometimes get away with it. Under CCP rule, that would be impossible. It was a matter of relativity. Political life under communism would be worse.[61]

Sympathy for the CCP was not lacking, however. The Chinese Communists, unlike their Russian counterparts, were thought to be land

---

the exception of Liang Shuming, the liberal intellectuals rarely suggested that British-style constitutionalism, or constitutional democracy, was unsuited to Chinese culture. It therefore came as a surprise that Zhang Dongsun, for all his exposure to Western philosophy, agreed with Liang on the question of elections. For that, Zhang and Liang were taken to task by a young economics professor at Beijing University. See Fan Hong, "Yu Liang Shuming, Zhang Dongsun liang xiansheng lun Zhongguo de wenhua yu zhengzhi" (Discussion with Mr. Liang Shuming and Mr. Zhang Dongsun about Chinese culture and politics), *GC* 3:14 (November 29, 1947): 5–8; and his "Wo duiyu Zhongguo zhengzhi wenti de genben kanfa" (My fundamental views on the question of Chinese politics), *GC* 3:18 (December 27, 1947): 5–6.

[57] Zou Wenhai, "Xingxian de tiaojian" (Conditions for constitutionalism), *Minzhu luntan* 1:4 (June 7, 1947): 11–12.

[58] Observations of Philip Sprouse of the American consulate in Shanghai. See *FRUS* (1947), VII, 677.

[59] Yang Renbian, "Ziyou zhuyizhe wang hechu qu?" p. 5.

[60] Zhou Shouzhang, "Lun shenhua zhengzhi" (Of myths and politics), *GC* 1:21 (January 18, 1947): 6.

[61] Chu Anping, "Zhongguo de zhengju," p. 6.

reformers not bent on achieving communism in the short or medium term. Many liberals could see that China was still a semifeudal and semicolonial society lacking the objective conditions for communism, notably an industrialized economy.[62] They could see also that the CCP was able to create a new social order in the "liberated areas" by tackling the land problem and to claim the countryside as the source of its political and military strength. Some liberals even accepted the necessity of class struggle in principle. What they opposed was the violent methods the Communists used in the implementation of the land reform program, especially in "settling accounts" with the landlords.[63] The CCP was different from orthodox Marxist communist parties that carried out proletarian revolutions. China did not have a proletarian industrial class, and the communist movement was, in the view of one prosocialist writer, a peasant movement led by the frustrated educated class, "an integration of off-production peasantry and extra-bureaucratic intellectuals," reflecting China's socioeconomic problems.[64]

Mao Zedong's treatises "On New Democracy" and "On Coalition Government" seem to have swayed them into accepting the CCP's now more moderate land policy and its united front strategy as a change of a fundamental nature rather than merely a tactical maneuver. Zhang Dongsun's change of attitude was instructive. Initially, he opposed the Communists' policy of making decisions on the basis of the short-lived impulses of the masses who engaged in class struggle and "liquidation" in the land reform program,[65] and he also found the CCP organization too strict and too disciplined to be appropriate for a democratic state. But by 1947, he no longer considered the CCP to be an impediment to democracy, for he had come to accept Mao's New Democracy, with which he was able to identify. Taking the words of the Communists at face value, he thought the CCP was superior to the GMD in one respect: "The CCP is sincere in what it proposes. Since it proclaims changing and

---

[62] See, for example, Huang Hai, "Ziyou fenzi neng lingdao Zhongguo ma?" (Can the liberal elements lead China?), *Minzhu banyuekan* 2 (January 25, 1947): 7.

[63] Pepper, *Civil War in China*, pp. 207–211.

[64] Yan Siping, "Zhongguo zhengzhi de qitu (xia)" (The crossroads of Chinese politics [part 2]), *Minzhu luntan* 2:7 (October 18, 1947): 8.

[65] *Zhonghua shibao* (Shanghai), August 3, 1946, cited in Anthony J. Shaheen, "The China Democratic League and Chinese Politics, 1939–1947," unpublished Ph.D. dissertation, University of Michigan, 1977, pp. 447–448.

adopting the New Democracy, then it is no longer an obstacle to a democratic nation. We must not doubt its New Democracy. Since the CCP has said that it will do it, then it will."[66] Although communism was the CCP's ultimate goal, none of the Communists with whom he had spoken expected to realize it in their lifetimes. Since communism was a problem for the distant future, he thought it "extremely possible" that China could avoid a communist revolution by rooting out the objective conditions for it with the "spirit of socialism." Because communism was avoidable, there was nothing to fear from the CCP.[67]

Many agreed that the CCP had no intention of realizing communism, not even socialism, at this point because the conditions were not ripe.[68] Luo Longji had come around to the view that the CCP deserved to be supported. His remark to the American consular officer John Melby in April 1947 was equally instructive: "even though Communism in China would allow no more scope for the activities of the liberals than does the [GMD], still Communism means greater good for the masses and should be supported."[69] These views, it may be noted, were similar to those of some American embassy officials in China.[70]

There is no way of establishing what proportion of liberal intellectuals was prepared to accept communist rule. The choice before them was not between democracy and dictatorship, but between two evils as far as individual liberty was concerned. The choice called for some theoretical rationalization. Thus, before making up their minds, some engaged in a discourse on the relationship between democracy and socialism, between political democracy and economic democracy, and between liberty and equality.

---

[66] Zhang Dongsun, "Zhuishu women nuli 'lianhe zhengfu' de yongyi," p. 7.

[67] Ibid.

[68] Pepper, *Civil War in China*, p. 225, citing Shi Fuliang.

[69] John Melby, *The Mandate of Heaven: Record of a Civil War, China, 1945–1949* (Toronto: Toronto University Press, 1968), p. 251.

[70] For example, John Davies, the Second Secretary of the American embassy had observed: "The Chinese Communists are backsliders. They still acclaim the infallibility of Marxian dogma and call themselves Communists. But they have become indulgent of human frailty and confess that China's communist salvation can be attained only through prolonged evolutionary rather than immediate revolutionary conversion. Like that other eminent backslider, Ramsay MacDonald, they have come to accept the inevitability of gradualness." *FRUS* (1944), VI, 669. Some other American observers also were fostering the widespread illusion that the Chinese Communists were not real Marxist–Leninists but rather "margarine Communists." See Melby, *Mandate*, pp. 253–256.

THE LIBERTY–EQUALITY DEBATE

The nexus between liberty and equality has been of interest t
and Chinese scholars alike. Giovanni Sartori holds that equali
poses freedom, that liberty must come first, in time or in fact, because
there could be no equality without freedom.[71] Liberty and economic conditions are related. The hungry person who wakes up in the morning
asking for breakfast may well call bread "liberty." However, "this is only,
and only in the short run, a way of asking for food. In the short run
because in illiberal systems the problem is not solved by giving more
bread but by taking away the right to ask for it." What troubles Sartori
is that "we are not free once our bellies are full." Political freedom does
not solve the problem of hunger. Equally, neither does bread solve the
problem of political freedom.[72]

Historically, the liberty–equality issue in China emerged early in the
twentieth century. Liang Qichao, apparently, fudged it, but Liu Shipei, the
anarchist, met it head on in a 1907 essay where he said he wanted both.
Liberty was an important value for Liu, but he treated it as an outcome
of equality, regarding the latter as the keystone of a just society. When they
clash, as they will, equality comes first, with liberties curtailed (the kind
of view that the CCP inherited). And yet, if people were not free, they
could not be equal. Equality also rested on a notion of concrete rights.[73]

In the immediate postwar period, the issue was discussed in terms of
the tension between "political" and "economic" democracies. Political
democracy, or political liberty, referred to systems serving the interests
of the rich and powerful at the expense of the poor and powerless. Economic democracy, or economic liberty, referred to economic equality and
social justice, often associated with the Soviet system, which gave a lower
priority to political rights. If only one kind of democracy were possible
at a time, which must come first? Was there a trade-off?

How to realize democracy in China without the "evils" of the capitalist system had long been a conundrum for modern Chinese intellectuals.
Before the end of the war, Luo Longji had begun to revisit the question.

---

[71] Giovanni Sartori, *The Theory of Democracy Revisited* (Chatham: Chatham House, 1987), p. 357.

[72] Ibid., p. 361.

[73] Peter Zarrow, "Citizenship and Human Rights in Early Twentieth-Century Chinese Thought: Liu Shipei and Liang Qichao," in Wm. Theodore de Bary and Tu Weiming, eds., *Confucianism and Human Rights* (New York: Columbia University Press, 1998), pp. 213–218.

He set out to debunk the myth that liberty and equality before the law ensured a commonality of well-being between the state and the people. He endorsed Marx's critique of capitalism, noting that the laws that protected the freedoms of speech, publication, assembly, and association, as well as the rights to vote and to be elected, worked only for the small minority of the population. This was because only the rich were able to publish, to form political parties, and to get elected to parliament, and they also controlled the law-making body in the state. "The rich enact the laws, the poor obey them. This is an undeniable fact. Consequently, in a democratic country, the state remains a tool in the hands of the rich, its well-being is still the well-being of a small minority."[74] Soviet Russia, he believed, had eliminated the capitalist class and established a new economic system whereby the people's rights to live and to work were safeguarded. Along with economic equality came economic liberty, hence the realization of economic democracy in Soviet Russia. But communism was not the only way of achieving economic democracy. Luo found other ways, such as the Roosevelt administration's "freedom from wants" program, the British Labour Party's nationalization policy, and the Anglo-American systems of social security. What was important for Luo was a society where the distribution of wealth was relatively even so that people, secure in their jobs and livelihood, could enjoy the *substance* of political liberty and equality. Industrialization was possible under an undemocratic regime as the cases of Japan and Germany demonstrated. But Luo called for industrialization under a democratic government. Because a capitalist class did not yet exist in China, he did not think Chinese industrialization and democratization need result in capitalist domination as in Britain, the United States, and France. To ensure that, it was necessary to learn from the experiences of both the West and Soviet Russia. Even though Chinese democracy would be enriched by industrialization, the capitalists should not drive the economy for their own benefits. Luo's premise was that there must be political liberty and equality first so that people could use their rights to steer the nation in the course of industrialization. There was no need for class dictatorship because economic democracy was not communism.[75]

Short of communism, China would need what one professor called "holistic social reform," which alone could guarantee the realization of

[74] Luo Longji, "Zhengzhi de minzhu yu jingji de minzhu" (Political democracy and economic democracy), *MZZK* 1:2 (December 16, 1944): 4.

[75] Ibid., pp. 4–5.

democracy. Widespread poverty was at the root of the "Chinese disease," and so industrialization was necessary to create wealth. However, wealth was to be created not for a small minority of capitalists but for the entire population whose living standard must be raised. Any democratic political construction, said the good professor, must focus on economic equalities.[76]

Writings like these set the tone for the postwar discourse on political and economic democracies. The shift in the rights thinking of the liberal intellectuals was unmistakable. In the 1930s, they had been concerned with civil and political rights, negative liberty that must be protected from the harmful action of the oppressive state. Now more attention was paid to economic and social rights, positive liberty that required positive state action for its realization. This shift from the first generation of rights to a second generation of rights was the result of two developments. The first was the devastation of the long war with Japan, which absolutely impoverished a population whose lives were hard enough in ordinary times. The DL, it will be recalled, felt compelled to state in the political report to its October 1945 Provisional National Party Congress that the economic welfare of the people was now a higher priority than political democracy. Second, the Soviet Union, having fought on the Allies' side, had grown significantly in international stature, creating a perception in some quarters that Soviet Russia had achieved for the Russians where Western democracies had failed for their citizens.

Thus, when the liberty–equality discourse was renewed after the war, the economist Qian Jiaju painted a rosy picture of the Soviet Union. He considered it the most democratic state in the world, one where there was no capitalist exploitation, no financial monopoly, no unemployment, and no beggars, and where political rights were exercised through worker–peasant participation. He differentiated between the "old democracy" of the nineteenth century and the "new democracy" of the 1940s, the former being the "bourgeois democracy of a minority" and the latter the "democracy of the vast majority of the people." Invoking President Franklin Roosevelt, he argued that political rights and personal freedoms were insufficient when the poor and starving man was not a free man, despite equality before the law. In the case of China, he equated economic democracy with the Principle of People's Livelihood, entailing land equalization and restriction of capital as well as the

[76] Cheng Zhi, "Zhanwang Zhongguo minzhu" (Looking at the prospect of Chinese democracy), *Ziyou luntan* 3:3 (November 1, 1944): 13.

elimination of official corruption and bureaucratic capitalism. He was not arguing for equality before rights; there could be no equality without basic freedoms. But he thought both were necessary and attainable simultaneously, adding that the current democratic movement should underscore the importance of people's livelihood.[77]

He was not alone in thinking that Soviet Russia was a democratic state. One writer believed that Soviet democracy was nonexploitative, nondiscriminatory, and nonantagonistic because the Soviet Union was a classless society. "It is true democracy, not paper democracy, and part of international democracy."[78] Another writer was convinced that the Soviet Union was democratic both politically and economically as well as with respect to national self-determination. Russians all had jobs, their livelihood was protected, there was no unemployment, social status and personal wealth were unimportant, equal opportunity existed for education, and so on. Soviet Russia was a success story of economic democracy.[79]

Such rosy views, however, were not widely shared. Drawing on Harold Laski's study of the Soviet system, one scholar reminded his fellow intellectuals of the dictatorial aspects of Soviet rule. He argued that the Soviet Union put economic equality ahead of personal freedoms, whereas Anglo-American democracy, currently of a bourgeois nature, was just about to move on to a higher stage of economic democracy. It followed that liberty would lead to equality. China needed both, which was possible only if the Three Principles of the People were implemented.[80] Others found that the Soviet system did not practice economic equality at all; it was merely an economic system under the dictatorship of the proletariat.[81]

To understand the Anglo-American and Soviet systems was to understand the nexus between liberty and equality. Both were important; having one without the other would make life miserable. Unfortunately for the Chinese, they had neither.[82]

---

[77] Qian Jiaju, "Lun jingji de minzhu" (On economic democracy), *Ziyou shijie banyuekan* 1:4 (December 16, 1945): 6–7.

[78] Yuan Xihua, "Sulian minzhu tezheng jiqi lishi fazhan" (Concrete evidence of Soviet democracy and its historical development), *MZZK* 2:1 (July 7, 1945): 11–12.

[79] Bo Han, "Cong zhidu shang kan Sulian de minzhu" (Soviet democracy seen from an institutional perspective), *MZZK* 2:3 (July 23, 1945): 8–9.

[80] Xiao Chun, "Hewei minzhu" (What is democracy?), *Minzhu yu tongyi* 8 (July 20, 1946): 6–7.

[81] Zhang Pijie, "Lun zhengzhi minzhu yu jingji pingdeng" (On political democracy and economic equality), *Gexin* 2:18 (July 31, 1947): 4–5.

[82] Wu Shichang, "Zhengzhi minzhu yu jingji minzhu" (Democratic politics and economic democracy), *GC* 1:5 (September 28, 1946): 5–7.

The relationship between liberalism and socialism also attracted scholarly attention. A view was gaining currency that they were both democratic, albeit in different ways, with the former putting more emphasis on "by the people," and the latter more on "for the people." More important, it was possible to reconcile their differences to produce the type of democratic institutions best suited to China.[83] The historian Xiao Gongquan thought that the "historical mission" of the twentieth century was not to create a new ideology, or to launch a new political movement, but to "harmonize" the special contributions of the eighteenth and nineteenth centuries. In this way, a new polity combining liberalism and socialism – what he called "liberal socialism" (*ziyou shehui zhuyi*) – could be created.[84] This new polity was not based on the Soviet model. It reflected the influence of Harold Laski.

Laski once wrote: "Political equality is never real unless it is accompanied by virtual economic equality; political power, otherwise, is bound to be the handmaid of economic power."[85] The Anglo-American model had much merit, but there could be no real political equality as long as it remained the handmaid of economic power. That model was critiqued in China for failing to control big business on which political parties depended for campaign funds.[86] One scholar noted that in Britain and the United States, under the domination of big business, liberty and equality for the ordinary people were a myth. He saw a lesson for China in the Anglo-American experience: it was important to narrow the gap between the rich and the poor, between the capitalists and the laboring classes; otherwise, China would suffer from what he called "social and economic autocracy."[87]

To say that both liberty and equality were attainable at the same time was to reject the either–or approach. Yet after an eight-year war, the Chinese people were demanding a better livelihood more than anything else. One impoverished professor, while wanting political rights, wished that there would be another July Seventh incident, this time to galvanize

---

[83] Xiao Gongquan, "Shuo minzhu" (On democracy), *GC* 1:7 (October 12, 1946): 3–7.

[84] Xiao Gongquan, "Ershi shiji de lishi renwu" (The historical mission of the twentieth century), *SJPL* 2:5 (August 2, 1947): 5–8.

[85] Harold J. Laski, *A Grammar of Politics*, 5th ed. (London: George Allen and Unwin, 1967), p. 162.

[86] See, for example, Fei Xiaotong, "Meiguo minzhu ruodian de baolu" (Exposure of the weaknesses of American democracy), *MZZK* 3:2 (March 6, 1946): 10–11.

[87] Zhang Yuanfeng, "Minzhu zhengzhi yu jiquan xingzheng" (Democratic politics and concentrated administration), *Minzhu luntan* 1:8 (July 5, 1947): 16–17.

the government into fighting a war against poverty.[88] There was a perception that liberty was contingent upon economic conditions, the vast majority of Chinese being denied liberty because of economic inequality. Wu Enyu, a professor at Beijing University, argued that liberty had become a preserve for the privileged classes, the landlords and the capitalists. He felt compelled to suggest a redistribution of wealth, or at least restricted accumulation of wealth, on the grounds that the right to property only benefited the rich at the expense of the poor. "Without the foundation of equality, there can be no real all-people liberty. Equality and liberty are not in conflict. Therefore, we should struggle for liberty on the one hand and promote equality as a basis for liberty on the other. The movement for liberty must spread to all levels [of society]."[89] In other words, liberty rested on a notion of equality. Wu was prepared to put equality before liberty because of his concern for the people's livelihood. He feared that in a society without an appropriate level of economic development, democracy could only be "unsatisfactory," "imperfect," and "unendurable."[90]

Some were quick to defend liberty as the source of, and safeguard for, equality. The historian Qian Shifu argued potently that equality could not exist without liberty because, first, equality is derived from liberty; second, equality is self-determined and a right, not a boon bestowed by the authorities; and, third, equality is incremental when liberty is enjoyed. "Equality without liberty is a skeleton without flesh, a form without substance, and a body without a soul."[91] Above all, liberty safeguards equality:

> Without liberty, there can be no self-determination, no self-protection. . . . Equality without liberty, we can only say, is a kind of "obedient equality." The individual who is not free cannot express

---

[88] Ding Hongfan, "Qidai yige minsheng zhuyi de qiqi shibian" (Looking forward to a July 7th incident of the principle of people's livelihood), *Minzhu luntan* 2:5 (October 4, 1947): 10–12.

[89] Wu Enyu, "Ziyou hu? pingdeng hu?" (Liberty? Equality?), *GC* 3:12 (November 15, 1947): 6–7.

[90] Drawing on Harold Laski, Wu saw capitalism as a system of minority ownership of production. It was impossible to abolish economic inequality, but it was possible to reduce substantially the gap between the rich and the poor by the equalization of land rights and the restriction of capital as Sun Yat-sen preached. See Wu Enyu, *Minzhu zhengzhi de jichu* (The foundations of democratic politics) (Chongqing: Shangwu yinshuguan, 1944), pp. 5–8.

[91] Qian Shifu, "Meiyou ziyou de pingdeng" (Equality without liberty), *Minzhu luntan* 2:1 (September 6, 1947): 17–18. The quote is on p. 18.

his or her will. . . . This kind of obedience is blind obedience allowing no room for demands or opposition. . . . Basically, it is inequality like slavery in a democracy.[92]

Sartori has written: "From liberty we are free to go on to equality; from equality we are not free to get back to liberty."[93] For Qian, too, equality presupposes freedom.

Not every liberal writer was so clear in his mind, one way or the other. Political philosopher Zou Wenhai, for one, did not think that political democracy and economic democracy were inherently contradictory; both were important, and liberty without equality was unjust. But he also appreciated that true equality required not only a narrowing of the economic disparities but also a proper working of democratic institutions. His view was that equality should be for all. In an unequal society, liberty nurtures a democratic culture, which in turn facilitates equality. In an already equal society, liberty helps to sustain equality. Historically, he conceptualized, if liberty without equality were a "positive" phase, equality without liberty was a "negative" one. There was a third "integrative" phase in which there was both liberty and equality. The negative phase was unavoidable, but it should not last long, and the challenge to the political leadership was to keep it short.[94] His point was implicit: China might well be entering the negative phase of liberty without equality, having bypassed the first positive phase; let it be brief so that the third phase could be reached before long.

The dominant view, therefore, was that the tension between liberty and equality could be resolved and their principles unified. In other words, there could be equality-based liberty and liberty-based equality.[95] Some found the socialism of the British Labour Party a source of inspiration.[96] British socialism demonstrated that "one can have a ballot paper and a bowl of rice at the same time."[97] The British model was inspiring because it appeared to be similar to what one professor called "new socialism" that "harmonized" capitalism and communism. It could succeed in China if only the GMD and CCP would reconcile their differences and coop-

---

[92] Ibid., p. 18.

[93] Sartori, *The Theory of Democracy Revisited*, p. 389.

[94] Zou Wenhai, "Minzhu zhengzhi shifou rengxu ziyou" (Does democratic politics still need liberty?), *GC* 1:10 (November 2, 1946): 3–5.

[95] Zhang Pijie, "Lun zhengzhi minzhu yu jingji pingdeng," pp. 3–5.

[96] Xiao Gongquan, for one, was impressed with the British Labour Party.

[97] Shang Zhi, "Zhengzhi minzhu yu jingji minzhu" (Political democracy and economic democracy), *SJPL* 1:11 (March 15, 1947): 11–13.

erate in a coalition government.[98] The British Labour Party was the subject of a couple of interesting articles in *Shiji pinglun* in the summer of 1948. One held it up as a model for party reform in China because of its democratic nature and identification with the people.[99] The other praised its organization, leadership, and democratic character, describing it as "a historical choice," "a necessity of the time," marking "an integration of the laboring classes and Fabianism," which "had freed Britons from hunger and fears." Fabianism was hailed as "the best cure of the time"; its integration with the laboring classes alone constituted "the mainstream of the twentieth century."[100]

The Chinese ideas of new liberalism, new democracy, and new socialism were reactions against the so-called classical liberalism that emphasized economic laissez-faire and unrestrained individualism. Chinese thinkers of the postwar period were not different from those in the West who attached as much importance to positive liberty as to negative liberty. Apart from the influence of Laski, H. G. Wells's ideas of social reform and collectivism, which distinguished themselves from the Soviet model by his emphasis on the juxtaposition of state powers, personal freedoms, and human rights (especially the right to subsistence and the right to work), seem to have made an impact on China's liberal intellectuals.[101]

Not everyone admired British socialism, though. Zhang Dongsun, rejecting both the Soviet and the British models in their existing forms, was more interested in the postwar Eastern European states, which he identified as coalition governments well served by private enterprise existing alongside state capitalism, cooperatives, and an equitable system of land redistribution. He found their systems somewhere between the Soviet and American models, all practicing new democracy, and was particularly impressed with the Czechoslovakia model;[102] however, there is no evidence that he had a good understanding of how it worked.

---

[98] Zhou Shouzhang, "Zhengzhi ziyou yu jingji pingdeng" (Political liberty and economic liberty), *SJPL* 1:20 (May 17, 1947): 13–15.

[99] Liu Naicheng, "Woguo zhengdang gaige yu Yingguo gongdang" (Party reforms in our country and the British Labour Party), *SJPL* 4:2 (July 10, 1948): 3–5.

[100] Li Shiyou, "Yingguo gongdang shi zenyang chengzhang de (san)" (How did the British Labour Party grow? [3]), *SJPL* 4:7 (August 14, 1948): 8–9; the quote is on p. 9.

[101] See, for example, Zhang Junmai, "Weiersishi zhengzhi sixiang ji qi jinzuo renquan xuanyan" (H. G. Wells's political thought and manifesto of human rights), *Minxian* 1:10 (December 20, 1944): 4–13.

[102] Zhang Dongsun, "Jingda Fan Hong xiansheng" (Respectful response to Mr. Fan Hong), *GC* 3:16 (December 13, 1947): 5–6; also "Guanyu Zhongguo chulu de kanfa" (On China's way out), *GC* 3:23 (January 31, 1947): 3–4.

As with other liberals, Zhang Dongsun had lost his faith in old democracy.[103] Even though he was a philosopher, he took an economist's approach to politics, seeing China's postwar problems as more economic than political. Production determined the scope for liberty and equality. If the imperatives of production dictated that limits be placed on both of them, so be it. To increase production – the only way to achieve liberty and equality in the long term – he called for a planned economy in an effort to rid China of its "remnant feudal forces" and to unleash "industrial energies."[104] Inequality was unjust. But strict equality could result in injustice, too. The problem with backward countries such as China, in his view, was not unequal distribution of wealth but lack of wealth itself (a controversial view among Chinese intellectuals in 1947–1948). Such countries faced problems when they tried to leapfrog from feudalism to socialism, bypassing the stage of capitalism. Although he had no objections to China's going down the socialist path, he insisted on wealth generation by enhancing and rewarding production through some form of capitalism. Exploitation would continue to exist during the transition to socialism, but it would not be a serious problem as long as it was contained.[105] He was prepared to restrict liberties for the sake of production, but he insisted on "cultural liberalism," meaning a spirit of tolerance and freedom of criticism – "the lifeline of cultural–intellectual development."[106] Differentiating between "political liberalism" and "cultural liberalism," he anticipated the collapse of the former under the weight of a planned economy and regarded the latter as his last line of defense. But this defense was untenable. As one reader was quick to point out, if "cultural liberalism" meant the freedoms of thought, speech, and publication and a critical mind, the juxtaposition of a liberal culture and a planned economy was inconceivable.[107]

Exploitation during the transition from feudalism to socialism was the subject of a debate in the pages of *Guancha* early in 1948. The debate was significant in that it went beyond the question of labor–management relations to an argument about the desirability of China's moving

---

[103] Zhang Dongsun, "Zhengzhi shang de ziyou zhuyi yu wenhua shang de ziyou zhuyi" (Political liberalism and cultural liberalism), *GC* 4:1 (February 28, 1948): 3.

[104] Ibid., pp. 3–5.

[105] Zhang Dongsun, "Jingji pingdeng yu feichu boxiao" (Economic equality and the abolition of exploitation), *GC* 4:2 (March 6, 1948): 3–4.

[106] Zhang Dongsun, "Zhengzhi shang de ziyou zhuyi yu wenhua shang de ziyou zhuyi," p. 4.

[107] Zheng Shenshan, "Shi ⟨liberal, liberalism⟩" (Interpreting liberal and liberalism), *GC* 4:6 (April 3, 1948): 5–6.

straight away into socialism. The debate followed an article by Shi Fuliang, who, agreeing with Zhang Dongsun on the need to generate wealth by increasing production, advanced the notion of new capitalism – a stage that China, lacking a material base, must go through before reaching socialism. This stage was characterized by a land to the tiller policy; an expanded nationalization regime of public utilities, banking, heavy industry, transport, and communication; protectionism; and a program of agricultural development. As Shi conceived it, this stage followed capitalist principles and methods of production, opposing imperialism, bureaucratic capitalism, comprador capitalism, and feudal exploitation. It was necessary not only to continue capitalist exploitation but also to expand it in order to increase production. Two safeguards, Shi believed, could ease the tension in worker–management relations. One was to guarantee a basic standard of living for the working class; another was to put in place policies designed to discourage the accumulation of excessive personal wealth and to encourage and reward the reinvestment of profits in productive enterprises in the public interest.[108]

Yan Rengeng, an economics professor at Zhejiang University, took Shi to task because he could see nothing new in Shi's new capitalism. Expansion of exploitation would neither alter the uneven distribution of wealth nor reduce the capitalist–worker disparity. Differentiating between capitalist forms of production and capitalism itself, Yan argued that the former was not a monopoly of capitalism and that there could be capitalist methods of production under socialism. (This sounded like Deng Xiaoping's contention that capitalism could be a tool in building socialism.) He advocated direct entry into the stage of socialism, convinced that the problems of production and uneven distribution of wealth could be resolved simultaneously.[109] Shi responded by saying that what was new in his new capitalism was the idea of correcting the wrongs of "old capitalism"; the economy of new capitalism could be achieved only after the laboring classes had come to power, thereby guaranteeing the transition to socialism. In other words, there would be a capitalist economy in a new democracy prior to socialism. Politics determined economics, Shi added, and the democratic revolution should now be led by the laboring classes because China lacked a powerful and effective national bourgeoisie

---

[108] Shi Fuliang, "Feichu boxiao yu zengjia shengchan" (Abolish exploitation and increase production), *GC* 4:4 (March 20, 1948): 7–9.

[109] Yan Rengeng, "Shehui zhuyi hu? 'Xin ziben zhuyi' hu?" (Socialism? "New capitalism"?), *GC* 4:17 (June 19, 1948): 5–8.

capable of national leadership.[110] Yan remained unconvinced, adamant that in new capitalism the laboring classes would not be free from oppression and stand united with the national bourgeoisie. The transitional period of new capitalism was unnecessary.[111] Calls for direct entry into the stage of socialism were supported by those who rejected exploitation categorically on the grounds that it was the source of all social evils that could be eliminated only by a change of regime. It followed that the only way was to seize power by revolutionary means.[112]

Discussions about direct entry into the stage of socialism immediately raised a question about the relationship between socialism and democracy.

THE SOCIALISM–DEMOCRACY RELATIONSHIP

Was socialism a negation of democracy or an advanced stage of it? Their ambiguous relationship prompted Zhang Dongsun to publish, in July 1948, a book treating them as essentially one thing rather than two separate things in an adversarial relationship. He held that both were the products of Western civilization, premised on liberty, equality, equity, the general will, universal principles, rationality, and human rights, and having the same ultimate goal. In this sense, Western civilization had been one long movement aimed at the attainment of liberty and equality for humankind, despite its occasional setbacks and zigzags. It was the "incompleteness" of the bourgeois–democratic revolution that led to the socialist revolution. Marxism was often thought to be antidemocratic because it advocated the dictatorship of the proletariat. But Marxism, Zhang insisted, was in fact concerned with liberty and equality for the great majority of the people. It was a mistaken view that capitalism emphasized liberty at the expense of equality, and it was equally false that socialism emphasized equality at the expense of liberty. He did not find himself impaled on the horns of the dilemma because he viewed their goals as essentially the same, despite differences over means and strategies. Liberty and equality could be "harmonized" to increase production in a planned economy. Thus, he redefined equality as equal

---

[110] Shi Fuliang, "Xin Zhongguo de jingji he zhengzhi" (New China's economy and politics), *GC* 4:21 (July 24, 1948): 4–6.

[111] Yan Rengeng, "Zai he Shi Fuliang xiansheng tan xin ziben zhuyi" (Again discussing new capitalism with Mr. Shi Fuliang), *GC* 4:23–24 combined (August 7, 1948): 15.

[112] Fan Hong, "Zhiyou liangtiao lu" (There are only two roads), *GC* 4:7 (April 10, 1948): 3–4.

opportunity, accepting that in a planned economy individual liberty would have to be incomplete.[113] He stopped short of advocating socialism, but by reconciling socialism with democracy, he seemed to be preparing himself for it. Moreover, he refused to be pessimistic about the prospect of academic freedom on the grounds that a culture of free thought had been fostered over the years and that a return to cultural repression was inconceivable.[114]

Shi Fuliang agreed that democracy and socialism were not adversarial, but he insisted that China's *chulu* lay in socialism. And socialism, the ultimate goal, was a process beginning with the "democracy of a minority" through the "democracy of a majority" to the "democracy of the entire population," the last stage being true democracy. Yet in the same breath, he seemed to contradict himself by saying that China's future lay between the Soviet system and the Anglo-American system,[115] a contradiction reflecting his lingering hopes for the middle path.

As a final CCP victory approached, many liberal intellectuals appeared to be preparing themselves for a new government. This is not to suggest that they were bending with the wind. They were genuinely sympathetic with the Communists who appeared to be concerned with the well-being of the people in sharp contrast to the Nationalists who had neglected them. Yan Siping called on the liberals to pay more attention to economics, particularly to industrialization, while not neglecting agriculture. He was confident that socialism – "the highest stage of human civilization" – would eventually be realized in China, and it would be socialism of the proletariat led by the intellectuals. By the proletariat, he meant not the working class alone but all property-less classes that could be united in undertaking reconstruction on a democratic basis.[116] If socialism could be achieved by peaceful means, so much the better. Many, however, remained unconvinced that it could.[117]

Many also held steadfastly to their liberal convictions, rejecting socialism and benevolent despotism and insisting that economic equality was

[113] Zhang Dongsun, *Minzhu zhuyi yu shehui zhuyi* (Democracy and socialism) (Shanghai: Guanchashe, 1948). I have had no access to this book. The information here is based on a review of his book by Xia Yande, in *SJPL* 4:5 (July 31, 1948): 13–14.

[114] Zhang Dongsun, "Zhishi fenzi yu wenhua de ziyou" (Intellectuals and cultural freedom), *GC* 5:11 (October 30, 1948): 5.

[115] Shi Fuliang, "Zhongguo wang nali qu" (Where is China going?), *Zaizao* 1:3 (July 25, 1948): 3–5.

[116] Yan Siping, "Zhongguo zhengzhi de qitu (xia), pp. 7–9.

[117] See the debate "Yong heping fangfa neng shixian shehui zhuyi?" (Can socialism be implemented by peaceful means?), *Xinlu* 6 (June 19, 1948): 3–7.

not democracy and that the gap between liberalism and communism was far too wide to be bridged.[118] Did that mean that there could be no compromise whatsoever? Not really, according to a young writer who argued, interestingly, that liberalism was not immutable. As "a view of life" and "an attitude toward society," he wrote, liberalism changed as society changed itself. It was inconceivable to speak of the liberal mission detached from Chinese society spatially and temporally. The goal of the mission was to destroy the semifeudal and semicolonial order, but so far it was a mission unaccomplished. Why? Because the liberals had failed to develop roots in the rural masses, because they had laid undue emphasis on personal freedoms, and because they did not understand China's problems. The solutions to those problems lay in land reform and the awakening of the peasantry. He also thought that liberalism and Chinese communism shared a belief in the necessity of destroying the feudal order, differing only over individual development. If the liberals wished to destroy the CCP merely for the sake of personal freedoms, history would be put back several decades. He emphasized that there could be no going back in history. Liberalism and communism were not mutually opposed. So only when feudalism was destroyed should liberalism and communism oppose each other. The CCP's violent methods were intolerable, but he thought that the liberals were utilitarian with a social conscience, which should provide the basis for a temporary compromise with communism. Finally, he believed, naïvely, that a CCP government would be more tolerant of political dissent because of the middle-class backgrounds of many of its leaders.[119]

By mid-1948, a significant number of noncommitted scholars appeared to have come around to the view that socialism was not antidemocratic and so was a possibility in China. Ultimately, the choice, for many, was reduced to one between bread and liberty. As Zhou Shouzhang, editor of Nanjing's *Xinminbao* (New People Daily), wrote, if both bread and liberty could be enjoyed at the same time, it was great; otherwise, those who provided bread would command "the basic forces of society" and go on to win power. Eventually, both must be enjoyed.[120] For the present,

---

[118] See, for example, Zhang Foquan, "Lun ziyou zhuyi yu zhengzhi" (On liberalism and politics), *Zaisheng* 1:6 (1948): 6–7.

[119] See, for example, Li Xiaoyou, "Du ⟨guanyu zhonggong wang hechu qu?⟩ jian lun ziyou zhuyizhe de daolu" (On reading "About where the CCP is headed" and comments on the road of the liberals), *GC* 3:19 (January 3, 1948): 7–9.

[120] Zhou thought that the CCP's land reform policy offered the only hope for China's future. Unlike Zhang Dongsun, he believed that uneven distribution of wealth was a

if one must choose between the freedom of the jungle and the security of the cage, many would choose the latter.

Others either had become resigned to their fate or remained confused. A vacillating Yang Renbian thought one moment that, in the existing circumstances, the ballot paper had to be sacrificed for a bowl of rice, and the next that a ballot paper in hand was extremely important because it was a right to ask for food. From the standpoint of an "economic revolution," he also found no reason to oppose communism. It was a significant personal concession when he wrote that liberals like him were not opposed to revolution, even if blood were shed. He had come to accept that although the pursuit of individual interests was the moving force in liberalism, it was not the only objective of the liberal endeavor; the progress to be achieved through liberalism should be the progress of society as a whole. As a self-styled true liberal, he was prepared to live with "other opposing forces."[121]

Yan Rengeng, the economist from Zhejiang University, had the last word at the end of 1948:

Some people are perhaps worried that when "economic democracy" is imposed, part of "political democracy" will inevitably be sacrificed, or even completely stripped off. Such worry is unnecessary. This is because political liberty and economic equality are not mutually exclusive. True Marxists not only advocate the realization of "economic democracy," they are also passionate about "political democracy," highly valuing individuality and the free will. In the [Communist] Manifesto [of 1848], Marx and Engels stated: "We are not those Communists who wish to destroy individual freedom. . . . We have no wish to secure equality by sacrificing liberty." Though advocating the dictatorship of the proletariat, they wanted to see in the peasantry and the laboring classes "a sense of dignity" and "independence of will." They considered "a sense of dignity" and "independence of will" more important than the daily necessity of bread. Therefore, their claim that their revolutionary movement was "a war that won democracy" was not without foundation. Moreover, they did not consider it absolutely impossible to attain socialism by peaceful means, even under a capitalist system. Wars are only the

more serious problem than scarcity of wealth. See Zhou Shouzhang, "Mianbao yu ziyou de jueze" (A choice between bread and liberty), *Shi yu wen* 3:18 (August 20, 1948): 1–2.
[121] Yang Renbian, "Zai lun ziyou zhuyi de tujing," pp. 3–5.

products of resistance to the oppression of the reactionary forces.
... Otherwise, wars are not the necessary road to communism or
socialism.[122]

THE FATE OF CIVIL OPPOSITION

What did all this – the liberty–equality and socialism–democracy discourse – mean for civil opposition? Momentous changes had taken place
since Hu Shi and Luo Longji raised the human rights issue in 1929. The
fall of the Nationalist government was imminent, but China had not
become more democratic, and the mainstream tradition of Chinese political culture still prevailed. What lay ahead was another one-party dictatorship, another party-state. The aspirations of civil opposition for the
freedoms of thought, speech, assembly, and association and political pluralism had not been fulfilled. Yet the shift in the rights thinking from the
first generation to a second generation had been complete. "The true
essence of democratic politics," wrote one liberal writer in 1948, "lies in
the priority of economic and social rights over civil and political rights."
But he had not been converted to Marxism. His democratic model was
President Roosevelt's New Deal and Henry A. Wallace's sense of social
justice.[123] Civil opposition could only hope that the new regime would
be a neo-dictatorship of the kind that Ding Wenjiang had advocated
fifteen years before.

The spirit of civil opposition did not dissipate, but support for the
Communists in 1948–1949 did mark a strategic retreat from liberalism.
Now that the liberal alternative had been rejected, the only road for
China, willy-nilly, was revolution. Zhang Shenfu, offering a prescription
for China's ills in a July 1948 essay entitled "On China's Alternative,"
had this to say:

In the past six months, there has been a great deal of discussion
about liberalism, about the middle path between Communists and
Nationalists, about the problem of intellectuals. But there has also
been much confusion, much muddled thinking that caused misun-
derstanding among various points of view. My own point of view is
that we must do everything possible to end the present situation of

---

[122] Yan Rengeng, "1848–1948 – lishi de liangge zhuanleidian" (1848–1948 – Two turning
points in history), *GC* 5:18 (December 25, 1948): 4.
[123] Li Xuan, "Minzhu zhengzhi de zhendi" (The true essence of democratic politics),
Zaisheng 203 (1948): 3.

national disaster. To accomplish this, we do not need liberalism – since it starts, all too often, with simple self-interest. Rather, we must struggle to implement democracy with its three preconditions: freedom, equality, and cooperation. It is also my conviction that there is only one real alternative in China today: revolution. Our current era is a revolutionary era, an era of science and democracy. Thus, only a revolutionary approach suits the current situation. Only a revolutionary approach will bring about a solution to our social and political problems.[124]

It would be difficult to reconcile a revolutionary era, Maoist style, with an era of science and democracy, liberal style. But retreating liberals were hoping that socialist democracy would be a real possibility under CCP rule.

If they were optimistic about their future in the revolutionary era, if they thought they understood the trends of the time, and if they felt able to contribute significantly to future change, it was probably because they had been influenced by Mao Zedong's writings as recently as January 1948.[125] Further, they had come to appreciate the importance of keeping pace with the masses as Mao did, which, as Zhang Shenfu discovered, was "the only alternative for the nation," "the only alternative for intellectuals, [and] the only kind of life possible in the future."[126]

The communist road to power was anything but peaceful. Those who greeted the communist victory were hoping that the CCP, once in power, would eschew the use of violence. In January 1949, Liang Shuming, blaming the Nationalists for the civil war, called on the Communists to put an immediate end to it and to all forms of violence:

I hope the CCP will complete peaceful unification with all the parties concerned, using its nonmilitant heart and its past spirit of accommodation. This is most important, because whoever have greater strength will have the heaviest responsibility thrust upon

---

[124] Quoted in Vera Schwarcz, *Time for Telling Truth Is Running Out: Conversations with Zhang Shenfu* (New Haven: Yale University Press, 1992), p. 188.

[125] Mao told the CCP that only a very small minority of intellectuals were counterrevolutionaries and that therefore the Party should "unite with them, educate them and give them posts according to the merits of each case, and only a tiny number of die-hard counter-revolutionaries among them will have to be appropriately dealt with through the mass line." See "On Some Important Problems of the Party's Present Policy," in Mao Tse-tung, *Selected Works of Mao Tse-tung* (Peking: Foreign Languages Press, 1967), IV, 184.

[126] Schwarcz, *Time for Telling Truth is Running Out*, pp. 188–189.

them. Those who fail to use their strength wisely will be culprits to the state. Therefore, all the people who have pinned high hopes on the GMD before now pin the same hopes on the CCP. Those who have indulged in war no longer exist today. There should be no more civil war. *Any problems should be resolved by political methods. No more force should be used* [emphasis added]. To achieve unification by force could only delay China's unification.[127]

Liang was concerned about recent CCP statements that the middle line and the liberals were not to be tolerated. On Christmas Eve 1948, the Communists had announced a list of "war criminals" (the forty-two figures on the list included Youth Party leader Zeng Qi and Democratic Socialist Party leader Zhang Junmai) who "should receive the just penalty."[128] This prompted Liang to plead for political tolerance. Even though he accepted the fact that mass psychology could be "unavoidably irrational" during a revolution, he strongly defended freedom of thought and independence of mind. Hoping that intolerance was not a feature of communist policy and politics, he "advised" the CCP leadership in an open letter not to repeat what the Nationalists had done.[129] Like many others, he tried to preserve a space for critical thought in a China torn by guns and revolution. His letter must be regarded as an extraordinary historical document just like Hu Shi's telegram to Mao Zedong in the late summer of 1945 asking him to build up a second major party in China by laying down its arms.[130] But Liang differed from Hu in that he wished to work with the CCP as a member of the "loyal opposition," a wish shared by those who chose to stay on the mainland after 1949.

China was in a big time, China was in a tragic time, and China had gone mad, lamented a newspaper editor. All those involved in the civil war had lost their sense of reasoning. Only a return to reason could emancipate them from the tragedy that was China, and only then could violence be avoided.[131] He voiced the sentiment of his fellow intellectu-

---

[127] Liang Shuming, "Guoqu neizhan de zeren zaishui," *LSMQJ*, VI, 795.

[128] Roger B. Jeans, *Democracy and Socialism in Republican China: The Politics of Zhang Junmai (Carsun Chang), 1906–1941* (Lanham: Rowman & Littlefield, 1997), p. 306.

[129] Liang Shuming, "Jinggao Zhongguo gongchandang" (Respectful advice to the CCP), *LSMQJ*, VI, 803–804.

[130] *Chinese Press Review* 238 (September 4, 1945): 6, cited in Chou Min-chih, *Hu Shih and Intellectual Choice in Modern China* (Ann Arbor: University of Michigan Press, 1984), p. 144.

[131] Zhou Shouzhang, "Fengkuang le de Zhongguo – yi ge mangdong de, beiju de da shidai" (Mad China – A blind, tragic era), *GC* 2:16 (June 14, 1947): 7–9.

als when he reaffirmed his belief in reason and rationalism as a means of conflict resolution, whatever the political color of the new regime.

On the eve of the communist takeover, the intellectual community was politically divided. Those who supported the Communists and the revolutionary road were still feeling much anxiety, confusion, and contradiction, looking forward to a new era with mixed feelings of fear and joy. And those who were committed to liberalism remained implacably opposed to the Communists. Hu Shi, after his return from the United States in June 1946, supported the government but refused to join it because of his desire to maintain his independence. He left for the United States again in April 1949. Zhang Junmai resigned himself to a lonely exile in the United States. Zuo Shunsheng, Li Huang, and others took refuge in Hong Kong, Europe, and elsewhere, whereas progovernment independents, such as Wang Yunwu and Fu Sinian, followed Chiang Kai-shek to Taiwan. Most of the professors whose ideas I have probed in this chapter chose to remain in Mao's New China. A few left permanently, starting a new life teaching in universities in the United States.

CONCLUSION

The final act in civil opposition was played out not by the DL but by the other component of the third force – the independent, nonparticipatory elite who regarded themselves as true liberals having neither political affiliations nor personal ambitions. They found themselves at a crossroads, pondering their future as well as China's. Acting in the time-honored tradition of the moral–intellectual elite, and showing disdain for power, they made a last stand for Chinese liberalism before coming to terms with the immediate prospect of CCP rule. The road to democracy was blocked long before they realized, and the search for middle-ground democracy had been in vain. Yet many still adhered to the elusive middle path, rationalizing their political impotence by a moral disclaimer of interest in power and assuming that they could exert their influence outside the government rather than within it. Pepper's judgment of them is harsh but correct: "Perhaps their greatest tragedy was, appropriately enough, more intellectual than political: they failed to comprehend the fact of their own irrelevance."[132] They were irrelevant in two senses. First, they were unable to keep pace with the masses, despite their pretensions to represent public opinion and the will of the people. Second, they had

---

[132] Pepper, *Civil War in China*, p. 194.

no bearing on the outcome of the civil war, which was determined purely by the two combatants. However, they were courageous and admirable for their unflagging spirit of criticism, their condemnation of political repression, and their continued clamor for liberty and democracy in the most adverse circumstances.

The postwar liberal forum devoted a great deal of attention to the liberty–equality nexus. The relative strengths and weaknesses of the Anglo-American and Soviet systems were examined and debated. The dominant view was that liberty and equality were both necessary and attainable. Moreover, liberty was defended as the source of, and a safeguard for, equality. But the stark reality was that China was crying out for help in feeding its population first and foremost. It was a powerful argument that, after an eight-year war, the people wanted a return to peace and considered the basic necessities of life and good governance more important than personal freedoms and political rights. Ultimately, it was a choice between bread and liberty. Many scholars both at home and abroad would have supported the view that, in a backward society with a low level of economic development, democracy could only be unsatisfactory and unendurable.

In socioeconomic terms, it was a matter of opinion whether China suffered from an unequal distribution of wealth or from a lack of wealth itself. To the CCP, it was the former. Zhang Dongsun took a different view, arguing for increased production even if exploitation was required and liberties curtailed. Shi Fuliang went further to contend that exploitation was not only necessary but should be expanded in a kind of new capitalism prior to socialism. But there was opposition in some quarters to exploitation altogether, wanting an immediate transition to socialism and seeing nothing to fear from the CCP.

Perhaps socialism and democracy need not be seen in adversarial terms. Zhang Dongsun was able to say in 1948 that both were the products of Western civilization, which had been one long movement aimed at the fulfillment of liberty and equality for humankind. Thus, there was no dilemma. Socialism and democracy shared an ultimate goal, and liberty and equality could be harmonized to increase production in a planned economy. If Zhang's acceptance of socialism was implicit, Yan Rengeng's was forthright because he was convinced that socialism was concerned with both liberty and equality. The last word was that socialism was necessary for China, provided that it was nonviolent.

Civil opposition was beating a strategic retreat from liberalism in the face of the CCP's rise to power. Perhaps China's ills really needed a revolutionary prescription requiring personal sacrifices. But no intellectuals would wish to forgo freedoms of thought, speech, and publication. National salvation in terms of resisting imperialism may have been accomplished, but enlightenment in term of democracy was still to be fulfilled. When the Nationalist government was overthrown in 1949, the tragedy was that liberalism and democracy went down with it.

Conclusion

CIVIL OPPOSITION has been studied in this book in the context of a continued search for Chinese democracy during a period when China was dominated by the politics of violence, war, and revolution. We have probed the thoughts and actions of China's "liberal democrats" who represented a minor but significant tradition of liberal opposition in juxtaposition against the mainstream authoritarian tradition of political culture represented by the GMD and the CCP. We have also documented the prodemocracy movement that unfolded amid mounting pressures from Japanese aggression that culminated in an eight-year war. Its starting point was a challenge to the political system characterized by political tutelage, one-party rule, official corruption, and political repression. The Nationalist regime was not merely a military dictatorship but also a personal dictatorship of Chiang Kai-shek. Yet it was a weak dictatorship, a weak garrison state, exercising ineffective control of the country, a fact that aided and abetted the growth of civil opposition.

Beginning in 1929 in protest against human rights violations, the opposition agenda was set for the next twenty years. Of course, civil opposition was not entirely concerned with democracy. To many, democracy simply meant unrelenting opposition to the government and everything it did. But the opposition found a cause dating back to the May Fourth period; this source was anchored in the belief that power could be won and conflict resolved without resorting to violence. In the process, civil opposition, identified with enlightenment (*qimeng*), became part of the movement for national salvation (*jiuwang*).

We have modified Li Zehou's thesis on the *jiuwang–qimeng* dichotomy to drive home the point that national salvation was not merely an external issue requiring armed resistance but also an internal one necessitating political and constitutional change. For the opposition

337

elite, *qimeng* was not about cultural iconoclasm; rather, it emphasized a democratic reordering of the political system. Consequently, they believed that *jiuwang* and *qimeng*, rather than being antagonistic, could be harmonized, that *jiuwang* presupposed *qimeng*, and that one could support the other without being suppressed. To demand political change in times of national crisis was not unpatriotic. Not all those with the anti-imperialist impulse were prepared to put aside liberal and democratic values in order to support any authoritarian regime that offered a decent hope for national fulfillment. Li Zehou's emphasis on revolution and war helps to explain the CCP's nationalistic appeal during the war period but fails to do justice to the prodemocracy movement. All the same, the opposition elite and their concerns ultimately lost, and the nationalism of the *jiuwang* type was at least partially to blame. The war with Japan constricted their space and hindered the influence of their ideas.

Following the Manchurian crisis, civil opposition underscored this interplay of internal and external forces as the GMD regime and Nanjing's nonresistance policy came under attack. From the opposition's point of view, the national emergency was no justification for continued monopoly of power and curtailment of the limited freedoms that the people enjoyed. On the contrary, widening the scope of political partic-ipation and putting an end to civil strife would enable the best minds around the country to rally behind the government in fighting the Japanese invasion. Because the government was inefficient, incompetent, and corrupt, the opposition held that democratic institutions could provide an answer to China's political problems that could not be sepa-rated from the external crisis.

The early Republican experience with democratic institutions, however, was a source of dismay and frustration to some erstwhile liberal intellectuals like Jiang Tingfu and Ding Wenjiang, who prescribed neo-dictatorship for China's ills. The prewar democracy versus dictatorship debate reflected the division within the intellectual community and the divergence of views on ways of leading China out of her crisis. In that debate, both neo-dictatorship and democracy were viewed as a response to *jiuwang*, to delayed development, and a means of modernization. There was no winner. Inconclusive, the debate did not polarize the intel-lectual community because the proponents of neo-dictatorship equally opposed political repression, pleading for civil liberties and viewing democracy as an ultimate goal. The choice was not cut and dried. As Japanese aggression intensified, a consensus emerged that a strong and effective government would best serve China's national interests. The challenge for the democracy advocates then was not merely to defend democracy in the midst of a national crisis but also to reconcile the needs of statism with the values of democracy.

At the outset of the war, the Nationalist government, making a virtue of necessity, called the People's Political Council into being in an effort to maintain a semblance of national unity. A "public opinion institution," a democratic experiment, and a useful experience for all the parties concerned, the PPC was the only public forum where opposition and government could debate a range of policy issues relating to war and reconstruction. It was also the venue for the constitutional movement, renewed vigorously after 1939, forcing the government to set up one committee after another to prepare for constitutional rule. It could have marked the beginning of a democratization project. But its powers were limited. After an initial period of goodwill, the government was unwilling to broaden political participation by increasing the number of non-GMD members and their powers. The democratic experiment was virtually aborted before the end of the war.

After the Japanese surrender, GMD–CCP differences threatened to plunge China into all-out civil war. Calls for an interim coalition government, conceived by the opposition parties as a mechanism for China's transition to democracy and a means of checks and balances, were rejected by the Nationalist leaders because the inclusion of the Communists posed a serious threat to their hold on power. Politics brought the PPC into being in 1938. Politics, including American pressures, led to the opening of the Political Consultative Conference early in 1946. And, in the end, politics blocked a democratic breakthrough – Chiang Kai-shek's dictatorship, the centrality of anticommunism to GMD politics, the consolidation of communist power in the "liberated areas," the complications of civil war, and the political culture of "win all or lose all." After 1945, imperialism was no longer to blame; party politics prevented a negotiated settlement. Failure to restore peace made any attempts at political reform ring hollow.

One crucial issue here was leadership and strategic decisions. Chiang Kai-shek could have expanded the powers of the PPC. He could have legalized the MPGs and the CCP at the outset of the war. He could have formed an interim coalition government under a dominant-party system and put in place some effective measures to make members of the regime accountable to the political constituencies or forces outside it. He could have liberalized the government by making better use of the progressive elements within the GMD and coopting others in or before 1946. To borrow Tang Tsou's idea again, Chiang's microactions and "rational strategic choice" could have changed the macrohistorical pattern of Chinese politics. In short, he could have begun a process of democratic change and still retained power. Decisions different from those he actually made and acted on could well have led to different outcomes. This is not to suggest that the absence of democratic change could be blamed on Chiang and the GMD alone. The point is that the Nationalist era contained the germs of a reformist, liberal order that had been prevented from growing by party politics, a lack of regime leadership, and bad strategic decisions.

The wartime literature on democracy was copious and fascinating. For the GMD, the promise of democracy was a means of elite mobilization. For the CCP, Mao's New Democracy was a vital part of the united front strategy designed to achieve hegemony in the long run. For the liberal intellectuals, democracy was desirable and attainable even in times of war. Conflating it with nationalism, they advocated democracy for what it could do for the nation. Apart from uniting the country in fighting the Japanese, democracy, we were told, could make a start of constitutional rule and allow the MPGs to operate legally, thereby institutionalizing opposition. Democracy could free the government from control by Chiang Kai-shek and the military, establish a rule of law, and protect human rights. It could produce an efficient, open, and responsible government, bring together the best intellects China had to offer, provide mechanisms for popular supervision of government, reduce official corruption, and enhance the government's capacity to undertake national reconstruction. Finally, democracy could ensure stability, provide peaceful means of conflict resolution, and facilitate institutional development. In short, democracy could lead China out of its predicament. When all that was said and done, democracy would earn international respect for China and transform her into a wealthy and powerful nation.

Some liberal thinkers did realize that the wartime situation was no help to democratization. Election of a new government under a new constitution was out of the question, and far-reaching change must await the return of peace. Thus, Luo Longji felt compelled to give a narrower meaning to "opening up the regime" in terms of personnel and administrative reforms bringing into the government virtuous and able people. Wartime democracy was then reduced to responsible and efficient administration, a rule of law, and respect for basic human rights. When Qian Duansheng, a long-time supporter of the GMD, spoke in favor of a single-party system, he also had these terms at the back of his mind, pleading for personnel reform, liberalization within the ruling party, and political institutionalization. His view that China could not be democratized until the ruling party democratized itself first was perceptive and realistic.

The opposition elite constituted a third force, claiming the middle ground between the two major parties. Intellectually, the middle ground reflected an interesting blend of Western and Chinese thought, as illustrated by the writings of Zhang Junmai, Zhang Shenfu, Zhang Dongsun, Pan Guangdan, Chen Qitian, and many others. Although they were attracted to Western political philosophy, they also held views consistent with the Confucian tradition in which politics was conceived in moralistic and paternalistic terms. Western democratic thought was not incompatible with Chinese values. Even Liang Shuming, "the last Confucian," was not opposed to democratic values. What he opposed was blind copying of foreign models that did not take account of Chinese culture and traditions. Responding to the challenge of modernity, third force intellectuals took a middle position between East and West, between democracy and socialism. Much as they admired the parliamentary system, few rushed to embrace liberal democracy, Anglo-American style; not even Luo Longji, who was unquestionably committed to the core values of liberalism, championed this form of democracy without reservations. But they distinguished themselves from both the liberal intellectuals of the late Qing and early Republican period and the Marxist and anarchist thinkers of the May Fourth era by their preoccupation with a search for a kind of middle-ground democracy suited to Chinese conditions and traditions.

In that search, they confronted the issue of how to balance rights with duties and how to reconcile the two values of statism and democracy. The relationship between the individual and the state, between the public sphere of community life and the pursuit of self-interest, and between public authority and popular power was a familiar question that had confronted Liang Qichao many years before.[1] Chinese intellectuals did not see those relationships in absolute or diametrically opposed terms. But, whereas Liang Qichao had stressed the *rhetoric* of the natural harmony of social roles and relations, the liberal intellectuals of the Nationalist period emphasized the *process* of reconciliation through social cooperation. This was a necessary process in the public interest, but it was neither automatic nor natural. The facile identification of individual

---

[1] See Andrew J. Nathan, *Chinese Democracy* (London: I. B. Tauris, 1986), pp. 49–62.

interests with those of the state rested on an assumption of their insep-
arability and complementarity rather than an assumption of natural
harmony. The desire for social harmony did not mean a failure to recognize conflicts of interests between the individual and the state,[2] despite
the fact that Chinese intellectuals generally were reluctant to discuss
them. Their continued clamor for political rights and civil liberties was
an acknowledgment of those conflicts. Democracy was valued precisely
for its capacity to reconcile differences, resolve conflicts, and protect
rights. Harmonization of interest was a process, attainable only through
social cooperation, which in turn was made possible not by following
instincts but by leading a civic life in a civil society.

Middle-ground democracy was a moderate critique as well as a
Sinification of liberal democracy. It presupposed the juxtaposition of
rational individualism and community rationality. It rejected the notion
of an intrinsically adversarial relationship between state and individual,
between state and society, and between rights and duties because that
notion fails to recognize sufficiently what Philip Huang calls "the third
realm,"[3] which has a capacity to foster a creative relationship between
them. That notion fails also to appreciate what philosopher Mou
Zongsan calls the "circuitous connection" between the values of freedom
and instrumental rationality on the one hand and the parameters of a
humane, civilized society on the other.[4] Chinese democracy did not
believe in a weak state. Few entertained Hu Shi's idea of *wuwei* government, or the American idea that the government that governs least
governs best. The dominant Chinese democratic thought was that China
needed a strong and effective government – wartime and peacetime alike
– one that was democratic and humanistic at once, protecting rights and
promoting the common good. In the sense that democracy pivots on
society and liberalism on the individual, China's "liberal democrats"
betrayed a penchant more for democracy than for liberalism.

During the civil war period, the liberty–equality dichotomy received
much attention, showing a shift in rights thinking from the first genera-

---

[2] Compare my view with that of Andrew Nathan (ibid., p. 57), who has written that modern
Chinese democratic thought, as reflected in the thought of Liang Qichao, did not admit
that individual interests might conflict in any fundamental way with those of the group.

[3] Philip Huang, " 'Public Sphere'/'Civil Society' in China? The Third Realm between State
and Society," *Modern China* 19:2 (April 1993): 216–240.

[4] Cited in Thomas A. Metzger, "Modern Chinese Utopianism and the Western Concept
of the Civil Society," in Chen Sanjing, ed., *Guo Tingyi xiansheng jiuxu danchen jinian
lunwenji* (Essays commemorating the ninetieth birthday of Professor Kuo Ting-yee)
(Nangang: Zhongyang yanjiuyuan jindaishi yanjiusuo, 1995), II, 311.

tion of civil and political rights to the second generation of economic and social rights. Facing a choice between Anglo-American democracy and Soviet socialism, and between bread and the right to ask for it, the non-committed intellectuals were still keen to follow the elusive middle path, which some located in British socialism, and others found in the Eastern European models. What they said about "new liberalism," "new democracy," and "new socialism" was a reaction against the so-called classical liberalism, which emphasized laissez-faire economics and unrestrained individualism. Many had come to reconcile democracy with socialism, identifying their ideas with Mao Zedong's New Democracy.

The third force intellectuals were loyal critics, occasional interlocutors of the government, and designers and promoters of constitutional schemes. They wanted the GMD to reform because they feared the CCP, which was violent and politically intolerant. Their self-proclaimed impartiality, combined with a desire for national unity, motivated them to play the role of a mediator in the renewed GMD–CCP conflict. But theirs was a factionalized movement, as demonstrated by the composition and history of the DL. Both the Youth Party and the Democratic Socialist Party broke away from the DL before 1945 was over, forcing what remained of it to form a full alliance with the Communists. Of course, the third force was larger than the DL and the minor parties. After 1946, the independent, nonparticipatory elite maintained a liberal forum, making a last stand for Chinese liberalism and continuing to peddle the middle line, even though the middle ground had already been lost.

Indeed, the liberals suffered from many weaknesses, some inherent in the Chinese situation and others relating to their mentality and political qualities generally. In a country dominated by militarists, and in an era of war and revolution, prospects for civil opposition were anything but bright. Political parties and groups that had no access to the country's military and financial resources were hopelessly ineffectual. Chinese intellectuals were a differentiated community with diverse interests and internal rivalries, and some were more politically engaged than others. Their political amateurism and poor organization detracted from their overall effectiveness as political operators. With the exception of the Rural Reconstructionists, few understood, or paid much attention to, rural problems. They were not populists. Worse of all, they were incapable either of producing strong leadership or of seeking such leadership around which to unite.

Perhaps they could be faulted for putting too much emphasis on democracy as a political system and not enough as a way of life and a culture that needed to be developed. Both in theory and practice, a democratic system does not automatically ensure, let alone guarantee, democracy; the system itself could easily be abused by those in authority who are either unwilling to act in a democratic manner or simply unaccustomed to democratic practice. Nor can democracy be realized just because there are formalistic democratic institutions and a constitution that provides for citizen's rights. Democracy is no guarantee for a rule of law, nor insurance for good governance, not to say reconstruction and development. There is a distinction between *being* and *becoming* democratic. What David Bachman and Dali Yang have written about Deng Xiaoping's China is equally relevant to China of the Nationalist era:

> China does not become democratic merely by proclaiming itself a democracy and laws do not become authoritative merely by their promulgation. Certain norms and expectations must be established if democracy and the rule of law are to take hold, such as impartiality in legal proceedings, equality among citizens, minority rights, etc. In the West, the struggle against traditional authority in the form of feudalism or the divine right of kings took centuries. It would be naïve to expect that traditional sources of power and authority will disappear in China merely through the formal establishment of new institutions and sets of rules.[5]

Yet if the democrats of the Nationalist era had emphasized cultural reform over political change, as did the intellectuals of the May Fourth period, they would have been faulted for political inertia. Even worse, they would have unwittingly endorsed political tutelage and neo-dictatorship. The DL's statement – that if democracy was not realized during the war then what the Chinese people would have after the war would not be democracy but the division and ruin of their country – did not mean that with democratic measures in place China would achieve democracy in one stroke. What civil opposition desired in the short term was a democratic breakthrough, in full knowledge that completion of the democratization project was a matter of years, if not decades. A little democracy was better than no democracy, and a little each time would amount to a great deal over time. The important thing for them was to start a process. Each step in the right direction, however small, could be a significant contribution.

---

[5] David Bachman and Dali L. Yang, eds. and trans., *Yan Jiaqi and China's Struggle for Democracy* (Armonk, NY: M. E. Sharpe, 1991), pp. xxx–xxxi.

Their functional approach, therefore, should not lead to the conclusion that Chinese intellectuals did not understand democracy. Such a judgment is too harsh and unfair. Most of them understood democracy as a political method, a procedure, a system of government, a political philosophy, a spirit, an ideal, and a way of life. To be sure, they did not and would not practice everything they preached. But what democrats in the West would, and what democrats do not talk about the uses of democracy? And if they had personal ambitions and sought high public office, they were being normal because pursuit of personal and sectional interests was legitimate in democratic societies the world over. Ambitions aside, some no doubt held liberal convictions. Functionalism did not preclude a normative understanding of democracy. Multiple commitments to democracy were possible. Contrary to conventional wisdom, Chinese conceptions of democracy were not significantly different from mainstream Western liberal conceptions that emphasized the protection of rights from the state. Where they differed was in their belief that strengthening state powers and protecting rights were not necessarily contradictory. Given the fact that the advanced countries of the West were all democratic and industrialized, it was only natural that they should view democracy as a world tide and a means of development. Even though few entertained the idea of "popular participation with influence," all believed in popular supervision of government, a possibility only with periodic elections and a free and independent press. What's more, they stood for institutionalized opposition either as loyal opposition because they were too weak to win power[6] or as an independent force maintaining checks and balances in a coalition government or as part of a two-party system that might be established.

Despite its weaknesses, civil opposition was taken seriously by the major parties for the best part of the period. The GMD found it necessary to accommodate the MPGs, though only up to a point, by forming the PPC. When the DL was growing in strength, Chiang Kai-shek tried to divide it by luring, successfully, the Youth Party and the Democratic Socialist Party to the government's side. In the summer of 1946, prominent dissidents like Li Gongpu and Wen Yiduo were assassinated because they were thought to be posing too much of a threat to the

---

[6] On his own admission Chen Qitian said that he was politically engaged in the knowledge that his party would never gain power. The Youth Party would content itself with being "a loyal critic." See Chen Qitian, *Jiyuan huiyilu* (The memoir of Chen Qitian) (Taibei: Taiwan Shangwu yinshuguan, 1972), p. 158.

authorities. For different reasons, the CCP made the MPGs part of the united front strategy and entered into an alliance with the DL. In 1946, amid hostilities in Manchuria, both major parties courted the third force and accepted its mediating role. Any suggestion that the third force was ignored or insignificant is wide of the mark.

The democratic movement had not been helped by a favorable international climate that did not exist. The 1930s and 1940s were not a liberal era in the world at large, with fascism on the rise in Europe and Japan. The end of the European War, greeted as a victory of democracy over fascism, was immediately followed by the Cold War, which polarized international politics. Nor did any foreign agents aid China's democrats. American policy in China was not designed to ensure a democratic government under Nationalist rule or under a coalition regime. The White House and the U.S. Congress were not vigorously campaigning for democracy and human rights as they have been doing since the end of the Cold War. Instead, they propped up the corrupt anticommunist regime of Chiang Kai-shek. There was no Amnesty International to monitor human rights violations around the globe, nor a Democratic International to counteract the weight of the Comintern.

In the final analysis, civil opposition failed to make a significant impact on Chinese political life in the sense that it did not change the nature of the Nationalist rule and the outcome of the civil war. The opposition elite had attempted to juxtapose their cultural vision against the dominant authoritarian culture of the GMD and the CCP. Their failure was that their cultural tradition ultimately could not stand up against the dominant political culture of the day, one that was armed and violent. But their thoughts and actions have a deeper significance than has been recognized. They sustained the late Qing and May Fourth democratic impulse, developed it further, and left a significant intellectual legacy to the democratic movement in the PRC. They fostered a tradition of liberal opposition by seeking changes to the political system and by maintaining a commitment to freedoms of thought, speech, and the press, and intellectual autonomy. Their argument – that a competitive party system, free speech, and a free press are necessary for democracy and popular supervision of government – was made long before the prodemocracy movement of the post-Mao era.[7] This tradition of liberal opposition,

---

[7] Contrast my view with that of Andrew Nathan, who, referring to the prodemocracy activists in the post-Mao era, says that such an argument "has rarely been made in China." See Nathan, *Chinese Democracy*, p. xiii.

which had only just begun, survived the repression of the Nationalist government but not that of the communist regime that followed. To ignore it just because it did not succeed is to engage in the teleological fallacy. Moreover, this tradition raises the possibility that contemporary Chinese intellectuals will once again take this intellectual legacy seriously and seek to change the rules of the game.

After 1949, those who remained in the country, such as Luo Longji, Zhang Bojun, Huang Yanpei, Liang Shuming, Shen Junru, Shi Liang, Chu Anping, Pan Guangdan, Zhang Shenfu, Qian Duansheng, and Fei Xiaotong, were coopted into the new government within a new framework of multiparty cooperation. Some of their political careers were spectacularly successful for a while.[8] What remained of the MPGs, including some new ones, became known in CCP parlance as *minzhu dangpai* (democratic parties and groups) – willing tools of the regime.[9] The intellectuals were compelled to undergo thought reform during the 1951–1952 period. Some found their way into what the Hungarian writer Miklos Haraszti calls the "velvet prison," where the Leninist state was able to domesticate them because they had already made the state their home.[10] Others maintained their liberal and democratic aspirations to which they gave full expression in the "Let a Hundred Flowers Blossom and a Hundred Schools Contend Campaign" before falling victim to the Anti-Rightist Campaign in 1957. A few outspoken critics of the regime were dubbed

---

[8] Zhang Bojun became Minister of Communications and also played an active role in the PRC's "people's diplomacy" programs. Huang Yanpei served as Minister of Light Industries until 1954 and also assisted in the founding of the Sino-Soviet Friendship Association, of which he was a vice-chairman. In 1954, he became a vice-chairman of the All-China Conference of Education Workers. Shi Liang was appointed Minister of Justice in 1950, one of the only two female ministers in the new government. Luo Longji, not particularly well treated by the new government, was appointed to the Government Administration Council (later reorganized as the State Council) and became a member of the Sino-Soviet Friendship Association and a director of the Chinese People's Institute of Foreign Affairs, representing the PRC at a number of important peace conferences. It was not until May 1956 that he was appointed Minister of Timber Industry.

[9] On the CCP's policy toward the MPGs since 1949, see Gerry Groot, "Managing Transitions: The Chinese Communist Party's United Front Work, Minor Parties and Groups, Hegemony and Corporatism," unpublished Ph.D. thesis, University of Adelaide, 1997, chs. 4–11.

[10] Miklos Haraszti, *The Velvet Prison: Artists under State Socialism*, Katalin and Stephen Landesman, trans. (New York: Noonday Press, 1989). The notion of the velvet prison argues that in a Leninist state, as the initial period of violence and overt repression dies away, it is replaced by a "soft" culture in which willing conformity to the requirements of the system by intellectuals is substituted for opposition and dissent. For an interpretation of this notion in a Chinese context, see Geremie Barmé, "The Chinese Velvet Prison: Culture in the 'New Age,' 1976–89," *Issues and Studies* 25:8 (August 1989): 54–79.

"cardinal rightists." Luo Longji and Zhang Bojun, in particular, were denounced, accused of forming the "Zhang–Luo Anti-Party, Anti-Socialist, Anti-People Alliance," and consequently stripped of all their important posts. Chu Anping, too, was purged, disappearing during the Cultural Revolution (1966–1976) and possibly committing suicide. Chairman Mao silenced the voice of loyal opposition with a ruthlessness that dwarfed the repression of the previous regime. For a short while after the Great Leap Forward of the late 1950s, the liberal intellectuals reemerged only to suffer a great deal more during the Cultural Revolution.[11] Civil opposition to the CCP regime was not to surface again until the Deng Xiaoping era.[12]

Students of contemporary China will find in the precommunist period historical antecedents to the prodemocracy movement in the post-Mao era. Forty-five years after Luo Longji and Hu Shi thrust the issue of human rights into political limelight, China saw the Li Yizhe Movement (1973–1974), the Democracy Wall Movement (1978–1979), and the formation of the Chinese Human Rights League early in 1979. After another ten years, public protests and demonstrations in the spring of 1989 culminated in the Tiananmen tragedy of June 4. Although the social, economic, and political contexts within which the search for democracy in the modern and the contemporary periods could not have been more different, there were continuities with the past and historical parallels.

Democracy means different things to different people at different times. In the Nationalist era, civil opposition spoke of constitutionalism, political pluralism, parliamentary democracy, expert politics, and so on – a model of bourgeois democracy, Chinese style. In the 1970s, the Li Yizhe Group tried to distill a theory of democracy from Marx's writings or from contemporary practice in the communist countries, particularly Yugoslavia – a model of participatory democracy, Marxist style. For the Group, democracy entailed a rule of law, a system of election, and safeguards for basic rights, including the power of the people to manage state affairs by electing representatives and supervising leaders at various levels.[13] In 1979, dissidents Wang Xizhe and Chen Erjin spoke of social-

[11] On the liberal intellectuals in Mao's China, see Merle Goldman, *China's Intellectuals: Advise and Dissent* (Cambridge, MA: Harvard University Press, 1981).

[12] On the democratic elite in the post-Mao era, see Merle Goldman, *Sowing the Seeds of Democracy in China: Political Reform in the Deng Xiaoping Era* (Cambridge, MA: Harvard University Press, 1994).

[13] He Baogang, *The Democratization of China* (London: Routledge, 1996), p. 24; Lei Guang, "Elusive Democracy: Conceptual Change and the Chinese Democracy Movement, 1978–79 to 1989," *Modern China* 22:4 (October 1996): 430–431.

ist, or populist, democracy modeled on the Paris Commune of 1871. Chen proposed a "proletarian–democratic system," different from the democracy of Marx and Mao in several important respects, including the replacement of the existing single-party system by a "proletarian" two-party system in which the two parties would represent not different classes, but different strategies and policy proposals.[14] The Chinese Human Rights League demanded freedoms of thought and speech, safeguards for the constitutional right to assess and criticize party and state leaders, elections of state and local leaders, and freedom of movement, including foreign travel. Wei Jingsheng called for a "Fifth Modernization" aimed at the realization of human rights and the kind of democracy that "recognizes the equal rights of all human beings and resolves all social problems on the basis of cooperation." And it was supported by "the kind of rule of law which is conducive to the realization of equal rights."[15] For Wei, true democracy meant "the right of the people to choose their own representatives to work according to their will and in their interests ... and to replace [them] anytime so that these representatives cannot go on deceiving others in the name of the people."[16] Some years later, the journalist Liu Binyan, stressing the importance of press freedom and party reform, advanced the idea of "a second kind of loyalty" based on political criticism, calling for the establishment of a multiparty system within the existing socialist framework.[17] Until the spring of 1989, the dissidents differed from the pre-1949 liberal intellectuals in their calls for socialist democracy. (One notable exception was the renowned astrophysicist Fang Lizhi, who considered that socialism, democratic or not, was no longer the answer to China's problems.) When Liu Binyan proclaimed that "there can't be socialism without democracy,"[18] he reminded us of those in 1947–1948 who were convinced that socialism was democratic.

Emphasis on a rule of law and respect for human rights were common elements in the movements of both periods. The CCP leaders, like those of the GMD before them, were virtually above the law; consequently, corruption was rampant and those in authority tended to act arbitrarily.

---

[14] For details, see He, *The Democratization of China*, pp. 24–26.
[15] James D. Seymour, ed., *The Fifth Modernization: China's Human Rights Movement, 1978–1979* (Stanfordville: Human Rights Publishing Group, 1980), pp. 65, 69.
[16] Ibid., p. 52.
[17] Cited in Ann Kent, *Between Freedom and Subsistence: China and Human Rights* (Hong Kong: Oxford University Press, 1991), p. 151.
[18] Quoted in ibid.

Communist politics were just as personalistic as politics had been in the Republican era, political interference with the judiciary being a perennial problem. A rule of law entailed the separation of party and government and institutional development about which both Luo Longji and the contemporary dissident political scientist Yan Jiaqi had written.

The dissidents of the late 1970s were interested in giving more power to the workers. Chen Erjin advocated universal suffrage, where every worker would be eligible to vote and to run for public office. But in the spring of 1989, as in the Nationalist era, the prodemocracy elements declared themselves in favor of elitist, paternalistic democracy. Joseph Esherick and Jeffrey Wasserstrom have discovered that the student leaders at Tiananmen Square did not trust the masses or believe in majority rule.[19] Likewise, James Seymour has observed that China's intellectuals in the 1980s, with the notable exception of the literary critic Liu Xiaobo, held an elitist view of the will of the people as the basis of government authority – a view that did not envisage every citizen to have the right to take part in government through democratic procedures.[20] The dissenting intellectuals were concerned not with popular participation in government but with an expanded leadership role for the intellectuals like themselves. As with Hu Shi and Luo Longji before them, they were not enthusiastic about the political empowerment of the ordinary people.

Democracy was approached from a functional premise. In the Nationalist period, it was connected with antiimperialist nationalism. In the post-Mao era, it was advocated as an aid to economic modernization and a mechanism for checking official corruption and abuses of power. It was linked with human rights in both. The notion of natural rights, rejected by Luo Longji in 1929, was a conviction held by prodemocracy activists in the late 1980s.[21]

There were also differences, of course. Pre-1949 opposition elites had little appeal for the masses, drawing most of their support from fellow intellectuals, university colleagues, and students. The dissidents of the post-Mao period included those who would not have been regarded as intellectuals in the traditional sense and who tried to reach out to the ordinary city dwellers. Theirs was a more broadly based movement,

[19] Joseph W. Esherick and Jeffrey N. Wasserstrom, "Acting Out Democracy: Political Theater in Modern China," *Journal of Asian Studies* 49:4 (November 1990): 837–838.

[20] James D. Seymour, "What the Agenda Has Been Missing," in Susan Whitfield, ed., *After the Event: Human Rights and their Future in China* (London: Wellsweep, 1993), pp. 38–39.

[21] See the human rights discourse in He, *The Democratization of China*, pp. 77–87.

begun by a few activists in Beijing like Wei Jingsheng, an electrician from working class background, and supported by university and college students as well as some establishment intellectuals. Before the Tiananmen crackdown, the support base was further broadened by city dwellers from different walks of life, although support from the rural areas was weak.

Second, the third force, squeezed between two authoritarian parties, had little political space in which to maneuver and, in the end, had no alternative but to choose between the two evils. Post-Mao dissidents had only the party government to contend with. There was no third force, only a second force emerging in search of a civil society. Unorganized, this second force had little political space in which to operate either, but it was helped by China's "open-door" policy and economic reforms.

Third, in the Nationalist period, economics was not an important factor in civil opposition, despite the plight of the Chinese masses and the corruption of bureaucratic capitalism. In the 1980s, economics was a very important issue. The demand for political reform stemmed from the country's economic development. As the economic reforms led to social and other changes, the desire for a civil society and personal freedoms grew.

Fourth, the international climate in the 1980s was very different. Momentous changes were taking place in the Soviet Union and Eastern Europe, democracy was the intellectual vogue around the world, and Chinese human rights advocates enjoyed the support of the West and such international organizations as Amnesty International. Post-Mao China was not threatened by imperialism; there was no Japanese invasion, no war, and no revolution. The Cold War was fast retreating to the background, eventually coming to an end early in the 1990s. The only foreign pressures were from countries that wished to see an improvement in China's human rights record. There was a resurgence of Chinese nationalism, but it was related to modernization and development, not antiimperialism, and was whipped up by the party leadership for neo-authoritarian purposes. Internally, the PRC was not a divided country dominated by regional militarism, despite the political upheavals, campaigns, and turmoil that characterized the CCP rule.

These differences notwithstanding, the similarities are significant, underscoring the continuities in the quest for democracy and human rights in twentieth-century China. Just as civil opposition failed to bring about a reform of the Nationalist government, so the dissidents of the 1980s failed to bring about a democratization of the communist regime.

But the quest goes on. The recent arrests, trials, and sentencing of three dissidents to over ten years in prison (December 1998) for trying to register a new opposition party, the Chinese Democratic Party, hammers home the message that there are limits to how far the CCP can be pushed. Despite signs of political relaxation under the current regime, multiparty politics remain taboo. The crackdown does not indicate that China is retreating from reform, but it is a stark reminder of the dominant authoritarian tradition of the Chinese political culture. The challenge for China's public intellectuals is to take the legacy of civil opposition seriously, to enrich it, and to uphold the values and virtues on which liberal intellectuals had insisted many decades before. One day, when democracy does come to China, some would hope, in the tradition of intellectual utopianism, that Chinese democracy, with its emphasis on a balance of competing interests and social cooperation, will be democratic and humanistic at once, combining principled participation in public life with the idea of public life as a sphere produced by state and society.

Selected Bibliography

Alitto, Guy S. *The Last Confucian: Liang Shu-ming and the Chinese Dilemma of Modernity*. Berkeley: University of California Press, 1979.

Bachman, David and Yang, Dali L., eds. and trans. *Yan Jiaqi and China's Struggle for Democracy*. Armonk, NY: M. E. Sharpe, 1991.

Bao Heping 包和平. "Lun 'Renquanpai' de zhengzhi zhuzhang" 论人权派的政治主张 (On the political platform of the Human Rights Group). *Mingguo dang'an* 民国档案 2 (1991): 79–87.

Barmé, Geremie. "The Chinese Velvet Prison: Culture in the 'New Age', 1976–89." *Issues and Studies* 25:8 (August 1989): 54–79.

Barry, Norman P. *An Introduction to Modern Political Theory*. 3rd ed. London: Macmillan, 1995.

Beetham, David. "Liberal Democracy and the Limits of Democratization." In David Held, ed., *Prospect for Democracy: North, South, East, West*, pp. 55–73. Cambridge: Polity Press, 1993.

Bo Han 伯韩. "Cong zhidu shang kan Sulian de minzhu" 从制度上看苏联的民主 (Soviet democracy seen from an institutional perspective). *Minzhu zhoukan* 民主周刊 2:3 (July 23, 1945): 8–9.

Bo Qi 伯奇. "Wei ziyou zhuyizhe de zhen mianmu" 伪自由主义者的真面目 (The real face of the fake liberal elements). *Shi yu wen* 时与文 1:22 (August 8, 1947): 9–10.

Bodde D., and Morris C. *Law in Imperial China*. Cambridge, MA: Harvard University Press, 1967.

Boorman, Howard L., ed. *Biographical Dictionary of Republican China*, 4 vols. New York: Columbia University Press, 1967–1971.

Burtt, Edwin A., ed. *The English Philosophers from Bacon to Mill*. New York: The Modern Library, 1939.

Chan Lau Kit-ching. *The Chinese Youth Party, 1923–1945*. Hong Kong: Centre of Asian Studies, University of Hong Kong, 1972.

Chang, Carsun. *The Third Force in China*. New York: Bookman, 1952.

Chang, Maria Hsia. "'Fascism' and Modern China." *China Quarterly* 79 (September 1979): 553–567.

Chang, Sidney, and Myers, Ramon, eds. *The Storm Clouds Clear Over China: The Memoir of Ch'en Li-fu, 1900–1993*. Stanford: Hoover Institution Press, 1994.

Chang Yansheng 常燕生. "Wei feizhi neizhanzhe jin yijie" 为废止内战者进一解 (A word on the cessation of civil war). *Minsheng zhoubao* 民生周报 28 (June 12, 1932): 1–2.

"Jianguo wenti pingyi" 建国问题平议 (Comment on the question of nation building). *Duli pinglun* 独立评论 88 (February 18, 1934): 9–16.

Chen Qitian 陈启天. "Liangchong guonan jiagong xia de Zhongguo" 两重国难夹攻下的中国 (China under the dual threat of national emergency). *Minsheng zhoubao* 民生周报 7 (November 14, 1931): 1–2.

"Guomin jiuwang yundong de sanda mubiao" 国民救亡运动的三大目标 (The three main goals of the national salvation movement). *Minsheng zhoubao* 12 (December 19, 1931): 1–2.

"Guomin jiuwang yundong" 国民救亡运动 (The national salvation movement). *Minsheng zhoubao* 11 (December 12, 1931): 1–2.

"Guonan yu dangzheng" 国难与党争 (The national emergency and party politics). *Minsheng zhoubao* 6 (November 7, 1931): 1–2.

"Guonan yu dangzhi" 国难与党治 (The national emergency and one-party rule). *Minsheng zhoubao* 21 (April 1, 1932): 3–9.

Jiyuan huiyilu 寄园回忆录 (The memoir of Chen Qitian). Taibei: Taiwan Shangwu yinshuguan, 1972.

Minzhu xianzheng lun 民主宪政论 (On constitutional democracy). Taibei: Taiwan Shangwu yinshuguan, 1966.

"Wei guonan gao guomin" 为国难告国民 (Advice to the citizens on the national emergency). *Minsheng zhoubao* 10 (December 5, 1931): 6–8.

"You manqing lishi shuodao dangguo xianzhuang" 由满清历史说到党国现状 (From Qing history to the present state of the party state). *Minsheng zhoubao* 26 (May 29, 1932): 5–6, continued in 27 (June 5, 1932): 7–9.

Chen Yishen 陈仪深. ⟨*Duli pinglun*⟩ *de minzhu sixiang* 独立评论的民主思想 (The democratic thought of the *Independent Critic*). Taibei: Lianjing chubanshe, 1989.

Chen Zhimai 陈之迈. "Lun zhengzhi de zheji" 论政制的设计 (On the design of political systems). *Duli pinglun* 独立评论 199 (May 13, 1934): 2–5.

"Lun zhengzhi tanwu" 论政治贪污 (On political corruption). *Duli pinglun* 184 (January 5, 1936): 2–6.

"Minzhu yu ducai de taolun" 民主与独裁的讨论 (Discourse on democracy and dictatorship). *Duli pinglun* 136 (January 20, 1935): 4–11.

"Shangguidao de zhengzhi" 上轨道的政治 (Politics on the right track). *Duli pinglun* 237 (June 6, 1937): 2–6.

"Xianzheng wenti yu dangzheng gaige" 宪政问题与党政改革 (The constitutional question and party reform). *Duli pinglun* 175 (November 3, 1935): 2–6.

"Zailun zhengzhi de sheji" 再论政治的设计 (Again on institutional designs). *Duli pinglun* 205 (June 14, 1936): 2–6.

"Zailun zhengzhi gaige" 再论政治改革 (Again on institutional reform). *Duli pinglun* 166 (September 1, 1935): 3–8.

"Zhengzhi gaige de biyao" 政治改革的必要 (The necessity of institutional reform). *Duli pinglun* 162 (August 4, 1935): 3–5.

Ch'en Yung-fa. *Making Revolution: The Communist Movement in Eastern and Central China 1937–1945*. Berkeley: University of California Press, 1986.

Cheng Chu-yuan, ed. *Sun Yat-sen's Doctrine in the Modern World.* Boulder: Westview Press, 1989.

Cheng Zhi 澄之. "Zhanwang Zhongguo minzhu" 展望中国民主 (Looking at the prospect of Chinese democracy). *Ziyou luntan* 自由论坛 3:3 (November 1, 1944): 11–13.

Chiang Kai-shek. *China's Destiny and Chinese Economic Theory.* New York: Roy Publishers, 1947.

Ch'ien Tuan-sheng. *The Government and Politics of China, 1912–1949.* Reprinted from 1950 Harvard University Press edition, Stanford: Stanford University Press, 1970.

"War-time Government in China." *American Political Science Review* 36:5 (October 1942): 850–872.

Chinese Ministry of Information, comp. *China Handbook, 1937–1945.* New York: Macmillan, 1947.

Chongqingshi zhengxie wenshi ziliao yanjiu weiyuanhui 重庆市政协文史资料研究委员会, ed. *Guomin canzhenghui jishi* 国民参政会记实 (A veritable record of the People's Political Council), 2 vols. Chongqing: Chongqing chubanshe, 1985.

Chou Min-chih. *Hu Shih and Intellectual Choice in Modern China.* Ann Arbor: University of Michigan Press, 1984.

Chu Anping 储安平. "Lun Zhang Junmai" 论张君劢 (On Zhang Junmai). *Guancha* 观察 1:19 (April 1, 1947): 3–4.

"Zhongguo de zhengju" 中国的政局 (China's political situation). *Guancha* 2:2 (March 8, 1947): 3–8.

Chu Yi 楚易. "Heping minzhu de guidao" 和平民主的轨道 (The right track of peace and democracy). *Minzhu banyuekan* 民主半月刊 1 (January 10, 1947): 2–5.

"Lun aiguo minzhu tongyi zhanxian 论爱国民主统一战线 (On the patriotic democratic united front). *Minzhu banyuekan* 3 (February 15, 1947): 2–10.

Coble, Parks M. *Facing Japan: Chinese Politics and Japanese Imperialism, 1931–1937.* Cambridge, MA: Council on East Asian Studies, Harvard University, 1991.

"The National Salvation Association as a Political Party." In Roger B. Jeans, ed., *Roads Not Taken: The Struggle of Opposition Parties in Twentieth-Century China,* pp. 135–147. Boulder: Westview Press, 1992.

The Shanghai Capitalists and the Nationalist Government, 1927–1937. Cambridge, MA: Council on East Asian Studies, Harvard University, 1980.

Cohen Paul A., and Goldman, Merle, eds. *Ideas Across Cultures.* Cambridge, MA: Harvard University Press, 1990.

Cui Zongfu 崔宗复, ed. *Zhang Lan xiansheng nianpu* 张澜先生年谱 (A chronology of Zhang Lan's life). Chongqing: Chongqing chubanshe, 1985.

Curran, Thomas D. "From Educator to Politician: Huang Yanpei and the Third Force." In Roger B. Jeans, ed., *Roads Not Taken: The Struggle of Opposition Parties in Twentieth-Century China,* pp. 85–110. Boulder: Westview Press, 1992.

Dagongbao 大公报 (Tianjin), relevant years.

Dahl, Robert A. *Preface to Democratic Theory.* Chicago: University of Chicago Press, 1963.

Who Governs?. New Haven: Yale University Press, 1961.

de Bary, Wm. Theodore. *The Liberal Tradition in China*. Hong Kong: Chinese University Press, 1983.

de Bary, Wm. Theodore and Tu Weiming, eds. *Confucianism and Human Rights*. New York: Columbia University Press, 1998.

Des Forges, Roger. "Democracy in Chinese History." In Roger Des Forges, ed. *Chinese Democracy and the Crisis of 1989: Chinese and American Reflections*, pp. 21–52. Albany: State University of New York Press, 1993.

Ding Hongfan 丁洪范. "Qidai yige minsheng zhuyi de qiqi shibian" 期待一个民生主义的七七事变 (Looking forward to a July 7th incident of the principle of people's livelihood). *Minzhu luntan* 民主论坛 2:5 (October 4, 1947): 10–12.

Ding Wenjiang 丁文江. "Feizhi neizhan de yundong" 废止内战的运动 (The movement for a cessation of civil war). *Duli pinglun* 独立评论 25 (November 6, 1932): 2–5.

——— "Gonggong xinyang yu tongyi" 公共信仰与统一 (A public faith and unification). Reprinted from *Dagongbao* 大公报 in *Guowen zhoubao* 国闻周报 11:5 (January 22, 1934): 1–2.

——— "Jiaru wo shi Jiang Jieshi" 假如我是蒋介石 (If I were Jiang Jieshi). *Duli pinglun* 35 (January 15, 1933): 3–4.

——— "KangRi jiaofei yu zhongyang de zhengju" 抗日剿匪与中央的政局 (Resistance to Japan, extermination of the Communists, and the political situation in the center). *Duli pinglun* 19 (September 25, 1932): 8–9.

——— "KangRi de xiaoneng yu qingnian de zeren 抗日的效能与青年的责任 (The capacity to resist Japan and the youth's responsibility). *Duli pinglun* 37 (February 12, 1933): 2–8.

——— "Minzhu zhengzhi yu ducai zhengzhi" 民主政治与独裁政治 (Democratic politics and dictatorial politics). Reprinted from *Dagongbao* in *Duli pinglun* 133 (December 30, 1934): 4–7.

——— "Pinglun gongchan zhuyi bing zhonggao Zhongguo gongchan dangyuan" 评论共产主义并忠告共产党员 (A critique of communism and advice to members of the Chinese Communist Party). *Duli pinglun* 51 (May 21, 1933): 5–14.

——— "Sue geming waijiao shi de yiye ji qi jiaoxun" 苏俄革命外交史的一页及其教训 (A page in the history of the foreign relations of the Russian revolution and its success). *Duli pinglun* 163 (August 11, 1935): 15.

——— "Suowei 〈jiaofei〉 wenti" 所谓〈剿匪〉问题 (On the so-called "bandit elimination" question). *Duli pinglun* 6 (June 26, 1932): 2–4.

——— "Wo de xinyang" 我的信仰 (My beliefs). Reprinted from *Dagongbao* in *Duli pinglun* 199 (May 13, 1934): 10–11.

——— "Zailun minzhi yu ducai" 再论民治与独裁 (Again on democracy and dictatorship). Reprinted from *Dagongbao* in *Duli pinglun* 137 (January 27, 1935): 19–22.

——— "Zhongguo zhengzhi de chulu" 中国政治的出路 (The exit for Chinese politics). *Duli pinglun* 11 (July 31, 1932): 2–6.

Ding Zuoshao 丁作韶. "Ping Sun Ke kangRi jiuguo gangling caoan 评孙科抗日救国纲领草案 (Comments on Sun Ke's anti-Japanese national salvation proposal). *Minsheng zhoubao* 民生周报 26 (29 May 1932): 7–11.

Dirlik, Arif. *Anarchism in the Chinese Revolution*. Berkeley: University of California Press, 1991.

"The Ideological Foundations of the New Life Movement: A Study in Counterrevolution." *Journal of Asian Studies* 34:4 (August 1975): 945–980.

The Origins of Chinese Communism. Oxford: Oxford University Press, 1989.

Domes, Jürgen. "China's Modernization and the Doctrine of Democracy." In Cheng Chu-yuan, ed., *Sun Yat-sen's Doctrine in the Modern World*, pp. 201–224. Boulder: Westview Press, 1989.

Du Guangxun 杜光埙. "Qingkan Ouzhou ducai zhengzhi de jieguo" 请看欧洲独裁政治的结果 (Please have a look at the consequences of European dictatorships). *Duli pinglun* 独立评论 146 (April 14, 1935): 9–13.

Duara, Prasenjit. *Culture, Power, and the State: Rural China, 1900–1942*. Stanford: Stanford University Press, 1988.

Duncan, Graeme, ed. *Democratic Theory and Practice*. Cambridge: Cambridge University Press, 1983.

Dutton, Michael R. *Policy and Punishment in China: From Patriarchy to "the People"*. Cambridge: Cambridge University Press, 1992.

Eastman Lloyd E. "China's Democratic Parties and the Temptations of Political Power, 1946–1947." In Roger B. Jeans, ed., *Roads Not Taken: The Struggle of Opposition Parties in Twentieth-Century China*, pp. 189–199. Boulder: Westview Press, 1992.

"Fascism and Modern China: A Rejoinder." *China Quarterly* 80 (December 1979): 838–842.

"Nationalist China During the Nanking Decade, 1927–1937." In Lloyd E. Eastman, Chen, Jerome, Pepper, Suzanne, and Van Slyke, Lyman P., *The Nationalist Era in China, 1927–1949*, pp. 115–176. Cambridge: Cambridge University Press, 1991.

"New Insights into the Nature of the Nationalist Regime." *Republican China* 9:2 (1984): 8–18.

"Regional Politics and the Central Government: Yunnan and Chungking." In Paul K. T. Sih, ed., *Nationalist China During the Sino-Japanese War, 1937–1945*, pp. 329–362. Hicksville, NY: Exposition Press, 1970.

Seeds of Destruction: Nationalist China in War and Revolution 1937–1949. Stanford: Stanford University Press, 1984.

The Abortive Revolution: China Under Nationalist Rule, 1927–1937. Cambridge, MA: Harvard University Press, 1974.

Eastman, Lloyd E., Chen, Jerome, Pepper, Suzanne, and Van Slyke, Lyman P. *The Nationalist Era in China, 1927–1949*. Cambridge: Cambridge University Press, 1991.

Edwards, R. Randle, Henkin, Louis, and Nathan, Andrew J. *Human Rights in Contemporary China*. New York: Columbia University Press, 1986.

Elleman, Bruce A. *Diplomacy and Deception: The Secret History of Sino-Soviet Diplomatic Relations, 1917–1927*. Armonk, NY: M. E. Sharpe, 1997.

Elvin, Mark. "The Gentry Democracy in Chinese Shanghai 1905–14." In Jack Gray, ed., *Modern China's Search for a Political Form*, pp. 41–65. London: Oxford University Press, 1969.

Esherick, Joseph W., and Wasserstrom, Jeffrey N. "Acting Out Democracy:

Political Theater in Modern China." *Journal of Asian Studies* 49:4 (November 1990): 835–865.

Fairbank, John K. *China: A New History*. Cambridge, MA: The Belknap Press of Harvard University Press, 1992.

Fairbank, John K., and Feuerwerker, Albert, eds. *Cambridge History of China*, vol. 13. Cambridge: Cambridge University Press, 1986.

Fan Hong 樊弘. "Wo duiyu Zhongguo zhengzhi wenti de genben kanfa" 我对于中国政治问题的根本看法 (My fundamental views on the question of Chinese politics). *Guancha* 观察 3:18 (December 27, 1947): 5–6.

"Yu Liang Shuming, Zhang Dongsun liang xiansheng lun Zhongguo de wenhua yu zhengzhi" 与梁漱溟张东荪两先生论中国的文化政治 (Discussions with Mr. Liang Shuming and Mr. Zhang Dongsun about Chinese culture and politics). *Guancha* 3:14 (November 29, 1947): 5–8.

"Zhiyou liangtiao lu" 只有两条路 (There are only two roads). *Guancha* 4:7 (April 10, 1948): 3–4.

Fan Yusui 范予遂. "Minzhu zhengzhi bixu you fanduidang" 民主政治必须有反对党 (Democratic politics must have an opposition party). *Minzhu luntan* 民主论坛 2:1 (September 6, 1947): 4–5.

Fei Xiaotong 费孝通. "Meiguo minzhu ruodian de baolu" 美国民主弱点的暴露 (Exposure of the weaknesses of American democracy). *Minzhu zhoukan* 民主周刊 3:2 (March 6, 1946): 10–11.

Fewsmith, Joseph. *Party, State, and Local Elites in Republican China: Merchant Organizations and Politics in Shanghai, 1890–1930*. Honolulu: University of Hawaii Press, 1985.

"Response to Eastman." *Republican China* 9:12 (1984): 19–27.

Fincher, John H. *Chinese Democracy: The Self-Government Movement in Local, Provincial and National Politics, 1905–1914*. Canberra: Australian National University Press, 1980.

Friedman, Edward, ed. *The Politics of Democratization: Generalizing East Asian Experiences*. Boulder: Westview Press, 1994.

Fu Mengzhen (Fu Sinian) 傅孟真 (傅斯年). "Lun haomen ziben zhi bixu chanchu" 论豪门资本必须铲除 (On the necessary elimination of noble house capitalism). *Guancha* 观察 2:1 (March 1, 1947): 6–8.

"Zhengzhi zhi jigouhua" 政治之机构化 (The institutionalization of politics). *Jinri pinglun* 今日评论 1:1 (January 1, 1939): 3–5.

"Zhongguoren zuoren de jihui dao le" 中国人做人的机会到了 (The opportunity for Chinese to be men has arrived). *Duli pinglun* 独立评论 35 (January 15, 1933): 7–8.

Fu Yushen 傅于深. *Minzhu zhengzhi yu jiuwang yundong* 民主政治与救亡运动 (Democratic politics and the national salvation movement). Shanghai: Guangming shuju, 1937.

Fudan daxue xinwenxi yanjiushi 复旦大学新闻系研究室, ed. *Zou Taofen nianpu* 邹韬奋年谱 (A chronology of Zou Taofen's life). Shanghai: Fudan daxue chubanshe, 1982.

Fukui, Haruhiro, ed. *Political Parties of Asia and the Pacific*. Westport: Greenwood Press, 1985.

Fung, Edmund S. K. *The Diplomacy of Imperial Retreat: Britain's South China Policy, 1924–1931*. Hong Kong: Oxford University Press, 1991.

"The Alternative of Loyal Opposition: The Chinese Youth Party and Chinese Democracy." *Modern China* 17:2 (April 1991): 260–289.

"The Human Rights Issue in Nationalist China, 1929–1931." *Modern Asian Studies* 32:2 (May 1998): 431–459.

"Recent Scholarship on the Minor Parties and Groups in Nationalist China." *Modern China* 20:4 (October 1994): 478–508.

Furth, Charlotte. *Ting Wen-chiang: Science and China's New Culture*. Cambridge, MA: Harvard University Press, 1970.

Gans, Gerald F. *The Modern Liberal Theory of Man*. New York: St. Martin's Press, 1983.

Gao Hua 高华. "Lun kangzhan houqi Sun Ke de 'zuoqing'" 论抗战后期孙科的 "左倾" (On Sun Fo's "leftist tendencies" during the latter part of the war of resistance). *Minguo yanjiu* 民国研究 2 (1995): 206–221.

Geisert, Bradley. "Probing KMT Rule: Reflections on Eastman's 'New Insights'." *Republican China* 9:2 (1984): 28–39.

Geming wenxian 革命文献 (Documents on the Chinese revolution), vol. 8, ed. Luo Jialun 罗家伦 (Taibei: Zhongguo Guomindang zhongyang weiyuanhui dangshi shiliao bianxuan weiyuanhui, 1955), and vol. 76, ed. Qin Xiaoyi 秦孝仪 (1978).

Geng Yunzhi 耿云志. *Hu Shi nianpu, 1891–1962* 胡适年谱 (A chronology of Hu Shi's life, 1891–1962). Hong Kong: Zhonghua shuju, 1966.

Gerth, H. H., and Mills, C. Wright, eds. and trans. *Max Weber: Essays in Sociology*. New York: Oxford University Press, 1964.

Gibson, Phillip. "Asian Values, Western Values and Human Rights." Keynote address delivered at the Twelfth New Zealand International Conference on Asian Studies, Massey University, November 26, 1997.

Goldman, Merle. *China's Intellectuals: Advise and Dissent*. Cambridge, MA: Harvard University Press, 1981.

"Human Rights in the People's Republic of China." *Daedalus* 112:4 (Fall 1983): 111–138.

Sowing the Seeds of Democracy in China: Political Reform in the Deng Xiaoping Era. Cambridge, MA: Harvard University Press, 1994.

Gregor, A. James. *Interpretations of Fascism*. Morristown, NJ: General Learning Press, 1974.

Greiff, Thomas E. "The Principle of Human Rights in Nationalist China: John C. H. Wu and the Ideological Origins of the 1946 Constitution." *China Quarterly* 103 (September 1985): 441–461.

Grieder, Jerome B. *Hu Shih and the Chinese Renaissance: Liberalism in the Chinese Revolution, 1917–1937*. Cambridge, MA: Harvard University Press, 1970.

Intellectuals and the State in Modern China. New York: The Free Press, 1981.

Groot, Gerry. "Managing Transitions: The Chinese Communist Party's United Front Work, Minor Parties and Groups, Hegemony and Corporatism." Unpublished Ph.D. thesis, University of Adelaide, 1997.

Guomin canzhenghui mishuchu 国民参政会秘书处, ed. *Diyijie dierci huiyi jilu*

第一届第二次会议 (Record of the second plenum of the First People's Political Council). Chongqing: Guomin canzhenghui mishuchu, 1938.

Diyijie disici huiyi jilu 第一届第四次记录 (Record of the fourth plenum of the First People's Political Council). Chongqing: Guomin canzhenghui mishuchu, 1939.

Diyijie diyici huiyi jilu 第一届第一次会议记录 (Record of the inaugural meeting of the People's Political Council). Chongqing: Guomin canzhenghui mishuchu, 1938.

Han Youtong 韩幽桐. "Renquan yundong yu minzhu zhengzhi" 人权运动与民主政治 (The human rights movement and democratic politics). In Zhou Jingwen 周鲸文, ed., *Renquan yundong zhuanhao* 人权运动专号 (Special issue on the human rights movement), pp. 37–39. Hong Kong: Shidai pipingshe, 1941.

Haraszti, Miklos. *The Velvet Prison: Artists under State Socialism*, Katalin and Stephen Landesman, trans. New York: Noonday Press, 1989.

Hayford, Charles W. *To the People: James Yen and Village China*. New York: Columbia University Press, 1990.

He Baogang. *The Democratization of China*. London: Routledge, 1996.

"A Methodological Critique of Lucian Pye's Approach to Political Culture." *Issues and Studies* 28:3 (March 1992): 92–113.

Held, David. *Models of Democracy*. Stanford: Stanford University Press, 1987.

ed. *Prospects for Democracy: North, South, East, West*. Cambridge: Polity Press, 1993.

Hu Daowei 胡道维. "Lun zhuanzhi yu ducai" 论专制与独裁 (On autocracy and dictatorship). *Duli pinglun* 独立评论 90 (March 4, 1934): 5–11.

"Quanli shi shenme 权利是什麼? (What are rights?). *Duli pinglun* 42 (March 26, 1933): 10–14.

"Zhongguo de qilu – wei minzhi yu ducai wenti jiushang yu Ding Wenjiang xiansheng ji shixia zhuxian" 中国的歧路 – 为民治与独裁问题就商于丁文江先生及时下诸贤 (China at a crossroads – a response to Mr. Ding Wenjiang and other scholars on the issue of democracy and dictatorship). *Guowen zhoubao* 国闻周报 12:6 (February 18, 1935): 1–10.

"Zhongguo de qilu (xu)" 中国的歧路 (续) (China's at a crossroads [continued]). *Guowen zhoubao* 12:7 (February 25, 1935): 1–9.

Hu Shi 胡适. "Baoquan huabei zhongyao" 保全华北重要 (The importance of protecting north China). *Duli pinglun* 独立评论 52–53 combined (June 4, 1933): 2–6.

"Cong minzhu dao ducai de taolun li qiude yige gongtong xinyang" 从民主到独裁的讨论裏求得一个共同信仰 (Seeking a common political belief from the democracy versus dictatorship debate). *Duli pinglun* 141 (March 10, 1935): 16–19. Reprinted from *Dagongbao* 大公报 (February 17, 1935).

"Da Ding Zaijun xiansheng lun minzhu yu ducai" 答丁在君先生论民主与独裁 (A response to Mr. Ding Zaijun on democracy and dictatorship). *Duli pinglun* 133 (December 30, 1934): 7–9.

"Geren ziyou yu shehui jinbu – zaitan wusi yundong" 个人自由与社会进步 – 再谈五四运动 (Individual liberty and social progress: The May Fourth Movement revisited). *Duli pinglun* 150 (May 12, 1935): 2–5.

"Jianguo yu zhuanzhi" 建国与专制 (Nation building and autocracy). *Duli pinglun* 81 (December 17, 1933): 2–5.

"Minquan de baozhang" 民权的保障 (The protection of civil rights). *Duli pinglun* 38 (February 19, 1933): 2–5.

"Renquan yu yuefa" 人权与约法 (Human rights and the provisional constitution). *Xinyue* 新月 2:2 (April 10, 1929): 1–7.

" 'Renquan yu yuefa' de taolun" 人权与约法的讨论 (On human rights and the provisional constitution). *Xinyue* 新月 2:4 (June 1929): 1–5.

"Wang Jiang tongdian li tiqi de ziyou" 汪蒋通电里的提起的自由 (The liberty mentioned in the telegram from Wang and Jiang). *Duli pinglun* 131 (December 16, 1934): 3–6.

"Women zou natiao lu" 我们走那条路 (Which way are we going?). *Xinyue* 2:10 (December 10, 1929): 1–16.

"Women keyi denghou wushinian" 我们可以等候五十年 (We can wait for fifty years). *Duli pinglun* 44 (April 2, 1933): 3–6.

"Women shenme shihou caike you xianfa?" 我们什么时候才可有宪法 (When can we have a constitution?). *Xinyue* 2:4 (June 1929): 1–8.

"Wuli tongyilun" 武力统一论 (On miltiary unification). *Duli pinglun* 85 (January 14, 1934): 2–7.

"Xianzheng wenti" 宪政问题 (The constitutional question). *Duli pinglun* 1 (May 12, 1932): 5–7.

"Xinwenhua yundong yu Guomindang" 新文化运动与国民党 (The New Culture Movement and the Guomindang). *Xinyue* 2: 6–7 combined (September 10, 1929): 1–15.

"Zailun jianguo yu zhuanzhi" 再论建国与专制 (Again on nation building and autocracy). *Duli pinglun* 82 (December 24, 1933): 2–5.

"Zhengzhi gaige de dalu" 政治改革的大路 (The wide road of political reform). *Duli pinglun* 163 (August 11, 1935): 2–9.

"Zhengzhi tongyi de tujing" 政治统一的途径 (The route to political unification). *Duli pinglun* 86 (January 21, 1934): 2–7.

"Zhengzhi tongyi de yiyi" 政治统一的意义 (The meaning of political unification). *Duli pinglun* 123 (October 21, 1934): 2–4.

"Zhinan, xing yi bu yi" 知难, 行亦不易 (To know is difficult, to act is not easy either). *Xinyue* 2:4 (June 10, 1929): 1–15.

"Zhongguo wu ducai de biyao yu keneng" 中国无独裁的必要与可能 (The unnecessity and impossibility of dictatorship in China). *Duli punglun* 130 (December 9, 1934): 4–5.

Hu Weixi 胡伟希, Gao Ruiquan 高瑞泉, and Zhang Limin 张利民. *Shizi jietou yu ta* 十字街头与塔 (Crossroads and the tower). Shanghai: Shanghai renmin chubanshe, 1991.

Hu Zuoying 胡卓英, ed. *Xianzheng wenti yanjiu* 宪政问题研究 (Study of constitutional issues). Chongqing: Xinyishishe, 1940.

Huang Ganyin 黄干因, ed. *Minmeng pipan* 民盟批判 (A critique of the Democratic League). Hong Kong: Zhongbaoshe, 1947.

Huang Hai 黄海. "Ziyou fenzi neng lingdao Zhongguo ma?" 自由份子能领导中国吗 (Can the liberal elements lead China?). *Minzhu banyuekan* 民主半月刊 2 (January 25, 1947): 6–7.

Huang Jianli. *The Politics of Depoliticization in Republican China: Guomindang Policy Towards Student Political Activism, 1927–1949.* Berne: Peter Lang, 1996.

Huang Yanpei 黄炎培. *Minzhuhua de jiguan guanli* 民主化的机关管理 (Organizational management of democratization). Shanghai: Shangwu yishuguan, 1948.

"Wo suo shenqin zhi Zhongguo zuichuqi ji zuijinqi xianzheng yundong" 我所身亲之中国最初期及最近期宪政运动 (My experience of the very early and the very recent Chinese constitutional movement). *Xianzheng yuekan* 宪政月刊 1 (1944): 10–11.

Huang, Philip C. C. "'Public Sphere'/'Civil Society' in China? The Third Realm between State and Society." *Modern China* 19:2 (April 1993): 216–240.

Hui Yiqun 珲逸群. "Tuixing xianzheng de jige juti wenti ji juti renwu" 推行宪政的几个具体问题及具体任务 (A few concrete questions and concrete tasks concerning the implementation of constitutionalism). In Hu Zuoying 胡卓英, ed., *Xianzheng wenti yanjiu* 宪政问题研究 (Study of constitutional issues), pp. 20–30. Chongqing: Xinyishishe, 1940.

Huntington, Samuel P. "Political Development and Political Decay." *World Politics* 17 (April 1965): 386–430.

Political Order in Changing Societies. New Haven: Yale University Press, 1968.

The Third Wave: Democratization in the Late Twentieth Century. Normal: University of Oklahoma Press, 1991.

Ip Hung-yok. "Liang Shuming and the Idea of Democracy in Modern China." *Modern China* 17:4 (October 1991): 469–508.

"The Origins of Chinese Communism: A New Interpretation." *Modern China* 20:1 (January 1994): 34–63.

Israel, John. *Lianda: A Chinese University in War and Revolution.* Stanford: Stanford University Press, 1999.

Student Nationalism in China, 1927–1937. Stanford: Stanford University Press, 1966.

"Southwest Associated University: Preservation as an Ultimate Value." In Paul K. T. Sih, ed., *Nationalist China During the Sino-Japanese War, 1937–1945*, pp. 131–154. Hicksville, NY: Exposition Press, 1977.

Jeans, Roger B. *Democracy and Socialism in Republican China: The Politics of Zhang Junmai (Carsun Chang), 1906–1941.* Lanham: Rowman & Littlefield, 1997.

"Last Chance for Peace: Zhang Junmai (Carsun Chang) and Third-Party Mediation in the Chinese Civil War, October 1946." In Larry I. Bland, ed., *George C. Marshall's Mission to China, December 1945–January 1947*, pp. 293–325. Lexington, Virginia: George C. Marshall Foundation, 1998.

"Third-Party Collaborators in Wartime China: The Case of the Chinese National Socialist Party." In Lawrence Shyu, ed., *China During the Anti-Japanese War, 1936–1945.* Berne: Peter Lang, forthcoming 2000.

ed. *Roads Not Taken: The Struggle of Opposition Parties in Twentieth-Century China.* Boulder: Westview Press, 1992.

Jiang Tingfu 蒋廷黻. "Canjia guonan huiyi de huigu" 参加国难会议的回顾 (Looking back at my participation in the National Emergency Conference). *Duli pinglun* 独立评论 1 (May 22, 1932): 9–12.

"Dui gongchandang bixu de zhengzhi celüe" 对共产党必须的政治策略 (The strategy necessary for dealing with the Communist Party). *Duli pinglun* 11 (July 31, 1932): 6–8.

"Geming yu zhuanzhi" 革命与专政 (Revolution and autocracy). *Duli pinglun* 80 (December 10, 1933): 2–5.

Jiang Tingfu huiyulu 蒋廷黻回忆录 (The memoir of Jiang Tingfu), Xie Zhonglin 谢钟琏 ed. Taibei: Zhuanji wenxue chubanshe, 1979.

Jiang Tingfu xuanji 蒋廷黻选集 (The collected works of Jiang Tingfu). Taibei: Zhuanji wenxue chubanshe, 1978.

"Lun zhuanzhi bing da Hu Shizhi xiansheng" 论专制并答胡适之先生 (On autocracy and a response to Mr. Hu Shi). *Duli pinglun* 83 (December 31, 1933): 2–6.

"Maodun de Ouzhou (shang)" 矛盾的欧洲 (上) (Europe in contradictions [part 1]). *Duli pinglun* 165 (August 25, 1935): 2–5.

"Maodun de Ouzhou (xia)" 矛盾的欧洲 (下) (Europe in contradictions [part 2]). *Duli pinglun* 166 (September 1, 1935): 8–10.

"Sanzhong zhuyi de shijie jingzheng" 三种主义的世界竞争 (The world competition of three ideologies). *Guowen zhoubao* 国闻周报 12:38 (September 30, 1935). 1–8.

"Wei shiqu de jiangtu shi women de chulu" 未失去的疆土是我们的出路 (The territory not yet lost is our way out). *Duli pinglun* 47 (April 23, 1933): 5–8.

"Zhengzhi ziyou yu jingji ziyou" 政治自由与经济自由 (Political liberty and economic liberty). *Shiji pinglun* 世纪评论 1:17 (April 26, 1947): 5–7.

"Zhishi jieji yu zhengzhi" 知识阶级与政治 (The intellectual class and politics). *Duli pinglun* 51 (May 21, 1933): 15–19.

"Zhongguo jindaihua de wenti" 中国近代化的问题 (On the question of China's modernization). *Dagongbao* 大公报 (October 10, 1936). Reprinted in *Duli pinglun* 225 (November 1, 1936): 10–13.

Jin Yaoji 金耀基. *Zhongguo minben sixiangshi* 中国民本思想史 (A history of the Chinese primacy-of-the-people thought). Taibei: Taiwan Shangwu yin-shuguan, 1993.

Jizhe 记者 (pen name). "Women yao shenmeyang de zhidu?" 我们要什么样的制度 (What sort of system do we want?). *Zaisheng* 再生 2:9 (June 1, 1934): 1–18. The authors were actually Zhang Junmai and Zhang Dongsun.

"Women dui yu 〈jiuguo〉 wenti de taidu" 我们对于〈救国〉的态度 (Our attitude toward the question of 〈national salvation〉). *Zaisheng* 2:8 (May 1, 1934): 1–18.

Kang Yongren 康庸人. "Cong renxin ji guoji jushi kan Zhongguo qiantu" 从人心及国际局势看中国前途 (China's future seen from public support and the international situation). *Shiji pinglun* 世纪评论 1:14 (April 5, 1947): 5–7.

Keanes, John. "Democracy and the Media: Without Foundations." *Political Studies* 40 (1992): 116–129.

Kennedy, Melville T., Jr. "The Chinese Democratic League." *Papers on China* 7 (1953): 136–175.

Kent, Ann. *Between Freedom and Subsistence: China and Human Rights*. Hong Kong: Oxford University Press, 1991.

Kirby, William C. *Germany and Republican China*. Stanford: Stanford University Press, 1984.

Laqueur, Walter, and Rubin, Barry, eds. *The Human Rights Reader*. New York: Meridian Book, 1977.

Laski, Harold J. *A Grammar of Politics*, 5th ed. London: George Allen and Unwin, 1967; originally published in 1925 by Columbia University Press.

Lei Guang. "Elusive Democracy: Conceptual Change and the Chinese Democracy Movement, 1978–79 to 1989." *Modern China* 22:4 (October 1996): 417–447.

Levine, Andrew. *Liberal Democracy: A Critique of Its Theory*. New York: Columbia University Press, 1981.

Levine, Marilyn A. "Zeng Qi and the Frozen Revolution." In Roger B. Jeans, ed., *Roads Not Taken: The Struggle of Opposition Parties in Twentieth-Century China*, pp. 225–240. Boulder: Westview Press, 1992.

Levine, Steven I. *Anvil of Victory: The Communist Revolution in Manchuria, 1945–1948*. New York: Columbia University Press, 1987.

Li Huang 李璜. *Xuedunshi huiyilu* 学钝室回忆录 (The memoir of Li Huang). Taibei: Zhuanji wenxue chubanshe, 1973.

"The Reminiscences of Li Huang," Lillian Chu Chin, trans., 1971. Chinese Oral History Project, Special Collections, Butler Library, Columbia University.

Li Huaxing 李华兴, ed. *Zhongguo xiandai sixiangshi ziliao jianbian* 中国现代思想史资料简编 (A brief compilation of materials on modern Chinese political thought), 5 vols. Hangzhou: Zhejiang renmin chubanshe, 1983.

Li, Lincoln. *Student Nationalism in China, 1924–1949*. Albany: State University of New York Press, 1994.

Li Pingxin 李平心. "Lun disan fangmian yu minzhu yundong" 论第三方面与民主运动 (On the third party and the democracy movement). In Li Huaxing 李华兴, ed., *Zhongguo xiandai sixiangshi ziliao jianbian* 中国现代思想史资料简编 (A brief compilation of materials on modern Chinese political thought), vol. 5, pp. 485–498. Hangzhou: Zhejiang renmin chubanshe, 1983.

Li Pusheng 李朴生. "Guomindang weishi jinbiaodui zige" 国民党未失锦标队资格 (The Guomindang has not yet lost its qualifications as a champion team). *Duli pinglun* 独立评论 176 (November 10, 1935): 6–9.

Li Shiyou 李时友. "Yingguo gongdang shi zenyang chengzhang de (san)" 英国工党是怎样成长的(三) (How did the British Labour Party grow [3]). *Shiji pinglun* 世纪评论 4:7 (August 14, 1948): 8–9.

Li Shuqing 李树青. "Lun minzhu zhuyi" 论民主主义 (On democracy). *Jinri pinglun* 今日评论 4:18 (November 3, 1940): 281–284.

Li Xiaoyou 李孝友. "Du 〈guanyu zhonggong wang hechuqu?〉 jian lun ziyou zhuyizhe de daolu" 读〈关于中共往何处去?〉兼论自由主义者的道路 (On reading "About where the CCP is headed" and comments on the road of the liberals). *Guancha* 观察 3:19 (January 3, 1948): 7–9.

Li Xuan 黎玄. "Minzhu zhengzhi de zhendi" 民主政治的真谛 (The true essence of democratic politics). *Zaisheng* 再生 203 (February 22, 1948): 3–5.

Li Yibin 李义彬, ed. *Zhongguo qingniandang* 中国青年党 (The Chinese Youth Party). Beijing: Zhongguo shehui kexue chubanshe, 1982.

Li Zehou 李译厚. *Li Zehou ji* 李译厚集 (The collected works of Li Zehou). Haerbin: Heilongjiang jiaoyu chubanshe, 1988.

Zhongguo xiandai sixiangshi lun 中国现代思想史论 (Discourse on modern Chinese intellectual history). Beijing: Dongfang chubanshe, 1987.

Liang Shiqiu 梁实秋. "Lun sixiang tongyi" 论思想统一 (On unity of thought). *Xinyue* 新月 2:3 (May 10, 1929): 1–10.

"Luo Longji lun" 罗隆基论 (On Luo Longji). *Shiji pinglun* 世纪评论 1:15 (April 12, 1947): 5–9.

"Sixiang ziyou" 思想自由 (Freedom of thought), in "Lingxing" 零星 (Miscellany). *Xinyue* 2:11 (January 10, 1930): 9–10.

"Sun Zhongshan xiansheng lun ziyou" 孙中山先生论自由 (Mr. Sun Zhongshan and liberty). *Xinyue* 2:9 (November 10, 1929): 1–10.

Liang Shuming 梁漱溟. *Liang Shuming quanji* 梁漱溟全集 (The collected works of Liang Shuming), 8 vols. Jinan: Shandong renmin chubanshe, 1993.

Yiwang tanjiu lu 忆往谈旧录 (Recollections of the past). Taibei: Li Ao chubanshe, 1991.

Lin Bu 林布. "Zhang Dongsun xiansheng de sixiang" 张东荪先生的思想 (The thought of Mr. Zhang Dongsun). *Shi yu wen* 时与文 12 (May 30, 1947): 7–10.

Lin Huanping 林焕平. "Renquan yundong yu tuanjie kangzhan" 人权运动与团结抗战 (The human rights movement and solidarity for the war of resistance). In Zhou Jingwen 周鲸文, ed., *Renquan yundong zhuanhao* 人权运动专号 (Special issue on the human rights movement), pp. 35–36. Hong Kong: Shidai pipingshe, 1941.

Lin Yu-sheng. *The Crisis of Chinese Consciousness: Radical Anti-traditionalism in the May Fourth Era*. Madison: University of Wisconsin Press, 1979.

Linebarger, Paul M. A. *Political Doctrines of Sun Yat-sen: An Exposition of the San Min Chu I*. Baltimore: John Hopkins University Press, 1937.

Lishi wenxianshe 历史文献社, comp. *Zhengxie wenxuan* 政协文选 (Documents on the Political Consultative Conference). N.p.: Lishi wenxianshe, 1946.

Liu Butong 刘不同. "Zhongguo zhi lu" 中国之路 (The China road). *Minzhu yu tongyi* 民主与统一 9 (July 30, 1946): 3–5.

Liu Jianqing 刘健清. "Renquanpai lunlüe" 人权派论略 (An outline of the Human Rights Group). *Nankai xuebao* 南开学报 2 (1987): 77–82.

Liu Naicheng 刘乃诚. "Woguo zhengdang gaige yu Yingguo gongdang 我国政党改革与英国工党 (Party reforms in our country and the British Labour Party). *Shiji pinglun* 世纪评论 4:2 (July 10, 1948): 13–15.

Liu Simu 刘思慕. "Xianzheng de 〈qicheng〉 yu 〈cujin〉" 宪政的〈期成〉与〈促进〉 (The promotion and implementation of constitutionalism). In Hu Zuoying 胡卓英, ed., *Xianzheng wenti yanjiu* 宪政问题研究 (Study of constitutional issues), pp. 15–19. Chongqing: Xinyishishe, 1940.

Liu Xia 柳下. *Shiba nian lai zhi Zhongguo qingniandang* 十八年来之中国青年党 (The Chinese Youth Party over the past eighteen years). Chengdu: Guoyun shudian, 1941.

Liu Zhi 刘志. "Shishu minmeng zai "yier.yi" yundong de zuoyong" 试述民盟在〈一二。一〉运动的作用 (An attempt to describe the Democratic League's role in the December First movement). In 〈Yier.yi〉 yundong yu xinan lianda bianweihui〈一二。一〉运动与西南联大编委会, ed., *〈Yier.yi〉 yundong yu xinan lianda*

〈一二。一〉运动与西南联大 (The December First movement and the Southwest Associated University). Kunming: Yunnan daxue chubanshe, 1996.

Lou Bangyan 楼邦彦. "Dangzhi yu fazhi" 党治与法治 (Party rule and rule of law). *Jinri pinglun* 今日评论 5:2 (January 1941): 10–12.

Lü Kenan 吕克难. "Wo dui yu Zhongguo minzhu de kanfa" 我对于中国民主的看法 (My views on Chinese democracy). *Minzhu luntan* 民主论坛 1:4 (June 7, 1947): 15–16.

"Zhongguo meiyou fanduidang le?" 中国没有反对党了? (China doesn't have an opposition party any more). *Minzhu luntan* 2:12 (November 25, 1947): 3–4.

Lü Shiqiang 吕实强. "Lun Sun Zhongshan xiansheng de jicheng Zhongguo datong yu fayang guangda" 论孙中山先生的继承中国大统与发扬光大 (On Sun Yat-sen's inheritance of Chinese traditions and their development). In Huang Wenfa 黄文法, ed., *Sun Zhongshan sixiang yu dangdai shijie yantaohui lunwenji* 孙中山思想与当代世界研讨会论文集研讨会论文集 (Essays on Sun Yat-sen's thought and the contemporary world), pp. 233–245. Taibei: Taipingyang wenhua jijinhui, 1990.

Lubot, Eugene. *Liberalism in an Illiberal Age: New Culture Liberals in Republican China, 1919–1937*. Westport: Greenwood Press, 1982.

Luo Longji 罗隆基. "Banian lai Zhongguo minzhu de dongxiang" 八年来中国民主的动向 (The Chinese democracy movement in the past eight years). *Minzhu zhoukan* 民主周刊 2:9 (September 16, 1945): 6–9.

"Cong canjia jiu zhengxie dao canjia Nanjing hetan de yixie huiyi" 从参加旧政协到参加南京和谈的一些回忆 (Some recollections of the events from my participation in the old Political Consultative Conference to my participation in the Nanjing peace negotiations). *Wenshi ziliao xuanji* 文史资料选集 No. 20, pp. 193–284. Beijing: Zhonghua shuju, 1961.

"Dui xunzheng shiqi yuefa de piping" 对训政时期约法的批评 (Critique of the Provisional Constitution). *Xinyue* 新月 3:8 (July 10, 1931): 1–20.

"Gao Riben guomin he Zhongguo de dangju" 告日本国民和中国的当局 (A word to the Japanese and also the Chinese authorities). *Xinyue* 3:12 (n.d. possibly November 1931): 1–20.

"Gao yabo yanlun ziyouzhe" 告压迫言论自由者 (Advice to those who suppress freedom of speech). *Xinyue* 2:6–7 (September 10, 1929): 1–17.

"Lun gongchan zhuyi: gongchan zhuyi lilun shang de piping" 论共产主义：共产主义上的批评 (On communism: A critique). *Xinyue* 3:1 (November 10, 1930): 1–22.

"Lun gongkai zhengquan" 论公开政权 (On the opening up of the regime). *Jinri pinglun* 今日评论 3:21 (May 26, 1940): 323–326.

"Lun renquan" 论人权 (On human rights). *Xinyue* 2:5 (July 10, 1929): 1–25.

"Lun Zhongguo de gongchan" 论中国的共产 (On the communization of China). *Xinyue* 3:10 (September 1931): 1–18.

"Minzhu de yiyi" 民主的意义 (The meaning of democracy). *Minzhu zhoukan* 1:1 (December 9, 1944): 3–5.

"Minzhu zhengzhi yu minyi zhengzhi" 民主与民意政治 (Democratic politics and the politics of public opinion). *Minzhu zhoukan* 1:6 (January 20, 1945): 3–6.

"Ouzhan yu minzhu zhuyi de qiantu" 欧战与民主主义的前途 (The European War and the future of democracy). *Jinri pinglun* 4:1 (July 7, 1940): 11–13.

"Qicheng xianzheng de wojian" 期成宪政的我见 (My view on the realization of constitutionalism). *Jinri pinglun* 2:22 (November 19, 1939): 339–344.

"Quanli yu xiaolü" 权力与效力 (Power and efficiency). *Jinri pinglun* 4:9 (September 1, 1940): 134–137.

"Renquan buneng liuzai yuefa li" 人权不能留在约法里 (Human rights cannot stay in the provisional constitution) in "Lingxing" 零星 (Miscellany). *Xinyue* 3:7 (August 1930): 3–7.

" 'Renquan' shiyi" 〈人权〉释疑 (Discourse on human rights) in "Taolun" 讨论 (Discussion). *Xinyue* 3:10 (November 1930): 5–10.

"Shenme shi fazhi?" 什么是法治 (What is rule of law?). *Xinyue* 3:11 (December 1930): 1–17.

"Wo de beibu de jingguo yu fan'gan" 我的被捕的经过与反感 (My arrest and my disgust at it). *Xinyue* 3:3 (January 10, 1931): 1–17.

"Wo dui dangwu shang de 'jinqing piping' " 我对党务上的〈尽情批评〉 (My "thorough criticism" of Party work). *Xinyue* 2:8 (October 10, 1929): 1–15.

"Wo dui Zhongguo ducai de yijian" 我对中国独裁政治的意见 (My opinions on Chinese dictatorship). *Yuzhou xunkan* 宇宙旬刊 2:3 (1935): 1–11.

"Women yao shenme de xianzheng?" 我们要什么的宪政? (What sort of constitutionalism do we want?). *Ziyou pinglun* 自由评论 1 (November 22, 1935): 3–9.

"Women yao shenmeyang de zhengzhi zhidu" 我们要什么样的政治制度 (What sort of political system do we want?). *Xinyue* 2:12 (February 10, 1930): 1–24.

"Zhengzhi de minzhu yu jingji de minzhu" 政治的民主与经济的民主 (Political democracy and economic democracy). *Minzhu zhoukan* 1:2 (December 16, 1944): 3–5.

"Zhongguo minzhu lucheng yaoyuan" 中国民主路程遥远 (The road to Chinese democracy is long). *Minzhu zhoukan* 1:19 (May 3, 1945): 4–5.

"Zhongguo muqian de zhengdang wenti (shang)" 中国目前的政党问题(上) (China's current problems with political parties [part 1]). *Jinri pinglun* 4:24 (December 18, 1940): 376–379.

"Zhongguo muqian de zhengdang wenti (xia)" 中国目前的政党问题(下) (China's current problems with political parties [part 2]). *Jinri pinglun* 4:25 (December 25, 1941): 392–397.

"Zhongguo xuyao disan ge da zhengdang" 中国需要第三个大政党 (China needs a third large political party). *Minzhu zhoukan* 1:16 (April 9, 1945): 4–7.

"Zhongguo yu minyi zhengzhi" 中国与民意政治 (China and the politics of public opinion). *Jinri pinglun* 4:21 (November 24, 1940): 329–331.

"Zhuanjia zhengzhi" 专家政治 (Expert politics). *Xinyue* 2:2 (April 10, 1929): 1–7.

Luo Wen'gan 罗文幹. "Lizhi zhiduhua" 吏治制度化 (The institutionalization of public administration). *Jinri pinglun* 今日评论 1:24 (June 13, 1939): 3–5.

Lutz, Jessie G. "The Chinese Student Movement of 1945–1949." *Journal of Asian Studies* 31:1 (November 1971): 89–110.

Ma Xulun 马叙伦. "Guomin de zeren yinggai shuohua" 国民的责任应该说话 (It is the citizen's duty to speak up). *Minzhu* 民主 8 (December 1, 1945): 173–181.

Macpherson, C. B. *Democratic Theory: Essays in Retrieval*. Oxford: Clarendon Press, 1973.

⸻ *The Life and Times of Liberal Democracy*. New York: Oxford University Press, 1977.

⸻ *The Real World of Democracy*. Oxford: Clarendon Press, 1966.

Mao Tse-tung. *Selected Works of Mao Tse-tung*, 4 vols. Peking: Foreign Languages Press, 1967.

Martin, Brian G. *The Shanghai Green Gang: Politics and Organized Crime*. Berkeley: University of California Press, 1996.

Melby, John F. *The Mandate of Heaven: Record of a Civil War, China, 1945–49*. Toronto: University of Toronto Press, 1968.

Metzger, Thomas A. "Continuities between Modern and Premodern China: Some Neglected Methodolgical and Substantive Issues." In Paul A. Cohen and Merle Goldman, eds., *Ideas Across Cultures*, pp. 263–292. Cambridge, MA: Harvard University Press, 1990.

⸻ "Did Sun Yat-sen Understand the Idea of Democracy? The Conceptualization of Democracy in the Three Principles of the People and in John Stuart Mill's 'On Liberty'." *American Asian Review* 10:1 (Spring 1992): 1–41.

⸻ *Escape from Predicament*. New York: Columbia University Press, 1977.

⸻ "Modern Chinese Utopianism and the Western Concept of the Civil Society." In Chen Sanjing 钱三井, ed., *Guo Tingyi xiansheng jiuxu danchen jinian lunwenji* 郭廷以先生九序诞辰记念论文集 (Essays commemorating the ninetieth birthday of Profesor Kuo Ting-yee), vol. 2, pp. 273–312. Nangang: Zhongyang yanjiuyuan jindaishi yanjiusuo, 1995.

Michael, Franz, and Wu Yuan-li. "Introduction: An Overview." In Franz Michael, Wu Yuan-li, and John F. Copper, *Human Rights in the People's Republic of China*, pp. 1–6. Boulder: Westview Press, 1988.

Michels, Robert. *A Sociological Study of the Oligarchical Tendencies of Modern Democracies*. New York: Collier Books, 1962.

Minsheng 民生 (pen name). "Shuangzhou xiantan (6)" 双周闲谈 (6) (Fortnightly talks [6]). *Duli pinglun* 独立评论 133 (December 30, 1934): 9–13.

Moore, Barrington, Jr. *Social Origins of Dictatorship and Democracy*. Boston: Beacon Press, 1966.

Mu Xin 穆欣. *Zou Taofen* 邹韬奋 (Zou Taofen). Hong Kong: Sanlian shudian, 1978.

Myers, Ramon H., and Metzger, Thomas A. "Sinological Shadows: The State of Modern China Studies in the US." *Australian Journal of Chinese Affairs* 4 (1980): 1–34.

Narramore, Terry. "Luo Longji and Chinese Liberalism, 1928–32." *Papers on Far Eastern History* 32 (1985): 165–195.

Nathan, Andrew J. *Chinese Democracy*. London: I. B. Tauris, 1986.

⸻ "Political Rights in Chinese Constitutions." In R. Randle Edwards, Louis Henkin, and Andrew J. Nathan, *Human Rights in Contemporary China*, pp. 77–124. New York: Columbia University Press, 1986.

⸻ "Some Trends in the English-language Historiography of Republican China." In Zhongyang yanjiuyuan 中央研究院, comp., *Dierjie guoji hanxue huiyi lunwenji* 第二届国际汉学会议论文集 (Proceedings of the Second International

Chinese Studies Conference), vol. 1, pp. 51–64. Taibei: Zhongyang yanjiu-yuan, 1989.

"Sources of Chinese Rights Thinking." In R. Randle Edwards, Louis Henkin, and Andrew J. Nathan, *Human Rights in Contemporary China*, pp. 125–164. New York: Columbia University Press, 1986.

"The Place of Values in Cross-Cultural Studies: The Example of Democracy in China." In Paul A. Cohen and Merle Goldman, eds., *Ideas Across Cultures*, pp. 293–314. Cambridge, MA: Harvard University Press, 1990.

Olenik, J. Kenneth. "Deng Yanda and the Third Party." In Roger B. Jeans, ed., *Roads Not Taken: The Struggle of Opposition Parties in Twentieth-Century China*, pp. 111–134. Boulder: Westview Press, 1992.

Ouyang Changhong 欧阳长虹. "Cong suowei 〈minzhu guoji〉 shuoqi" 从所谓〈民主国际〉说起 (Speaking on the so-called Democratic International). *Shi yu wen* 时与文 1:22 (August 8, 1947): 7–8.

Pan Guangdan 潘光旦. "Geren, shehui, yu minzhi" 个人，社会与民治 (The individual, society, and democracy). *Minzhu zhoukan* 民主周刊 1:4 (December 30, 1944): 3–7.

"Minzhu zhengzhi yu Zhongguo shehui sixiang beijing (shang)" 民主政治与中国社会思想背景（上） (Democratic politics and the background of Chinese social thought [part 1]). *Ziyou luntan* 自由论坛 2:3 (March 1, 1944): 8–16.

"Yousheng de chulu" 优生的出路 (Eugenics as a way out). *Xinyue* 新月 4:1 (December 1931): 1–33.

Parekh, Bhikhu. "The Cultural Particularity of Liberal Democracy." In David Held, ed., *Prospects for Democracy: North, South, East, West*, pp. 156–175. Cambridge: Polity Press, 1993.

Pateman, Carole. *Participation and Democratic Theory*. Cambridge: Cambridge University Press, 1970.

Pepper, Suzanne. *Civil War in China: The Political Struggle, 1945–1949*. Berkeley: University of California Press, 1978.

"The KMT–CCP Conflict, 1945–49." In Lloyd E. Eastman, Jerome Chen, Suzanne Pepper, and Lyman P. Van Slyke, *The Nationalist Era in China, 1927–1949*, pp. 291–356. Cambridge: Cambridge University Press, 1991.

Plamenatz, John. *Democracy and Illusion: An Examination of Certain Aspects of Modern Democratic Theory*. London: Longman, 1973.

Poe, Dison Hsueh-feng. "Comments on Lawrence N. Shyu, 'China's 'Wartime Parliament': The People's Political Council, 1938–1945.'" In Paul K. T. Sih, ed., *Nationalist China During the Sino-Japanese War, 1937–1945*, pp. 314–325. Hicksville, NY: Exposition Press, 1977.

Premont, D., ed. *Essays on the Concept of a "Right to Live."* Brussels: Bruylant, 1988.

Price, Don C. "Constitutional Alternative and Democracy in the Revolution of 1911." In Paul A. Cohen and Merle Goldman, eds., *Ideas Across Cultures*, pp. 199–260. Cambridge, MA: Harvard University Press, 1990.

Przeworski, Adam. *Democracy and the Market: Political and Economic Reforms in Eastern Europe and Latin America*. Cambridge: Cambridge University Press, 1991.

Pye, Lucian W. *The Spirit of Chinese Politics: A Psychocultural Study of the*

Authority Crisis in Political Development. Cambridge, MA: M.I.T. Press, 1968.

"Tiananmen and Chinese Political Culture: The Escalation of Confrontation." In George Hicks, ed., *The Broken Mirror: China After Tiananmen*, pp. 162–179. Harlow: Longman, 1990.

"How China's Nationalism Was Shanghaied." In Jonathan Unger, ed., *Chinese Nationalism*, pp. 86–112. Armonk, NY: M. E. Sharpe, 1996.

Qian Duansheng 钱端升. "Duiyu liuzhong quanhui de qiwang" 对于六中全会的期望 (My expectations of the sixth plenum). *Duli pinglun* 独立评论 162 (August 4, 1935): 6–8.

"Guojia jinhou de gongzuo yu zeren" 国家今后的工作与责任 (The task and responsibility of the nation from now on). *Jinri pinglun* 今日评论 4:13 (September 29, 1940): 197–198.

"Kangzhan zhisheng de tujing" 抗战致胜的途径 (The path to war victory). *Jinri pinglun* 1:11 (December 3, 1939): 5–7.

"Lun dang" 论党 (On political parties). *Jinri pinglun* 3:23 (June 9, 1940): 355–358.

"Lun dangwu" 论党务 (On party affairs). *Jinri pinglun* 5:14 (April 13, 1941): 234–236.

"Minzhu zhengzhi hu? Jiquan guojia hu?" 民主政治乎？极权国家乎？ (Democracy? Dictatorship?). *Dongfang zazhi* 东方杂志 31:1 (January 1, 1934): 17–25.

"Wei heping keyi tongyi lun" 唯和平可以统一论 (Only peace can achieve unification). *Guancha* 观察 2:4 (March 22, 1947): 3–7.

"Women xuyao de zhengzhi zhidu" 我们需要的政治制度 (The political system we need). *Jinri pinglun* 4:15 (October 13, 1940): 228–230.

"Yidang yu duodang" 一党与多党 (Single party and multiple parties). *Jinri pinglun* 4:16 (October 20, 1940): 246–248.

"Zhengzhi de zhiduhua" 政治的制度化 (The institutionalization of politics). *Jinri pinglun* 1:7 (February 12, 1939): 4–5.

Qian Jiaju 千家驹. "Ping zhengzhi xieshanghui" 评政治协商会 (Comments on the Political Consultative Conference). *Ziyou shijie banyuekan* 自由世界半月刊 1:5 (January 1, 1946): 11–12.

"Lun jingji de minzhu" 论经济的民主 (On economic democracy). *Ziyou shijie banyuekan* 1:4 (December 16, 1945): 6–7.

Qian Shifu 钱实甫. "Meiyou ziyou de pingdeng" 没有自由的平等 (Equality without liberty). *Minzhu luntan* 民主论坛 2:1 (September 6, 1947): 16–18.

Qin Yingjun 秦英君. "Zhongguo renquanpai sixiangqianxi" 中国人权派思想浅析 (A brief analysis of Chinese human rights thought). *Shixue yuekan* 史学月刊 6 (1986): 63–68.

Qiu Qianmu 邱钱牧. *Zhongguo minzhu dangpaishi* 中国民主党派史 (A history of the Chinese democratic parties and groups). Hangzhou: Zhejiang jiaoyu chubanshe, 1987.

Rosinger, Lawrence K. *Wartime Politics in China, 1937–1944.* Princeton: Princeton University Press, 1945.

Rubin, Vitaly A. *Individual and State in Ancient China: Essays on Four Chinese Philosophers*, Steven I. Levine, trans. New York: Columbia University Press, 1976.

Russell, Bertrand. *Power: A New Social Analysis.* London: Allen and Unwin, 1938.

Sartori, Giovanni. *Democratic Theory.* New York: Praeger, 1967.

The Theory of Democracy Revisited. Chatham: Chatham House, 1987.

Schram, Stuart R. *The Political Thought of Mao Tse-tung,* revised and enlarged edition. New York: Praeger, 1969.

The Thought of Mao Tse-tung. Cambridge: Cambridge University Press, 1989.

ed. *Mao's Road to Power: Revolutionary Writings.* Armonk, NY: M. E. Sharpe, 1992.

Schumpeter, Joseph. *Capitalism, Socialism and Democracy,* 3rd ed. New York: Harper and Row, 1962.

Schwarcz, Vera. *The Chinese Enlightenment: Intellectuals and the Legacy of the May Fourth Movement of 1919.* Berkeley: University of California Press, 1986.

Time for Telling Truth Is Running Out: Conversations with Zhang Shenfu. New Haven: Yale University Press, 1992.

Seymour, James D. *China's Satellite Parties.* Armonk, NY: M. E. Sharpe, 1987.

"What the Agenda Has Been Missing." In Susan Whitfield, ed., *After the Event: Human Rights and Their Future in China,* pp 36–49. London: Wellsweep, 1993.

ed. *The Fifth Modernization: China's Human Rights Movement, 1978–1979.* Stanfordville: Human Rights Publishing Group, 1980.

Shaheen, Anthony Joseph. "The China Democratic League and Chinese Politics, 1939–1947." Unpublished Ph.D. dissertation, University of Michigan, 1977.

Shang Zhi 商治. "Zhengzhi minzhu yu jingji minzhu" 政治民主与经济民主 (Political democracy and economic democracy). *Shiji pinglun* 世纪评论 1:11 (March 15, 1947): 10–13.

Sharman, Lyon. *Sun Yat-sen: His Life and Its Meaning.* Reprinted from the 1934 ed. Stanford: Stanford University Press, 1968.

Shen Pu 沈谱 and Shen Renhua 沈人骅, eds. *Shen Junru nianpu* 沈钧儒年谱 (A chronology of Shen Junru's life). Beijing: Zhongguo wenshi chubanshe, 1992.

Shen Yunlong 沈云龙. *Minguo shishi yu renwu luncong* 民国史事与人物论丛 (Reflections on republican historical events and personalities). Taibei: Zhuanji wenxue chubanshe, 1981.

Sheridan, James E. *Chinese Warlord: The Career of Feng Yu-hsiang.* Stanford: Stanford University Press, 1966.

Shi Fuliang 施复亮. "Feichu boxiao yu zengjia shengchan" 废除剥削与增加生产 (Abolish exploitation and increase production). *Guancha* 观察 4:4 (March 20, 1948): 7–9.

"Hewei zhongjianpai" 何谓中间派 (What is meant by middle party?). *Wenhuibao* 文汇报 (July 14, 1946). Reprinted in Li Huaxing 李华兴, ed., *Zhongguo xiandai sixiangshi ziliao jianbian* 中国现代思想史资料简编 (A brief compilation of materials on modern Chinese political thought), vol. 5, pp. 485–498. Hangzhou: Zhejiang renmin chubanshe, 1983.

"Lun zhongjianpai" 论中间派 (On the middle party). *Guoxun* 国讯 405 (January 1, 1946): 12–13.

"Lun ziyou zhuyi de daolu" 论自由主义的道路 (On the road of liberalism). *Guancha* 3:22 (January 24, 1948): 3–5.

Minzhu kangzhan lun 民主抗战论 (On democracy in the war of resistance). Shanghai: Jinhua shuju, 1937.

"Xin Zhongguo de jingji he zhengzhi" 新中国的经济和政治 (New China's economy and politics). *Guancha* 4:21 (July 24, 1948): 4–6.

"Zhongguo wang naliqu" 中国往哪里去 (Where is China going?). *Zaizao* 再造 1:3 (July 25, 1948): 3–5.

"Zhongjianpai de zhengzhi luxian" 中间派的政治路线 (The political line of the middle party). *Shi yu wen* 时与文 1 (March 14, 1947): 6–10.

"Zhongjianpai zai zhengzhi shang de diwei he zuoyong" 中间派在政治上的地位和作用 (The position and role of the middle party in politics). *Shi yu wen* 1:5 (April 1, 1947): 3–5.

Shuo Ren 硕人 (pen name). "Zhengzhi wenti de taolun" 政制问题的讨论 (Discussion of the question of political institutions). *Duli pinglun* 独立评论 164 (August 18, 1935): 17–19.

Shyu, Lawrence N. "China's 'Wartime Parliament': The People's Political Council, 1938–1945." In Paul K. T. Sih, ed., *Nationalist China During the Sino-Japanese War, 1937–1945*, pp. 273–325. Hicksville, NY: Exposition Press, 1977.

"China's Minority Parties in the People's Political Council." In Roger B. Jeans, ed., *Roads Not Taken: The Struggle of Opposition Parties in Twentieth-Century China*, pp. 151–169. Boulder: Westview Press, 1992.

Sichuan shifan xueyuan 四川师范学院, comp. *Zhang Lan wenji* 张澜文集 (The collected works of Zhang Lan). Chengdu: Sichuan jiaoyu chubanshe, 1991.

Sih, Paul K. T., ed. *Nationalist China During the Sino-Japanese War, 1937–1945*. Hicksville, NY: Exposition Press, 1977.

Situ Yiheng 司徒伊衡. "Zhongguo minzhu de zhanwang" 中国民主的展望 (The prospect of Chinese democracy). *Minzhu luntan* 民主论坛 2:3 (September 20, 1947): 9–11.

So Wai-chor. *The Kuomintang Left in the National Revolution, 1924–1931*. Hong Kong: Oxford University Press, 1991.

Solomon, Richard. *Mao's Revolution and the Chinese Political Culture*. Berkeley: University of California Press, 1971.

Song Shiying 宋士英. "Zhongguo xianzheng zhi qiantu" 中国宪政之前途 (The future of Chinese constitutionalism). *Duli pinglun* 独立评论 234 (May 16, 1937): 15–18.

Spar, Frederic J. "Human Rights and Political Engagement: Luo Longji in the 1930s." In Roger B. Jeans, ed., *Roads Not Taken: The Struggle of Opposition Parties in Twentieth-Century China*, pp. 61–81. Boulder: Westview Press, 1992.

"Liberal Political Opposition in Kuomintang and Communist China: Lo Lung-chi in Chinese Politics, 1928–1958." Unpublished Ph.D. dissertation, Brown University, 1980.

"Human Rights and Political Activism: Luo Longji in Chinese Politics, 1928–1958." A 1993 manuscript based on his Ph.D. dissertation.

Strauss, Julia C. *Strong Institutions in Weak Polities: State Building in Republican China, 1927–1940*. Oxford: Clarendon Press, 1998.

"The Evolution of Republican Government." *China Quarterly* 150 (June 1997): 329–351.

Stromberg, Ronald N. *Democracy: A Short, Analytical History.* Armonk, NY: M. E. Sharpe, 1996.

Su Mingxian. "The Regional Faction and Chinese Nationalism: A Case Study of Li Zongren and the Guangxi Clique During the Nanjing Decade." Unpublished Ph.D. thesis, Griffith University, 1996.

Sun Fo. *China Looks Forward.* London: George Allen and Unwin, 1944.

Sun Jiyi 孙几伊. "Zhanhou Zhongguo zhengzhi wenti" 战后中国政治问题 (The question of postwar Chinese politics). *Minzhu zhengzhi* 民主政治 6–7 combined (November 1945): 25–28.

Sun Ke 孙科. "Youguan xianzheng zhu wenti" 有关宪政诸问题 (Various questions concerning constitutionalism). *Xianzheng yuekan* 宪政月刊 3 (1944): 5–13.

"Zhixian jingguo ji xianfa zhong de jige zhongyao wenti" 制宪经过及宪法中的几个重要重要问题 (The constitution-making process and a few important issues). In Hu Zuoying 胡卓英, ed., *Xianzheng wenti yanjiu* 宪政问题研究 (Study of constitutional issues), pp. 1–12. Chongqing: Xinyishishe, 1940.

Sun Youli. *China and the Origins of the Pacific War.* New York: St. Martin's Press, 1993.

Svensson, Marina. "The Chinese Conception of Human Rights: The Debate on Human Rights in China, 1898–1949." Unpublished Ph.D. dissertation, Lund University, 1996.

Symposium. "Yong heping fangfa neng shishi shehui zhuyi?" 用和平方法能实施社会主义？ (Can socialism be implemented by peaceful means?). *Xinlu* 新路 6 (June 19, 1948): 3–7.

Tao Menghe 陶孟和. "Minzhu yu ducai" 民主与独裁 (Democracy and dictatorship). *Guowen zhoubao* 国闻周报 12:1 (January 1, 1935): 1–4.

Tao Xisheng 陶希圣. "Budangzhe de liliang" 不党者的力量 (The strength of the non-Party elements). *Duli pinglun* 独立评论 242 (July 11, 1937): 9–11.

"Lun kaifang dangjin" 论开放党禁 (On lifting the ban on political parties). *Duli pinglun* 237 (June 6, 1937): 9–11.

"Minzhu yu ducai de zhenglun" 民主与独裁的争论 (The debate between democracy and dictatorship). *Duli pinglun* 136 (January 20, 1935): 11–12.

"Yige shidai cuowu de yijian" 一个时代错误的意见 (A view on the error of an era). *Duli pinglun* 20 (October 2, 1933): 2–4.

"Zailun dangjin wenti" 再论党禁问题 (Again on the ban on political parties). *Duli pinglun* 239 (June 20, 1937): 13–14.

Tien Hung-mao. "Factional Politics in Kuomintang China, 1928–1937: An Interpretation." In Gilbert Chan, ed., *China at the Crossroads: Nationalists and Communists, 1927–1949*, pp. 19–35. Boulder: Westview Press, 1980.

Government and Politics in Kuomintang China, 1927–1937. Stanford: Stanford University Press, 1972.

Tseng Chao-lun (Zeng Zhaolun). "The Chinese Democratic League." *Current History* 1:33 (1946): 31–37.

Tsou Tang. "The Tiananmen Tragedy: The State–Society Relationship, Choices, and Mechanisms in Historical Perspective." In Brantly Womack, ed.,

Contemporary Chinese Politics in Historical Perspective, pp. 265–327. New York: Cambridge University Press, 1991.

Tui Zhi 退知. "Lianhe zhengfu" 联合政府 (Coalition government). *Minzhu zhoukan* 民主周刊 2:8 (September 8, 1945): 10–11.

U.S. Department of State. *Foreign Relations of the United States.* Washington, DC: Government Printing Office, relevant years.

The China White Paper (August 1949), orginally issued as *United States Relations with China with Special Reference to the Period 1944–1949*, reissued with a new introduction by Lyman P. Van Slyke. Stanford: Stanford University Press, 1967.

Van Slyke, Lyman P. *Enemies and Friends: The United Front in Chinese Communist History.* Stanford: Stanford University Press, 1967.

ed. *Marshall's Mission to China, December 1945–January 1947: The Report and Appended Documents.* Arlington, VA: University Publications of America, 1976.

Wakeman, Frederic, Jr. *Policing Shanghai, 1927–1937.* Berkeley: University of California Press, 1995.

"A Revisionist View of the Nanjing Decade: Confucian Fascism." *China Quarterly* 150 (June 1997): 395–432.

Wang Fei 王飞. "Minzhu tongmeng jiepou" 民主同盟解剖 (Anatomy of the Democratic League). *Ziyou tiandi* 自由天地 1:8 (30 April 1947): 6–7, 9.

Wang Gongliang 王公亮. "Ziyou zhuyizhe yu zhongli taidu" 自由主义者与中立态度 (The liberal elements and their neutral attitude). *Shiji pinglun* 世纪评论 4:20 (November 13, 1948): 9–10.

Wang Gongyu 王贡愚. "Fazhi minzhu yu tongyi" 法治民主与统一 (Rule of law, democracy, and unification). *Jinri pinglun* 今日评论 1:16 (April 16, 1939): 6–8.

"Jiquan yu minzhu" 集权与民主 (Concentrated powers and democracy). *Jinri pinglun* 3:17 (January 7, 1940): 9–11.

"Tantan ducai zhengzhi" 谈谈独裁政治 (On dictatorship). *Jinri pinglun* 5:9 (March 9, 1941): 143–144.

"Zoushang xianzheng zhi lu" 走上宪政之路 (Going down the constitutional road). *Jinri pinglun* 2:23 (November 26, 1939): 357–359.

Wang Gungwu. *Power, Rights and Duties in Chinese History: The 40th George Ernest Morrison Lecture in Ethnology.* Canberra: Australian National University, 1979.

Wang Huabin 王华斌. *Huang Yanpei zhuan* 黄炎培传 (Biography of Huang Yanpei). Jinan: Shandong wenyi chubanshe, 1992.

Wang Tianwen 王天文 and Wang Jichun 王继春. *Zhongguo minzhu dangpai shigang* 中国民主党派史纲 (Outline of the Chinese democratic parties and groups). Kaifeng: Henan daxue chubanshe, 1988.

Wang Yunsheng 王芸生. "Zhongguo shiju qiantu de sange quxiang" 中国时局前途的三个去向 (Three trends for China's current situation and future). *Guancha* 观察 1:1 (September 1, 1946): 5–6.

Wang Yunwu 王云五. *Youlu lun guoshi* 岫庐论国事 (Wang Yunwu on national affairs). Taibei: Taiwan Shangwu yinshuguan, 1965.

Wang Zaoshi 王造时. "Duiyu xunzheng yu xianzheng de yijian" 对于训政与宪政的

意见 (My views on political tutelage and constitutionalism). *Zaisheng* 再生 1:2 (June 20, 1932): 1–10.

"Wo weishenme zhuzhang shixing xianzheng" 我为什么主张实行宪政 (Why do I advocate the implementation of constitutional rule?). *Zaisheng* 1:5 (September 20, 1932): 1–10.

Wang, Y. C. *Chinese Intellectuals and the West, 1872–1949*. Chapel Hill: University of North Carolina Press, 1966.

Wasserstrom Jeffrey N. *Student Protests in Twentieth-Century China: The View from Shanghai*. Stanford: Stanford University Press, 1991.

Wei Hongyun 魏宏运. *Zhongguo jindai lishi de guocheng* 中国近代历史的过程 (The process of Chinese history in recent times). Guangzhou: Guangdong renmin chubanshe, 1989.

Wen Liming 闻黎明. "Huang Yanpei yu kangRi zhanzheng shiqi de dierci xianzheng yundong" 黄炎培与抗日战争时期的第二次宪政运动 (Huang Yanpei and the second constitutional movement during the war against Japan). *Jindaishi yanjiu* 近代史研究 5 (1997): 147–165.

"Wang Shijie yu guomin canzhenghui (1938–1944)" 王世杰与国民参政会 (Wang Shijie and the People's Political Council, 1938–1944). *KangRi zhanzheng yanjiu* 抗日战争研究 3 (1993): 170–190.

White, Theodore H., and Jacoby, Annalee. *Thunder Out of China*. New York: William Sloane Associates, 1946.

Womack, Brantly. "In Search of Democracy: Public Authority and Popular Power in China." In Brantly Womack, ed., *Contemporary Chinese Politics in Historical Perspective*, pp. 53–89. Cambridge: Cambridge University Press, 1991.

Wong Young-tsu. "The Fate of Liberalism in Revolutionary China." *Modern China* 19:4 (October 1993): 457–490.

Wu Dange 伍丹戈. "Minzhu luxian yu zhongjian luxian" 民主路线与中间路线 (The democratic line and the middle line). *Shi yu wen* 时与文 1:8 (May 2, 1947): 3–4, 15.

Wu Enyu 吴恩裕. *Minzhu zhengzhi de jichu* 民主政治的基础 (The foundations of democratic politics). Chongqing: Shangwu yinshuguan, 1944.

"Ziyouhu? pingdenghu?" 自由乎？平等乎？ (Liberty? Equality?). *Guancha* 观察 3:12 (November 15, 1947): 6–7.

Wu Guanyin 吴贯因. "Minguo chengli ershiernian shang zai taolunzhong zhi xianfa" 民国成立二十二年尚在讨论中之宪法 (The constitution still talked about twenty years after the establishment of the Republic). *Zaisheng* 再生 1:11 (March 20, 1933): 1–10, continued in the next two issues.

Wu Han 吴晗. "Lun kuoda zhengfu zuzhi fang'an" 论扩大政府组织方案 (A proposal on the enlargement of the governmental structure). *Minzhu zhoukan* 民主周刊 2:24 (January 20, 1946): 3–4.

"Zhiren yu zhifa" 治人与治法 (Rule of man and rule of law). *Ziyou luntan* 自由论坛 2:3 (March 1, 1944): 17–18.

Wu Jingchao 吴景超. "Geming yu jianguo" 革命与建国 (Revolution and nation building). *Duli pinglun* 独立评论 84 (January 7, 1934): 2–5.

"Zhongguo de zhengzhi wenti" 中国的政制问题 (The question of China's political system). *Duli pinglun* 134 (January 6, 1935): 17–19.

Wu Jingxiong 吴经熊 and Huang Gongjue 黄公觉. *Zhongguo zhixianshi*

中国制宪史 (A history of Chinese constitution making). Shanghai: Shangwu yinshuguan, 1937.

Wu Shichang 吴世昌. "Hetan yinian" 和谈一年 (One year after the peace talks). *Guancha* 观察 1:24 (February 8, 1947): 2–3.

"Lun ⟨minzhu guoji⟩" 论⟨民主国际⟩ (On the Democratic International). *Guancha* 2:22 (July 26, 1947): 5.

"Minzhu zhengzhi yu fanduidang" 民主政治与反对党 (Democratic politics and opposition party). *Minzhu luntan* 民主论坛 2:8 (October 26, 1947): 3–4.

"Zhengzhi minzhu yu jingji minzhu" 政治民主与经济民主 (Democratic politics and economic democracy). *Guancha* 1:5 (28 September 1946): 5–7.

Wu Wenzao 吴文藻. "Minzhu de yiyi" 民主的意义 (The meaning of democracy). *Jinri pinglun* 今日评论 4:8 (August 23, 1940): 116–120.

Wu Zhizhuang 吴之桩. "Zhongguo de fazhi yu minzhu" 中国的法治与民主 (China's rule of law and democracy). *Ziyou luntan* 自由论坛 1:1 (February 15, 1943): 3–5.

"Zhuanbian shehui zhong de Zhongguo xianfa yu xianzheng" 转变社会中的中国宪法与宪政 (The Chinese constitution and constitutionalism in a changing society). *Ziyou luntan* 2:3 (March 1, 1944): 2–7.

Xiao Chun 晓春. "Hewei minzhu" 何谓民主 (What is democracy?). *Minzhu yu tongyi* 民主与统一 8 (July 20, 1946): 6–7.

Xiao Gongquan 萧公权. "Ershi shiji de lishi renwu" 二十世纪的历史任务 (The historical mission of the twentieth century). *Shiji pinglun* 世纪评论 2:5 (July 26, 1947): 5–8.

"Shuo minzhu" 说民主 (On democracy). *Guancha* 观察 1:7 (October 12, 1946): 3–7.

Xiao Zhongna 萧仲纳. "Dangqian renquan yundong de tezheng ji qi zhongxin renwu" 当前人权运动的特征及其中心任务 (The current human rights movement and its characteristics and central tasks). In Zhou Jingwen 周鲸文, ed., *Renquan yundong zhuanhao* 人权运动专号 (Special issue on the human rights movement), pp. 88–89. Hong Kong: Shidai pipingshe, 1941.

Xiong Yuezhi 熊月之. *Zhongguo jindai minzhu sixiangshi* 中国近代民主思想史 (History of modern Chinese democratic thought). Shanghai: Shanghai renmin chubanshe, 1986.

Xu Daolin 徐道邻. "Xianfa caoan chugao shangdui" 宪法草案初稿商兑 (On the draft constitution). *Duli pinglun* 独立评论 94 (April 1, 1934): 10–12.

Xu Hansan 许汉三, ed. *Huang Yanpei nianpu* 黄炎培年谱 (A chronology of Huang Yanpei's life). Beijing: Wenshi ziliao chubanshe, 1985.

Yan Rengeng 严仁赓. "1848–1948 – lishi de liangge zhuanliedian" 历史的两个转捩点 (1848–1948 – Two turning points in history). *Guancha* 观察 5:18 (December 25, 1948): 2–4.

"Lun fandui zhengfu" 论反对政府 (On opposition to the government). *Guancha* 3:20 (January 10, 1948): 10–11.

"Shehui zhuyi hu? 'xin ziben zhuyi' hu?" 社会主义乎？新资本主义乎？ (Socialism? "New capitalism"?). *Guancha* 4:17 (June 19, 1948): 5–8.

"Zai he Shi Fuliang xiansheng tan xin ziben zhuyi" 再和施复亮先生谈新资本主义 (Again discussing the new capitalism with Mr. Shi Fuliang). *Guancha* 4:23–24 combined (August 7, 1948): 15.

Yan Siping 晏嗣平. "Zhongguo zhengzhi de qitu (shang)" 中国政治的歧途（上）(The crossroads of Chinese politics [part 1]). *Minzhu luntan* 民主论坛 2:6 (October 18, 1947): 12–14.

"Zhongguo zhengzhi de qitu (xia)" 中国政治的歧途（下）(The crossroads of Chinese politics [part 2]). *Minzhu luntan* 2:7 (October 18, 1947): 6–9.

Yang Guangshi 杨光时 et al. "Women duiyu daju de kanfa yu duice" 我们对于大局的看法与对策 (Our views and strategies on the current situation). *Guancha* 观察 2:21 (July 19, 1947): 3–4.

Yang Renbian 杨人㛃. "Guanyu ⟨Zhonggong wang hechu qu?⟩" 关于⟨中共往何处去？⟩ (About "Where the CCP is going?"). *Guancha* 观察 3:10 (November 1, 1947): 11–12.

"Zailun ziyou zhuyi de tujing" 再论自由主义的途径 (Again on the path of liberalism). *Guancha* 5:8 (October 16, 1948): 3–5.

"Ziyou zhuyizhe wang hechu qu?" 自由主义者往何处去？(Where are the liberals headed?). *Guancha* 2:11 (May 10, 1947): 3–6.

Yang Tianshi 杨天石. "Hu Shi yu Guomindang de yiduan jiufen" 胡适与国民党的一段纠纷 (Hu Shi's differences with the Nationalist Party). *Zhongguo wenhua* 中国文化 9 (Spring 1991): 119–132.

YCS (pseudonym). "Renquan yundong yu kangzhan" 人权运动与抗战 (The human rights movement and the war of resistance). In Zhou Jingwen 周鲸文, ed., *Renquan yundong zhuanhao* 人权运动专号 (Special issue on the human rights movement), pp. 88–89. Hong Kong: Shidai pipingshe, 1941.

Ye Qing 叶青. *Tongyi yu minzhu* 统一与民主 (Unification and democracy). N.p.: Duli chubanshe, 1940.

Yi Qiwen 伊其文. "Yizai suowei ⟨minzhu guoji⟩!" 异哉所谓⟨民主国际⟩! (Wonderful! The so-called Democratic International). *Shi yu wen* 时与文 1:21 (August 1, 1947): 10–11.

Yi Sheng 毅生. "Zhongguo minzhu tongmeng" 中国民主同盟 (The Chinese Democratic League). *Zaisheng* 再生 104 (May 1, 1946): 14–15.

Yishibao 益世报 (Social Welfare) (Tianjin), revelant years.

You Huansheng 忧患生. "Minzhu zhengzhi hu?" 民主政治乎？(Democratic politics?). *Duli pinglun* 独立评论 135 (January 13, 1935): 7–9.

Young, Ernest P. *The Presidency of Yuan Shih-k'ai: Liberalism and Dictatorship in Early Republican China*. Ann Arbor: University of Michigan Press, 1977.

Yu Ying-shih. "Sun Yat-sen's Doctrine and Traditional Chinese Culture." In Cheng Chu-yuan, ed., *Sun Yat-sen's Doctrine in the Modern World*, pp. 79–102. Boulder: Westview Press, 1989.

Yuan Xihua 袁西华. "Sulian minzhu tezheng jiqi lishi fazhan" 苏联民主特征及其历史发展 (Concrete evidence of Soviet democracy and its historical development). *Minzhu zhoukan* 民主周刊 2:1 (July 7, 1945): 11–12.

Zarrow, Peter. *Anarchism and Chinese Political Culture*. New York: Columbia University Press, 1990.

"Citizenship and Human Rights in Early Twentieth-Century Chinese Thought: Liu Shipei and Liang Qichao." In Wm Theodore de Bary and Tu Weiming, eds., *Confucianism and Human Rights*, pp. 209–233. New York: Columbia University Press, 1998.

Historical Perspectives on Public Philosophy in Modern China. New York: Carnegie Council on Ethics and International Affairs monograph, 1997.

Zeng Zhaolun 曾昭伦. "Banian lai de shijie minzhu langchao" 八年来的世界民主浪潮 (The world democratic tide over the last eight years). *Minzhu zhoukan* 民主周刊 2:1 (July 7, 1945): 7–8.

Zhang Dongsun 张东荪. "Dang de wenti" 党的问题 (The party's problem). *Zaisheng* 再生 1, 3 (July 20, 1932): 1–12.

"Guanyu Zhongguo chulu de kanfa" 关于中国出路的看法 (On China's way out). *Guancha* 观察 3:23 (January 31, 1947): 3–4.

"Guomin wuzui: ping Guomindang de xianzheng lun" 国民无罪: 评国民党的宪政论 (The people are innocent: a critique of the Guomindang's theory of constitutionalism). *Zaisheng* 1:8 (December 20, 1932): 11–10.

"Heping heyi hui si le?" 和平何以会死了? (Why is peace dead?). *Shi yu wen* 时与文 1:3 (March 28, 1947): 3–4.

"Jingda Fan Hong xiansheng" 敬答樊弘先生 (Respectful response to Mr. Fan Hong). *Guancha* 3:16 (December 13, 1947): 5–6.

"Jingji pingdeng yu feichu boxiao" 经济平等与废除剥削 (Economic equality and the abolition of exploitation). *Guancha* 4:2 (March 6, 1948): 3–5.

Lixing yu minzhu 理性与民主 (Reason and democracy). Hong Kong: Longmen shudian, 1968. Originally published by Shangwu yinshuguan in Shanghai in 1946.

"Minzhu yu zhuanzhi shi bu xiangrong de me?" 民主与专制是不相容的么? (Are democracy and autocracy mutually exclusive?). *Zaisheng* 1:7 (November 20, 1932): 1–11.

Sixiang yu shehui 思想与社会 (Thought and society). Hong Kong: Longmen shudian, 1968. Originally published by Shangwu yinshuguan in Shanghai in 1946.

"Wo yi zhuilun xianzheng jianji wenhua de zhenduan" 我亦追论宪政兼及文化的诊断 (I also want to talk about constitutionalism and cultural diagnosis). *Guancha* 3:7 (October 11, 1947): 3–6.

"Yige zhongjian xing de zhengzhi luxian" 一个中间性的政治路线 (A political line of a middle nature), *Zaisheng*, 118 (June 22, 1946). Reprinted in Li Huaxing 李华兴, ed., *Zhongguo xiandai sixiangshi ziliao jianbian* 中国现代思想史资料简编 (A brief compilation of materials on modern Chinese political thought), vol. 5, pp. 202–207. Hangzhou: Zhejiang renmin chubanshe, 1983.

"Zhengzhi shang de ziyou zhuyi yu wenhua shang de ziyou zhuyi" 政治上的自由主义与文化上的自由主义 (Political liberalism and cultural liberalism). *Guancha* 4:1 (February 28, 1948): 3–5.

"Zhishi fenzi yu wenhua de ziyou" 知识份子与文化的自由 (The intellectuals and cultural freedom). *Guancha* 5:11 (October 30, 1948): 3–5.

"Zhuishu women nuli jianli 'lianhe zhengfu' de yongyi" 述说我们努力建立〈联合政府〉的用意 (An account of the purpose of our efforts at establishing a "coalition government"). *Guancha* 2:6 (April 5, 1947): 5–7.

Zhang Foquan 张佛泉. "Jianguo yu zhengzhi wenti" 建国与政制问题 (Nation building and the question of political institutions). *Guowen zhoubao* 国闻周报 11:26 (July 2, 1934): 1–8.

"Jidian piping yu jianyi: zaitan zhengzhi gaige wenti" 几点批评与建议: 再谈政治

改革问题 (A few criticisms and suggestions: Again on the question of political reform). *Guowen zhoubao* 12:38 (August 13, 1935): 1–6.

"Jinhou zhengzhi zhi zhanwang" 今后政治之展望 (A look at the future of politics). *Duli pinglun* 独立评论 219 (September 20, 1936): 2–5.

"Lun zhengzhi zhi zhiduhua 论政治之制度化 (On the institutionalization of politics). *Jinri pinglun* 今日评论 1:19 (May 7, 1939): 4–5.

"Minyuan yilai woguo zai zhengzhi shang de chuantong cuowu" 民元以来我国在政治上的传统错误 (The traditional error we have made in politics since the beginning of the Republic). *Guowen zhoubao* 10:44 (November 6, 1933): 1–8.

"Women jiujing yao shenmeyang de xianfa?" 我们究竟要什么样的宪法？ (What sort of constitution do we really want?). *Duli pinglun* 236 (May 30, 1937): 2–4.

"Women wei shenme yao shuochang daoduan" 我们为什么要说长道短 (Why should we be talking long and short?). *Duli pinglun* 230 (April 18, 1937): 12–14.

"Xunzheng yu zhuanzhi" 训政与专政 (Political tutelage and autocracy). *Guowen zhoubao* 11:36 (September 10, 1934): 1–4.

"Zhengzhi gaizao de tujing" 政治改造的途径 (The path of institutional reform), *Guowen zhoubao* 12:34 (September 2, 1935): 1–10.

Zhang Hong 张弘. "Zhuanzhi wenti pingyi" 专制问题评议 (An appraisal of the question of dictatorship). *Duli pinglun* 独立评论 104 (June 10, 1934): 4–11.

Zhang Jinjian 张金鉴. "Minzhu zhuyi zai jinri" 民主主义在今日 (Democracy today). *Dongfang zazhi* 东方杂志 31:4 (February 16, 1934): 43–47.

Zhang Junmai 张君劢. "Da aiguoxin" 大爱国心 (Great patriotism). *Minxian* 民宪 1:2 (May 31, 1944): 1–4.

"Guojia minzhu zhengzhi yu guojia shehui zhuyi" 国家民主政治与国家社会主义 (National democracy and national socialism). *Zaisheng* 再生 1:2 (June 20, 1932): 1–38; continued in 3 (July 20, 1932): 1–38.

"Guomindang dangzheng zhi xin qilu" 国民党党政之新歧路 (Guomindang rule at a new crossroads). *Zaisheng* 1:2 (June 29, 1932): 1–15.

Liguo zhi dao 立国之道 (The way to build the nation). Chongqing: Zhongguo minzhu shehuidang zhongyang zongbu, 1938.

"Minzhu ducai yiwai zhi disanzhong zhengzhi" 民主独裁以外之第三种政治 (A third kind of politics besides democracy and dictatorship). *Zaisheng* 3:2 (April 15, 1935): 1–24.

"Minzhu zhengzhi de zhexue jichu" 民主政治的哲学基础 (The philosophical basis of democracy). In Li Huaxing 李华兴, ed., *Zhongguo xiandai sixiangshi ziliao jianbian* 中国现代思想史资料简编 (A brief compilation of materials on modern Chinese political thought), vol. 5, pp. 363–368. Hangzhou: Zhejiang renmin chubanshe, 1983.

"Weiersishi zhengzhi sixiang ji qi jinzuo renquan xuanyan" 威尔斯氏政治思想及其近作人权宣言 (H. G. Wells's political thought and manifesto on human rights). *Minxian* 1:10 (December 20, 1944): 4–13.

Zhang Pengyuan 张朋园. *Liang Qichao yu minchu zhengzhi* 梁启超与民初政治 (Liang Qichao and early Republican politics). Taibei: Shihuo chubanshe, 1981.

Zhang Pijie 张丕介. "Lun zhengzhi minzhu yu jingji pingdeng" 论政治民主与经济平等 (On political democracy and economic equality). *Gexin* 革新 2:18 (July 31, 1947): 3–5.

Zhang Qifeng 张起凤. "Huang Yanpei: Zhongguo zhiye jiaoyu zhi xianju" 黄炎培: 中国职业教育之先躯 (Huang Yanpei: Pioneer in Chinese vocational education). Unpublished MA thesis, National Taiwan Normal University, 1990.

Zhang Shenfu 张申府. "Minzhu tuanjie de jingshen tiaojian" 民主团结的精神条件 (The spiritual conditions for democratic unity). *Wencui* 文粹 1:1 (October 9, 1945): 2.

"Minzhu yu zhexue" 民主与哲学 (Democracy and philosophy). *Ziyou luntan* 自由论坛 3:3 (November 1, 1944): 9–10.

"Women wei shenme yao minzhu yu ziyou" 我们为什么要民主与自由 (Why do we want democracy and liberty). *Xinhua ribao* 新华日报 (September 12, 1944).

Zhang Xiaofang 张晓芳. "Zhongguo minzhu tongmeng zhi yanjiu" 中国民主同盟之研究 (A study of the Chinese Democratic League). Unpublished MA thesis, National Taiwan Normal University, 1991.

Zhang Xiruo 张奚若. "Guomin renge zhi peiyang" 国民人格之培养 (Cultivation of national integrity). *Duli pinglun* 独立评论 150 (May 12, 1935): 14–16.

"Minzhu zhengzhi dangzhen shi youzhi de zhengzhi ma?" 民主政治当真是幼稚的政治吗? (Is democracy really kindergarten politics?). *Duli pinglun* 239 (June 20, 1937): 3–6.

"Wo wei shenme xiangxin minzhi" 我为什么相信民治 (Why do I believe in democracy?). *Duli pinglun* 240 (June 27, 1937): 2–5.

"Yiqie zhengzhi zhi jichu" 一切政治之基础 (The foundations of all politics). *Guowen zhoubao* 国闻周报 12:6 (February 18, 1935): 1–4.

"Zailun guomin renge" 再论国民人格 (Again on national integrity). *Duli pinglun* 152 (May 26, 1935): 2–5.

"Zhengzhi xieshang huiyi yinggai jiejue de wenti" 政治协商会应该解决的问题 (The questions that should be resolved in regard to the Political Consultative Conference). *Minzhu zhoukan* 民主周刊 2:24 (January 20, 1946): 9–12.

Zhang Yuanfeng 章元凤. "Minzhu zhengzhi yu jiquan xingzheng" 民主政治与集权行政 (Democratic politics and concentrated administration). *Minzhu luntan* 民主论坛 1:8 (July 5, 1947): 16–17.

Zhang Zhenzhi 张振之. *Ping Hu Shi fandang yizhu* 评胡适反党义著 (A critique of Hu Shi's anti-Party doctrine writings). Shanghai: Guangming shuju, 1929.

Zhang Zhirang 张志让. "Zhongguo xianzheng yundong yu shijie minzhu chaoliu" 中国宪政运动与世界民主潮流 (The Chinese constitutional movement and the democratic world tide). *Xianzheng yuekan* 宪政月刊 1 (1944): 2–6.

Zhao Suisheng. *Power by Design: Constitution-making in Nationalist China.* Honolulu: University of Hawaii Press, 1996.

Zhao Xihua 赵锡骅. *Minmeng shihua, 1941–1949* 民盟史话 (History of the Democratic League, 1941–1949). Beijing: Zhongguo shehui kexue chubanshe, 1992.

Zheng Shenshan 郑慎山. "Shi ⟨liberal, liberalism⟩" 释 ⟨liberal, liberalism⟩ (Interpreting liberal and liberalism). *Guancha* 观察 4:6 (April 3, 1948): 5–6.

Zhengzhi xieshang huiyi ziliao 政治协商会议资料 (Source materials on the Political Consultative Conference), no editor. Chengdu: Sichuan renmin chubanshe, 1981.

Zheng Xuejia 郑学稼. "Lun minzhu yu jingji jianshe" 论民主与经济建设 (On democracy and economic construction). *Minzhu yu tongyi* 民主与统一 4 (June 10, 1946): 3–4.

Zhonggong Yunnan shengwei tongzhanbu 中共云南省委统战部, comp. *Yunnan tongyi zhanxian ziliao huibian* 云南统一战线资料汇编 (Collection of materials on the CCP's Yunnan provincial committee's united front), *neibu ziliao* 内部资料 (for internal distribution). Kunming, 1992.

Zhongguo dier lishi dang'anguan 中国第二历史档案馆, ed. *Zhongguo minzhu shehuidang* 中国民主社会党 (The Chinese Democratic Socialist Party). Beijing: Dang'an chubanshe, 1988.

Zhongguo Guomindang zhongyang weiyuanhui dangshi weiyuanhui 中国国民党中央委员会党史委员会, ed. *Guofu quanji* 国父全集 (The complete works of Sun Yat-sen), 6 vols. Taibei: Zhongguo Guomindang zhongyang weiyuanhui dangshi weiyuanhui, 1981.

Zhongguo kexueyuan jindaishi yanjiusuo 中国科学院近代史研究所, ed. *Zhongguo minquan baozhang tongmeng* 中国民权保障同盟 (The Chinese League for the Protection of Civil Rights), 2nd ed. Beijing: Zhongguo shehui kexue chubanshe, 1984.

Zhongguo minzhu tongmeng zhongyang wenshi ziliao weiyuanhui 中国民主同盟中央文史资料委员会, ed. *Zhongguo minzhu tongmeng lishi wenxian, 1941–1949* 中国民主同盟历史文献 (Documents on the Chinese Democratic League, 1941–1949). Beijing: Wenshi ziliao chubanshe, 1983.

Zhongguo minzhu tongmeng 中国民主同盟, comp. *Heping minzhu tongyi jianguo zhilu* 和平民主统一建国之路 (The road to peace, democracy, reunification, and national reconstruction). Chongqing: Minxian yuekanshe, 1945.

Zhongguo shehui kexueyuan jindaishi yanjiusuo Zhonghua minguo shiliaoshi 中国社会科学院近代史研究所中华民国史料室, comp. *Hu Shi laiwang shuxinxuan* 胡适来往书信选 (Selected correspondence of Hu Shi). Hong Kong: Zhonghua shuju, 1983.

Zhou Jingwen 周鲸文, ed. *Renquan yundong zhuanhao* 人权运动专号 (Special issue on the human rights movement). Reprinted from *Shidai piping* 时代批评 nos. 73–74. Hong Kong: Shidai pipingshe, 1941.

Zhou Shouzhang 周绶章. "Fengkuang le de Zhongguo – yi ge mangdong de, beiju de da shidai" 疯狂了的中国 – 一个盲动的, 悲剧的大时代 (Mad China – A blind, tragic era). *Guancha* 观察 2:15 (June 7, 1947): 7–9.

"Lun shenhua zhengzhi" 论神话政治 (Of myths and politics). *Guancha* 1:21 (January 18, 1947): 5–7.

"Mianbao yu ziyou de jueze" 面包与自由的抉择 (A choice between bread and liberty). *Shi yu wen* 时与文 3:18 (August 20, 1948): 1–2.

"Wei zhenzheng de ziyou zhuyi fenzi daqi" 为真正的自由主义份子打气 (Cheering for the true liberal elements). *Shiji pinglun* 世纪评论 4:10 (September 4, 1949): 5–7.

"Zhengzhi ziyou yu jingji pingdeng" 政治自由与经济平等 (Political liberty and economic liberty). *Shiji pinglun* 1:20 (May 17, 1947): 13–15.

Zhou Tiandu 周天度, ed. *Qi junzi zhuan* 七君子传 (The seven honorable persons). Beijing: Zhongguo shehui kexueyuan chubanshe, 1988.

——— ed. *Shen Junru wenji* 沈君儒文集 (The collected works of Shen Junru). Beijing: Renmin chubanshe, 1994.

Zhu Qinglai 诸青来. "Xianzheng pingyi" 宪政评议 (A critique of constitutionalism). *Minsheng zhoubao* 民声周报 27 (June 5, 1932): 12–14.

Zhu Weiru 朱蔚如. "Demo kelaxi de qiantu" 德谟克拉西的前途 (The future of democracy). *Shidai gonglun* 时代公论 3:7 (May 11, 1934): 8–14.

Zhu Yisong 朱永松. "Guanyu minzhu yu ducai de yige da lunzhan (shang)" 关于民主与独裁的一个大论战 (上) (The great democracy versus dictatorship debate [part 1]). *Zaisheng* 再生 3:2 (April 15, 1935): 1–16.

——— "Guanyu minzhu yu ducai de yige da lunzhan (xia)" 关于民主与独裁的一个大论战 (下) (The great democracy versus dictatorship debate [part 2]). *Zaisheng* 再生 3:4–5 combined (July 15, 1935): 1–49.

——— "Xinshidai de minzhi zhuyi" 新时代的民治主义 (Democracy in a new era). *Zaisheng* 1:9 (January 1, 1933): 1–82.

Zou Dang 邹谠. Ershi shiji Zhongguo zhengzhi: cong hongguan lishi yu weiguan xingdong de jiaodu kan 二十世纪中国政治：从宏观历史与微观形动的角度看 (Twentieth-century Chinese politics viewed from the perspective of macro history and micro action). Hong Kong: Oxford University Press, 1994.

Zou Taofen 邹韬奋. *Taofen wenji* 韬奋文集 (The collected works of Zou Taofen). Hong Kong: Sanlian shudian, 1959.

——— "Dangpai yu renquan" 党派与人权 (Parties, groups, and human rights). In Zhou Jingwen 周鲸文, ed. *Renquan yundong zhuanhao* 人权运动专号 (Special issue on the human rights movement), pp. 5–7. Hong Kong: Shidai pipingshe, 1941.

Zou Wenhai 邹文海. "Minzhu zhengzhi yu ziyou" 民主政治与自由 (Democratic politics and liberty). *Guancha* 观察 1:13 (November 23, 1946): 9–12.

——— "Minzhu zhengzhi shifou rengxu ziyou?" 民主政治是否仍需自由 (Does democratic politics still need liberty?). *Guancha* 1:10 (November 2, 1946): 3–5.

——— "Xingxian de tiaojian" 行宪的条件 (Conditions for constitutionalism). *Minzhu luntan* 民主论坛 1:4 (June 7, 1947): 11–12.

——— "Xuanju yu daibiao zhidu" 选举与代表制度 (Elections and the representative system). *Zaisheng* 再生 2:5 (February 1, 1934): 1–32.

Zuo Shunsheng 左舜生. *Jin sanshinian jianwen zaji* 近三十年见闻杂记 (A record of the events of the last thirty years). Taibai: Zhonghua yilin wenwu chubanshe, 1976.

——— "The Reminiscences of Tso Shun-sheng," as told to Julie Lien-ying How, 1965. Chinese Oral History Project, Special Collections, Butler Library, Columbia University.

——— "Wenti zainei bu zaiwai" 问题在内不在外 (The problem is internal, not external). *Minsheng zhoubao* 民声周报 15 (January 9, 1932): 1–2.

Glossary

This glossary does not include the proper names that appear in the Selected Bibliography.

B

Bai Chongxi 白崇禧
Baohuangdang 保皇党
baojia 保甲
baonue 暴虐
buke qinfan 不可侵犯
buke yirang 不可移让
buzhi bujuezhe 不知不觉者

C

Cai Yuanpei 蔡元培
caifa 财阀
Chang Naide 常乃德
Chen Bulei 陈布雷
Chen Dezheng 陈德徵
Chen Duxiu 陈独秀
Chen Erjin 陈尔晋
Chen Jitang 陈济棠
Chen Lifu 陈立夫
Chen Mingshu 陈铭枢
Chen Shaoyu 陈绍禹
Chen Youren 陈友仁
chengren pangren 承认旁人
Chiang Kai-shek 蒋介石
chongtu 冲突

Chu Fucheng 褚辅成
chulu 出路

D

da aiguoxin 大爱国心
dadao zhi xing ye, tianxia weigong, xuanxian yu neng
大道之行也，天下为公，选贤与能
Dai Li 戴笠
dang gao yu guo 党高于国
danghua 党化
dangnei minzhu 党内民主
dangwai wudang 党外无党
dangzhi 党治
dangzhu 党主
datong 大同
Dazhong shenghuo 大众生活
Deng Xiaoping 邓小平
Deng Yanda 邓演达
Deng Yingchao 邓颖超
Disandang 第三党
Disan fangmian 第三方面
Dong Biwu 董必武
Dong Shijin 董时进
Duan Qirui 段祺瑞
ducai 独裁

E

erchong zuzhi 二重组织

F

Fang Lizhi 方励之
fangdang buji 放荡不羁
fazhi 法治
fazhi shenghuo 法治生活
fei 匪
Feng Yuxiang 冯玉祥

G

Gaizupai 改组派
gede qisuo 各得其所

geren benwei 个人本位
gong 公
gongmin shenghuo 公民生活
gongtong guize 共同规则
Guangmingbao 光明报
guanxi 关系
gua yangtou mai gouro 挂羊头卖狗肉
Guo Moruo 郭沫若
Guofang canyihui 国防参议会
guofang zhengfu 国防政府
Guojia shehuidang 国家社会党
Guomin canzhenghui 国民参政会
Guomin daibiao dahui 国民代表大会
Guomin jingshen zongdongyuan gangling 国民精神总动员纲领
Guominbao 国民报
Guomindang 国民党
Guomindang linshi xingdong weiyuanhui 国民党临时行动委员会
Guomindang minzhu cujinhui 国民党民主促进会
guonan 国难
Guonan huiyi 国难会议

H
He Xiangning 何香凝
houzhi houjuezhe 后知后觉者
Hu Hanmin 胡汉民
Hu Lin 胡霖
Hu Zhaoxiang 胡兆祥
Hua Gang 华岗
huanzheng yu min 还政于民

J
Jiang Baili 蒋百里
Jiang Hengyuan 江恒源
Jiang Menglin 蒋梦麟
Jianguo dagang 建国大纲
Jianguo fanglüe 建国方略
jianu 家奴
Jiefang ribao 解放日报
Jinbudang 进步党
jinqi zaiwu 尽其在吾

jiquan 极权
jiuguo 救国
Jiuguo tongxun 救国通讯
Jiuguohui 救国会
Jiusan xueshe 九三学社
jiuwang 救亡
Jiuwang ribao 救亡日报
jizhong xinli zhi guojia minzhu zhengzhi 集中心力之国家民主政治
juguo yizhi zhi zhengfu 举国一致之政府

K

kaifang zhengquan 开放政权
KangRi jiuguo gangling 抗日救国纲领
kangzhan 抗战
Kong Geng 孔庚
Kong Xiangxi (K. K. Kung) 孔祥禧
kuoda 扩大

L

laibin 来宾
lao baixing 老百姓
Leng Yu 冷遹
Li Dazhao 李大钊
Li Gongpu 李公朴
Li Jishen 李济深
Li Yizhe 李义哲
Li Zhuchen 李烛尘
Li Zongren 李宗仁
Liang Qichao 梁启超
Liao Zhongkai 廖仲恺
Lin Boqu 林伯渠
Lin Sen 林森
Lin Zuhan 林祖涵
Liu Binyan 刘宾雁
Liu Shipei 刘师培
Liu Wenhui 刘文辉
Liu Xiang 刘湘
Liu Xiaobo 刘晓波
lixiang 理想
lixing 理性

Lixingshe 力行社
Long Yun 龙云
Lu Dingyi 陆定一
lunli 伦理

M
Ma Junwu 马君武
Ma Zemin 马哲民
Mao Zedong 毛泽东
minben 民本
Mingri zhi Zhongguo wenhua 明日之中国文化
minquan 民权
Minquan chubu 民权初步
minquan zhuyi 民权主义
minsheng zhuyi 民生主义
minyi jiguan 民意机关
minyi zhengzhi 民意政治
minzhu dangpai 民主党派
minzhu de lianhe zhuanzheng 民主的联合专政
Minzhu guoji 民主国际
Minzhu shehuidang 民主社会党
Minzhu xianzhengdang 民主宪政党
minzu 民族
Mo Dehui 莫德惠
Mou Jiaming 缪嘉铭

P
peike 陪客
pengdang 朋党
pingmin geming 平民革命
putong 普通

Q
qi junzi 七君子
qian 谦
Qian Yongming 钱永铭
qimeng 启蒙
Qin Bangxian 秦邦宪
quan–neng 权能
Quanguo gejie jiuguo lianhehui 全国各界救国联合会

quanli 权力
quanli 权利
quanmin geming 全民革命
Quanmin zhoukan 全民周刊
quanshu 权术
quanying quanshu 全赢全输
Qunzhong zhoukan 群众周刊

R

rang 让
ren 仁, also 人
ren'ai 仁爱
renge 人格
renmin canzheng 人民参政
renqing 人情
renquan 人权
renqun 人群
renzhi 人治

S

sandang sanpai 三党三派
Sanmin zhuyi 三民主义
Sanmin zhuyi tongzhihui 三民主义同志会
Sha Qianli 沙千里
Shao Congen 邵从恩
Shao Lizi 劭力子
shehui xianda 社会贤达
Shen Congwen 沈从文
shengguan facai 升官发财
Shenghuo zhishi 生活知识
shenglijun 生力军
shengming 生命
shengwang 圣王
Shi Liang 史良
Shi Zhaoji 施肇基
shijie datong 世界大同
Shishi xinbao 时事新报
shu 恕
si 私
sixiang tongyi 思想统一

Song Jiaoren 宋教仁
Song Qingling 宋庆龄
Song Ziwen (T. V. Soong) 宋子文
Sun Fo (Sun Ke) 孙科
Sun Hongyi 孙洪伊
Sun Yat-sen 孙逸仙

T

Tan Pingshan 谭平山
Tao Xingzhi 陶行知
tebie 特别
tianfu renquan 天赋人权
tianxia weigong 天下为公
Tongmenghui 同盟会
Tongyi jianguo tongzhihui 统一建国同志会
tongyi zhengfu 统一政府

W

Wang Chonghui 王宠惠
Wang Jingwei 汪精卫
Wang Ruofei 王若飞
Wang Shijie 王世杰
Wang Xizhe 王希哲
Wang Yangming 王阳明
wangdao 王道
weichi shengming 维持生命
Wei Jingsheng 魏京生
Wen Yiduo 闻一多
wenhua shitiao 文化失调
Weng Wenhao 翁文灏
Wu Jingxiong 吴经熊
Wu Tiecheng 吴铁城
Wu Yifang 吴贻芳
Wu Yuzhang 吴玉章
Wu Zhihui 吴稚晖
wudang wupai 无党无派
Wuhan ribao 武汉日报
wuwei 无为

X

xian 县

xiandai shijie chaoliu 现代世界潮流

xianfa 宪法

Xiangcun jianshepai 乡村建设派

xianren zhengzhi 贤人政治

xianzheng 宪政

Xianzheng qichenghui 宪政期成会

Xianzheng shishi xiejinhui 宪政实施协进会

xianzhi xianjuezhe 先知先觉者

xiao shimin 小市民

Xiaoxi 消息

Xin Zhonghuabao 新中华报

Xinhua ribao 新华日报

Xingzheng dagang 行政大纲

xinnian 信念

xinyi 信义

xinyue 信约

Xinyueshe 新月社

xiuzheng minzhu zhengzhi 修正民主政治

Xu Deheng 徐德珩

Xu Zhimo 徐志摩

Y

Yan Fu 严复

Yan Jiaqi 严家其

Yan Xishan 严锡山

Yan Yangchu 晏阳初

Yang Yongjun 扬永浚

Yanjiuxi 研究系

Ye Chucang 叶楚苍

Ye Gongchao 叶公超

Ye Jianying 叶剑英

yiduo xiangrongzhi 一多相容制

yiguo yizhi zhi zhengfu 一国一致之政府

Yu Jiaju 余家菊

Yuan 院

Yuan Shikai 袁世凯

yuren weishan 与人为善

Z

Zaishengshe 再生社

zaoshu 早熟

Zeng Guofan 曾国藩

Zeng Qi 曾琦

Zhang Bojun 章伯钧

Zhang Boling 张伯苓

Zhang Fakui 张发奎

Zhang Jia'ao 张嘉璈

Zhang Lisheng 张厉生

Zhang Naiqi 张乃器

Zhang Qun 张群

Zhang Yaozeng 张耀曾

Zhang Zhiben 张知本

Zhang Zhizhong 张治忠

zhanshi juguo yizhi zhengfu 战时举国一致政府

zhengquan 政权

zhengtuan 政团

Zhengxuexi 政学系

Zhengzhi xieshang huiyi 政治协商会议

zhengzhi zhiduhua 政治制度化

zhiguo 治国

zhiquan 治权

zhong 忠

Zhongguo gongxue 中国公学

Zhongguo minzhu cujinhui 中国民主促进会

Zhongguo minzhu tongmeng 中国民主同盟

Zhongguo minzhu zhengtuan tongmeng 中国民主政团同盟

Zhongguo nonggong minzhudang 中国农工民主党

Zhongguo qingniandang 中国青年党

Zhonghua gemingdang 中华革命党

Zhonghua minzu 中华民族

Zhonghua zhiye jiaoyushe 中华职业教育社

zhongjian 中间

zhongjianpai 中间派

zhongyang 中央

Zhongyang ribao 中央日报

zhongyong zhi dao 中庸之道

Zhou Enlai 周恩来

Zhou Lan 周览

Zhou Xinmin 周新民
Zhu Ziqing 朱自清
zhuanjia zhengfu 专家政府
zhuanjia zhengzhi 专家政治
zhuanmen kexue 专门科学
zhuanzhi 专制
zhuhui weiyuanhui 驻会委员会
ziyou 自由
ziyou shehui zhuyi 自由社会主义
ziyou zizai 自由自在
zongcai 总裁
zongli 总理
zuigao lingxiu 最高领袖
zuoren 做人

Index

An "f" after a number indicates a separate reference on the next page, an "ff" indicates separate references on the next two pages. Continuous discussion over two or more pages is indicated by a span of numbers, for example, 1–5.